BEYOND ARCHITECTURE

IMAGINATIVE BUILDINGS AND FICTIONAL CITIES

Edited by Robert Klanten and Lukas Feireiss

gestalten

INTRODUCTION

by Lukas Feireiss

Follow the White Rabbit

In Lewis Carroll's famous children's novel *Alice in Wonderland*, a little girl follows a white rabbit into an improbable world of paradox and the absurd. With reference to the curious pursuit down the rabbit-hole, this book sees itself as a portal into an equally unpredictable and marvellous realm. Yet not a dreamy underworld populated by talking playing cards, grinning cats or riddling caterpillars, but a wizarding world of expressive experimentation and reflection in architecture and beyond architecture. Artistic visions of imaginary buildings that transform and interact, illusive urban scenarios of teeming energy and density, fantastically fictitious cities and curiously moving landscapes that unlock the imagination and spur original exploration of architecture's motivational power.

Beyond Architecture presents an eclectic survey on architecture and the city as a primary source of inspiration and stimulation in the contemporary arts. The featured projects I have brought together in this erratic compilation range from miniscule city sculptures to room-filling installations of urban networks, and from minimalistic illustrations to strikingly excessive paintings and strangely familiar photo-collages of architecture that offer a conspicuously unconventional view on the city. The book features the work of more than hundred young and upcoming as well as internationally renowned artists from around the world who display a heightened level of creative reflection on the subject. *Beyond Architecture* examines the original responses of artists to the influential strength of architecture in visual culture and explores how built forms are being used and abused in their work, thereby distending and extending space, and perhaps offering alternatives to the autonomous presumptions of architecture. At this point, my sincere gratitude goes to all contributing artists who made this book possible through their unfailing support.

Outland

The numerous projects collected in this book are brought together under three thematic headings, shifting from micro to macro-scale as the spectator's perspective moves from single houses and bottom-up street scenes to top-down views of entire city grids. Two and three-dimensional projects using most diverse materials can be found encompassing everything from cardboard to jelly, soap and chocolate.

The first chapter, Home Alone, looks at works of art that ironically and formalistically play with the elementary idea of single buildings. Take for example Erwin Wurm's tongue-in-cheek meltdown of Modern Architecture's icons in *Mies van der Rohe – melting* and *Fat-house Moller/Adolf Loos* or Constantin and Laurence Boym's dark-humoured *Buildings of Disaster* that showcase historically terrifying buildings such as Chernobyl's nuclear power-plant, Ted Kacinsky's uncanny reinterpretation of Thoreaux's *Walden* hut or even the Twin Towers after the attack. But there are also works such as Mike Perry's friendly *Alphabet Town* or Lindsey Lesh's strolling habitats that emphasise, in their poetic simplicity, another side of this ludic take on basic living units.

The next chapter, Street Dreams, proceeds from the singular to the multiple as it depicts the intoxicating diversity and vitality of street life. This change from single residence to settlement is probably best demonstrated by works such as Nathan Coley's and Edouard Sautai's cardboard house accumulations or Rachel Whiteread's installation of 200 doll houses, clustered together like a village. An abundance of colourful details can also be found in the close-packed street scenarios by Apfel Zet and eBoy or the captivating works of Isidro Blasco, who successfully moves from the two to the three-dimensional in his photo installations. Equally transcending the real and the virtual, photography and collage are the street depictions of Dionisio Gonzalez and Laura Kicey.

The third and concluding chapter, City High, concentrates on larger urban structures. The city offers a reality too complex and diverse, too disparate and plural, in order to be represented as a whole. This observation is valid for the city from its very beginning until the present day. And it holds all the more true for the numerous cityscapes presented in this chapter. What we are witnessing here is the creative emergence of profoundly new fantastic types of cities beyond the blueprint, such as Andreas Zimmermann's enthralling urban Lego worlds, the almost autistic cardboard models by Matias Bechtold or Body Isek Kingelez's hallucinogenic Las Vegas-like Dream City structures. The ever-changing nature of cities can also be traced in many of the works ranging from Michael Najjar's multiply-exposed black-and-white photo series *Netropolis* on numerous cities of the world to Eamon O'Kane's series of paintings on the development over time of a rural area into a industrial zone and its regeneration back to nature.

CONTRIBUTORS

You must realize that all this is only a glimpse of the fabulous world you are about to witness, and nothing but the beginning.

Finding Neverland But just as all dream worlds commonly serve to teach some lessons, this book would like to advocate to the reader a free, unbiased blending and ardent experimentation with and within the discipline of architecture. By doing so, *Beyond Architecture* charts novel ways of discovering and negotiating the potential of the urban in visual culture, thus also providing alternative and valid critical insights into understanding the city.

However, on reintroduction to the real world, the question often arises of what exactly constitutes reality, as a result of the vivid recollection and experience of the dream world. And secondly, how to return there. Now, the first answer I will wisely leave open for the reader and for the second I will do nothing but refer to one who knows. So in the words of the boy who wouldn't grow up: "Second star to the right, and straight on till morning."

Lukas Feireiss is an artist, curator and writer deeply involved in the discussion and mediation of architecture, art and media beyond their disciplinary boundaries. He teaches at various universities worldwide.

21_21 Design sight
Akim
Alekos Hofstetter
Ana Serrano
Andi Zimmermann
Andreas Gefeller
Andreas Koch
Andy Council
Apfel Zet
Arne Quinze
Asif Mian
Asmund H.-Mikkelsen
Atelier Van Lieshout
BIG / Bjarke Ingels Group
Björn Hegardt
Body Isek Kingelez
Bompas & Parr
Boym Partners
Brian Dettmer
Camille Rousseau
Cathelijne Montens
Chris Dent
Christian Hellmich
Constantin Luser
Cord Woywodt
David Herbert
David Keating
David Thorpe
Dionisio González
Do-Ho Suh
Droog Design
Eamon O'Kane
eboy
Edouard Sautai
Erik Göngrich
Erik Olofsen
Erwin Wurm
Evol / Ct'ink
Faculty of Architecture/ Univ. of Technology Munich: (Annika Sophia Dreyer, Monika Grandl, Antje Luckhardt & Nikolas Witte)
Filip Dujardin
Frank Kunert
Franz Höfner & Harry Sachs
George Hadjimichalis
Hans Op De Beeck
Hema Upadhyay
Hiroki Tsukuda
Holger Lippmann
Hvass&Hannibal
Isidro Blasco
J. Davis Studio
J. Michael Birn
Jake & Dinos Chapman
Jakob Kolding
Jan Brokof
Jan Feindt
Jenny Berntsson
Jens Reinert
Jeremias Böttcher
Jörn Gerstenberg
Jonas Liveröd
Jordi Colomer
Joshua Callaghan
J, P: A Jones, Partners
Karsten Konrad
Kobas Laksa
Kramer van der Veer
Larissa Fassler
Laura S. Kicey
Lizzie Mary Cullen
Lok Jansen
London Fieldworks
Luc Deleu & T.O.P. office
Lukas Feireiss
Lyndsey Lesh
M-City
Marcus Tremonto
Mario Wagner
Marko Mäetamm
Mathilde Nivet
Matias Bechtold
Matthew Picton
Michael Najjar
Mieke Driessen
Mike Kelly
Mike Perry
Moga Mobo Studio
Mounir Fatmi
Nan Na Hvass
Nathan Coley
Nigel Peake
NotedCo.
Olafur Eliasson
Olof Bruce, Tom Eriksson & Liv Wadström
Oscar Lourens
Pablo Valbuena
Paul Eachus
Paul Hollingworth
Peach Beach
Peter Callesen
Pezo von Ellrichshausen
Philip Wiegard
Pipilotti Rist
Rachel Whiteread
Raumlabor Berlin
realities:united
Rhoads Clarke Design
Rob Voerman
Romain Laurent
Sandra Rauch
Serge Seidlitz
Simon Bent
Simon Boudvin
Slinkachu
Sotiria Kornaropoulou
Squint / Opera
Stephanie Backes
Stephen Willats
Studio Job
Sven Drühl
Theo Deutinger
Thomas Demand
Till Gerhard
Tim Dinter
Titus Matiyane
Tom Sachs
Tonk
Unfold
Vangelis Vlahos
Vasco Mourao
Veron Urdarianu
Wang Qingsong

HOME ALONE

The first chapter, Home Alone, looks at works of art that ironically and formalistically play with the elementary idea of the single house.

Softly coloured miniature soap buildings by Belgium artist Chatelijne Montens as well as jelly architectures of London's St. Paul's Cathedral by Bombas & Parr can be found here. Naoto Fukasawa of 21_21 Design Sight curates an entire exhibition on chocolate buildings and Brooklyn-based artist Jill K. Davis ornaments miniscule houses on silver rings. Austrian artist Erwin Wurm ironically melts down icons of modern architecture from Mies van der Rohe to Adolf Loos while the American artist couple Constantin and Laurence Boym create strangely familiar revenants of anti-symbols of contemporary culture such as Chernobyl's atomic reactor or 9/11's Twin Towers. Droog Design, Harry Sachs and Franz Höffner and Lindsey Lesh display inspiring overlappings of content as they all send anthropomorphic buildings on a playful stroll. The same kind of creative interference goes for the many works that take cathedral-and-fairy-tale-castle-like buildings as their object of inspiration: Whether it be Jonas Liverod's black-and-white drawings and Alekos Hofstetter's colourful paintings or David Herbert's plexiglass rendition of the famous Sleeping Beauty castle from Disneyland. An equally iconic discussion is presented by David Keating's *Seven Wonders* installation in which he combines the seven world wonders in one architectonic model and Hans Op de Beeck's series of sculptures that is inspired by architectural archetypes of modernity such as a residential complex, a sports arena and an observatory. Yet at closer look the sculptures of the latter show silent signs of decay and deterioration. These subversive notes of social criticisms are also tangible in Atelier van Lieshout's Female and Male Slave University models which represent elegant and efficiently designed education centres within a fictional slave city and contemporary labour camp. All of the above are, however, only snapshots of the myriad of artistic variations on somewhat detached dwellings and separate, free-standing buildings that appear in this chapter.

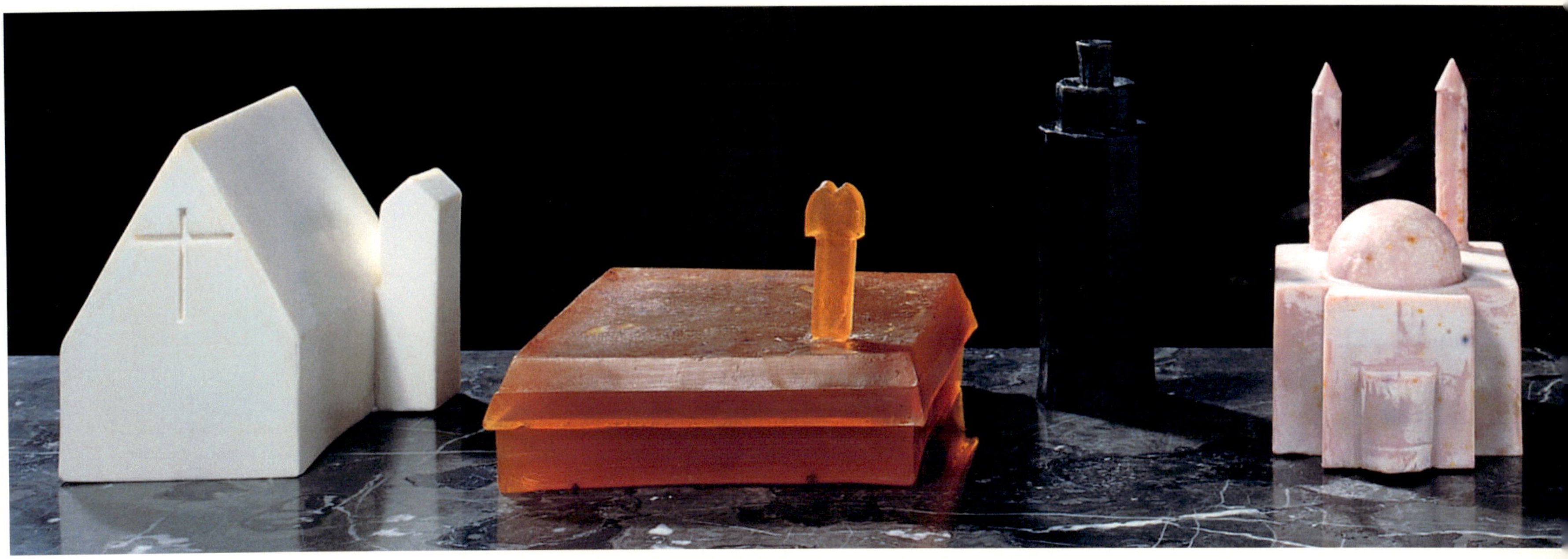

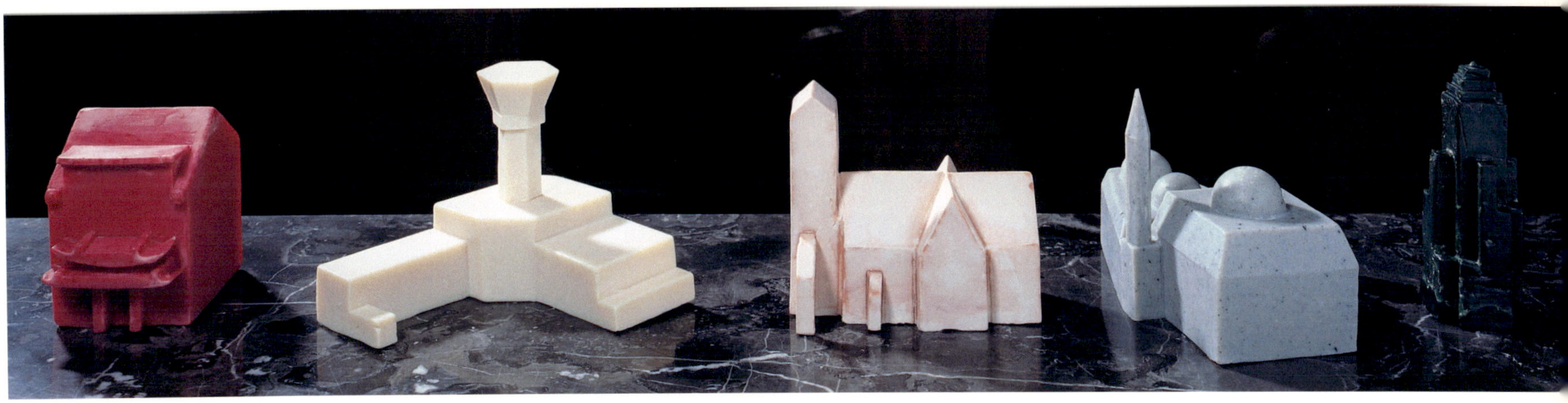

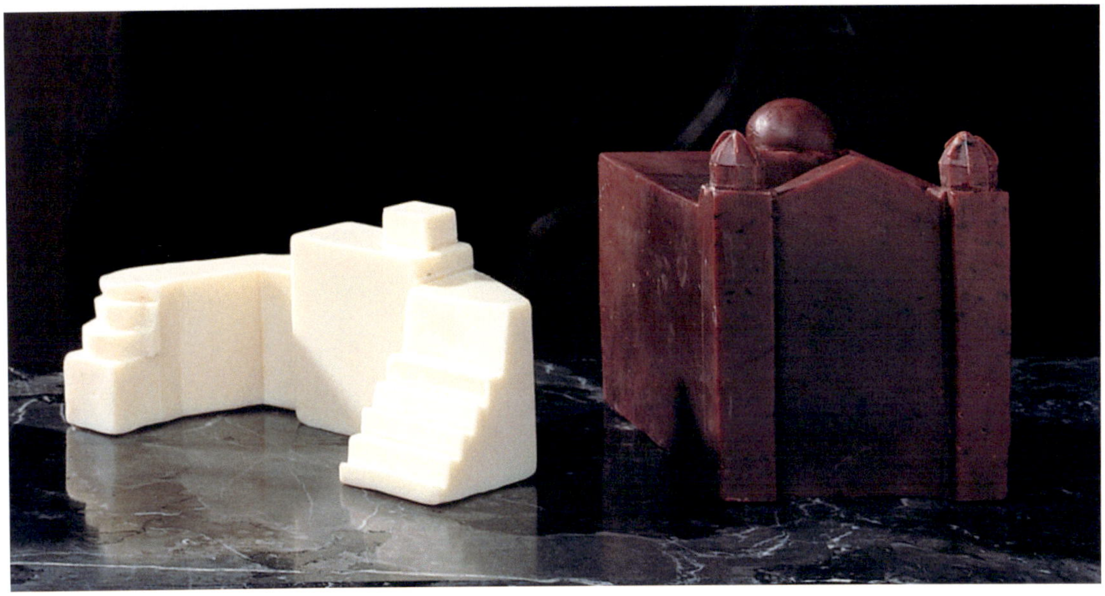

Cathelijne Montens

A COLLECTION OF SOAP BUILDINGS

Miniature mouldings of religious and commercial buildings form a contemporary variation on the seventeenth-century tradition of knick-knack collections. These collections are attempts to gather the main curiosities of the world in such a way that they fit nicely into one cabinet.

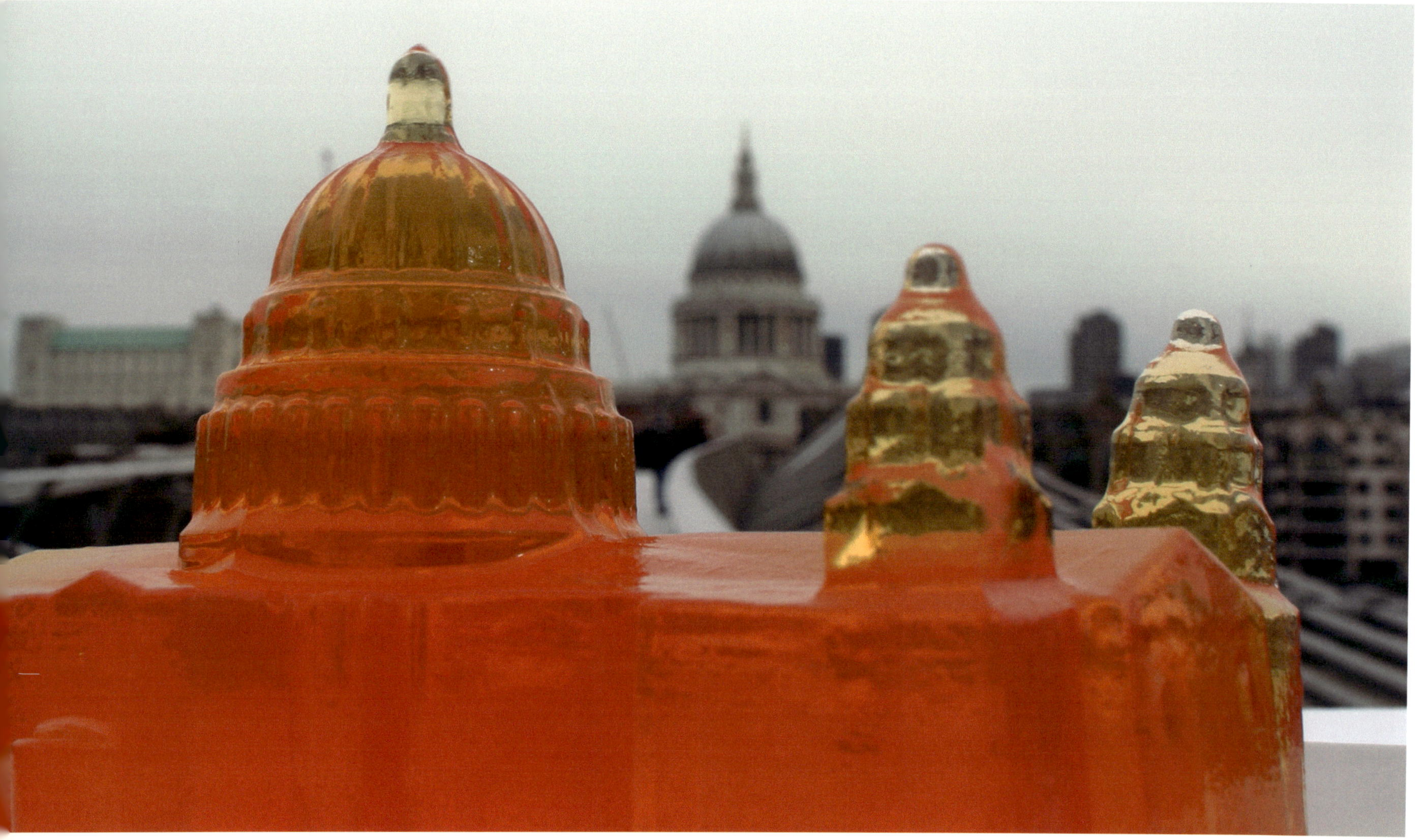

Bompas & Parr

JELLYMONGERS

London-based Bompas & Parr creates English jellies, designs bespoke jelly moulds and curates culinary events. Bompas & Parr's work operates in the space between food and architecture. As part of the London Festival of Architecture 2008, Bompas & Parr invited architects to design a jelly. The jellies were later displayed at the Architectural Jelly Banquet and the moulds auctioned to raise money for building aid charities.

Copper St. Paul's Jelly Mould *(top)*
Barajas Jelly Airport, 2008 *(right)* – Rogers Stirk Harbour + Partners designed a jelly version of their Barajas Airport for the architectural jelly design competition.

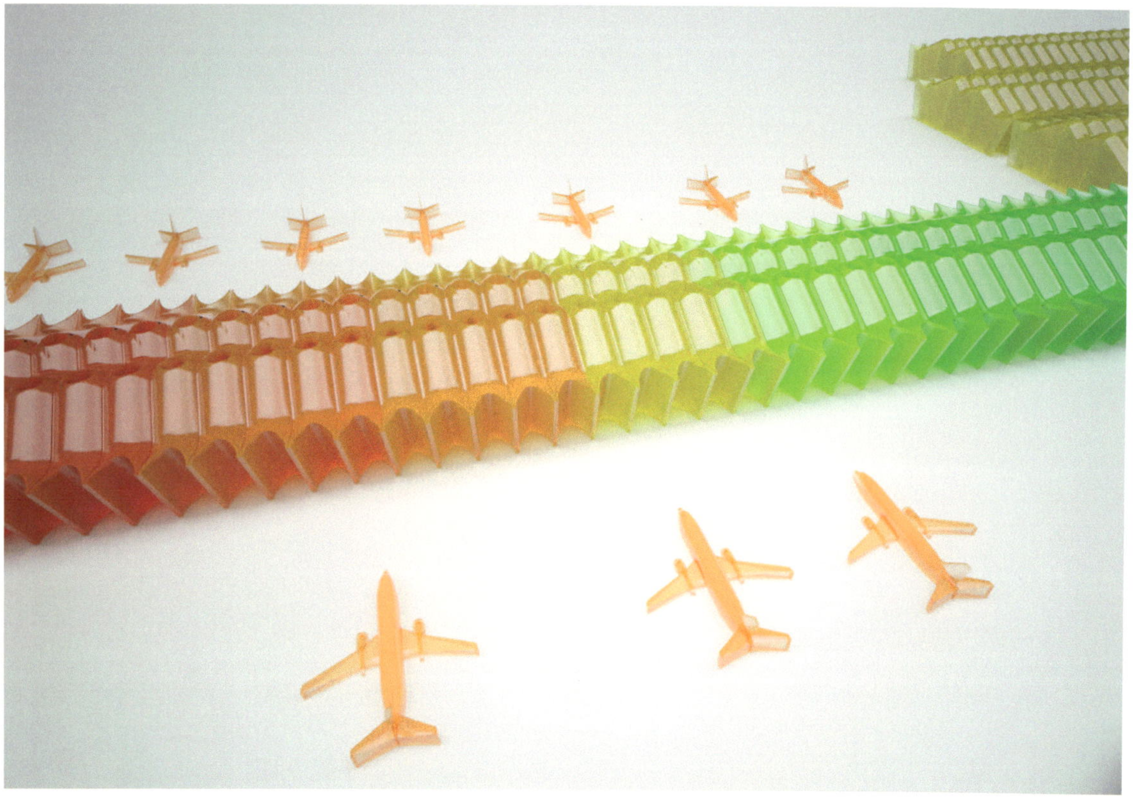

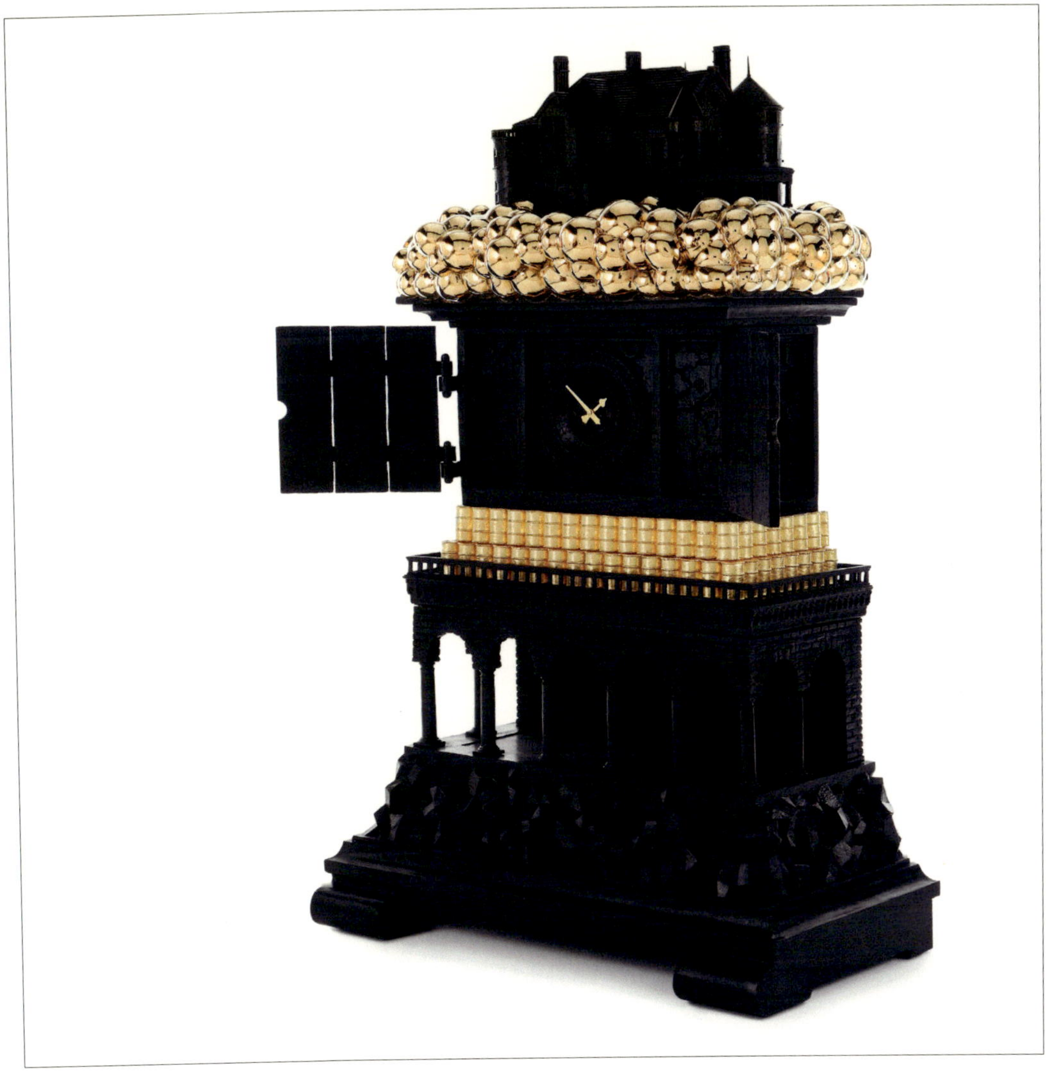

Studio Job JOB SMEETS + NYNKE TYNAGEL

ROBBER BARRON

These three monumental pieces from a series of fire by Studio Job, cast in bronze, combine stylised elements from famous landmarks around the world and represent industrial power, wealth and corruption. They are part of a suite of five cast-bronze furnishings, each to be offered in a limited edition, exclusive to Moss. Their mirror finish is intended to reflect the excesses of America's 19th century tycoons and Russia's new oligarchs. With clouds of pollution belching from towering smoke stacks, and missiles, hawks, gas masks, warplanes, and wrenches adorning golden surfaces, Robber Baron celebrates and shames both art and industry.

Robber Barron Clock *(left)*
Robber Barron Table *(bottom)*

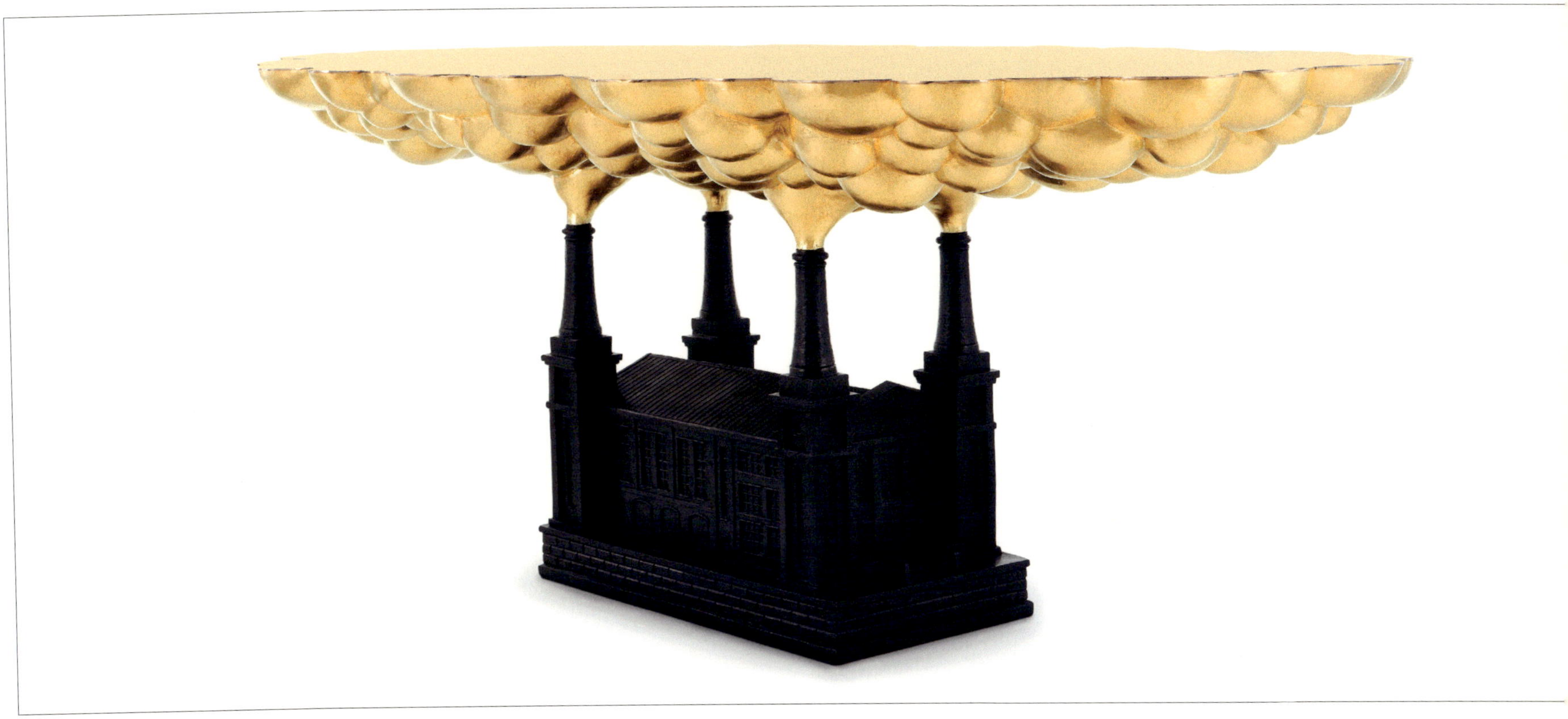

Studio Job JOB SMEETS + NYNKE TYNAGEL

Robber Barron Lamp

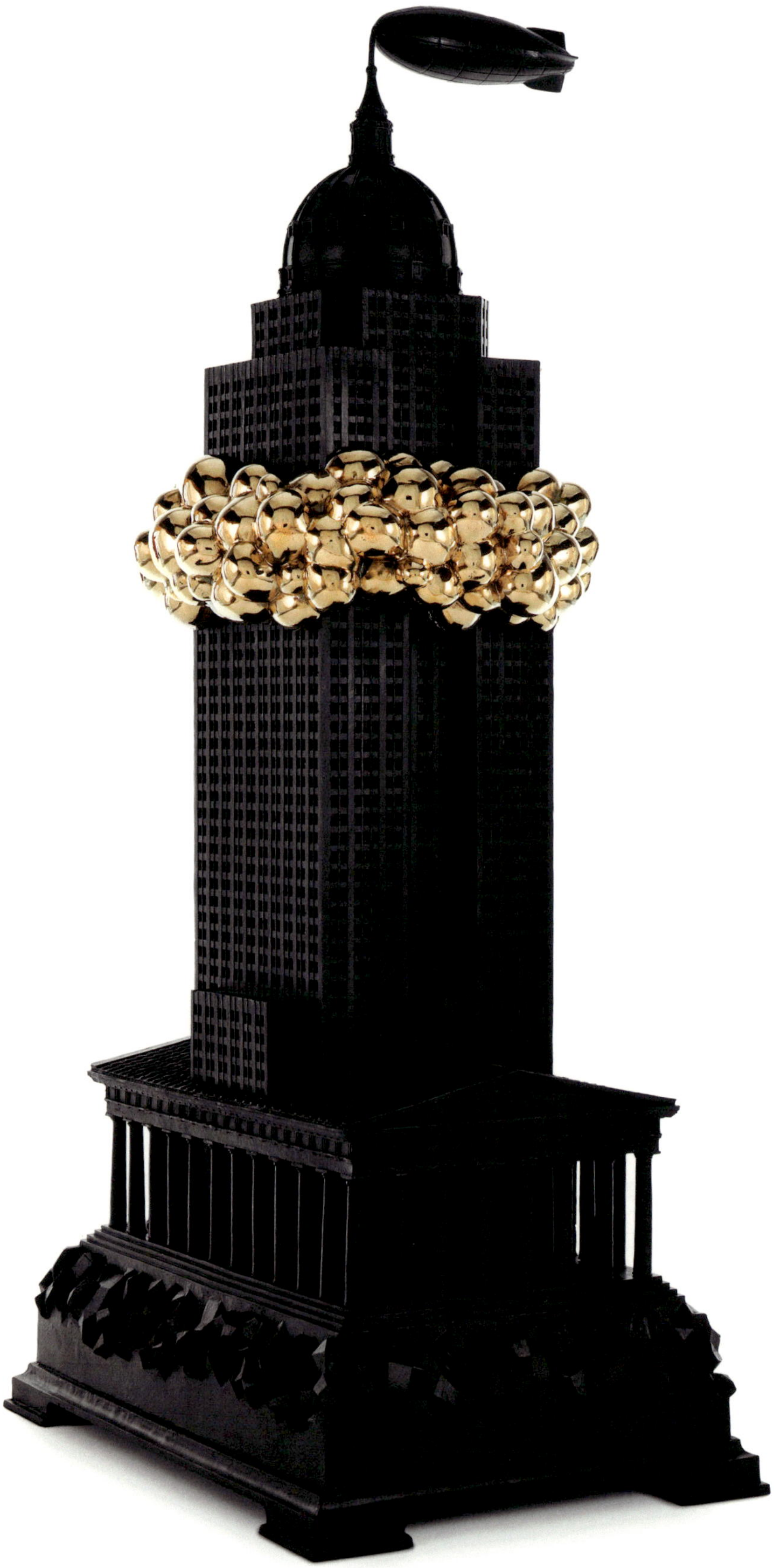

Constantin and Laurence Boym

BUILDINGS OF DISASTER

Twin Towers, September 11, 2001

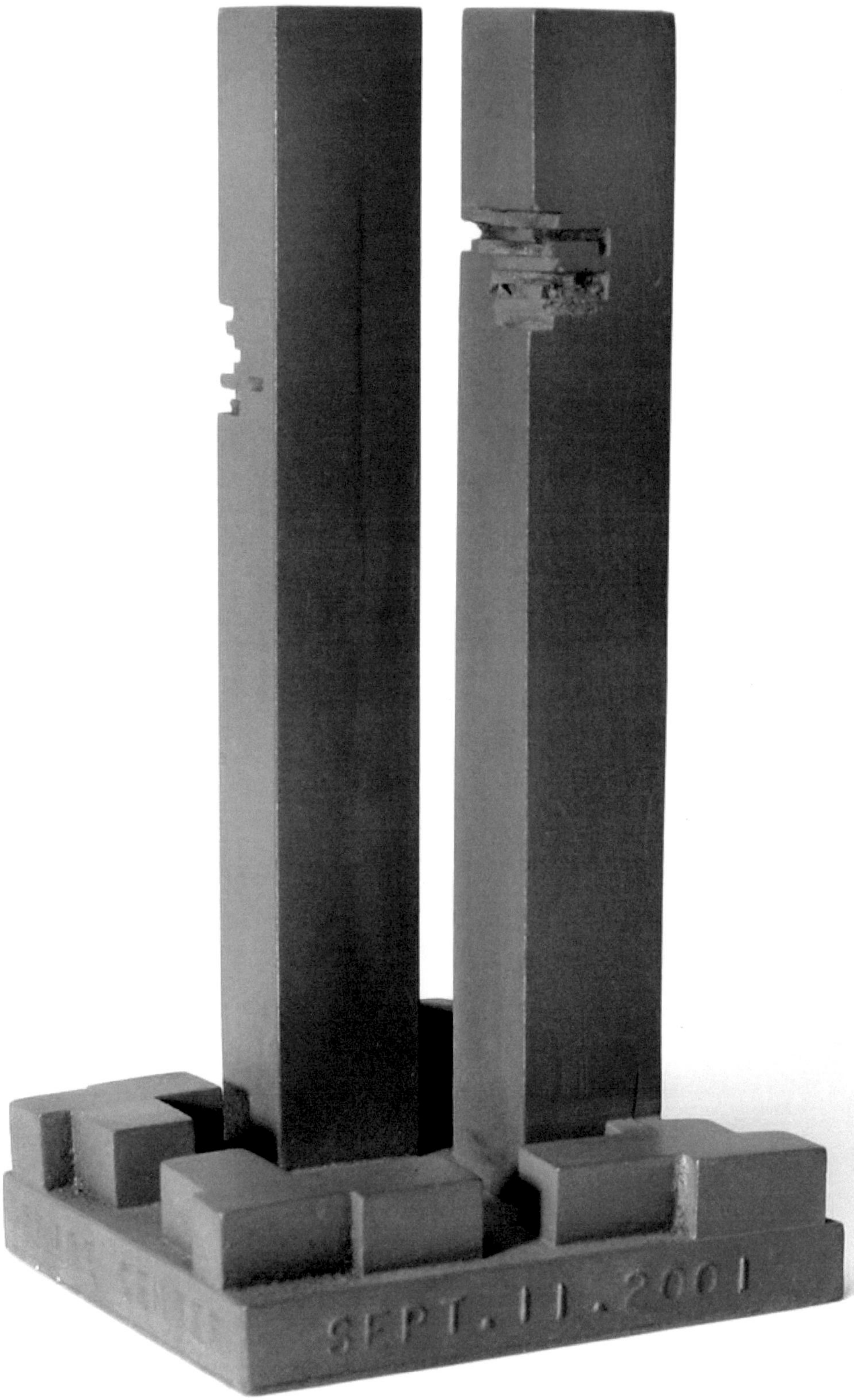

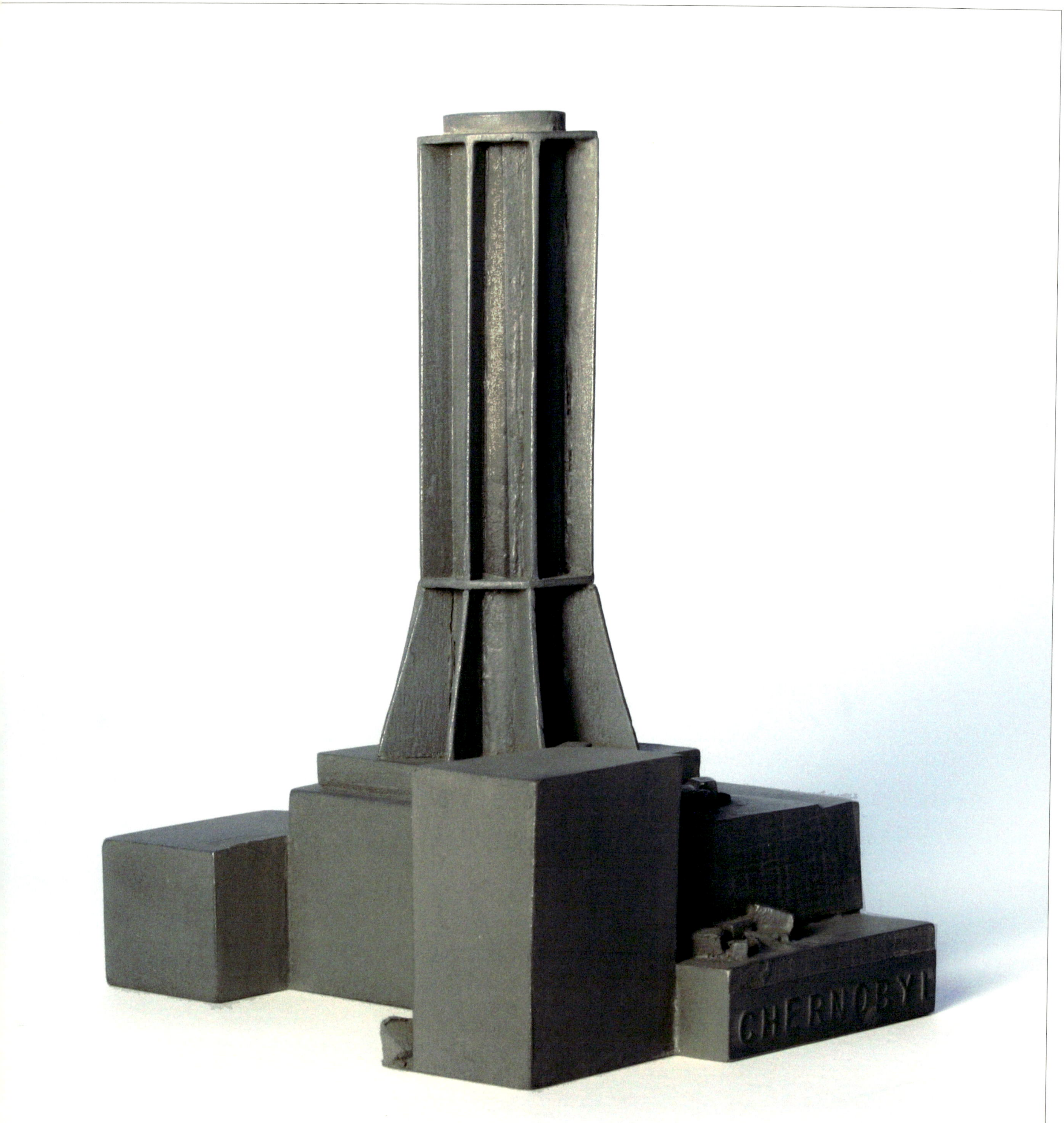
CHERNOBYL

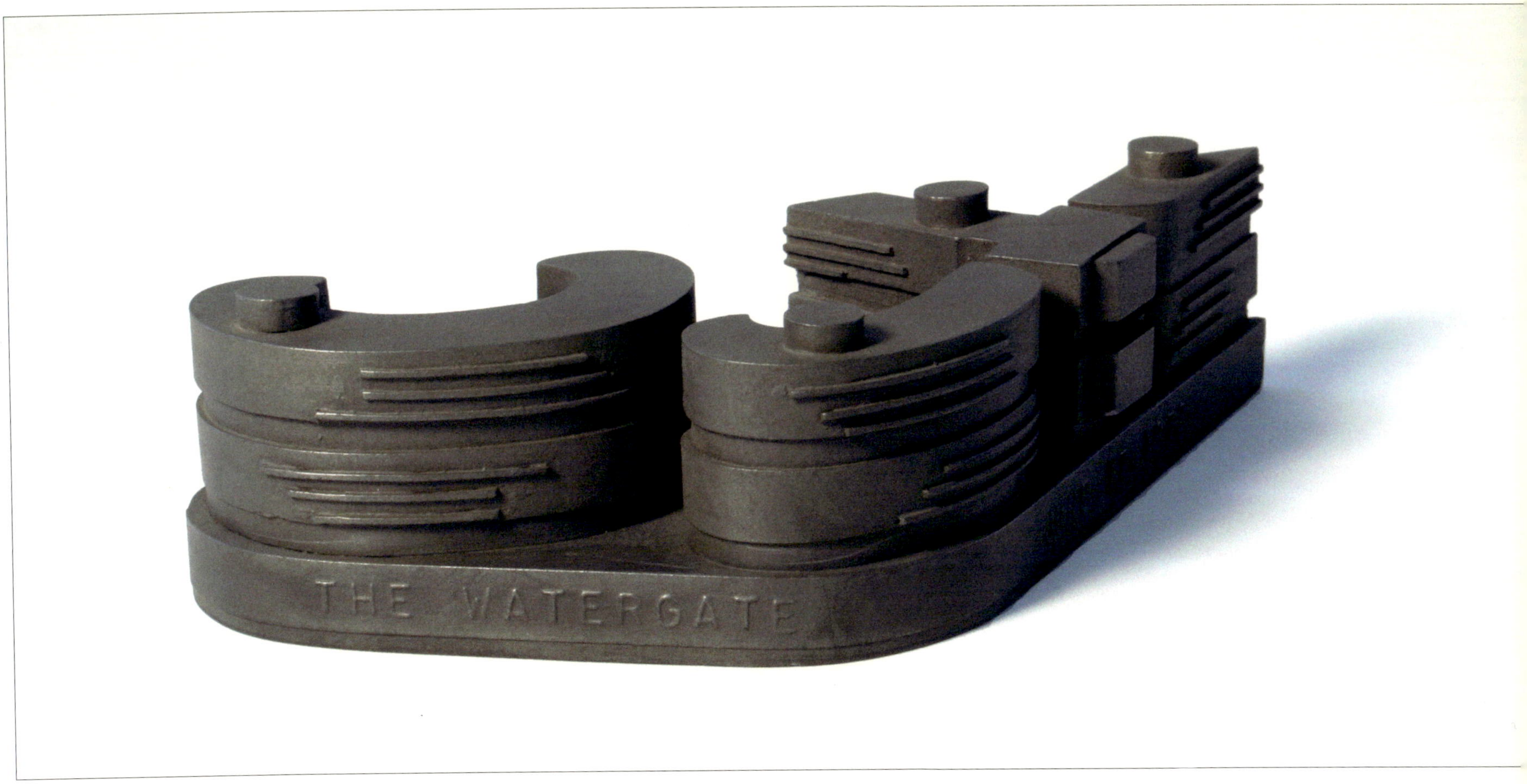

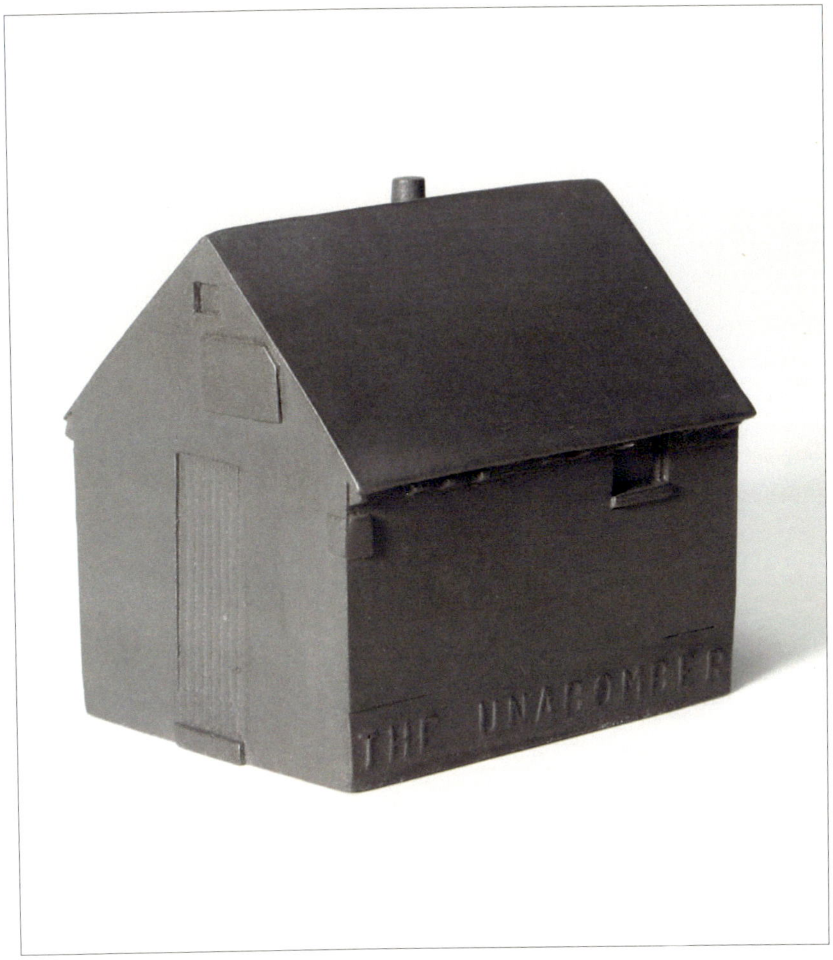

Constantin and Laurence Boym

BUILDINGS OF DISASTER

Buildings of Disaster are miniature replicas of famous structures where tragic or terrible events happened to take place. These small monuments create a different populist history of architecture, based on emotional involvement rather than on scholarly appreciation.

Chernobyl, April 26, 1986 *(left page)*
The Watergate, June 17, 1972 *(top)*
Unabomber's Cabin, April 3, 1996 *(left)*
Neverland Ranch, 1993–2005 *(bottom)*

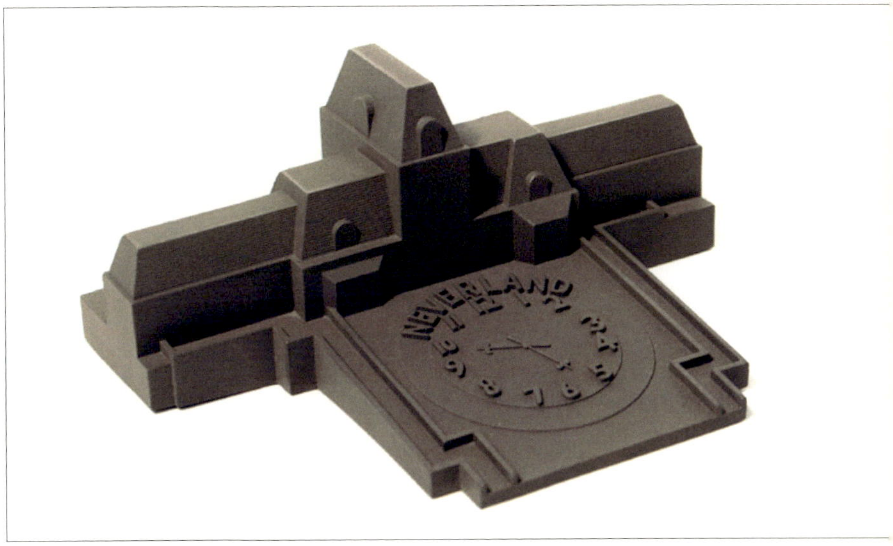

Erwin Wurm

KUHFLADE (COWPAT)

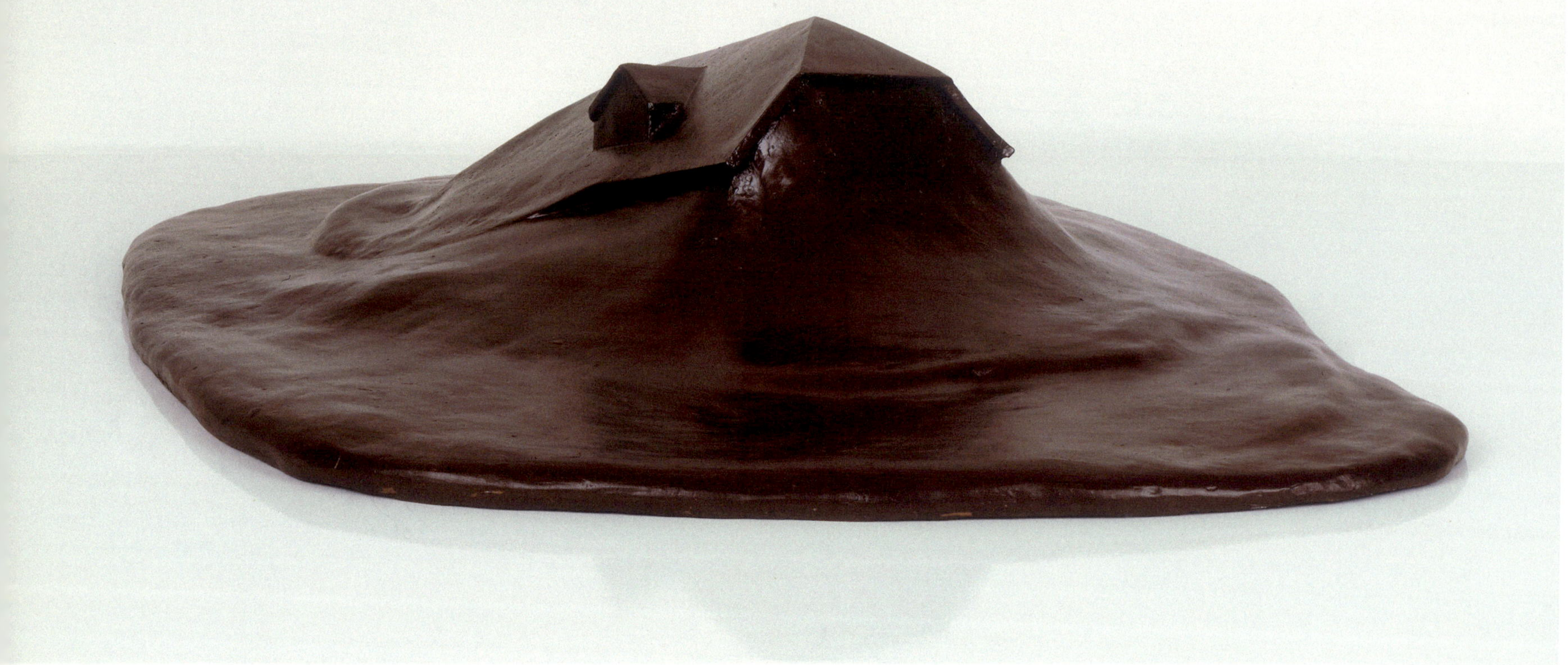

21_21 Design Sight MAKOTO HASHIKURA

CHOCOLATE WITH FLASH

21_21 Design Sight YASUHIRO SUZUKI

CHOCOLATE GINKAKU-JI

For the Chocolate exhibition curated by Naoto Fukasawa at 21_21 Design Sight/The Miyake Issey Foundation in Tokyo, artists have been invited to create buildings made from chocolate.

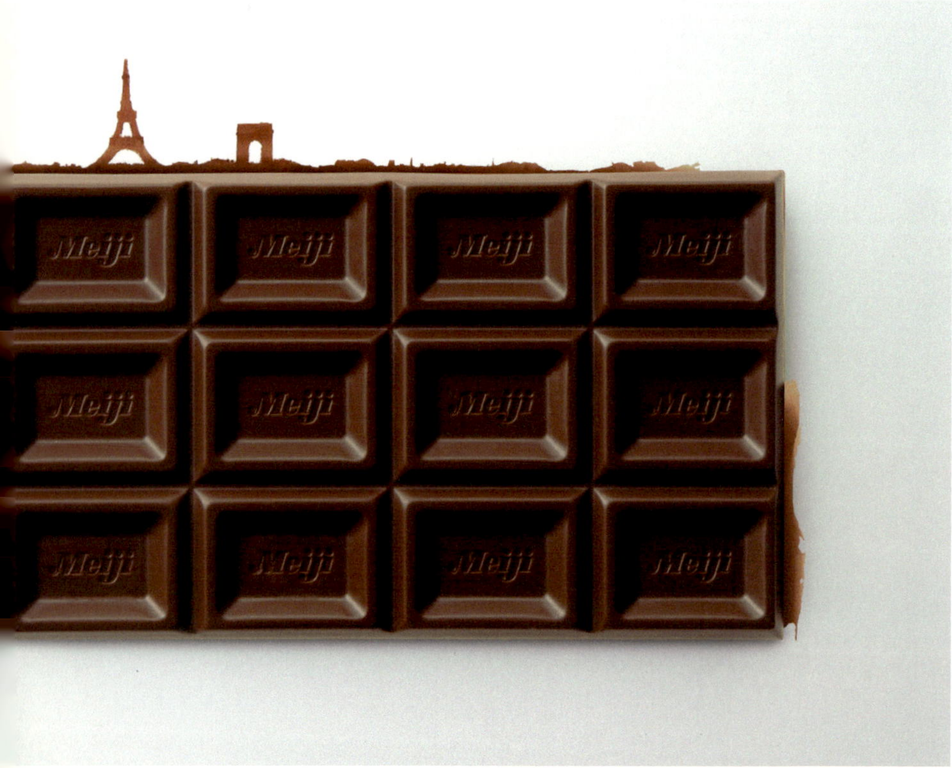

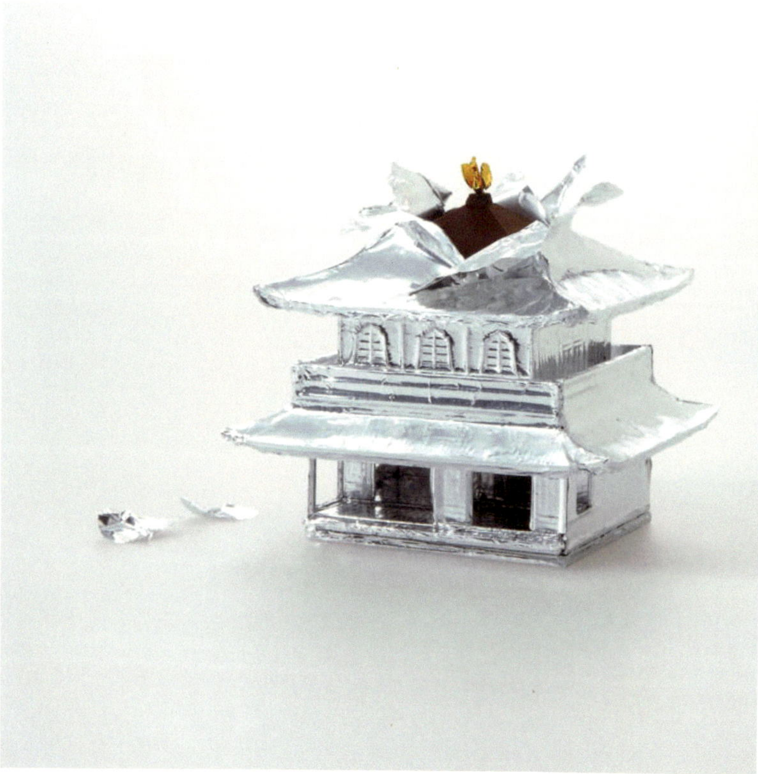

Erwin Wurm

MIES VAN DER ROHE – MELTING

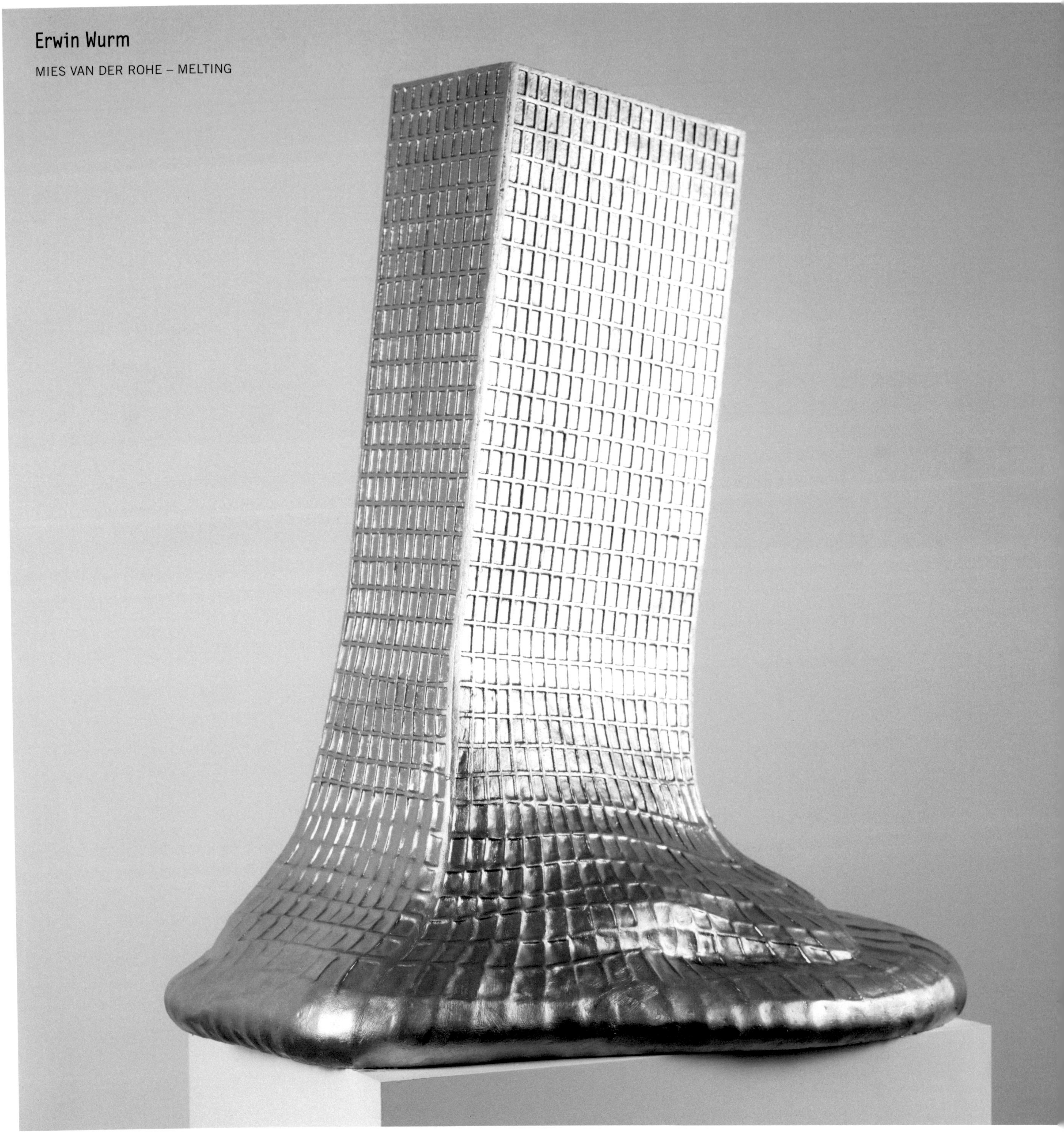

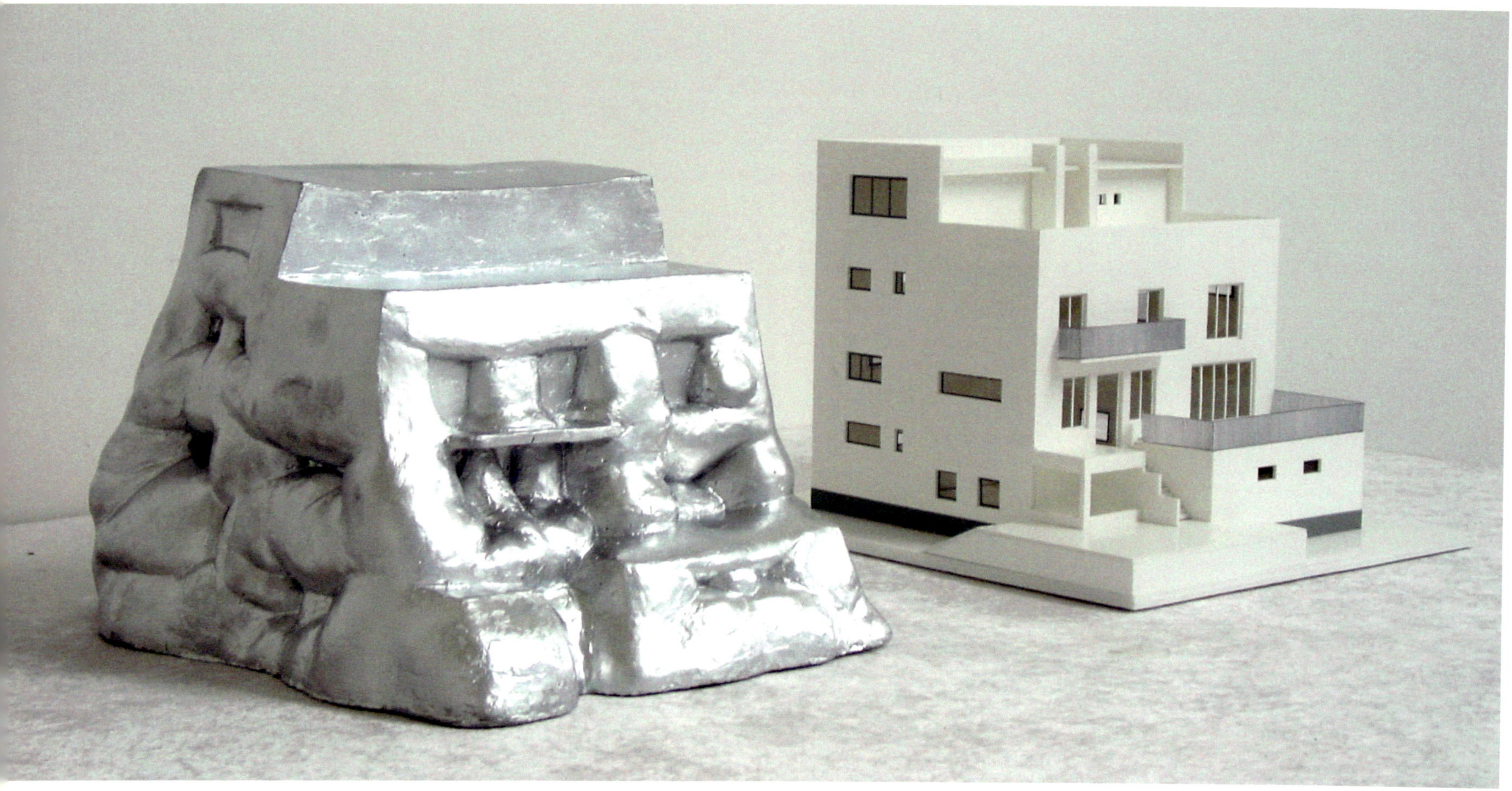

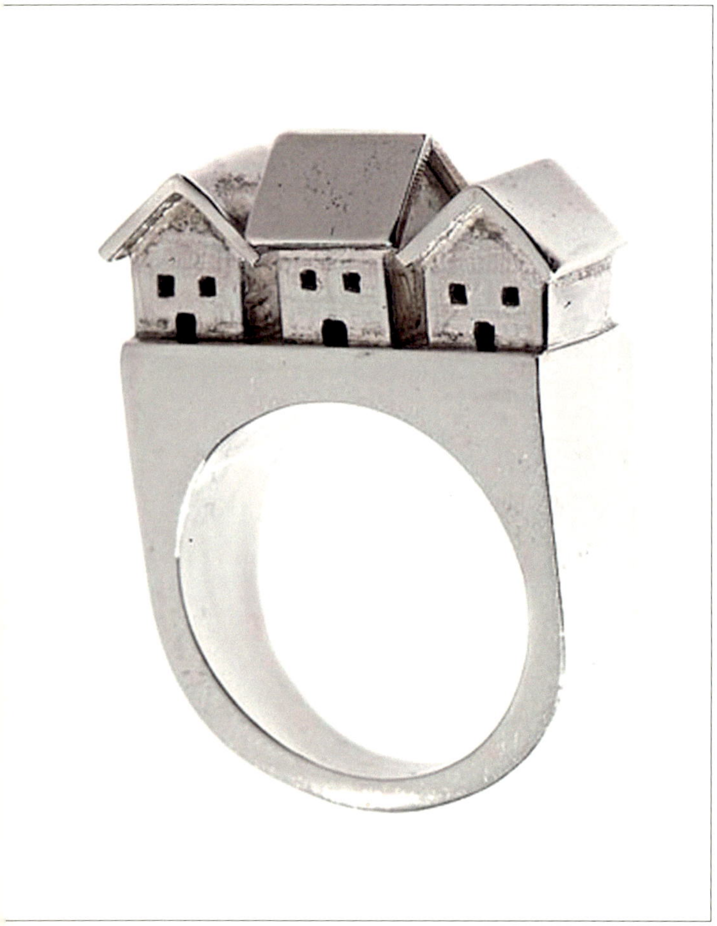

Erwin Wurm

FAT HOUSE MOLLER / ADOLF LOOS

J. Davis Studio

TINY HOUSE RING *(bottom)*
NEIGHBORHOOD RING *(left)*

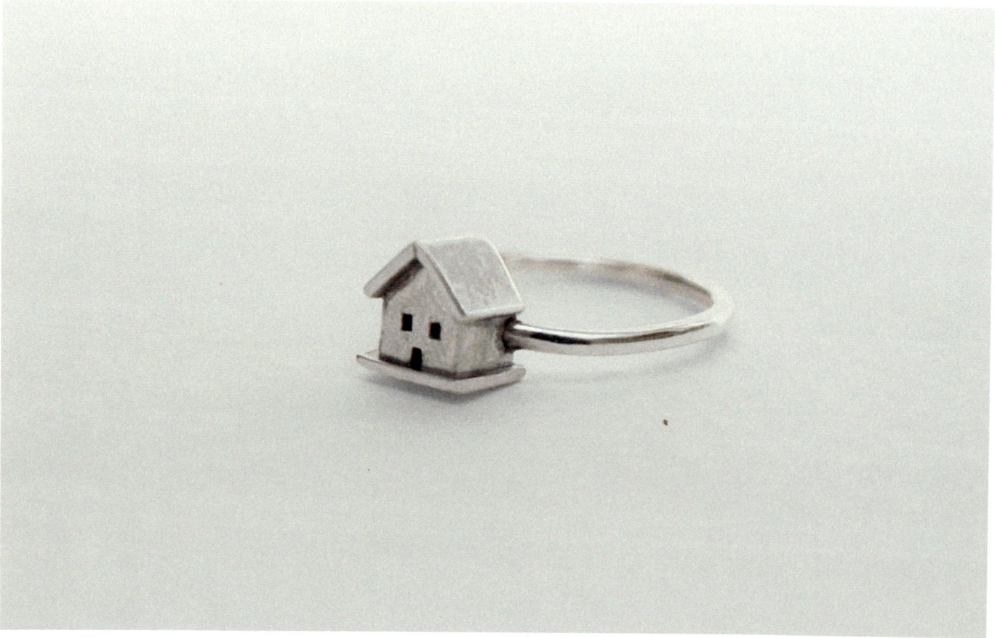

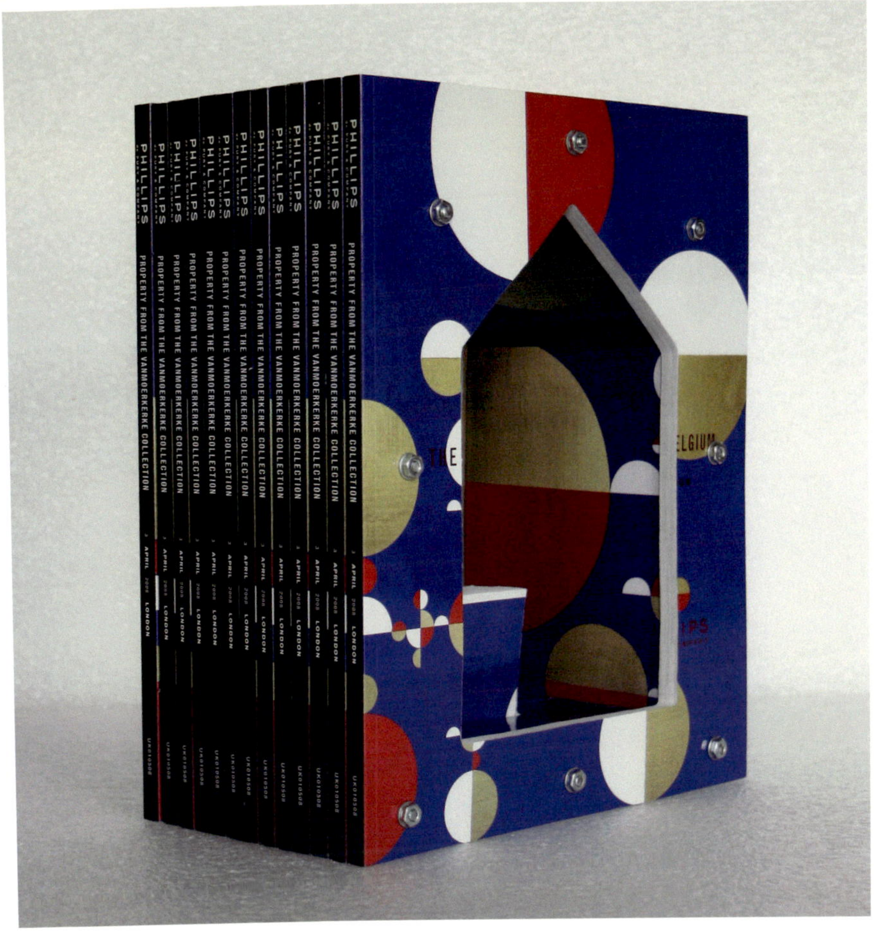

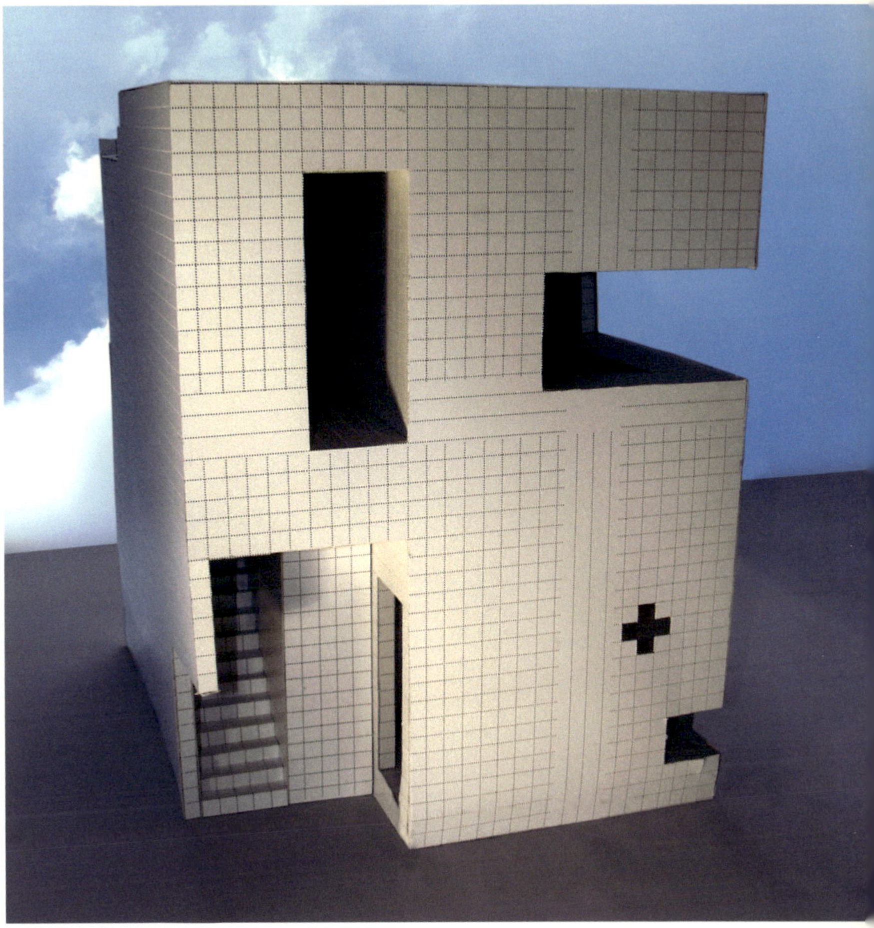

Marcus Tremonto

CAT HOUSE

Cat house, referring to catalogues, is Marcus Tremonto's response to the brief of designing a habitat for birds/bats/bees using waste material from Phillips de Pury & Company. Tremonto's bird house design is created by hand cutting old catalogues from the auction house that would otherwise be thrown away or just left in boxes.

Unfold DRIES VERBRUGGEN

XS,M,XL *(top right, bottom)*

XS, M, XL is a study in the twilight zone between interior and architecture; a volume, comparable to the block of stone with which a sculptor begins and that ends up as his work of art. The occupant digs out his own living environment, just as a mole digs its nest from a mass of dirt.

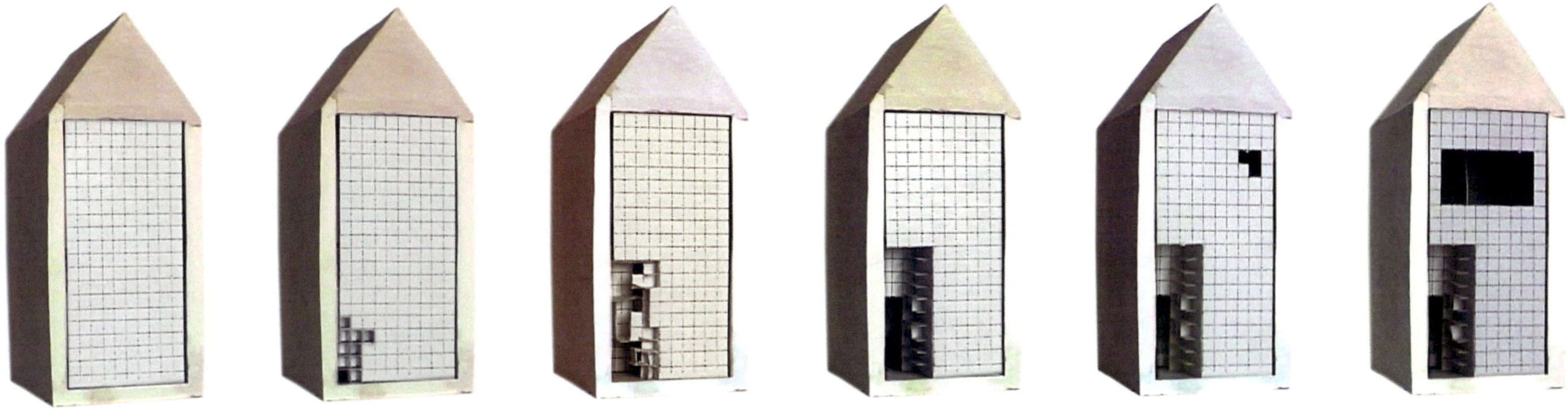

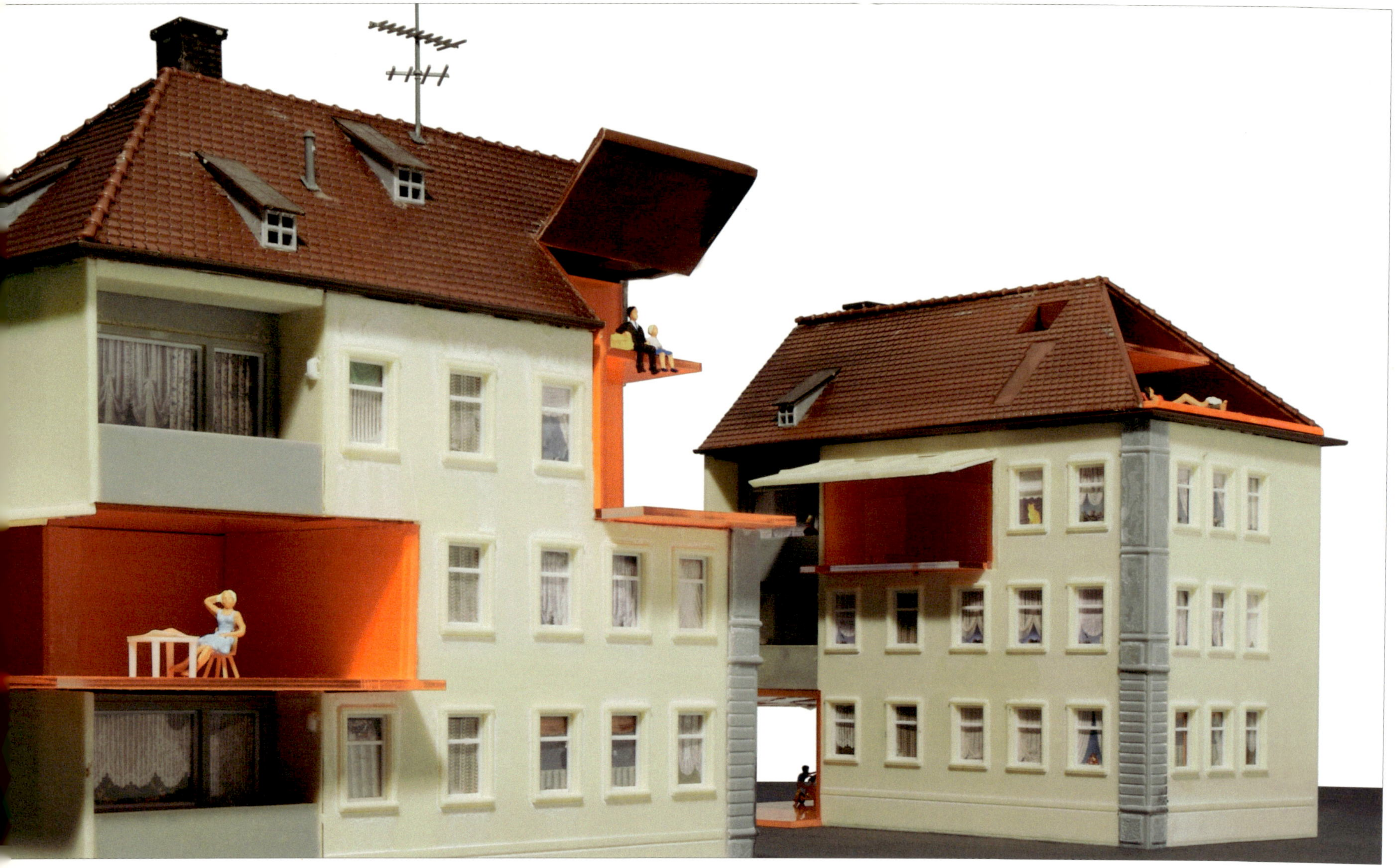

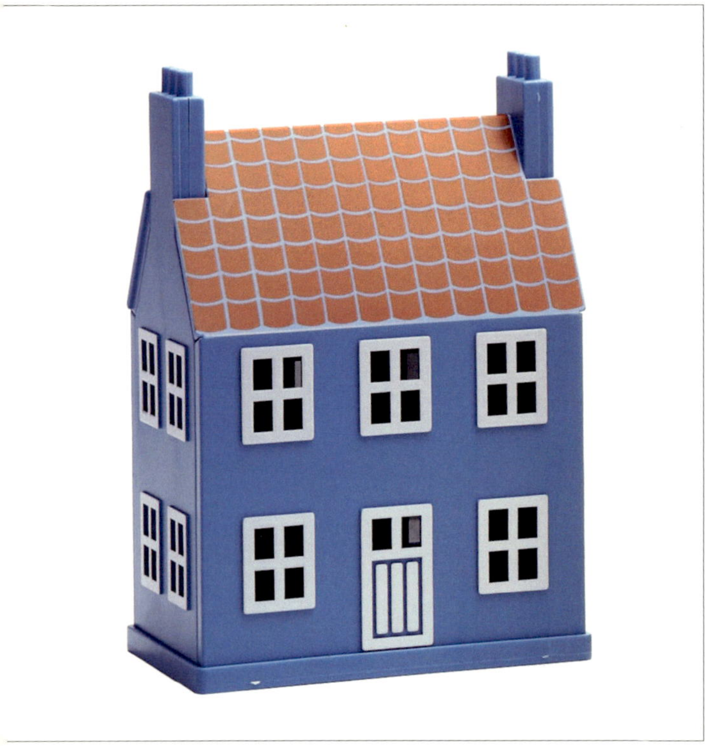

realities:united

OPEN THE HOUSE *(top)*

Open the House is an alternative concept to living in closed spaces. The house is finally freed from its task of creating an artificial climatic zone, thus liberating the inhabitants from their isolation. Envisioning clothing that regulates body temperature in almost any climate, this project by Berlin-based realities:united frees architecture from the tyranny of enclosed, air-conditioned spaces to create more open, economical structures that are integrated with their surroundings.

NotedCo. DOUG WOLSKE

DOMUS BUILT-IT COIN BANK *(left)*

Danish designed and made, this coin bank made of plastic was created by Paul Willumsen and is inspired by a variety of traditional European architecture, resulting in a cross between farmhouse and townhouse.

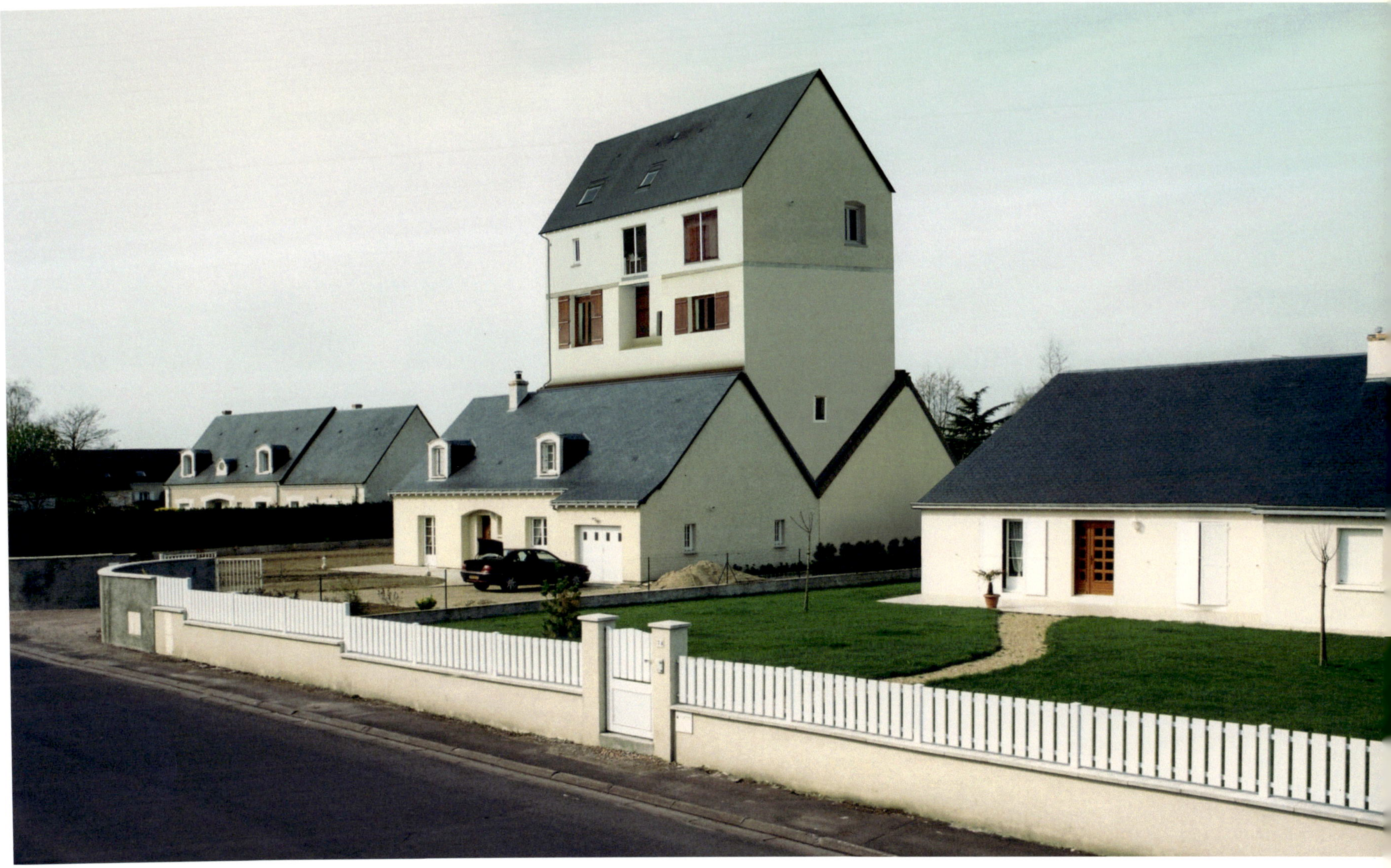

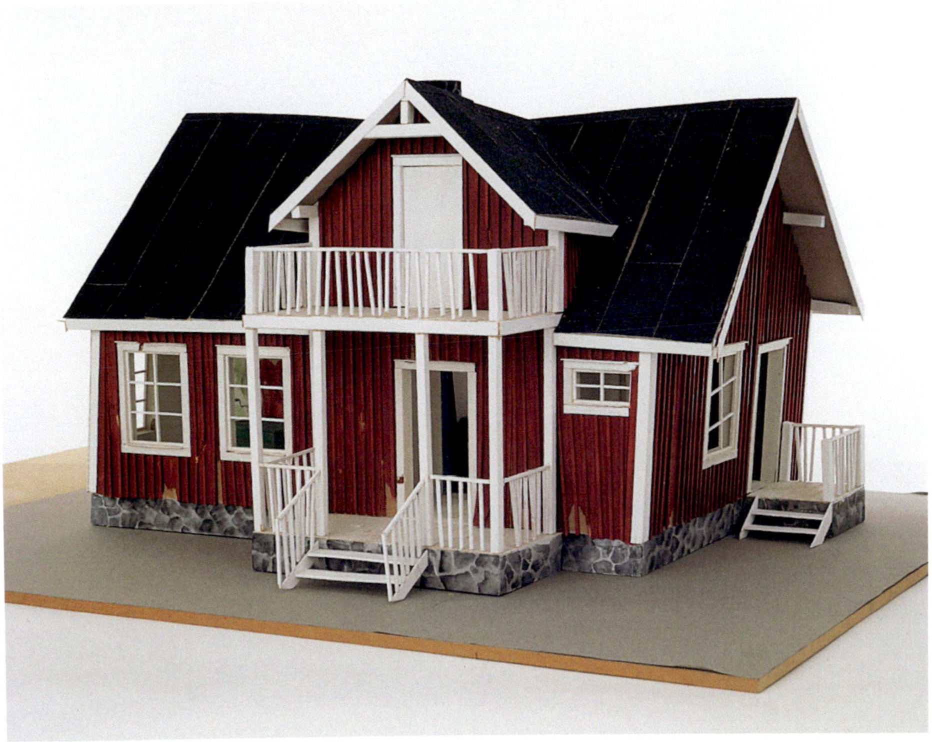

Simon Boudvin

SEMI-COLLECTIF *(top)*

In his photomontage works French artist Boudvin ironically converts architectural readymades.

Faculty of Architecture / University of Technology Munich ANNIKA SOPHIE DREYER

DIE VILLA KUNTERBUNT *(left)*

This model house of Astrid Lindgren's famous child heroine Pippi Longstocking arose as part of a seminar at the Faculty of Architecture of the University of Technology, Munich. The students were asked to replicate a building or architecture from a piece of literature of their choice. Some of the resulting works were presented in an exhibtion and accompanying publication entitled *Architektur wie sie im Buche steht* (a textbook example of architecture) edited by Winfried Nerdinger.

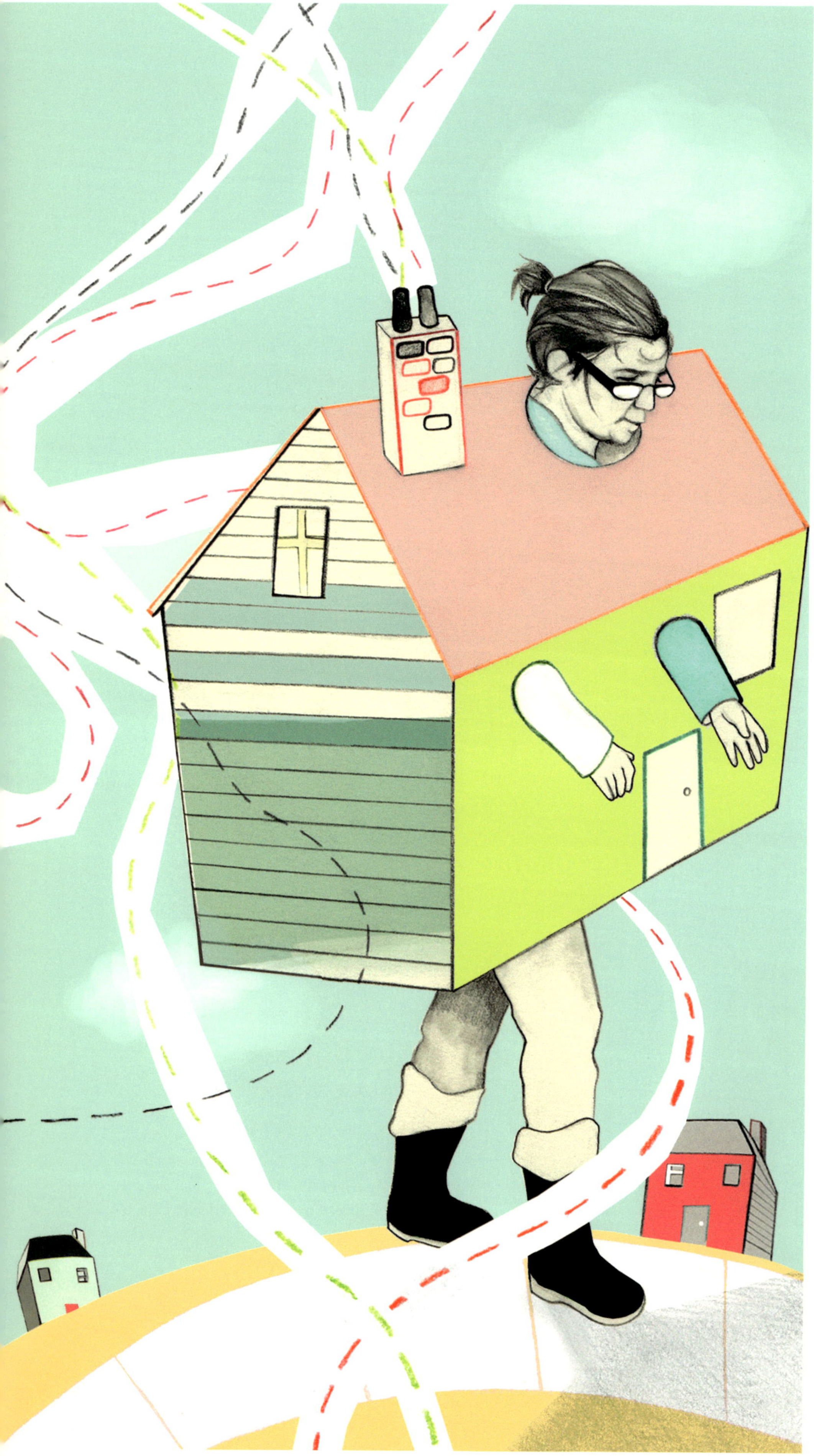

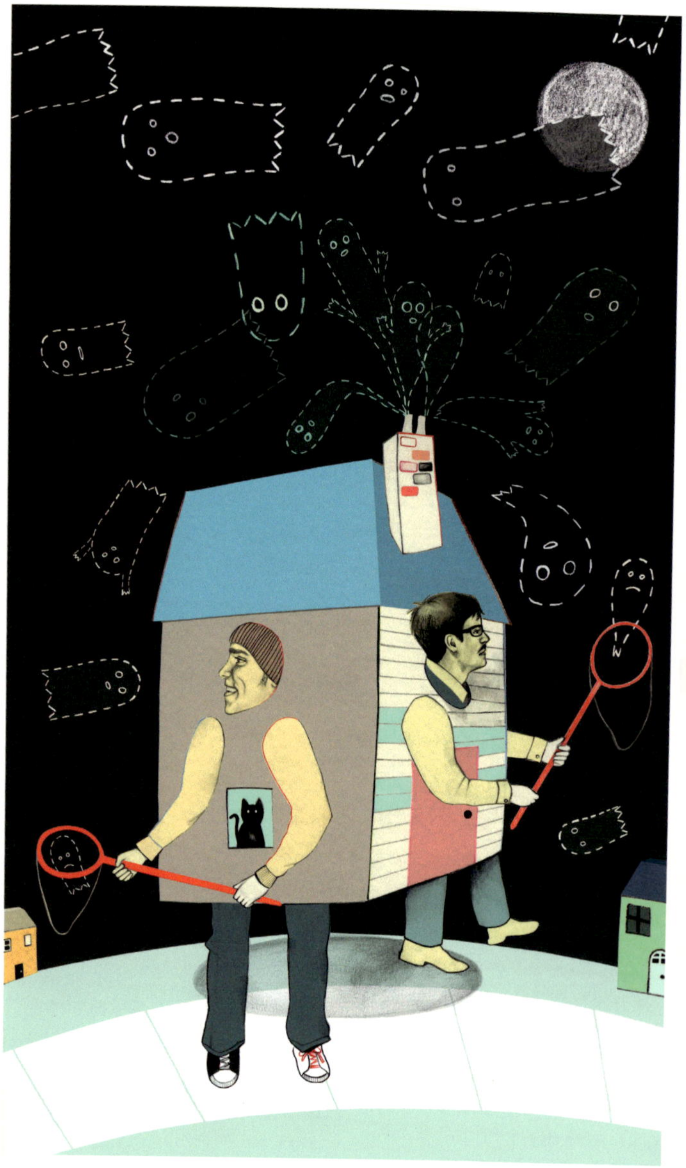

Lyndsey Lesh

GONE FOR A STROLL SERIES (2 OF 3):

We Have a Ghost Problem *(top)*
Restless *(left)*

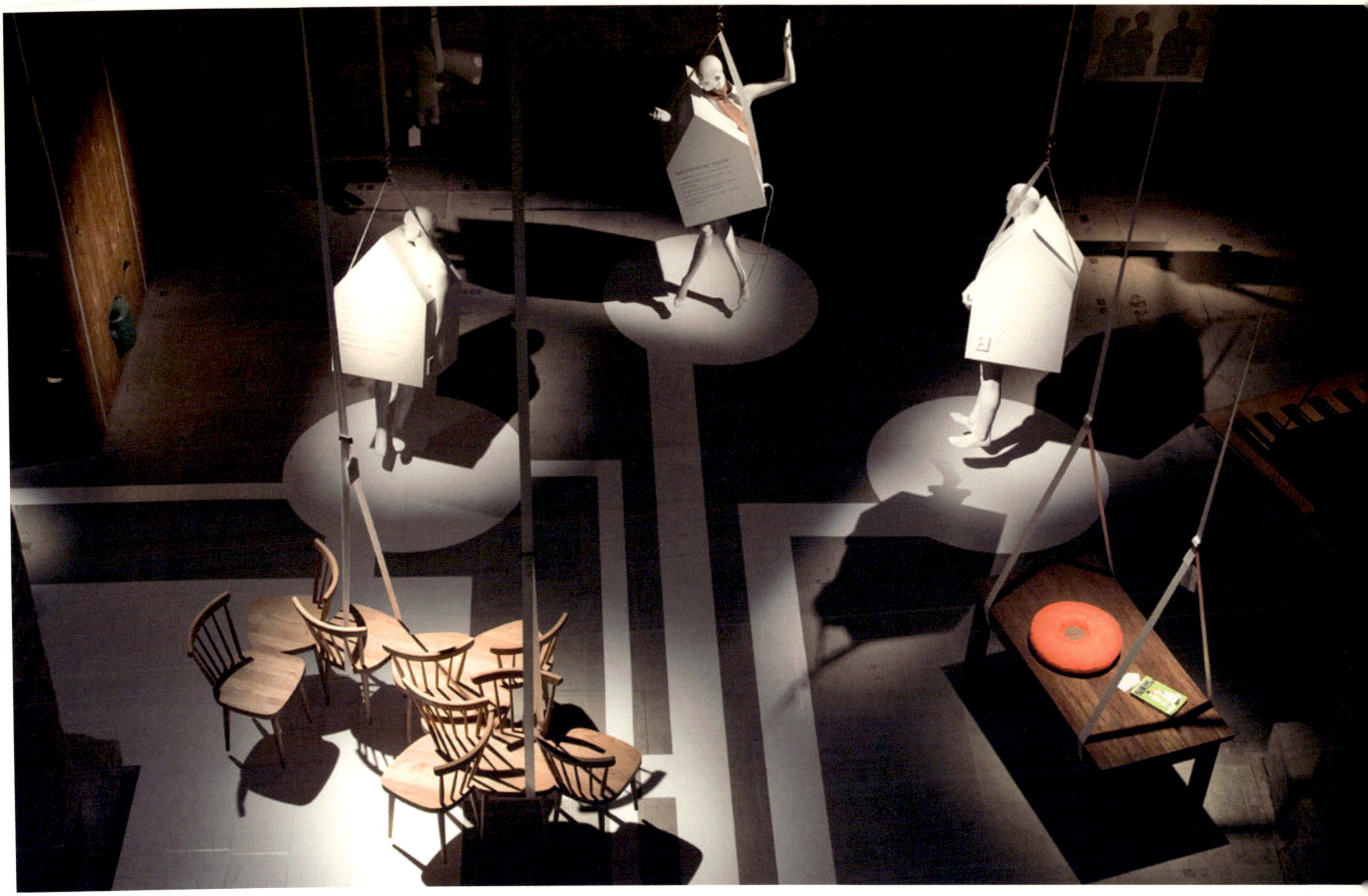

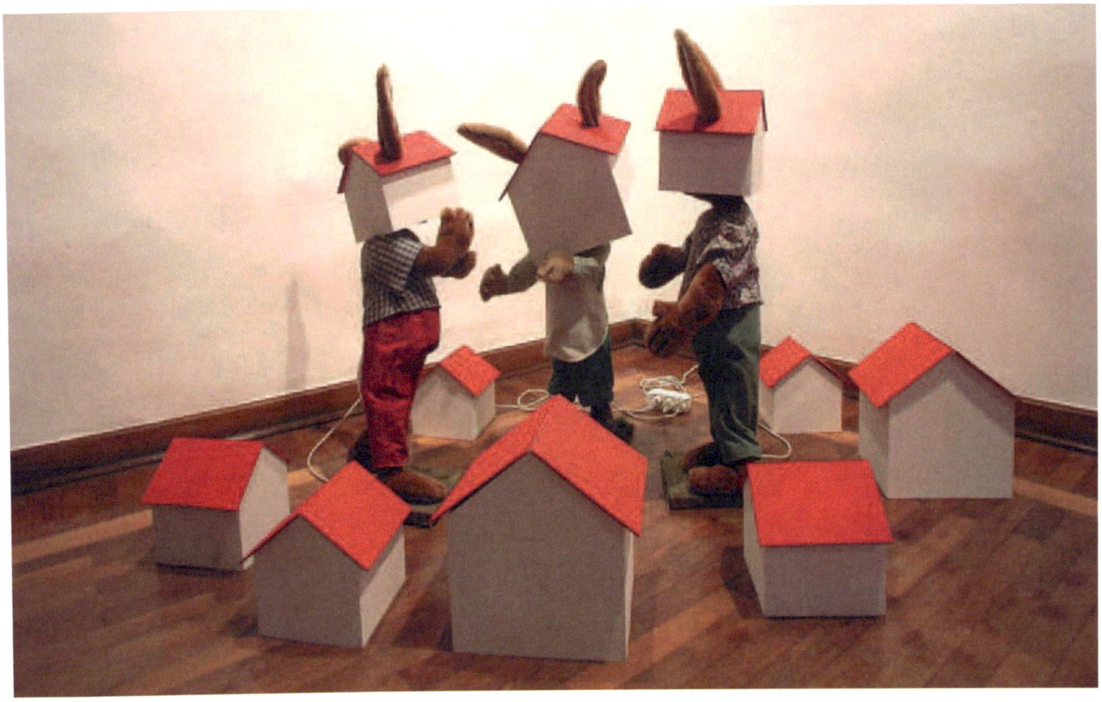

Droog Design WITH KESSELSKRAMER

S1NGLETOWN *(top)*

This project focuses on the world of contemporary singles and is based on the prediction that a third of people in developed countries will be living alone by 2026. S1NGLETOWN is an exhibition that's also a town, an abstract interpretation of a new kind of urban space. Visitors can walk its streets and interact with its products and citizens, and view their homes.

Franz Höfner & Harry Sachs

HAUSEN *(left)*

For this installation at the Kunstverein Göttingen, the German artist duo created a city model with moving bunnies.

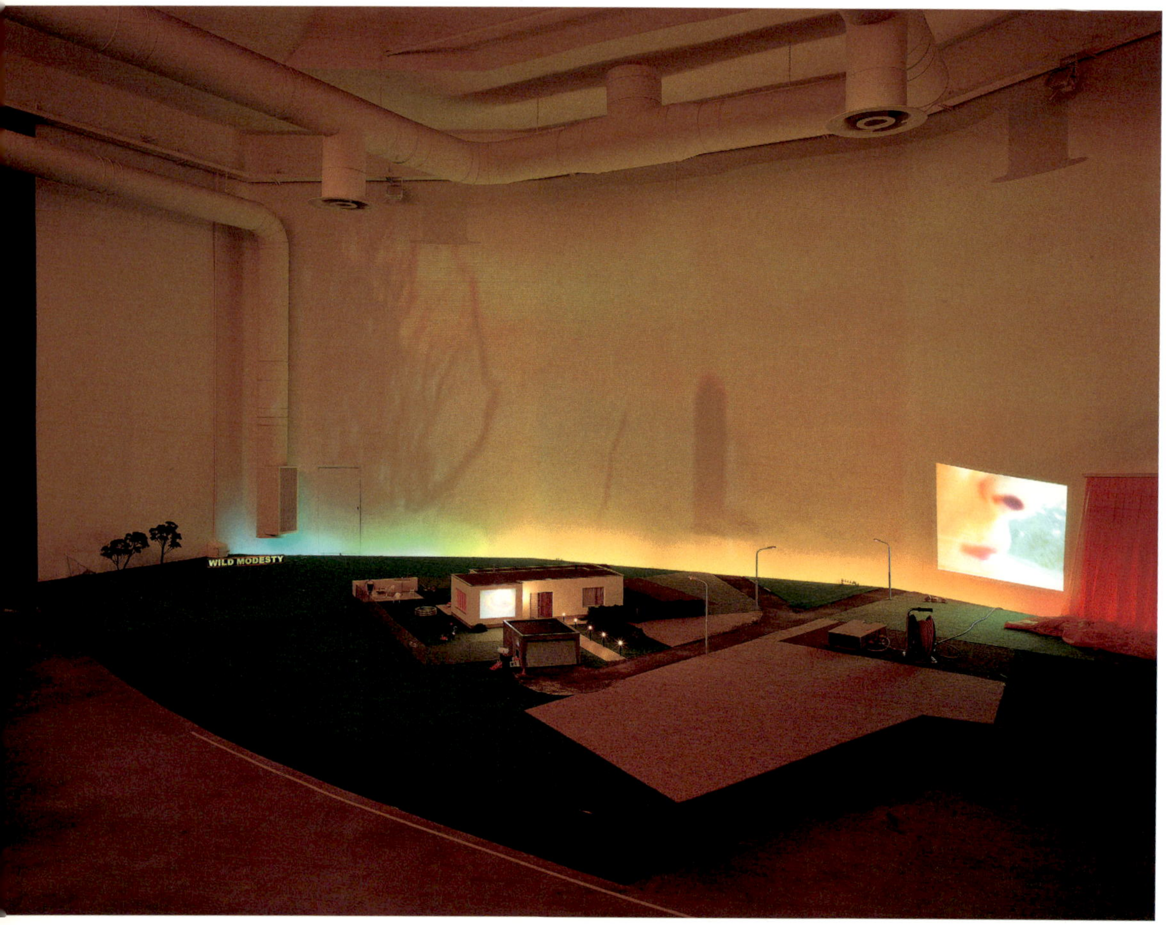

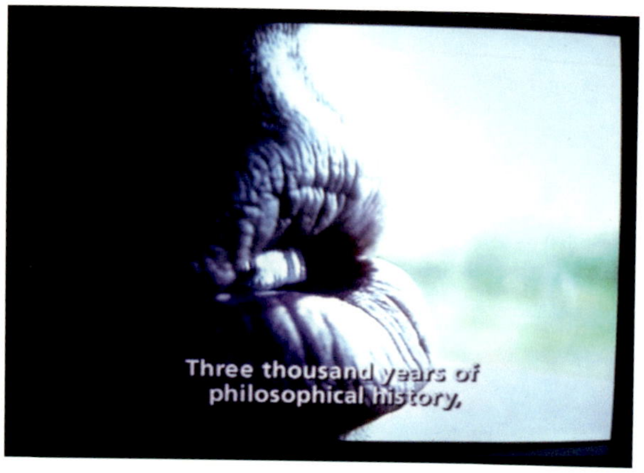

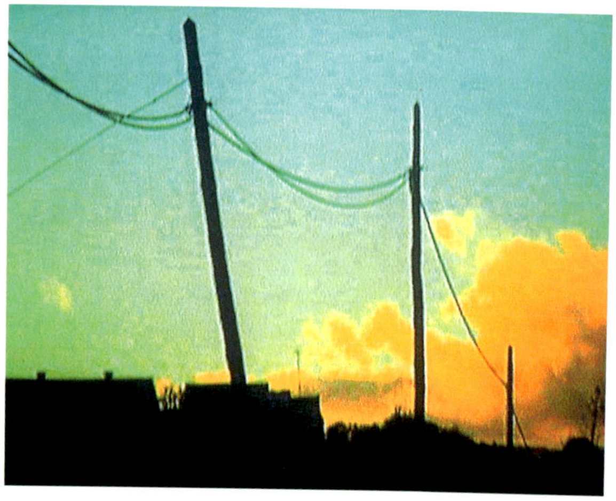

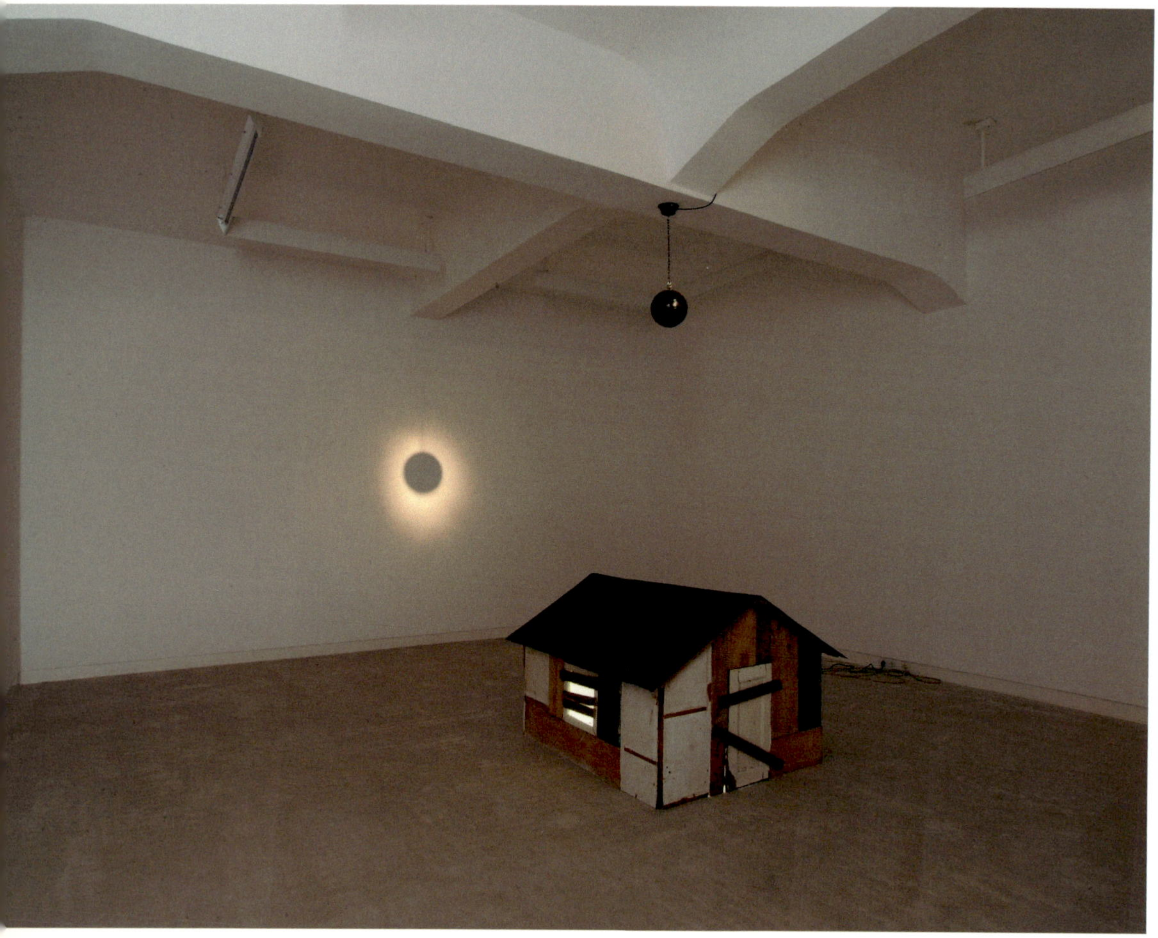

Pipilotti Rist

SUBURB BRAIN *(top)*

This audio video installation by Swiss artist Pipilotti Rist was presented at the 48th Venice Biennial in Italy and depicts a miniaturised model of a suburban residential area situated near the highway, containing various objects and lettering that state "wild modesty".

Till Gerhard

FAITH, HOPE AND CHARITY *(left)*
Orakelstätte (Oracelsite)

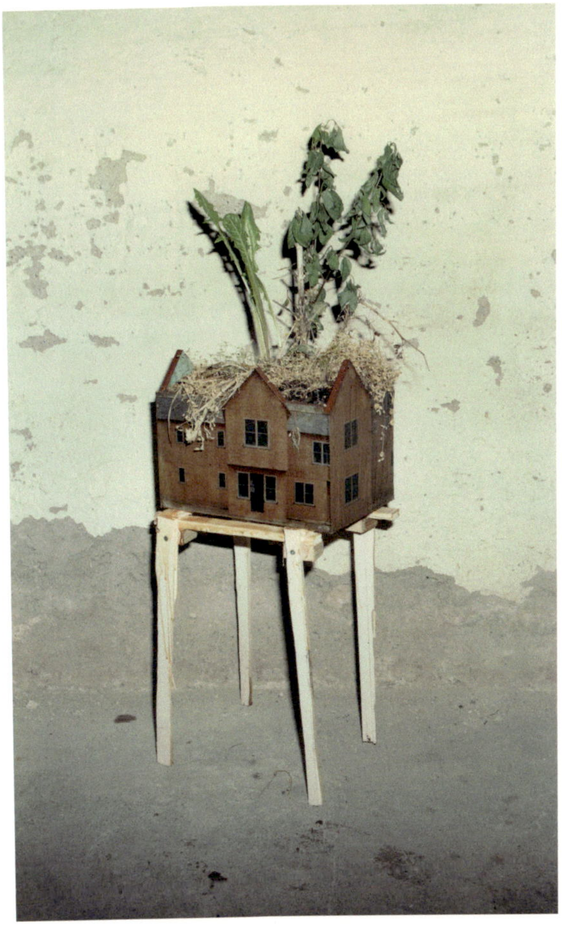

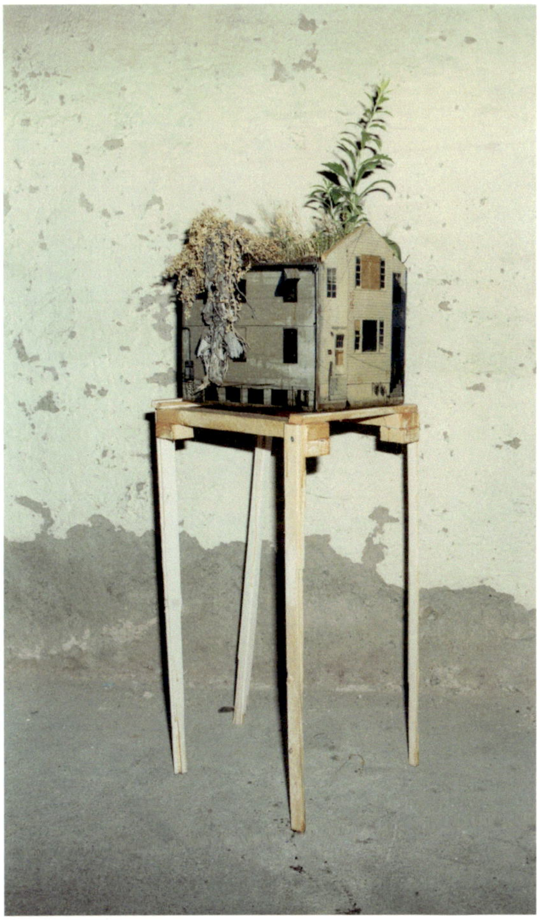

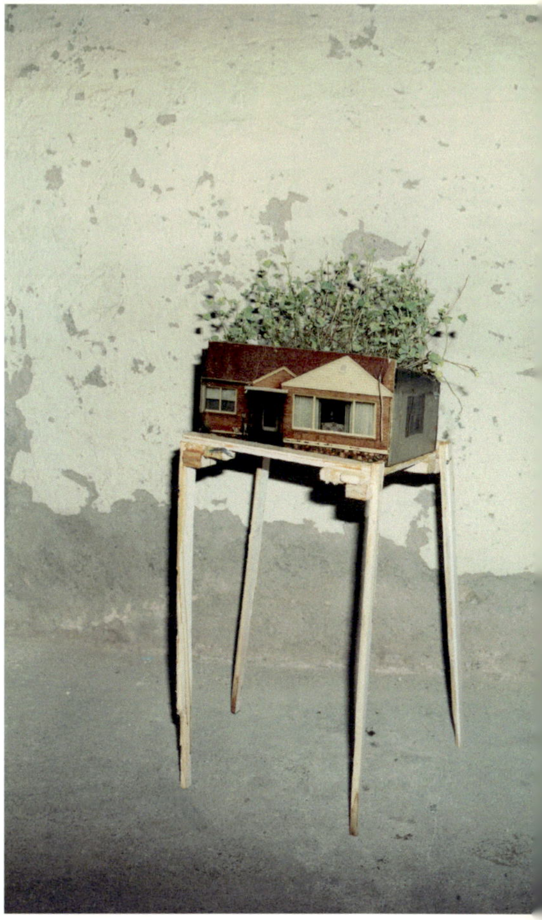

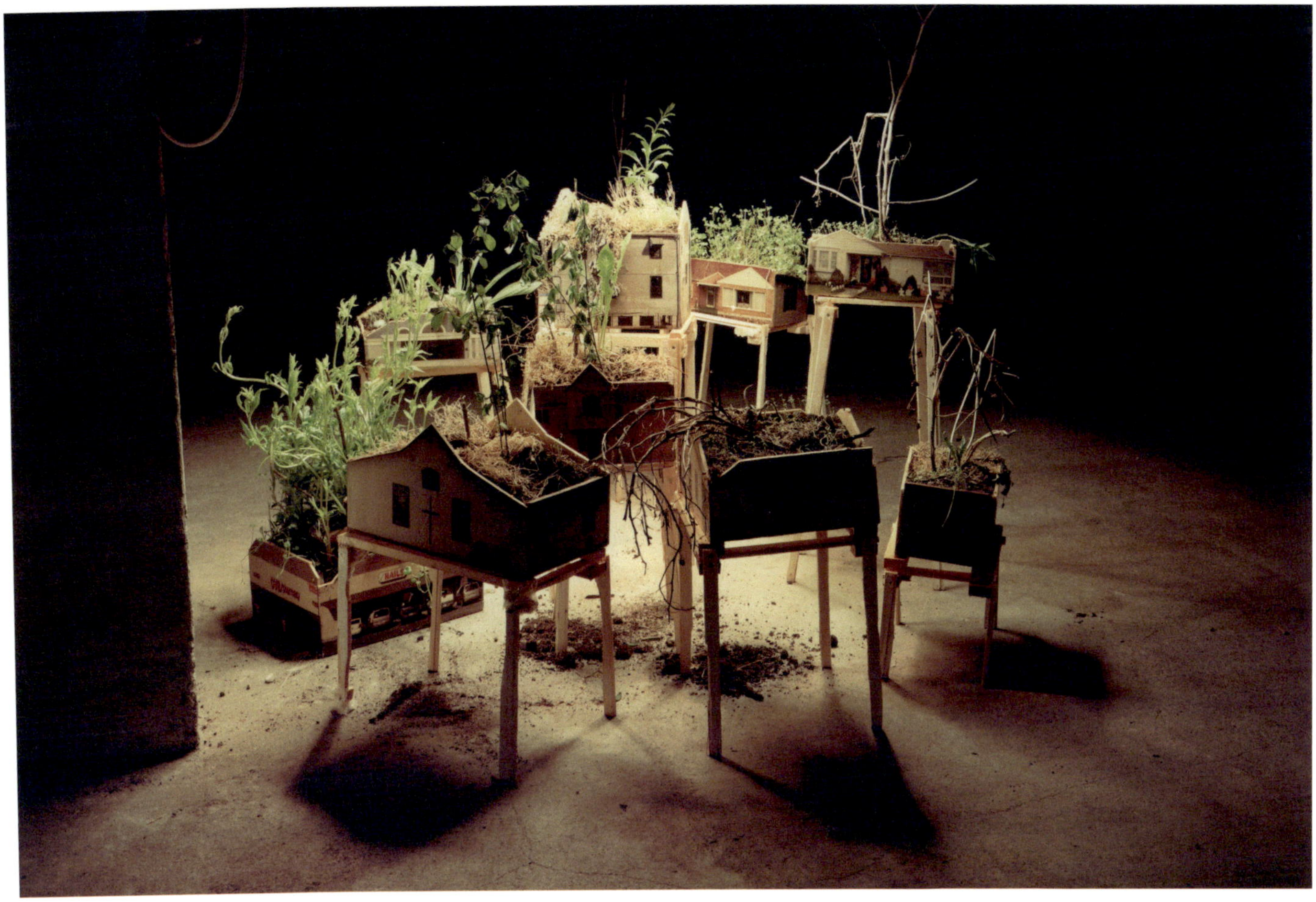

Tonk

TAIYO ONORATO & NICO KREBS

GROW HOMES

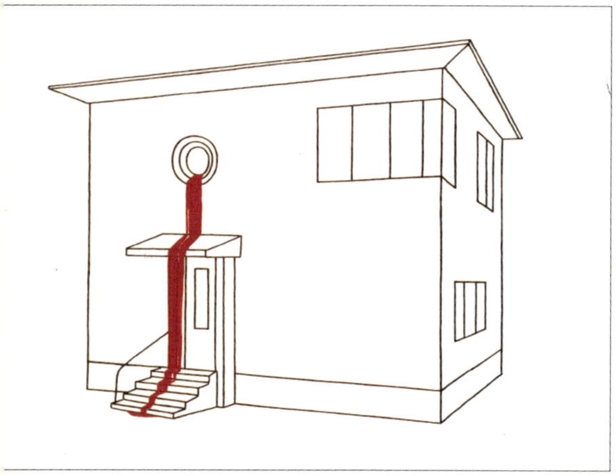

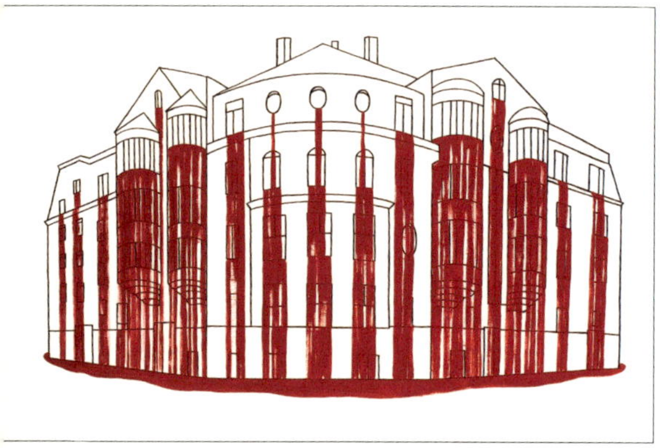

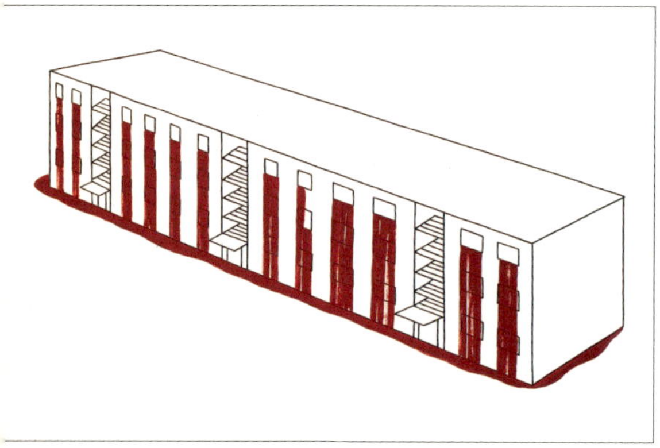

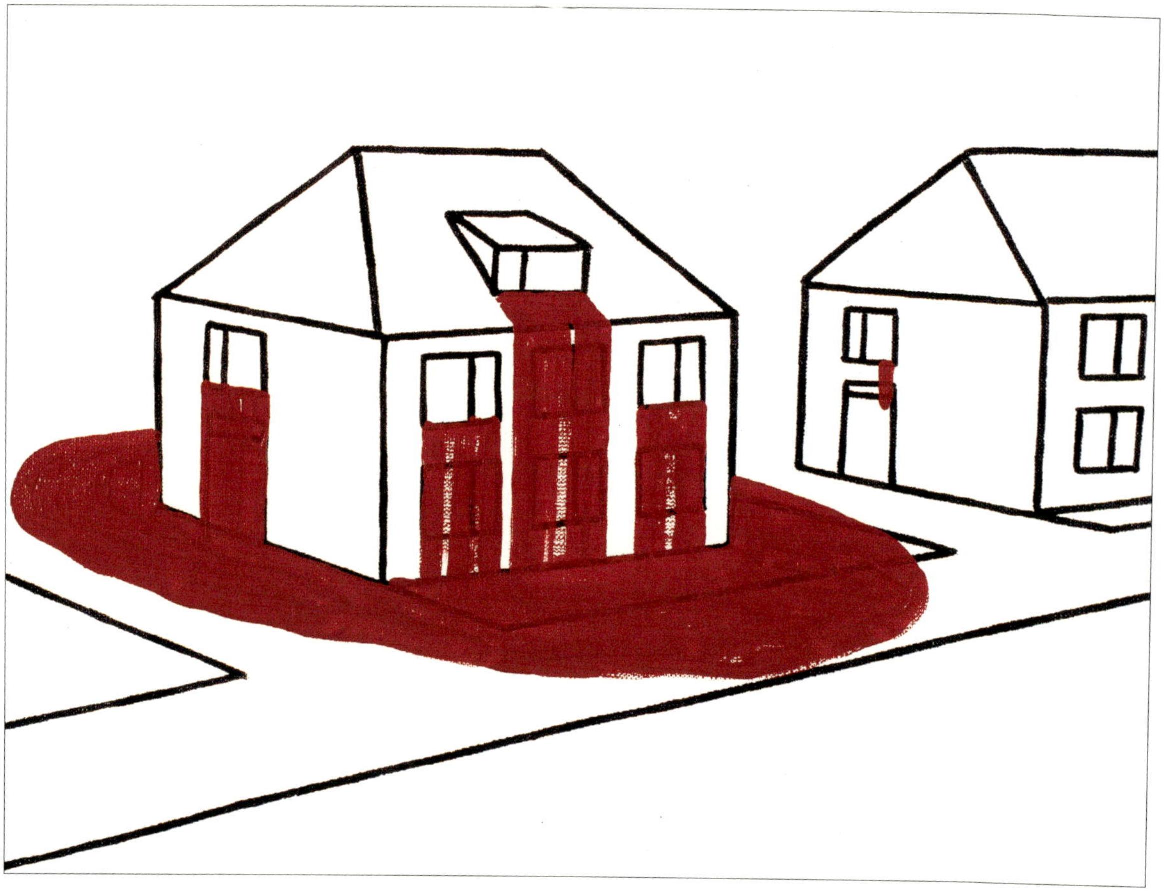

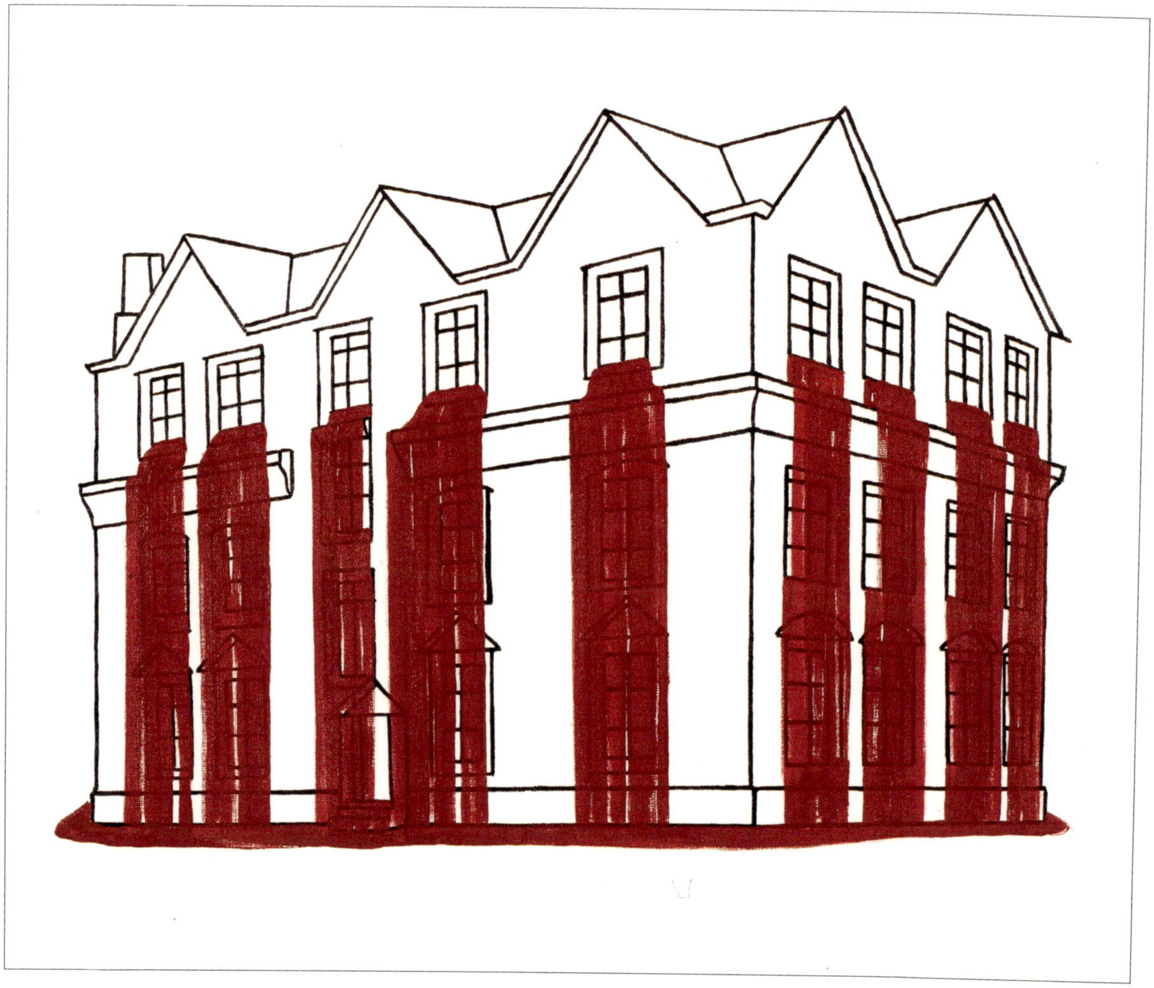

Marko Mäetamm

BLEEDING HOUSES

These are some works of a series of Bleeding Houses, painted on canvas and paper.

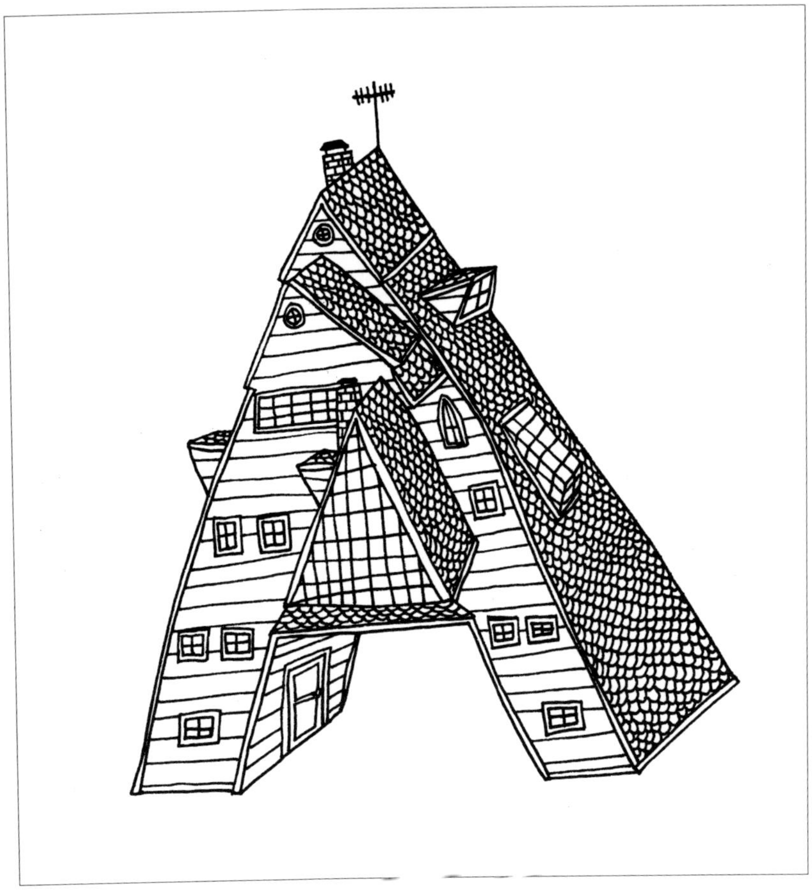

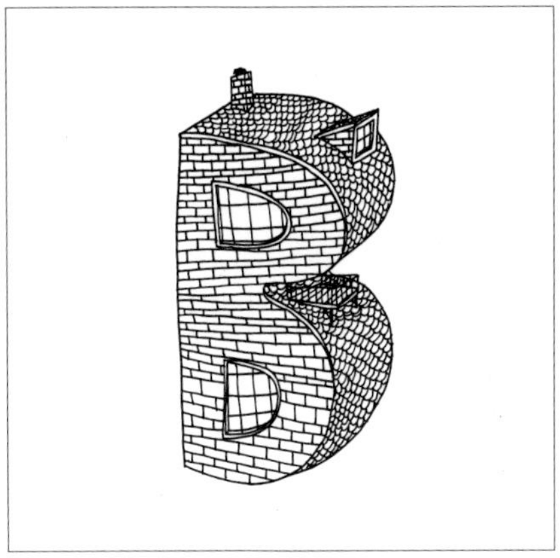

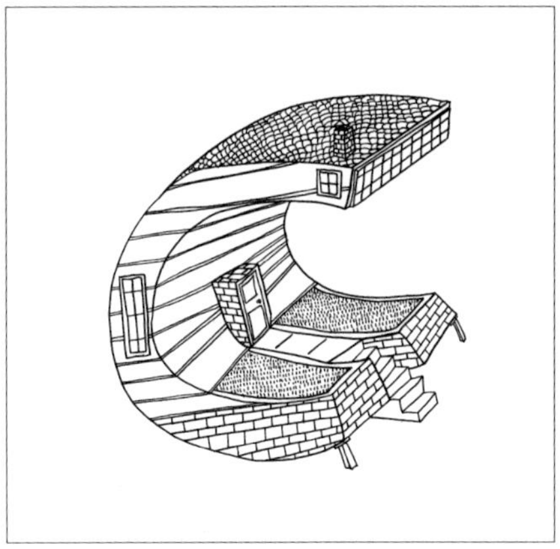

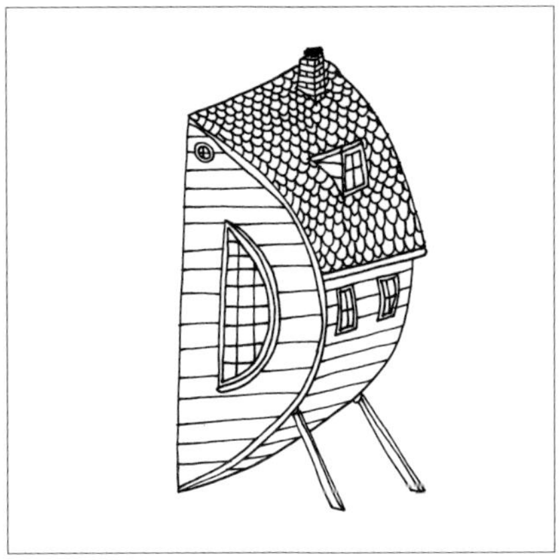

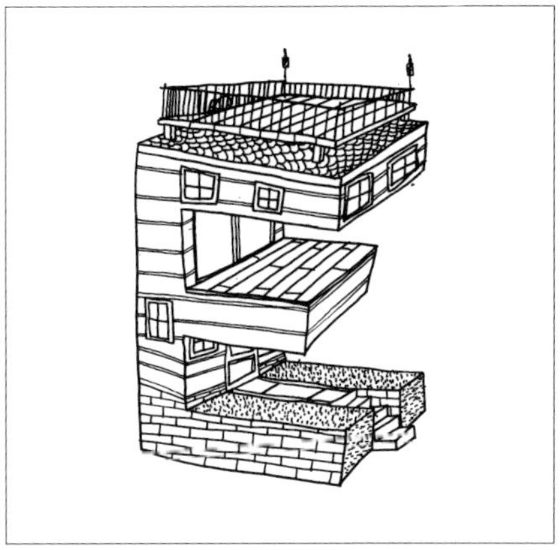

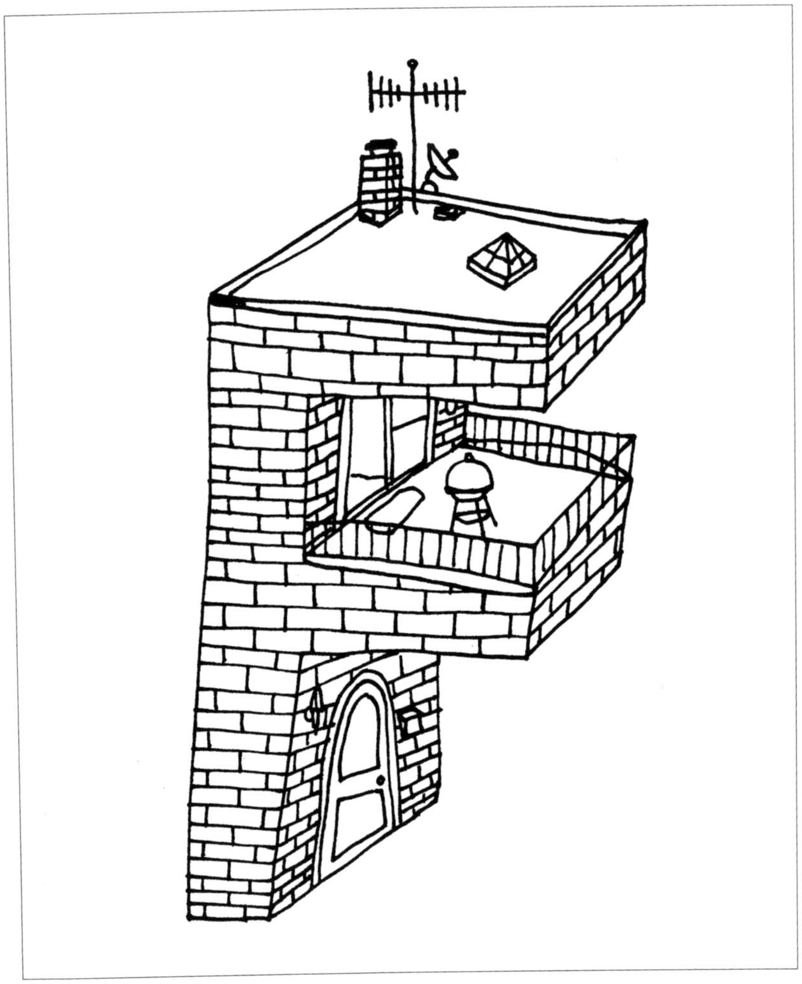

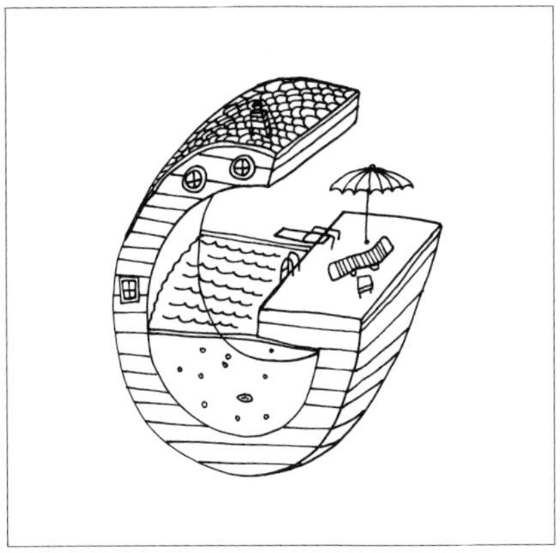

Mike Perry

ALPHABET TOWN

In Mike Perry's Alphabet Town, letter design becomes illustration rather than typography.

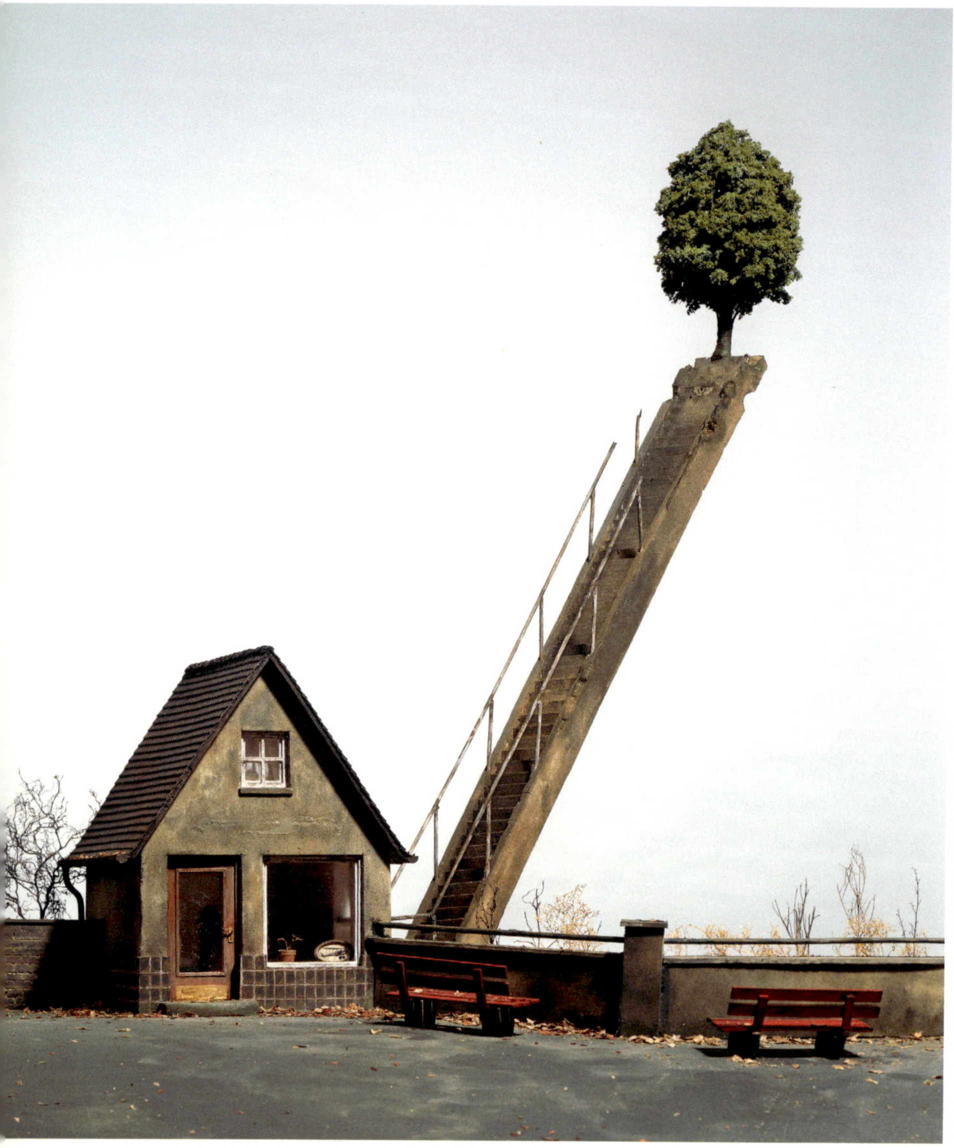

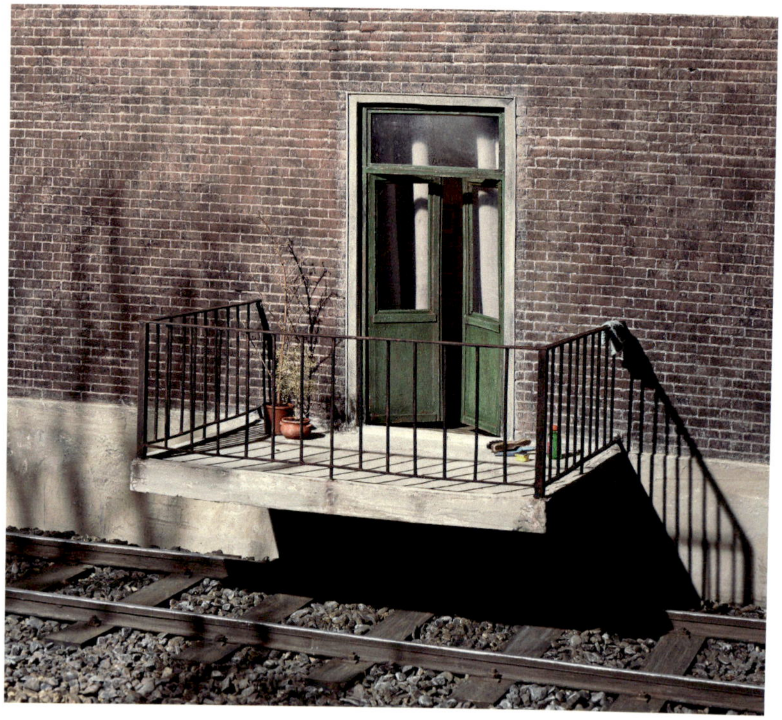

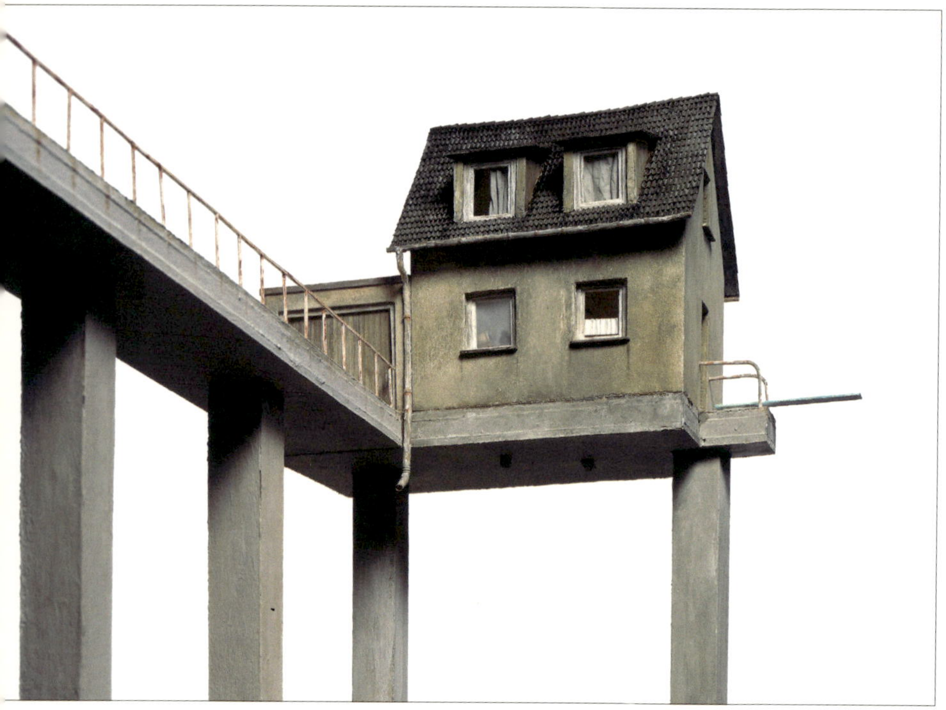

Frank Kunert

SMALL WORLDS

Frank Kunert's Small Worlds series is far from being mere photographic satire. In order to construct his scenic models, Kunert spends weeks and months, working with deco boards, plasticine and paint. His work thereby deliberately oscillates between humour, wit, scurrility and the grotesque.

Sunny Side *(top)*
Almost Heavenly *(bottom left)*
Hope is Green *(top left)*

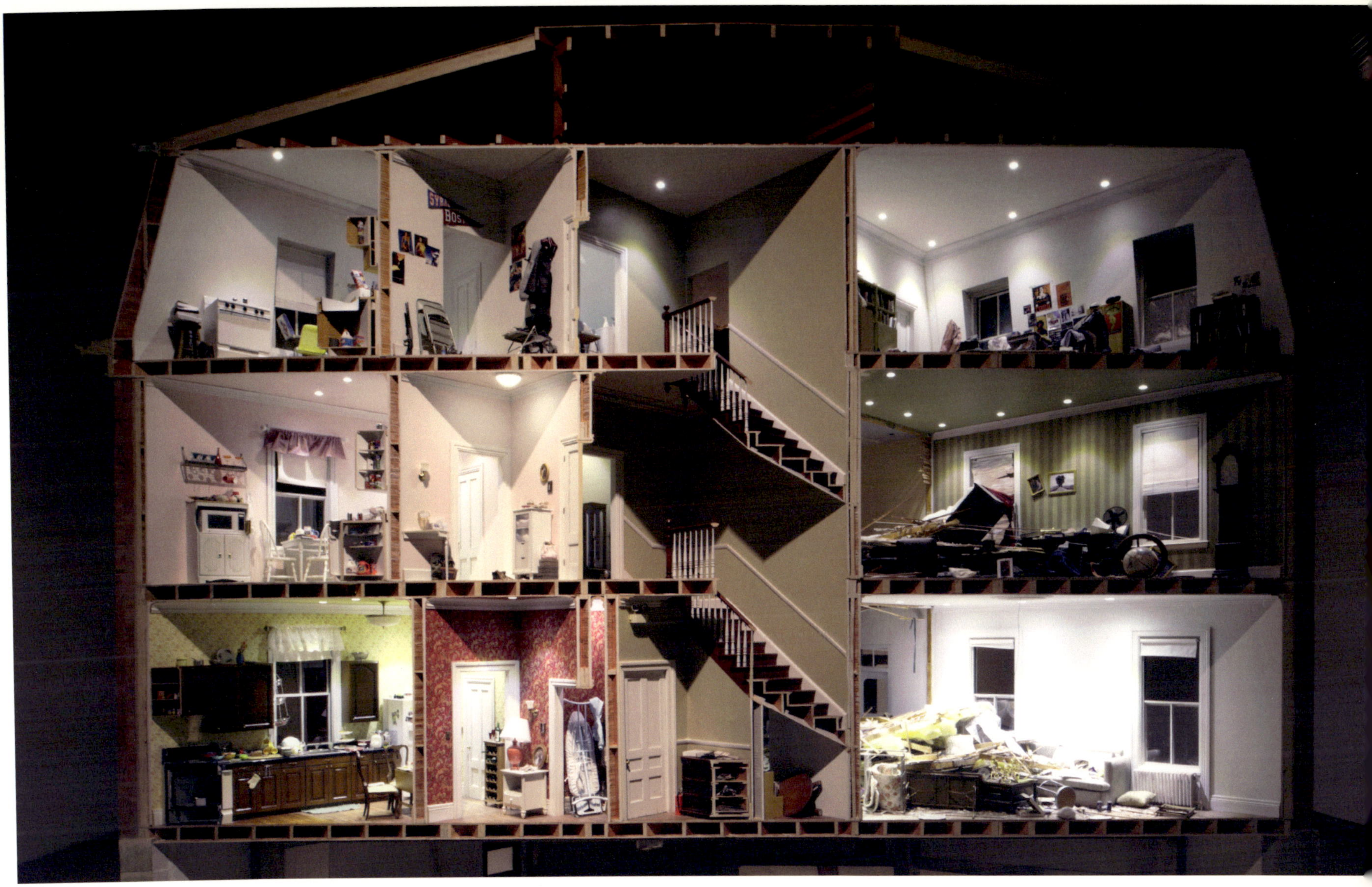

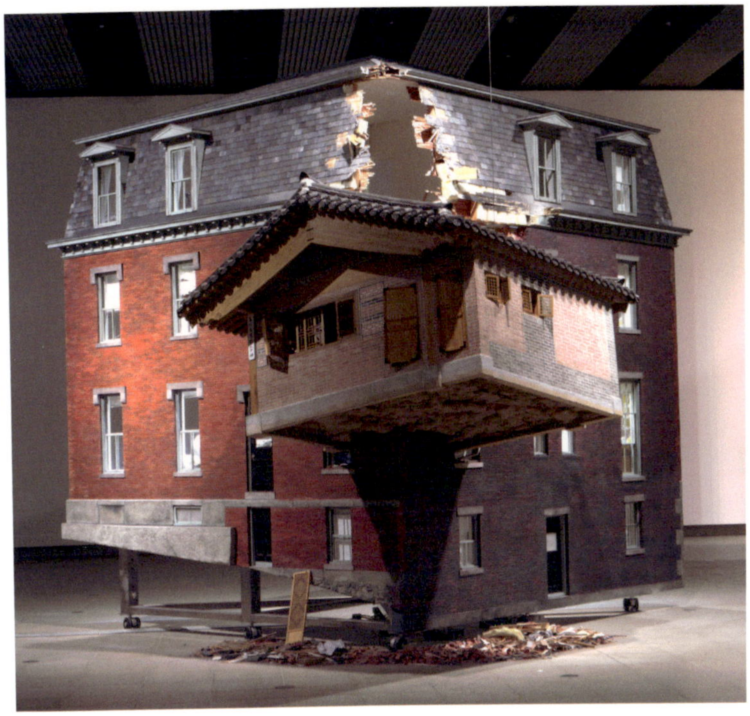

Do Ho Suh

FALLEN STAR 1/5

This autobiographical work features an extraordinarily detailed 1:5 scale model of the artist's childhood home in Korea colliding into the New England apartment where he lived as an art student. The intricately recreated contents of both houses merged together on impact.

Jake & Dinos Chapman

ARBEIT MCFRIES

This installation by the London-based artist duo seems to equate Nazi fascism and American consumerism by displaying members of the infamous Waffen SS – Hitler's heavily armed special forces, feared for their brutality – engaged in massacres in front of a wrecked mill building adorned with the McDonald's trademark. This hellish site is littered with dying men, corpses and skeletons.

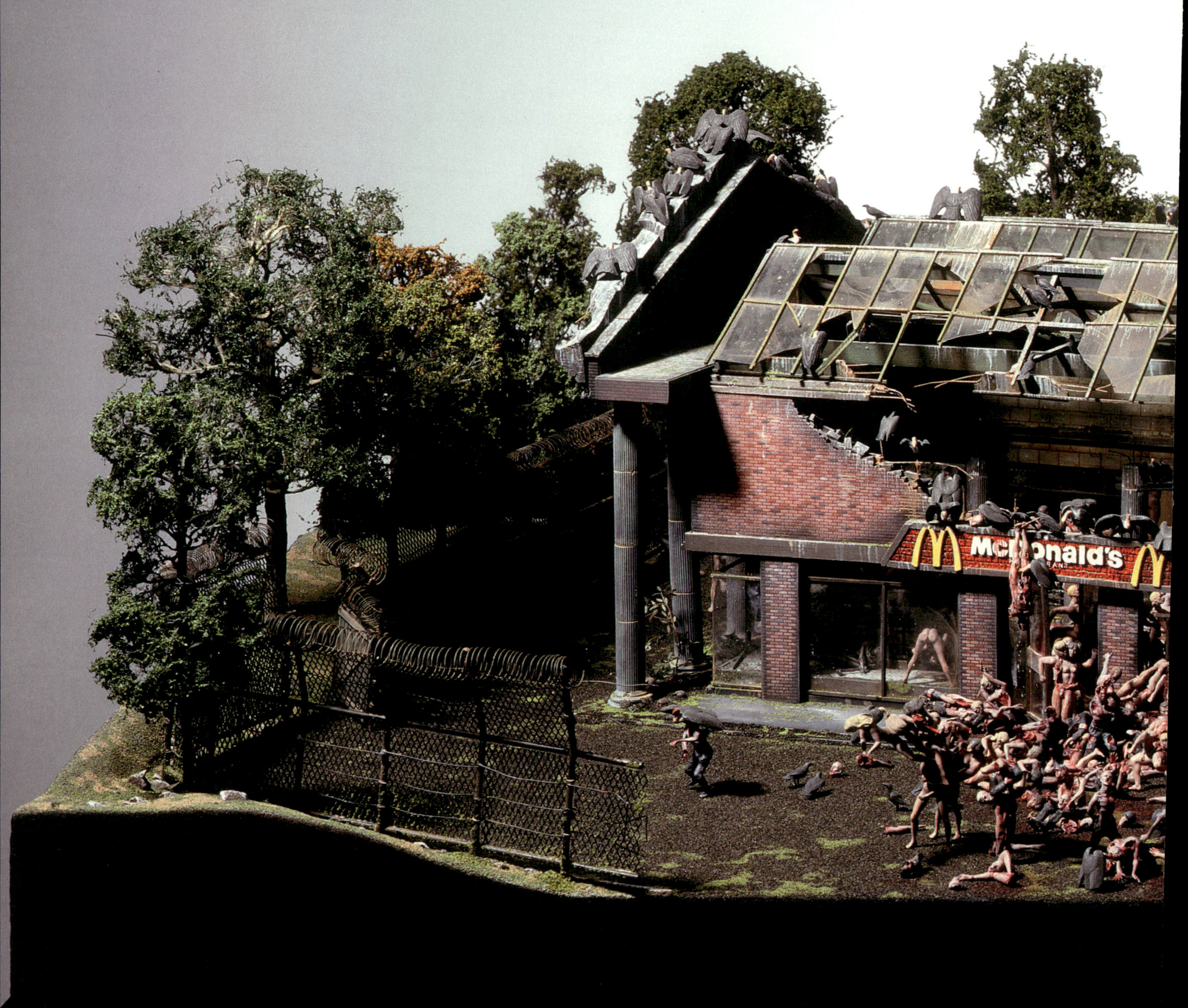

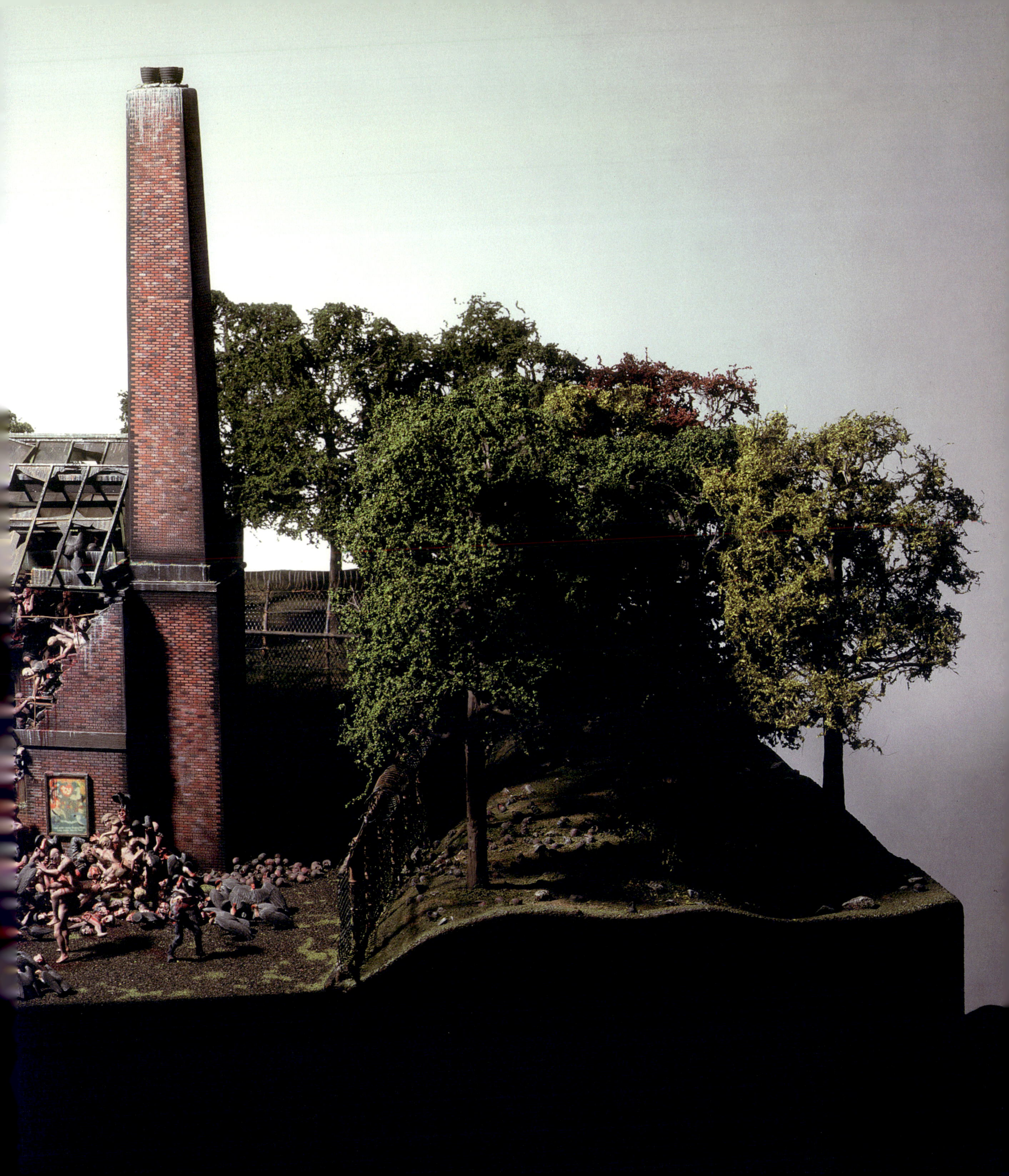

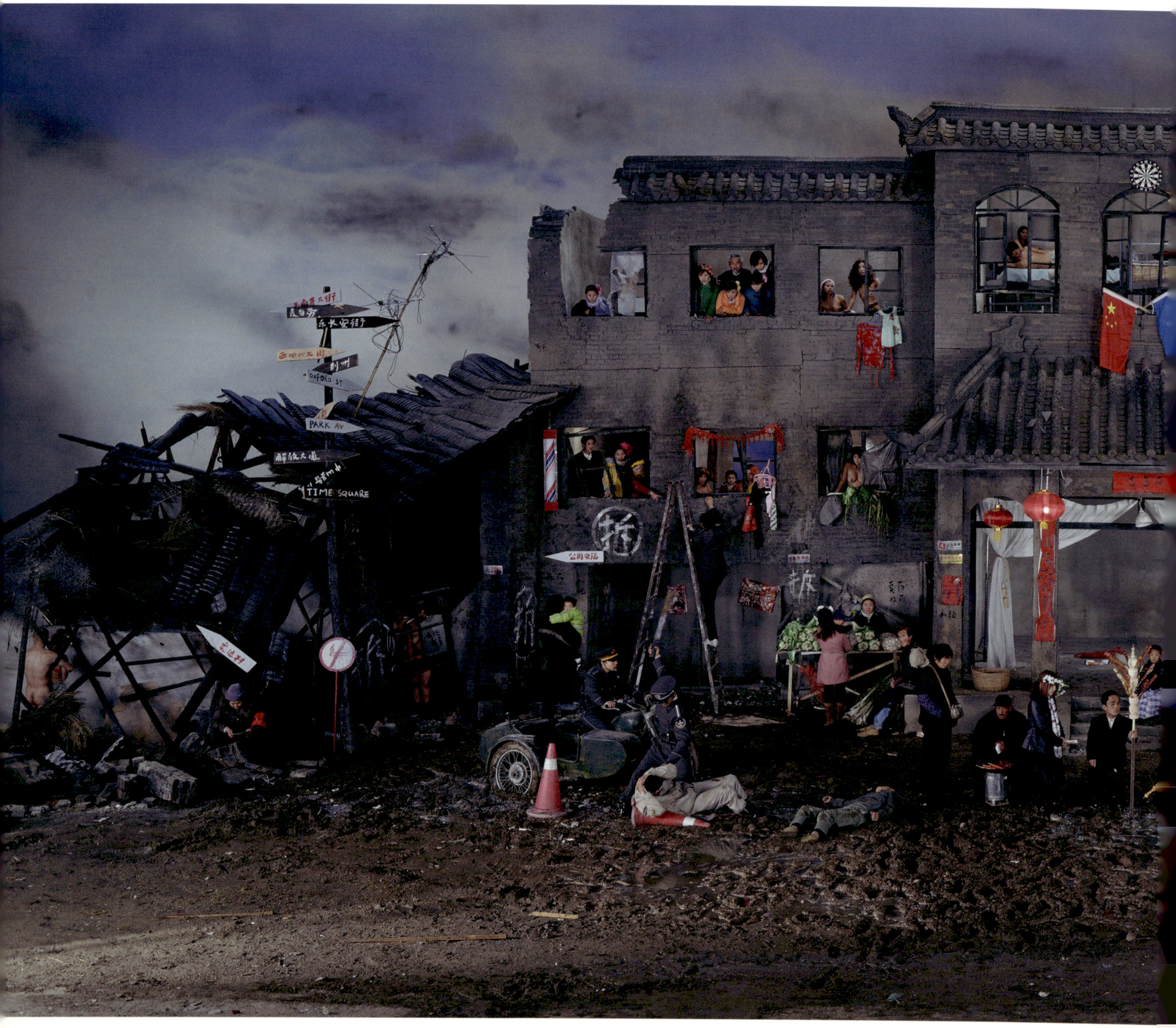

Wang Qingsong

DREAM OF MIGRANTS

Dream of Migrants seems to show us a derogatory China, where aimlessly drifting population move from one place to another – mostly from countryside to big cities to look for jobs: In Beijing, there are nearly three million such people. In this monumental work, Wang Qingsong expresses this pursuit of dreams and opportunities in bigger cities. For this work the artist built up a three-storey building in Beijing movie studio that combines Chinese, Soviet and European-style architecture.

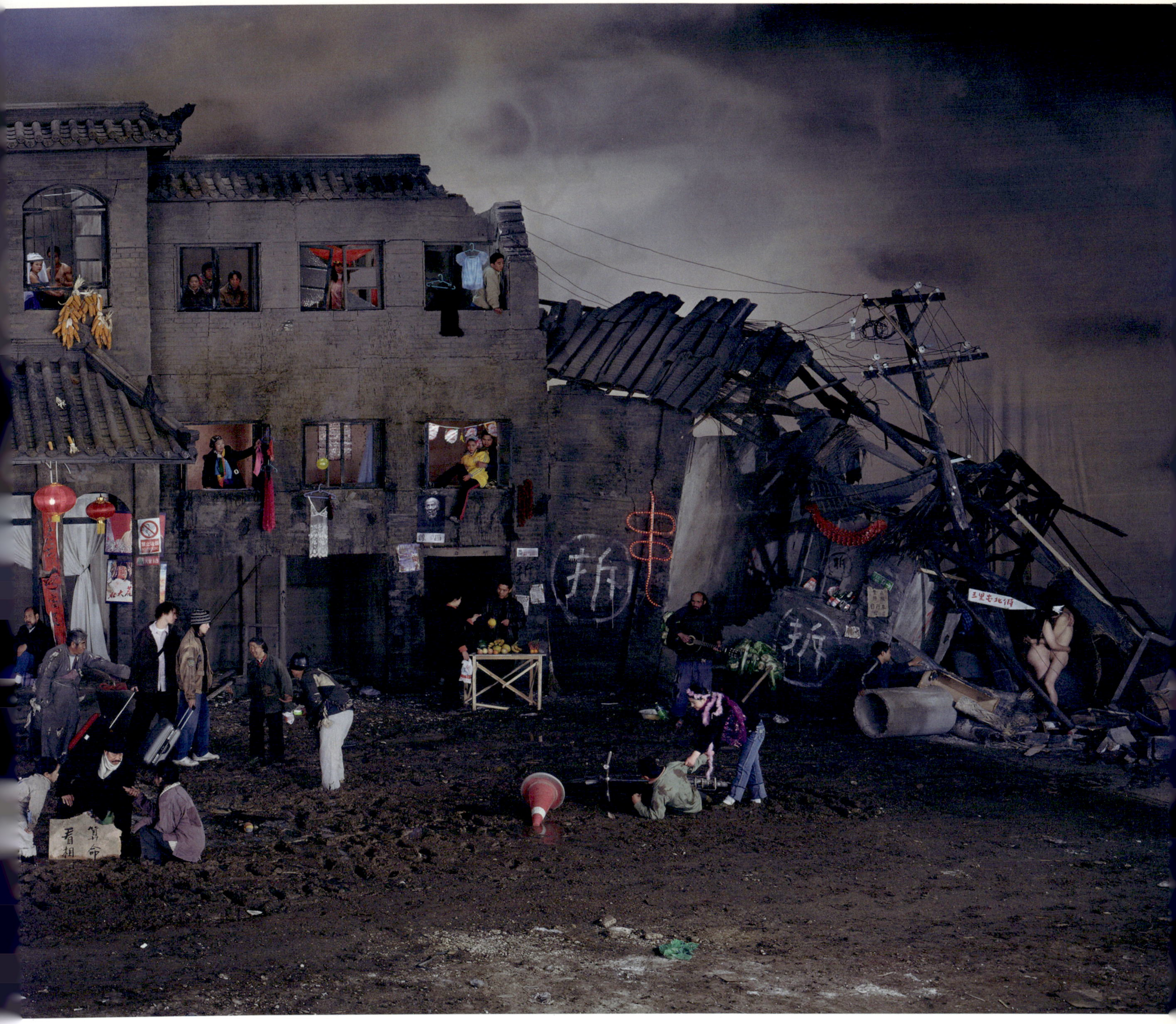
拆
拆
三里屯北街
算命
看相

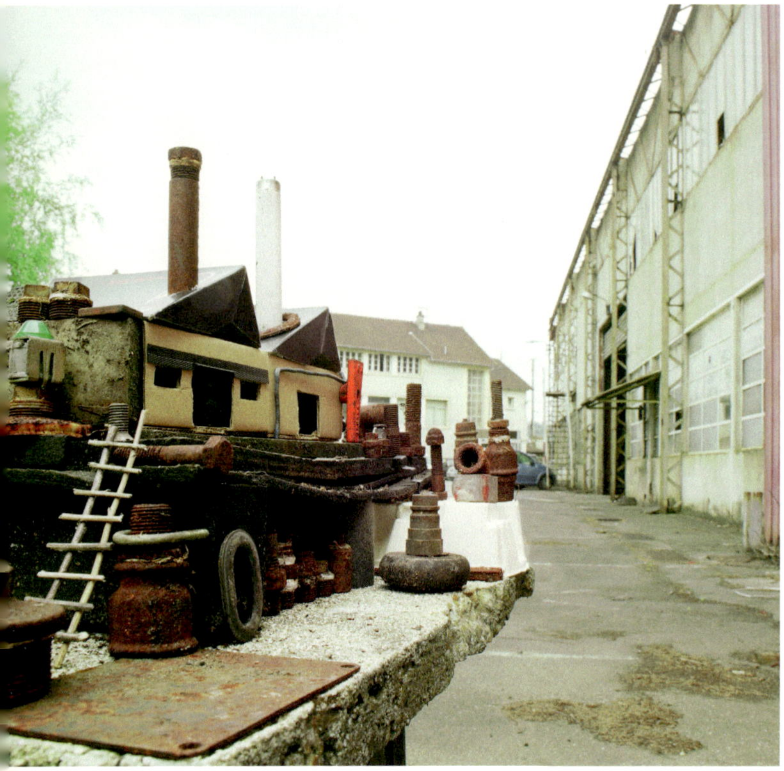

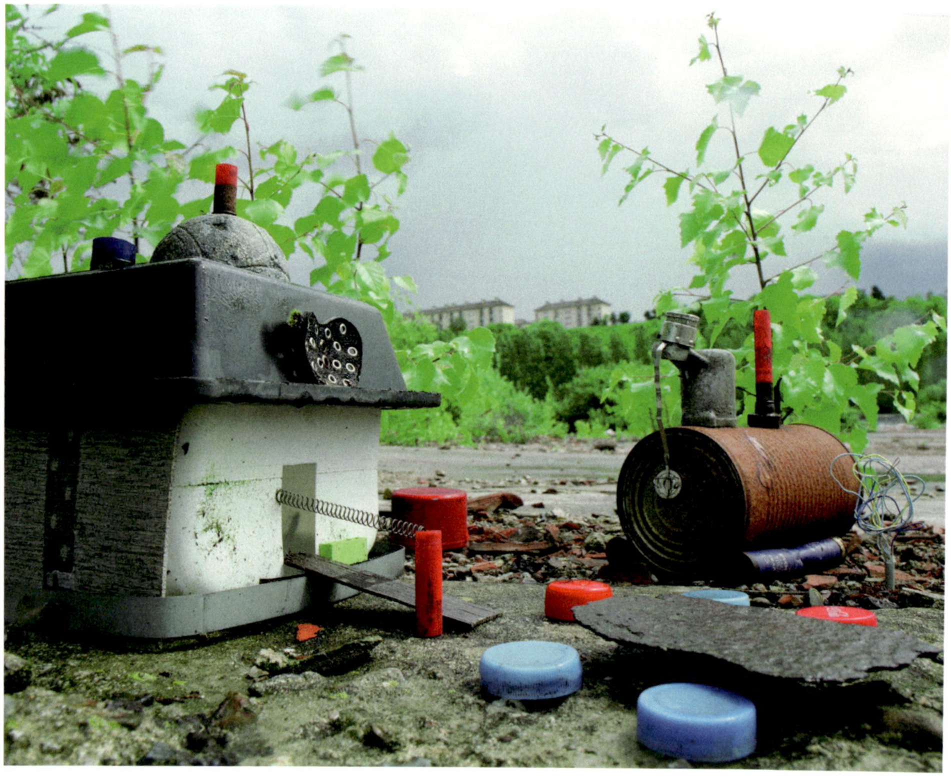

Edouard Sautai

CONSTRUCTION À SÉOUL HWANGHAK DONG II

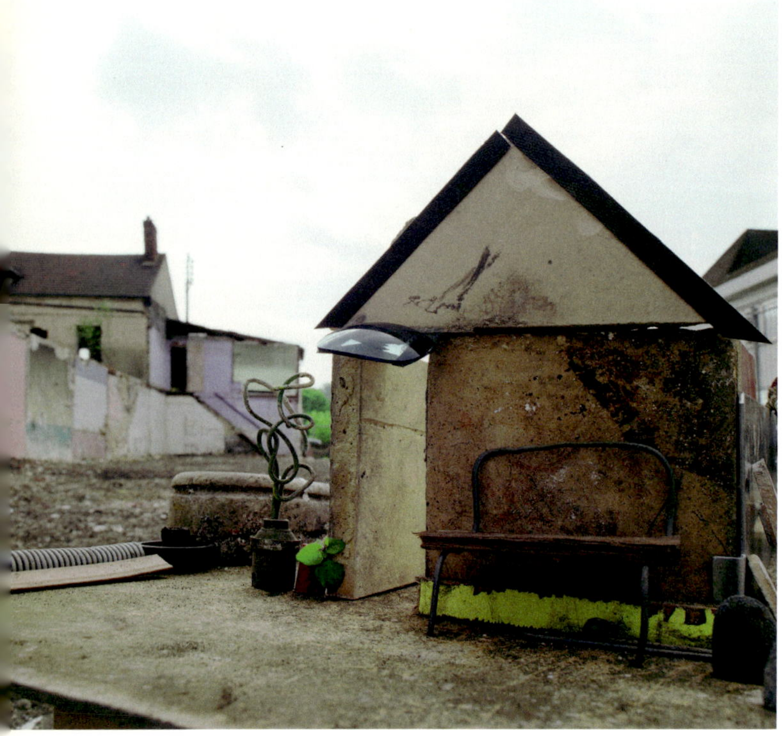

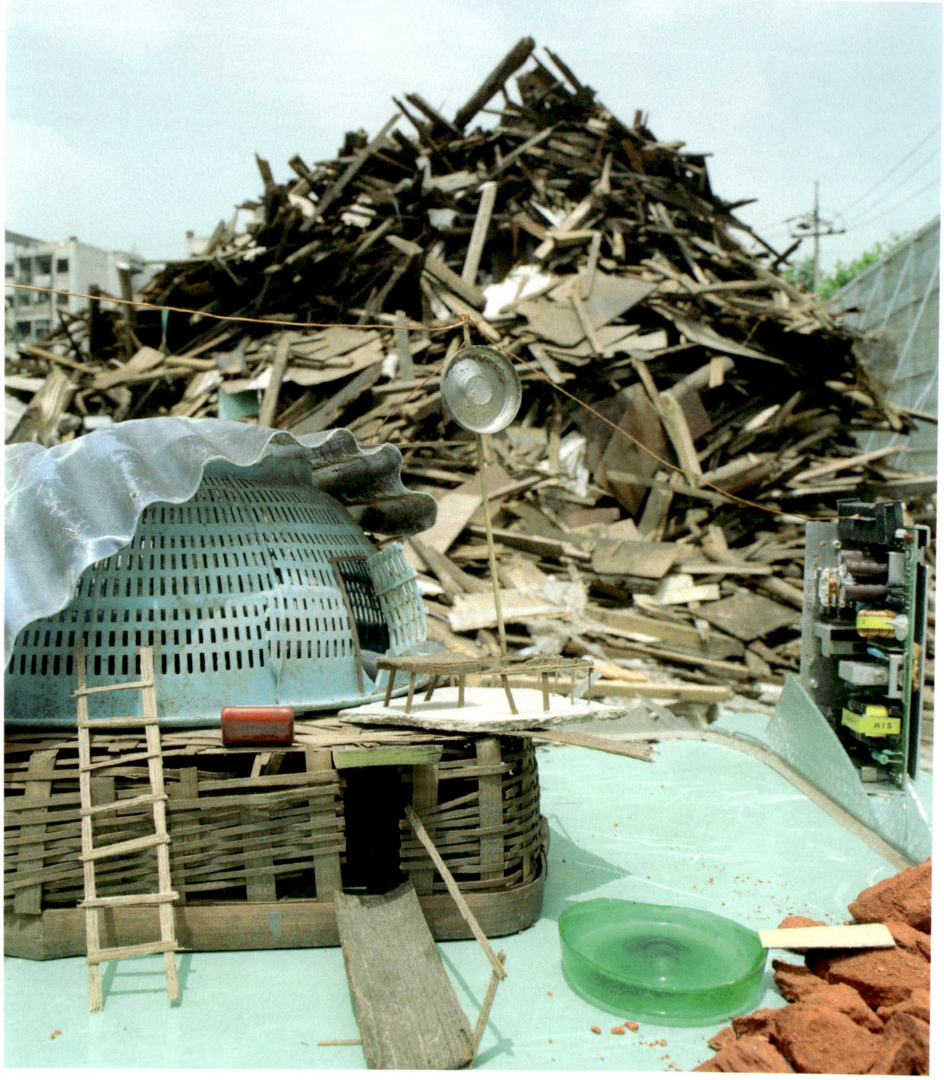

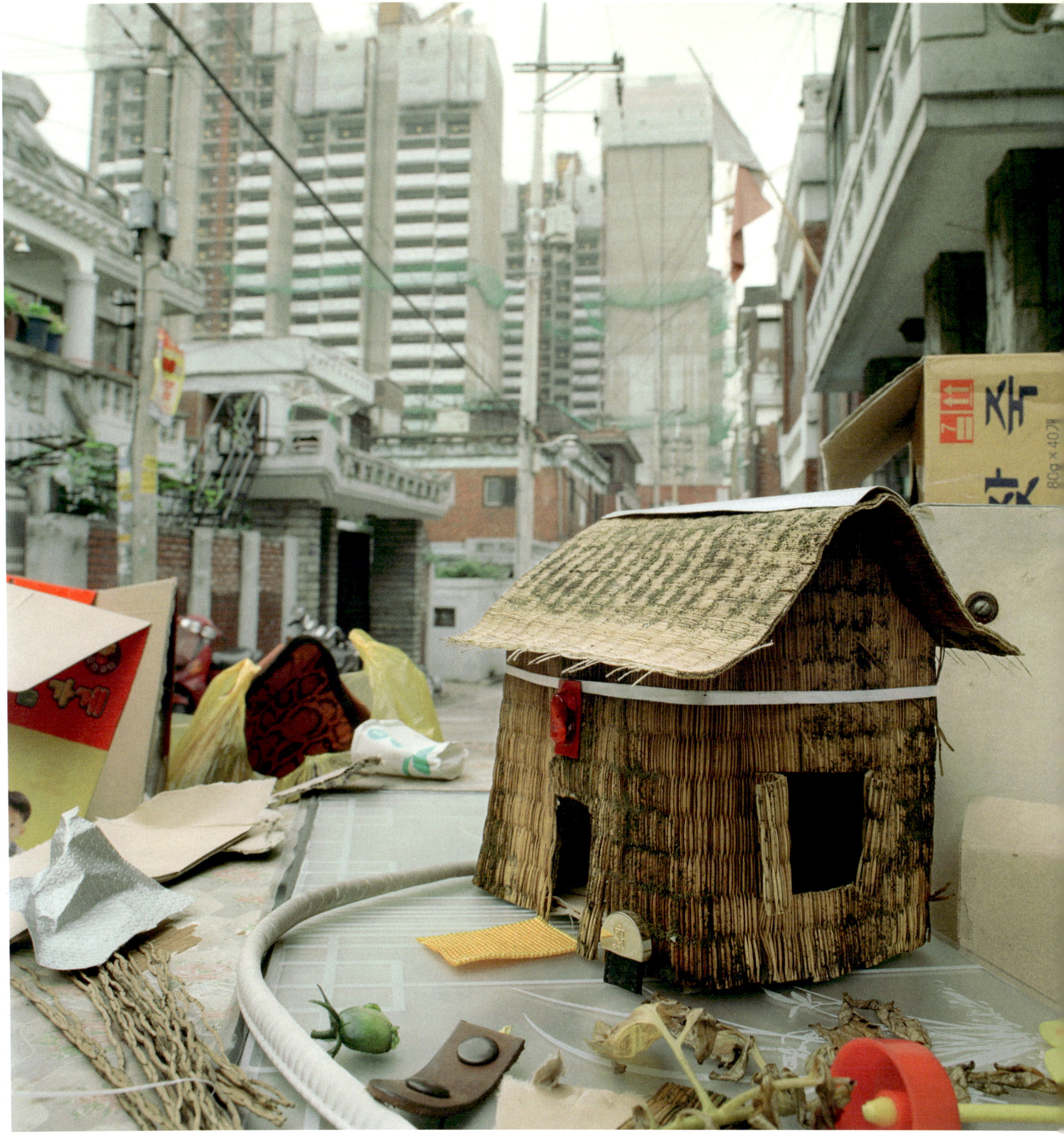

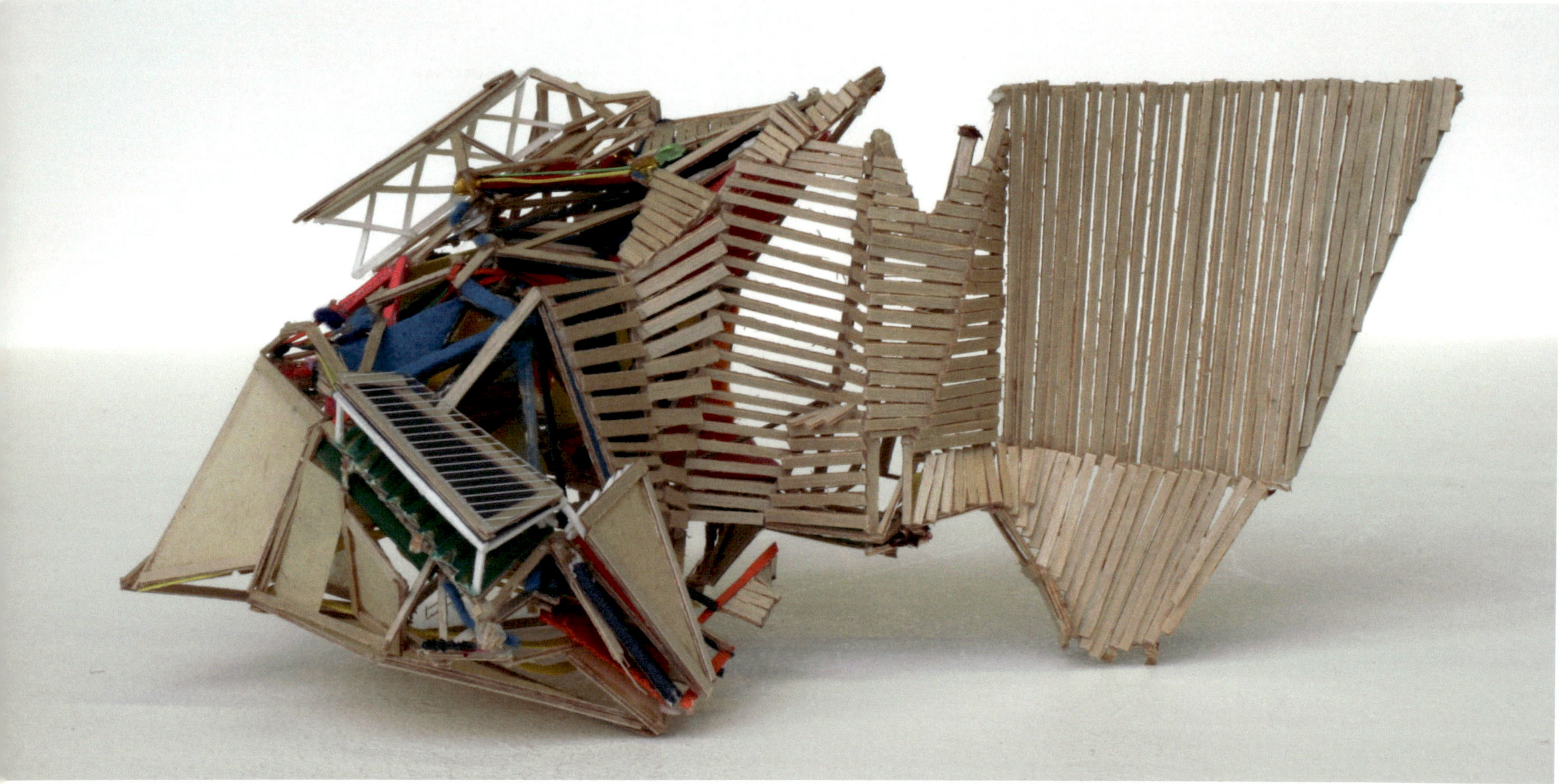

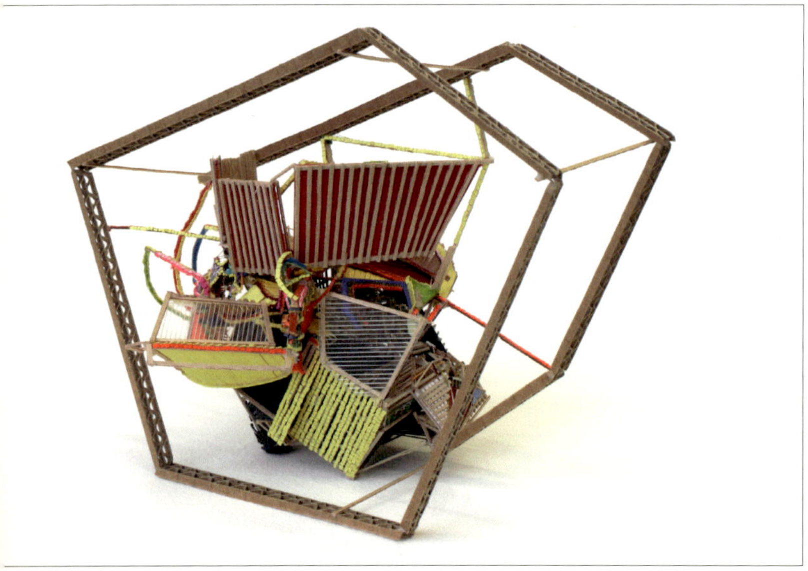

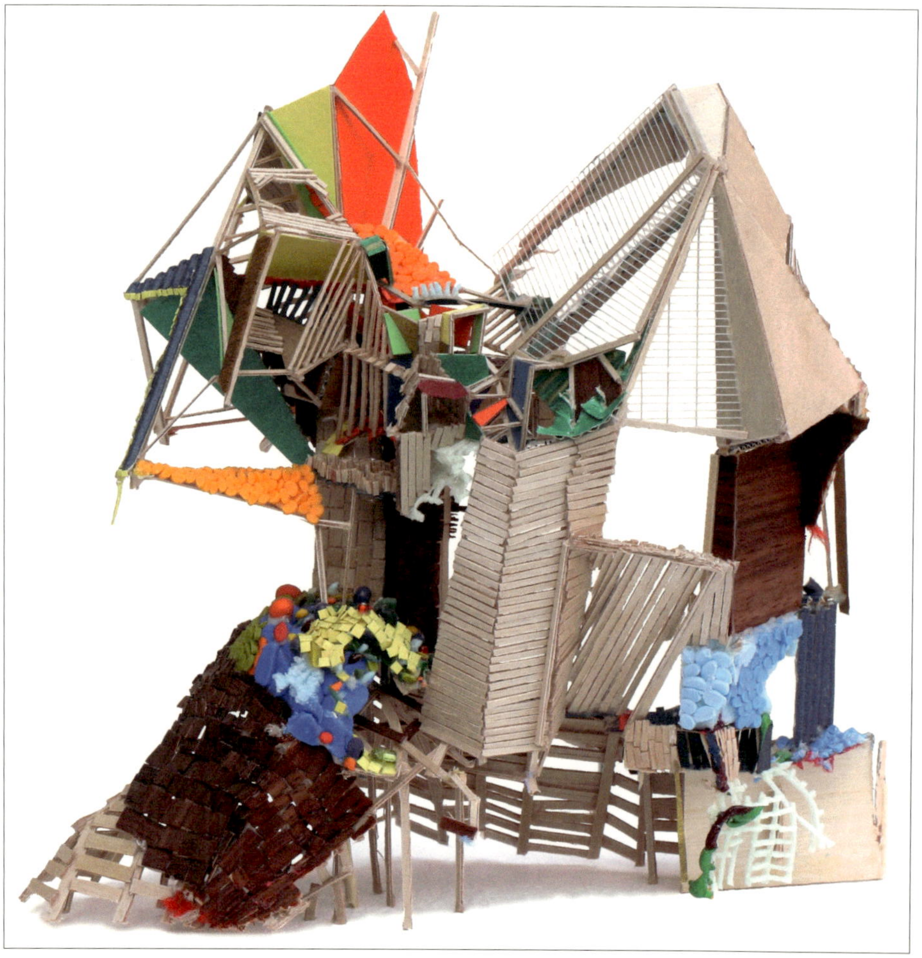

Stephanie Backes

SCHWIMMER *(top)*
KLAPPANZER *(left)*
WANDLER *(right)*

Karsten Konrad

IMMEUBLE SAR LE SABLE *(left)*
DELTA 2 *(bottom)*

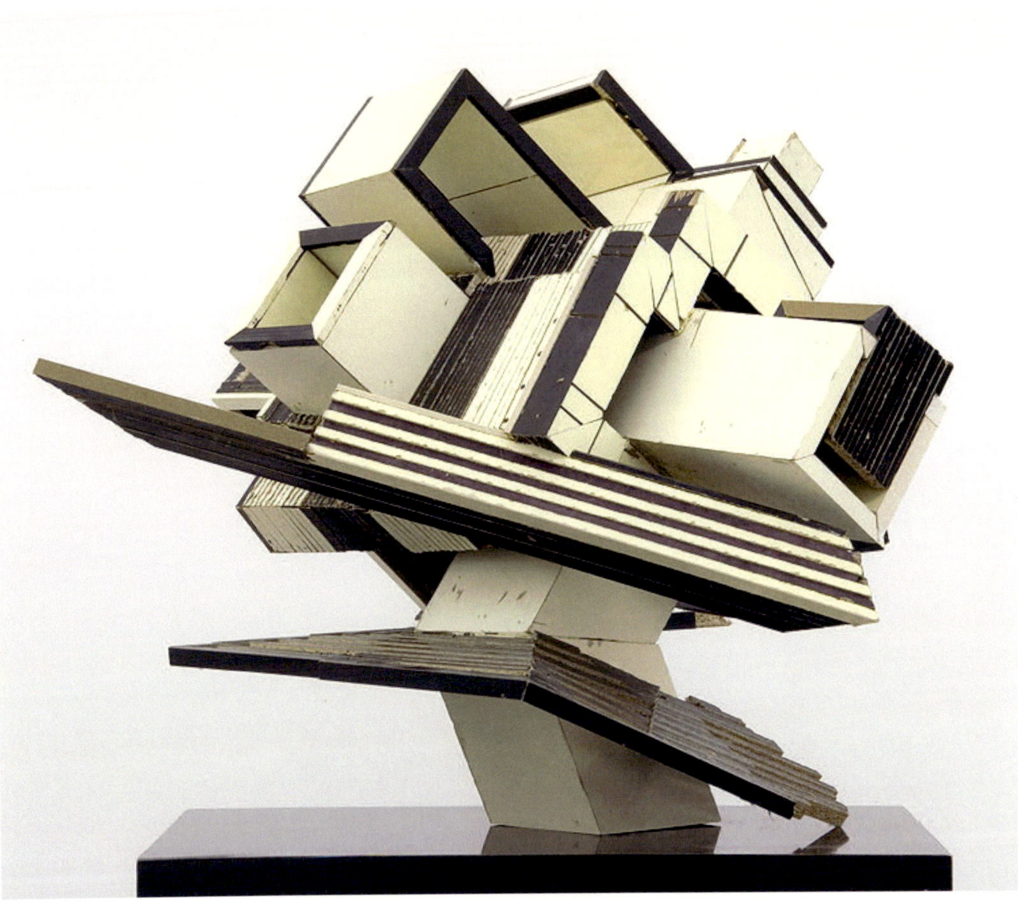

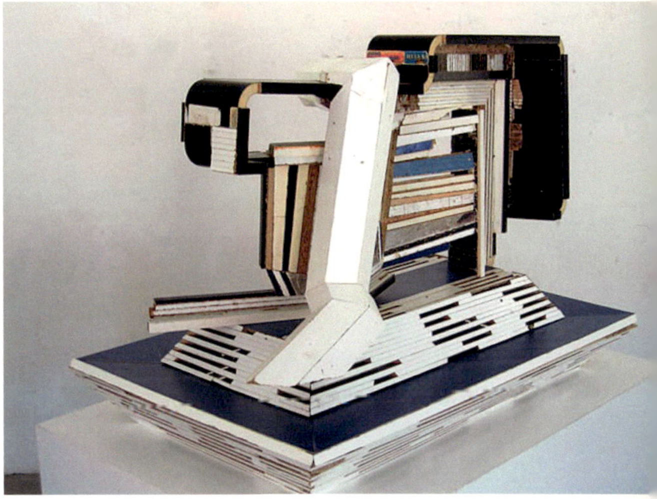

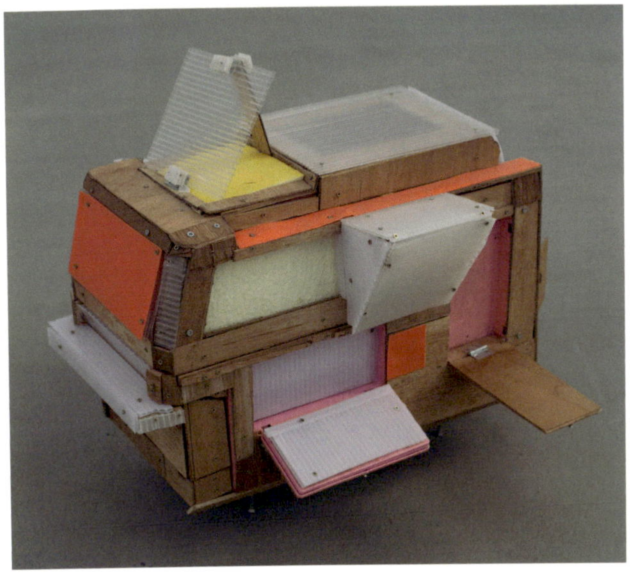

Veron Urdarianu

SURVIVAL HOUSE *(top)*
SCHUIFHUIS 3 *(right)*

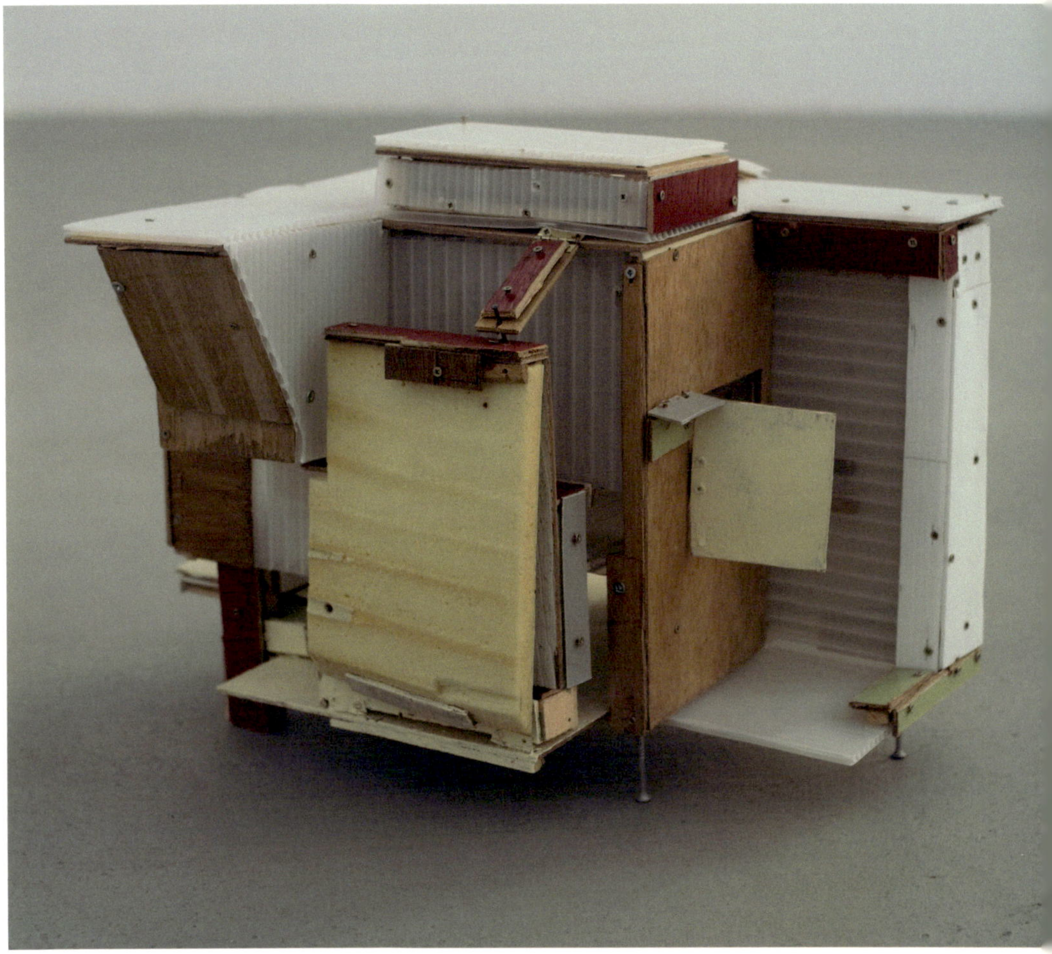

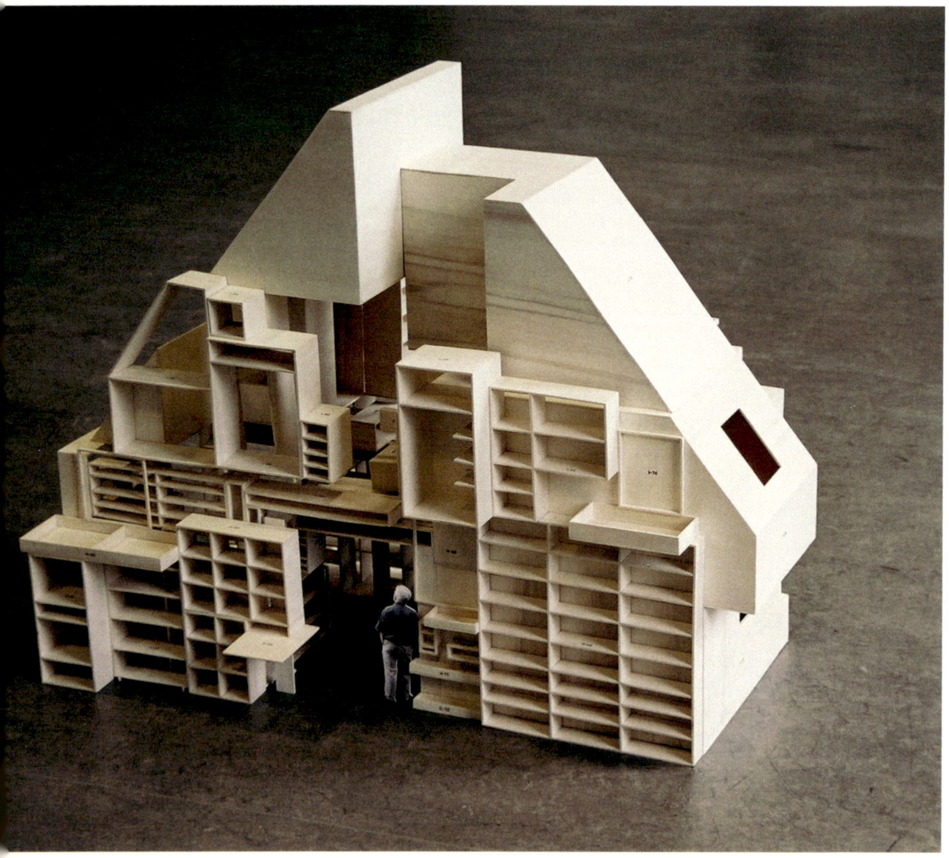

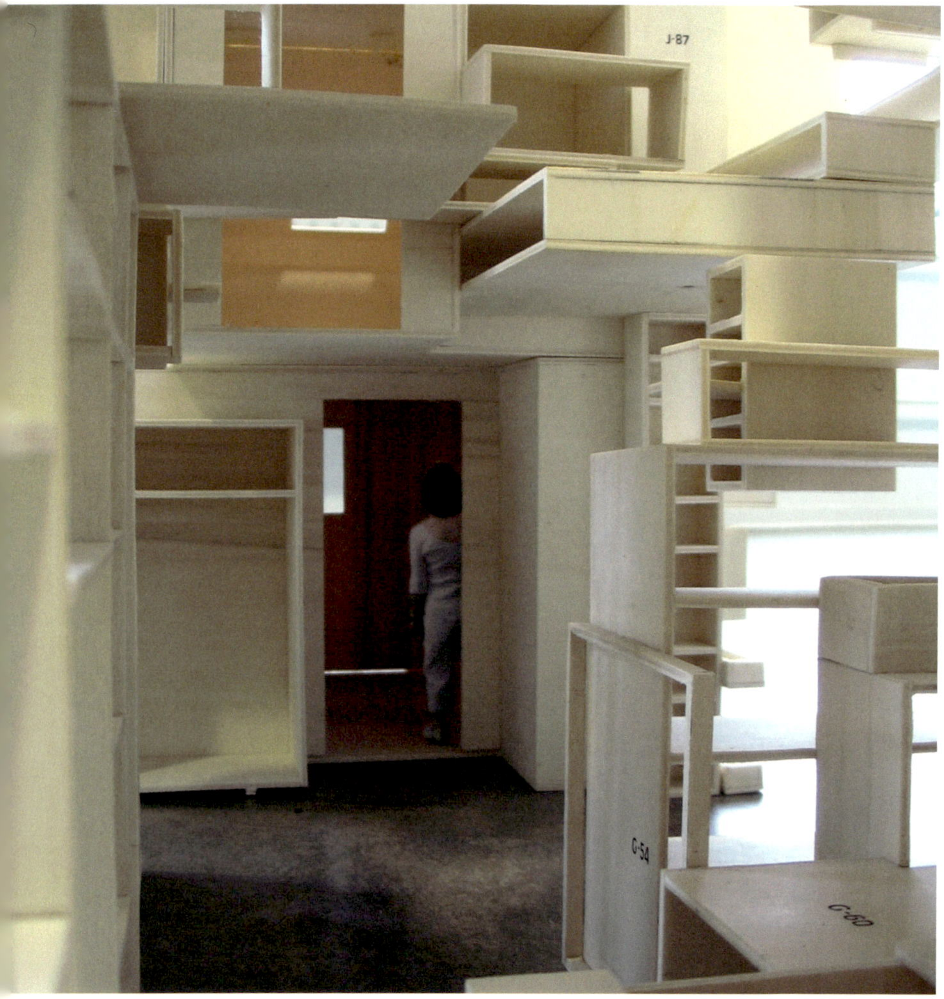

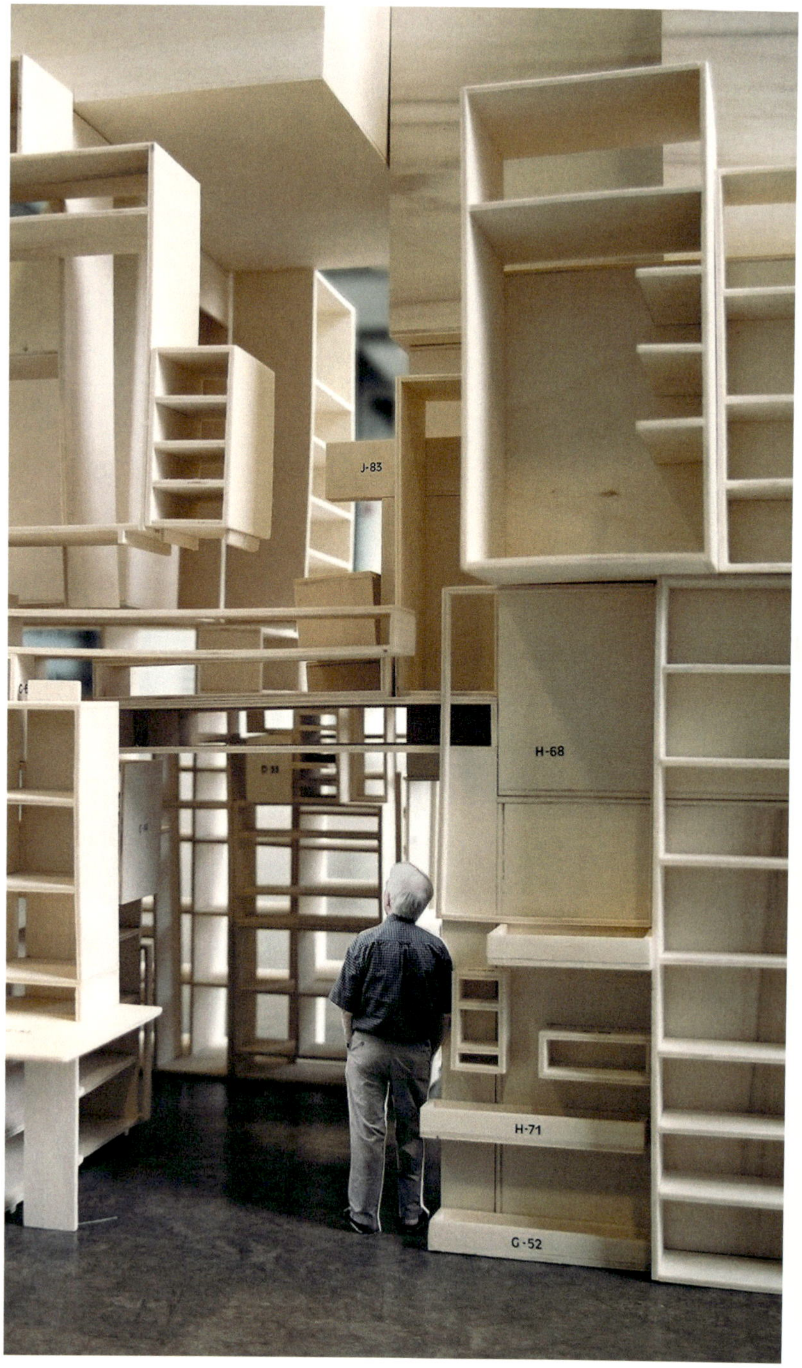

Sotiria Kornaropoulou

THE HEART OF THE HOME: THE CUPBOARD HOUSE

A Dutch, single-family house in a village of 9,000 people was studied with regard to the possessions of its four inhabitants. The items accumulated during the 25 years of family life were analysed and recomposed in a structure that plays a double role: It confronts the viewer with the volume of the items in stand-by mode and the labyrinth they produce, but at the same time brings in a new order of hiding or displaying the items and celebrates the richness of detail.

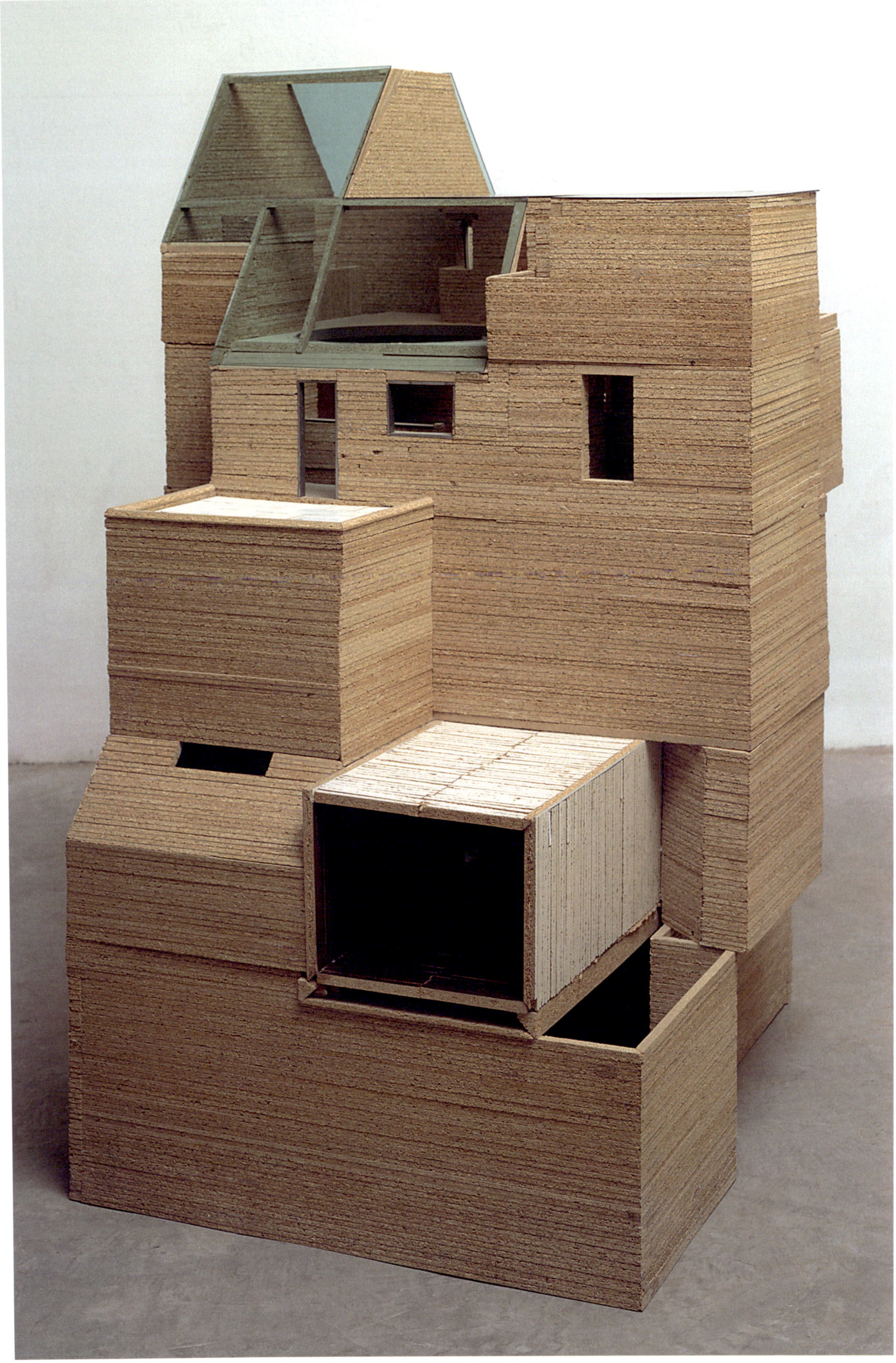

Karsten Konrad

ALDOS' HOUSE

Berlin-based artist Karsten Konrad creates sculptural illustrations of the balance between model and object. Konrad's sculptural powers of imagination are always accompanied by the pronounced suggestion, in planning terms, that everything could be otherwise; everything might have, or could still be, developed differently.

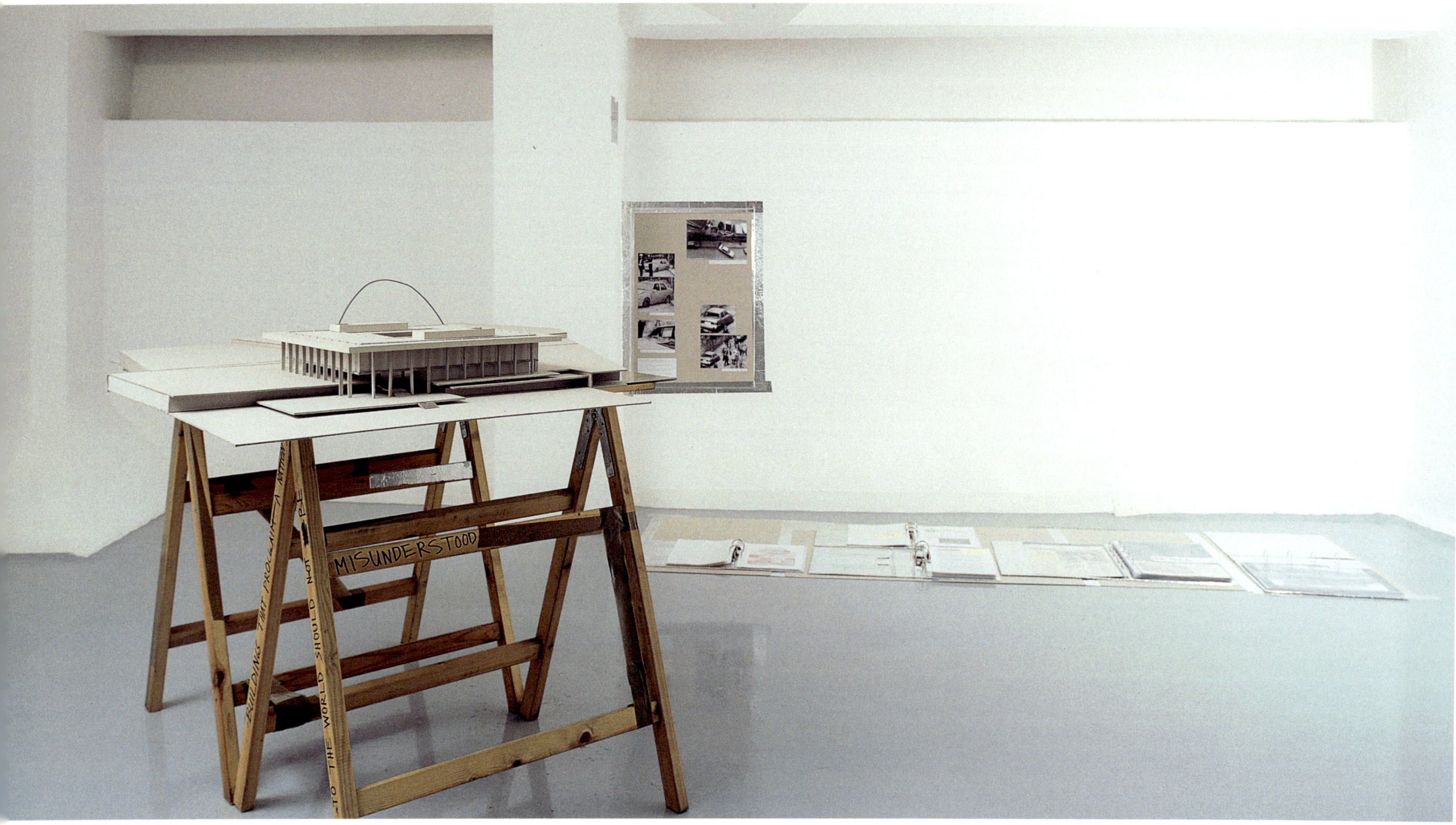

Vangelis Vlahos

BUILDINGS THAT PROCLAIM A NATION'S IDENTITY
TO THE WORLD SHOULD NOT BE MISUNDERSTOOD

In this installation, Greek artist Vangelis Vlahos portrays the rocket attack against the US embassy building – designed by Walter Gropius – in Athens in 1996. Made out of cardboard, the 1:150 scale model of the building is done in such a way that it is very much in line with the newspaper graphic illustrations of that time. The curved metal wire represents the trajectory of the rocket. Located on the floor, beside the table, are five bulky volumes with various newspaper clippings, photographs that reconstruct the embassy's complex history up to the attack. There are collages on the walls are collages and stylised architectural drawings of the embassy building.

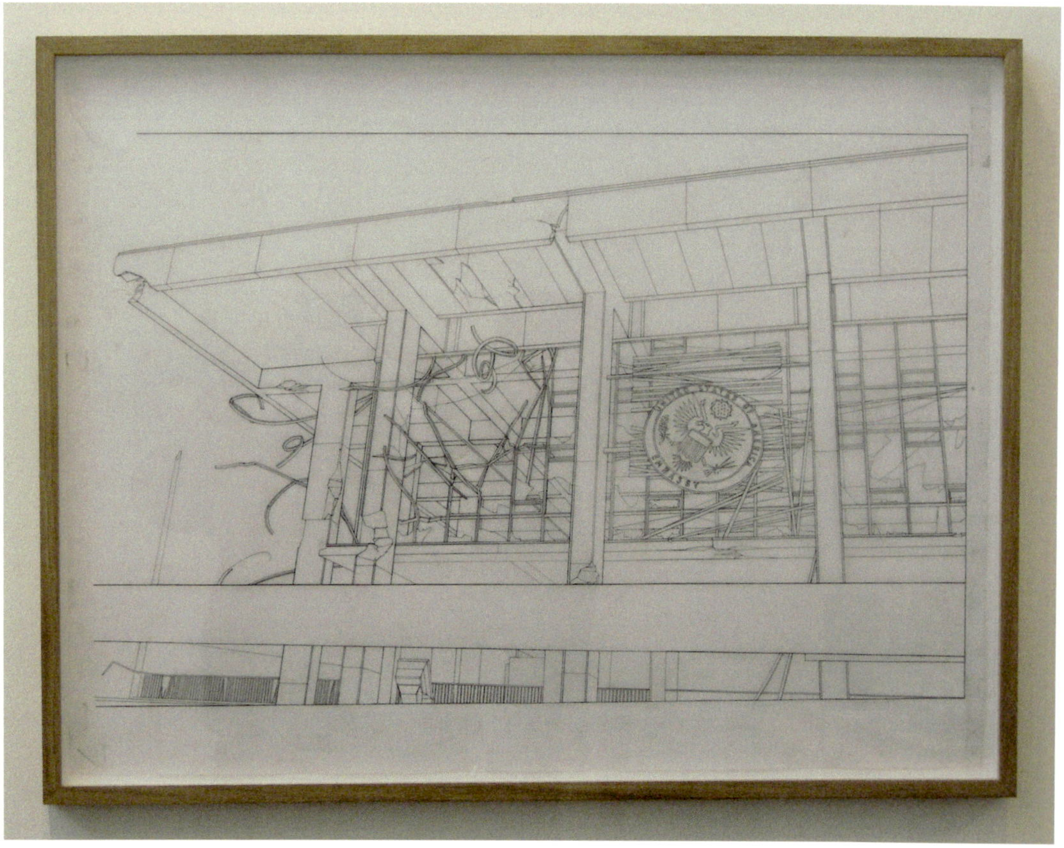

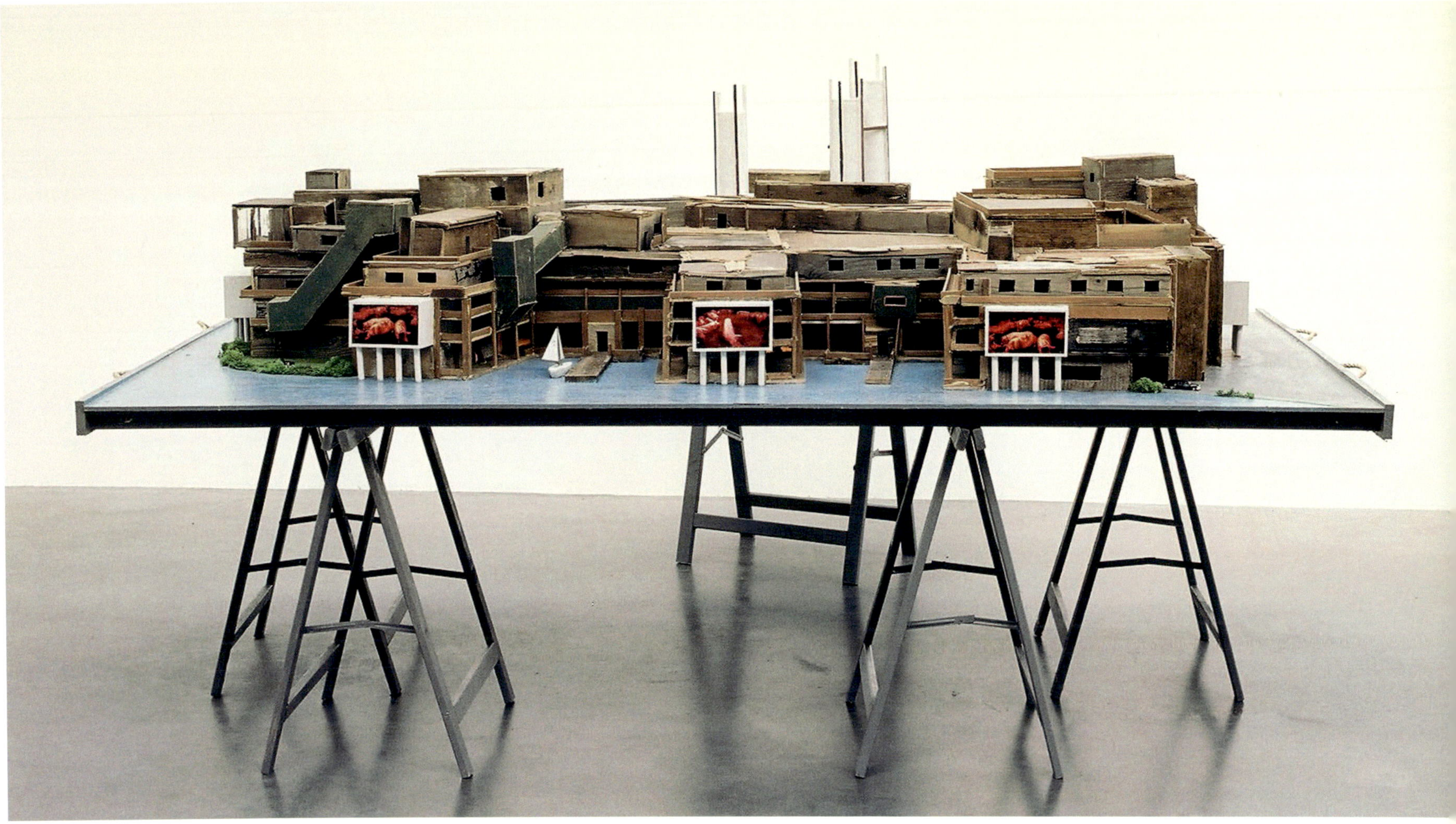

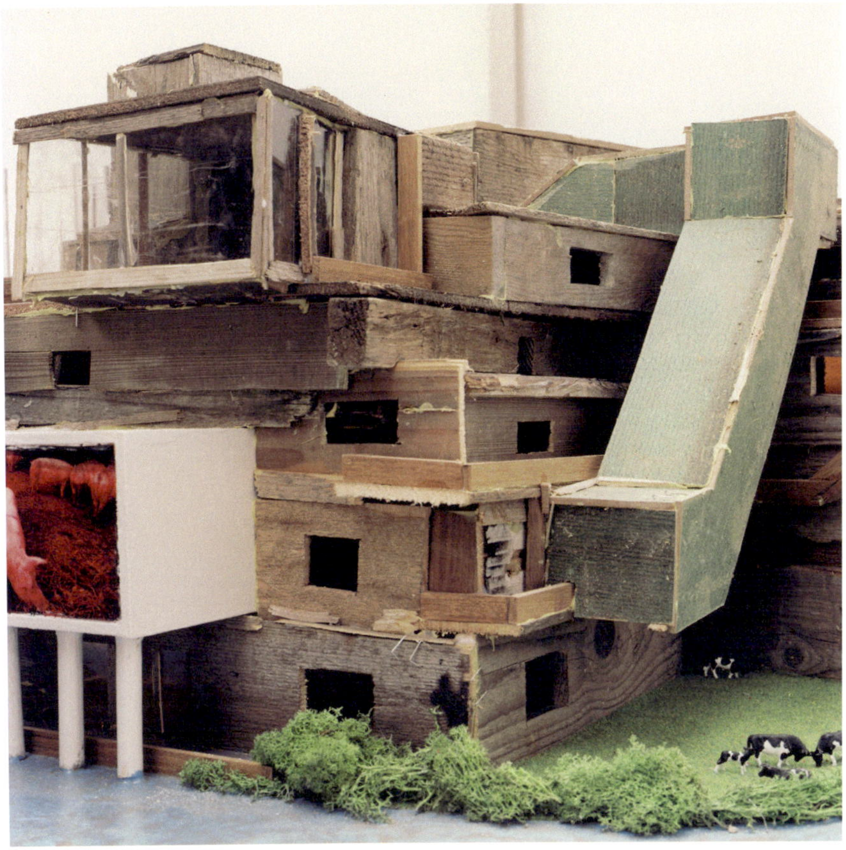

Rob Voerman

MEGAFARM

Under the auspices of a large-scale architecture exhibition project, Archipuncturale 2004, Voerman was invited to make a maquette taking the problems of Dutch agricultural regions as its starting point. Voerman proposed to build a superfarm. A farm for pigs that also includes everything from various living units to a museum and restaurant as well as a power generator and funeral parlour.

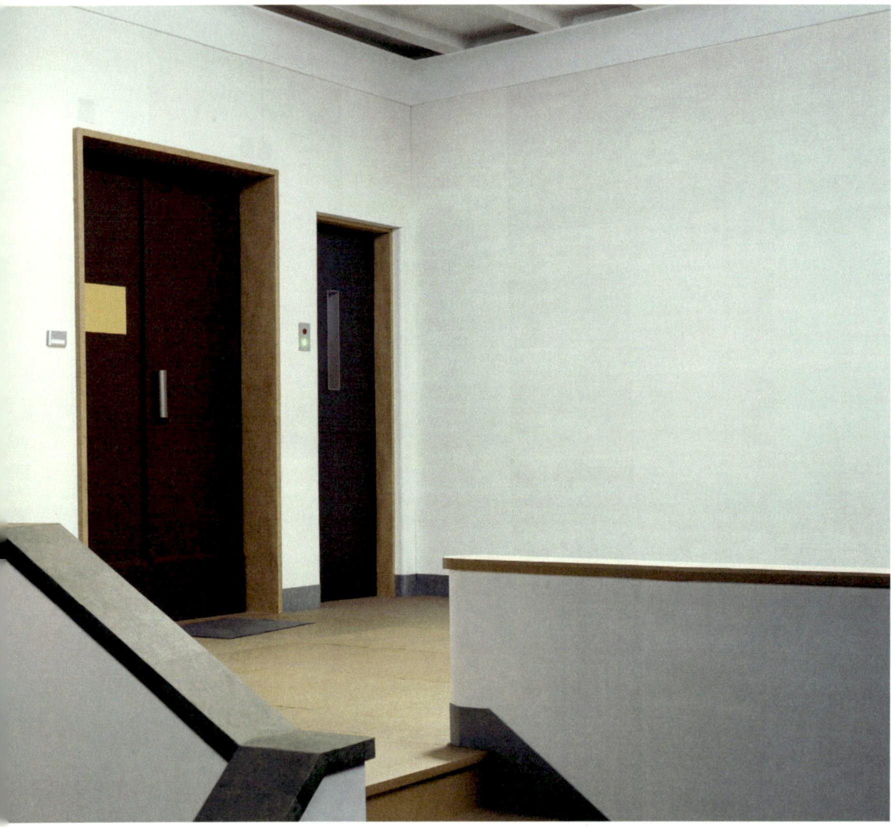

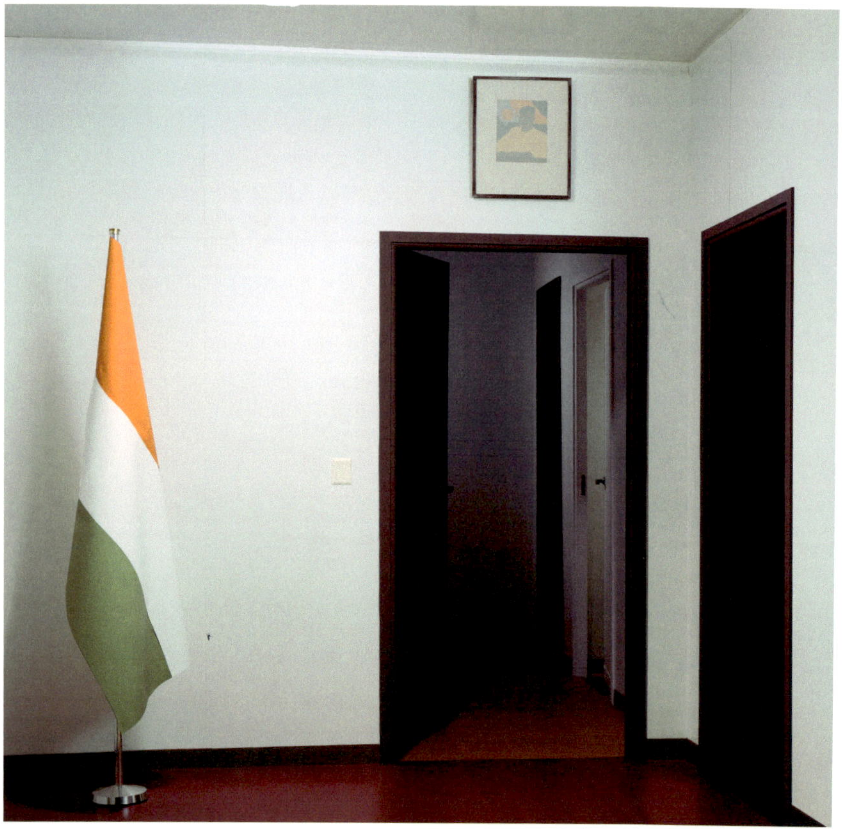

Thomas Demand

EMBASSY

Often starting from a pre-existing image referring to controversial socio-political events, Thomas Demand proceeds to reconstruct the scene with a cardboard model. The photograph he takes of this model is the final stage of his work, and it is only this image that is exhibited, not the models. The Embassy project is part of Demand's Yellowcake series. Yellowcake denotes a concentrated form of uranium, which when enriched may be used to make nuclear weapons. This word emerged in mainstream political discourse because it was the fulcrum of US President George Bush's famous accusation that the British government had learned that Saddam Hussein had recently sought significant quantities of uranium in Africa. The evidence was paperwork supposedly stolen from the Embassy of the Republic of Niger in Rome and passed on to British and American intelligence by SISMI, their Italian counterparts. The documents, which soon turned out to be obvious forgeries, were supposedly a contract for the sale of hundreds of tons of yellowcake to the Iraqi authorities.

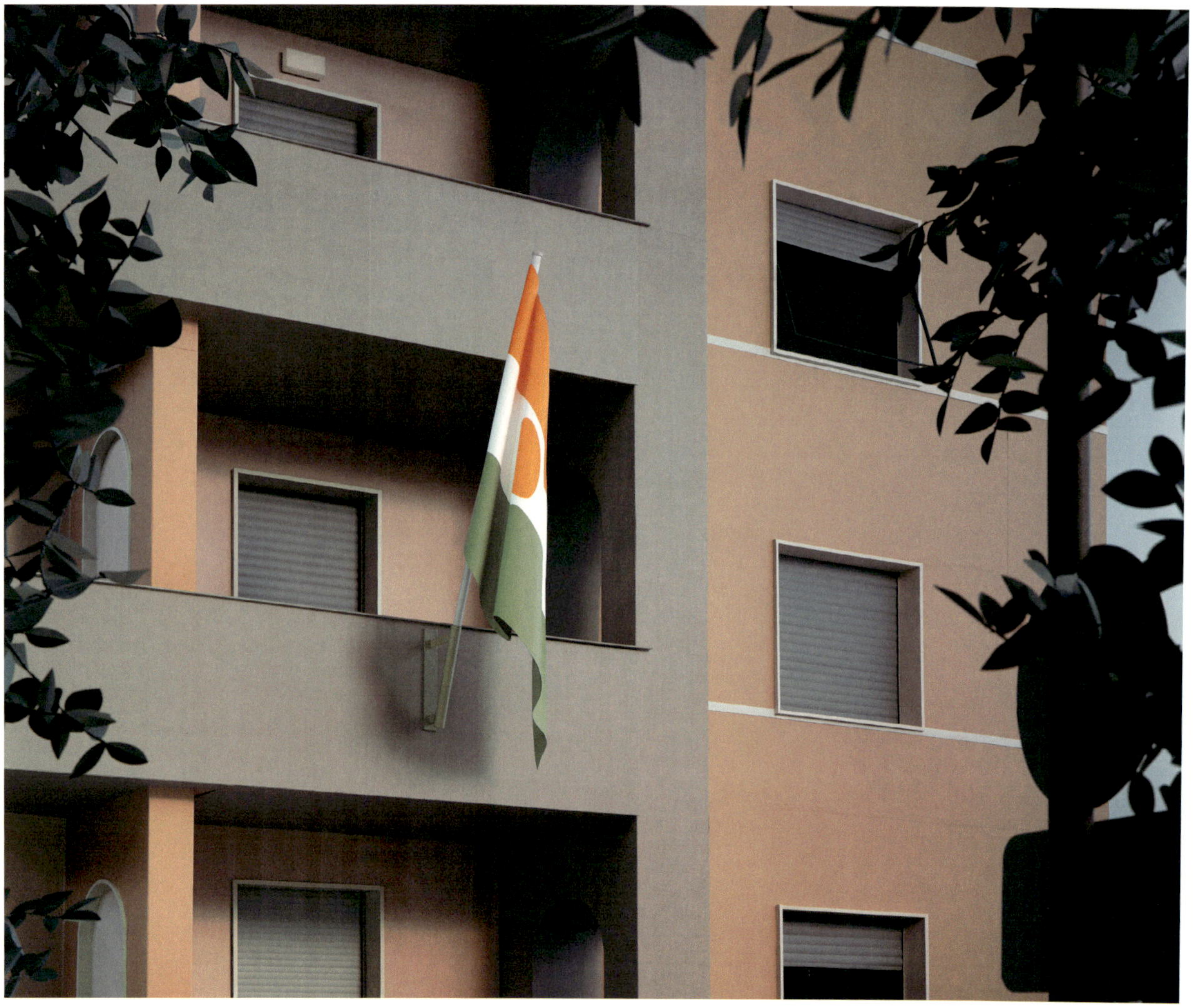

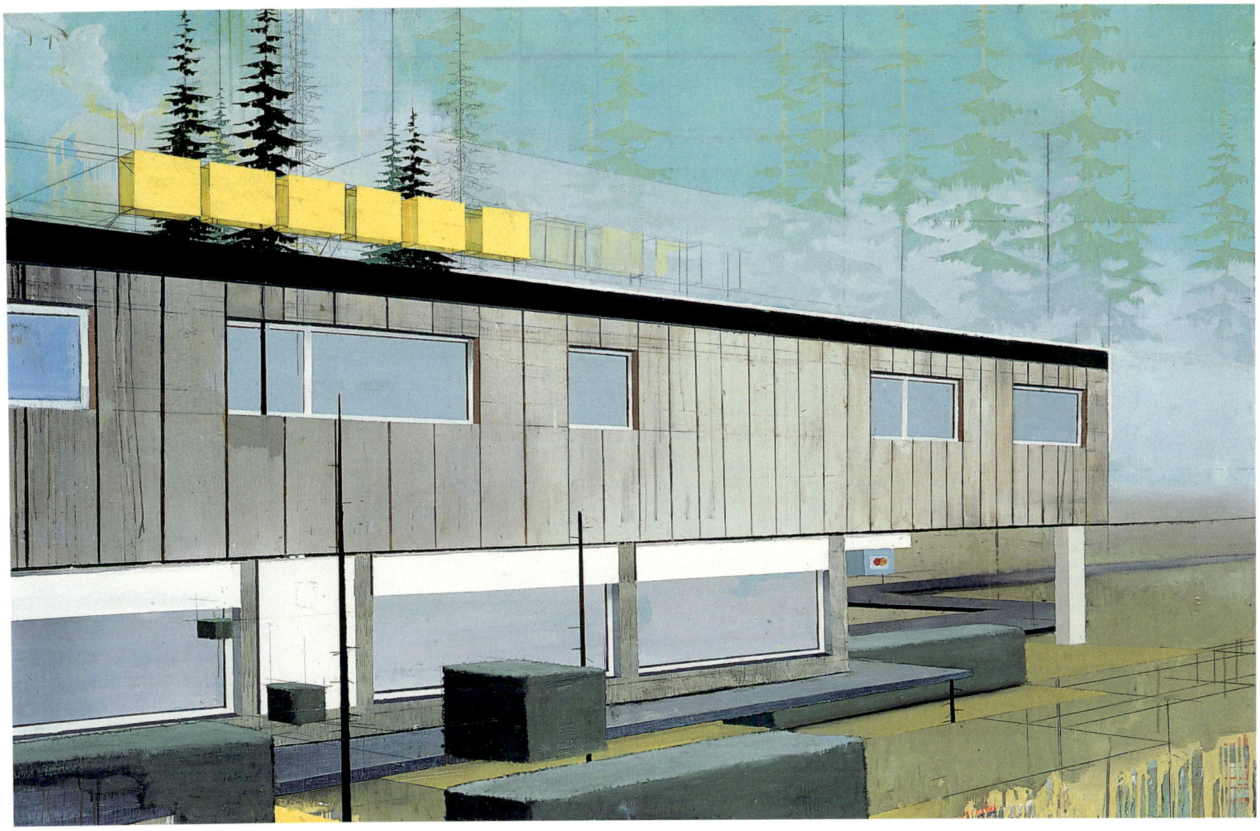

Christian Hellmich

BANK *(left)*
KIOSK II *(bottom)*

For Hellmich, painting is an exercise in taxonomy rather than storytelling. His buildings and landscapes emphasize texture, form and geometry, with rigorous investment in the materiality of his surfaces.

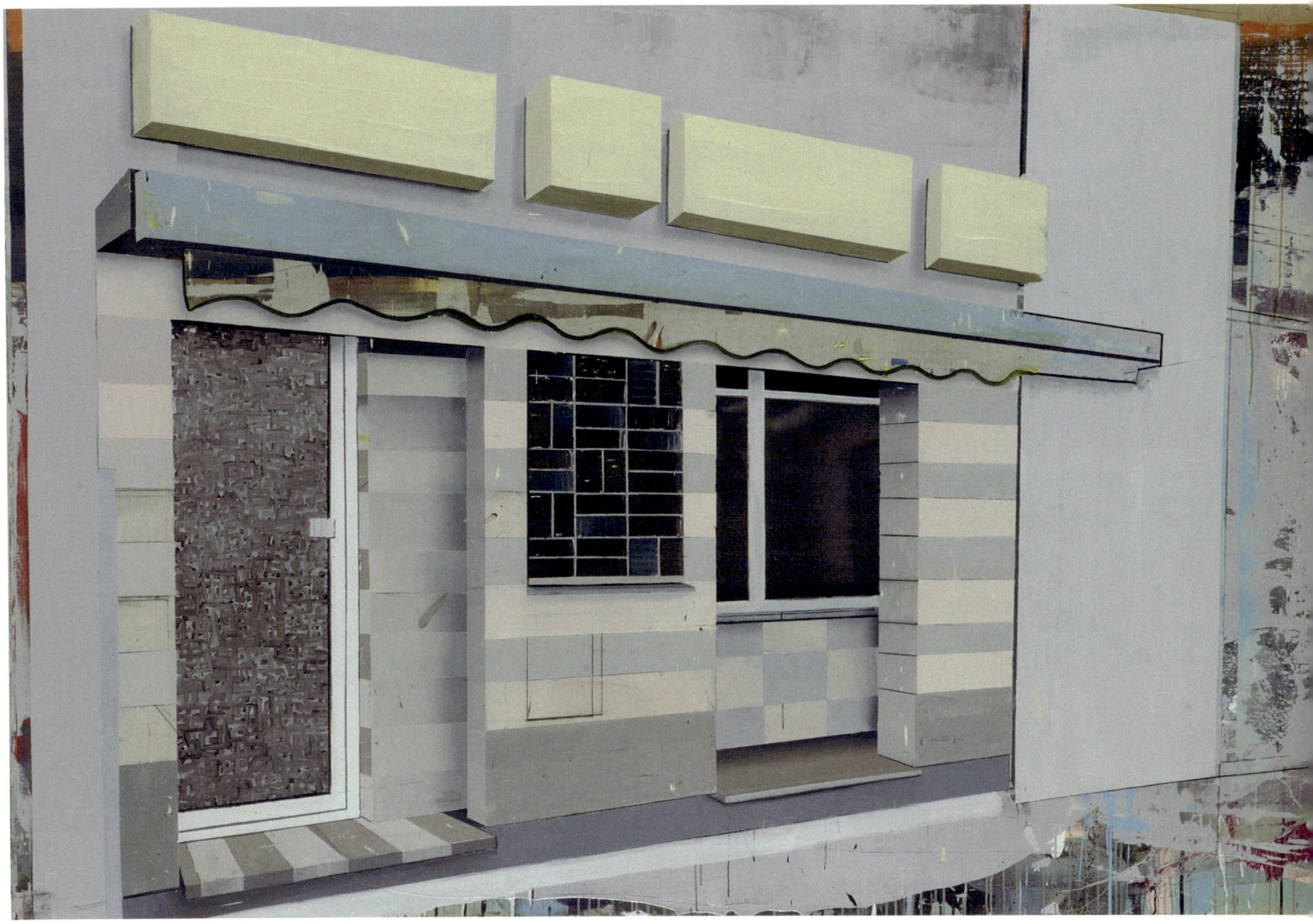

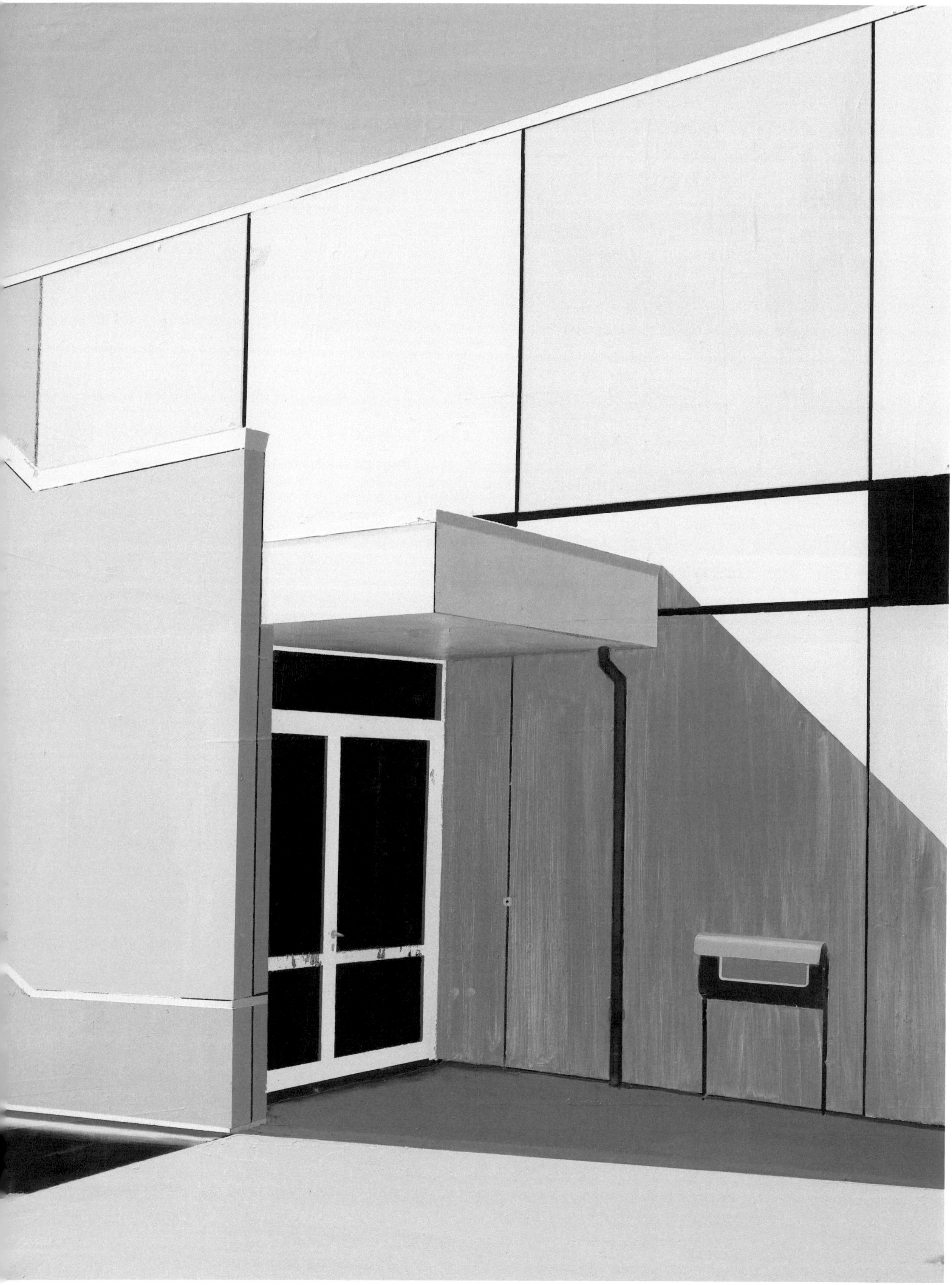

Asmund Havsteen-Mikkelsen

OFFICE *(left)*
TOWER *(right page, top)*

In his work, Havsteen-Mikkelsen exlores painterly space, drawing inspiration from the built-environment via photography and models.

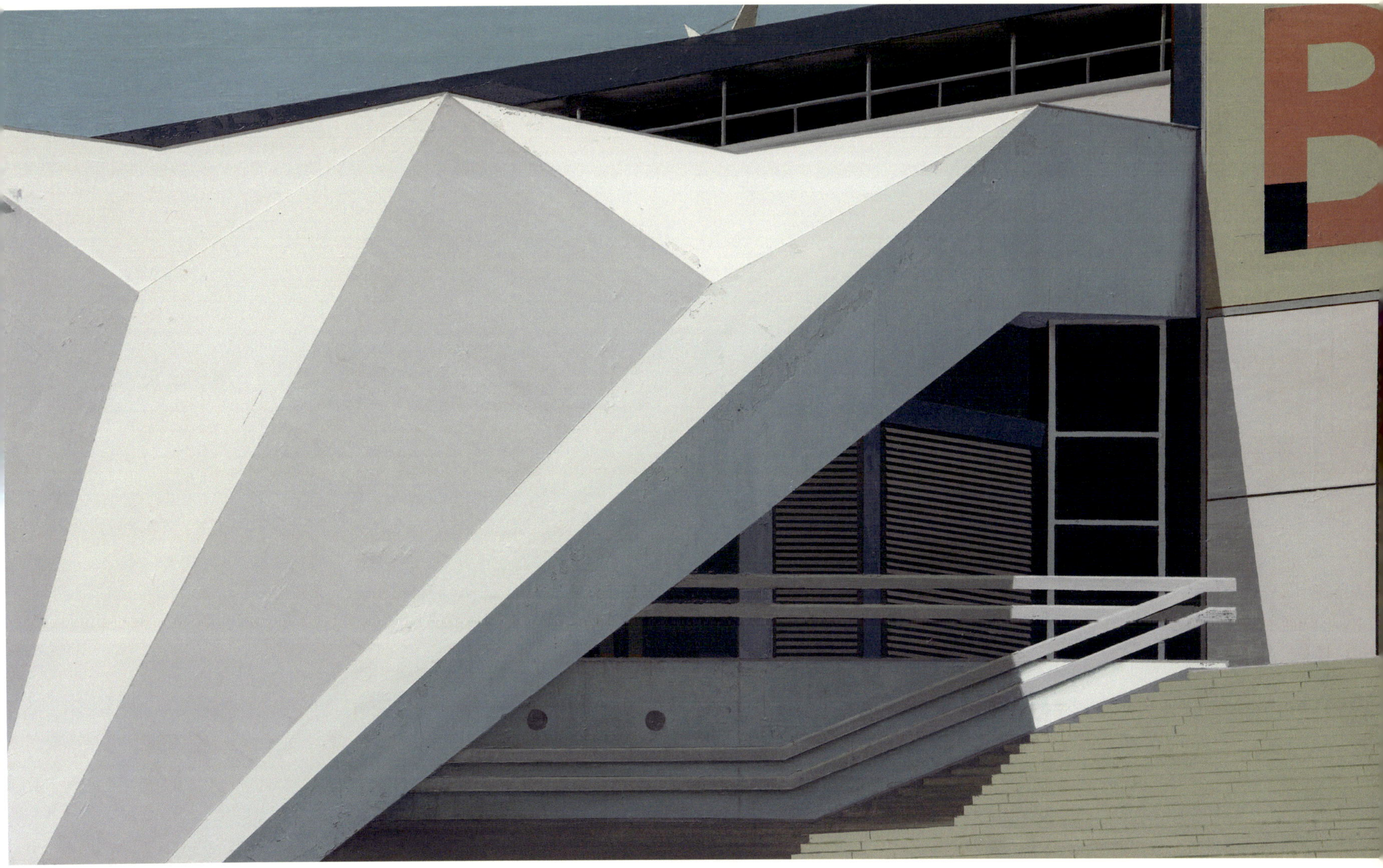

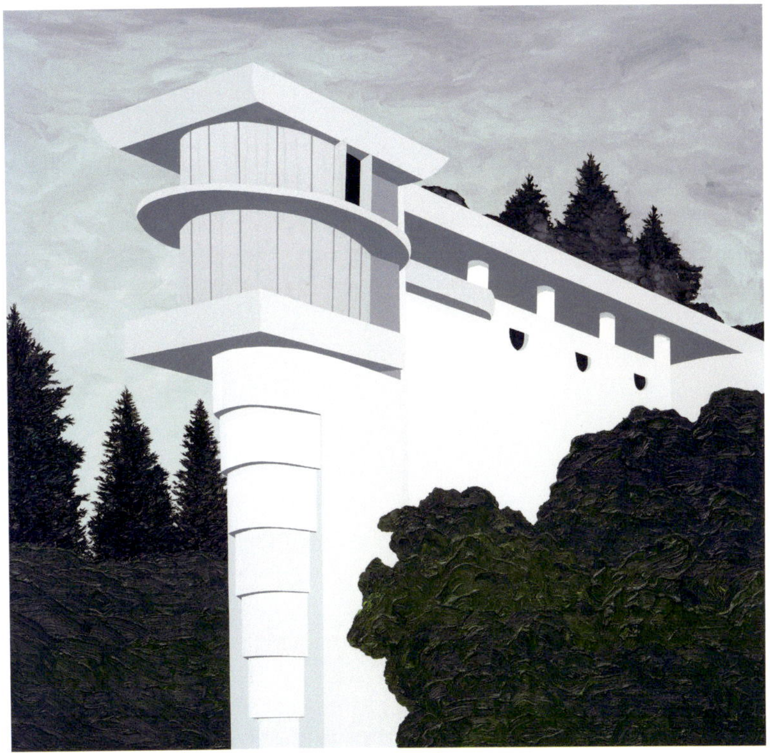

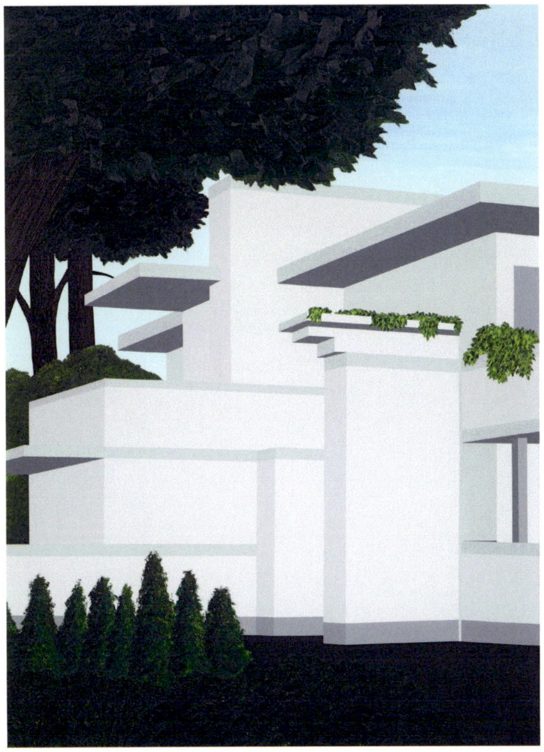

Sven Drühl

S.D.F.L.W. II *(left)*
S.D.F.L.W. III *(right)*

Drühl approaches painting as a conceptual endeavor and often appropriates popular art and historical imagery.

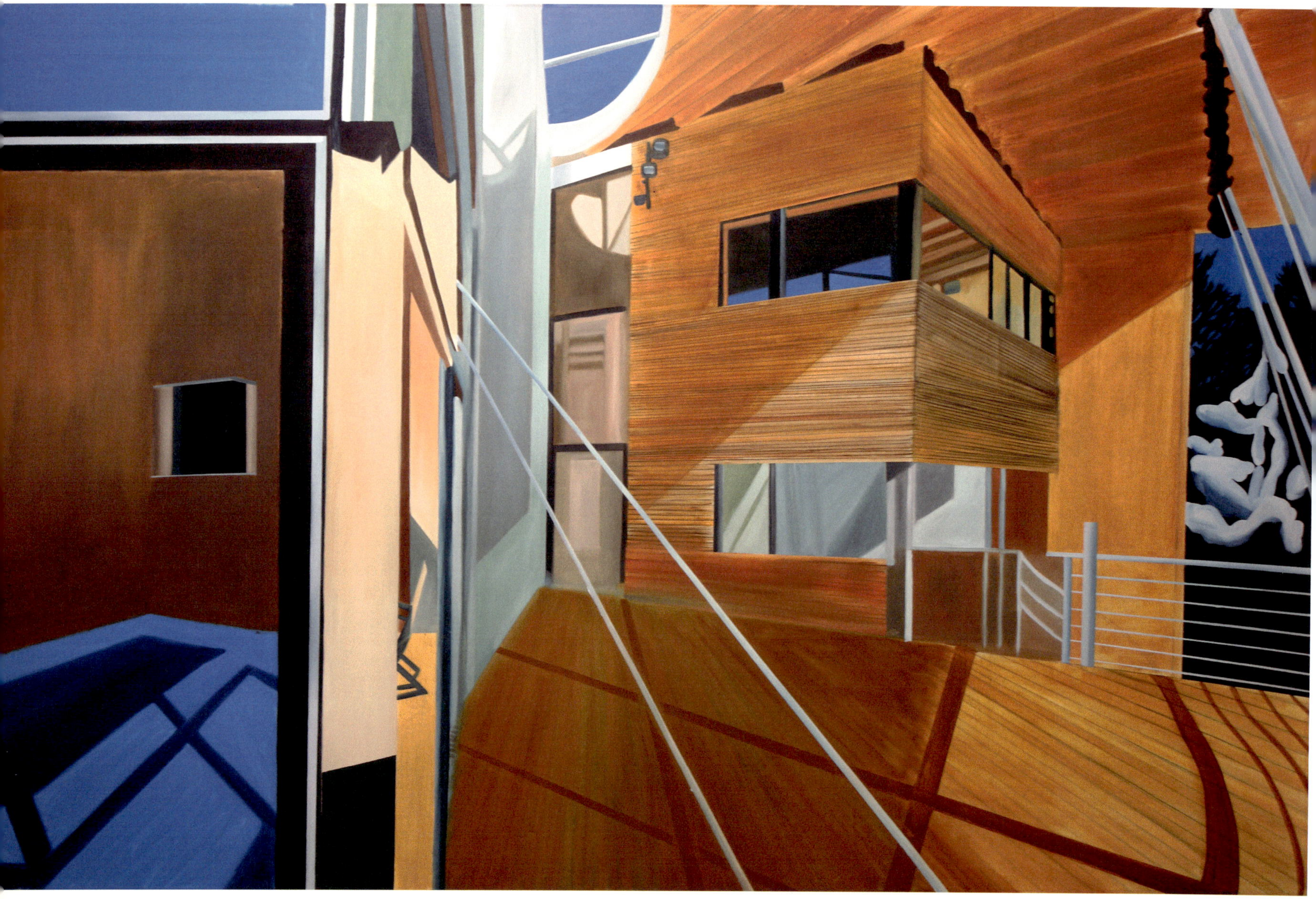

Eamon O'Kane

HOUSE MORNING EAST VIEW *(top)*
LLOYD WRIGHT DREAMS *(right)*

This large-scale oil painting on canvas by O'Kane is part of the artist's The Architect's House series which explores and reflects Modernist architecture, cinema and literature.

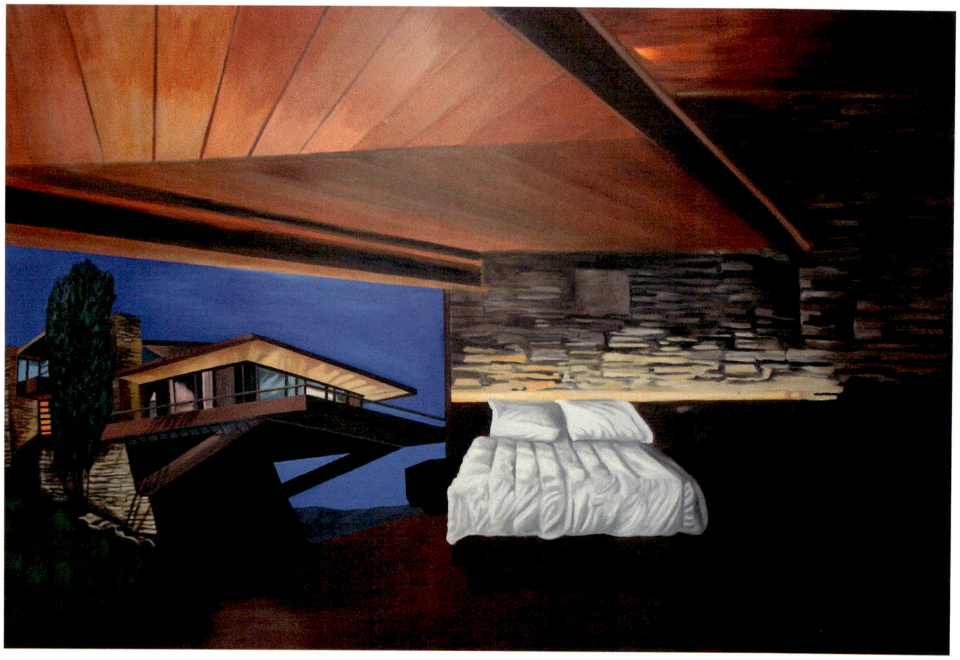

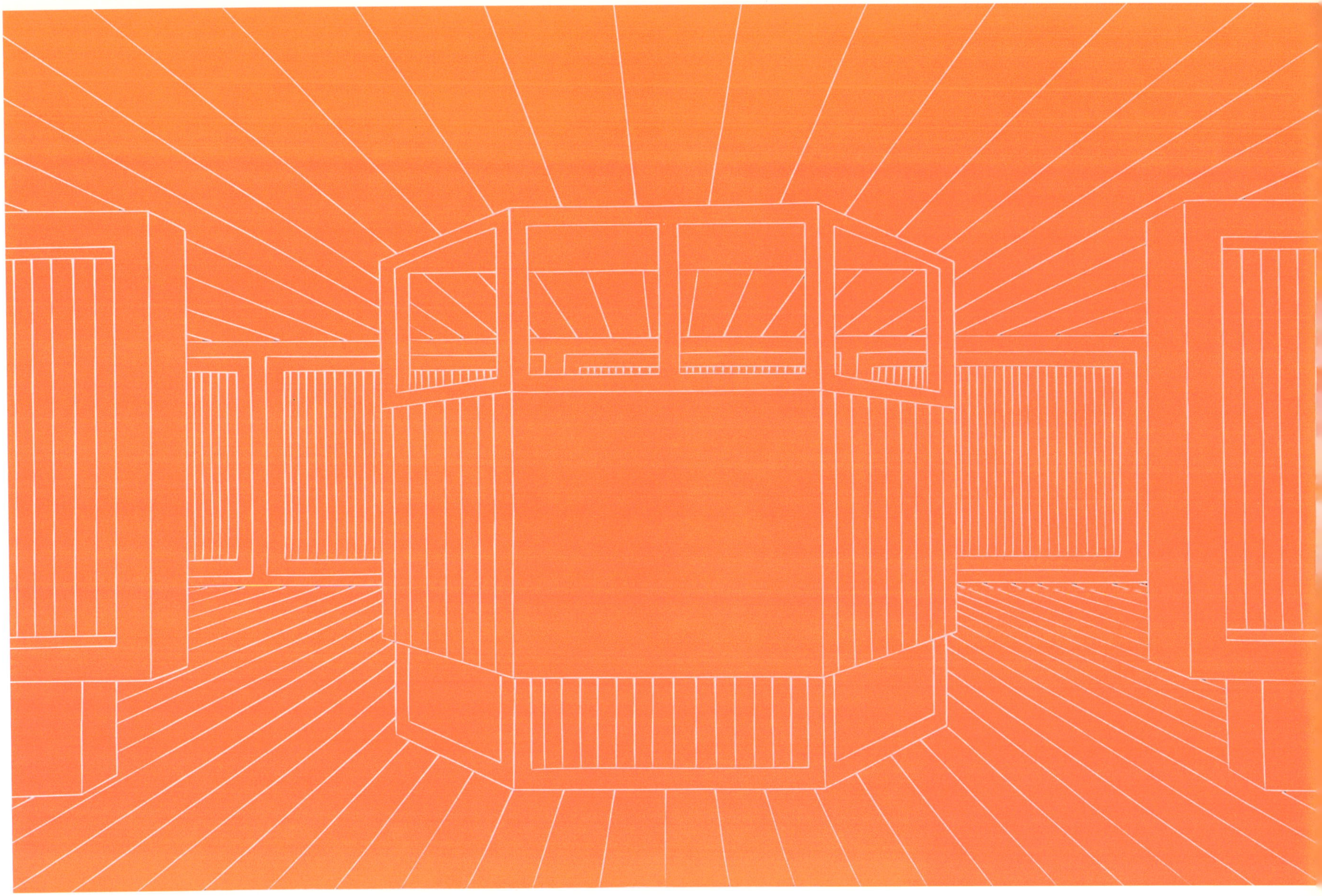

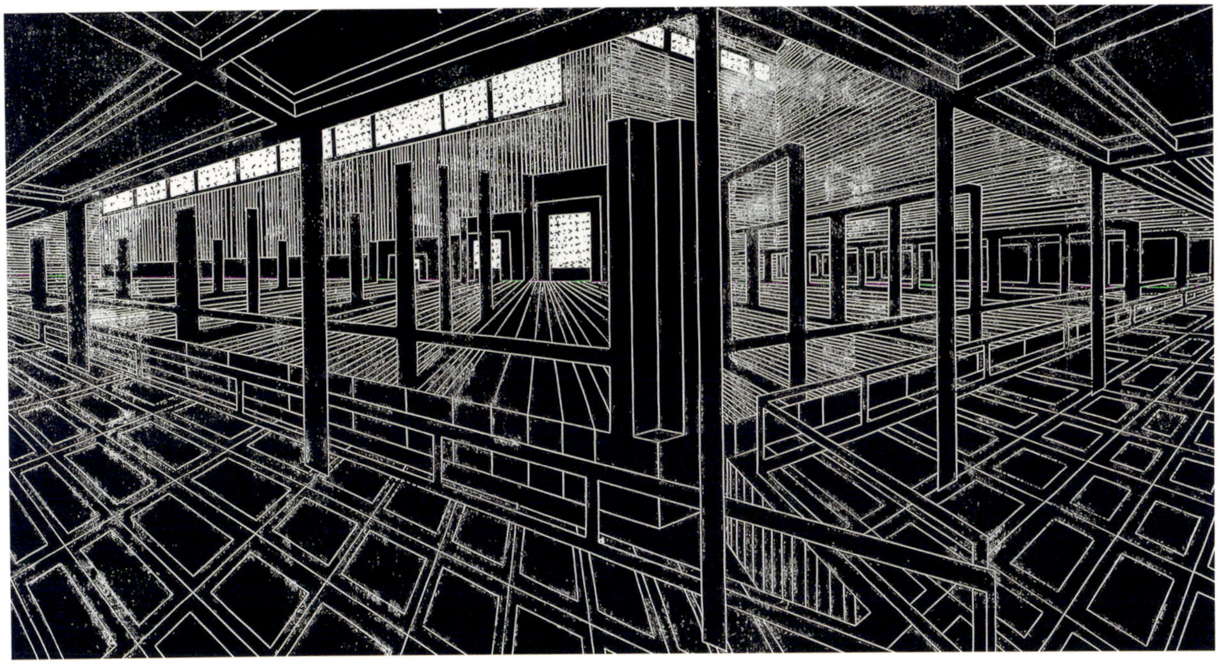

Jörn Gerstenberg

PLATFORM (top)
ELEPHANTHOUSE (left)

The PVC-prints by Berlin-based artist Jörn Gerstenberg display interior spaces that merge reality and imagination.

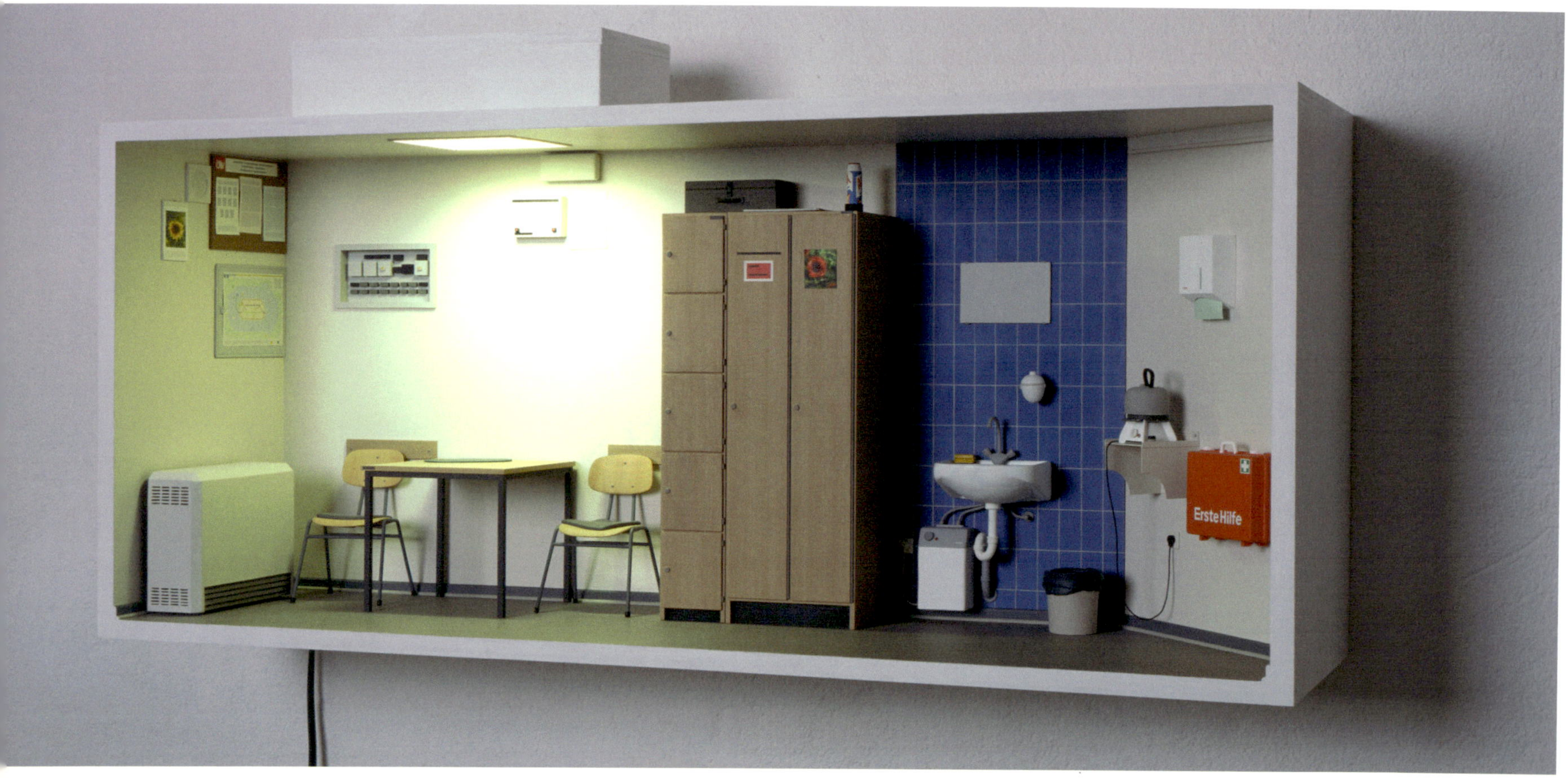

Eamon O'Kane

MOBILE STUDIO *(right)*

Eamon O'Kane's portable studio, approximating in size to a shipping container, filled with finished pieces and works in progress.

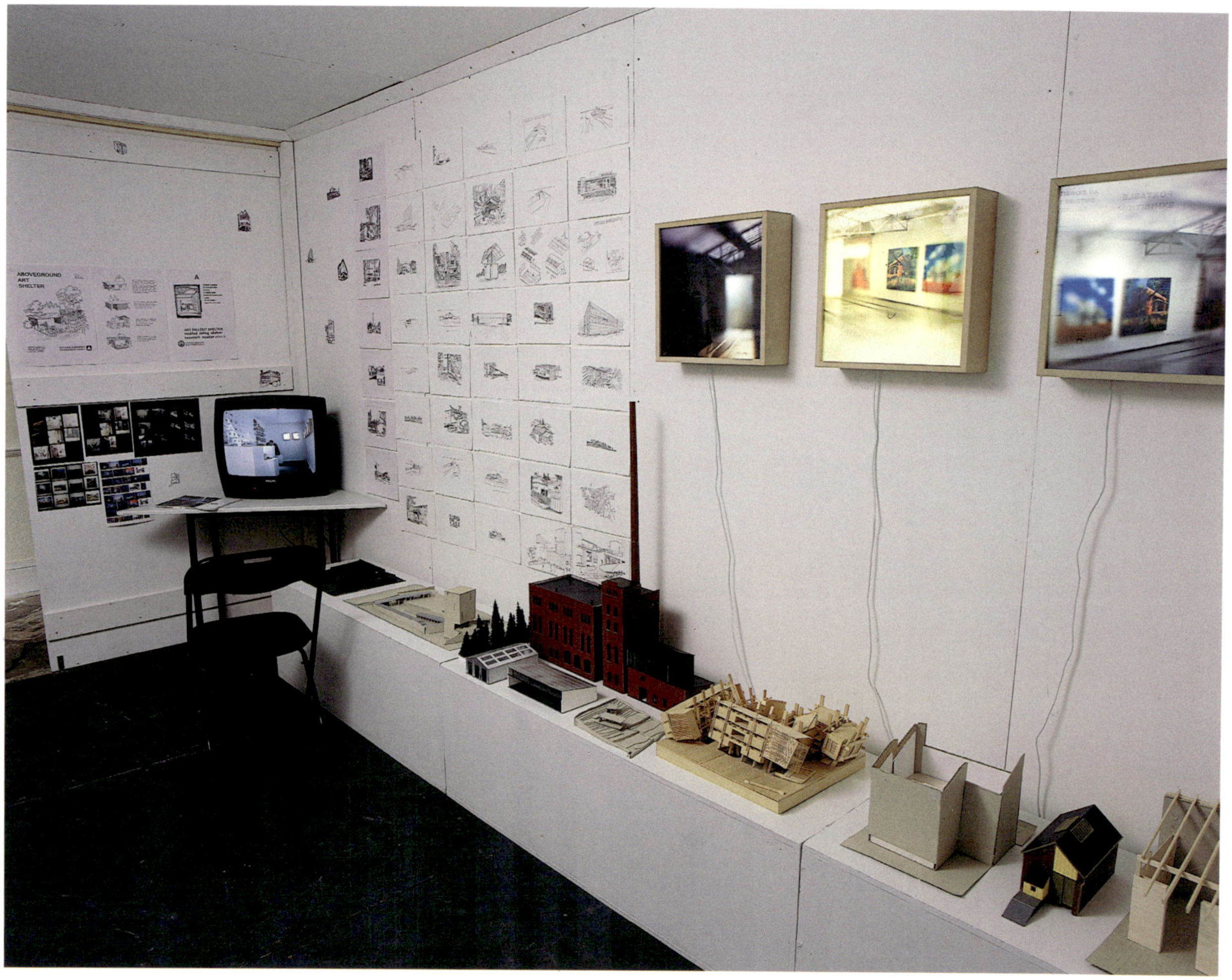

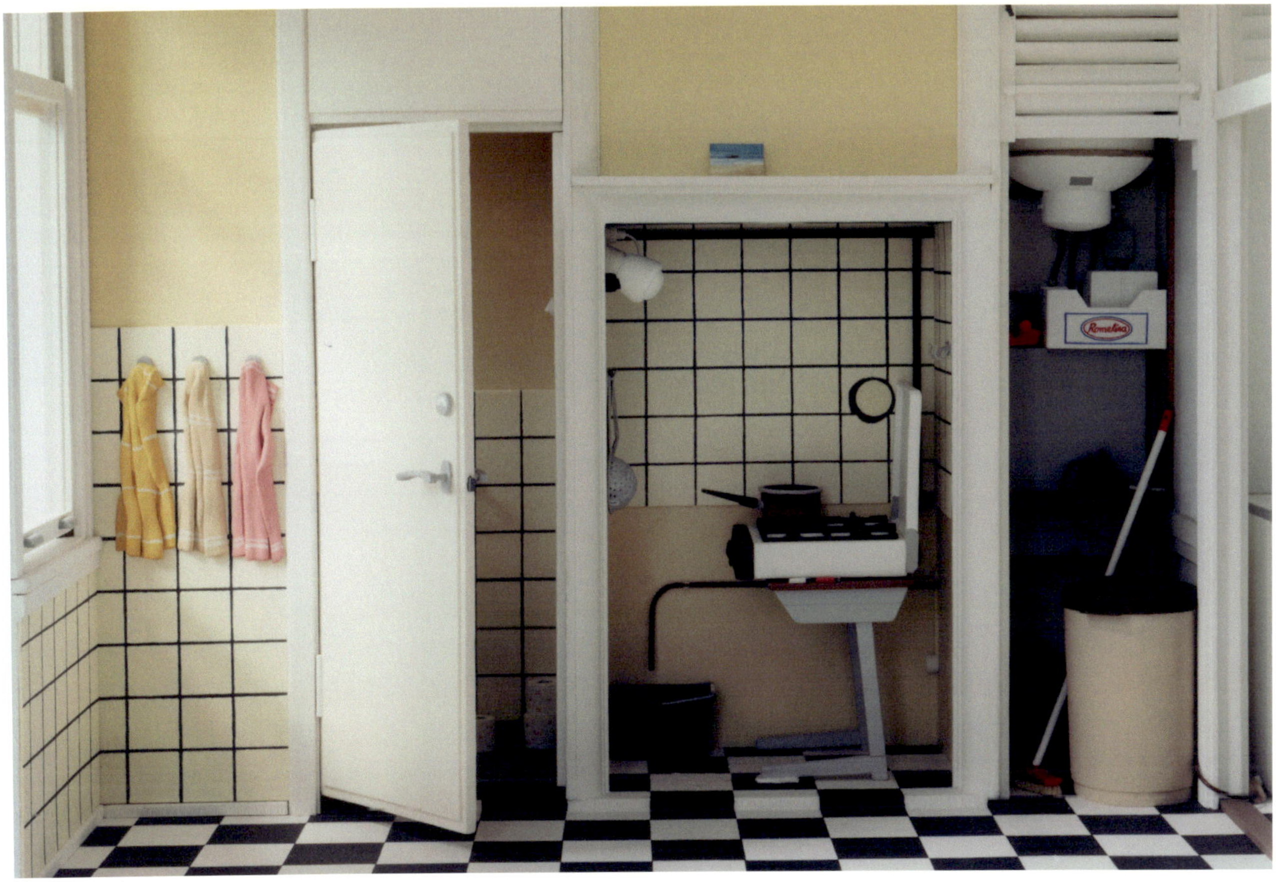

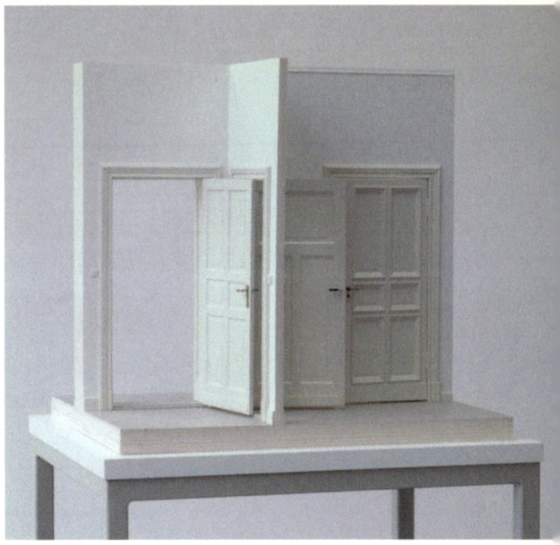

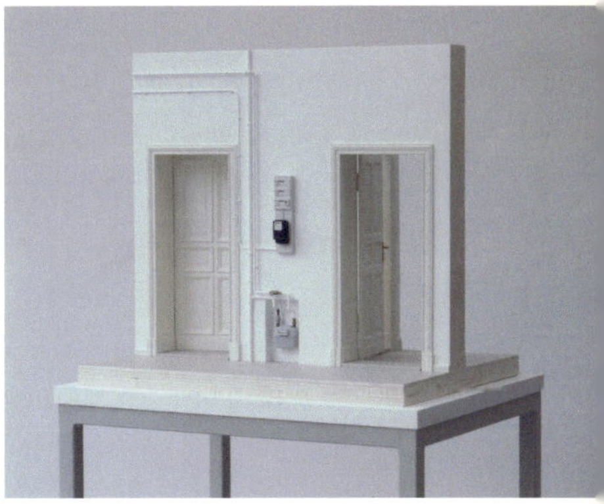

Jens Reinert

BUREAU *(left page, top)*
PAUL'S APARTMENT *(top, left)*
PORTER'S OFFICE *(left)*
3 DOORS *(top)*
ENTRY/EXIT *(bottom)*

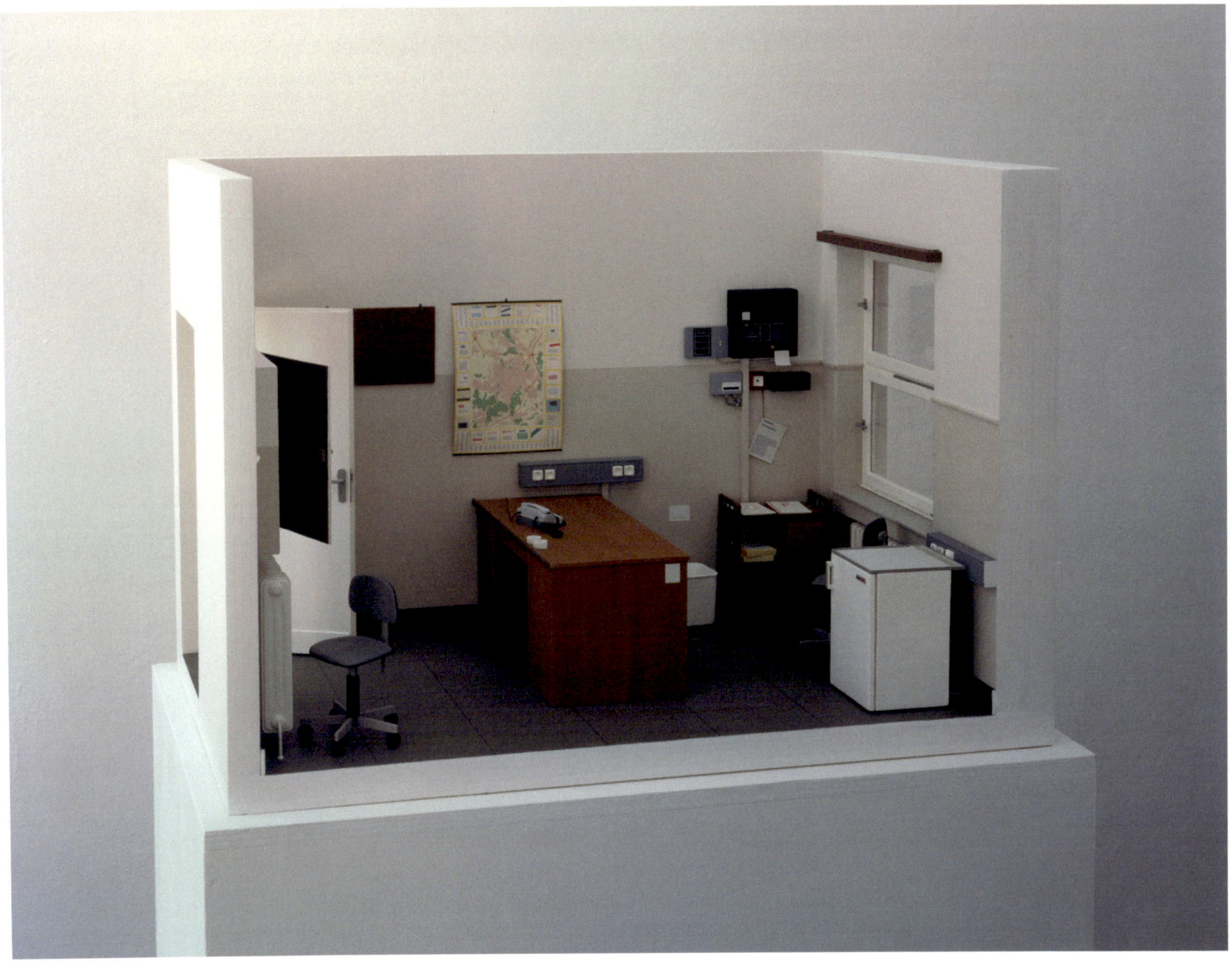

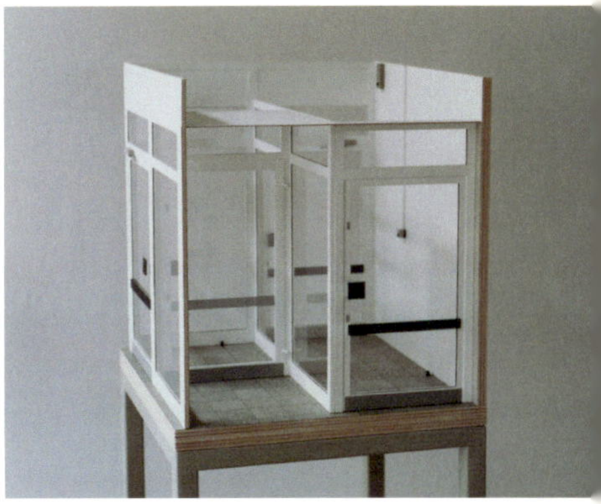

Andreas Koch

APARTMENT

Andreas Koch's work is mainly about space, which he reorganises and makes visible using different media such as photography, film, sculpture and mixed media. Therefore, he often changes the scale and relations between objects and works by transforming two-dimensional surfaces into three-dimensional sculptures or films.

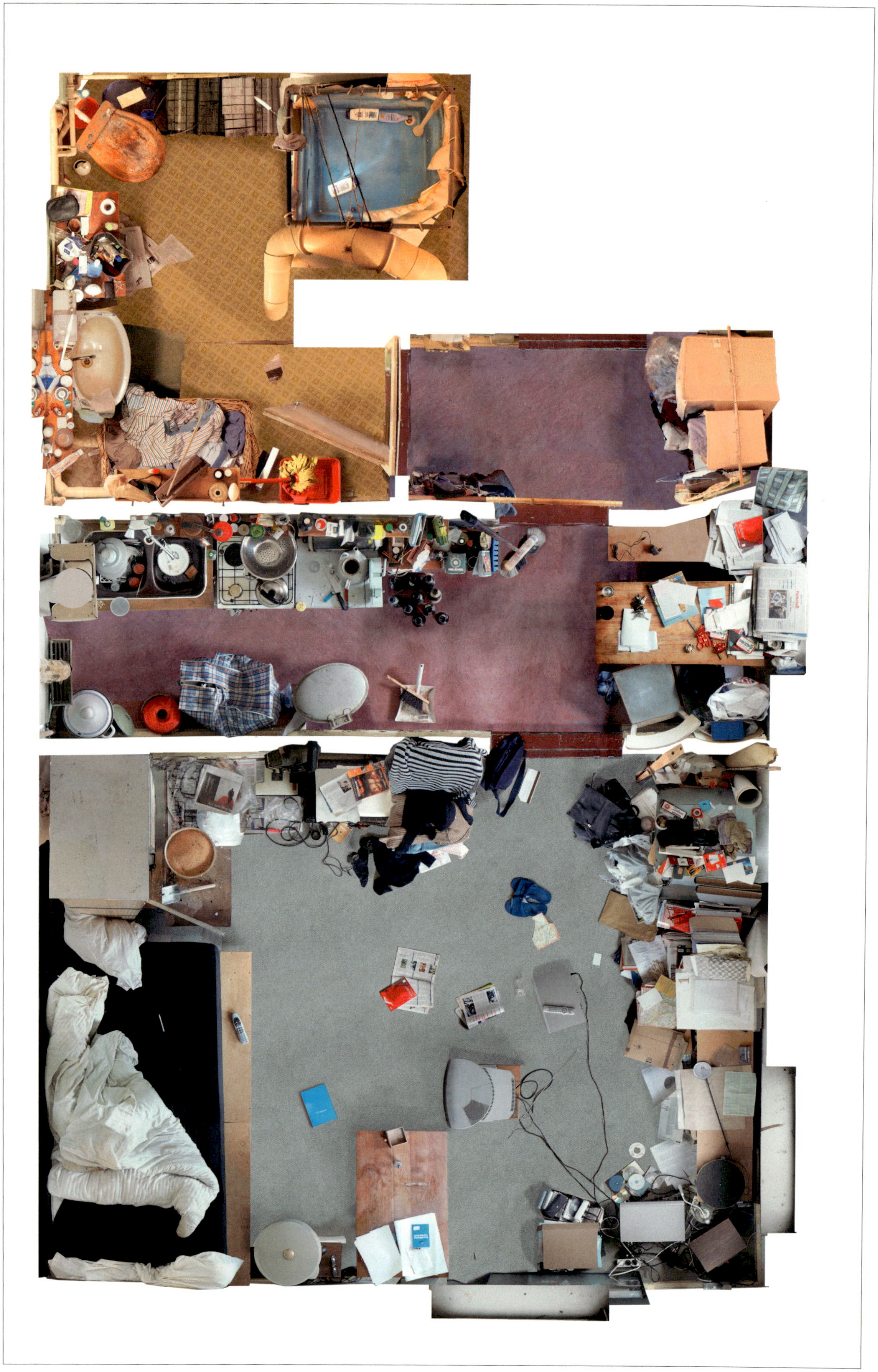

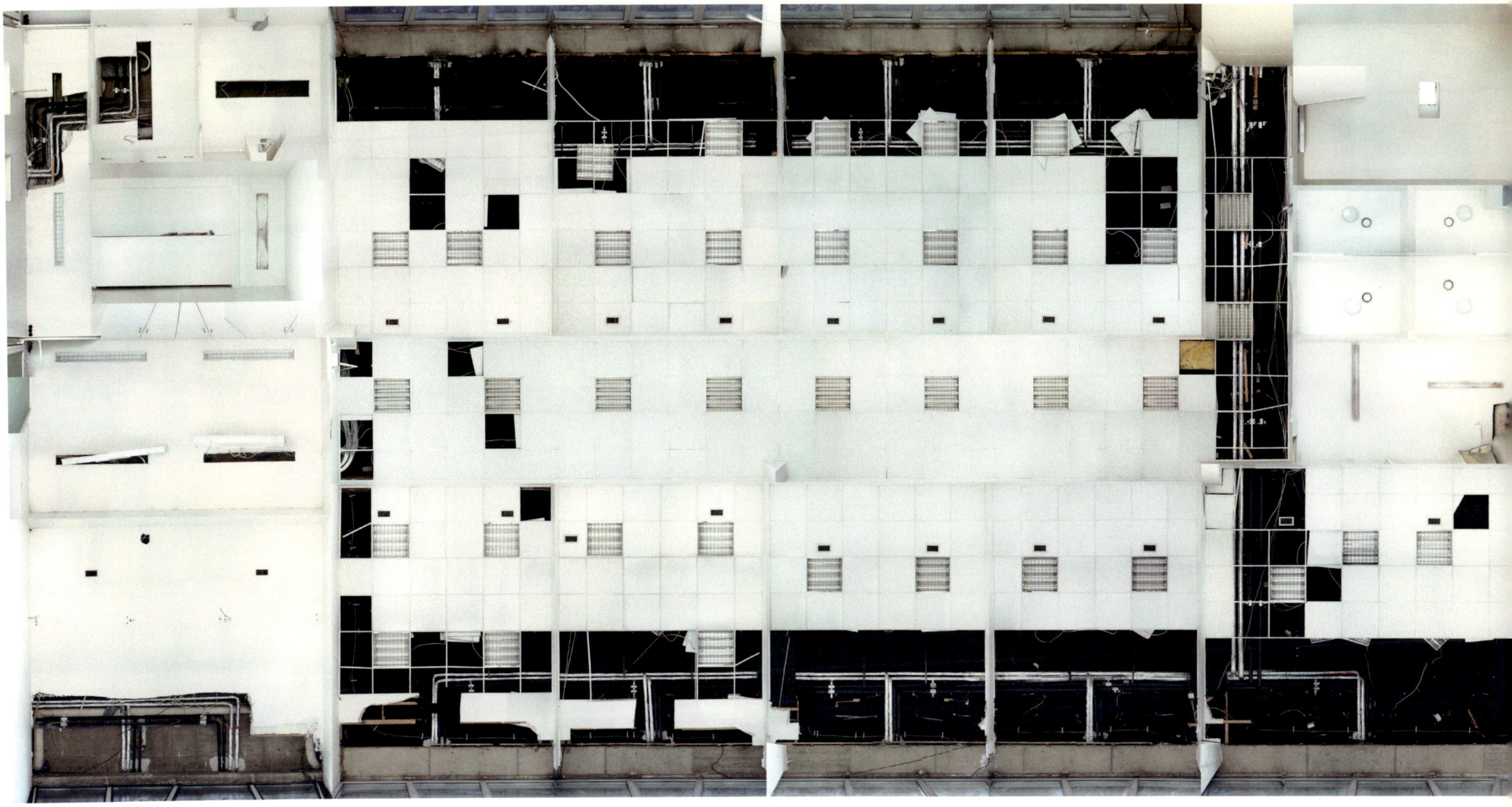

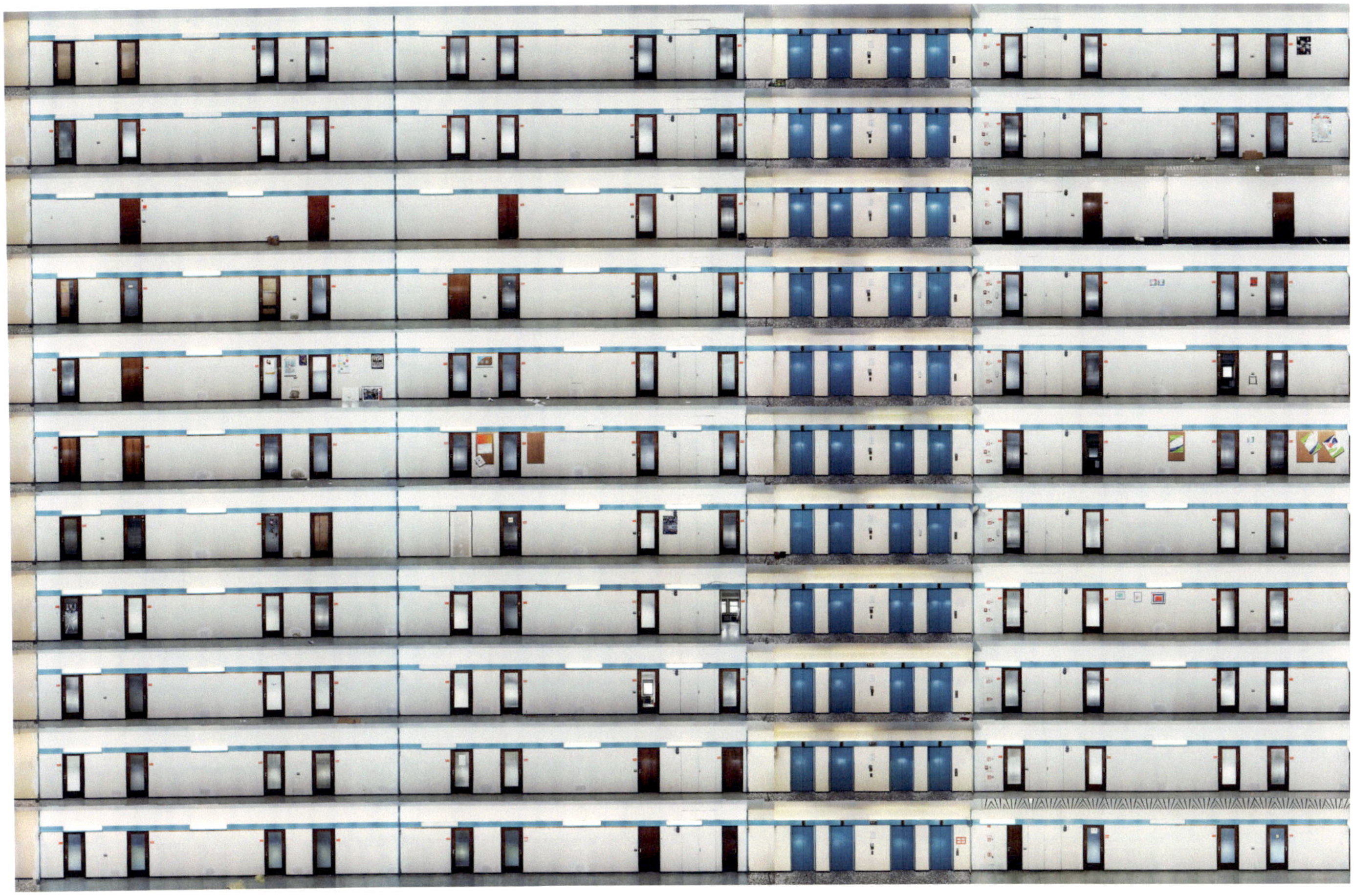

Andreas Gefeller

UNTITLED
(CEILING 3, DÜSSELDORF)
UNTITLED (OFFICE)

In the series Supervisions, Gefeller employs a technically elaborate method to scan the surface of urban sites.

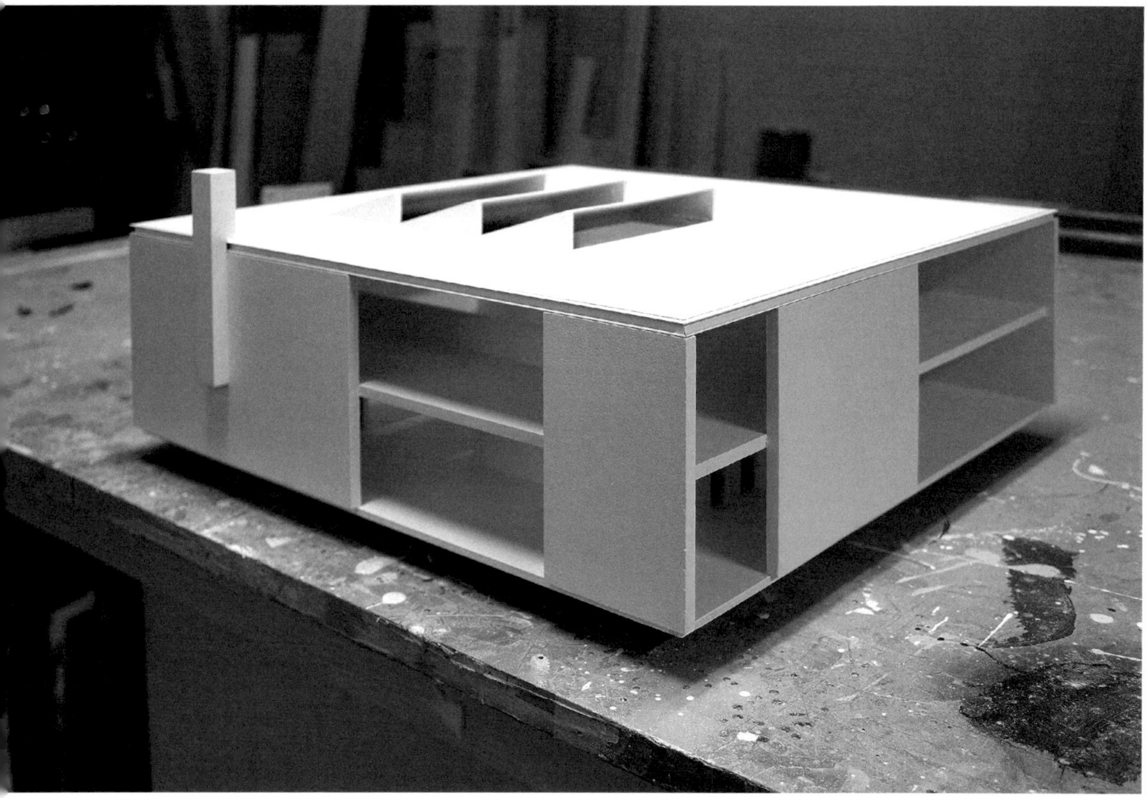

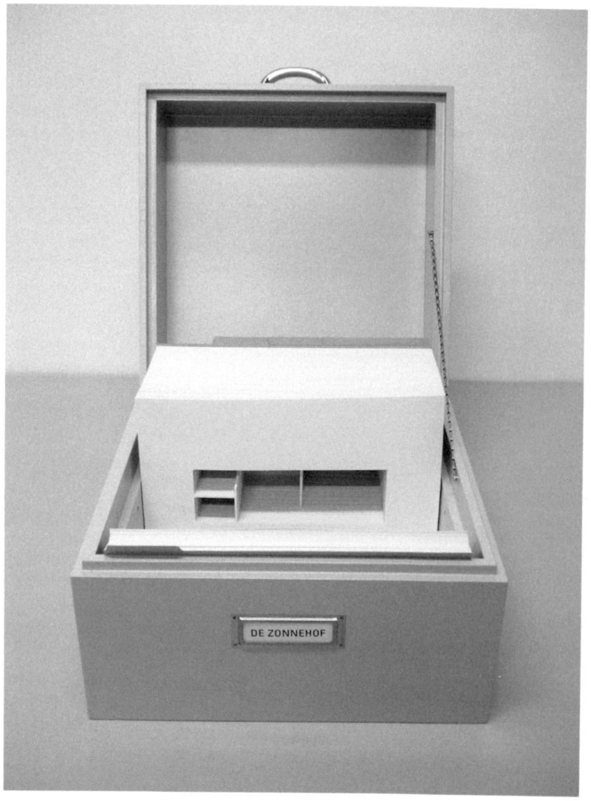

Oscar Lourens

UNTITELD (DE ZONNEHOF)

De Zonnehof is an exhibition pavilion designed by Gerrit Rietveld in 1958. In these works by Dutch artist Oscar Lourens, the geometrical properties of the building have been meticulously copied and converted to cheesecloth works, architectural models and an index card box. The cheesecloth works depict the façades and the floor plan of the pavilion. The three-dimensional relations are investigated in three models that depict the entire building as well as the exterior and interior of the De Zonnehof. Finally, in the index card box, the cross sections of the interior space of the building have been combined in almost 700 cards.

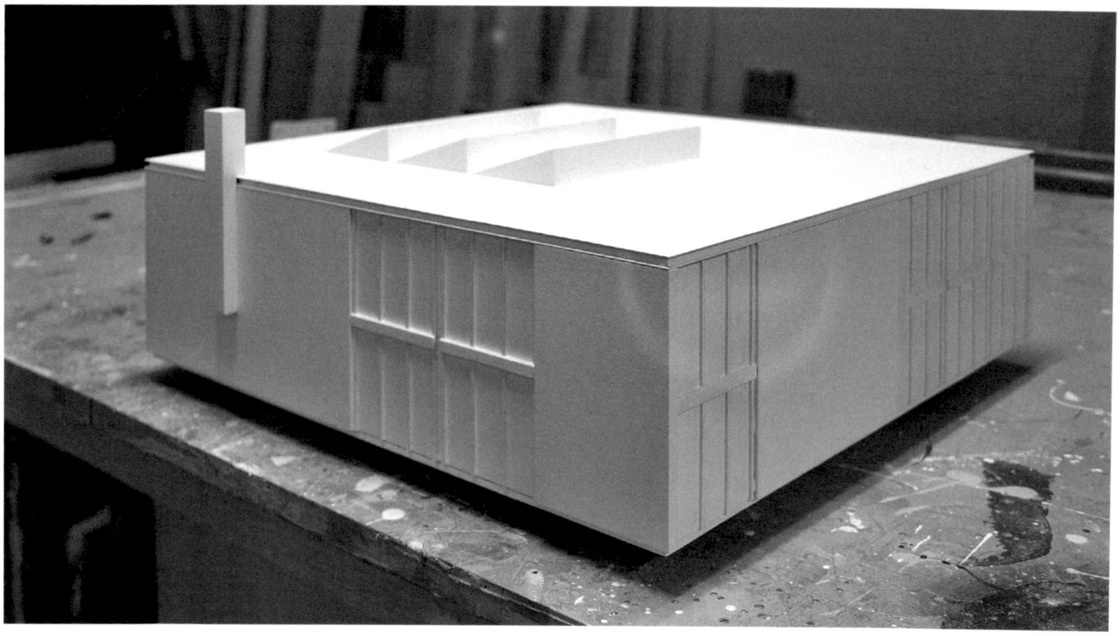

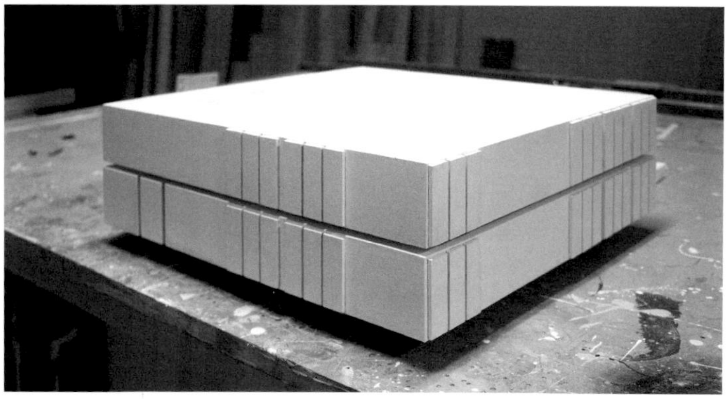

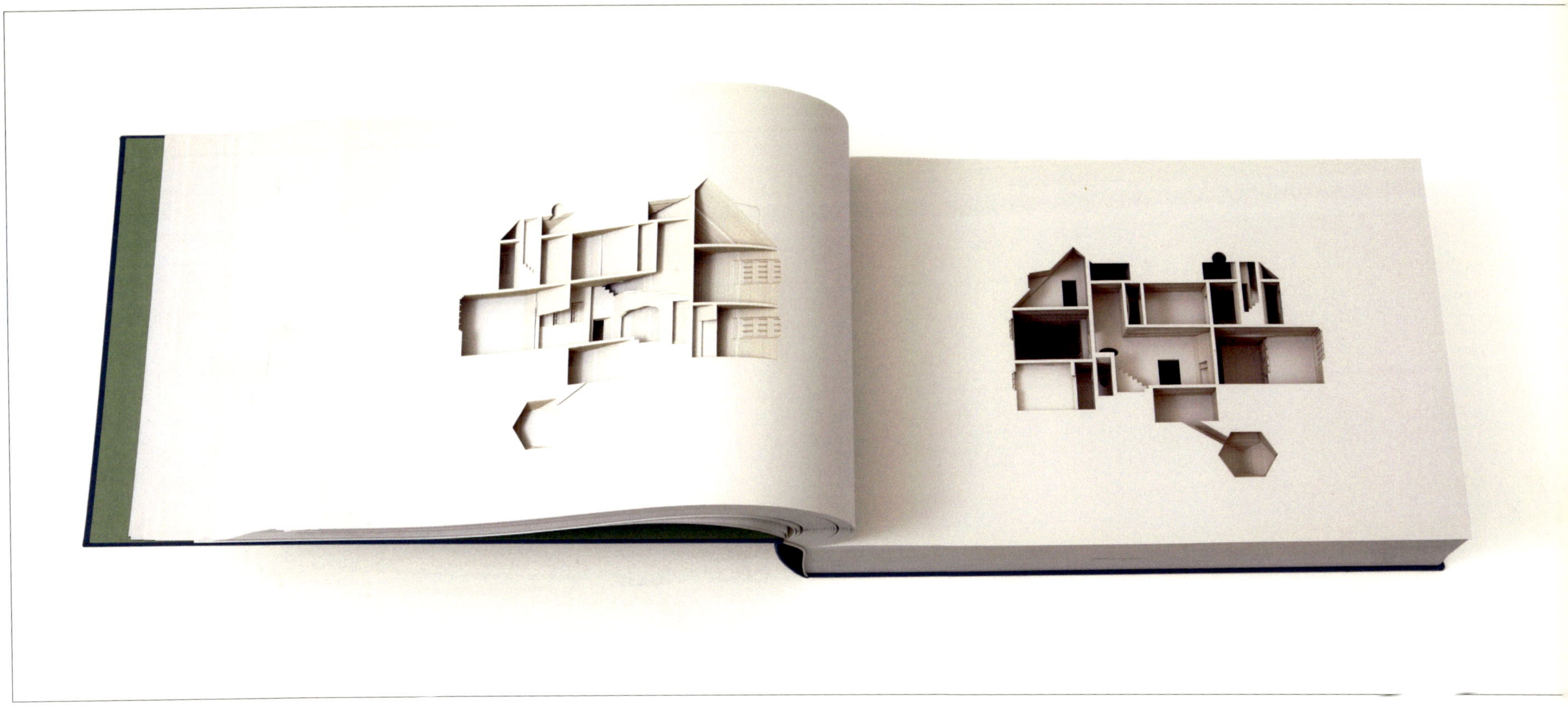

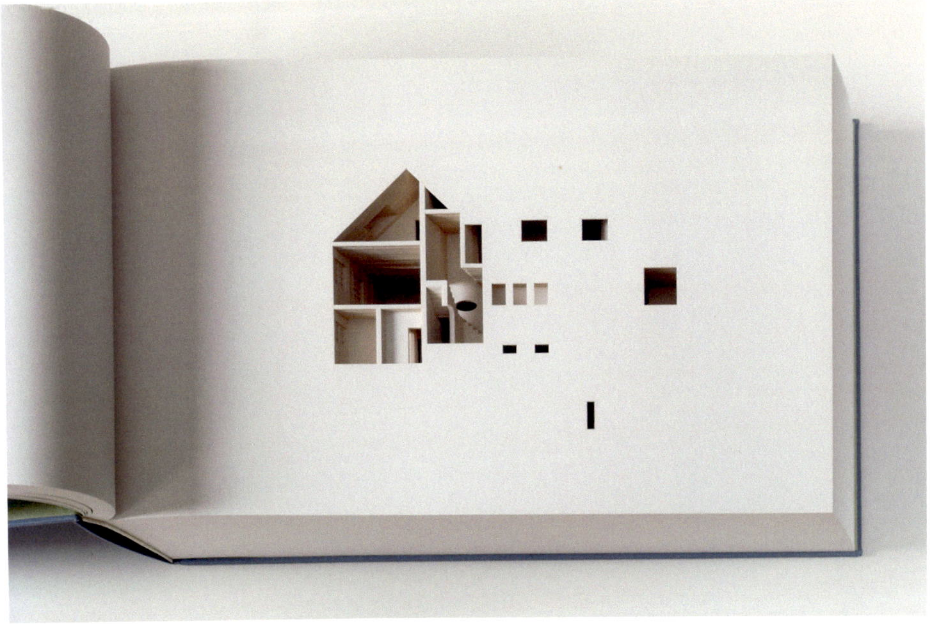

Olafur Eliasson

YOUR HOUSE

Olafur Eliasson's Your House is an oversized sculptural volume evoking a tour through a turn of the century European house – the artist's own home in Copenhagen, Denmark. The book's 454 hand-bound leaves, layouted by Michael Heimann, digitally reproduce a series of vertical cross-sections of the house. In addition, each leaf is individually laser-cut to create negative spaces in the paper.

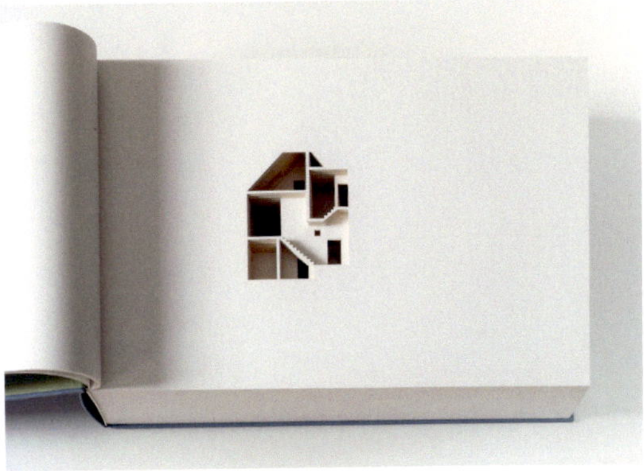

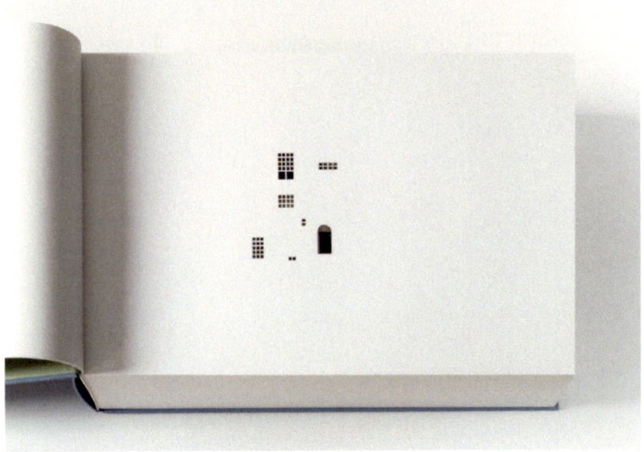

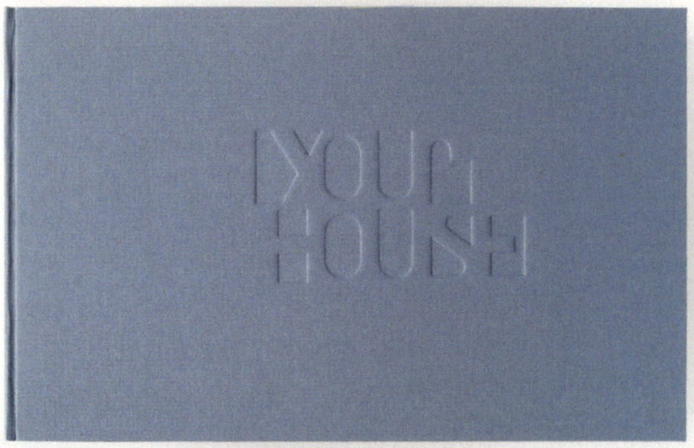

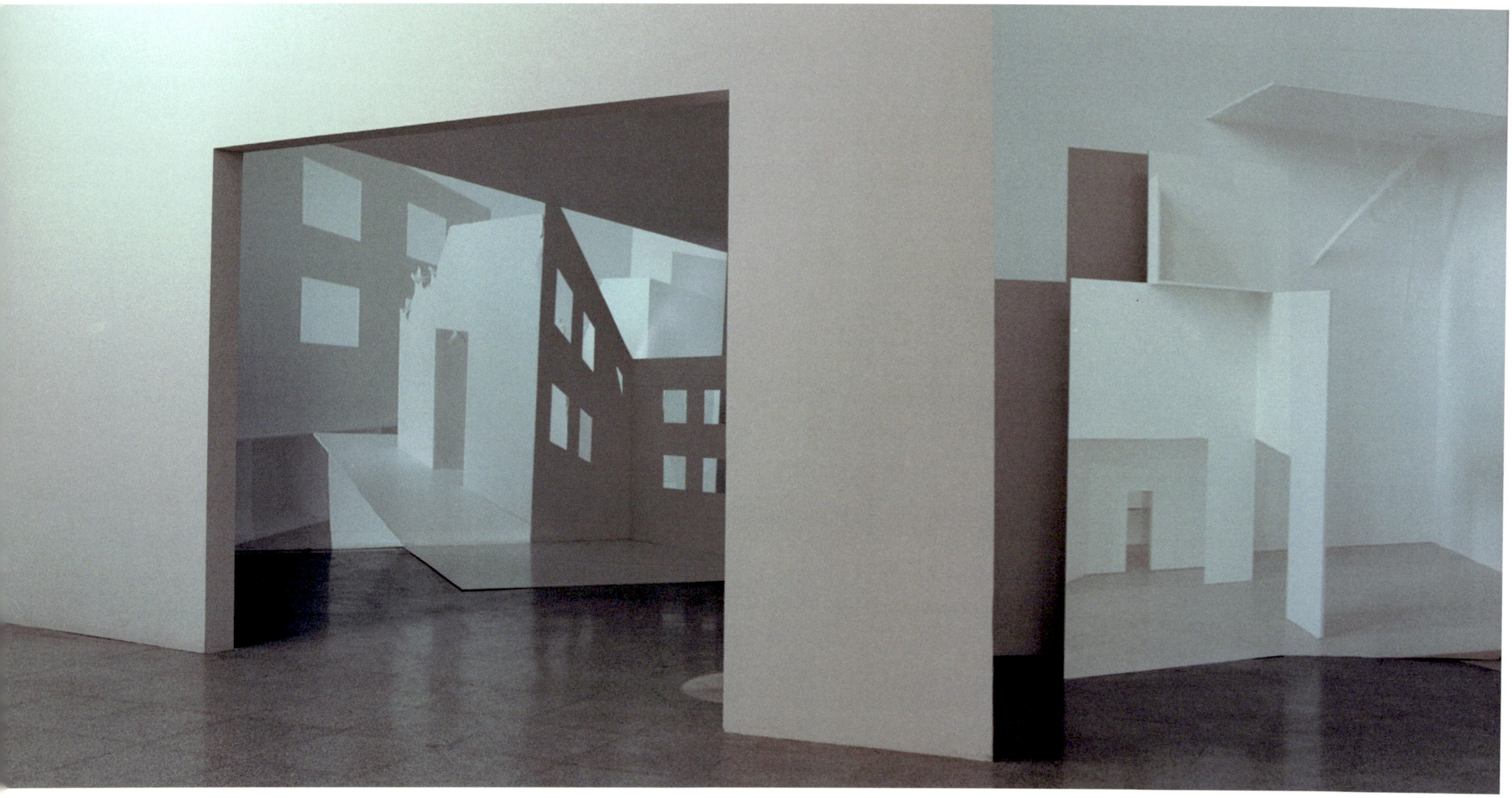

Erik Olofsen

STATE OF DELUSION

State of Delusion is built in close consideration of its surrounding environment. Measured, studied, re-arranged, the space is this artist's canvas. The walls are slanted to give a false sense of perspective. The optical illusions, the distorted images, the play of light and shadow generated by the projectors, make crossing the exhibition hall a new sensory – almost dizzying – experience. Erik Olofsen manipulates the physical space that houses them with walls and wood, video projections and other perceptual means.

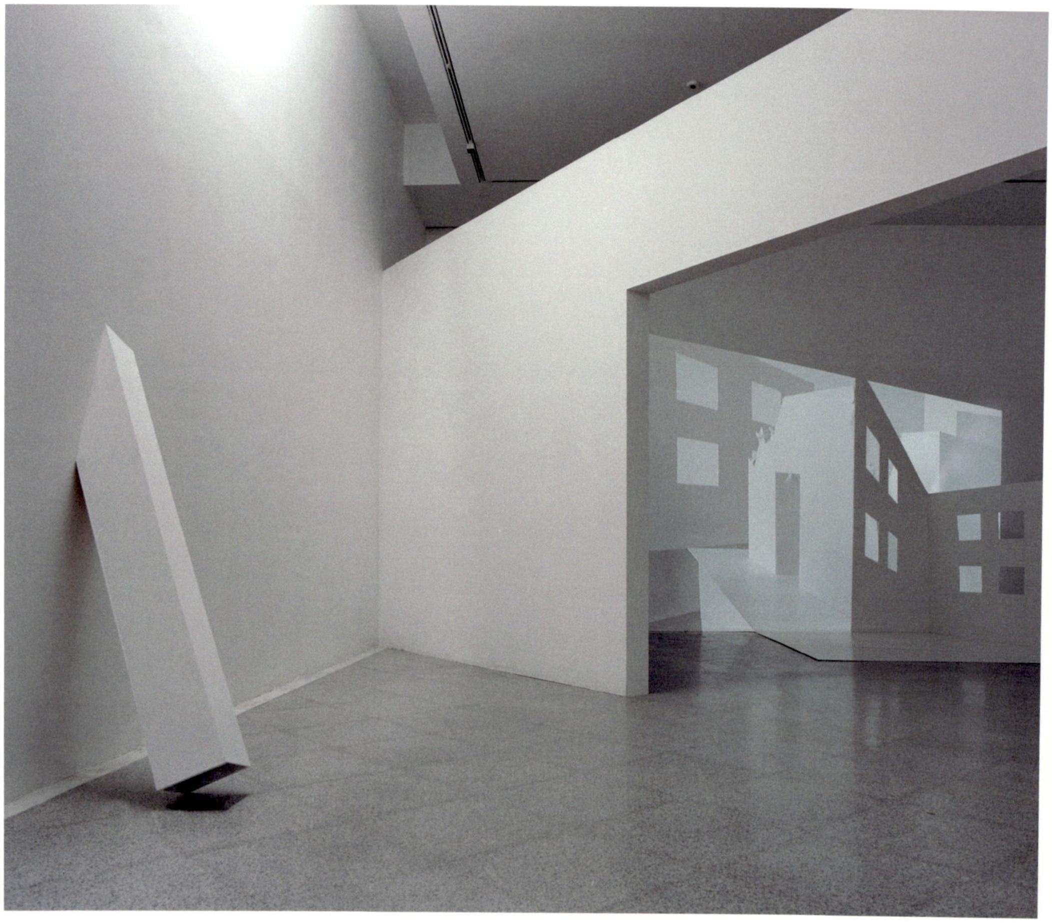

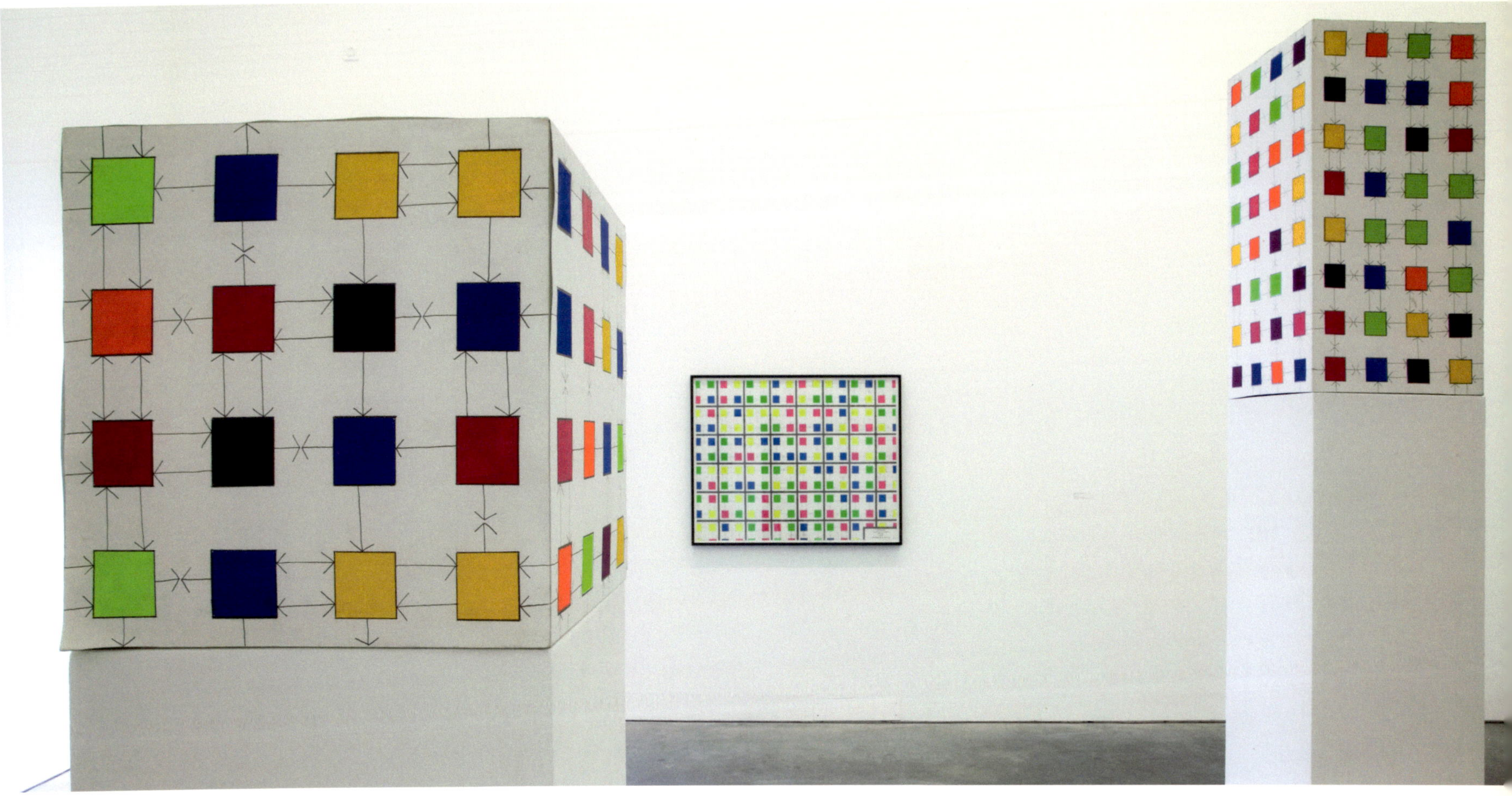

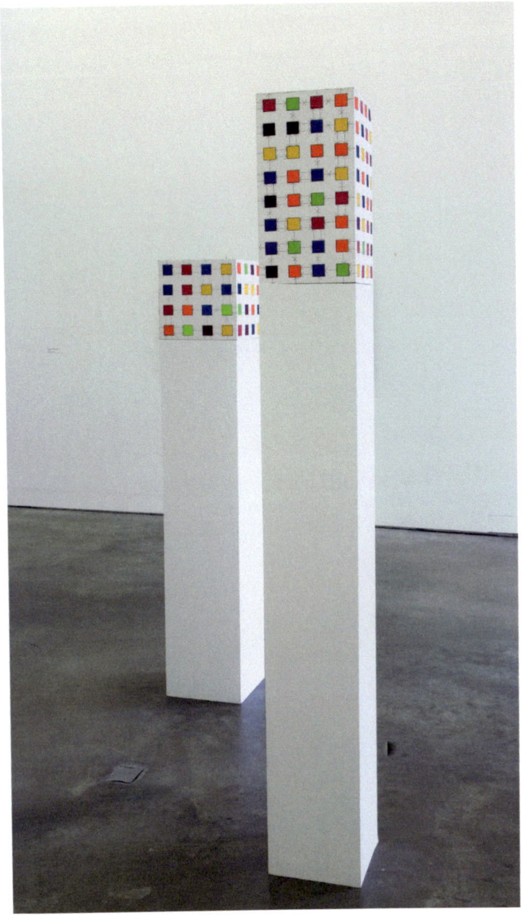

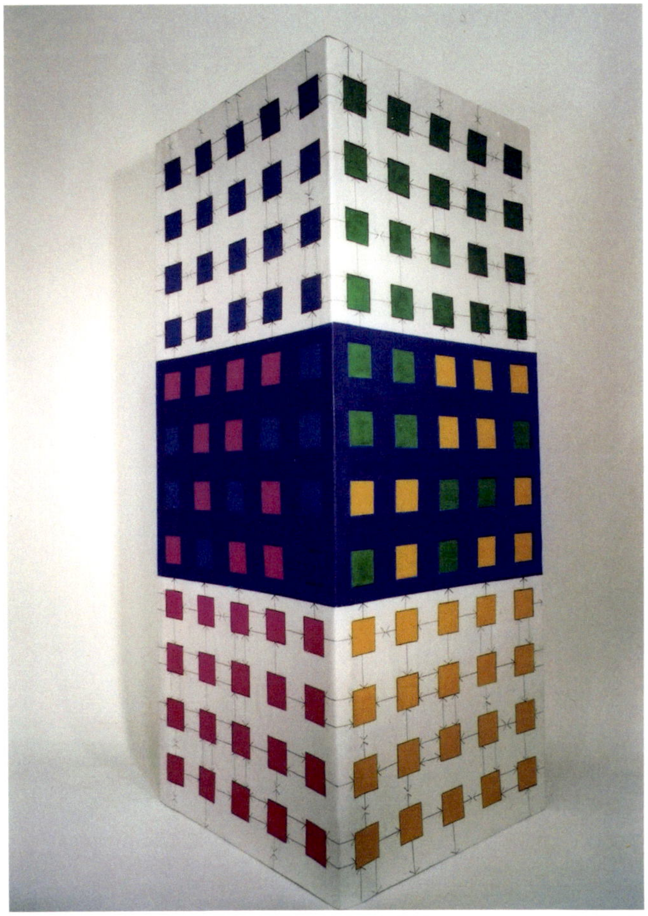

Stephen Willats

DEMOCRATIC GRID SERIES NO. 14 & 15
NETWORK INTERVENTIONS NO. 7

Since the 1960s, London-based Stephen Willats has been one of the most important representatives of Great Britain's progressive art scene. In his Democratic Grids, he depicts social models as window-like views from an endlessly large structure, while the drawings of his Ideological Towers series play with the abstraction of architecture and modernistic everyday objects as emblems of social and individual self-identification.

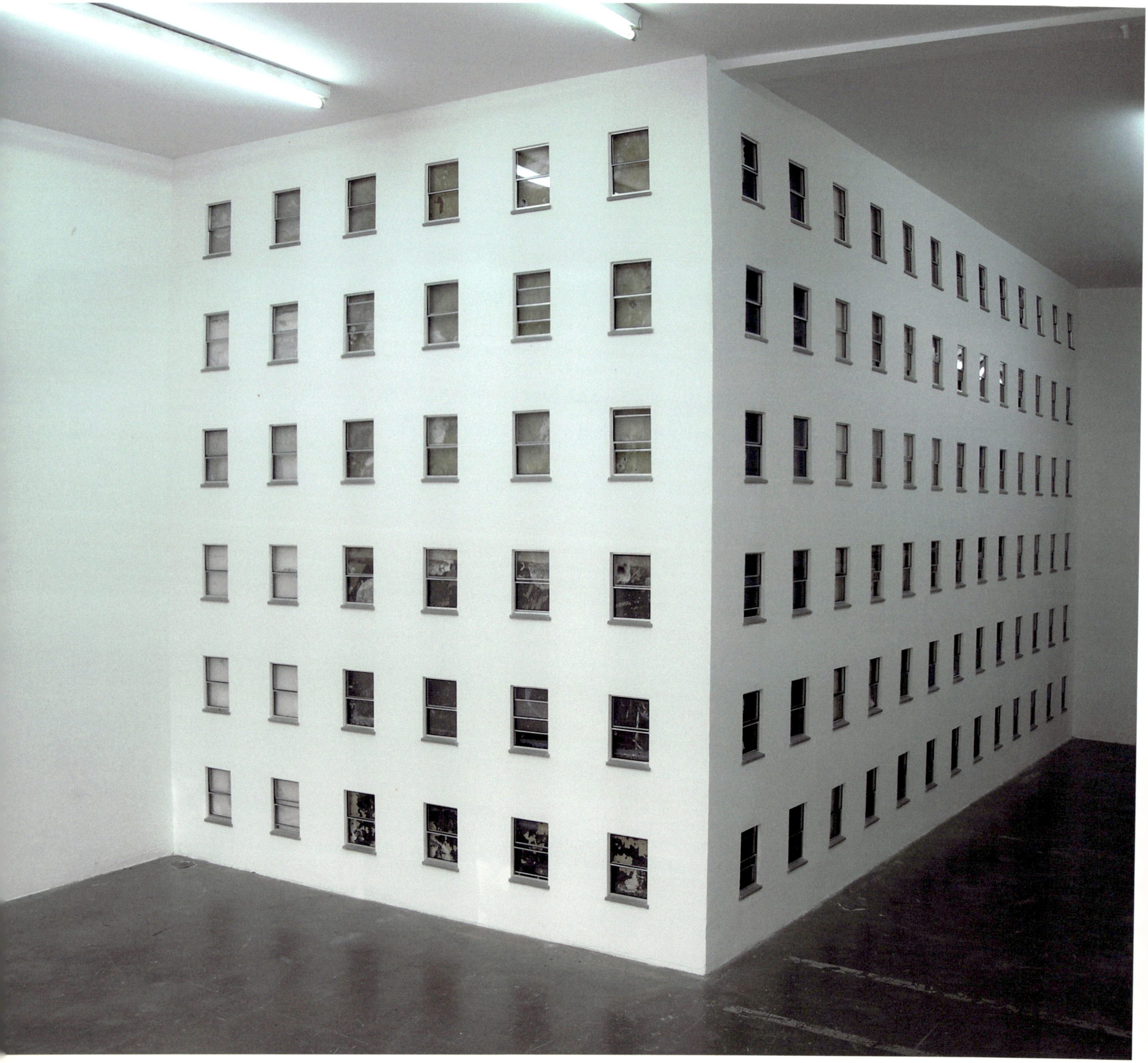

Simon Boudvin

FACES

Installation view at Coretin Hamel gallery. The apparent natural quality of Boudvin's work hides something unexpected and abnormal.

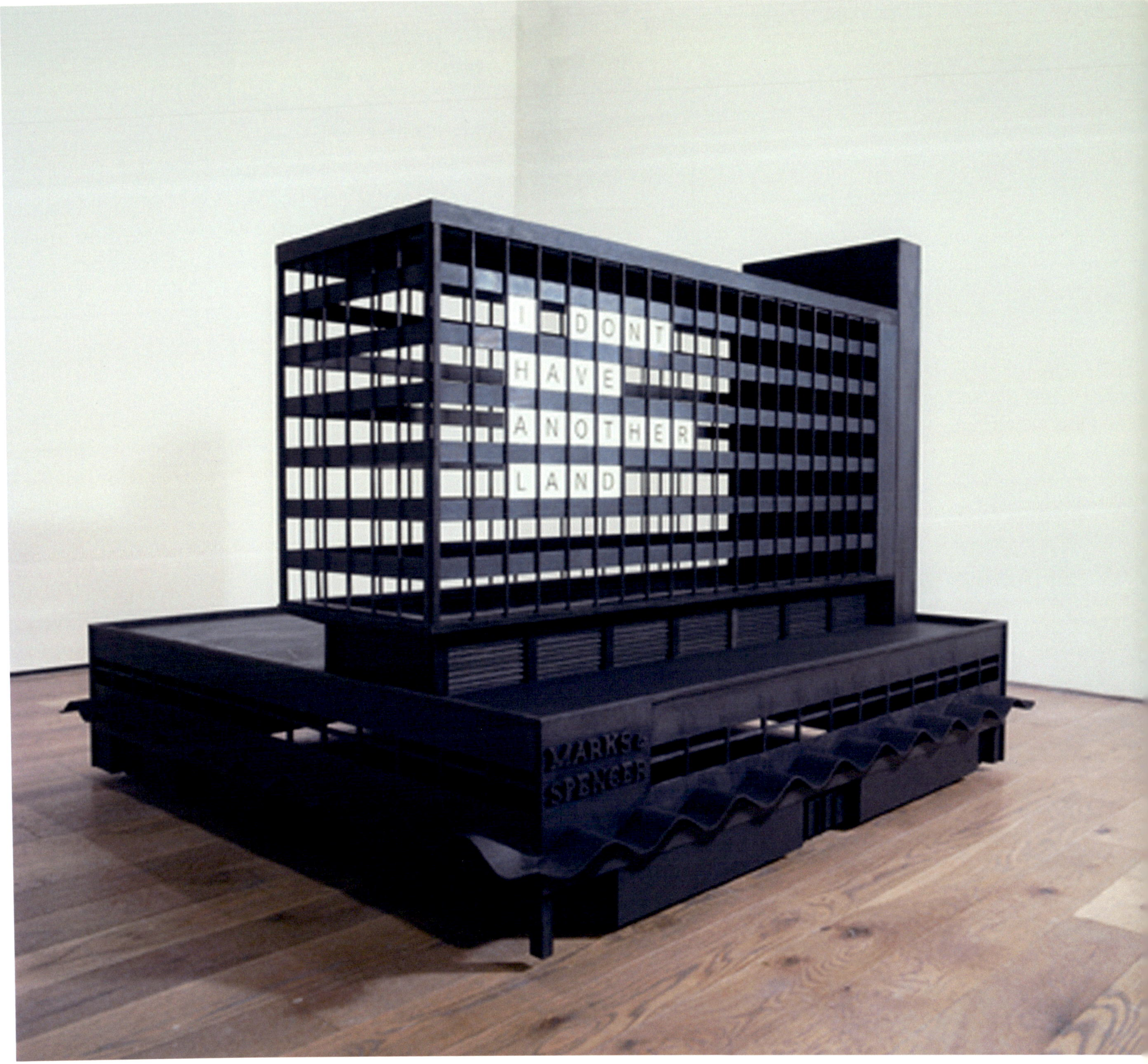

Nathan Coley

I DON'T HAVE ANOTHER LAND

I Don't Have Another Land, a site-specific work in the form of an architectural model of the modernist Marks & Spencer building in Manchester, which was the city's architectural heart until an IRA bomb did away with it in 1996. "I Don't Have Another Land", it says on the side of Coley's charred reconstruction of the building. It's a quote from an Israeli folk song – introducing a whole new set of complexities into an already loaded artwork.

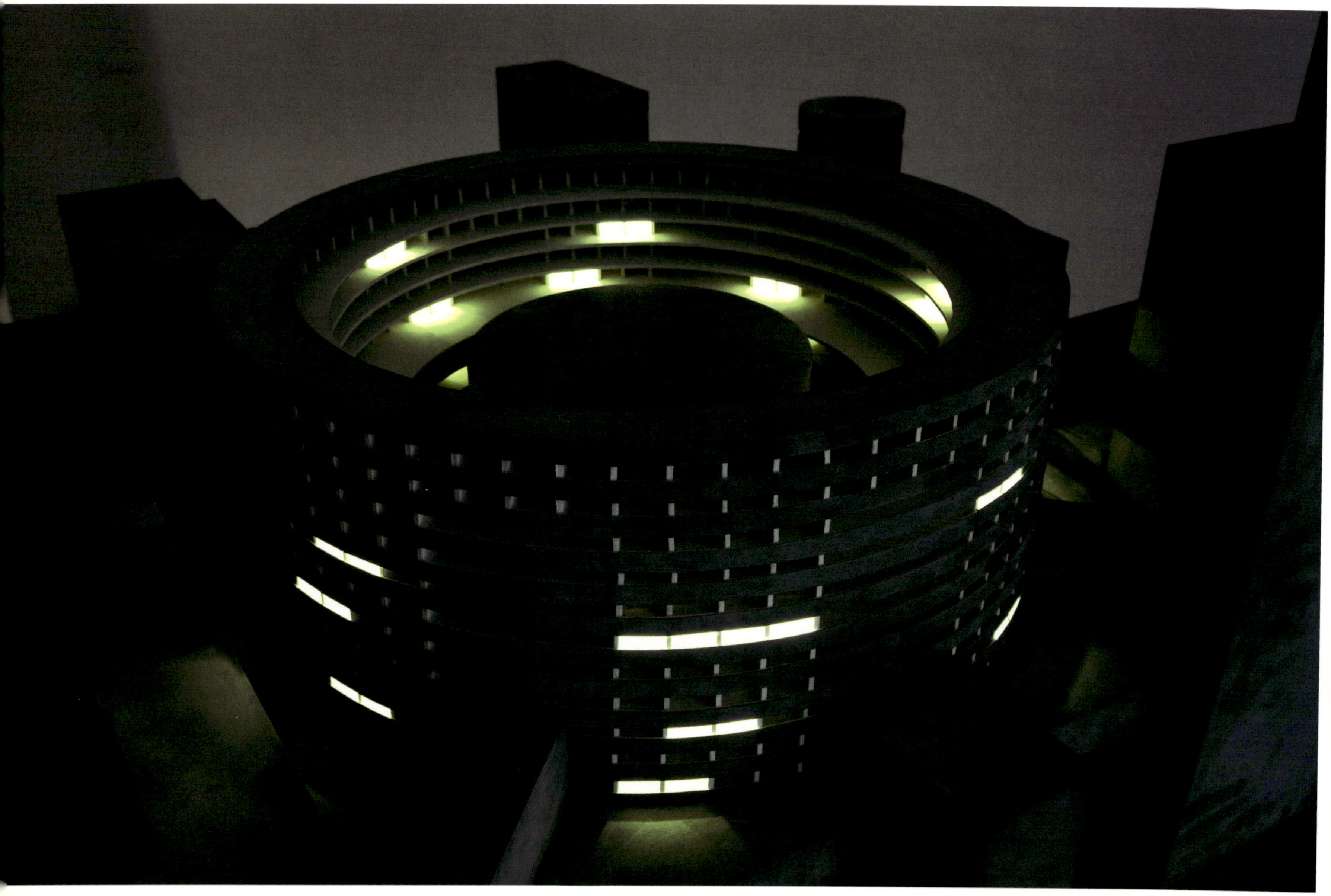

Hans Op De Beeck

ACCUMULATION (DESIGN FOR THE BUILDING)

Accumulation (Design for The Building) is a medium-sized sculpture, a combination of architectural cardboard, steel, cement sealant, and electronics. This architectural sculpture evokes a fictitious postmodern complex of buildings. The building is a preliminary model for the film *The Building*, in which the artist sends the viewer on a virtual, nocturnal walking tour of a fictitious hospital complex.

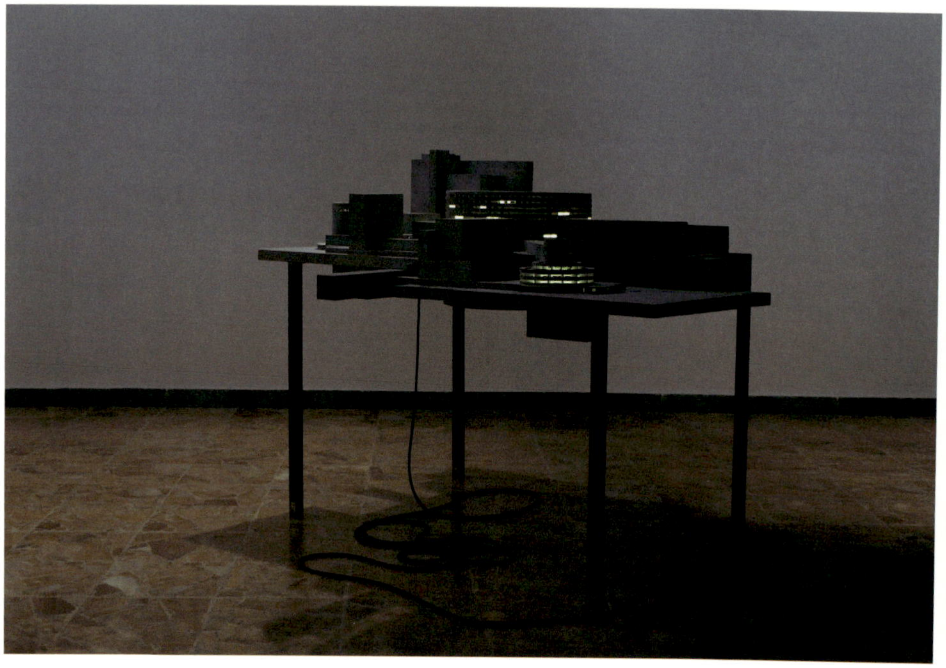

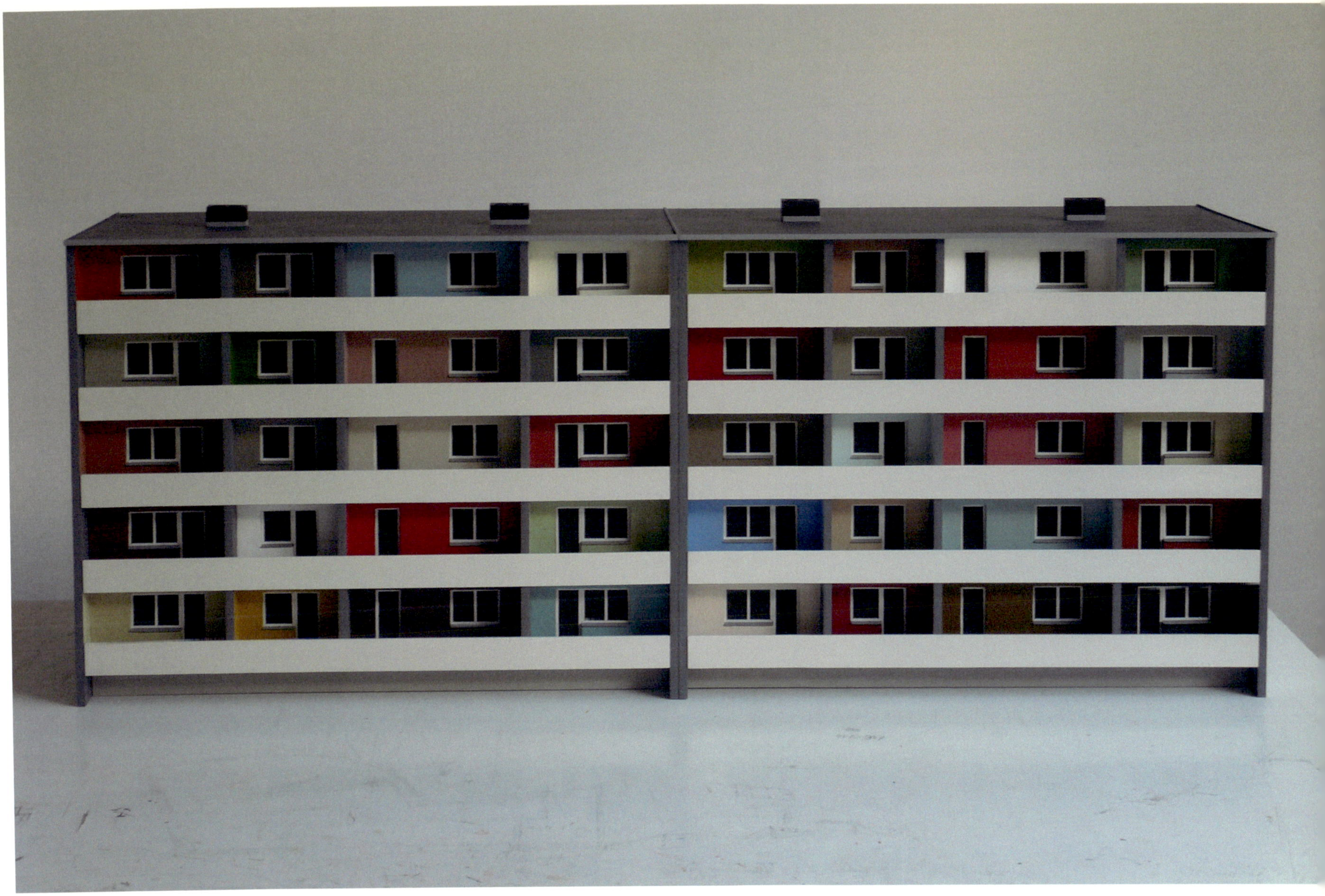

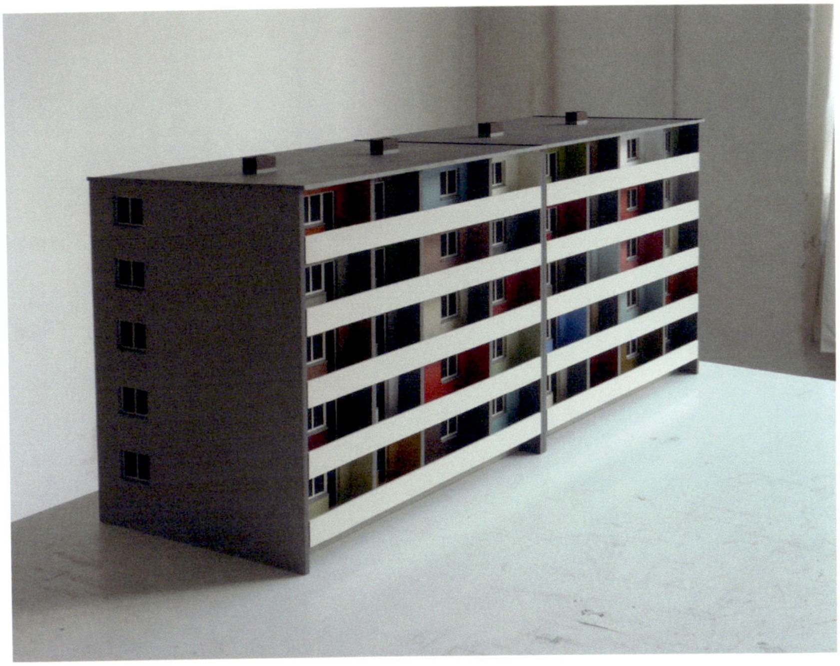

Jens Reinert

COLOURFUL BALCONIES

German artist Jens Reinert finds his motives in average places familiar to everyone in the urban landscape, such as a gatekeeper's lodge, a coffee-break niche, an apartment or a pedestrian underpass, and creates realistic dollhouse-scale models of these public and private places.

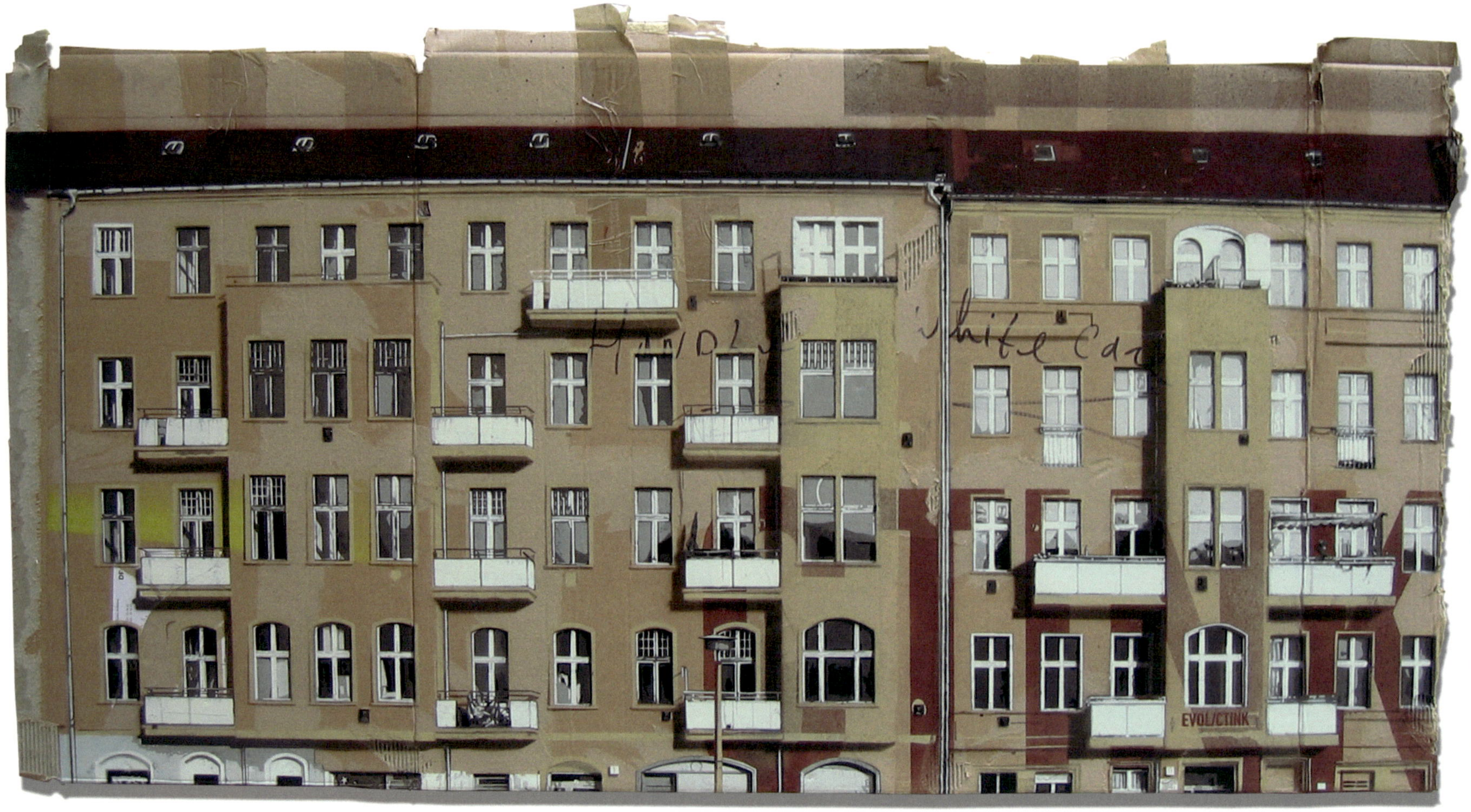

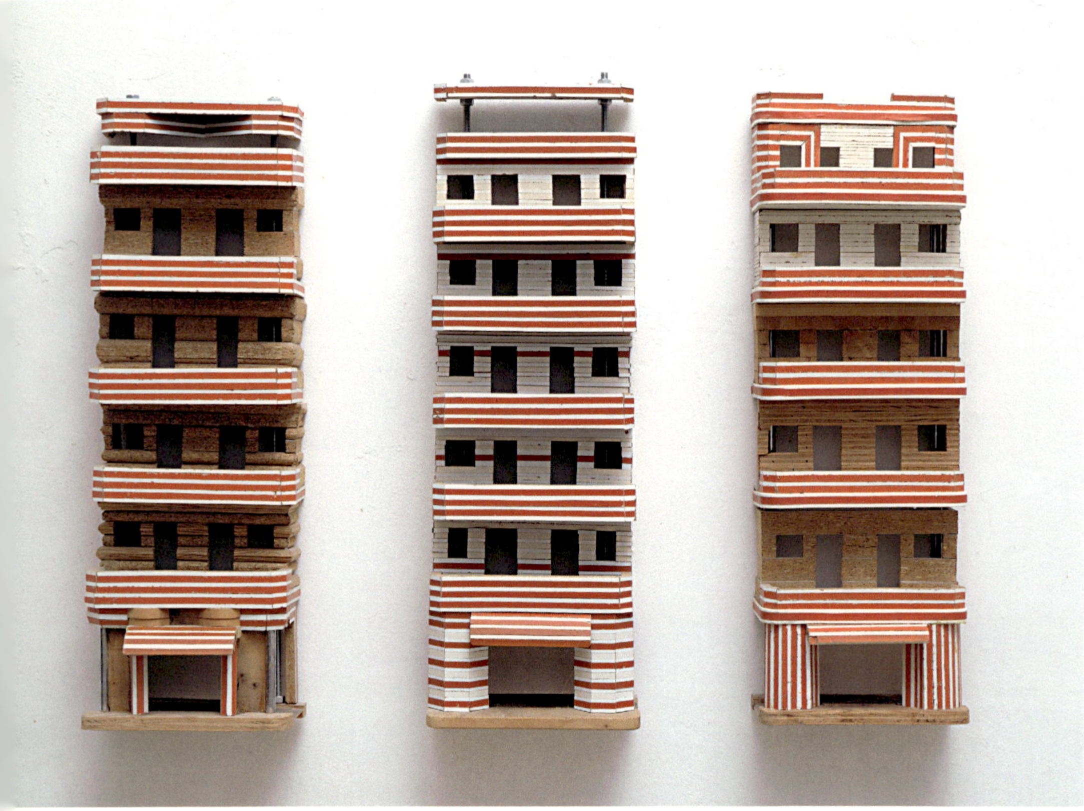

Evol / Ct'ink

HANDLE WITH CARE [LEHMBRUCK 9-11 #3] *(top)*

Berlin-based artist Evol uses spray-paint, adhesive tape and stencil on cardboard to create these images.

Karsten Konrad

APARTHOTEL ISTANBUL *(left)*

Simon Boudvin

HAUSMANN

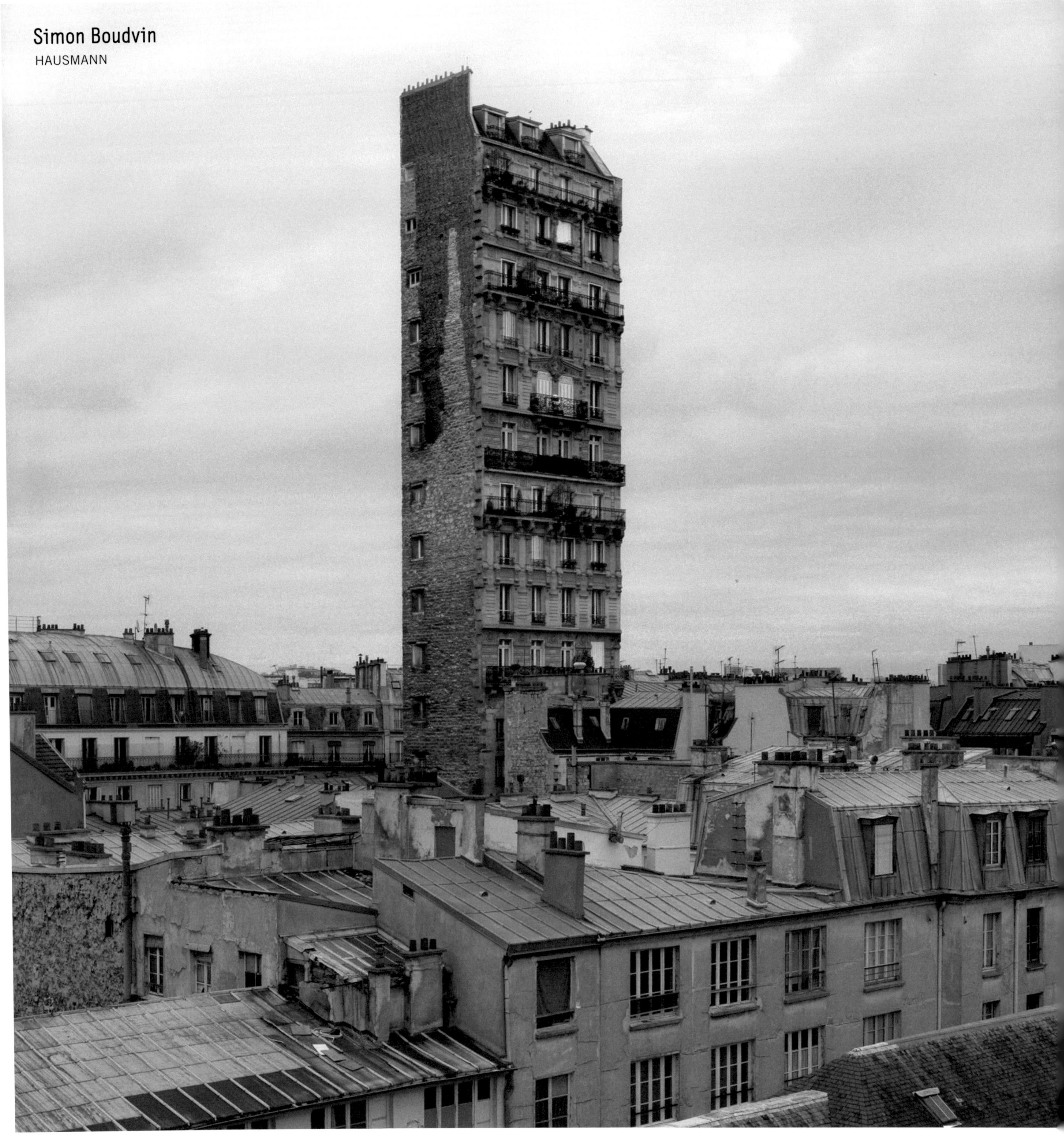

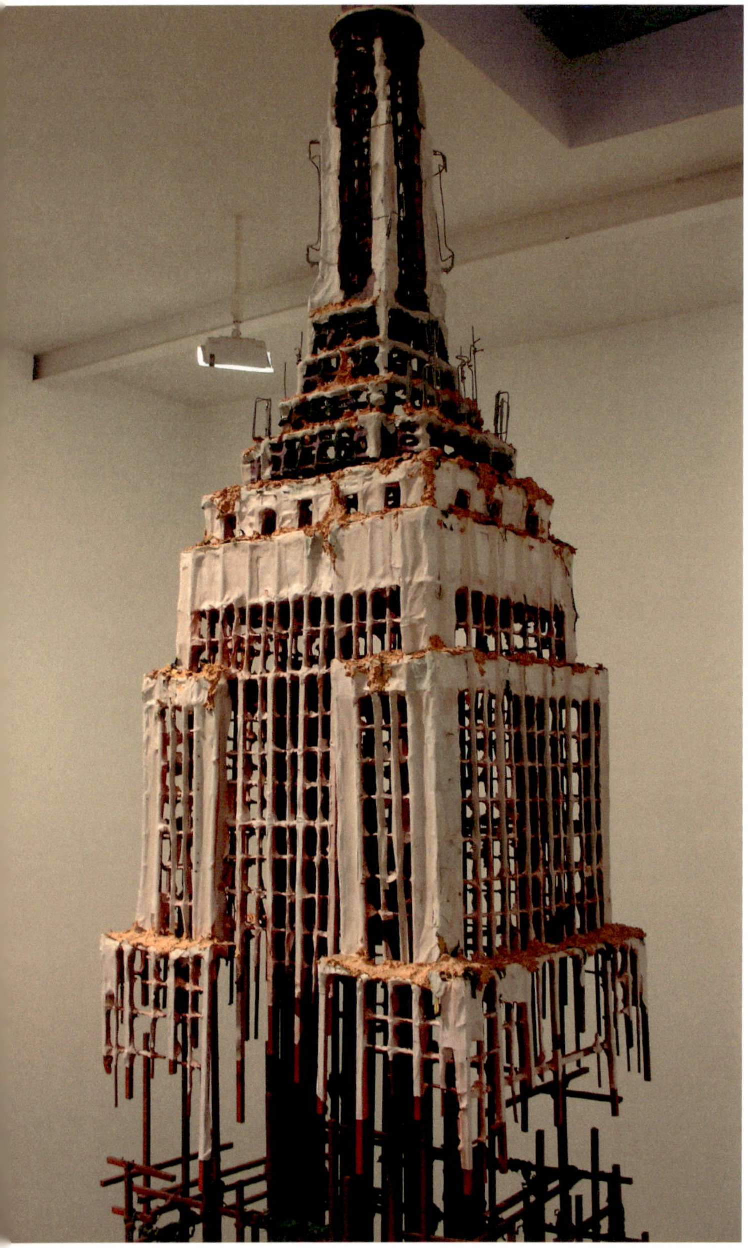

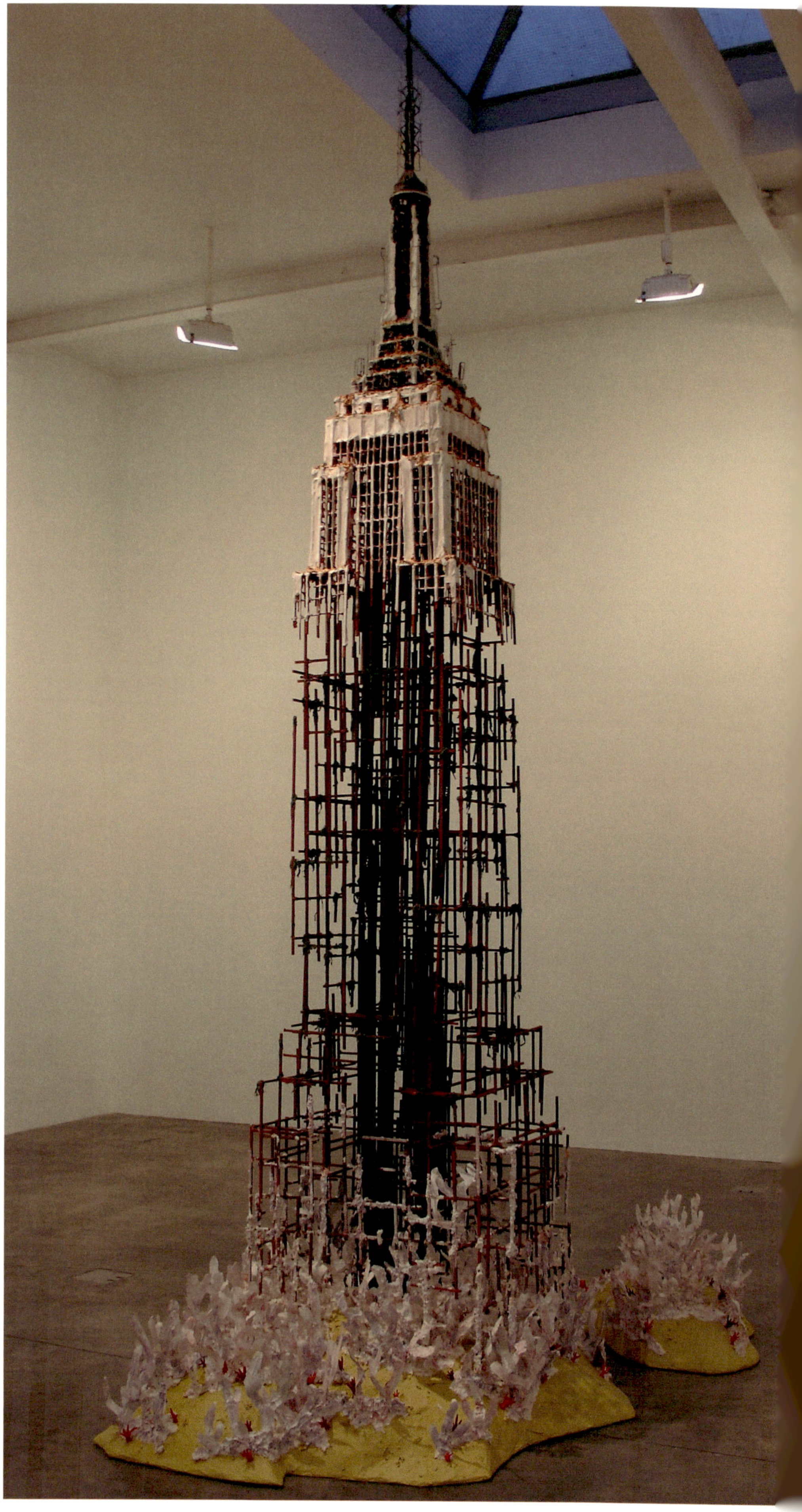

David Herbert

EMPIRE

Herbert explores the idea of great metropolis in final stages of collapse and disintegration in this large-scale sculpture of the Empire State Building in a state of progressive decay.

Matias Bechtold

RAKETE (MISSILE)

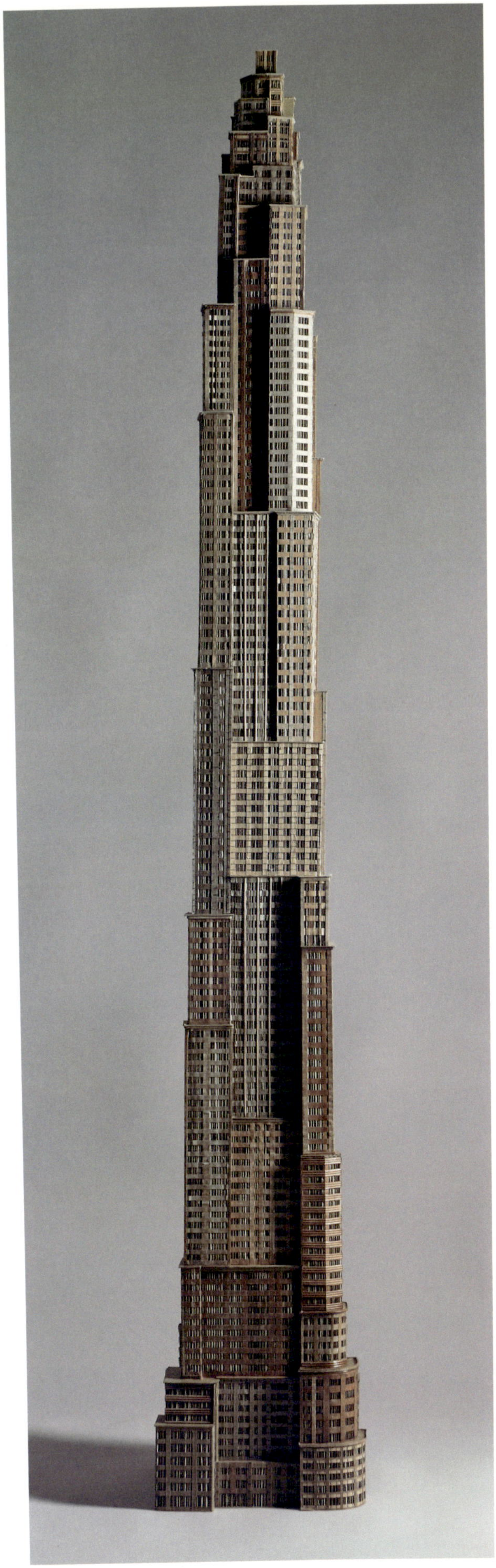

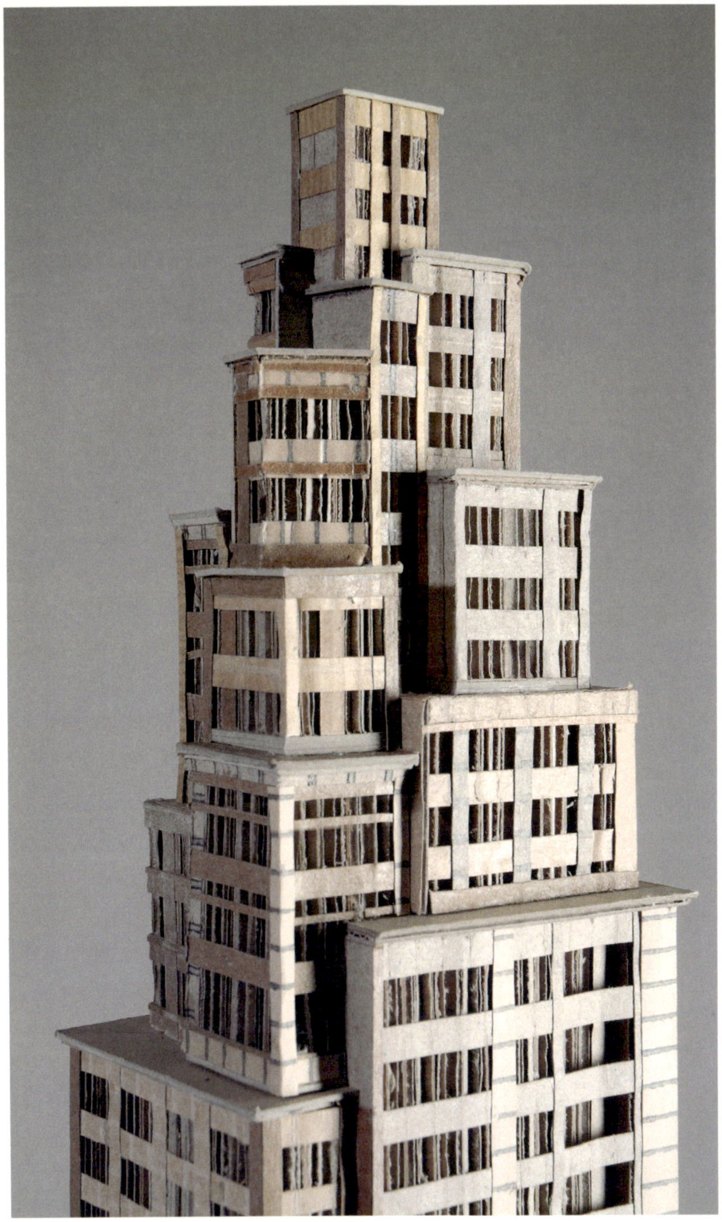

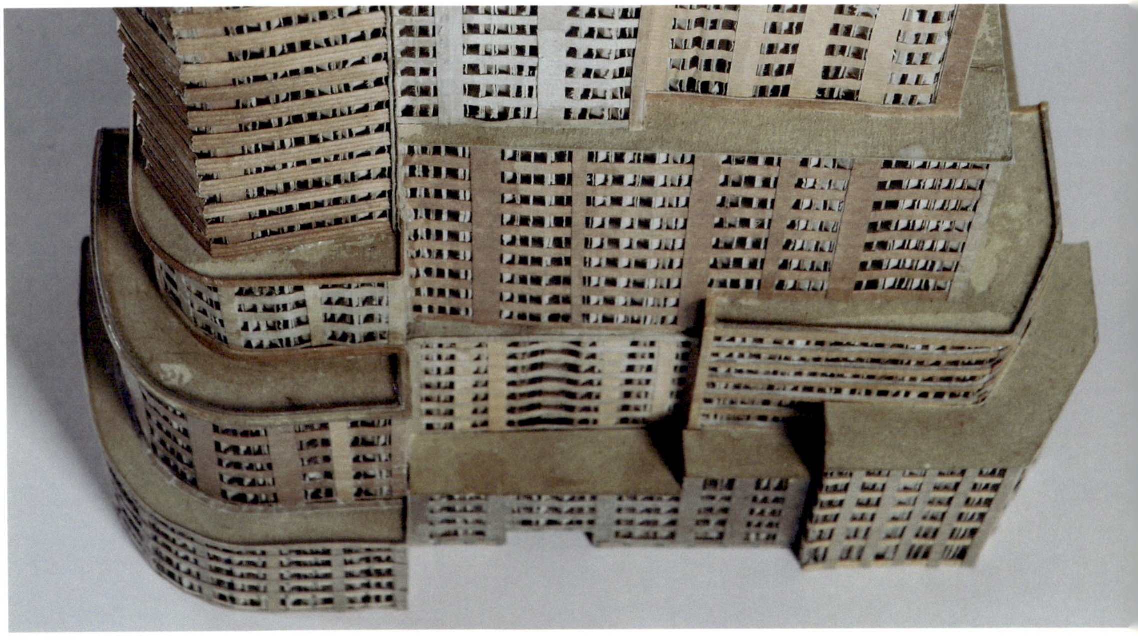

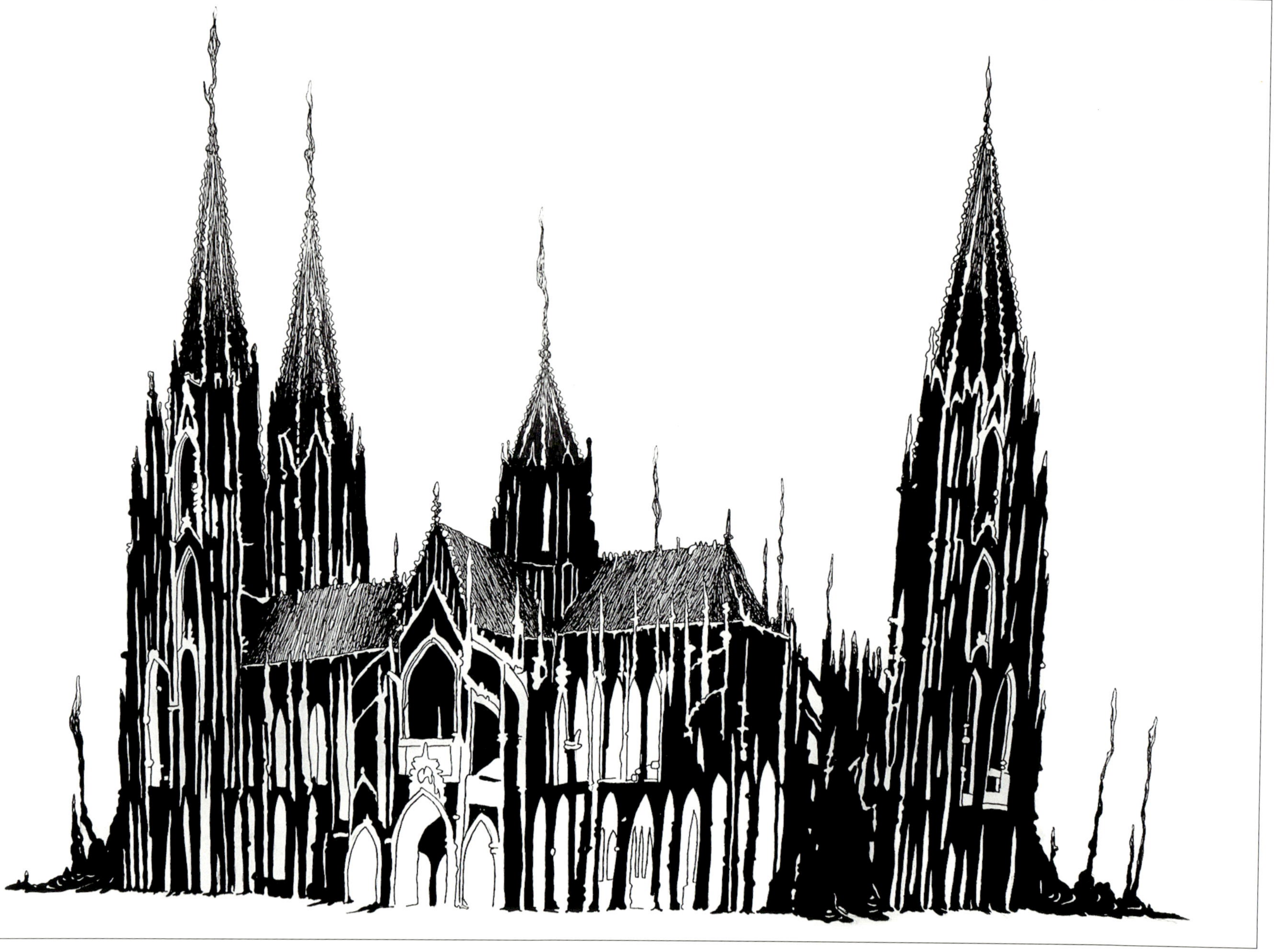

Jonas Liveröd

MELTING CATHEDRAL *(top)*

David Herbert

CRYSTAL PALACE *(right)*

A Plexiglass rendition of the iconic Sleeping Beauty castle from Disneyland.

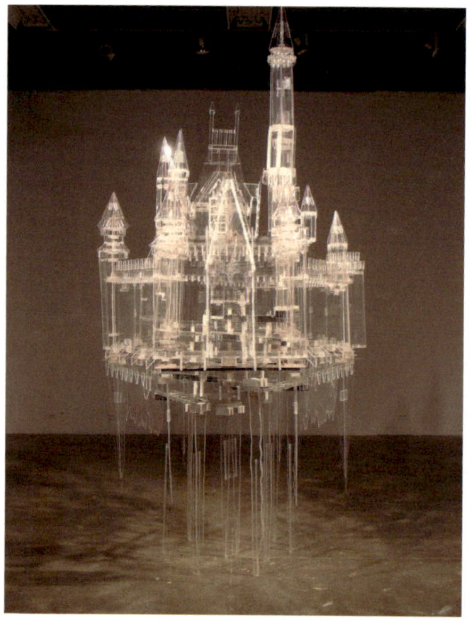

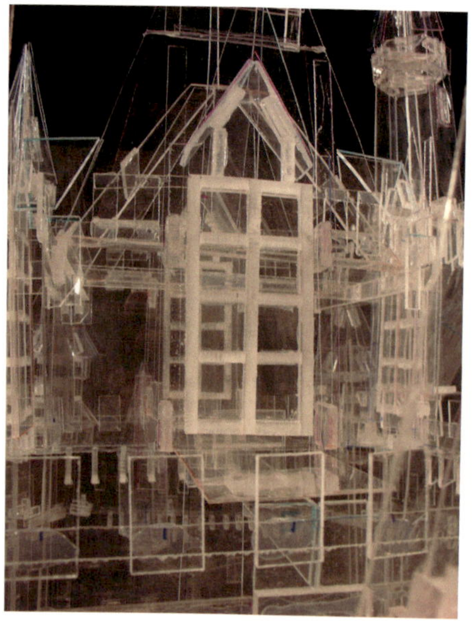

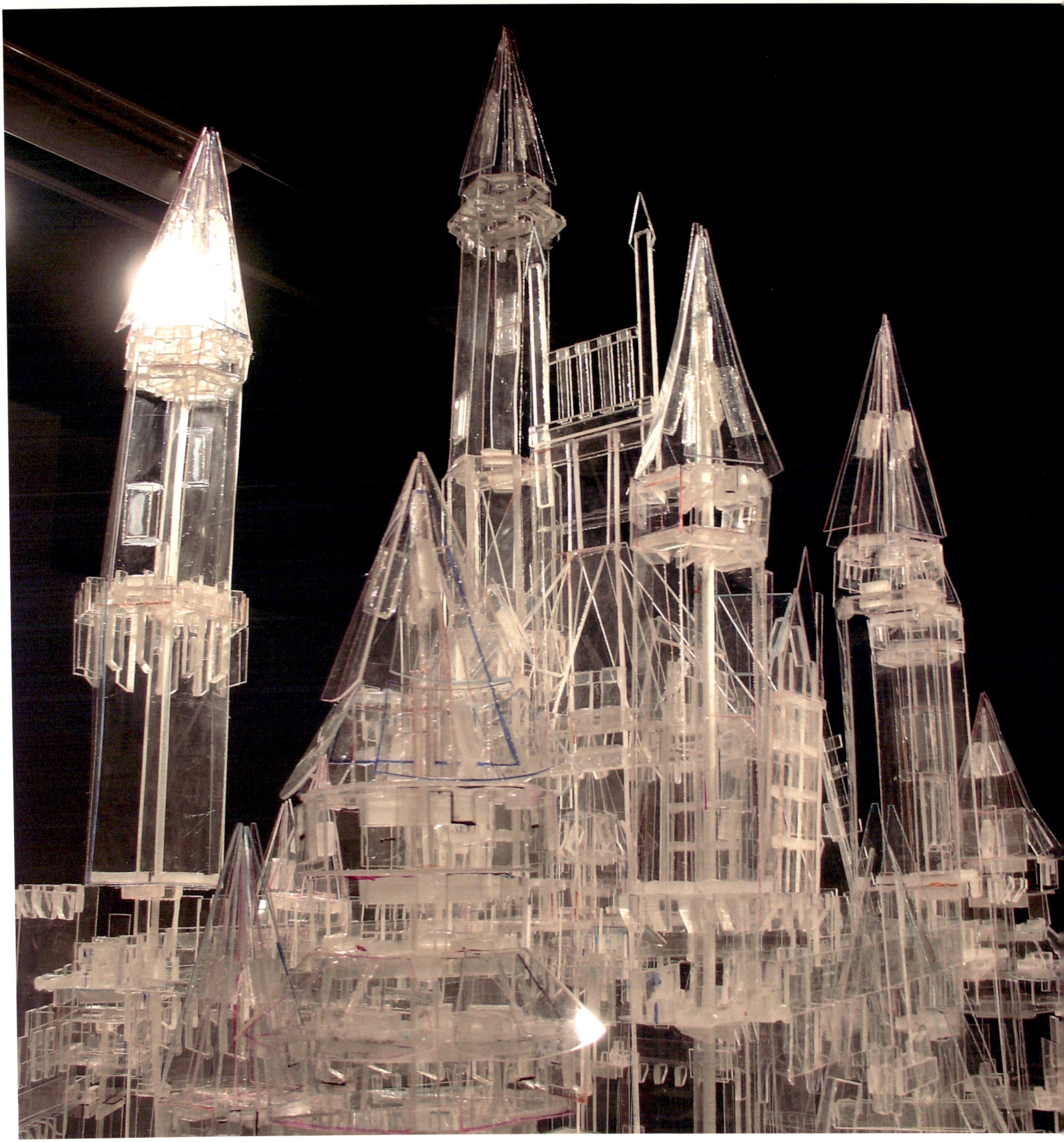

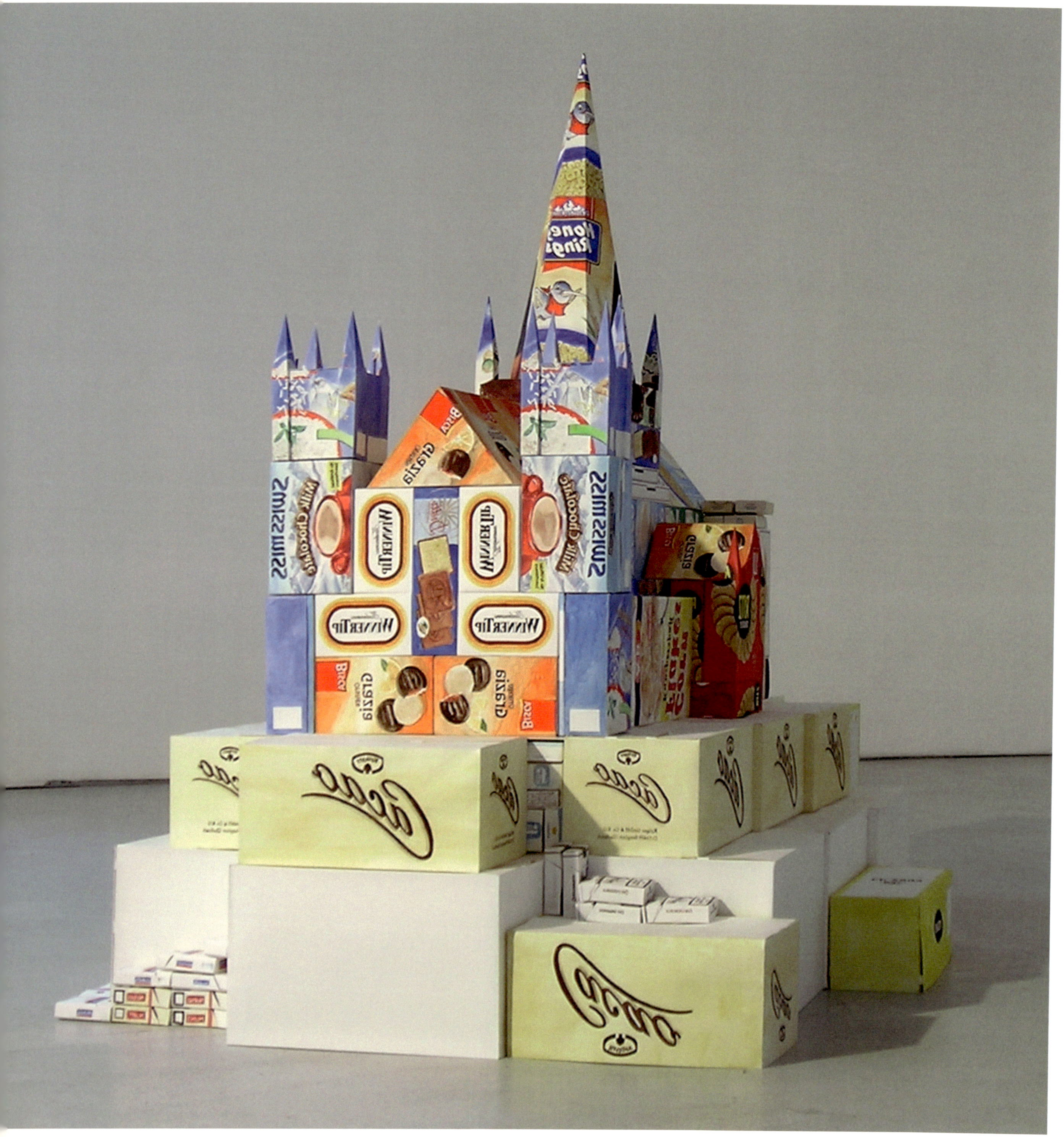

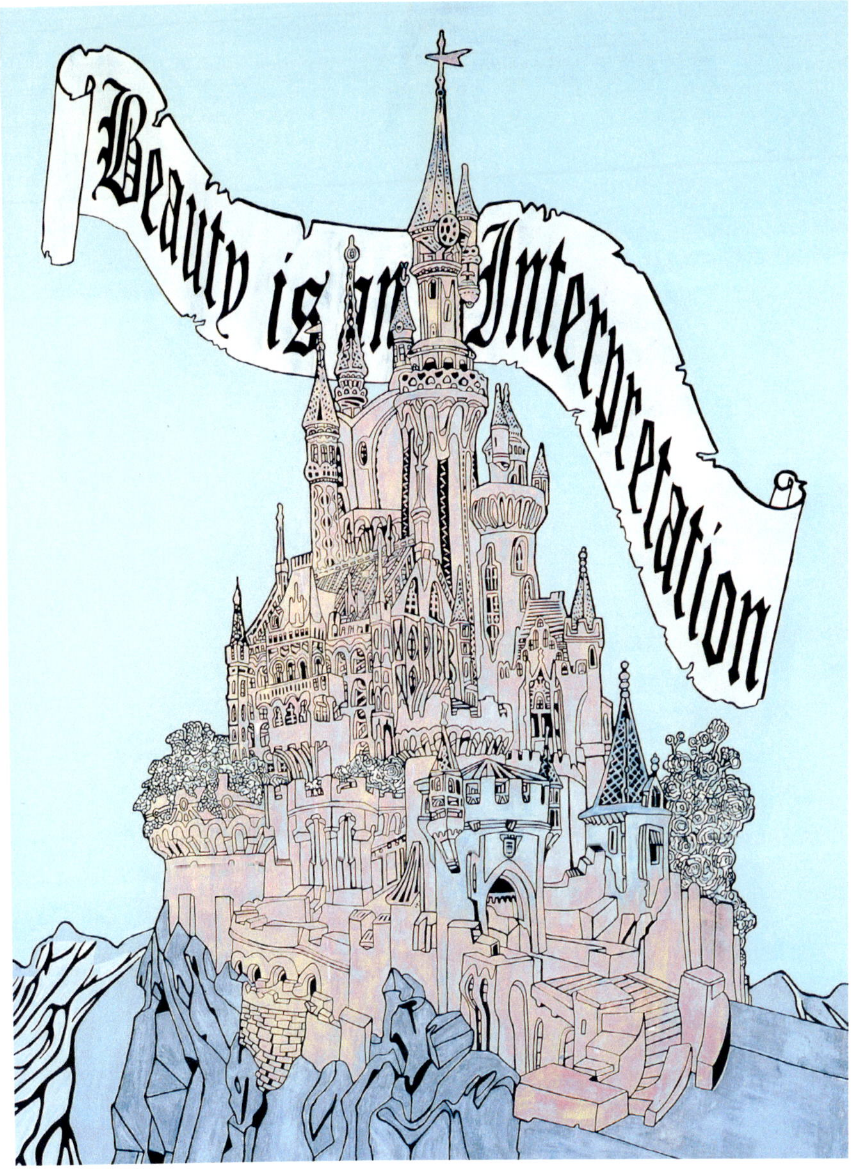

Alekos Hofstetter

FALKENSTEIN

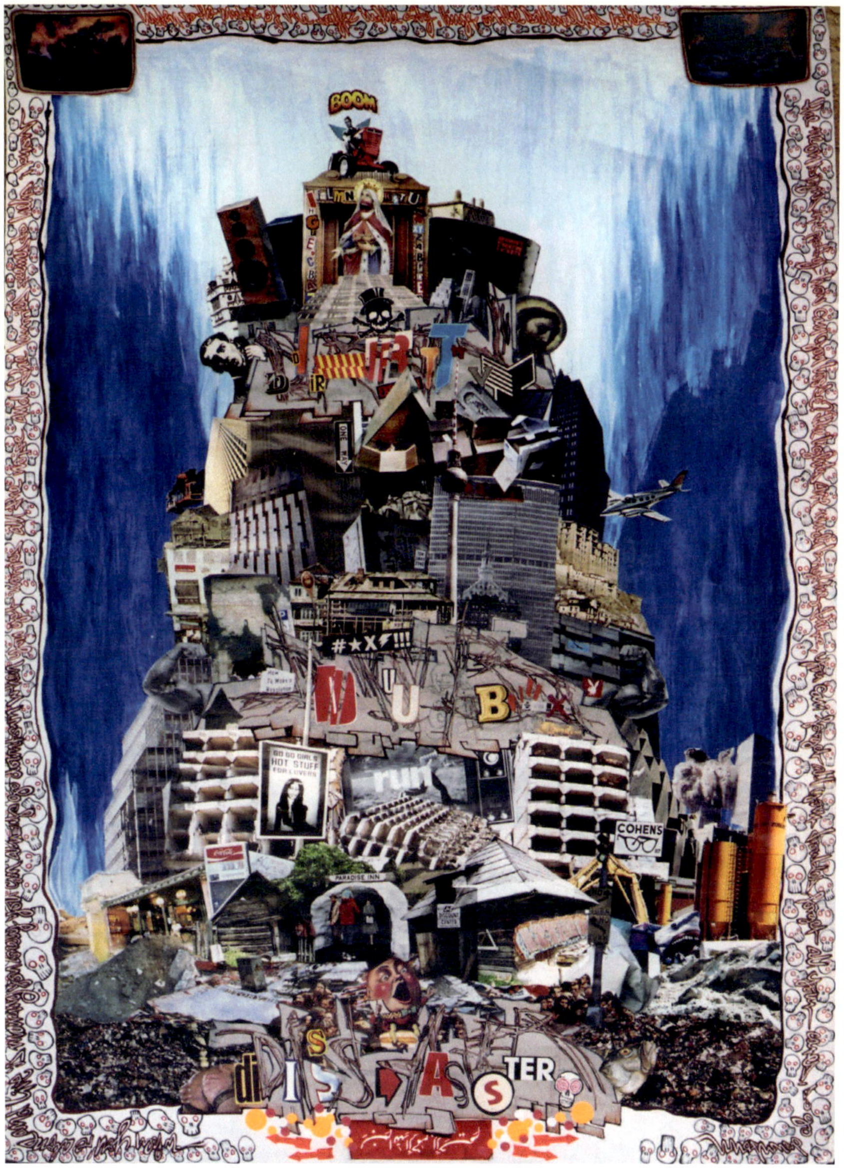

Lukas Feireiss

DIRTY DUB DISASTER

This mixed-media collage ironically plays with the Babylonian confusion of tongues and urban life. City scenes are merged with the lyrics of Petula Clark's hit single *Downtown* and images of the Great Hore of Babylon.

David Keating

GLOBAL VILLAGE IDIOT

A sculptural installation constructed from handmade reproductions of consumer packaging, collected from a variety of countries investigating notions such as Global Village consumerism and artistic practice in the age of mechanical reproduction.

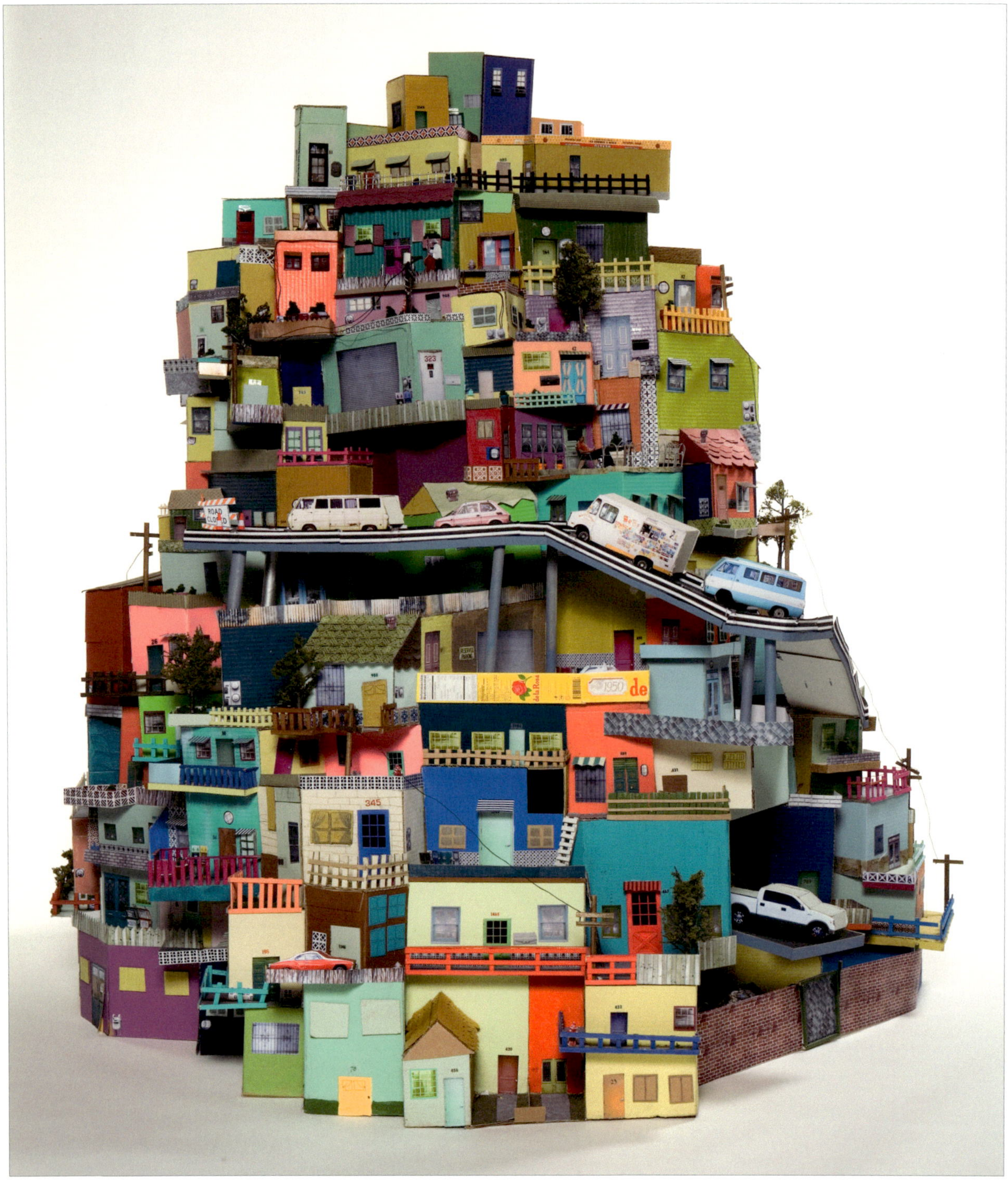

Ana Serrano

CARTONLANDIA

This playful sculpture work of Ana Serrano is a vibrant cardboard microcosm of perfect little houses and vehicles.

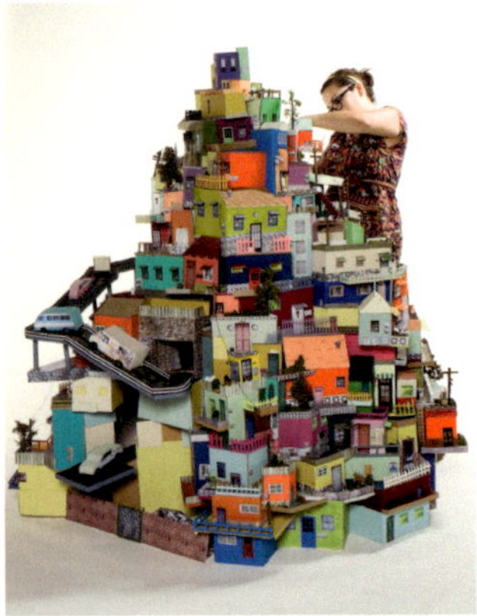

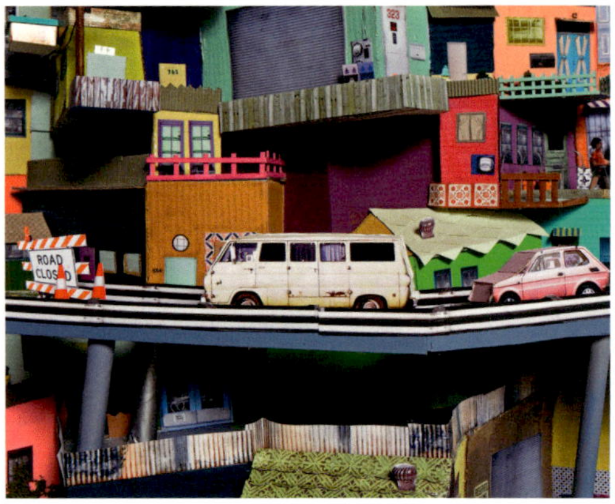

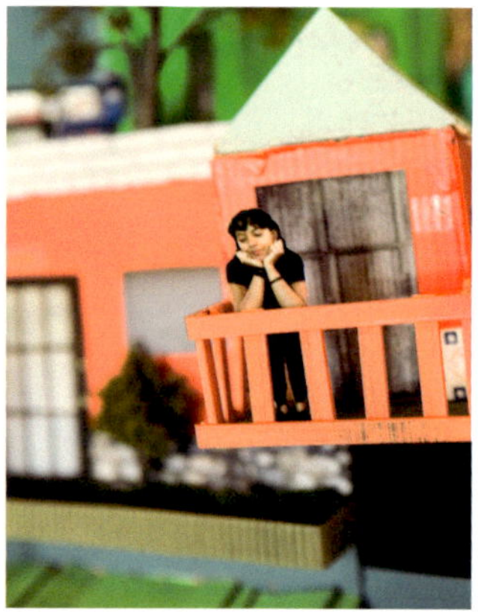

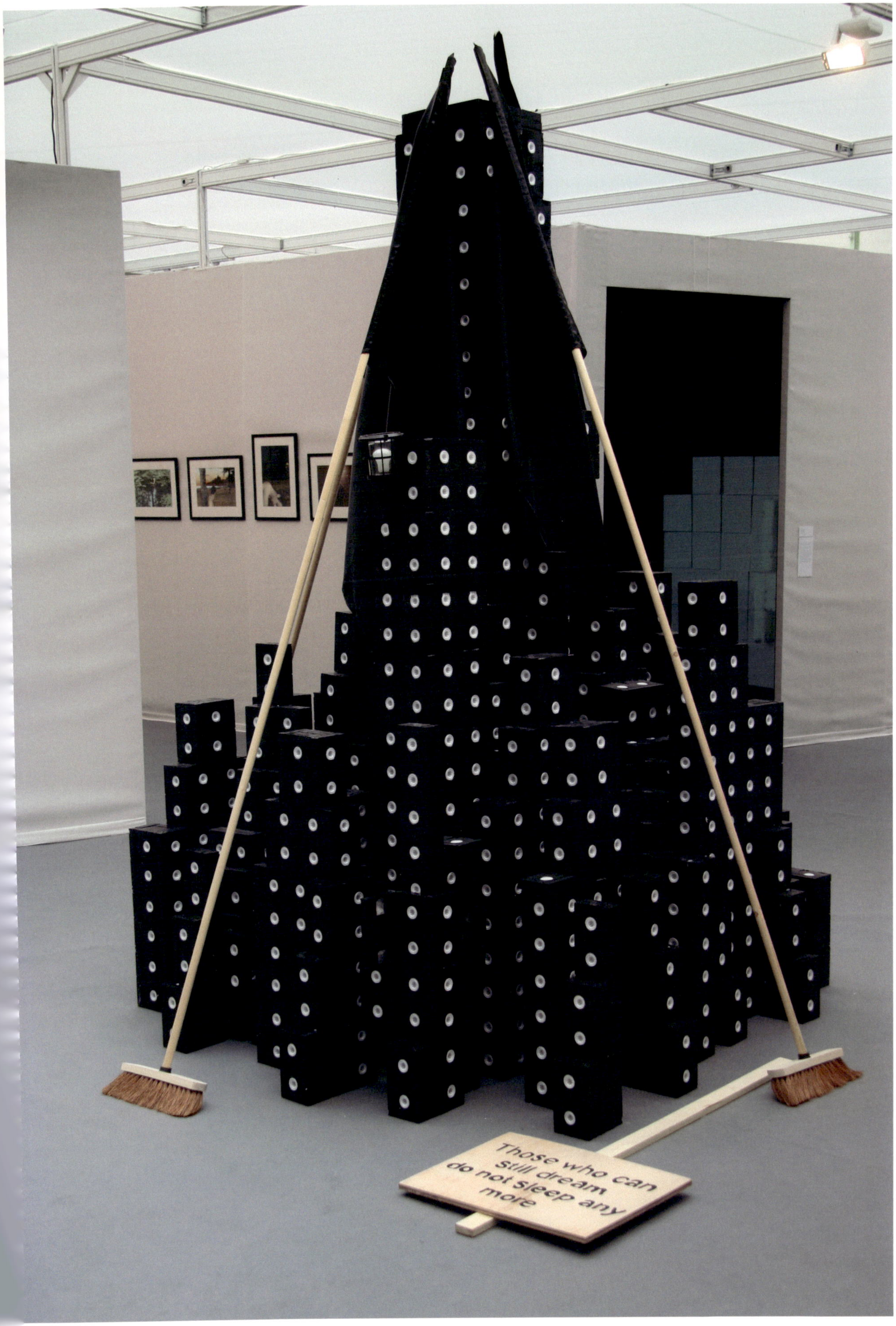

Mounir Fatmi

BABEL HOUSE

Tangiers-born Mounir Fatmi constructs visual spaces and linguistic games that aim to free the viewer from their preconceptions of politics and religion, and allows them to contemplate these and other subjects in new ways.

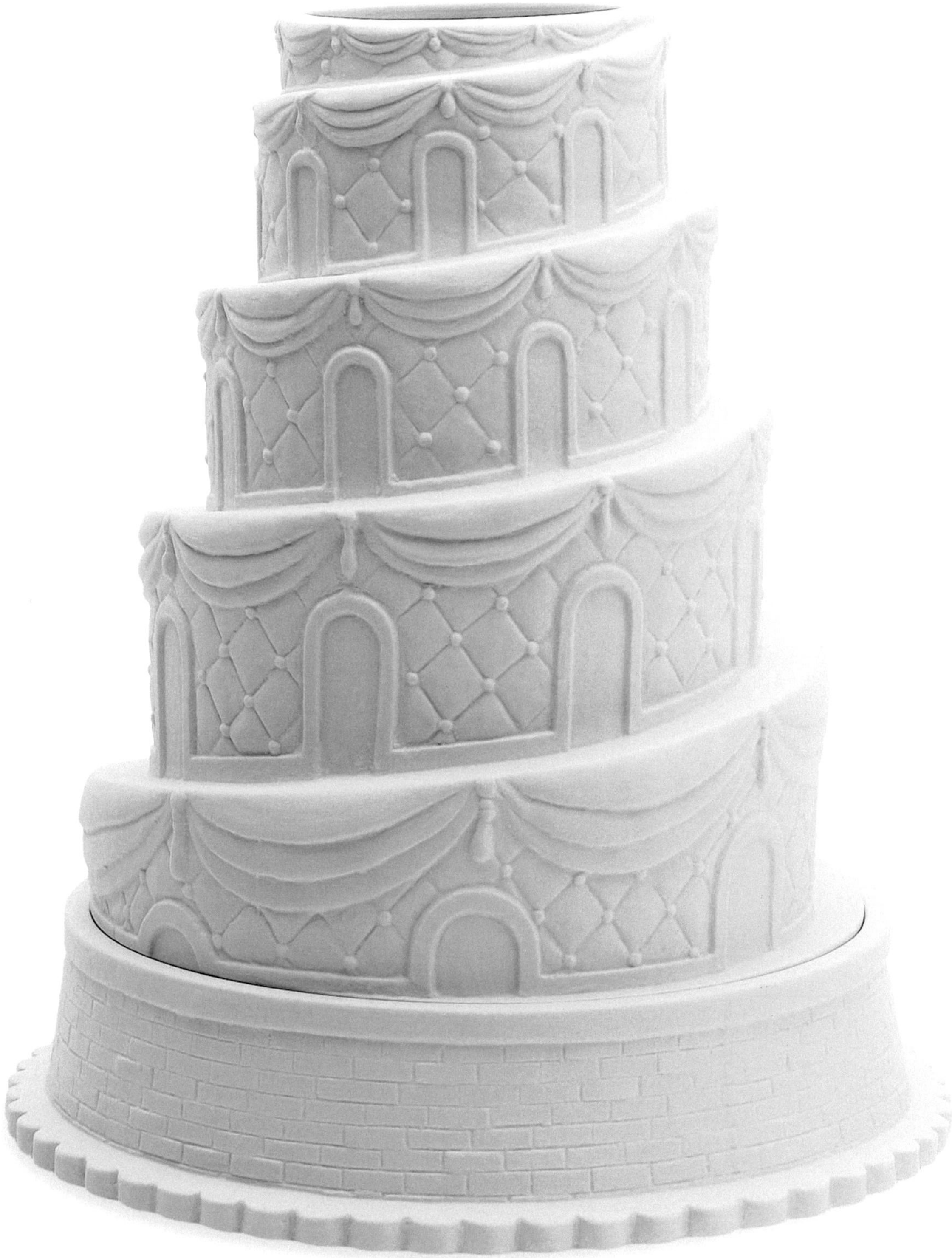

Studio Job
JOB SMEETS + NYNKE TYNAGEL

VASE OF BABEL

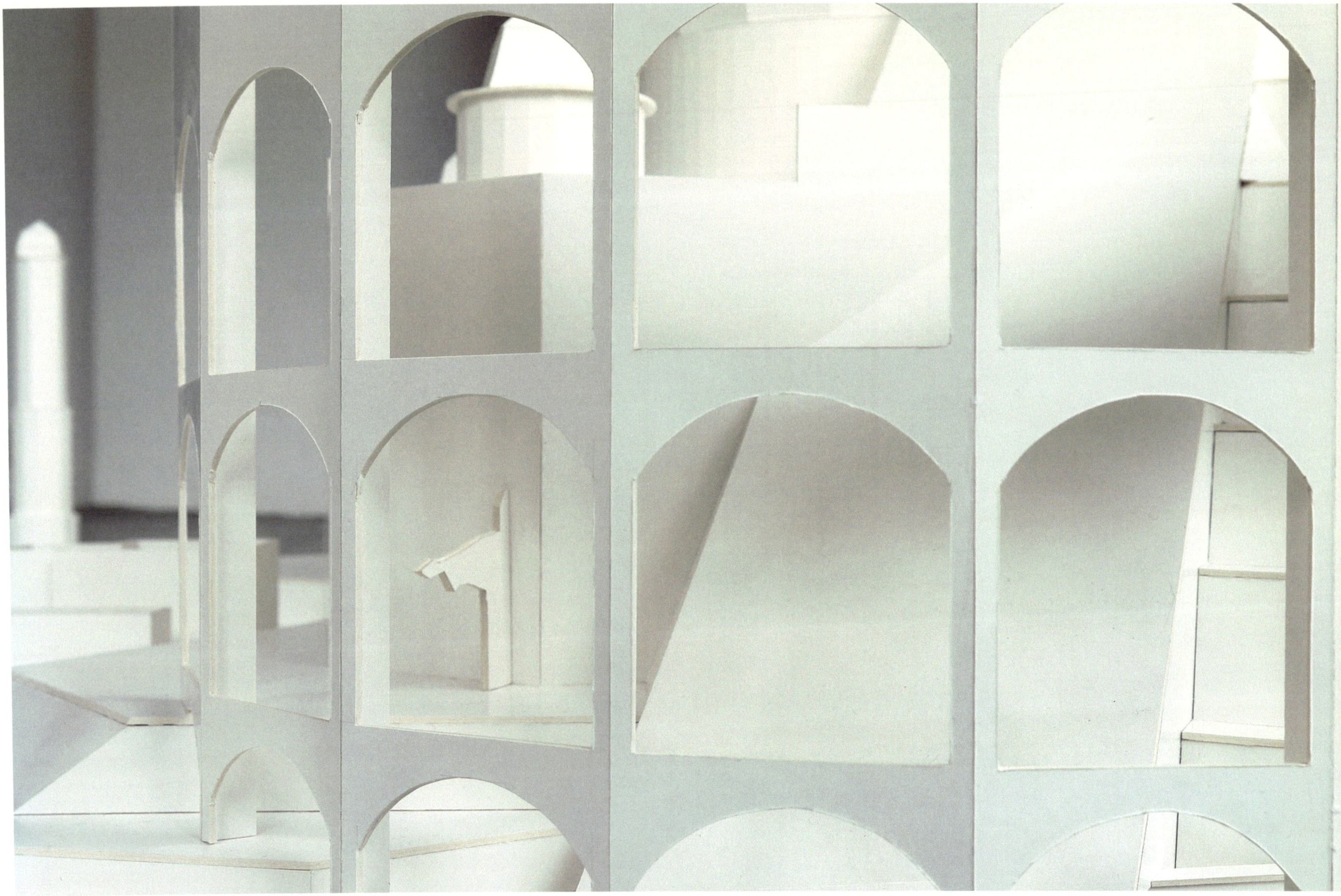

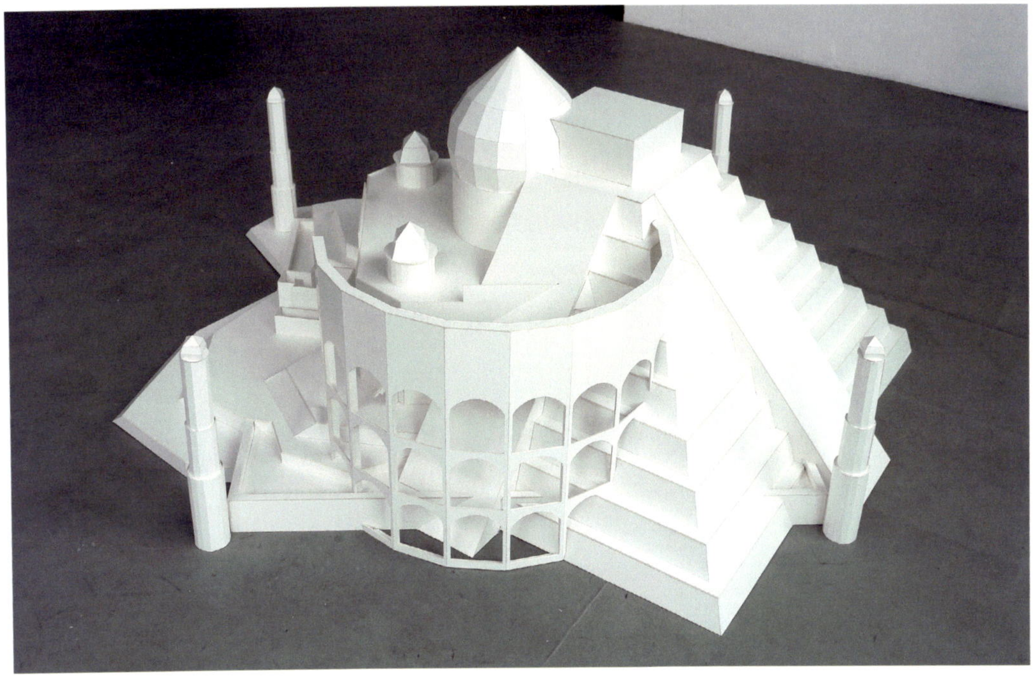

David Keating

SEVEN WONDERS

In 2007, a Swiss foundation held an open call to identify seven noteworthy cultural monuments to be classified as "world wonders" for architectural, cultural and sensational reasons. Over 100,000 people around the world participated in the unofficial poll, naming Chichén Itzá, Christ the Redeemer, the Colosseum, the Taj Mahal, the Great Wall of China, Macchu Picchu and Petra in Jordan as the most fitting manifestations of "esteemed" global heritage. In his eponymous Seven Wonders Keating examines the implications of the programmatic selection process, whose result came to better reflect a global cultural smorgasboard than an open representation of world monuments.

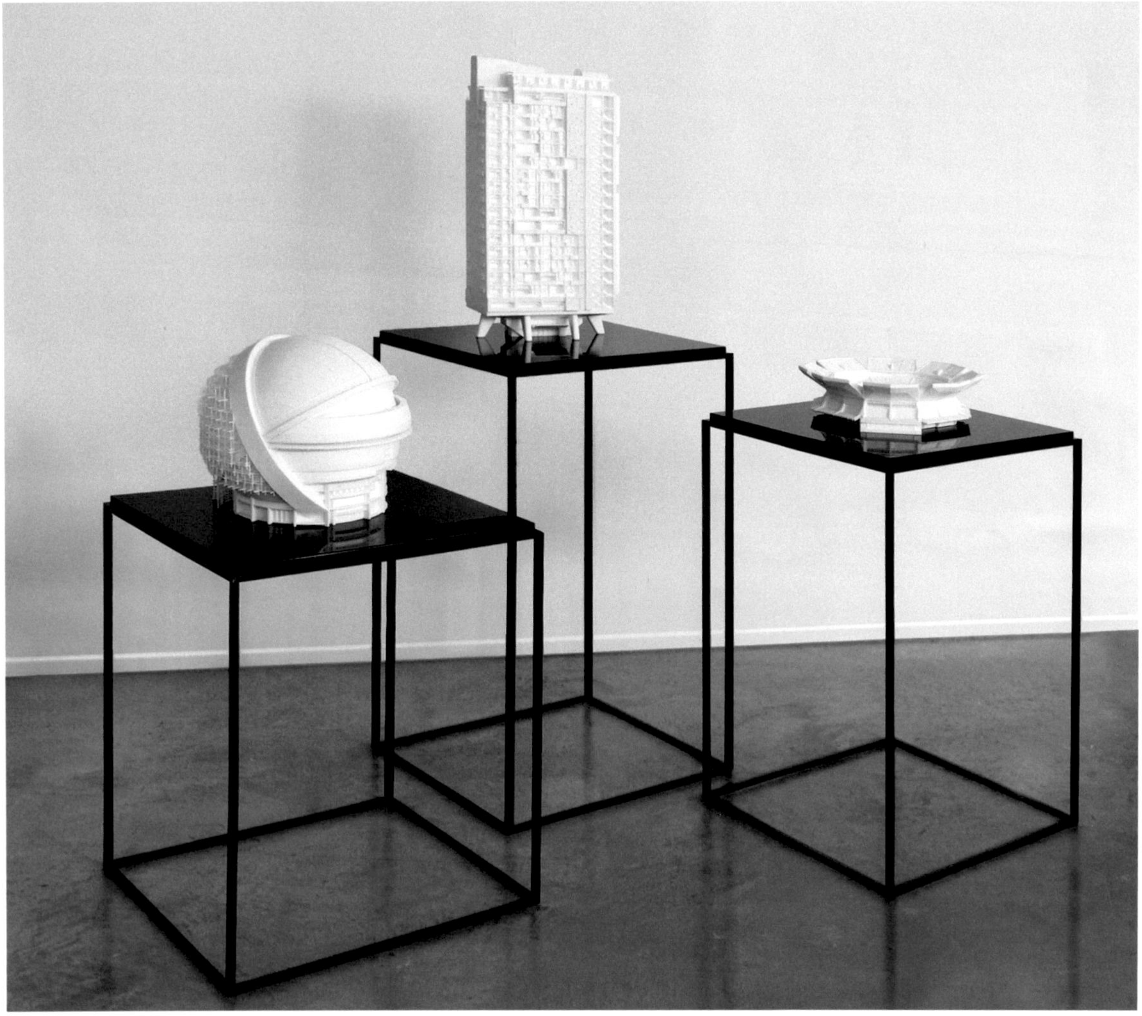

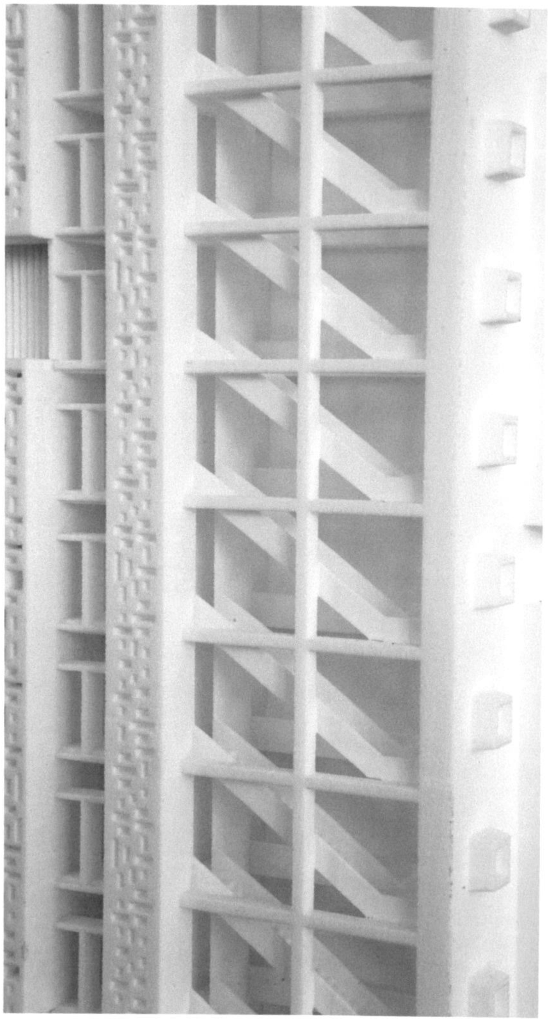

Hans Op De Beeck

OBSERVATORY, SOCIAL HOUSING, ARENA *(this page)*

The inspiration for these autonomous sculptures came from three architectural archetypes: a residential complex, a tennis arena and an observatory. They represent living, free time and science. The three non-existent buildings are clear references to modern architecture. Yet at closer look, the spectator finds cracks and fissures, signs of decay and detoriation.

PANORAMIC CONSTRUCTIONS *(right page)*

Each of these three sculptures is an architectural study for a panorama and offers the spectator a 360° view of an artificial exterior. They show three different styles: Neoclassicism, early Industrial architecture and 1950s Modernism.

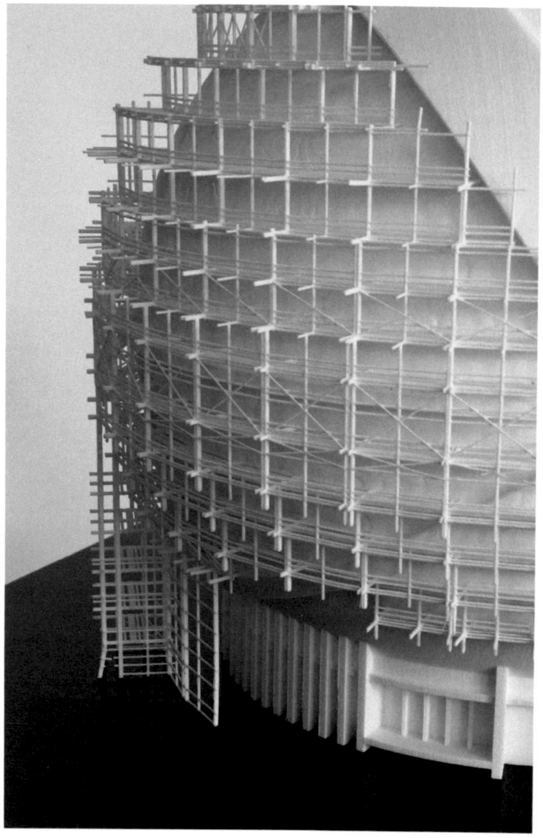

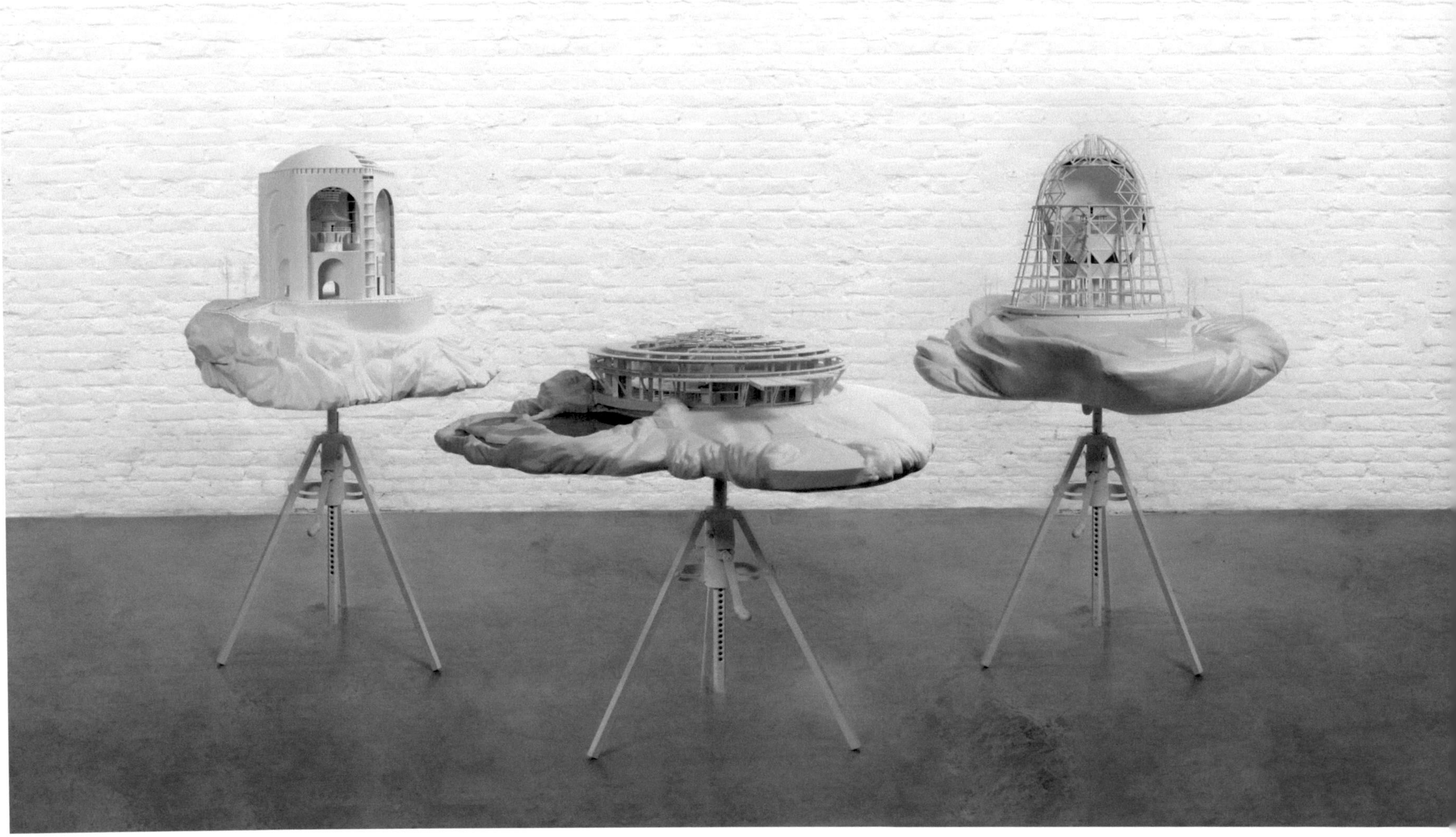

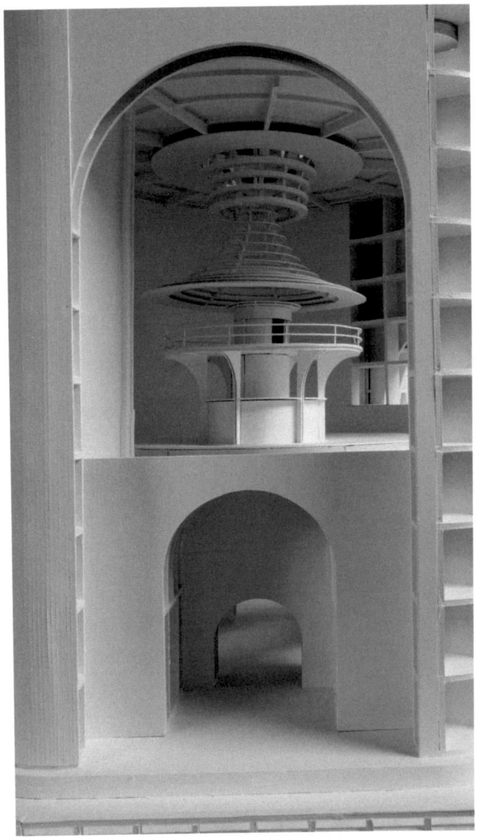

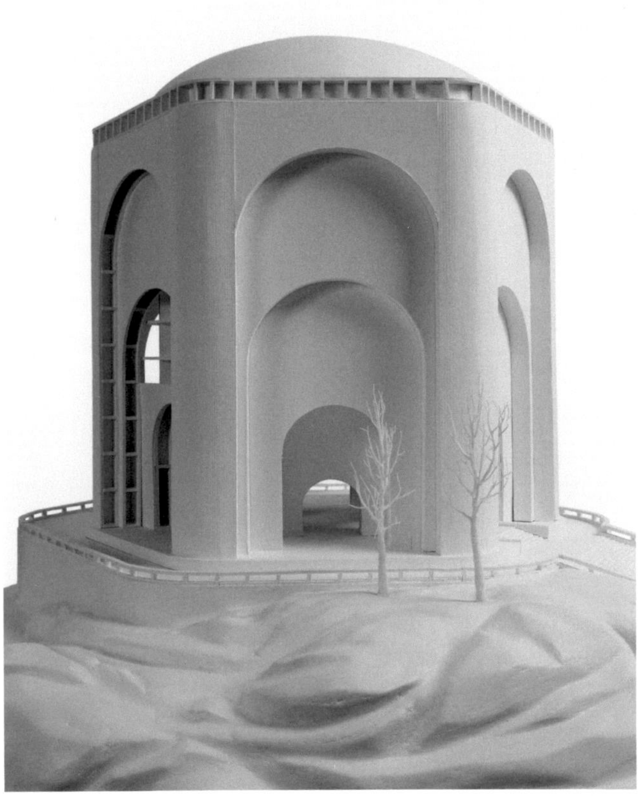

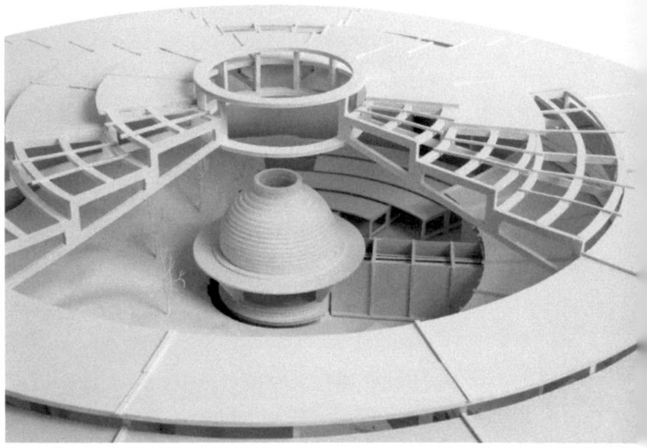

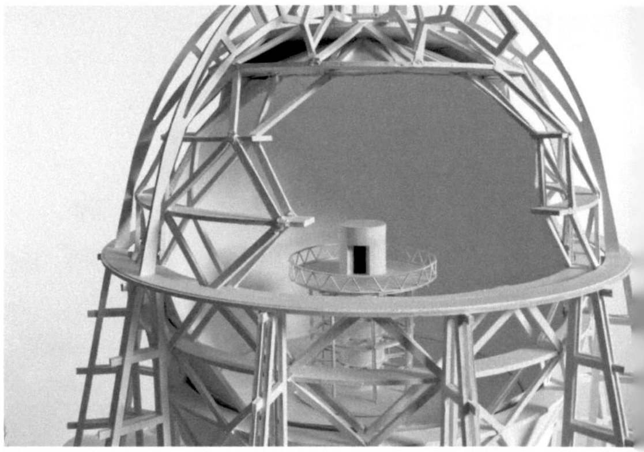

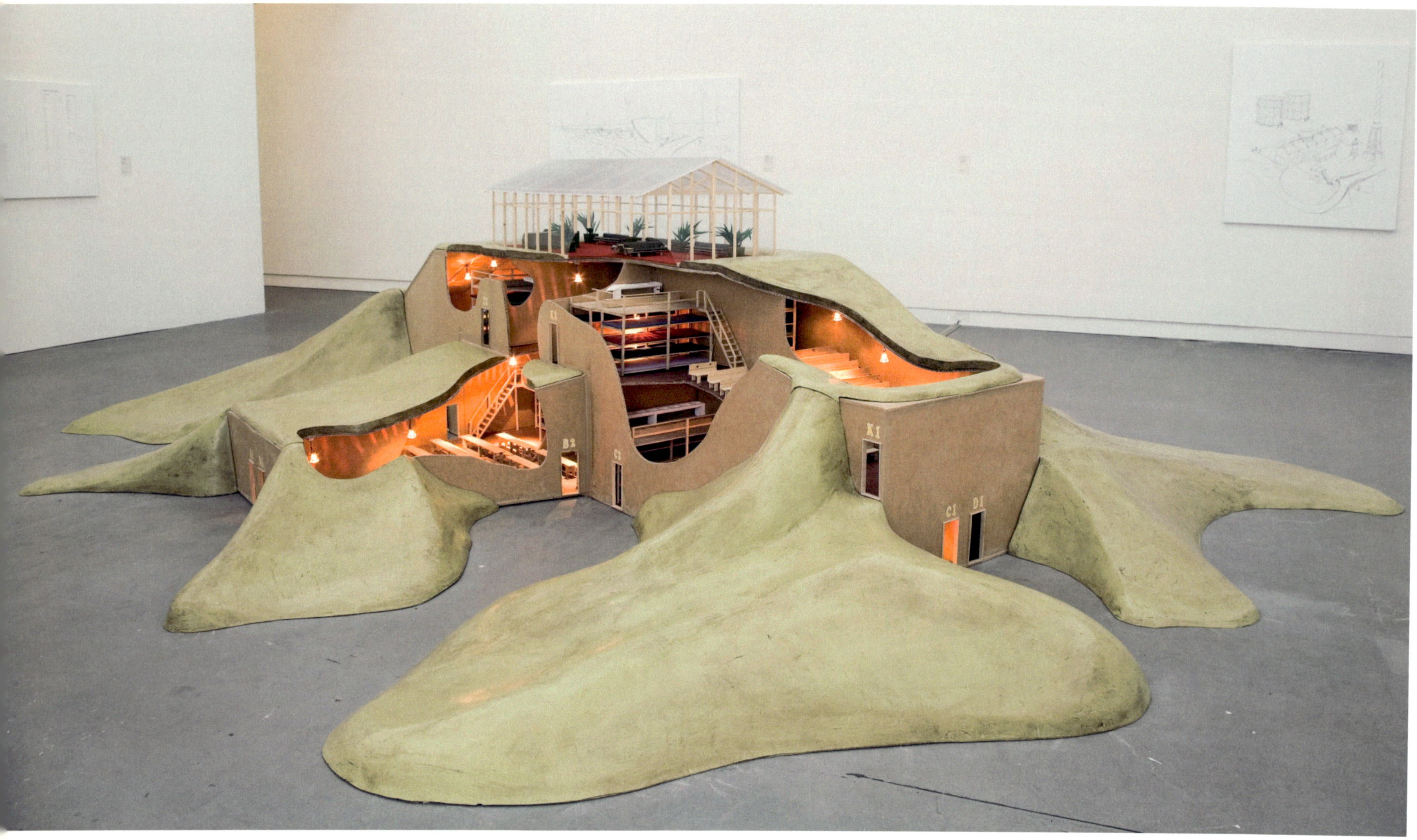

Atelier Van Lieshout

FEMALE & MALE SLAVE UNIVERSITY

The Female and Male Slave University is a model of the elegant and efficiently designed education centre within Atelier van Lieshout's fictious Slave City, a contemporary labour camp. It consists of 12 auditoriums piled up and surrounded by slopes. There are two Slave Universities, one for the males and one for the females. On top of the Slave University is a meeting room for the professors, who are the only ones receiving payment for their work, in this building. The other rooms are for the slaves who are being educated to function well and efficiently within the objectives of Slave City.

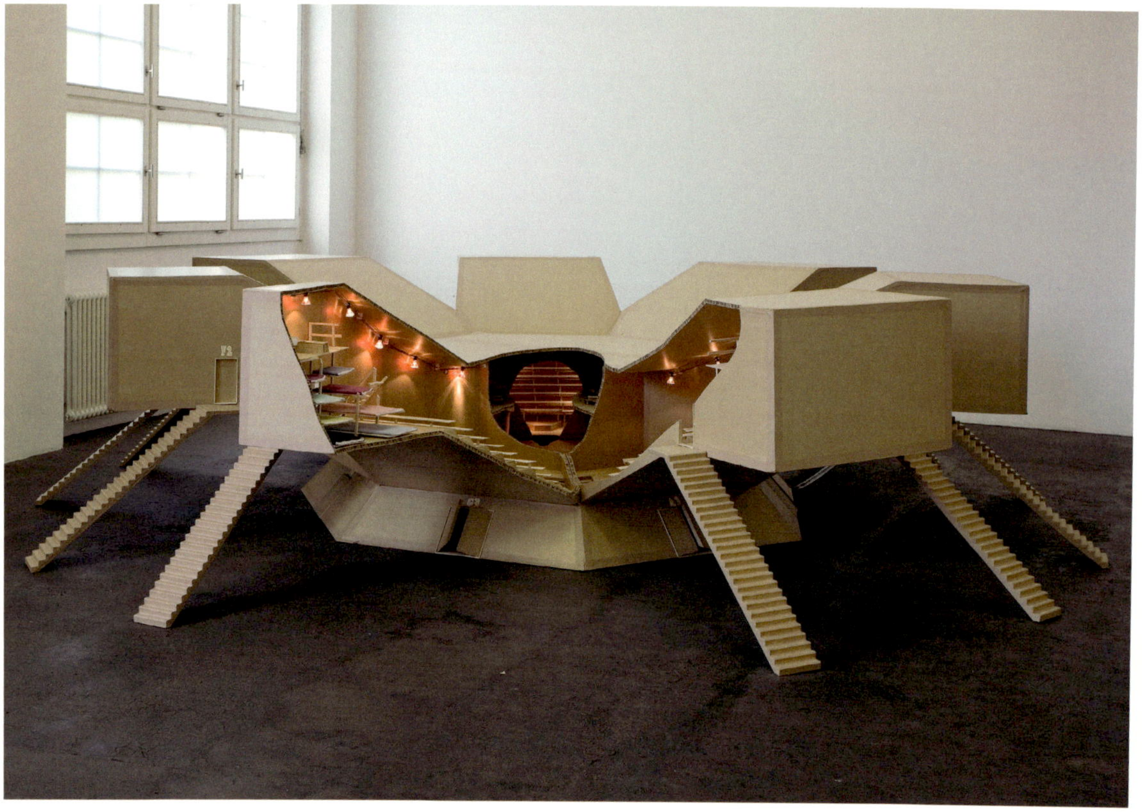

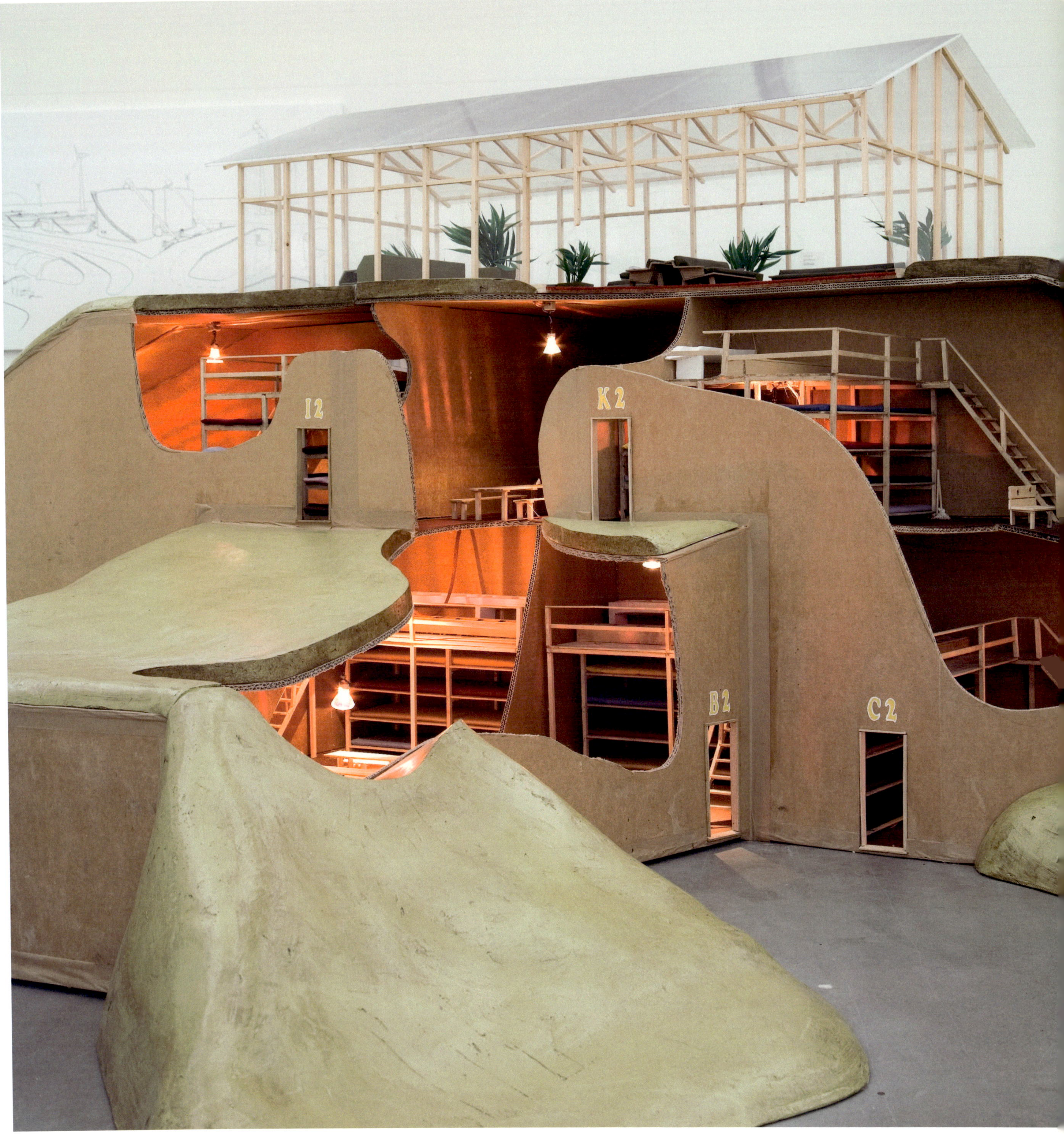
I2
K2
B2
C2

STREET DREAMS

The following Street Dreams chapter chooses the multiple over the singular as it depicts the intoxicating diversity and vitality of street life and leaves the domestic particularity of the previous chapter.

Growing in physical scale as well, the projects here encompass miniature street scenarios embedded in a small transistor radio by Samuel Rhoads Clarke as well as detailed views through cardboard street canyons by Matias Bechtold, Nathan Coley and Edouard Sautai. British artist Rachel Whiteread's *Village* links itself to these residential accumulations with a cluster of 200 illuminated doll houses whereas the work of Björn Hegardt and Erik Olofsen seems to move free of any gravitational restrictions troughout the city. Another take on the urban terrain, are the infinite examples that provide a new perspective on the architectural phenomena of social housing. The dismal nature of these seemingly hopeless settlements gives way to the tongue-in-cheek architectural photo-renderings by Filip Dujardin and Paul Hollingworth, collages by Mario Wagner and Jakob Kolding's and Stephen Willats's empathetic urban explorations. Other artists such as Jens Reinert, Larissa Fassler and Jeremias Böttcher inquire into the city's transitory spaces and public transportation systems, making amazingly accurate models of pedestrian underpasses and entire subway stations. Yet another totally different approach to depicting the abundance and vitality of street and city life, are the tantalising forms that collide in the chromatic and captivating photo-collages of Laura S. Kicey and Dionisio Gonzáles and the spectacular photo-installations by Isidro Blasco. The illustrations of Apfel Zet and eBoy reveal equally close-packed street scenes that ardently commit themselves to the full spectrum of colours.
All in all, the projects in this chapter not only transcend the real and virtual, but also offer a refreshing perspective on the vital creativity of street life and its reflection in visual culture.

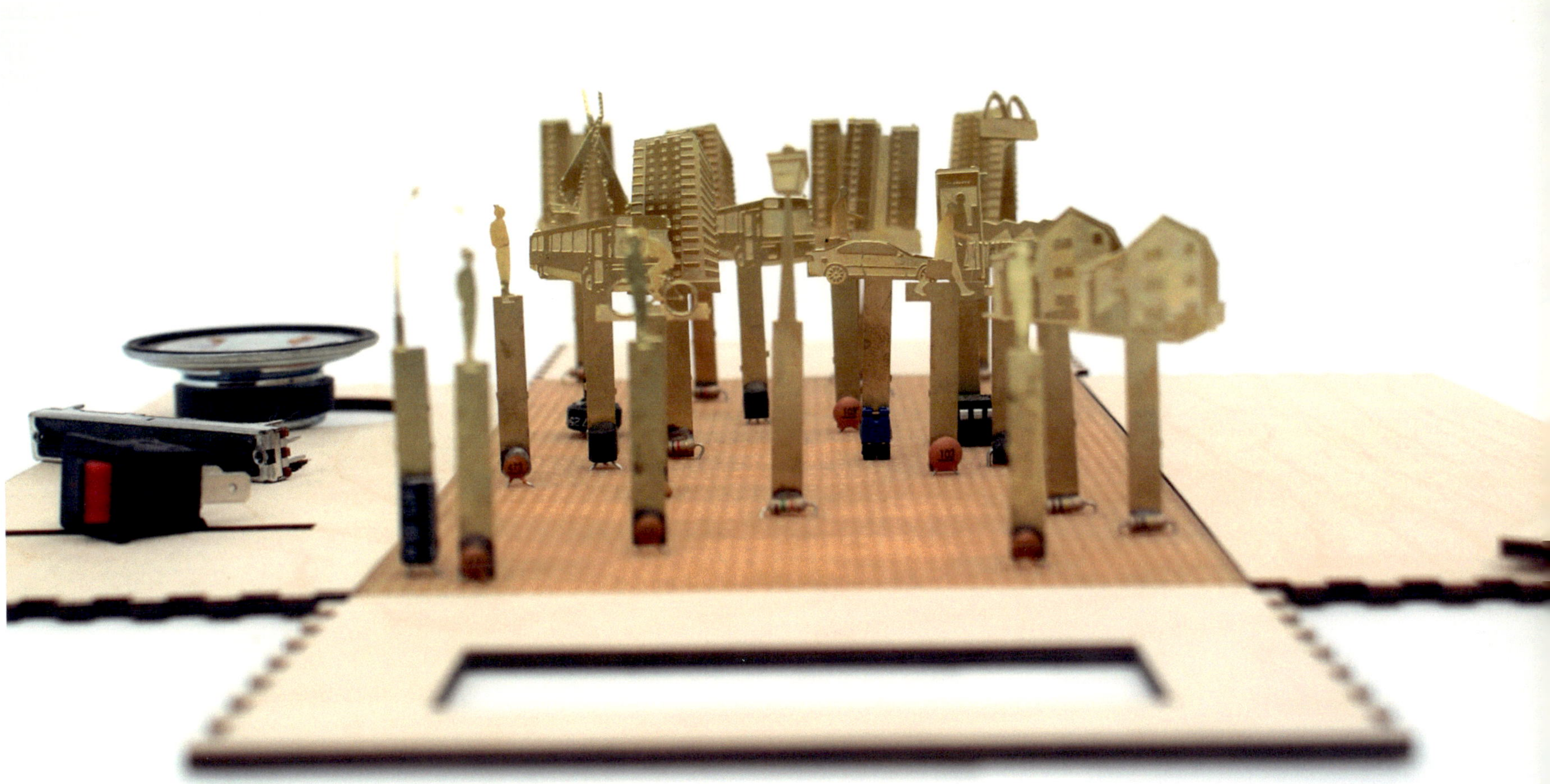

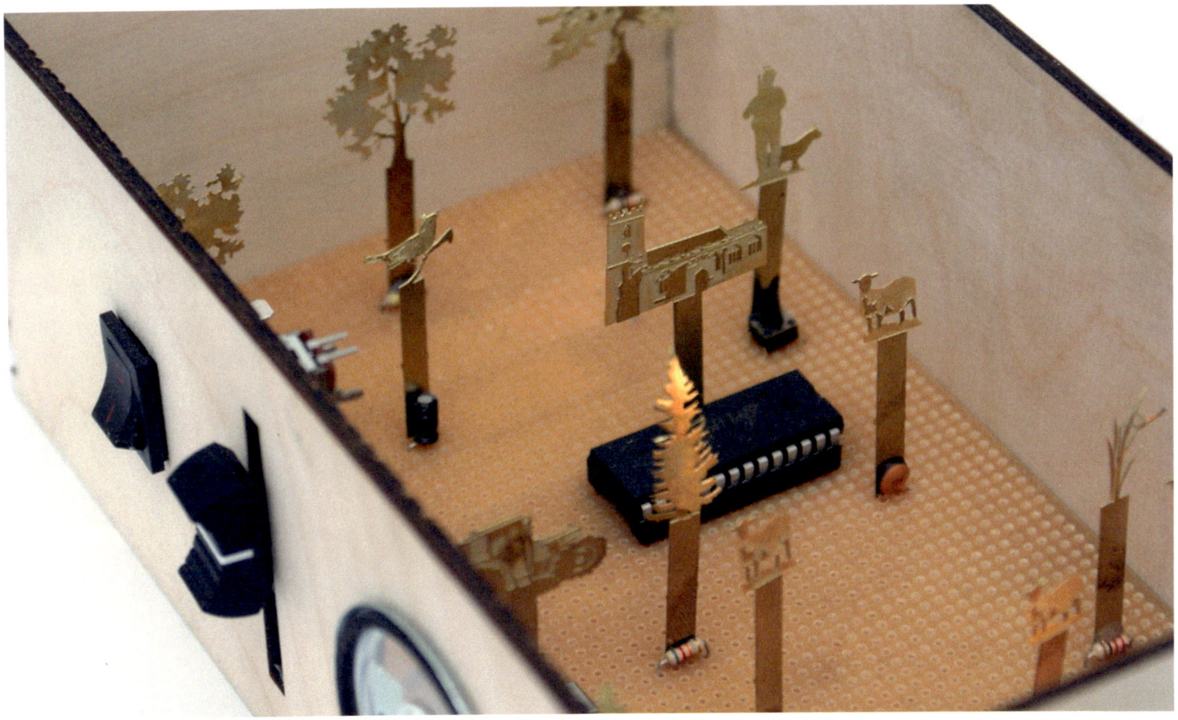

Rhoads Clarke Design

KITRADIO

Samuel Rhoads-Clarke has designed a build-it-yourself radio with electronic components that combine to create urban or farm scenes. By assembling the parts manually, Rhoads-Clarke hopes consumers will have a longer-lasting relationship with products. By re-educating the user to feel comfortable towards digital processes, the user is able to reconnect with products once again.

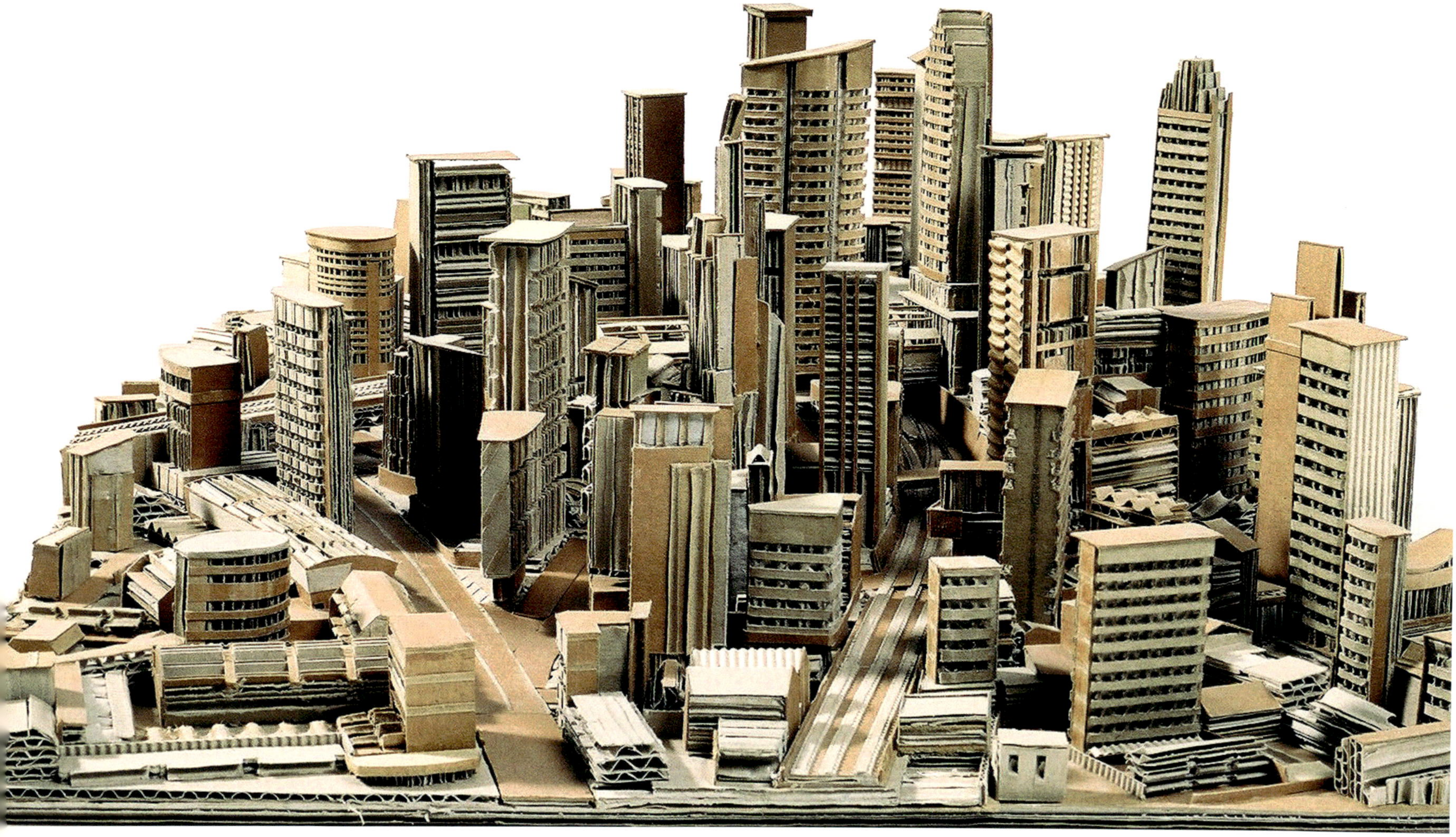

Matias Bechtold

UNTITLED *(top)*

Peach Beach

WEMIX CITY *(right)*

A little cardboard city which was used for a DVD menu for WeMixTV.

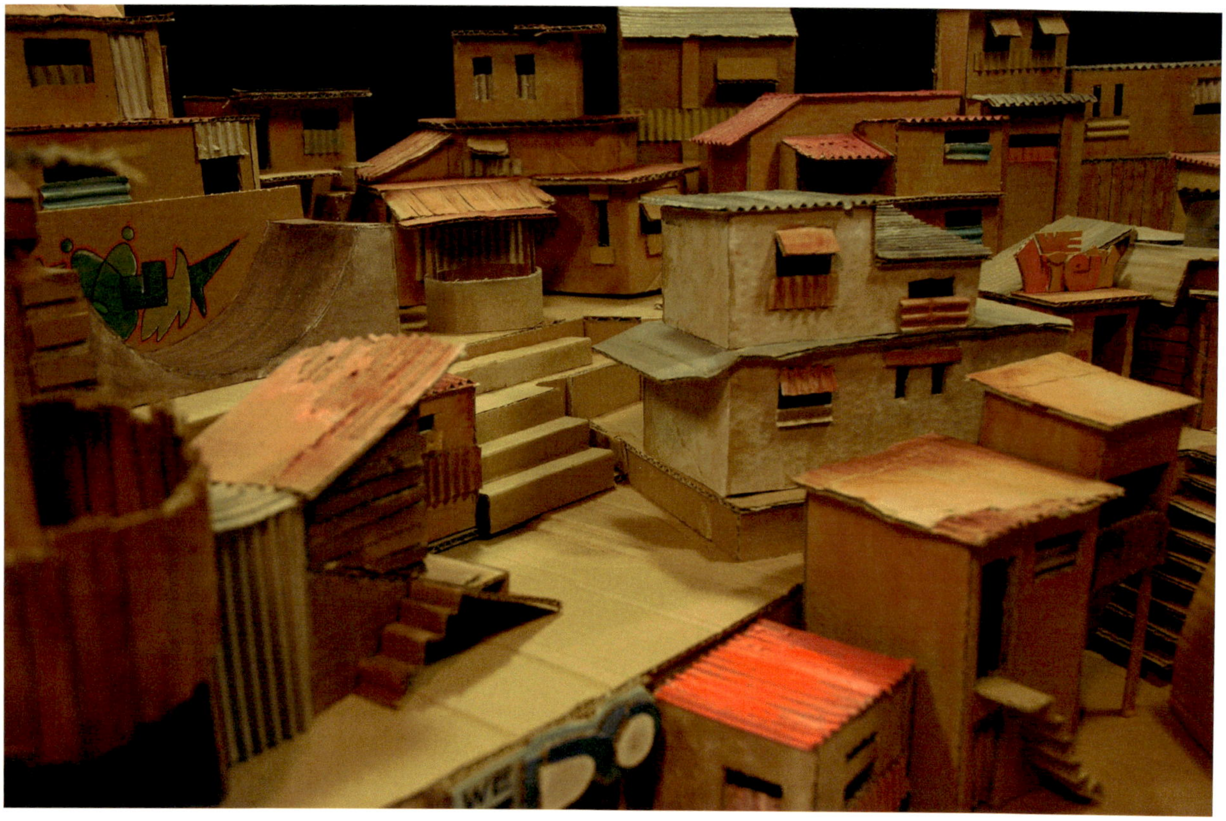

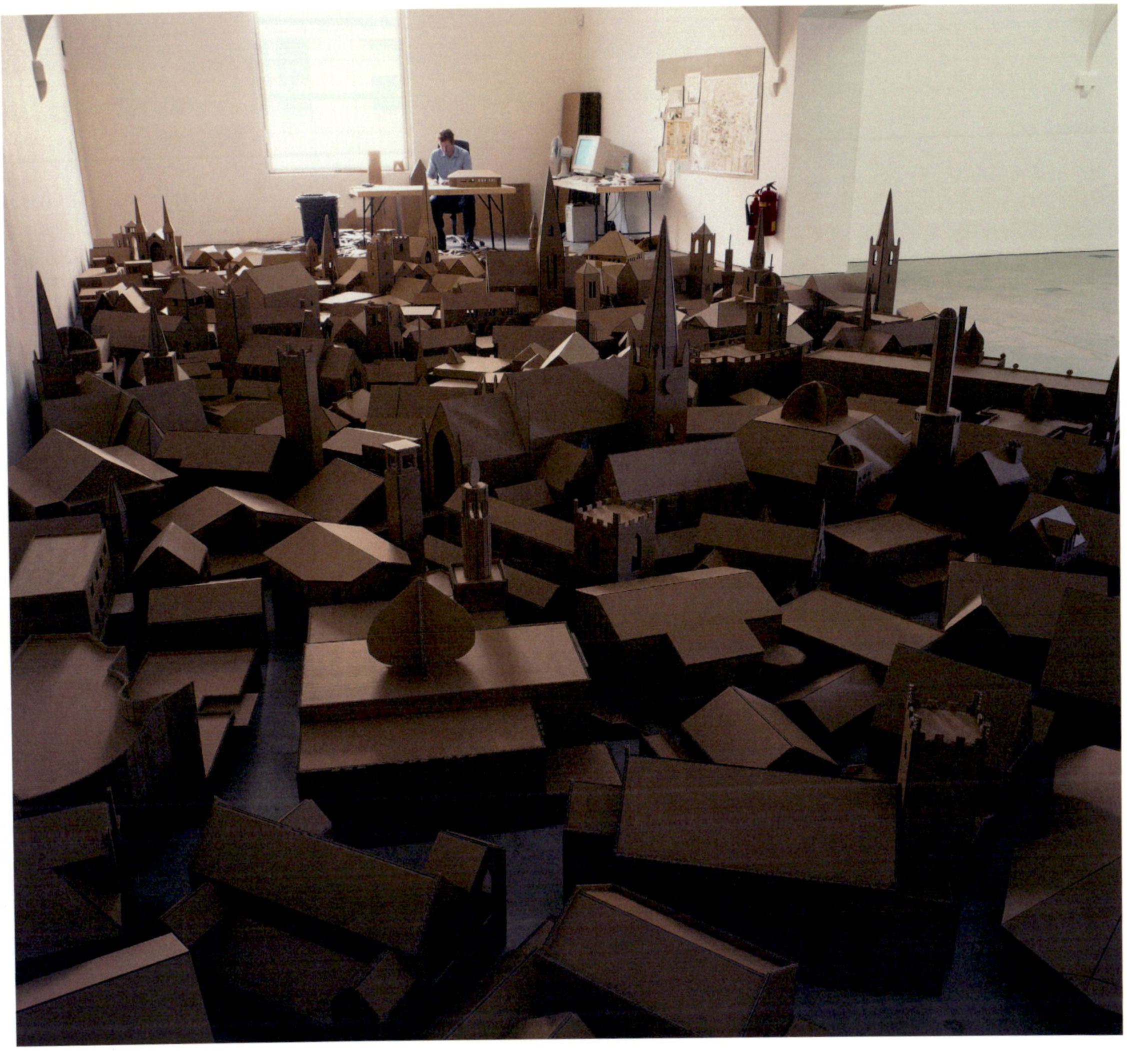

Nathan Coley

THE LAMP OF SACRIFICE,
161 PLACES OF WORSHIP, BIRMINGHAM *(left, bottom left)*

Coley's work is concerned with revealing the unwritten codes of convention surrounding physical structures. For this project he hand-made, in full view of the visiting public, perfectly scaled cardboard models of 161 Places of Worship in central Birmingham, accumulating and eventually recycling the cardboard.

TOWER AND WALL (1937 PREFABS) *(bottom)*

For Coley, buildings are empty vessels given significance by their social history and by the communities that populate them. Tower and Wall is a group of five single storey buildings, erected during the settlement of Palestine by the Israelis during the 1930s. Like the buildings they are based on, the models in the work were built in a day. Coley sites them on a blue tarpaulin with a ten-metre rope, giving the models' positioning a sense of impermanence.

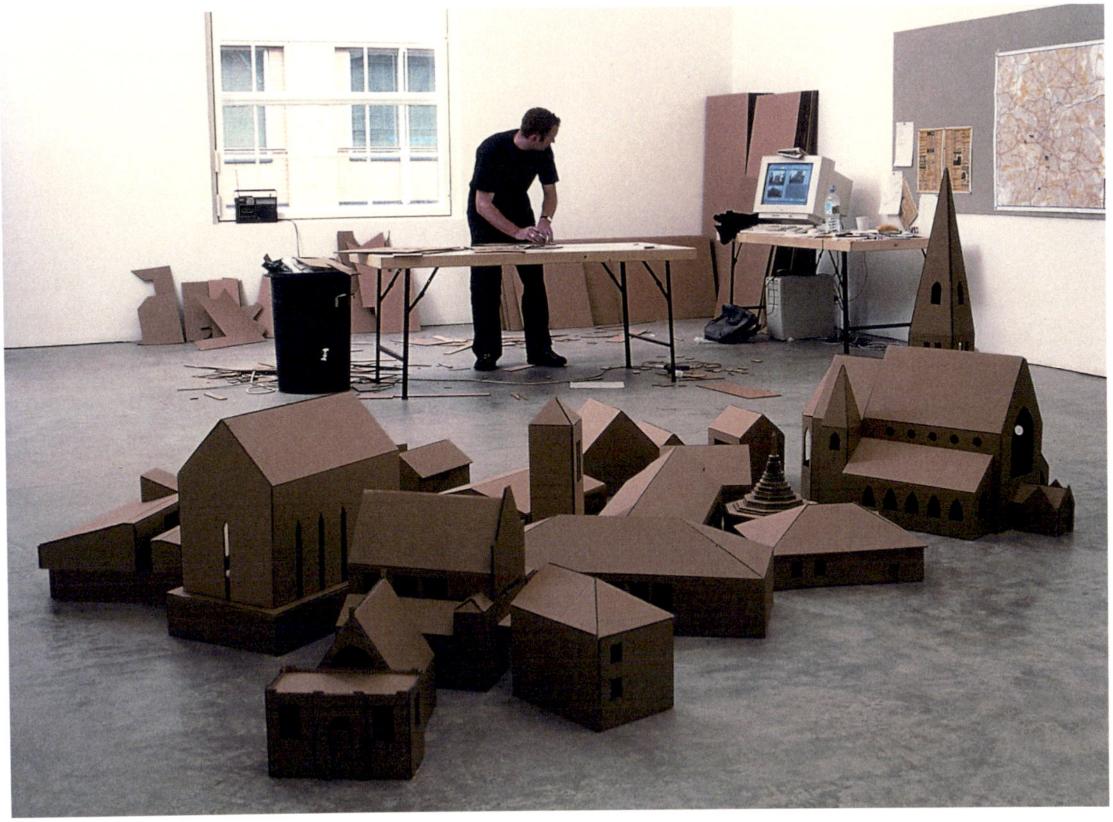

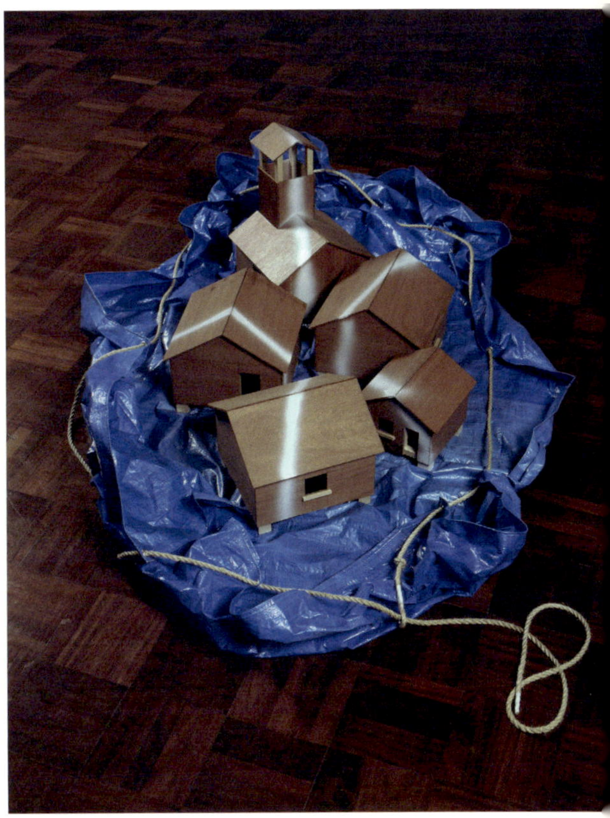

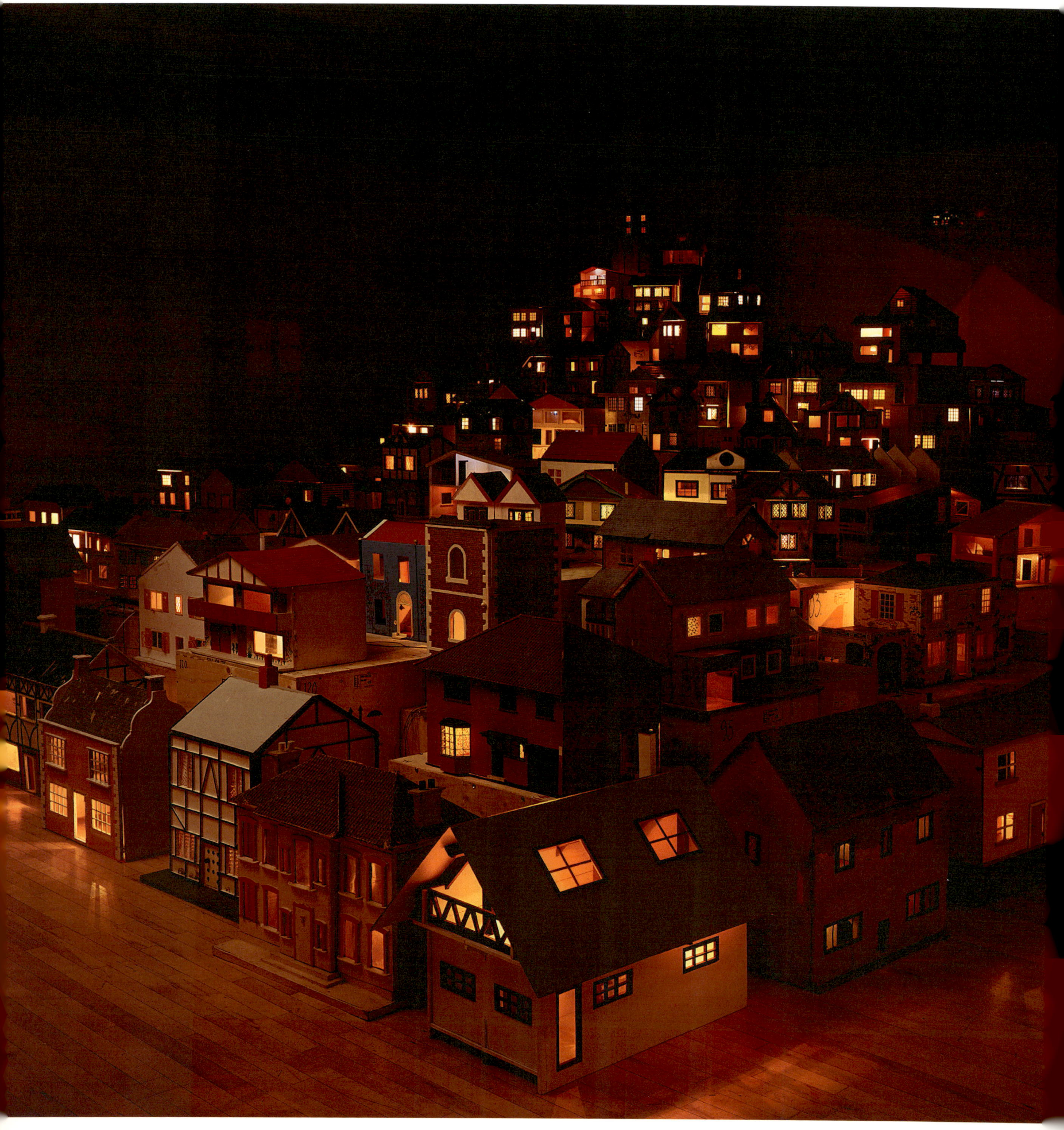

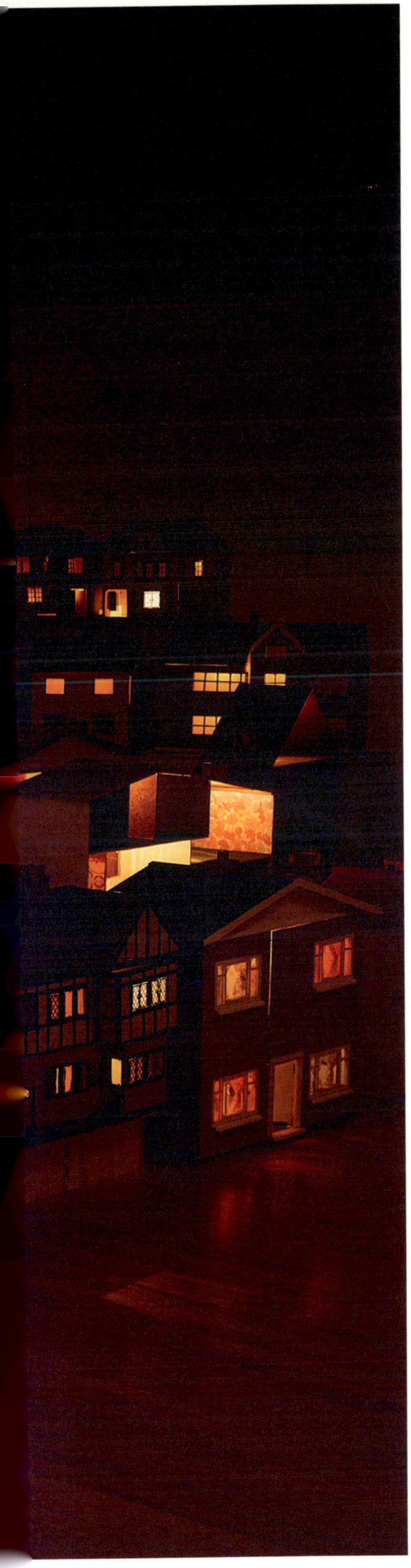

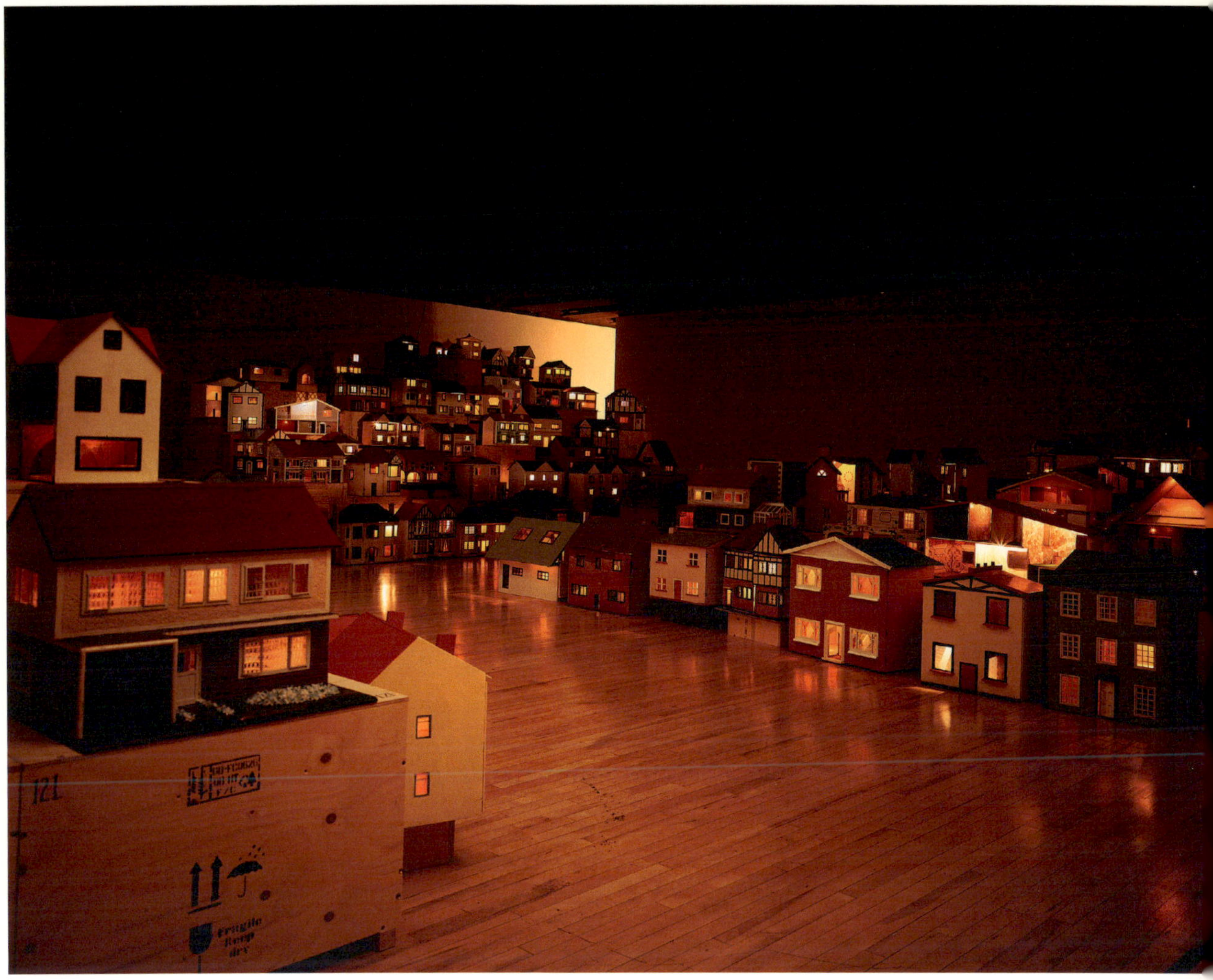

Rachel Whiteread

PLACE (VILLAGE)

As part of the Psycho Buildings Exhibition at The Hayward Gallery in London, Rachel Whiteread clustered 200 illuminated doll houses together like a village.

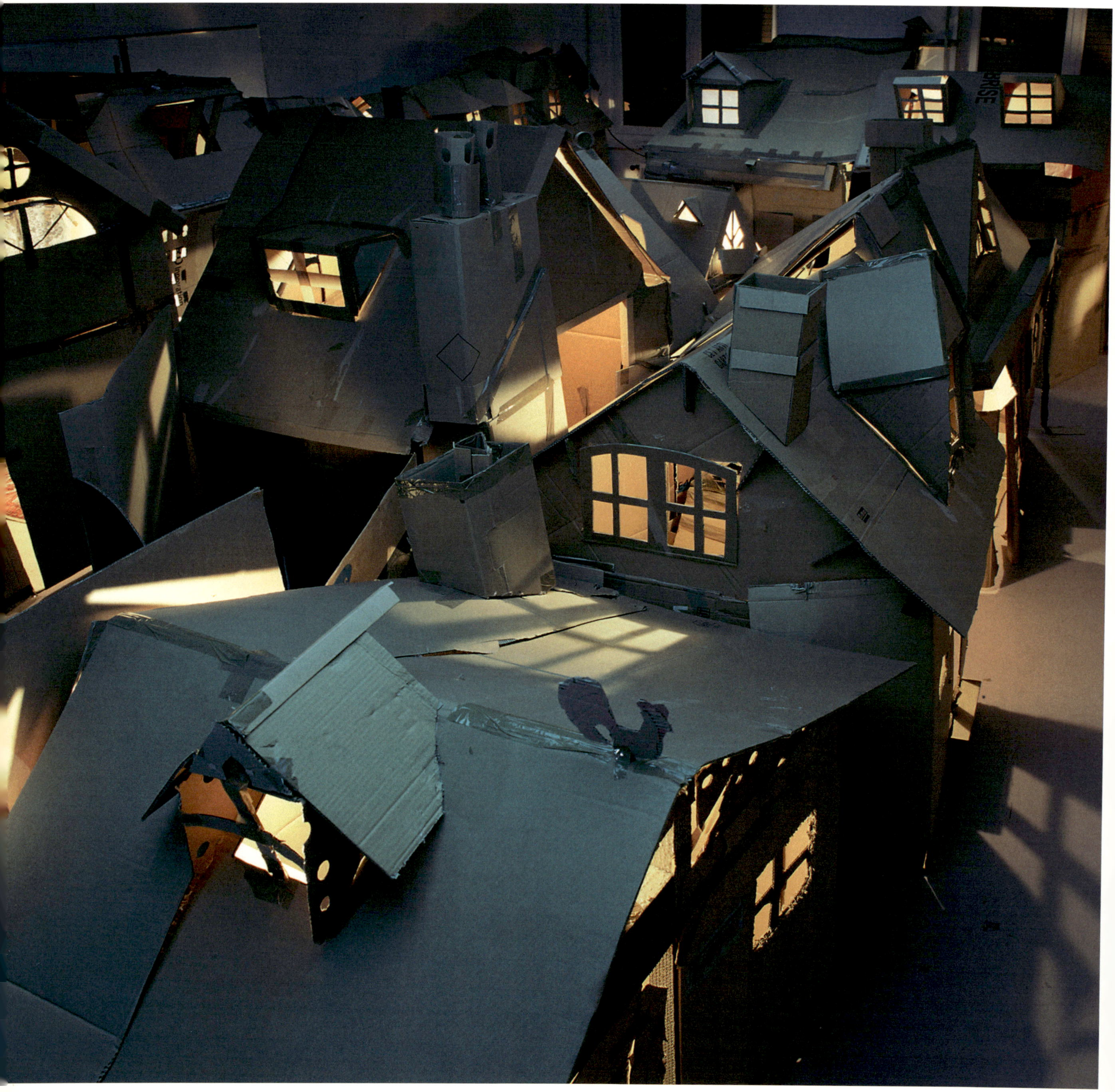

Edouard Sautai CARDBOARD CITY

This cardboard city by French artist Edouard Sautai is the result of a two-week workshop with students of the Collège Chateaubriand, Vielleneuve sur Yonne.

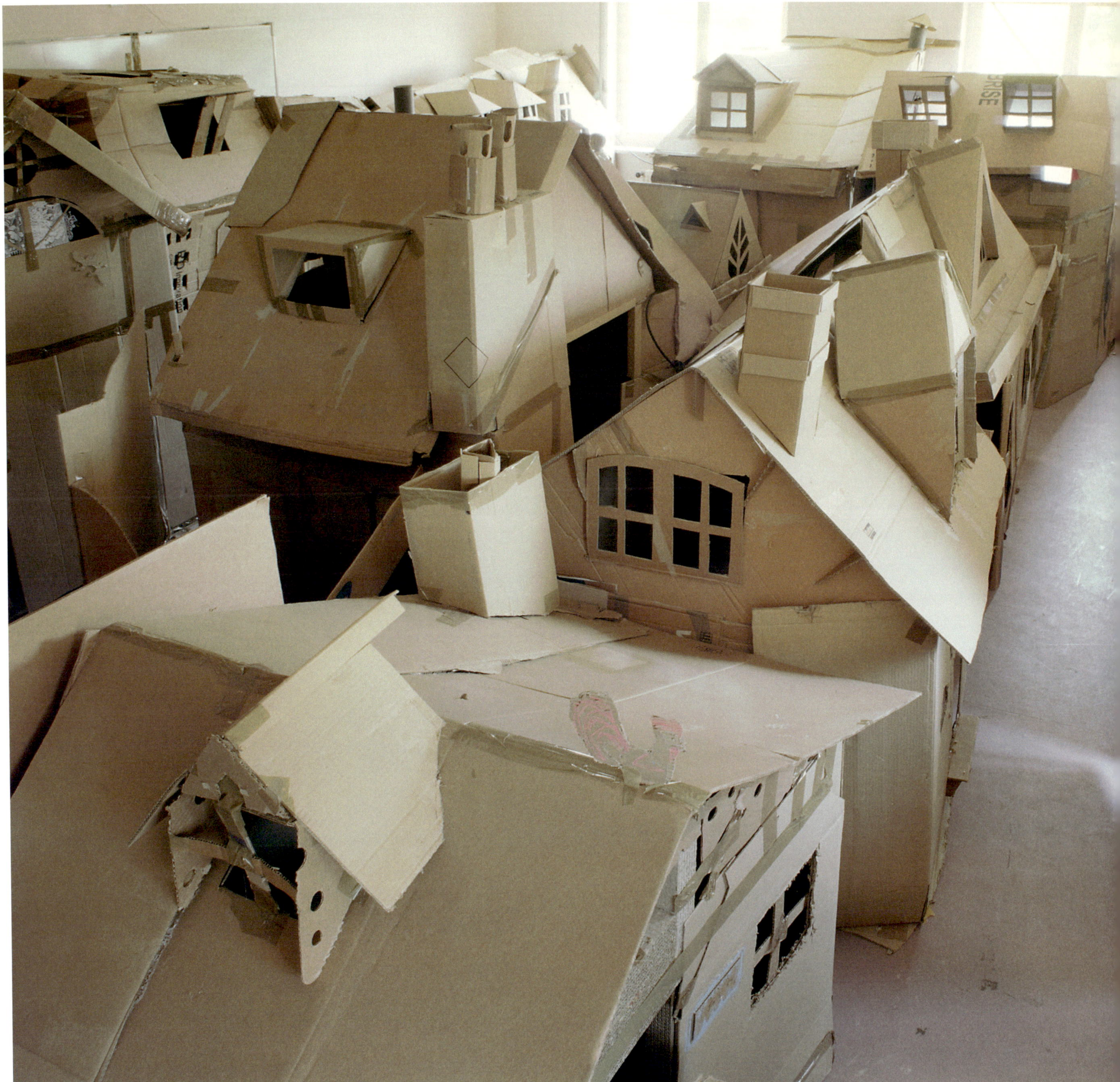
BRISE

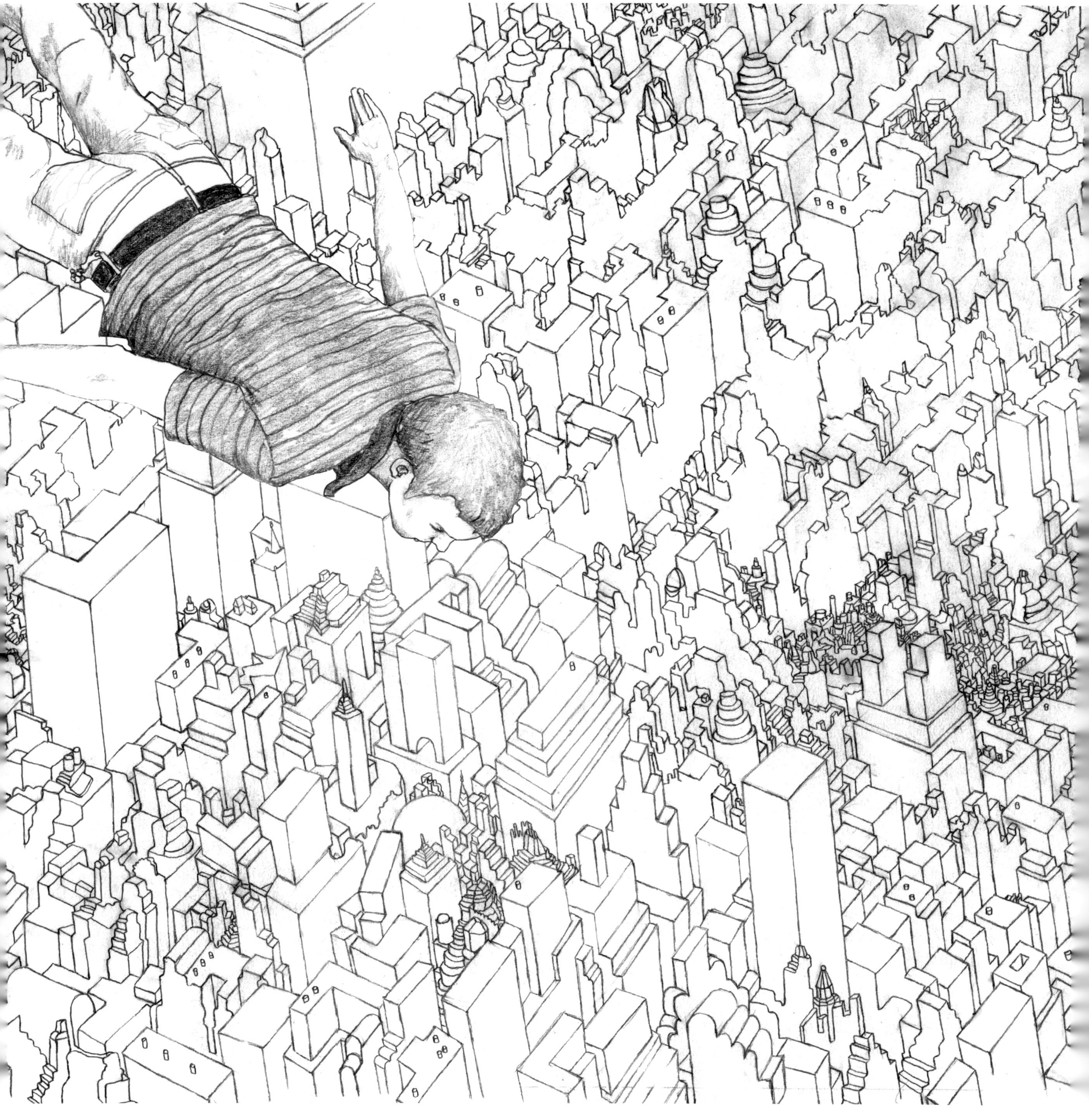

Björn Hegardt A DREAM WOKE ME

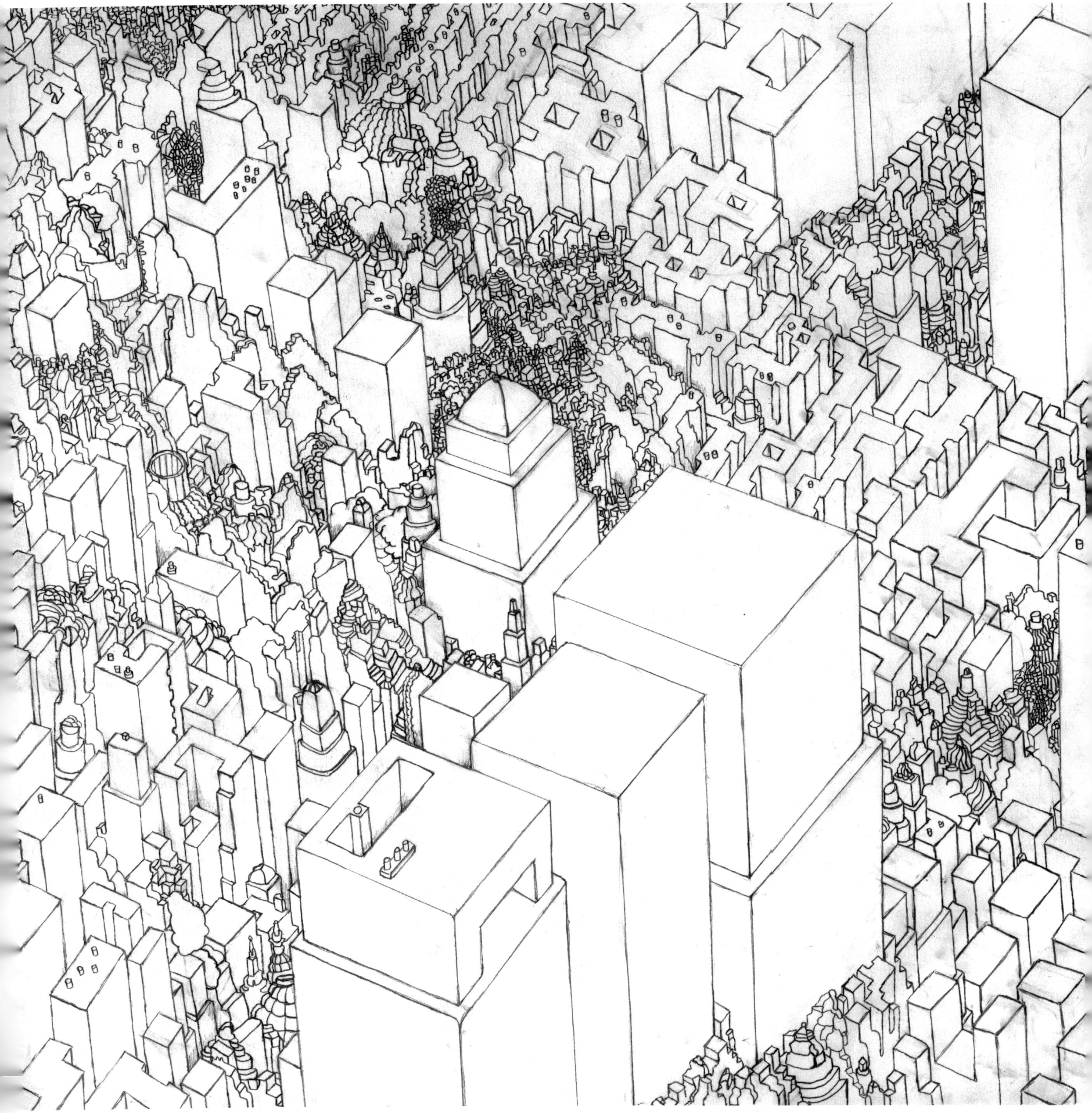

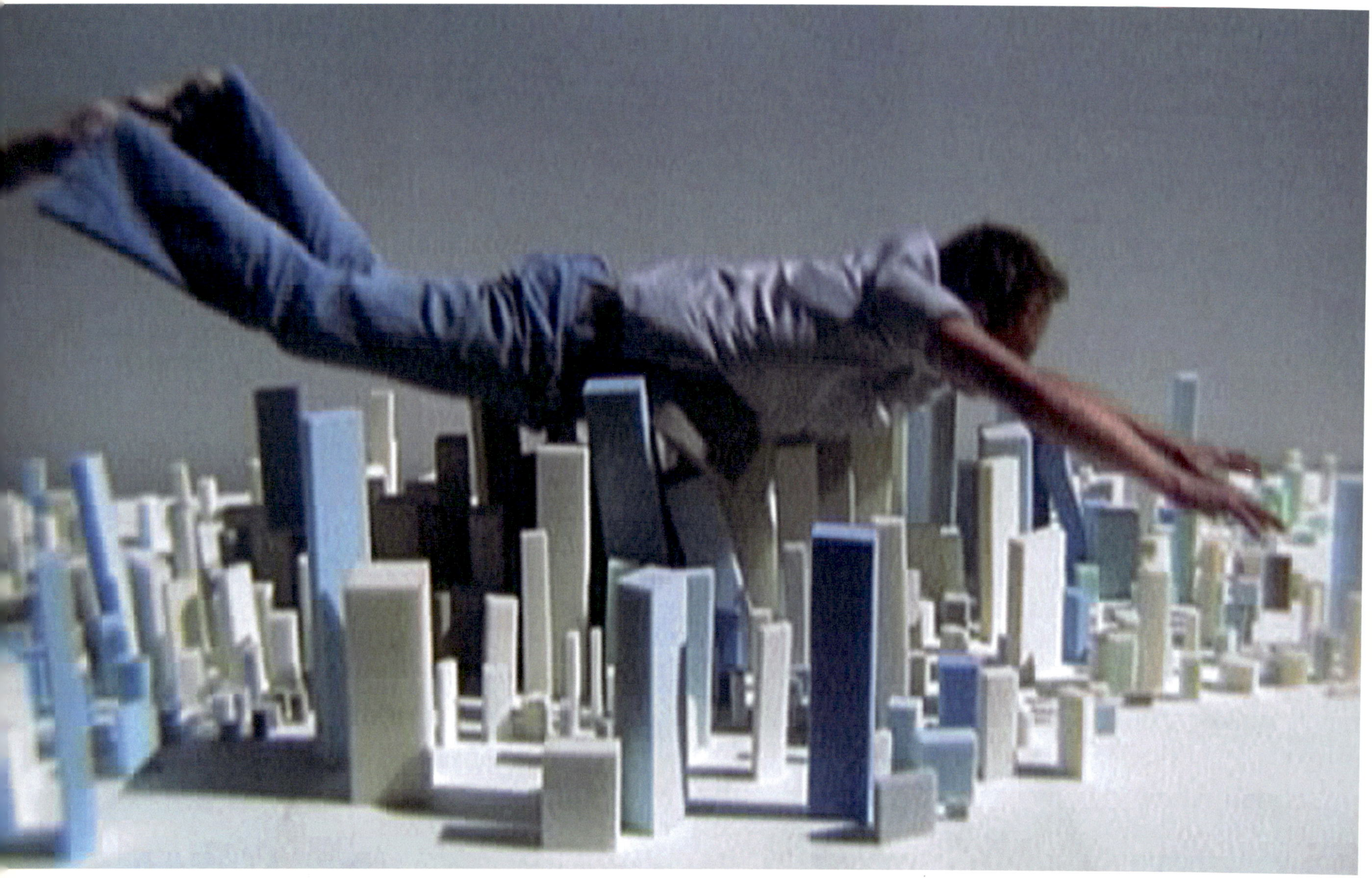

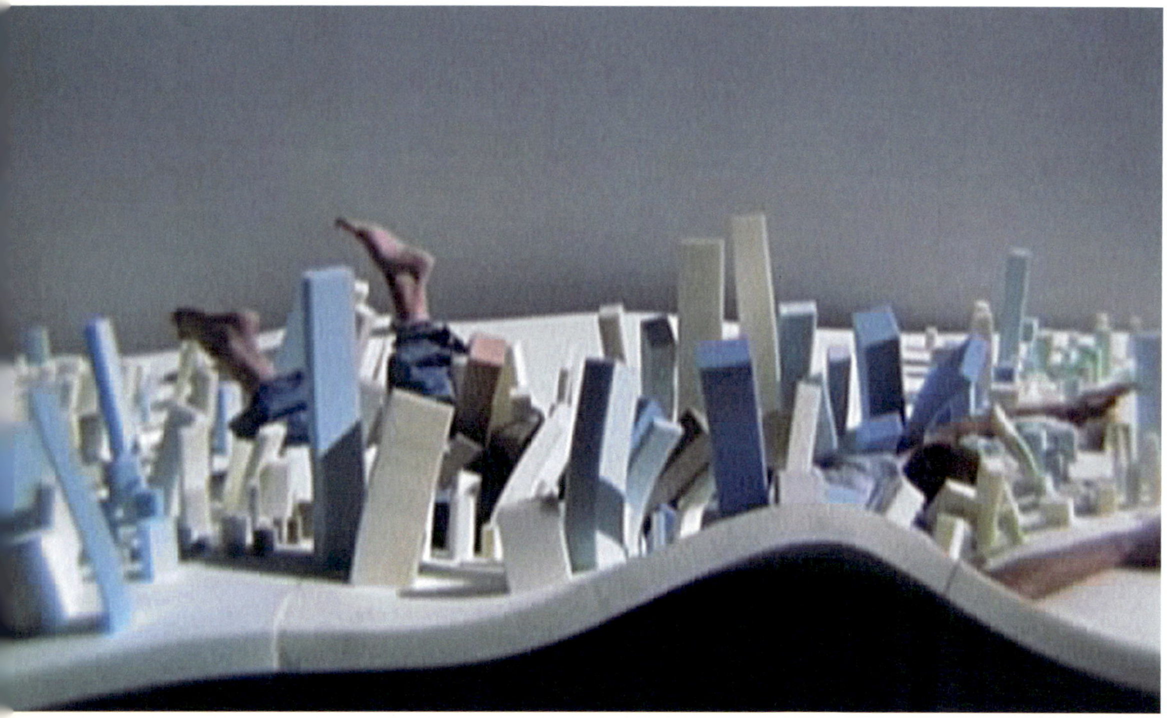

Erik Olofsen

IN PLACES

A super slow-motion camera captures the artist's fall into a cityscape of soft skyscrapers.

Rachel Whiteread

EMBANKMENT *(right page)*

For this installation in the Turbine Hall of the Tate Modern in London, Rachel Whiteread created a modular landscape from 14,000 polyethylene boxes.

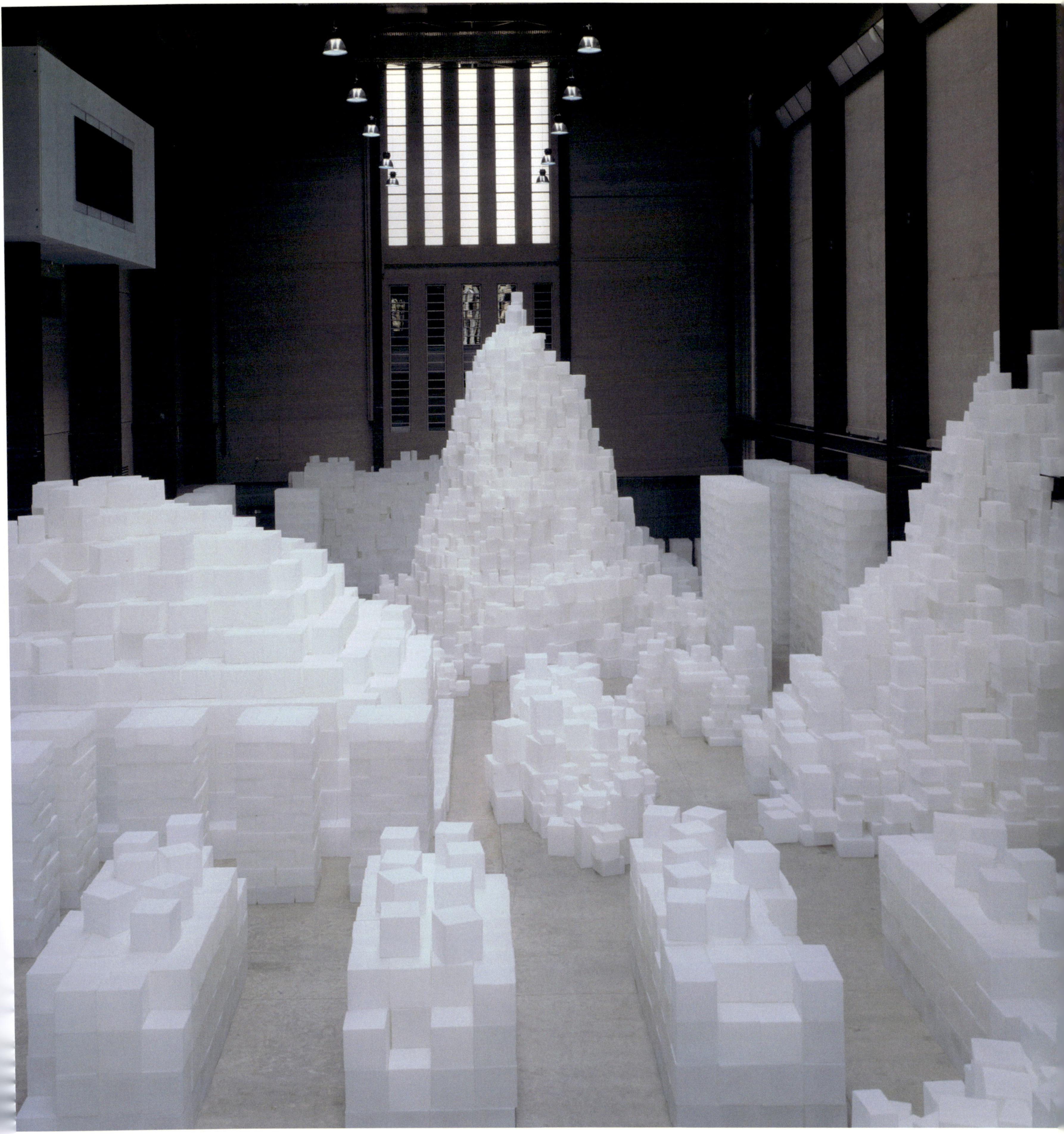

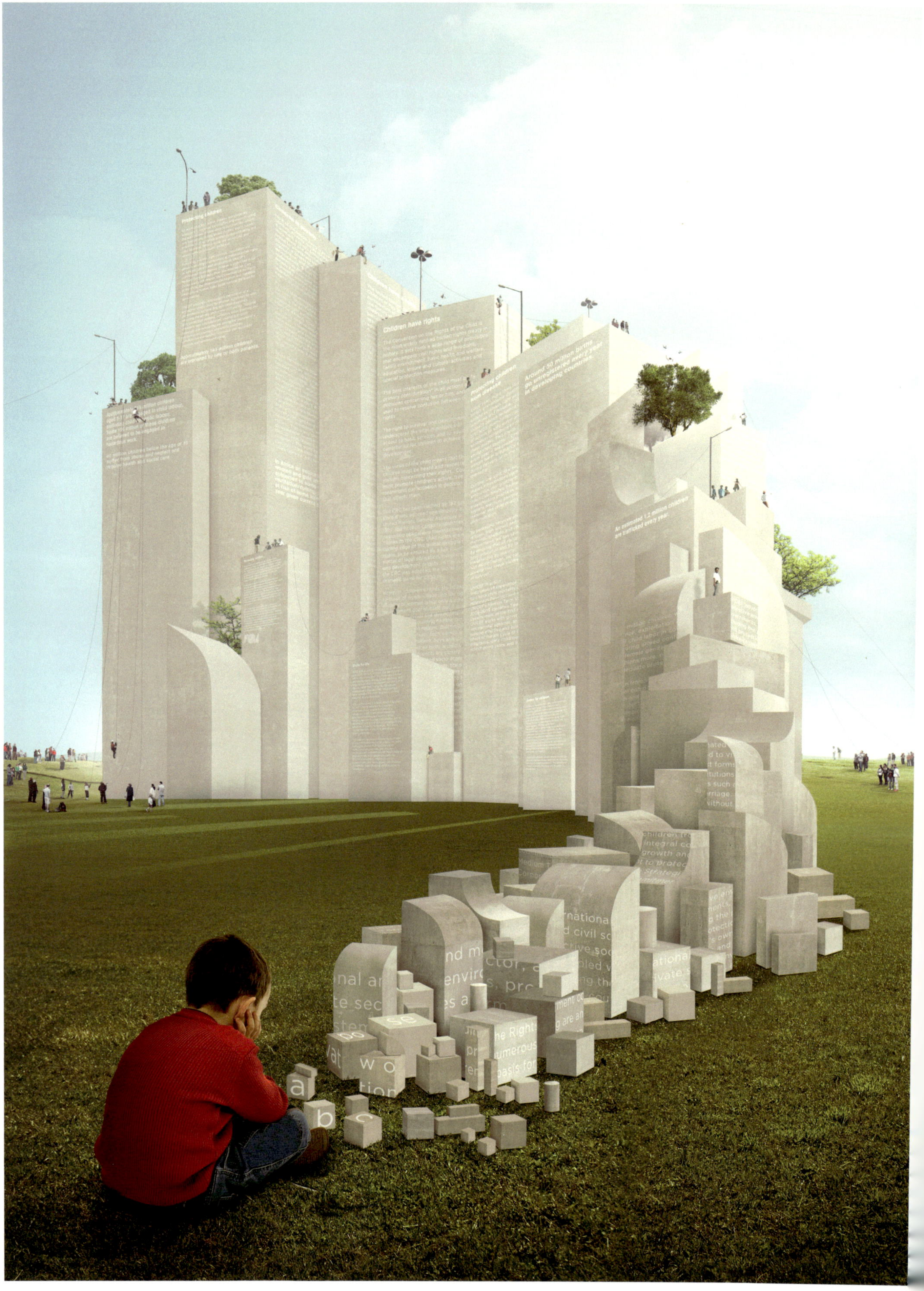

Paul Hollingworth

POTENTIAL

This digitally crafted artwork was generated specifically for UNICEF as part of a graphic project titled *60 Unite for Children*. 60 artists from around the world came together to create a book dedicated to highlighting UNICEF's actions. This contribution in particular was intended to demonstrate the potential within every single child worldwide. All children are born with the same potential, however, not all have the same opportunity to exhaust this potential.

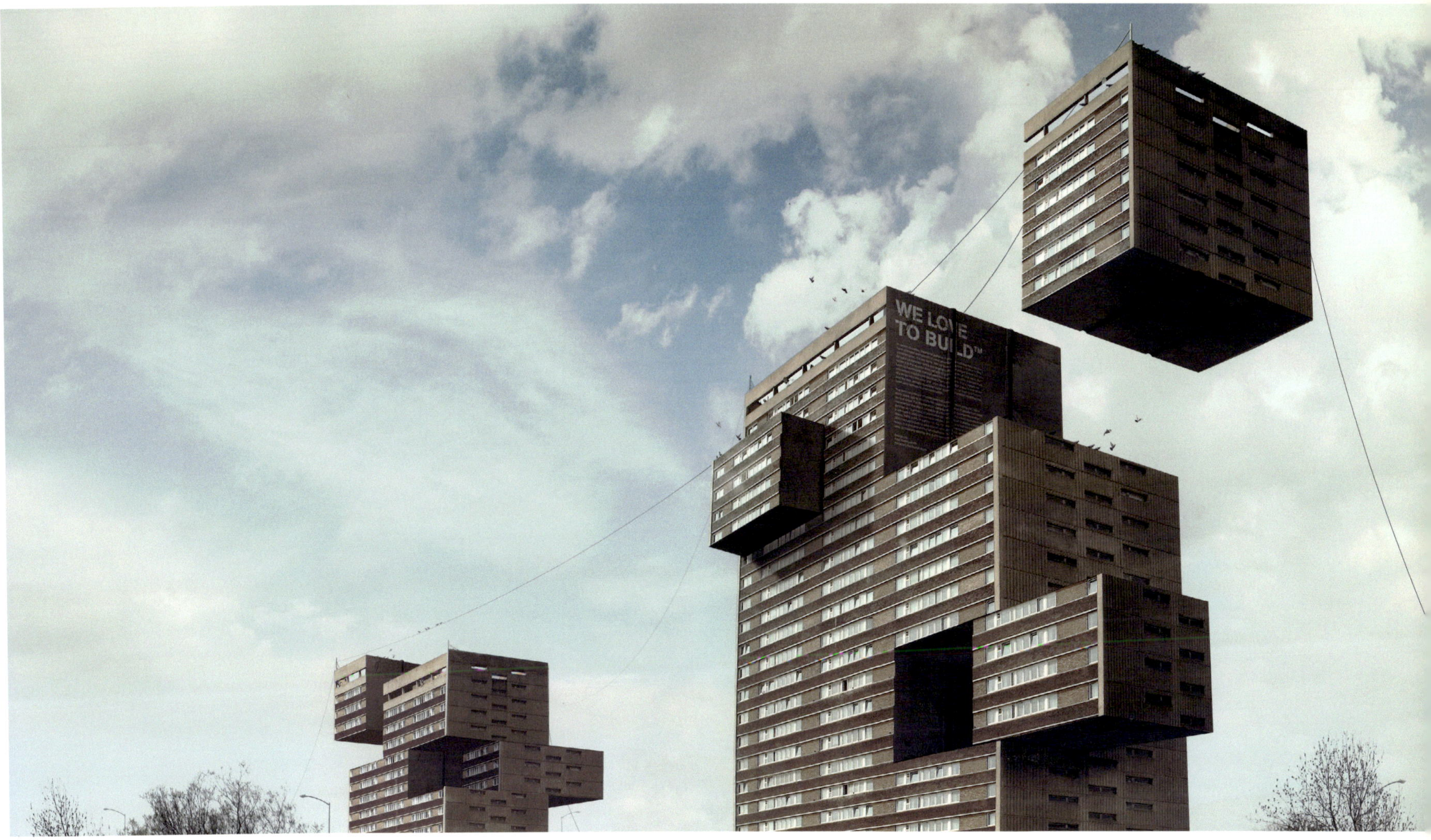

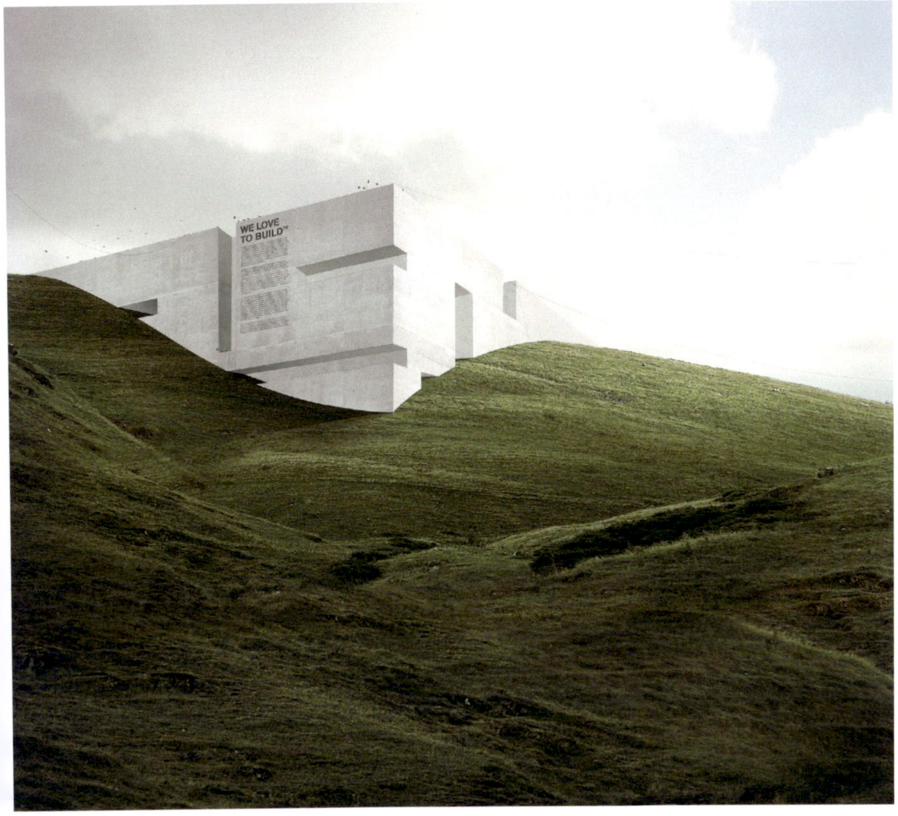

Paul Hollingworth

WE LOVE TO BUILD™

This is a series of images devoted to playing with architecture. Regular concrete structures from everyday urban landscapes are dissected and digitally re-constructed, generating new and interesting monolithic art pieces that appear surreal and intriguing.

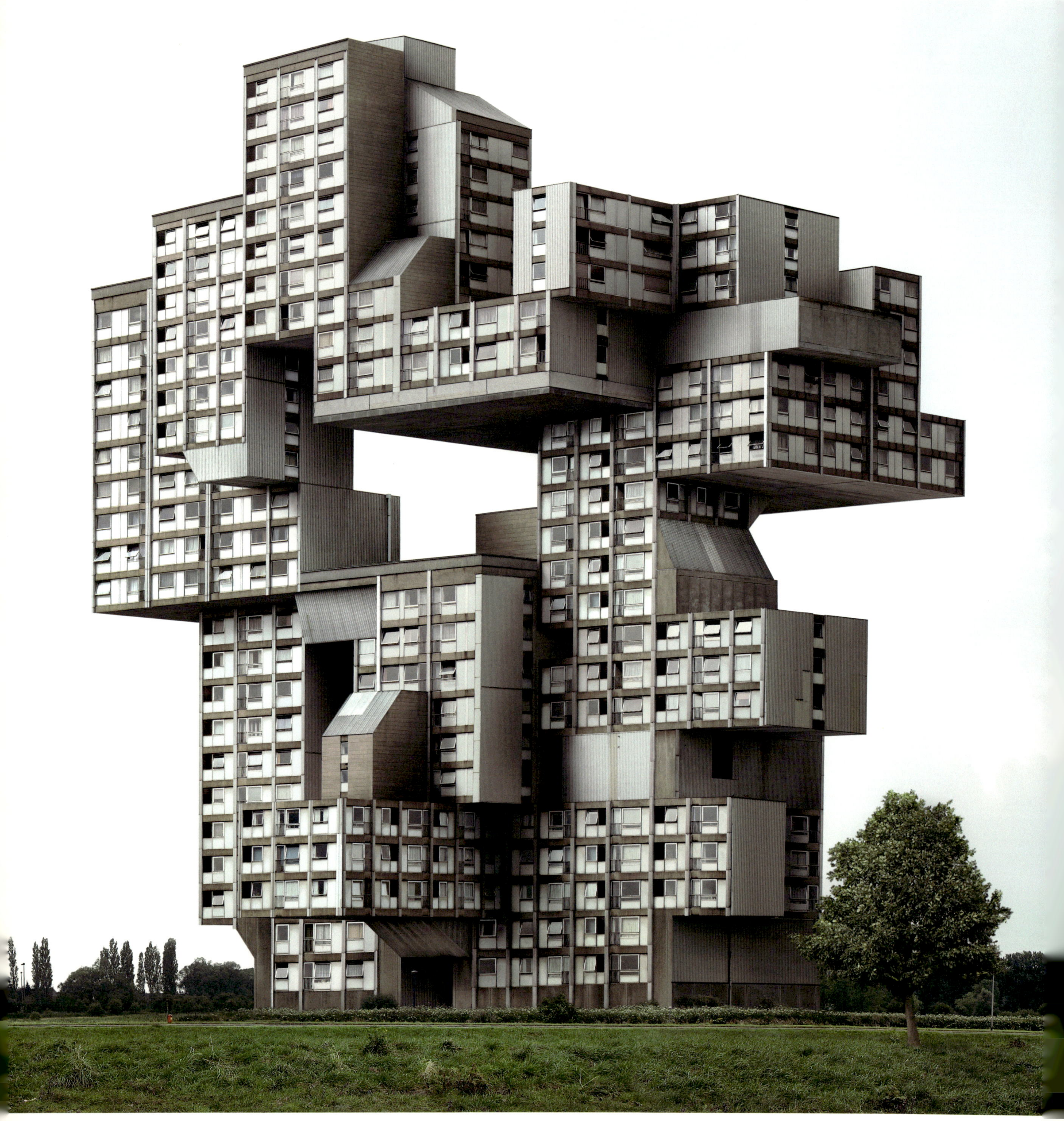

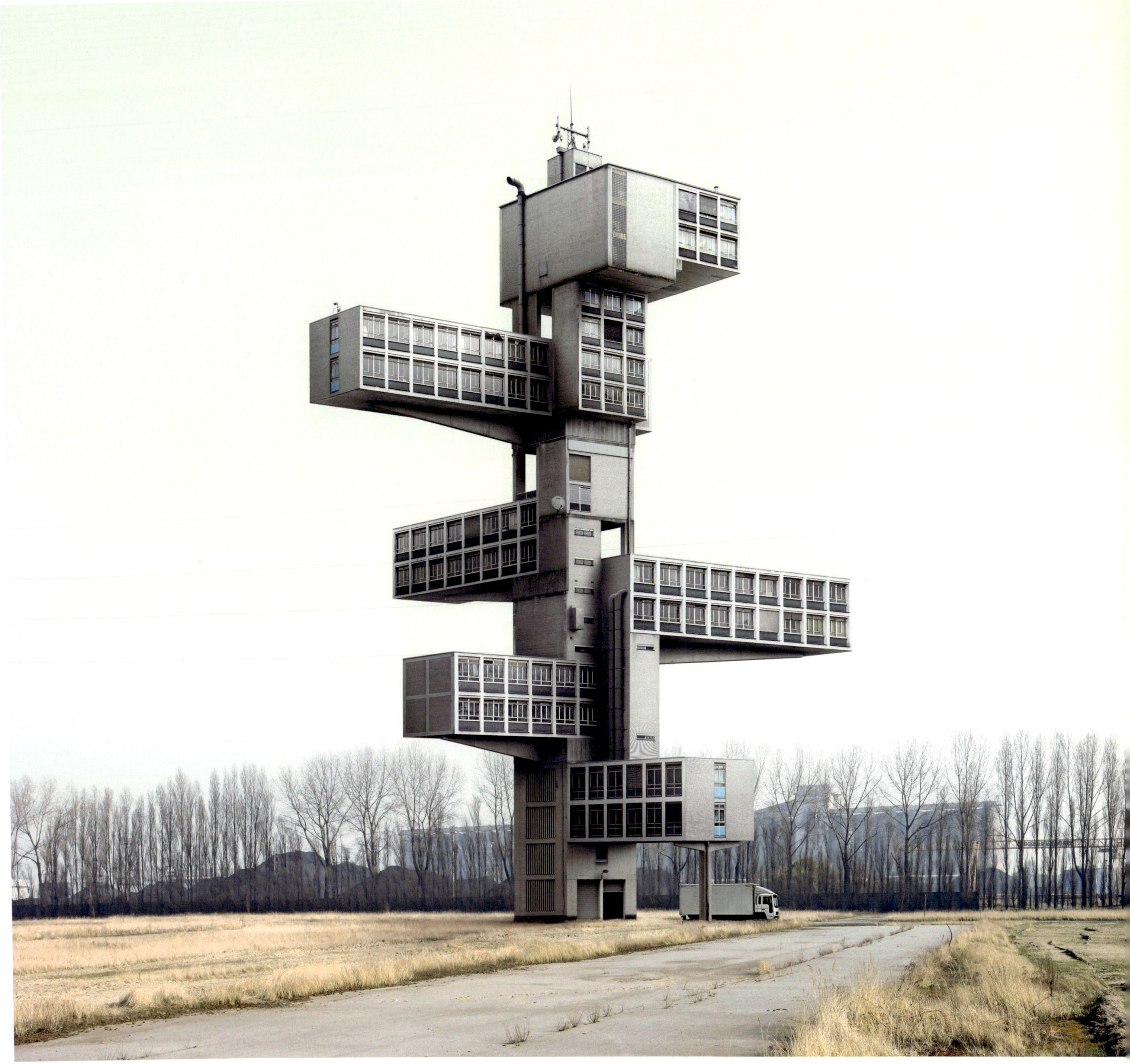

Filip Dujardin

UNTITLED *(left page, this page, next page)*

Belgian photographer Filip Dujardin creates unique and bizarre building montages from photographs of different buildings.

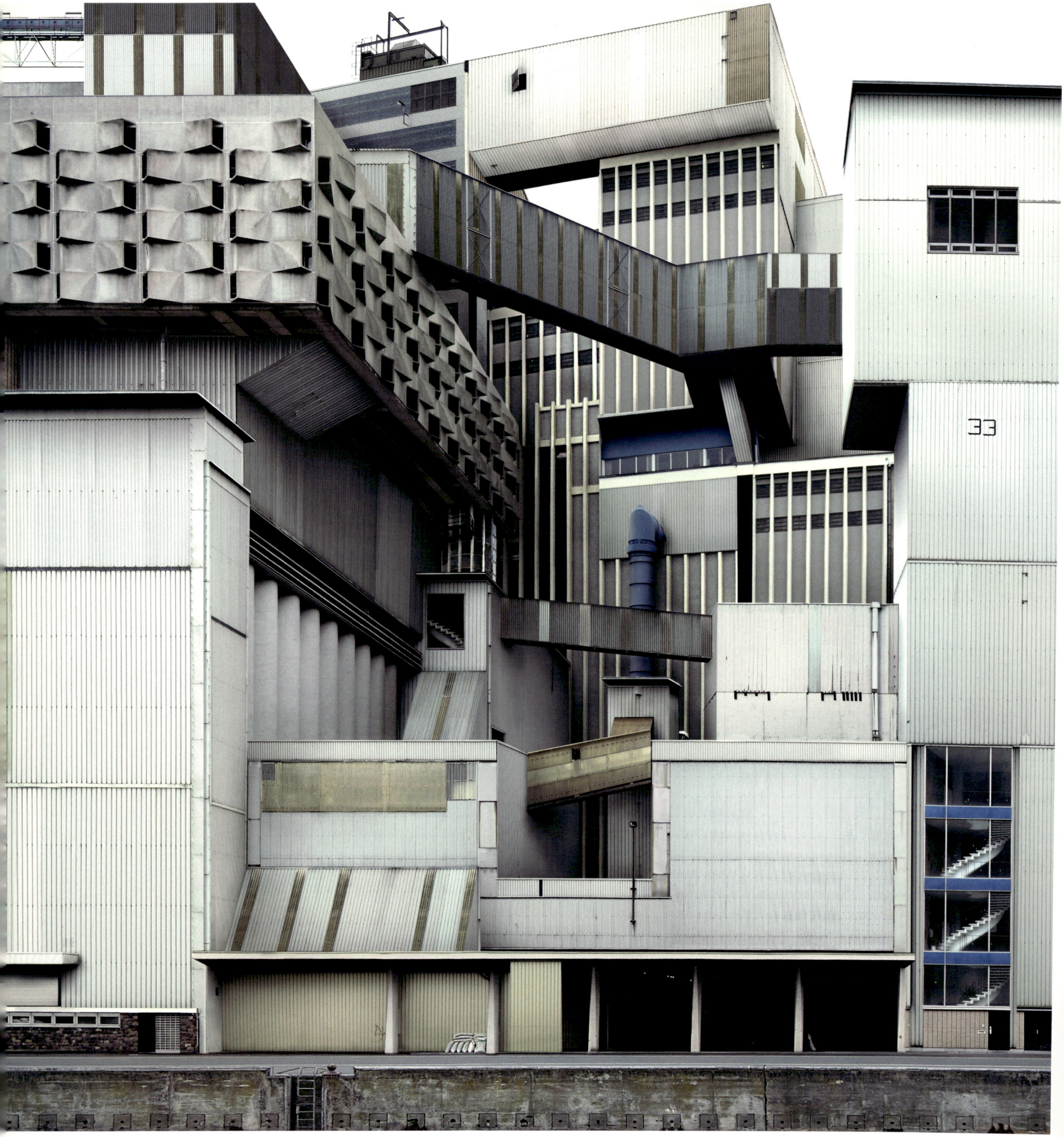
33

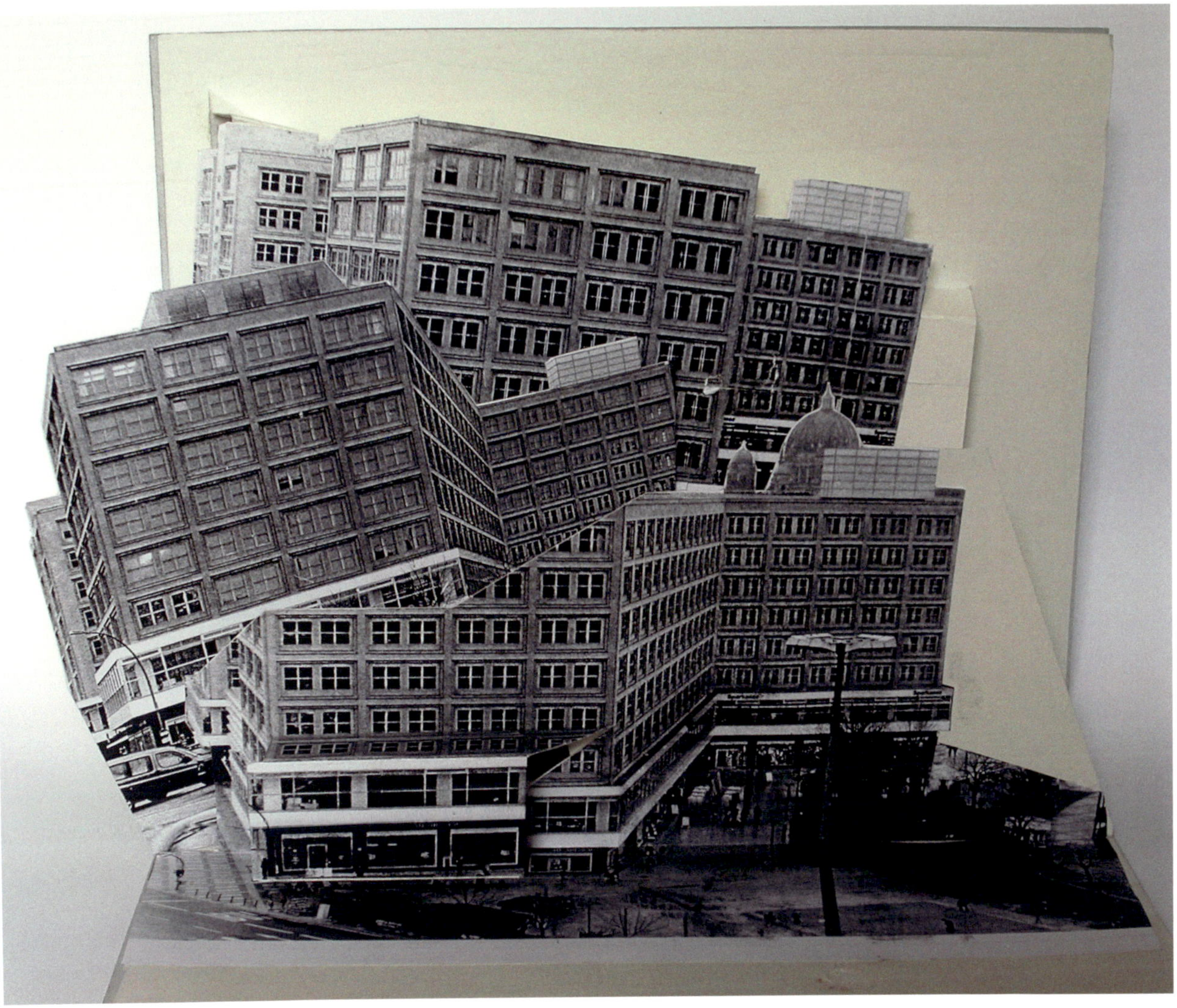

Philip Wiegard

BERQLINA

For this project, the Berlin-based artist and sculptor created a pop-up of the Berolina building at Alexanderplatz in Berlin, Germany.

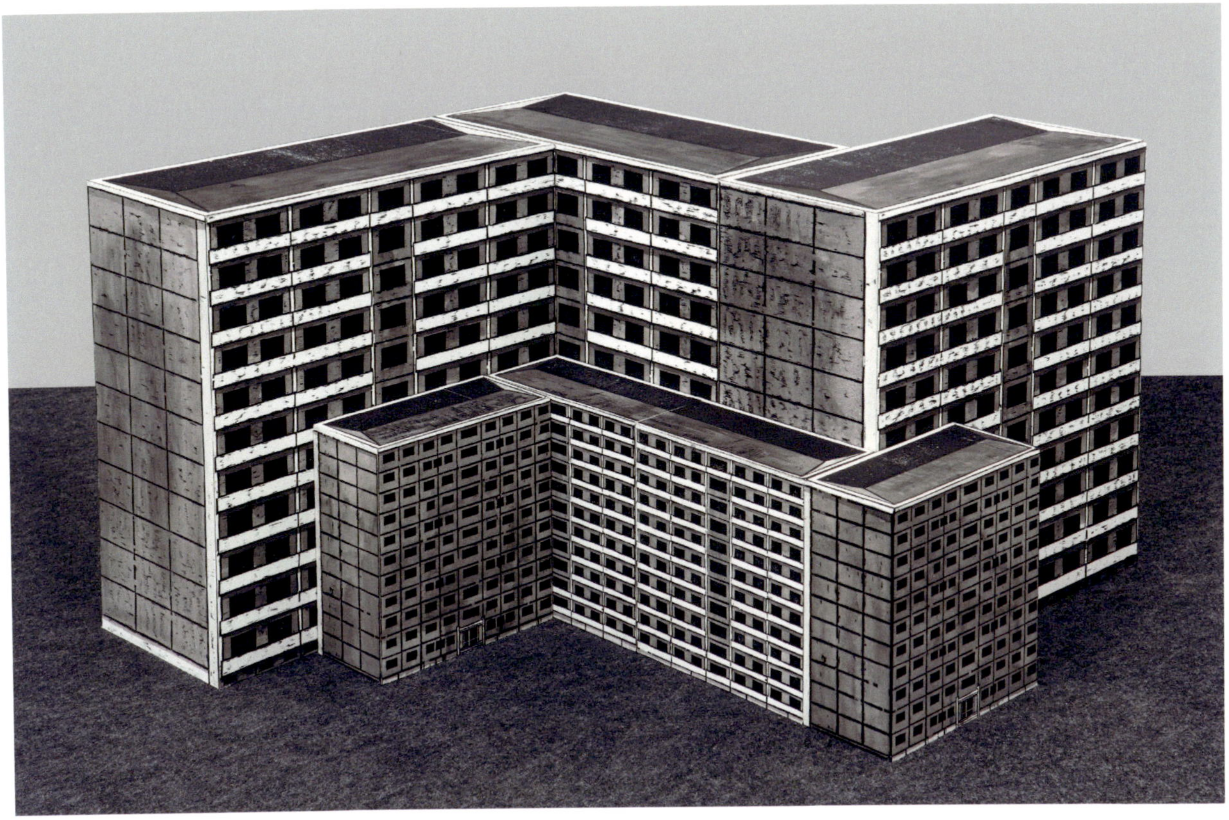

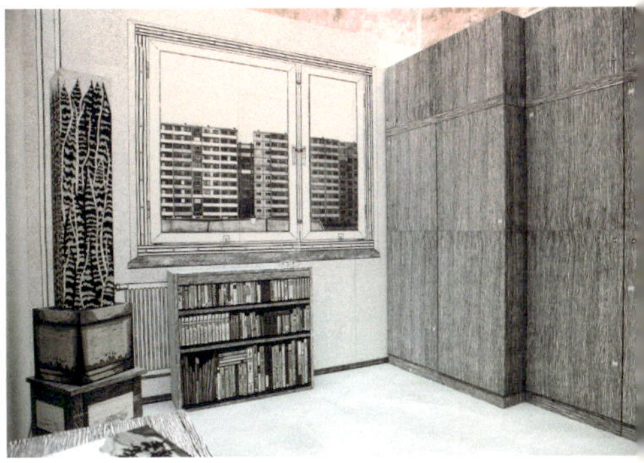

Jan Brokof

SYMMETRIE UND ALLTAG *(left)*
JUGENDZIMMER *(top)*

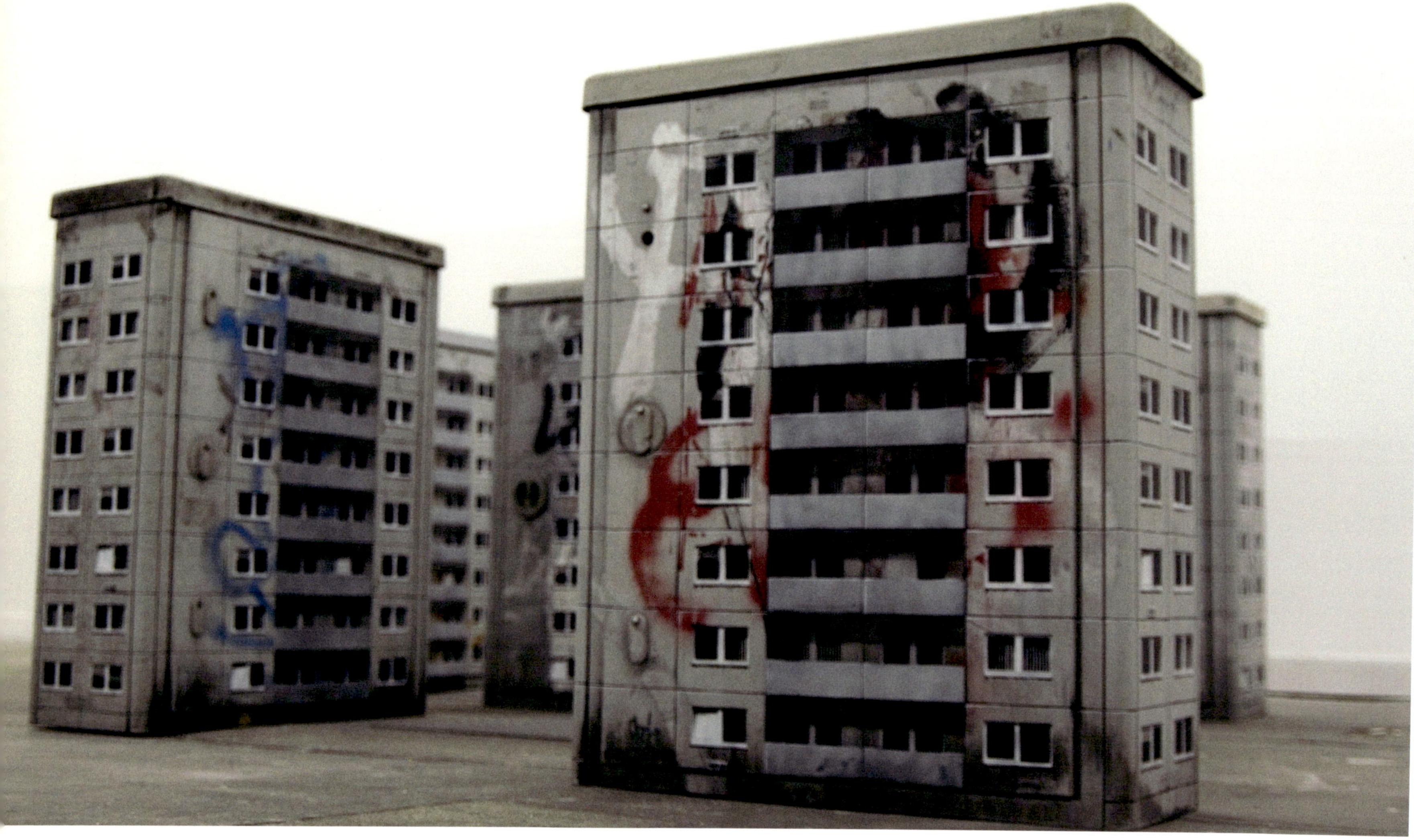

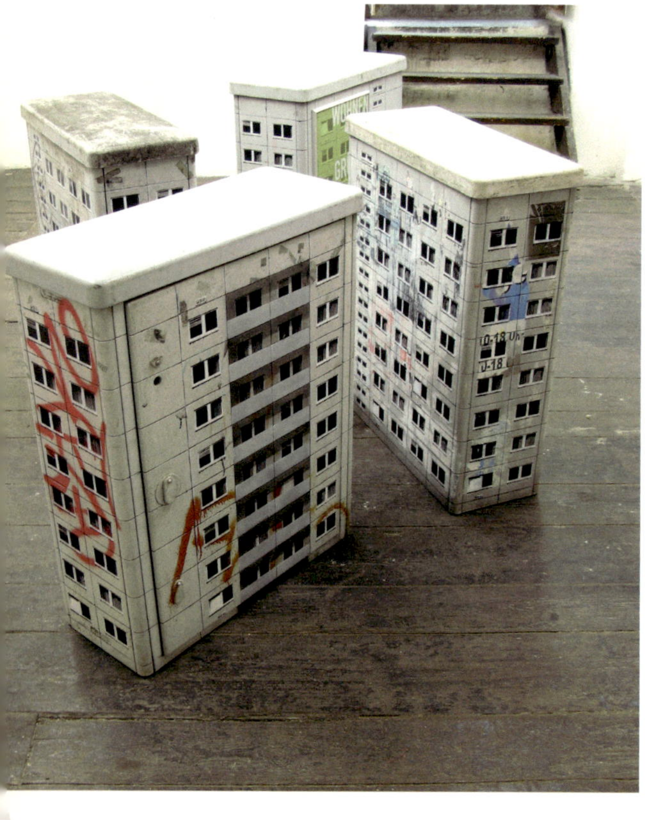

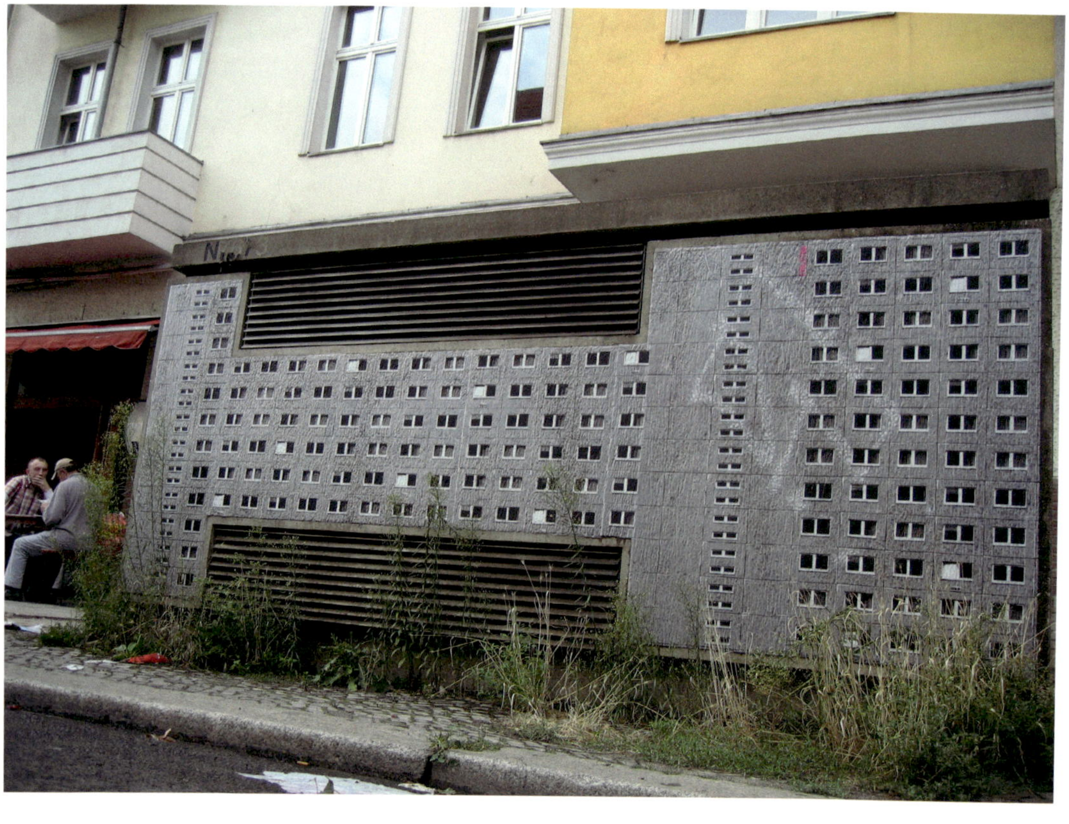

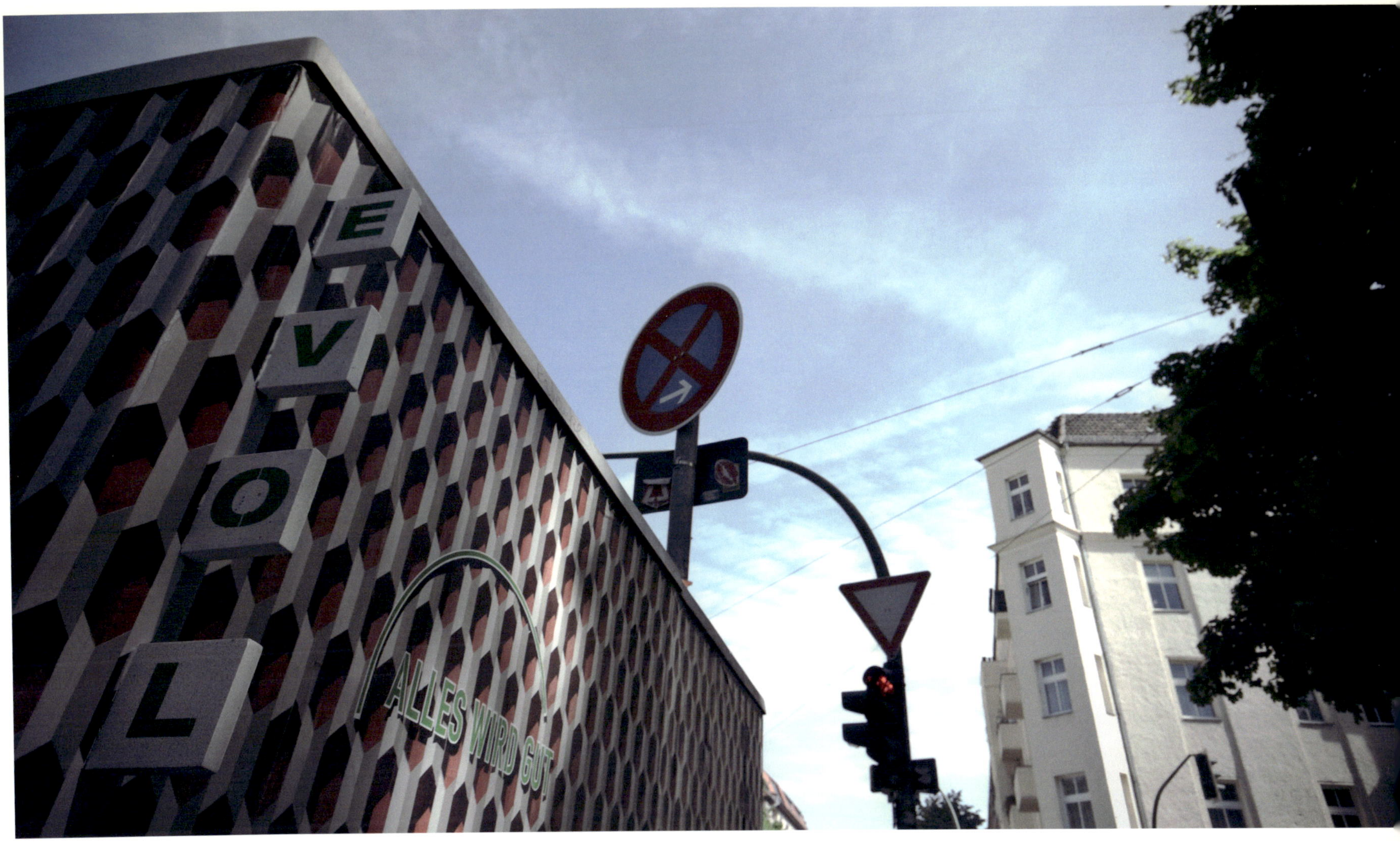

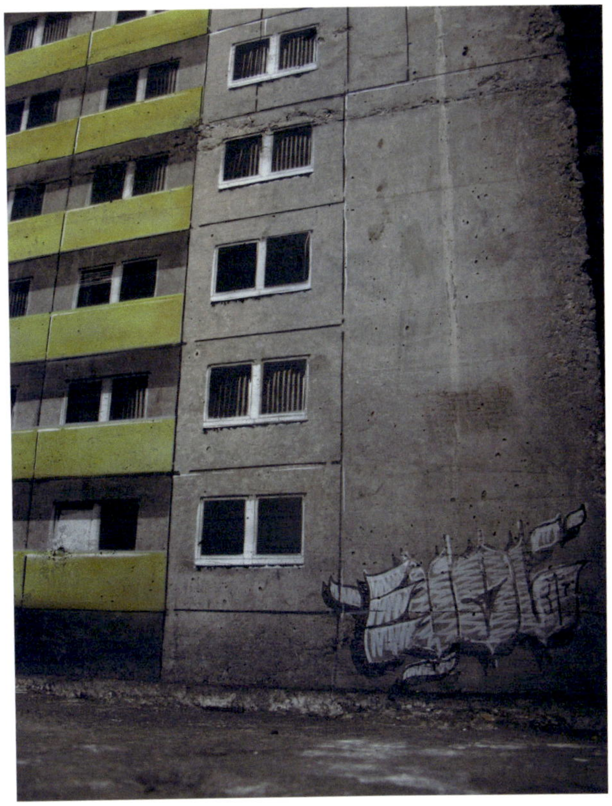

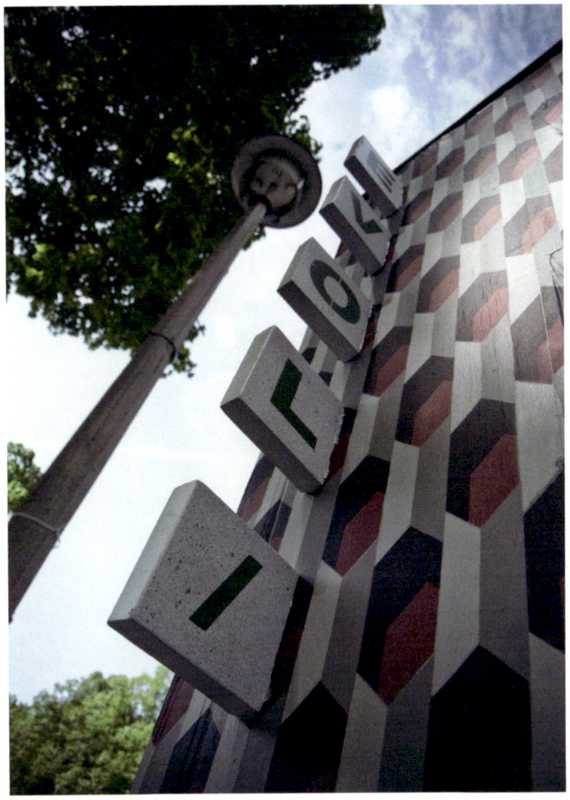

Evol / Ct'ink

PLATTENBAUTEN

Blocks *(left page top, left)*
Wohnmaschine *(left page, right)*
Alles wird gut *(top + below right)*
Concrete Wall *(below left)*

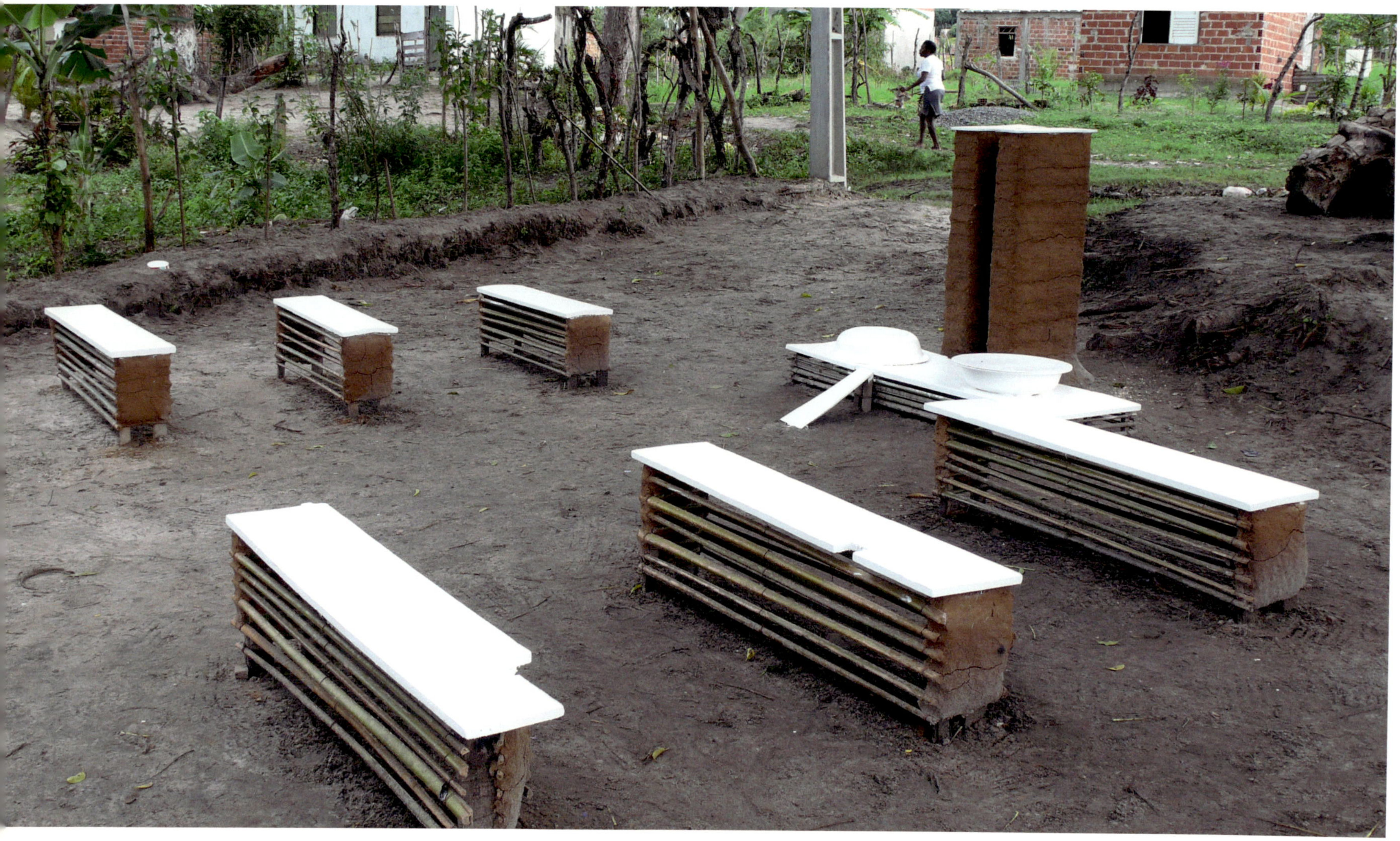

Erik Göngrich

PRACA NUEVA BRASILIA

For this project, Göngrich rebuilt Oscar Niemeyer's futuristic Brasilia, the national capital of Brazil, from simple everyday materials.

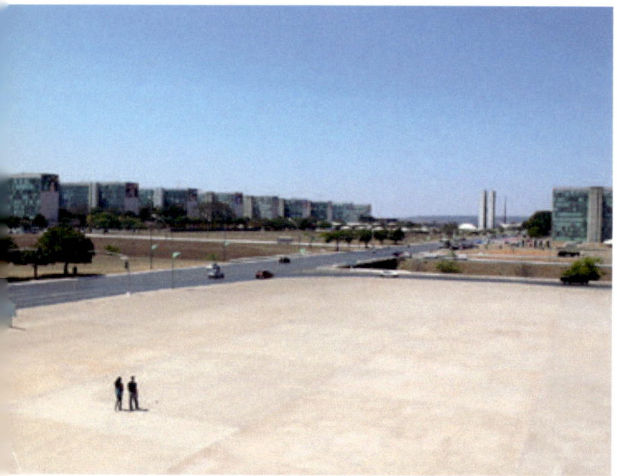

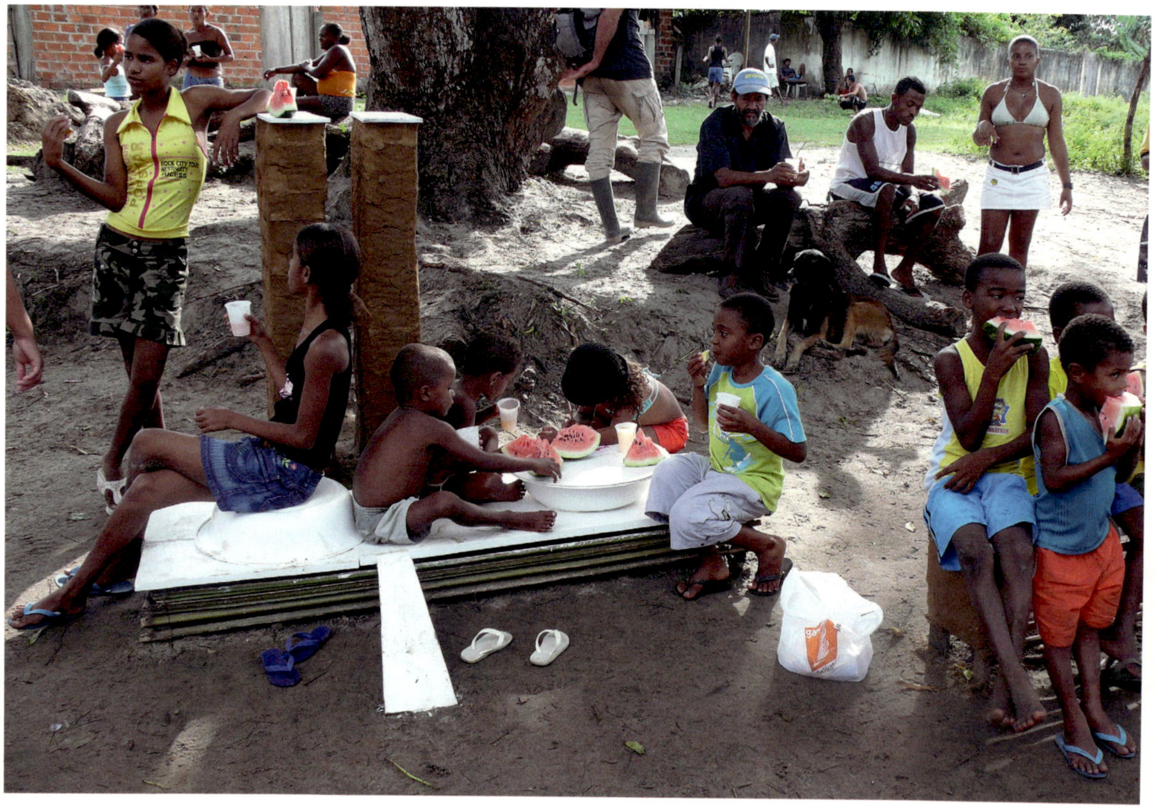

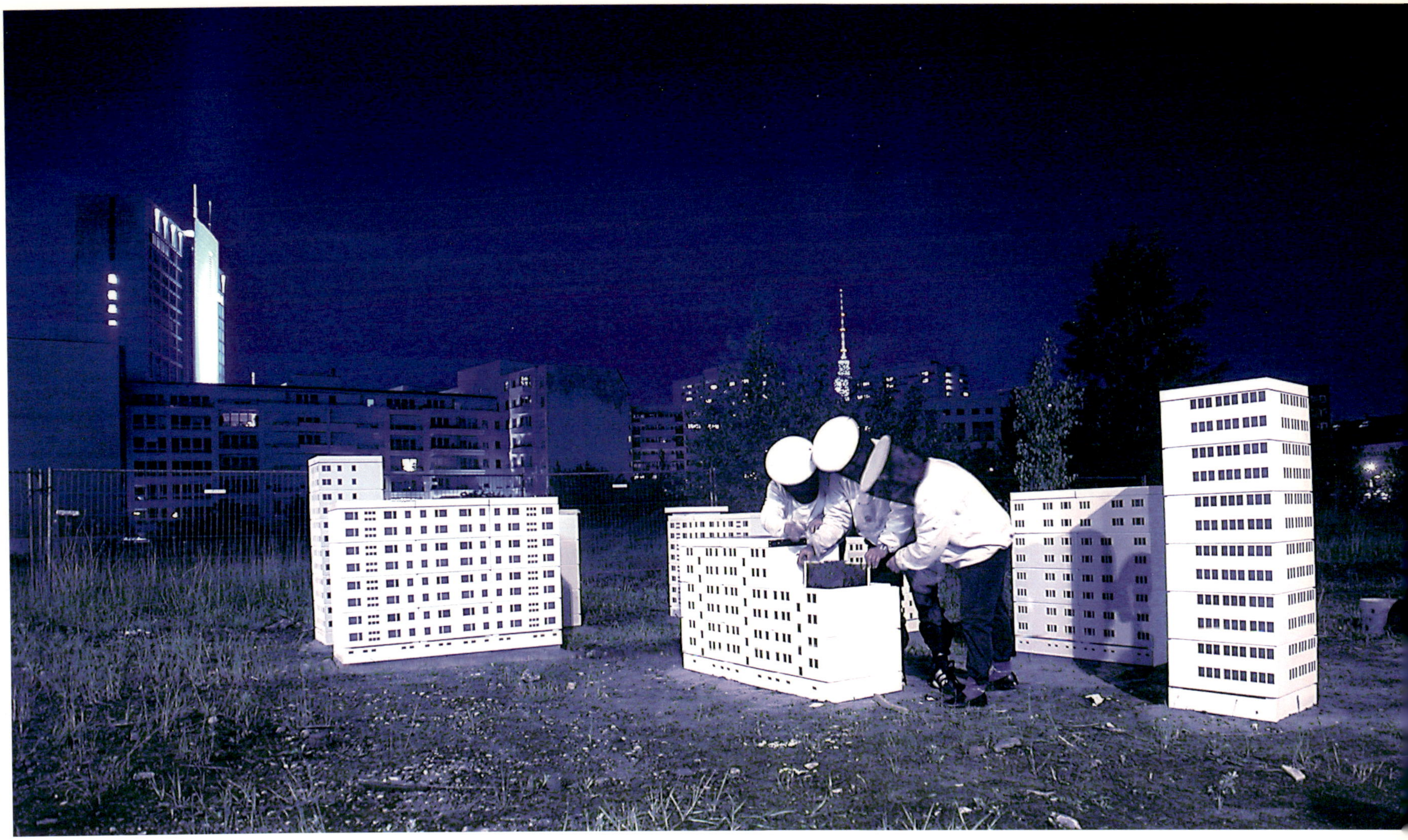

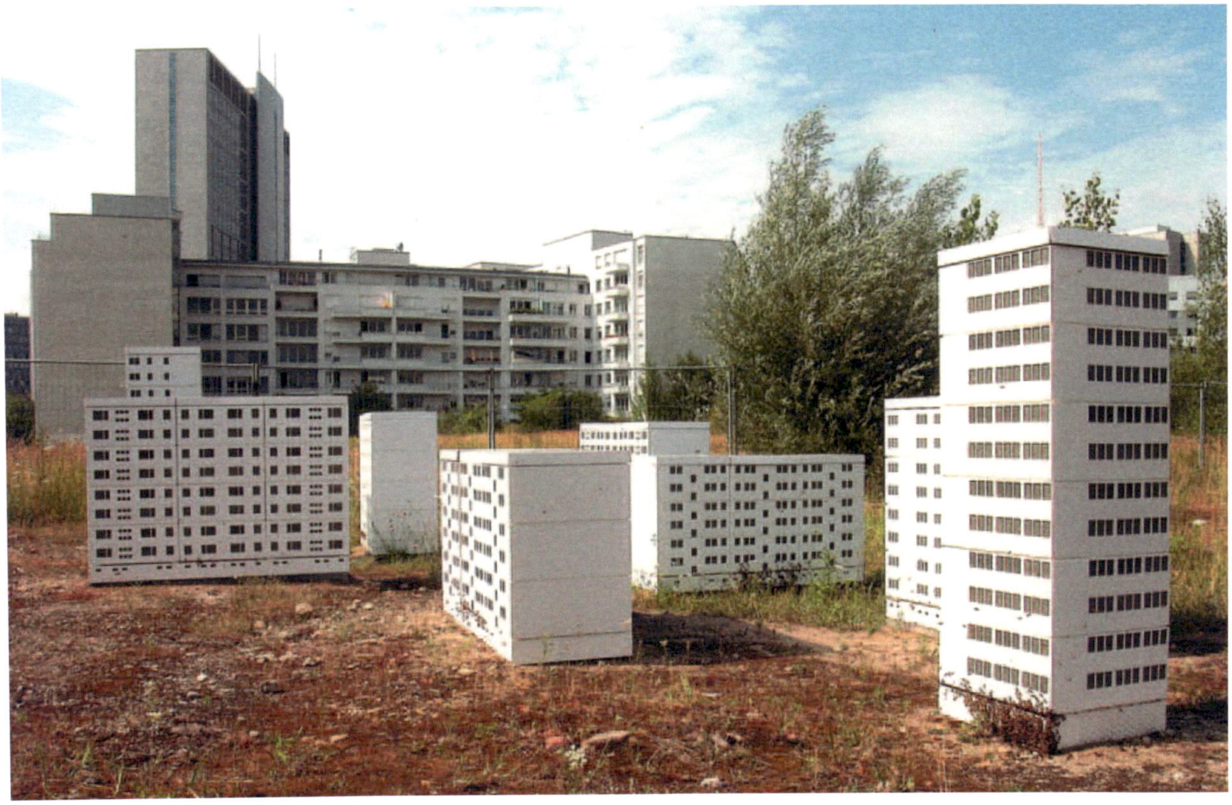

Franz Höfner & Harry Sachs

HONEY NEUSTADT

Honey Neustadt is a city model with one million bees in the shrinking city of Halle-Neustadt in Eastern Germany. The beehives with their honey production can be seen as an analogy for dormitory towns, for instance like in Halle-Neustadt, where chemical workers previously commuted daily to chemical factories. The bees' honey production provides an analogy, in that it is also a chemical process. The project can be seen as a miniature memorial for the former workers there.

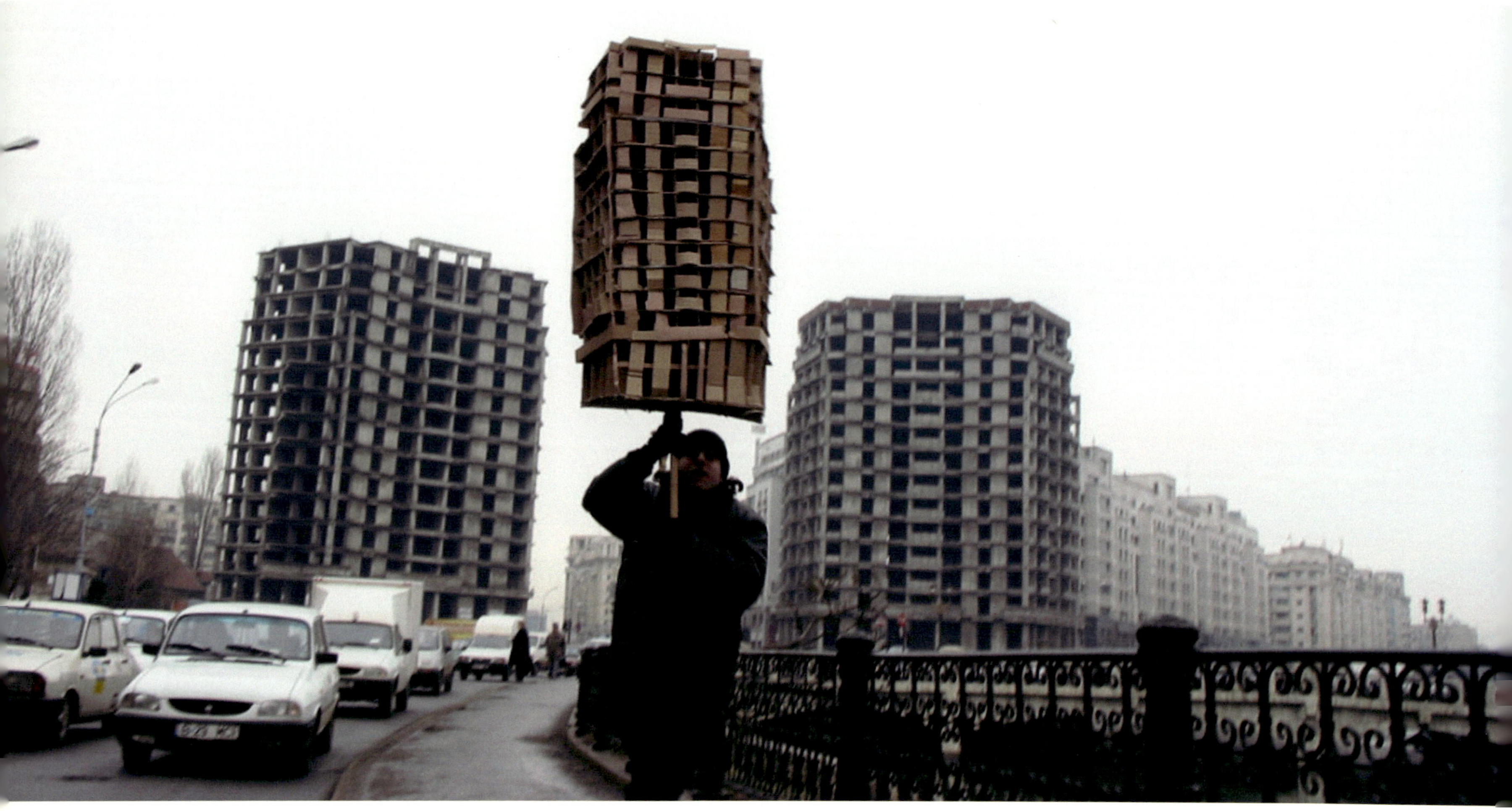

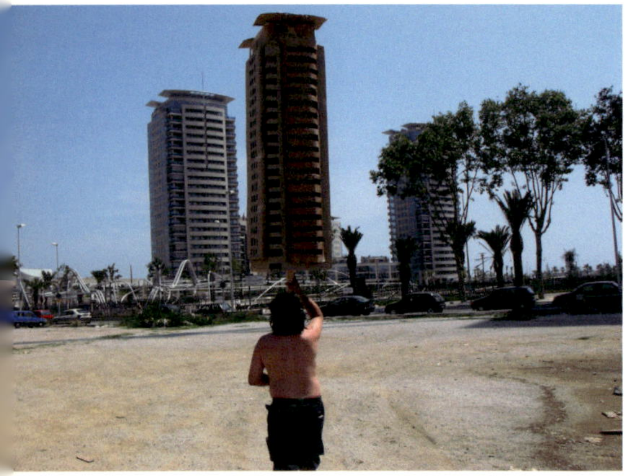

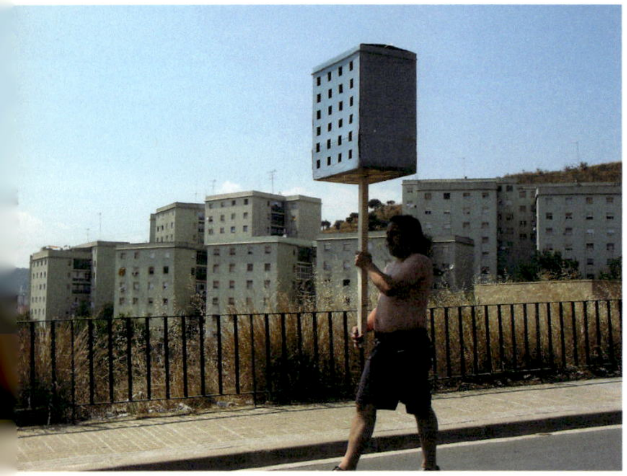

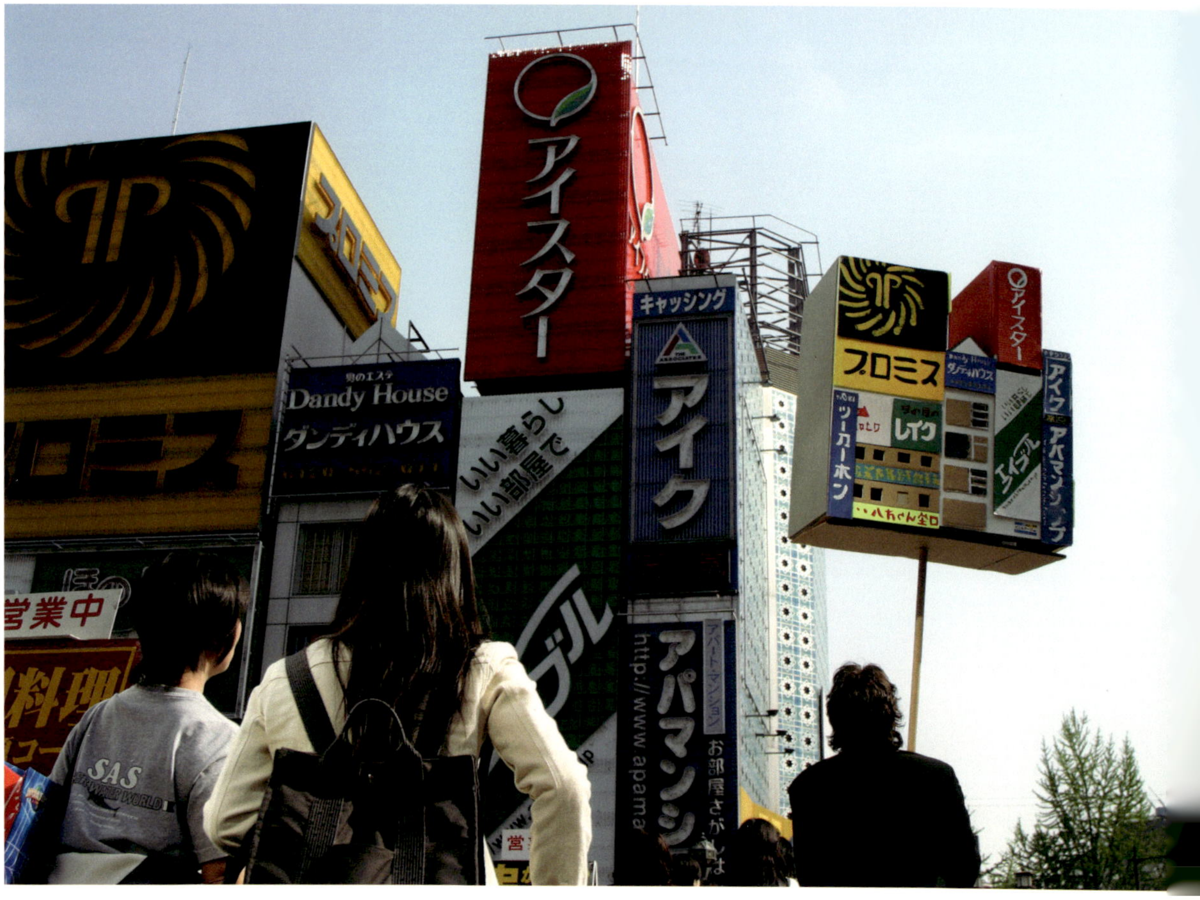
アイスター
プロミス
キャッシング
アイク
男のエステ
Dandy House
ダンディハウス
いい暮らし
いい部屋で
営業中
http://www.apama
SAS

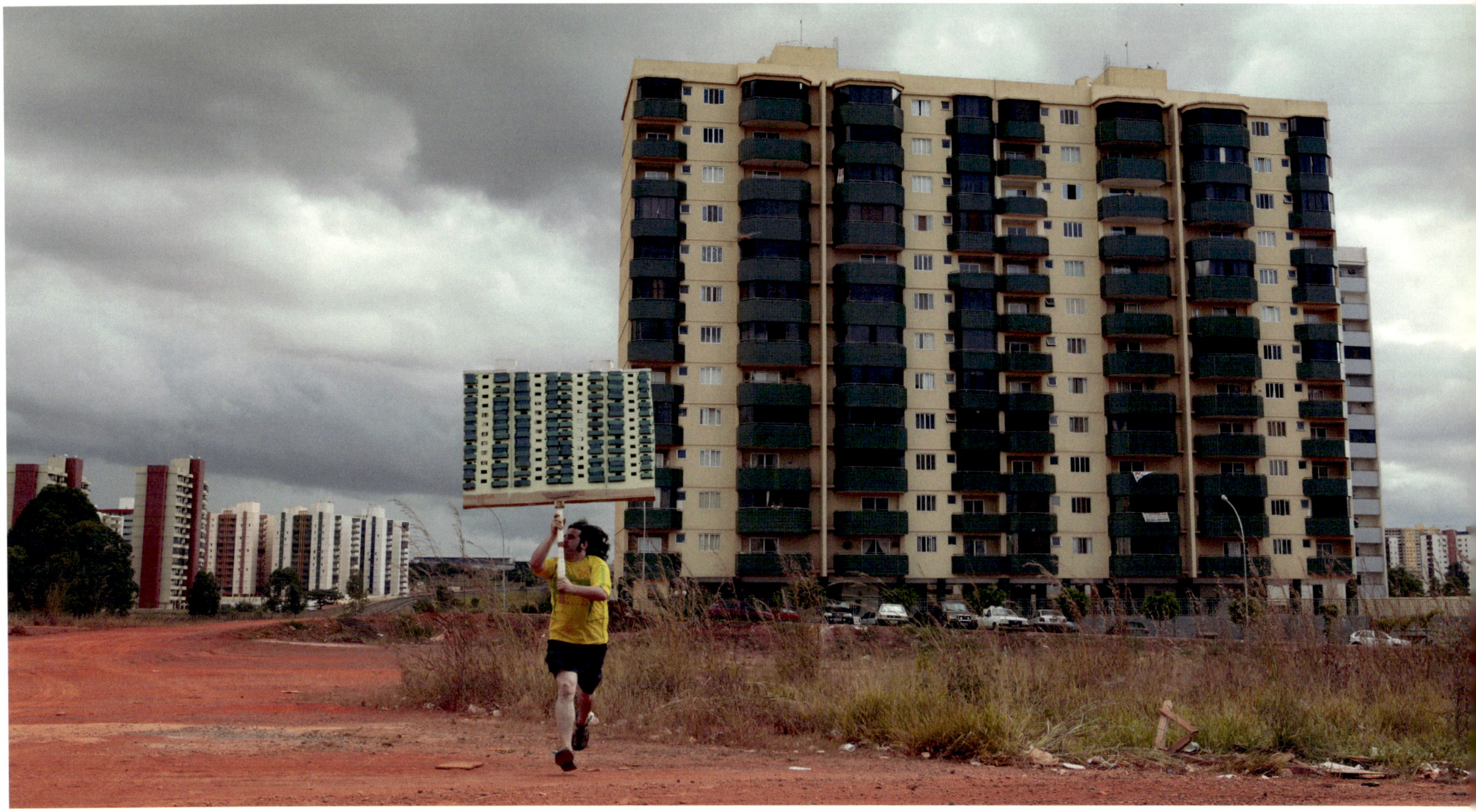

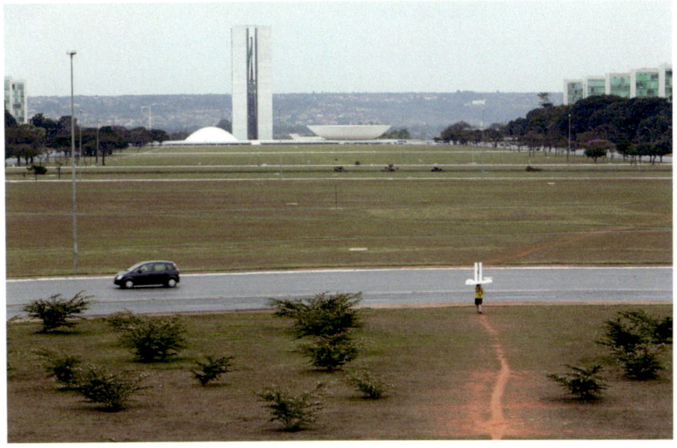

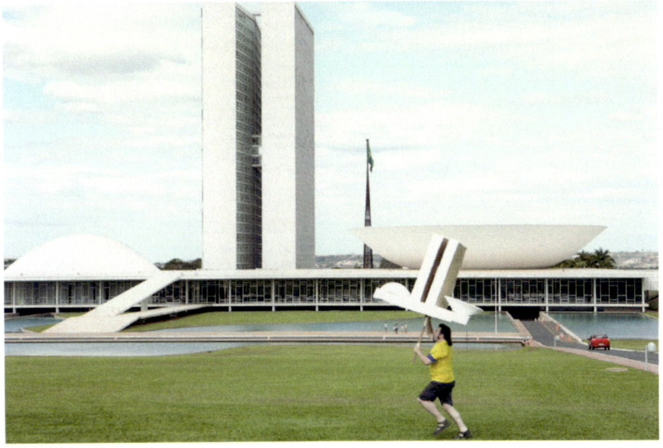

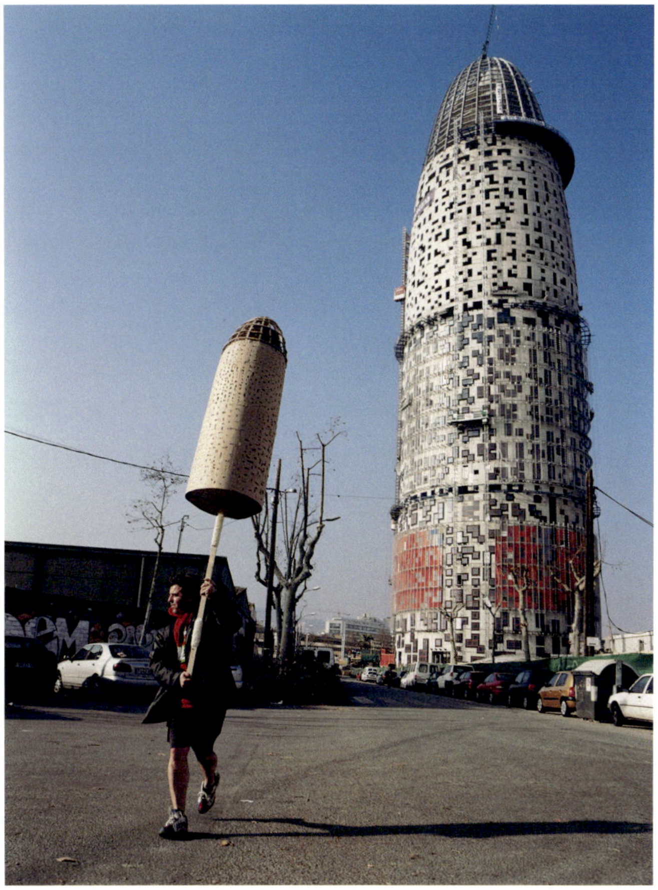

Jordi Colomer

ANARCHITEKTON

Anarchitekton is the generic title of a video series by Jordi Colomer made as a work in progress in Barcelona, Bucarest, Brasilia and Osaka. A man can be seen carrying models of buildings like a flag that reflect the surrounding cityscapes. The models of the builidings appear like grotesque banners or utopian provocations.

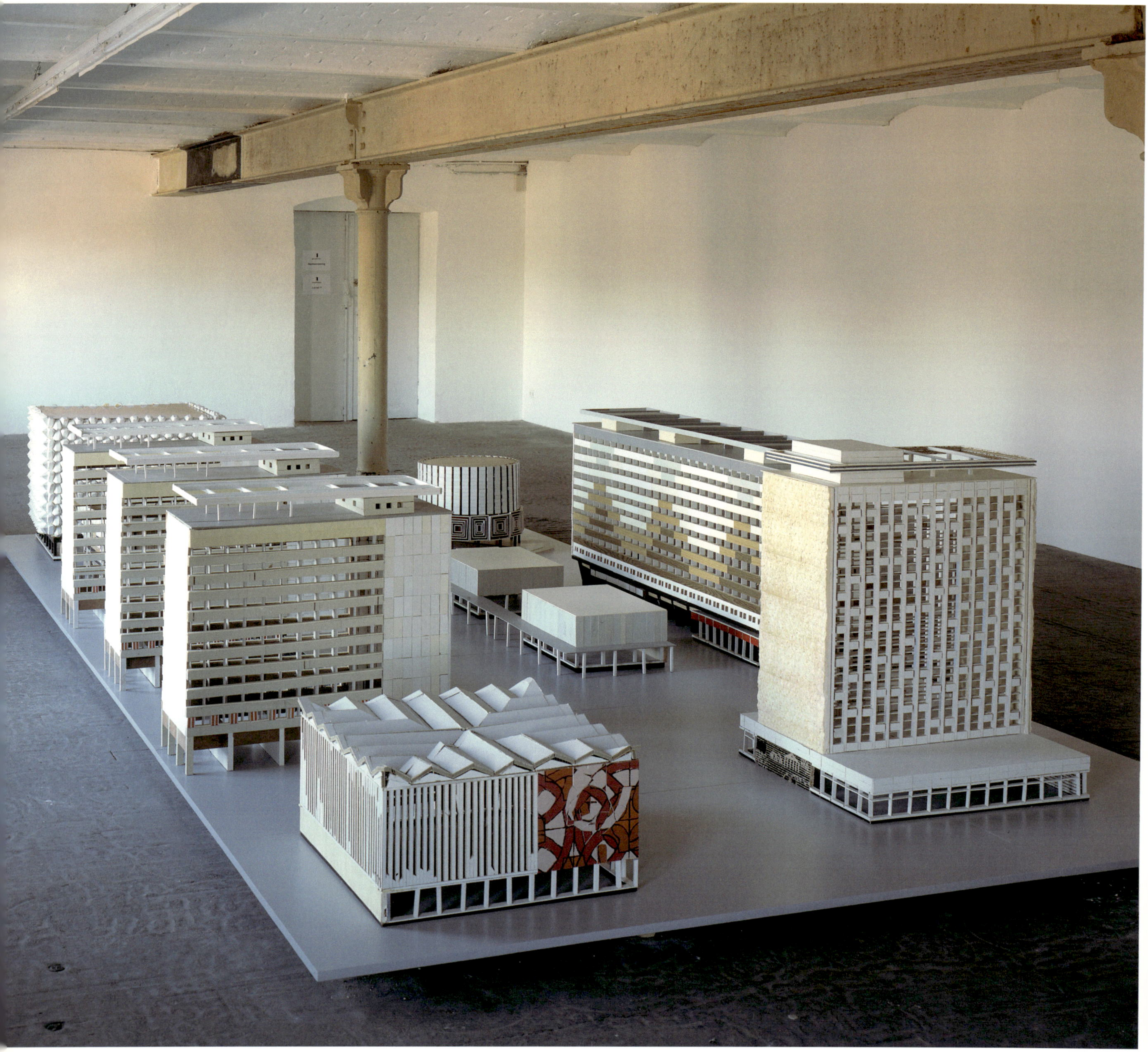

Karsten Konrad

DRESDEN

Karsten Konrad's fictional scale model of Prager Straße in Dresden. The street is a major pedestrian thoroughfare and one of the key examples of modern GDR city planning, currently facing demolition and restructuring as part of efforts to reconstruct the historic (medieval) city blueprint. Konrad's model, made of recycled materials found on the site in Dresden, investigates the open-plan impression of Prager Straße, which will soon be part of history.

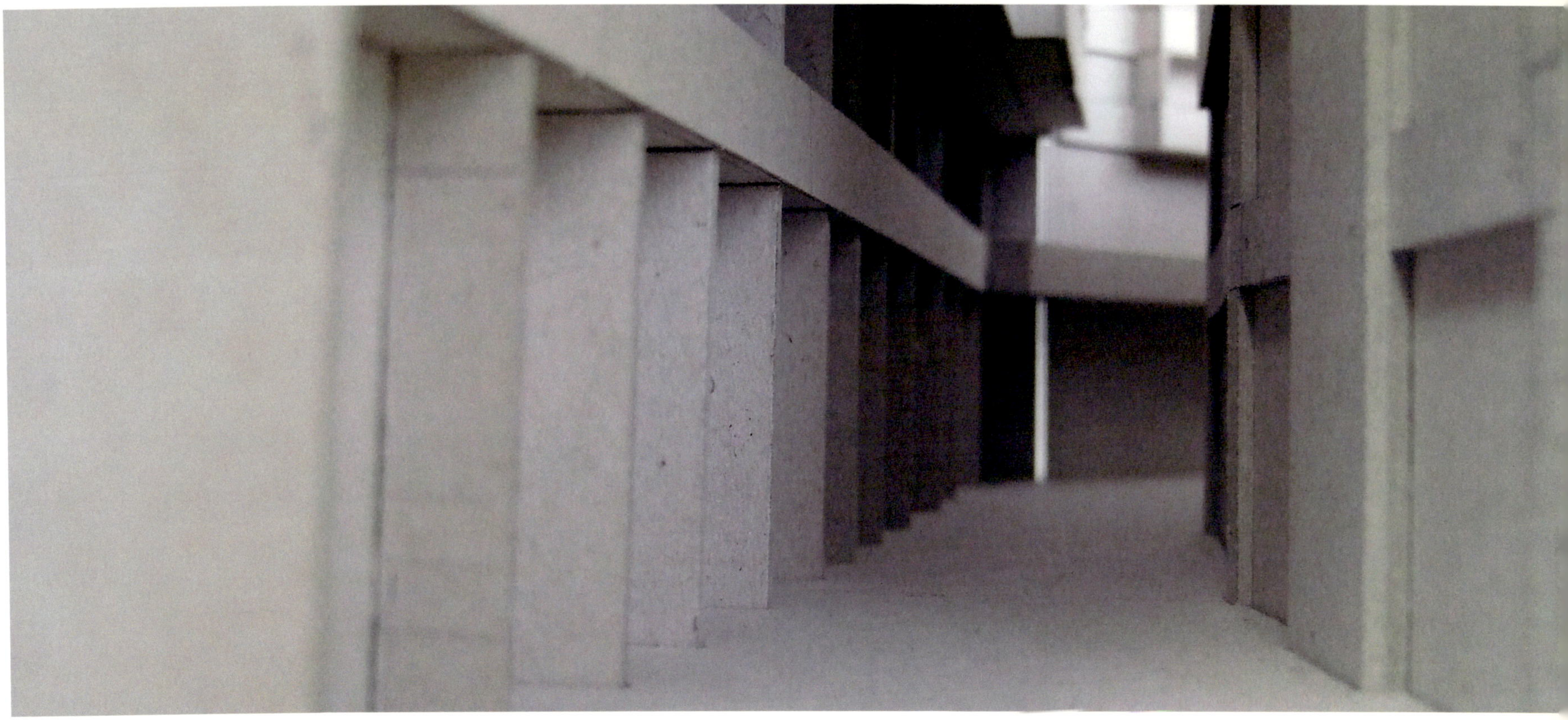

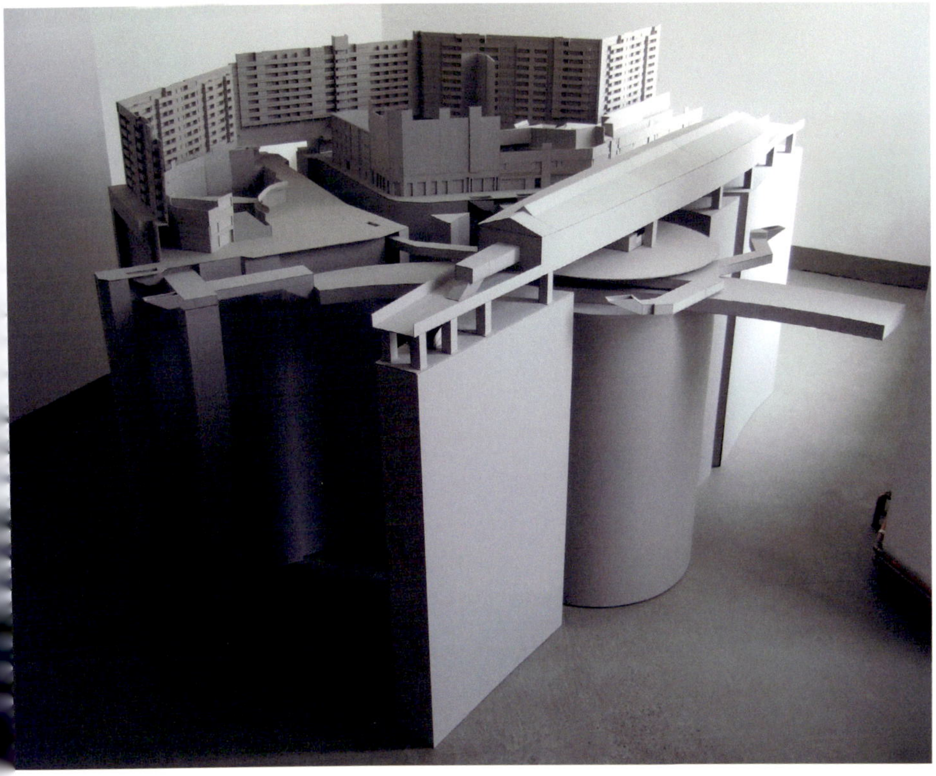

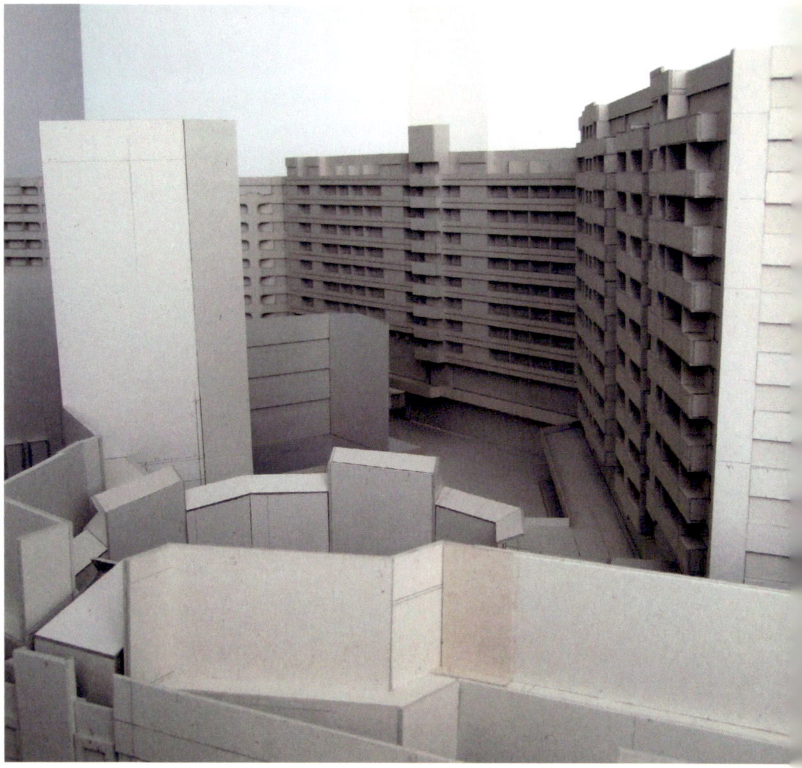

Larissa Fassler

KOTTI

Kotti is a model representation of the publicly accessible areas of the Zentrum Kreuzberg (ZK) housing estate and its surroundings in Berlin, Germany. Rather than constructing a model based on the positive masses of the buildings, Fassler has measured and built the negative volumes – in the tunnels and between façades, following the surfaces of sidewalks and plazas, and leaving the rest as empty space. By creating an inversion of the classic planning model, she seeks to challenge the omnipresence of the master plan and to make visible the in-between, uncertain and transient areas that make up public space.

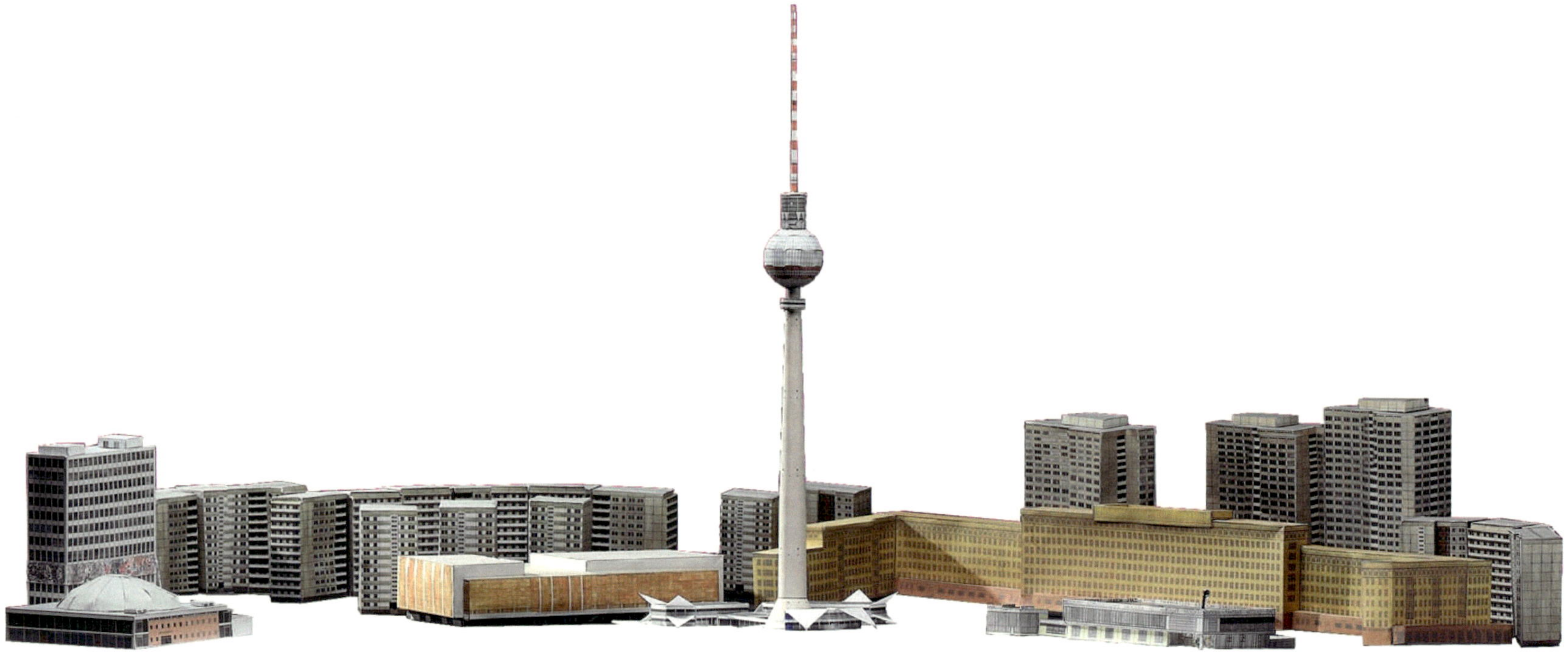

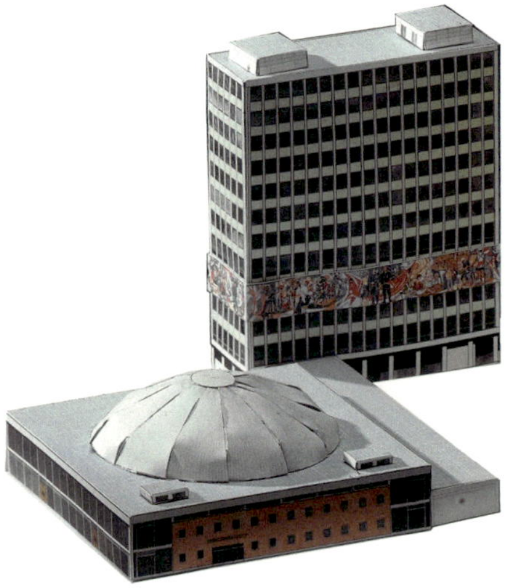

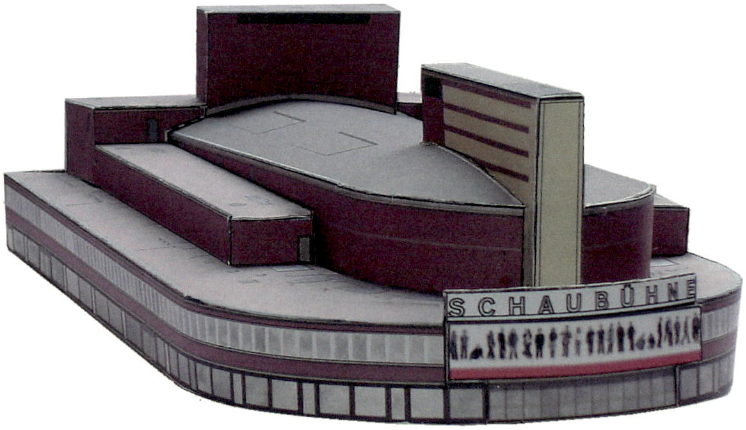

Cord Woywodt

FALTPLATTE

Inspired by the architecture of the former GDR, Cord Woywodt established the edition faltplatte in 2002 – extraordinary pieces of architecture as cardboard cutouts. Starting with two different models of East German prefabricated housing blocks, he now includes more models like the Berlin TV tower and the Bauhaus in Dessau. Faltplatte enables a different view on architectural structures by scaling them down.

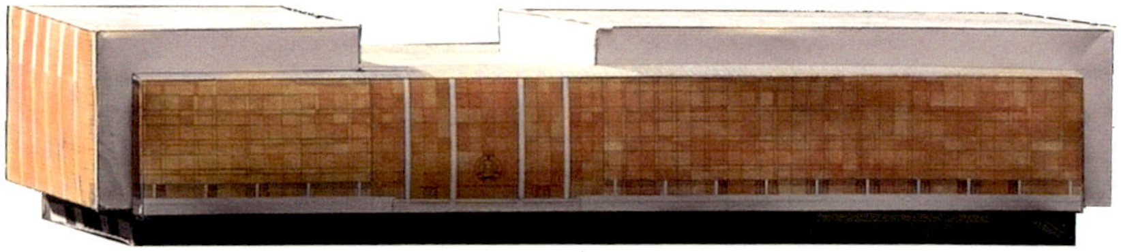

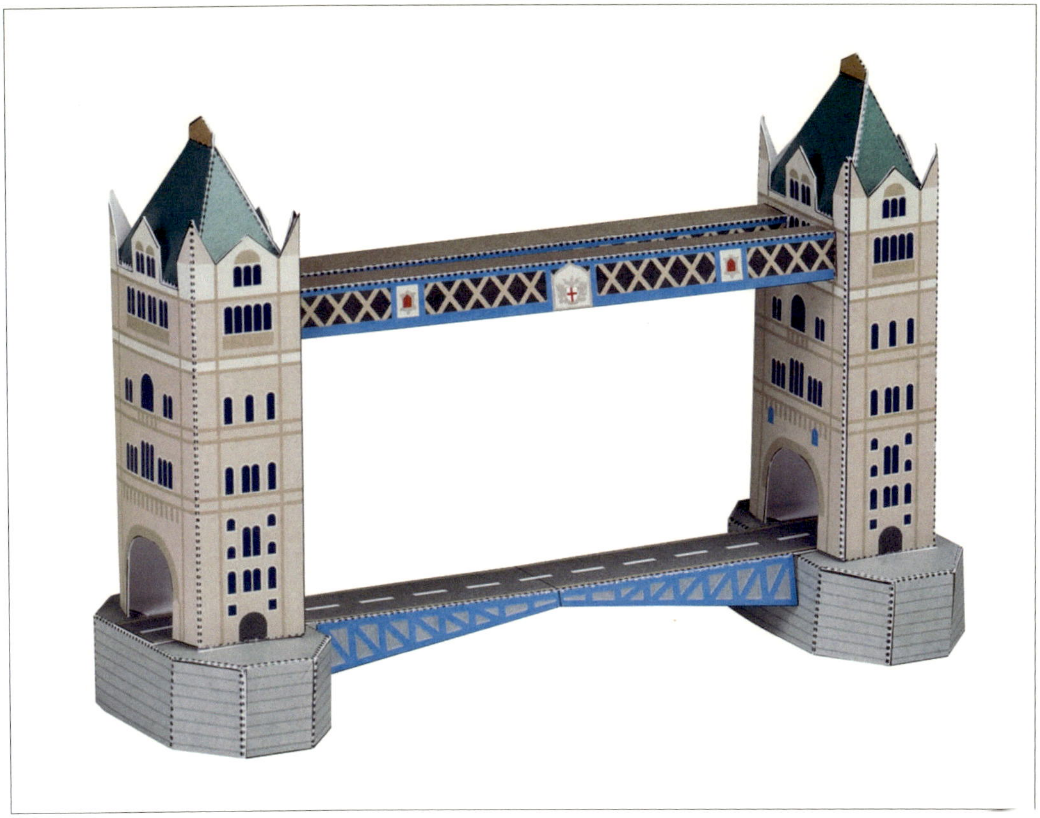

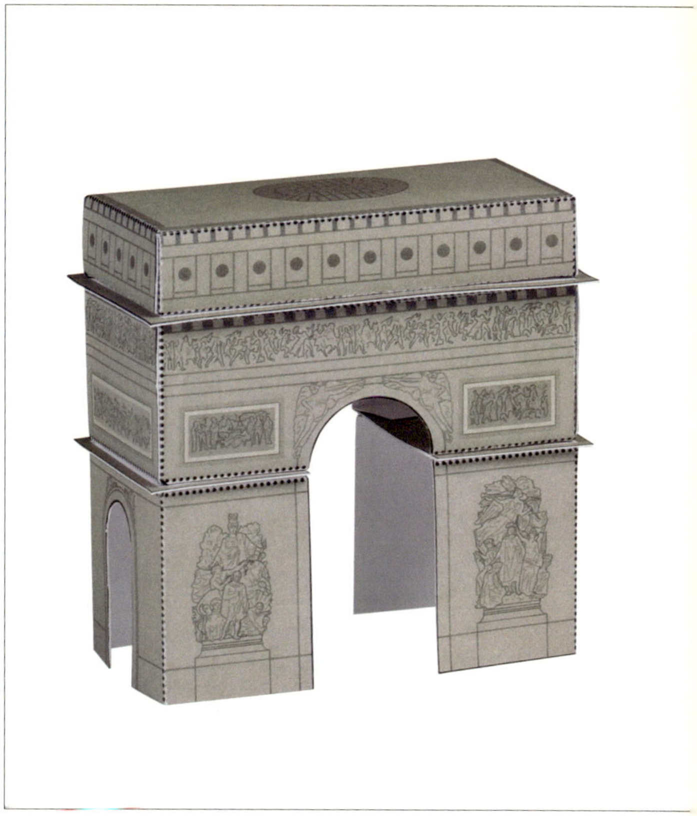

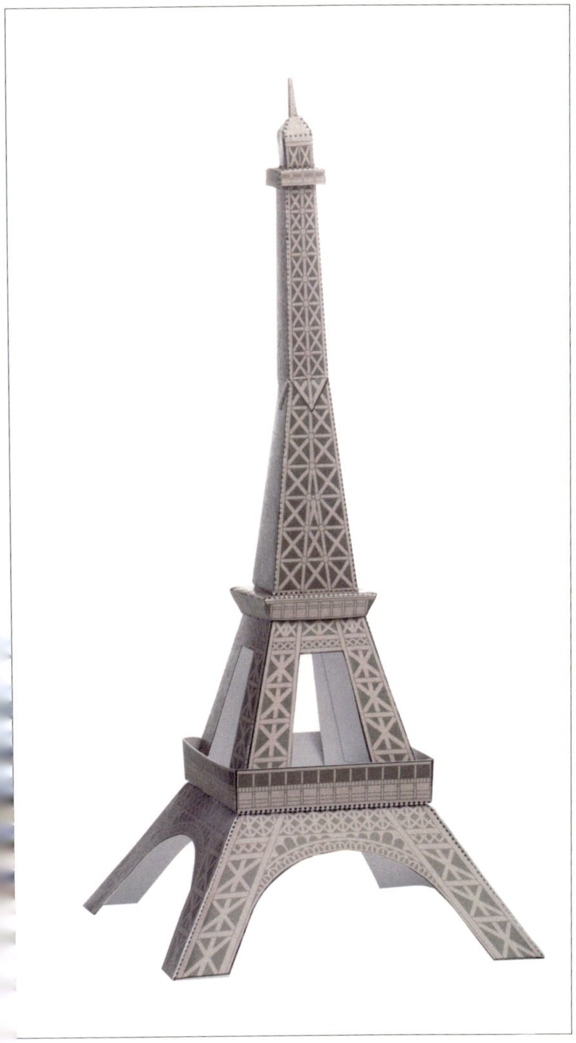

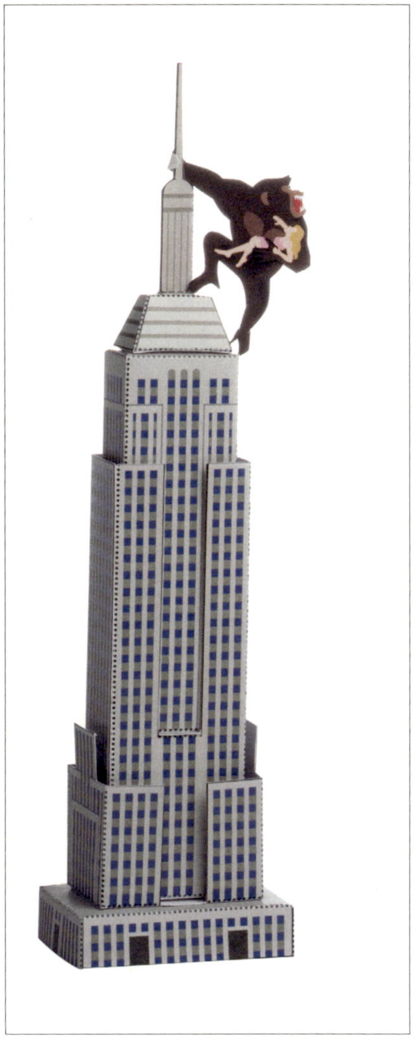

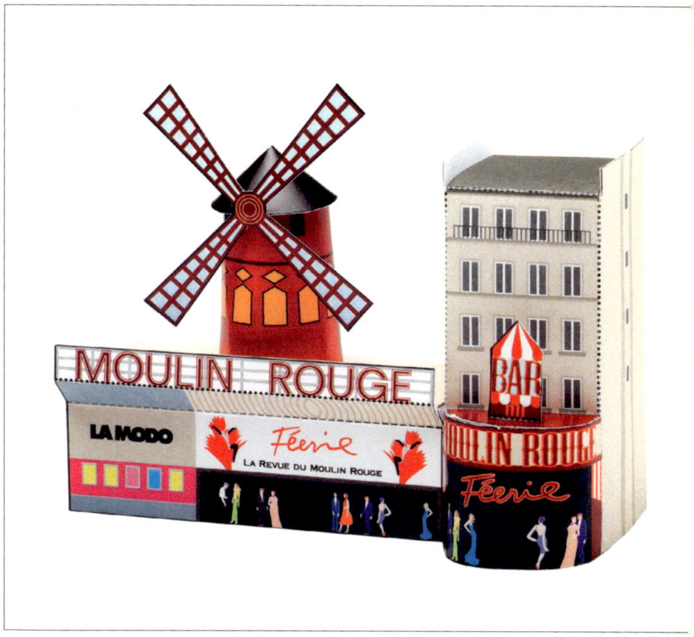

NotedCo. KEISUKE SAKA

MAKE CITY

A trio of the world's most beloved cities are featured in the Make City postcard sets. Designed by Keisuke Saka, each Make City set has five cards that can be cut and assembled into miniature models of famous city icons.

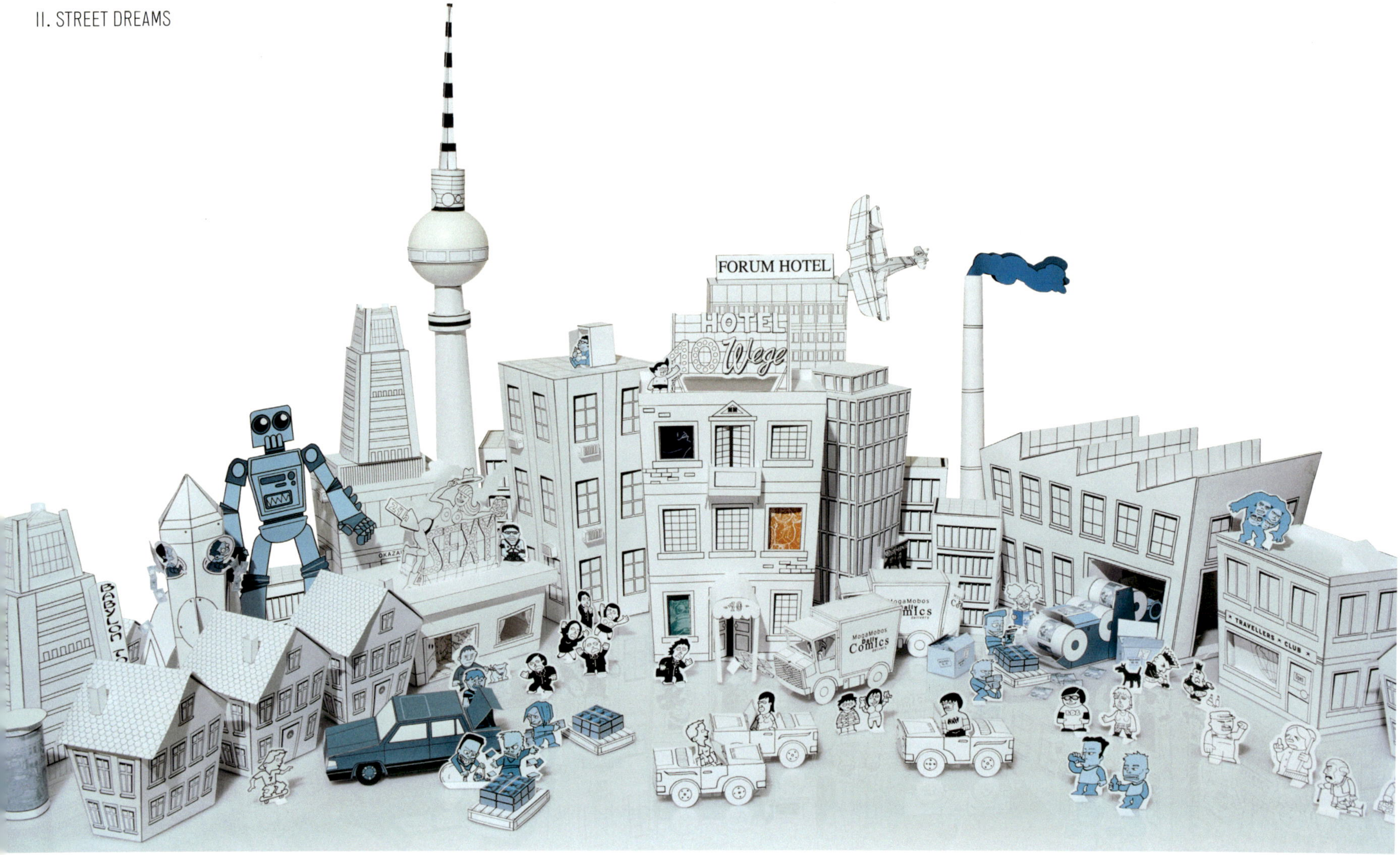

Moga Mobo Studio

MOGA MOBO PAPER CITY *(top)*
TOKYO VS. BERLIN – A CULTURE CLASH *(bottom)*

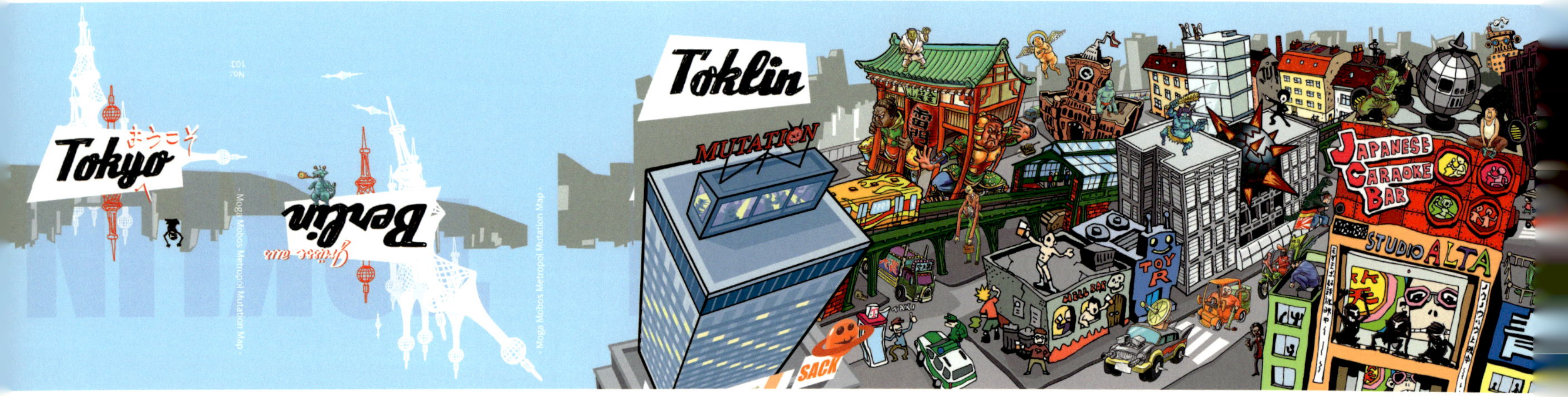

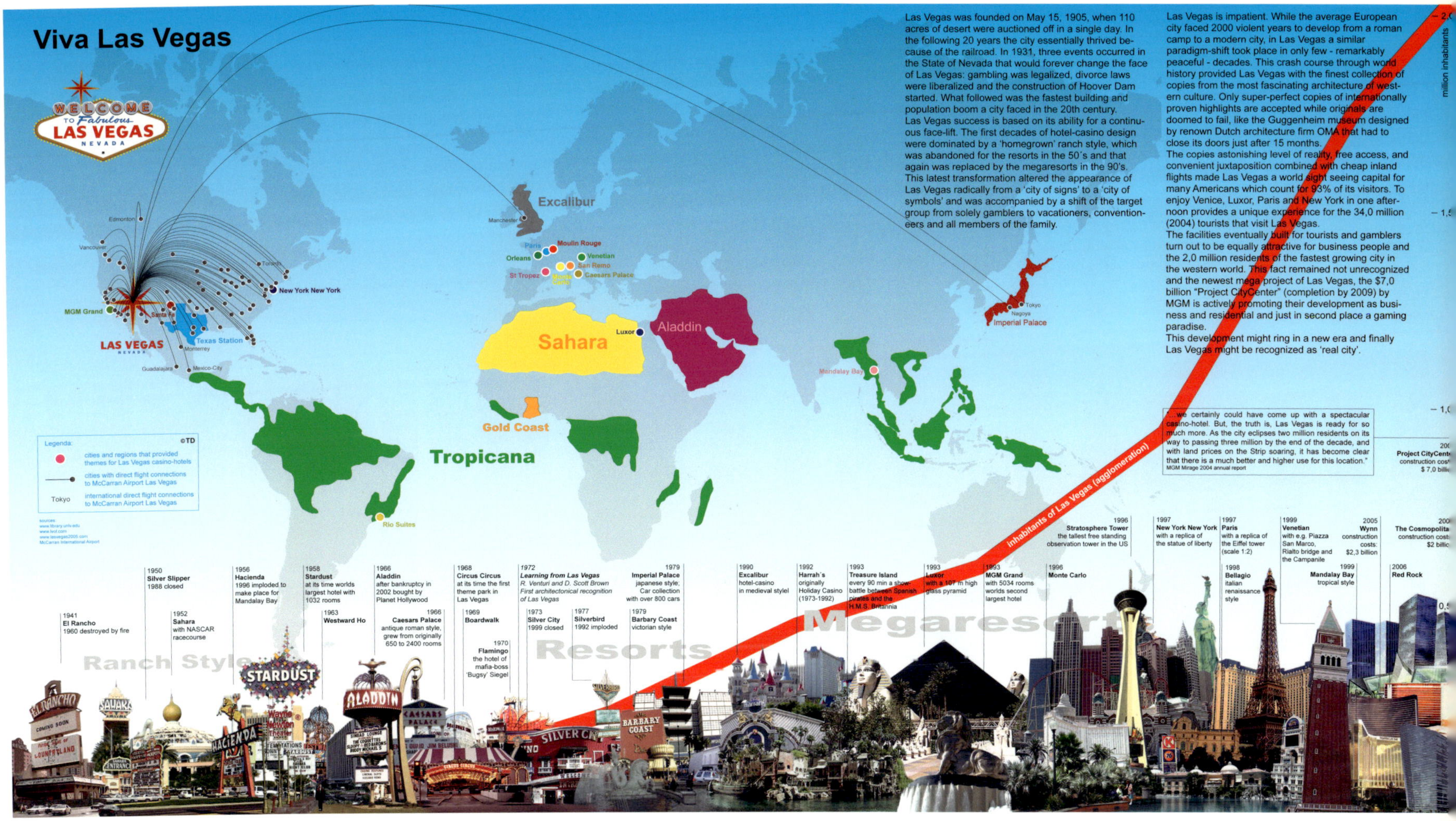

Theo Deutinger

VIVA LAS VEGAS

Rotterdam-based, Austrian-born architect Theo Deutinger describes his critical data-art as SNOGs: Snapshots of Globalization. Viva Las Vegas illustrates the development of the city's architectural language from signs to symbols to sameness over the course of the last century.

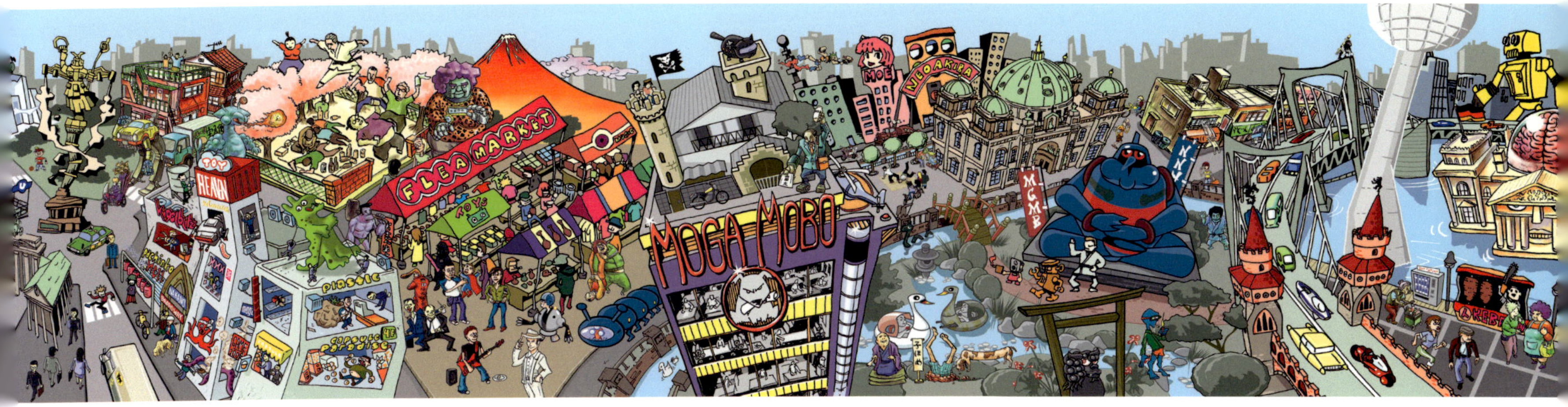

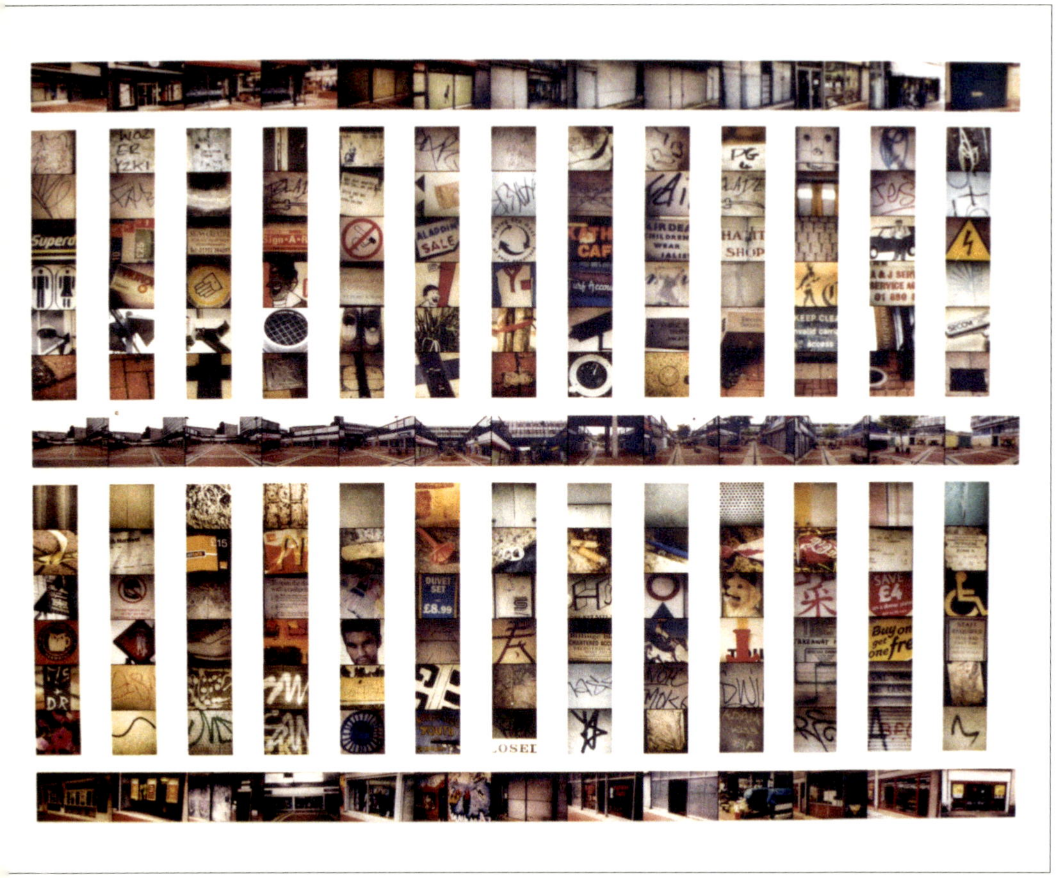

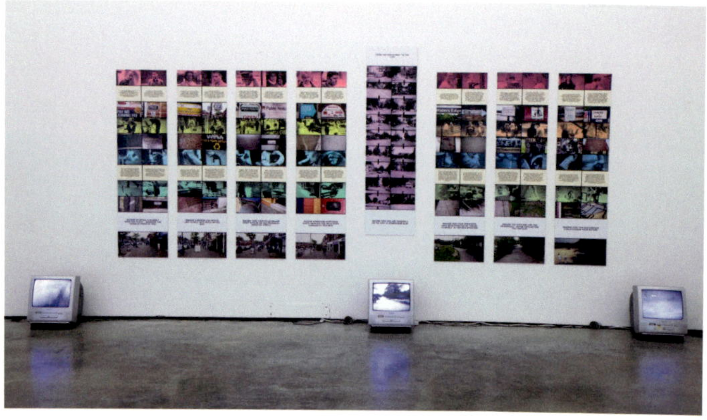

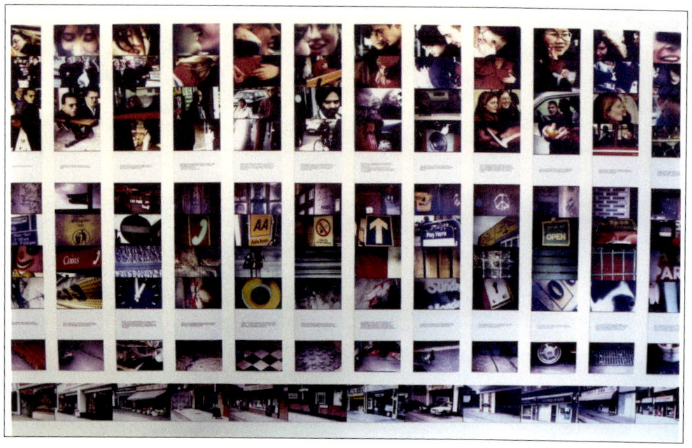

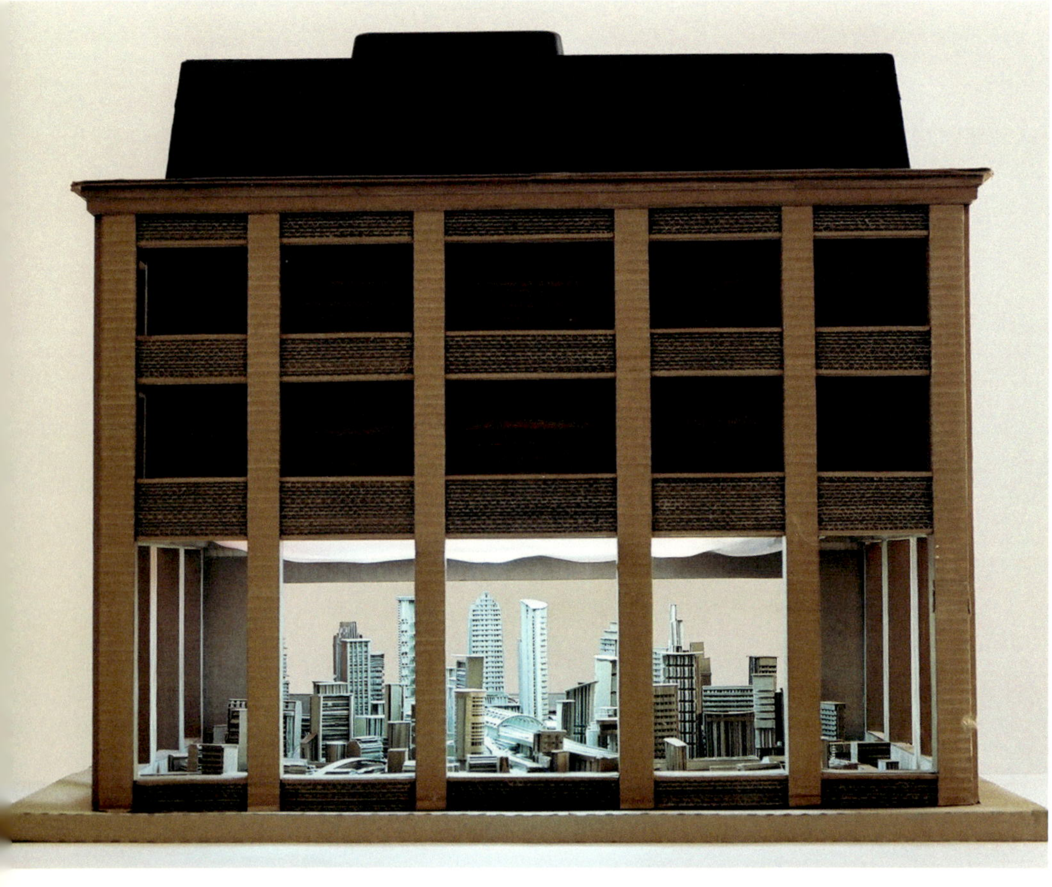

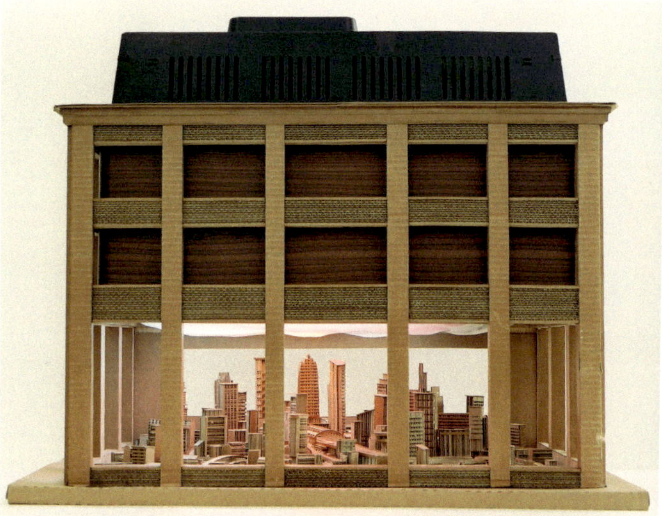

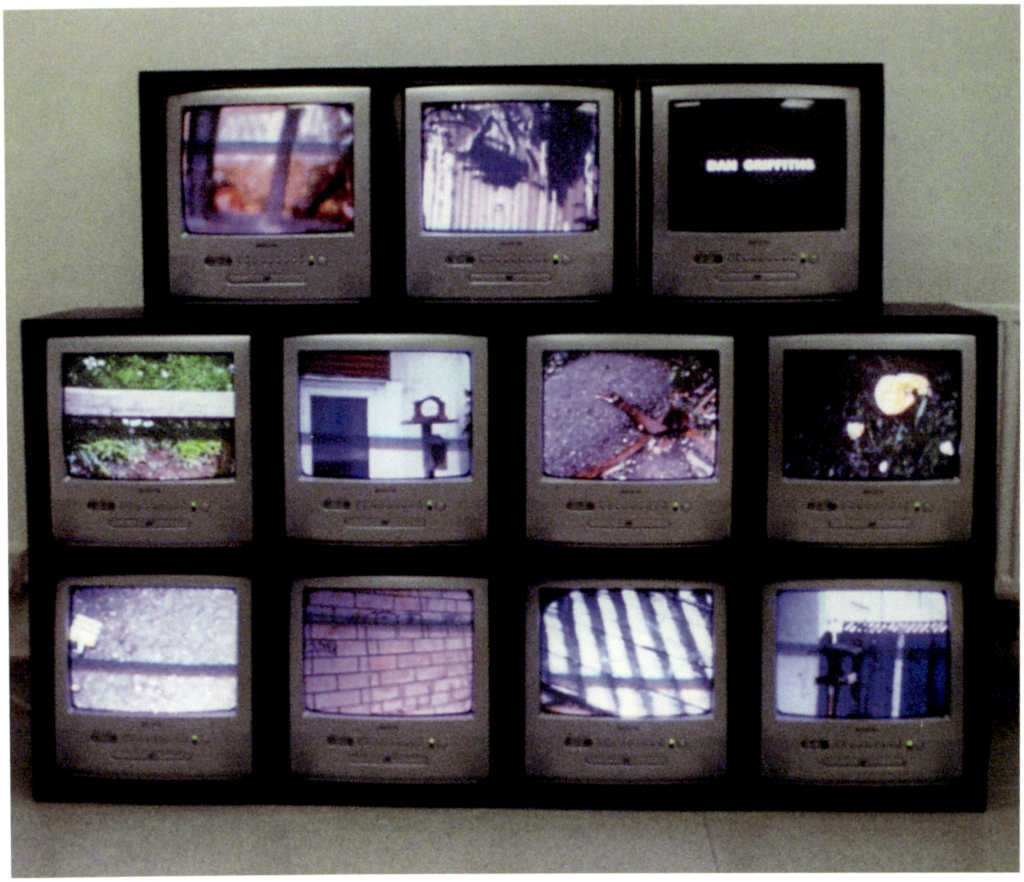

Stephen Willats

The work of Willats primarily addresses the role of the artist and the opportunities to effect social transformation. Willats makes socially engaged, multi-media art projects in areas and communities of all sorts. Working with small groups of volunteers, the artist encourages participants to look at their surroundings in a different way, capturing their environments through text, sound, photography and film.

SPACE TIME FRAGMENTS *(left)*
MACRO TO MICRO *(middle bottom)*

For this, an invited group of actors was filmed and recorded by the artist and a group of participants. The whole group collectively edited the material over the course of a couple of months. The selected frames were then made into one still and laser printed.

IMAGINARY JOURNEY *(middle top)*

Imaginary Journey focusses on typical outer London suburbs, looking at how interpretations of reality come from interactions with other people or are socially constructed.

PERSON TO PERSON, PEOPLE TO PEOPLE *(right)*

Person to Person, People to People is the result of a 12-month engagement with the people of the Netherfield estate, Milton Keynes.

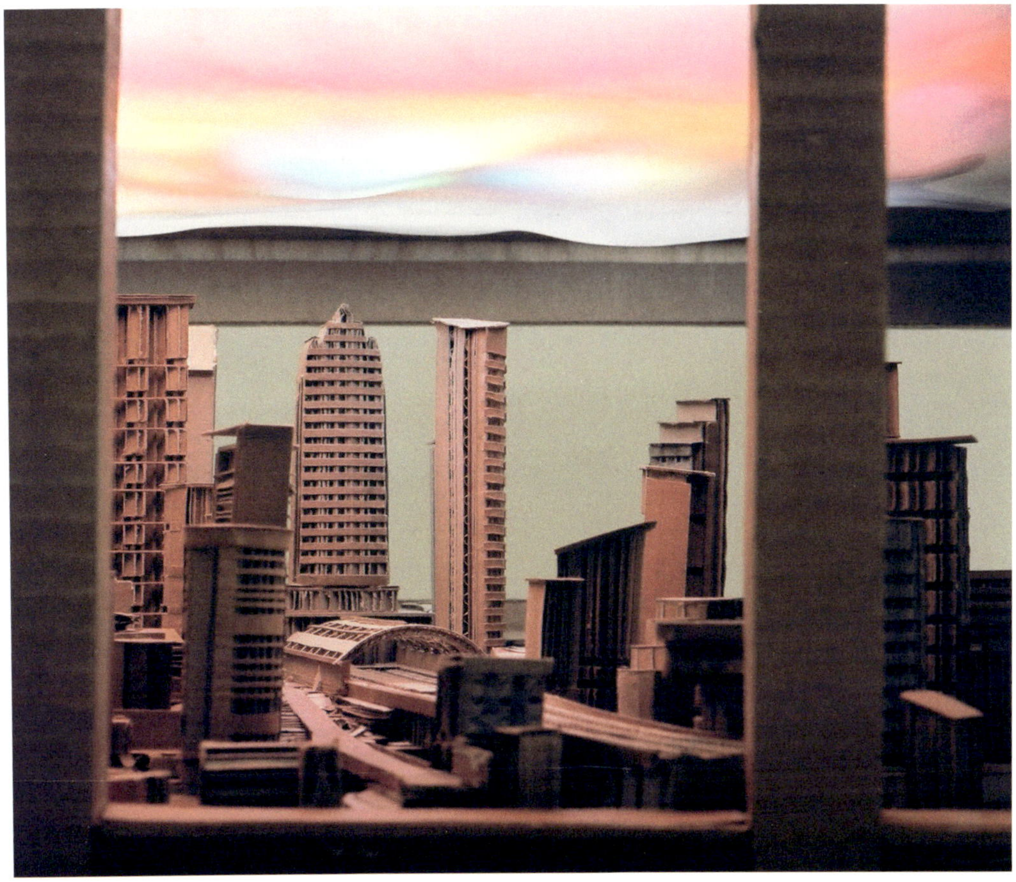

Matias Bechtold

MODEL IN A MODEL

For this series of installations made from corrugated card board and an upside down television, Berlin-based artist Matias Bechtold created a miniature cityscape illuminated by the television's flickering screen.

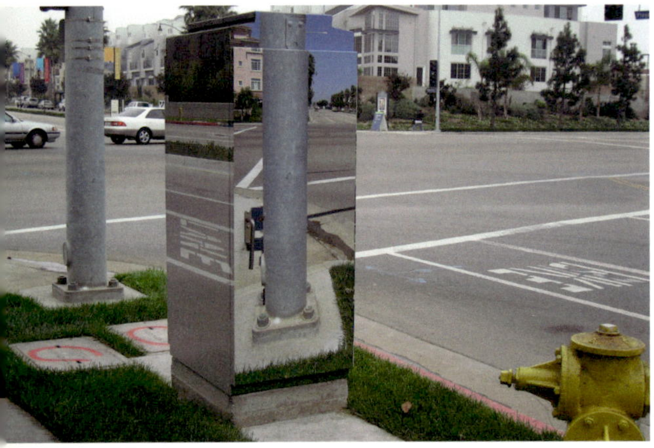

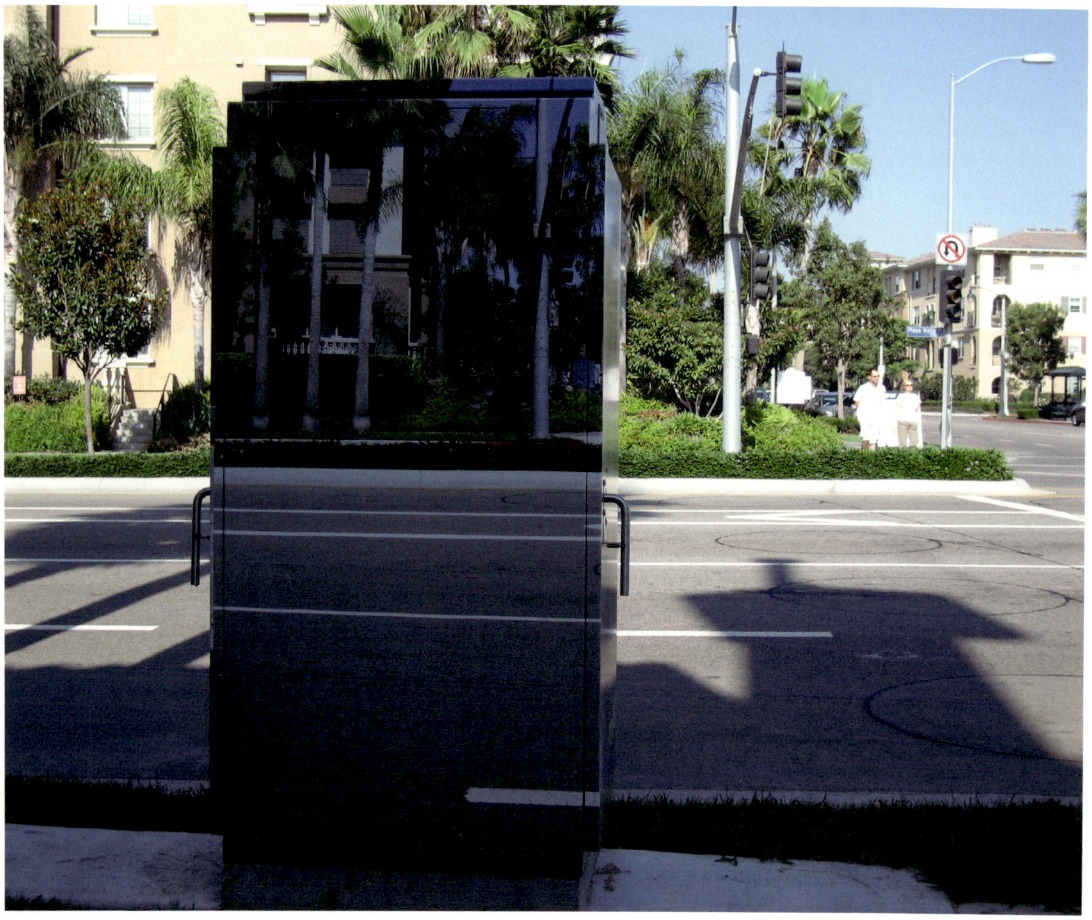

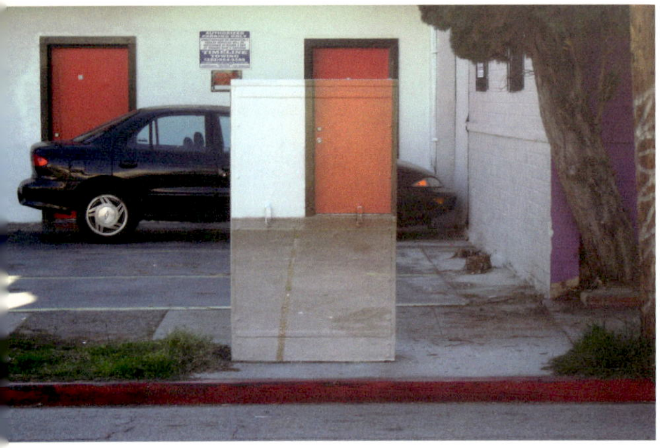

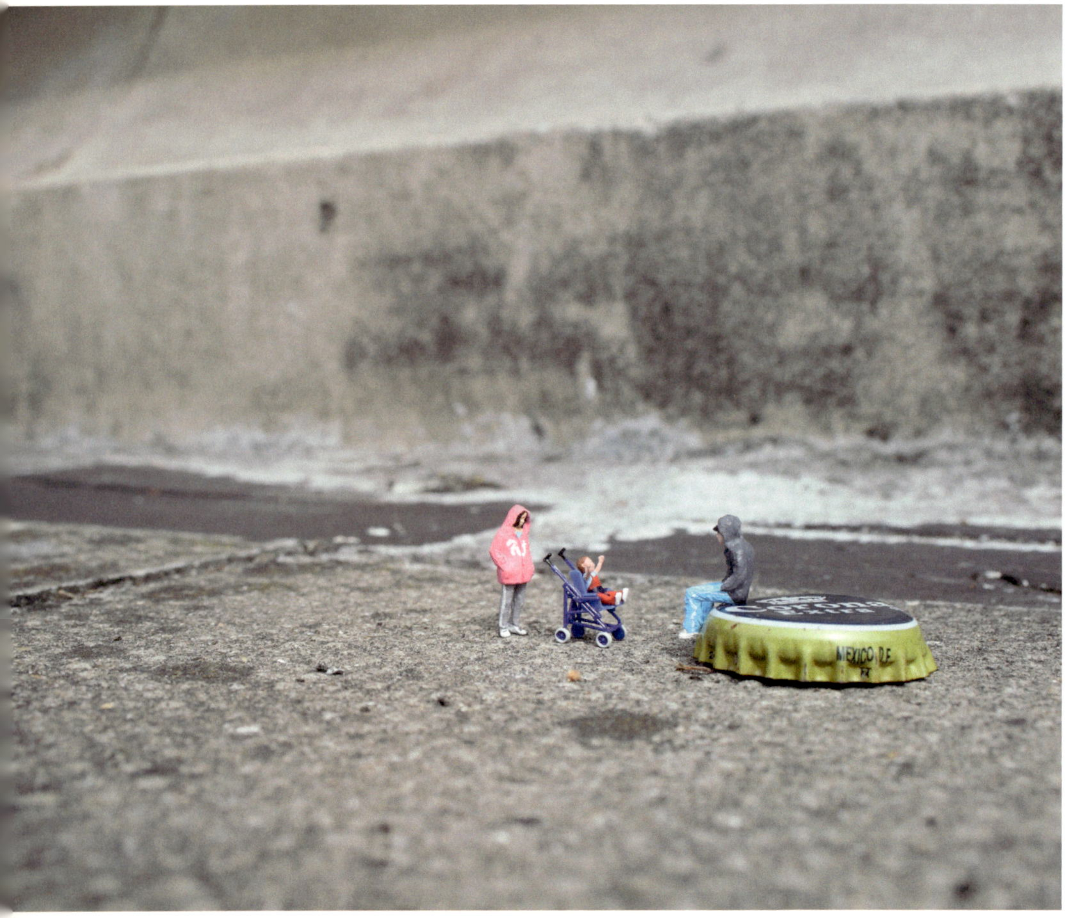

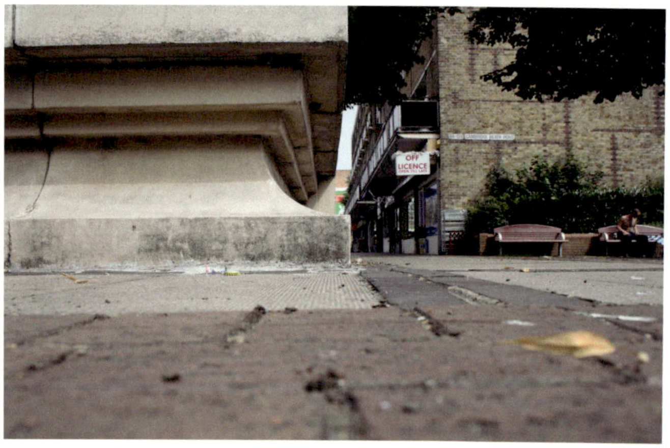
OFF
LICENCE

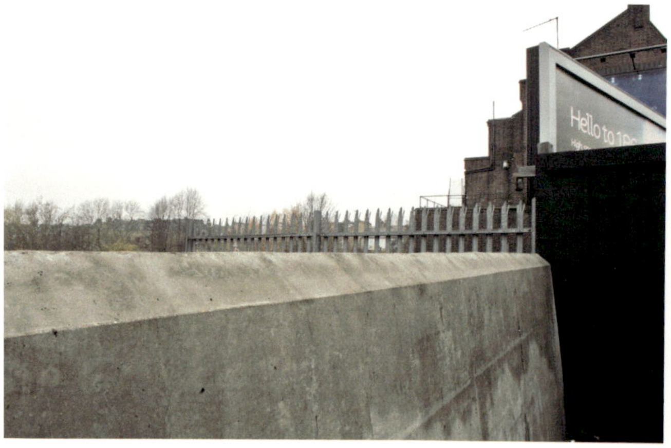

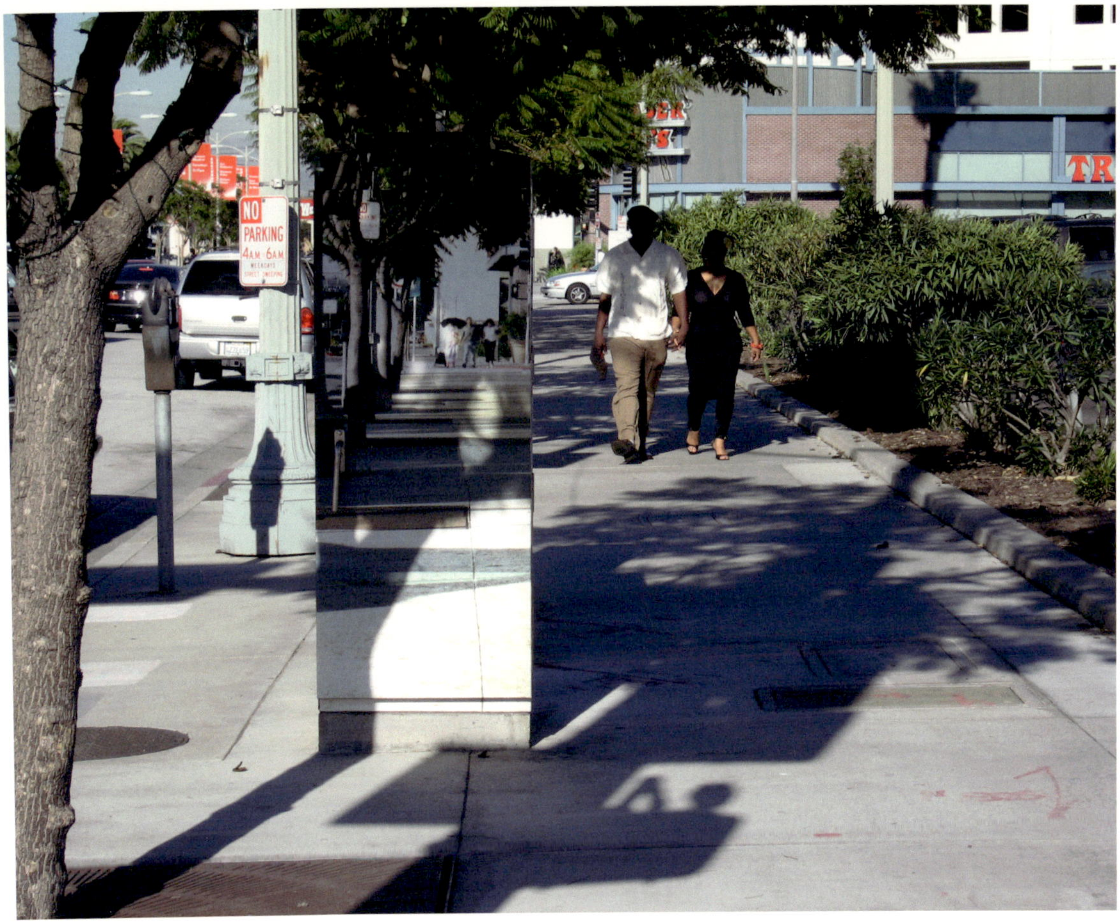

Joshua Callaghan

PLAYA VISTA PROJECT *(left top, middle)*
HOLLYWOOD PROJECT *(left bottom)*
CULVER CITY TOWN SQUARE PROJECT *(right)*

Typical for his public art projects, Callaghan here applied digital images of the immediate environment to utility boxes throughout various communities in California. His trompe l'oeil approach integrate the boxes into the surrounding landscape in a curious fashion.

Slinkachu

UNTITLED

Slinkachu is an artist who installs tiny figurines around the city. Slinkachu modifies and paints figurines made for model train sets before installing them in streets and parks, where he photographs the scene and leaves the characters behind.

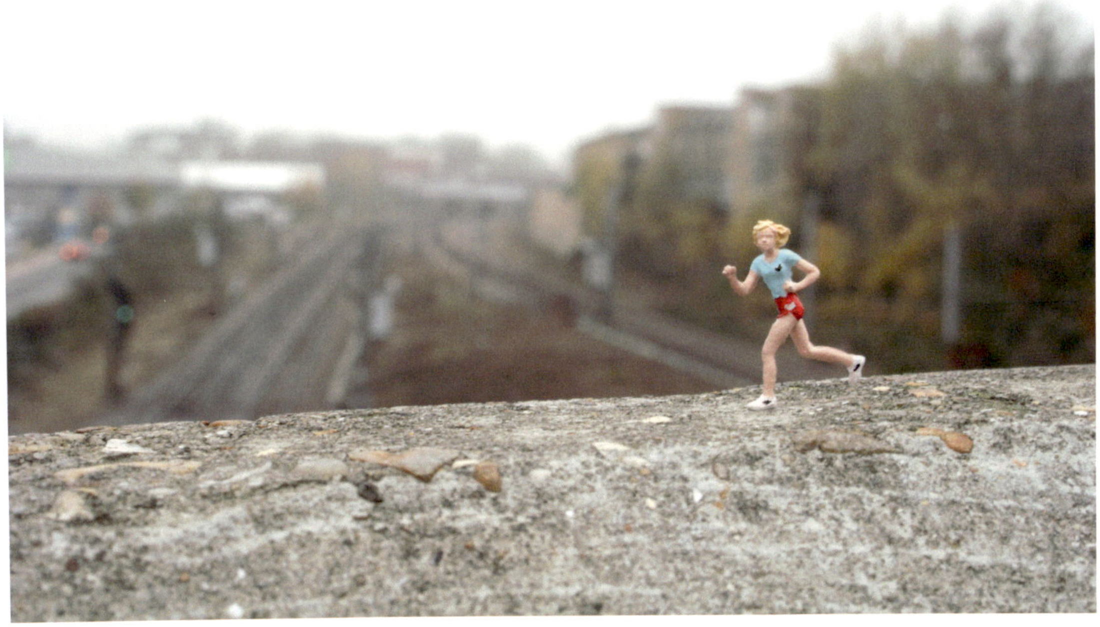

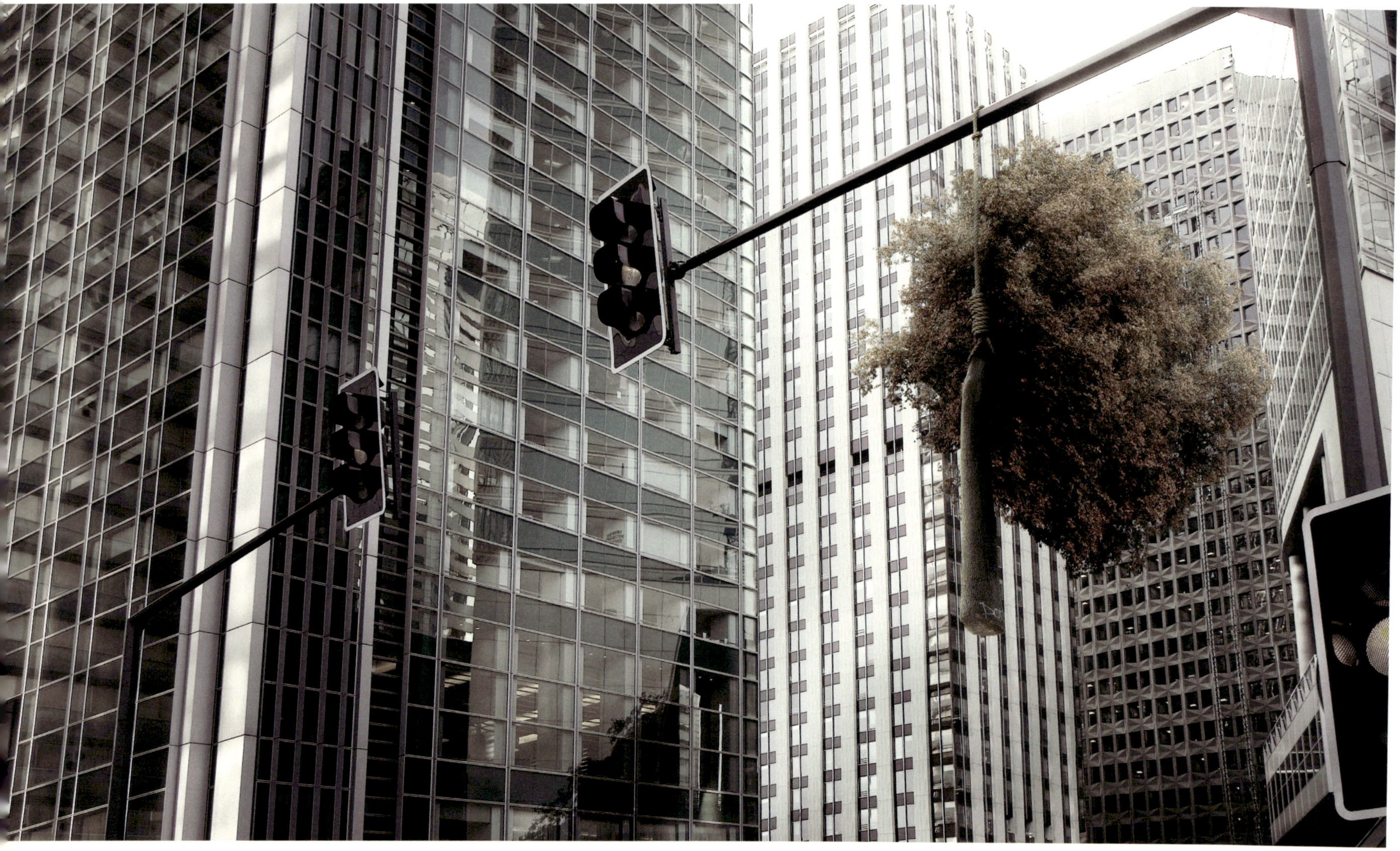

Romain Laurent

WHAT IF TREES CAN DECIDE
WHAT THEY REALLY WANT *(top)*

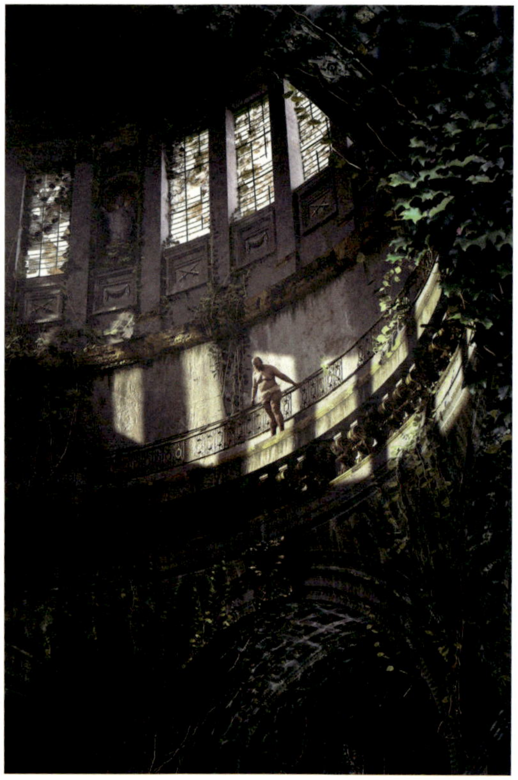

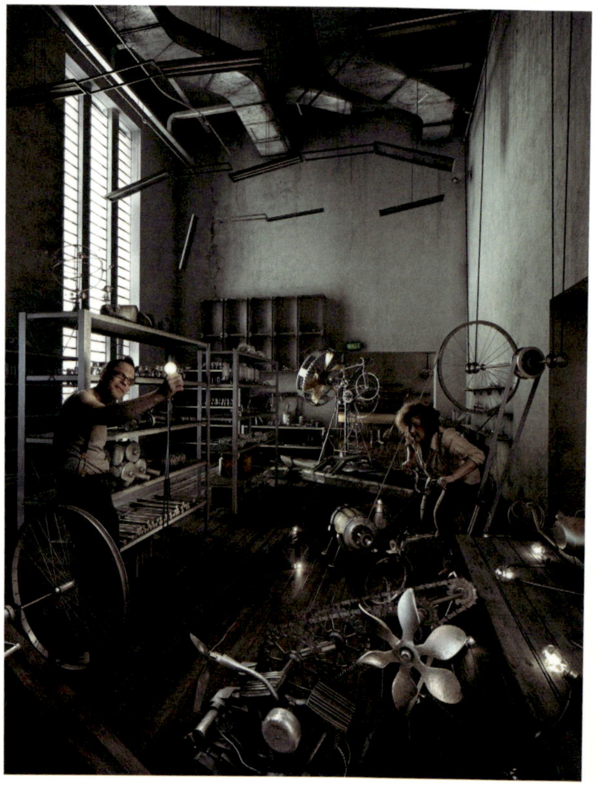

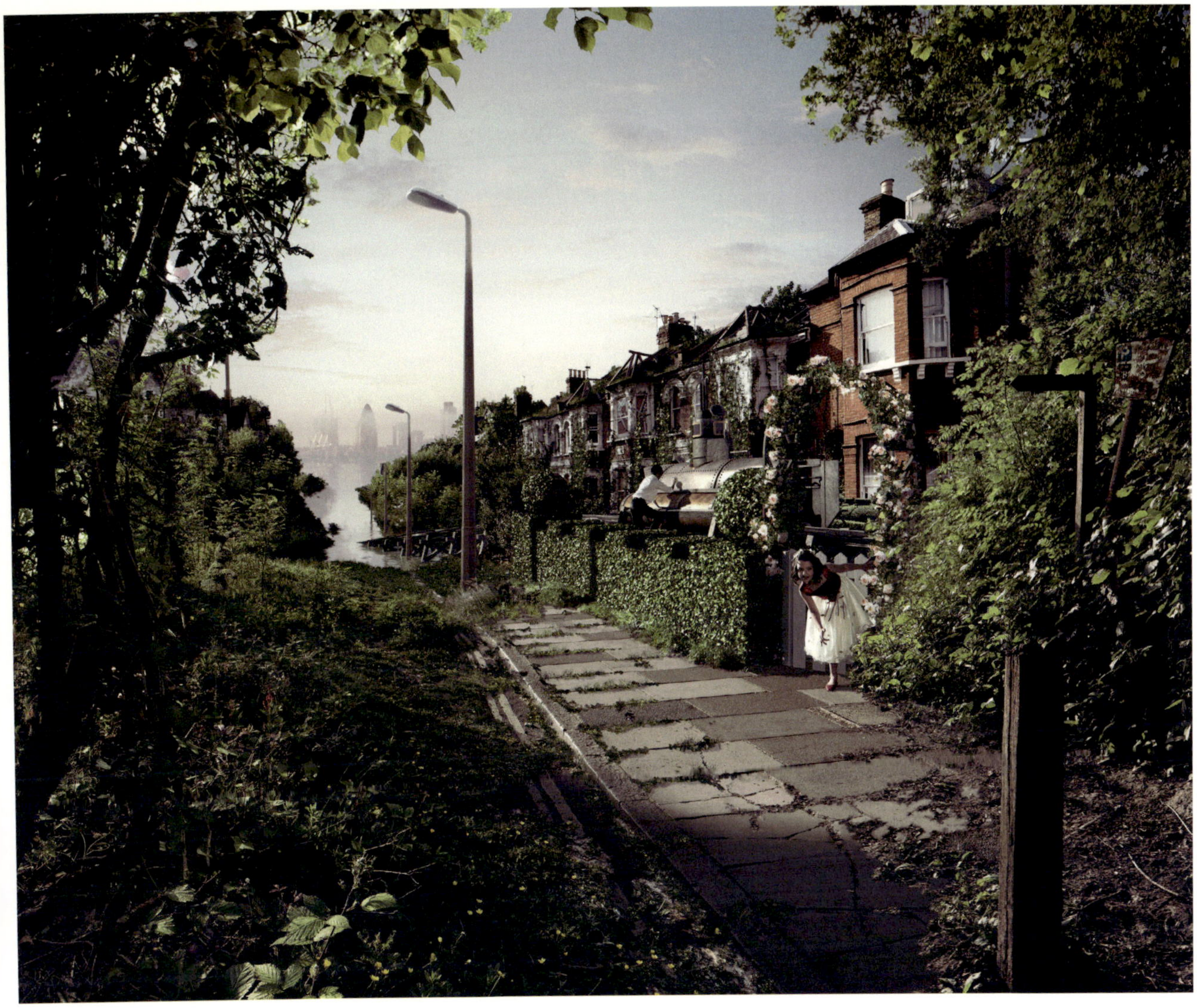

Squint / Opera

HONOR OAK – SUBURBAN BUCOLIA/ FLOODED LONDON *(four images)*

The images of Flooded London are snapshots of London lives some time after a catastrophe, obliquely depicting adaptations to a near-deserted urban environment. Originally presented on lightboxes, Squint used photography, 3D modelling and image manipulation to imitate the techniques and aesthetic of Victorian landscape painters.

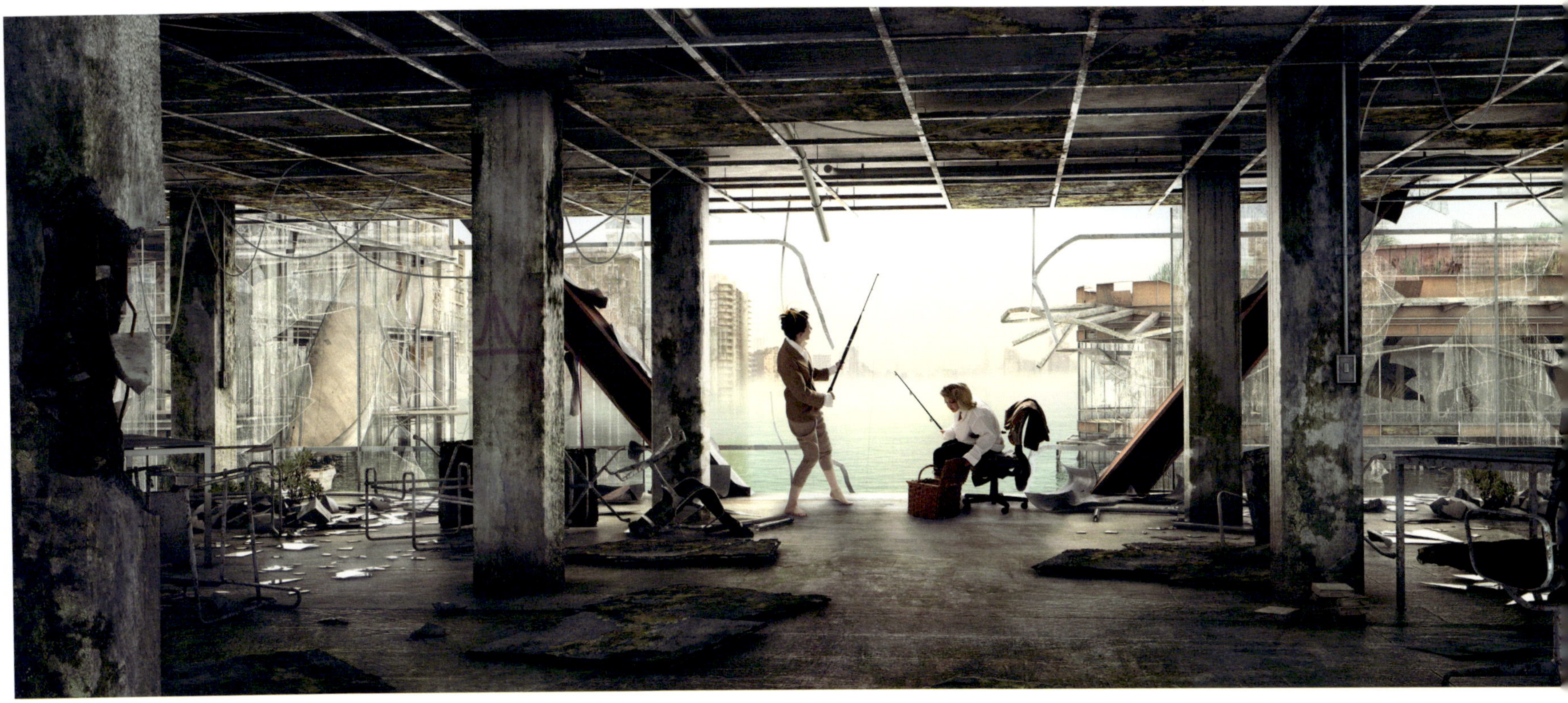

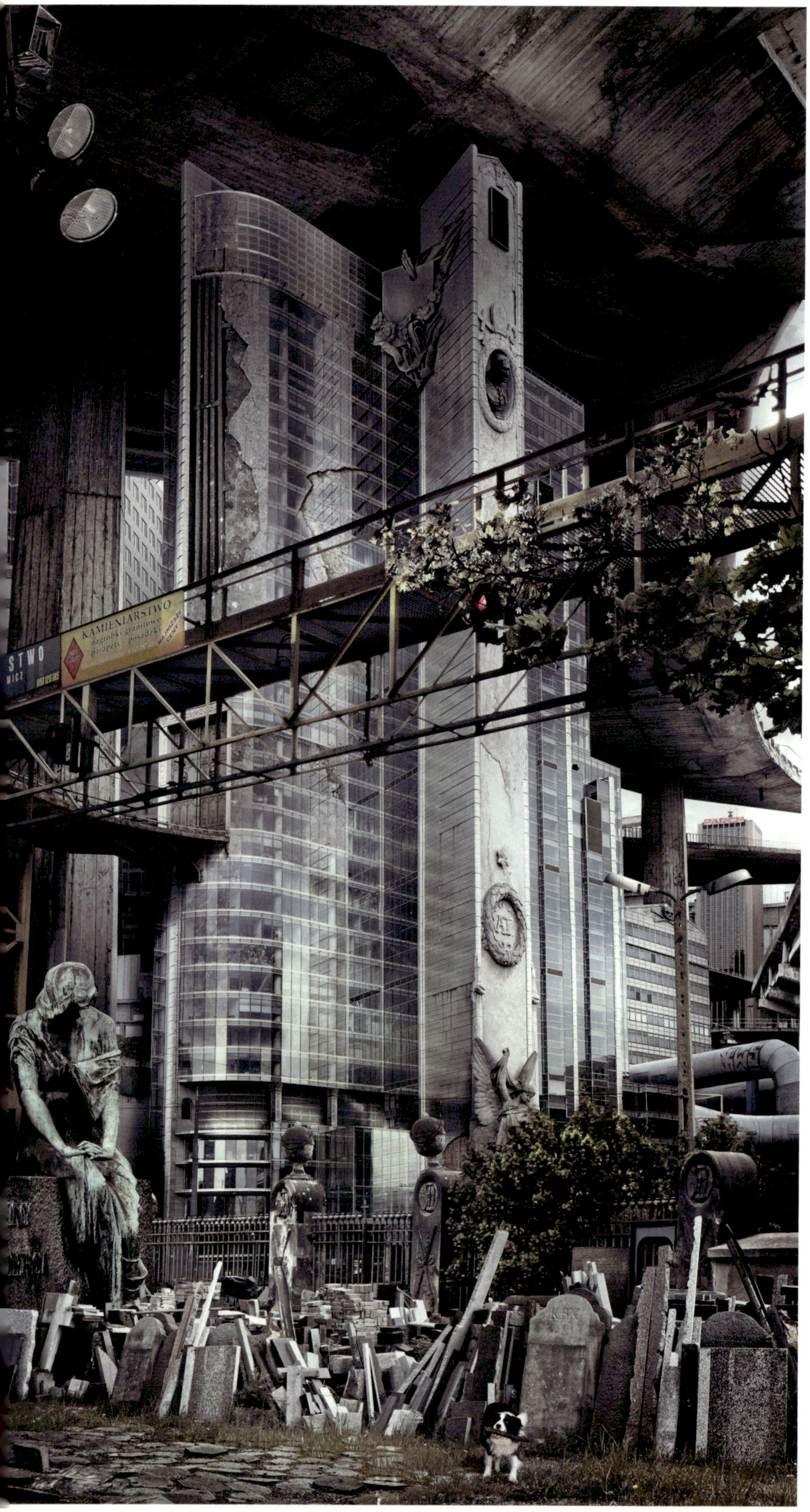

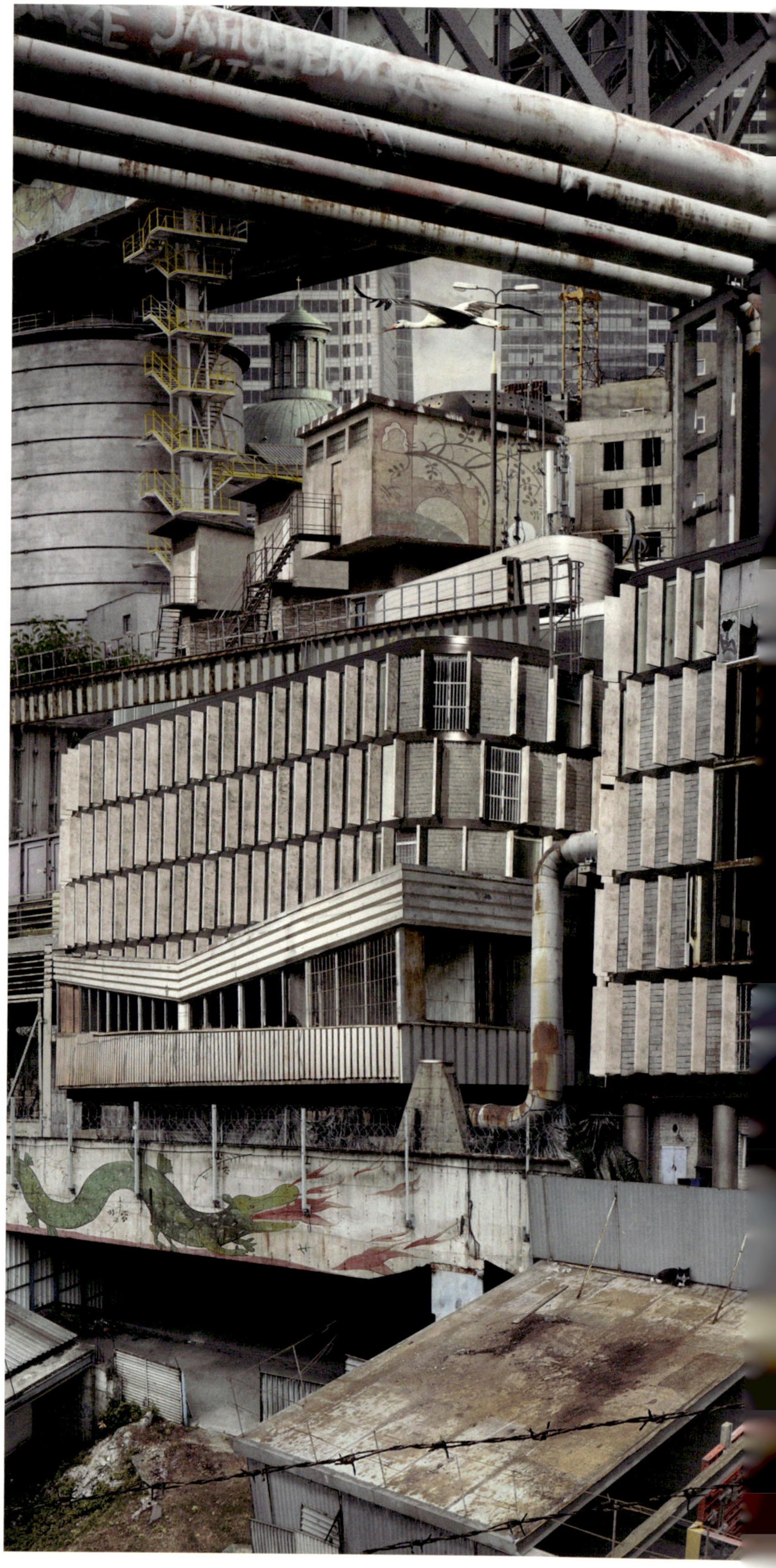

Kobas Laksa URBAN GANGRENE/ARCHITECTURE BEYOND BUILDING

The photomontages by Kobas Laksa show possible transformations of recently built architecture in Poland that has changed its function: Among others, an office building is transformed into a columbarium, a church is transformed into a water park, an airport is transformed into a slaughterhouse. This project shown in the Polish pavilion as Hotel Polonia in Venice, 2008 was awarded the Golden Lion.

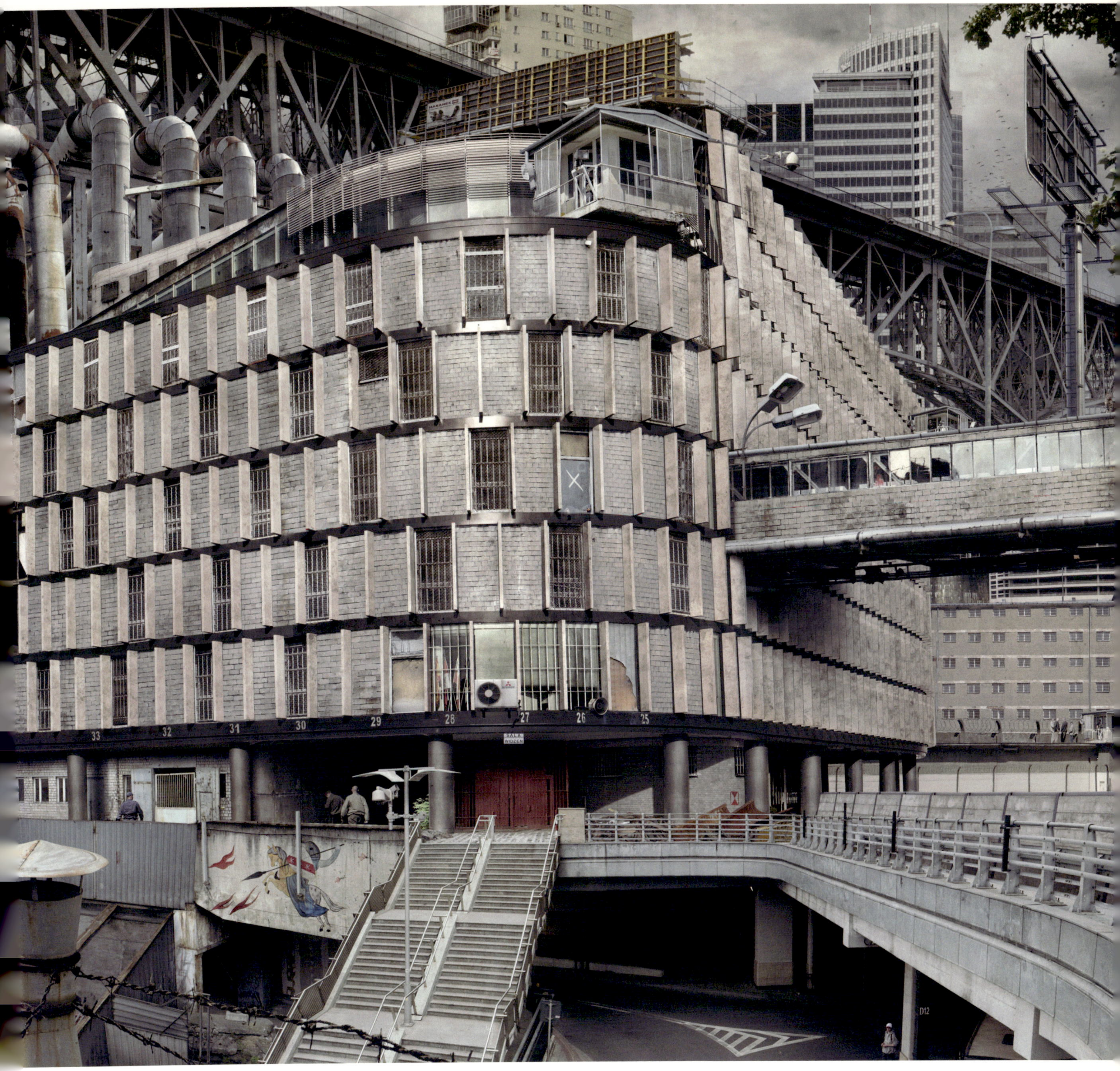
33
32
31
30
29
28
27
26
25
WIDZEN
D12

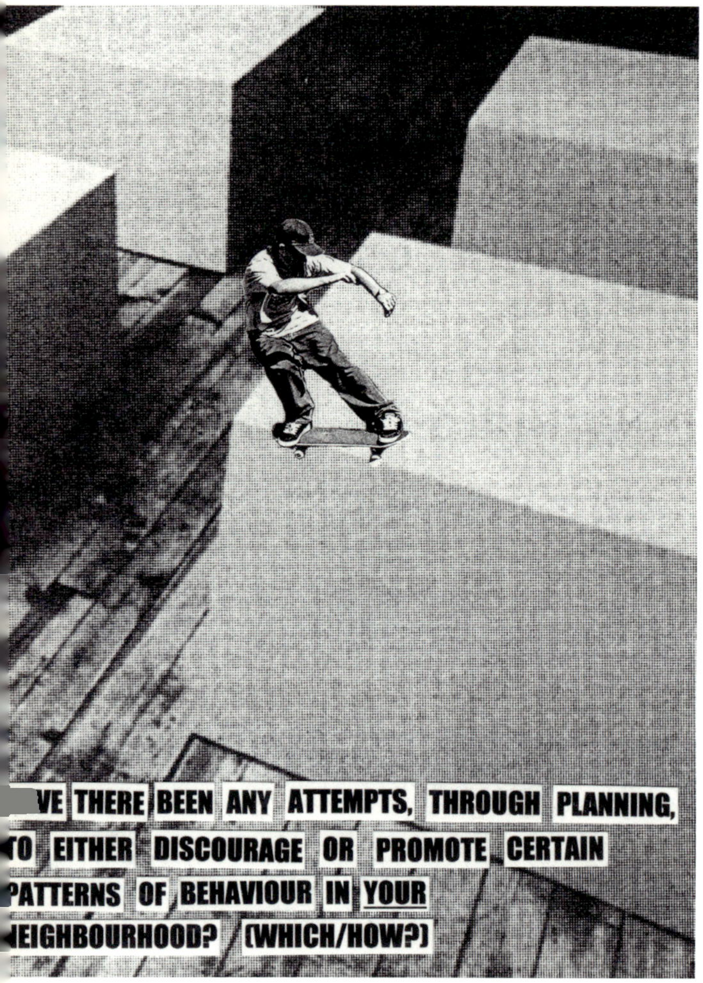

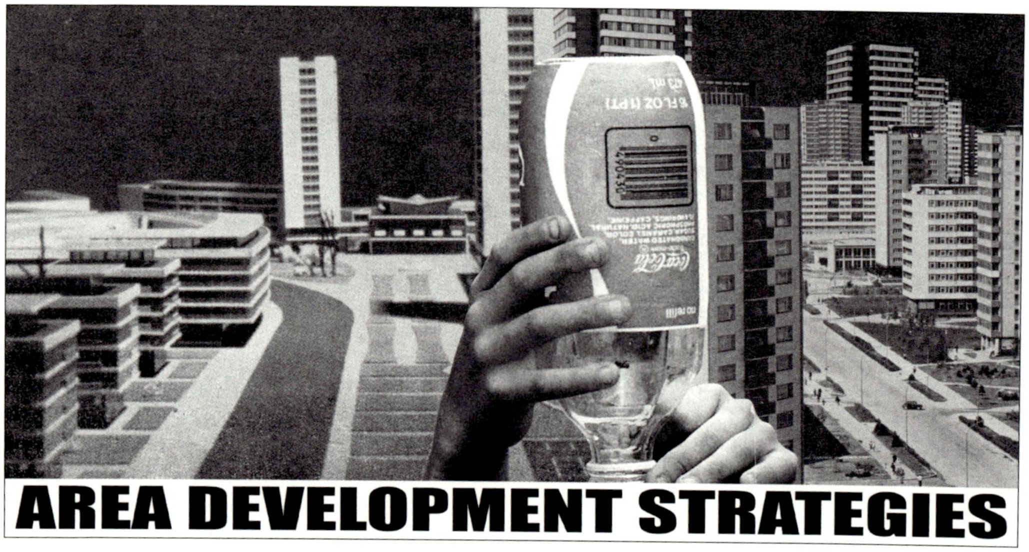

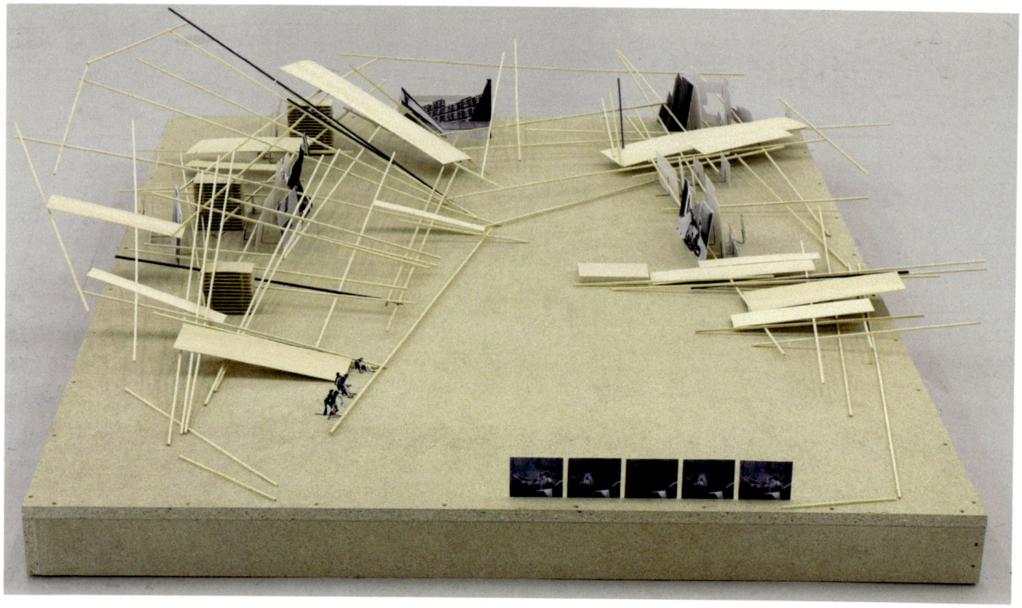

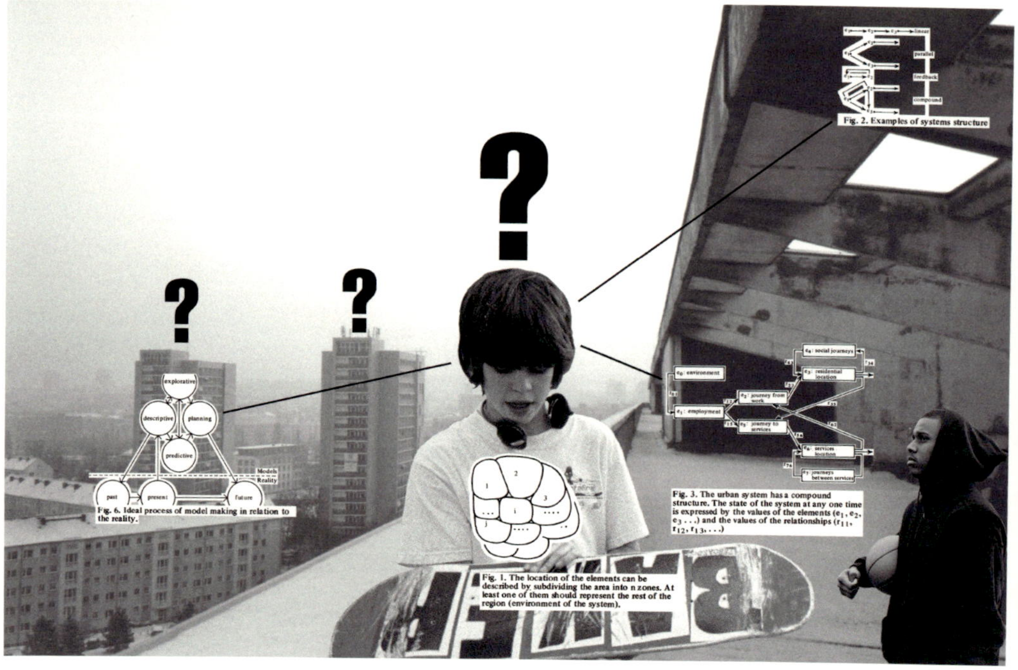

Jakob Kolding

UNTITLED

Jakob Kolding makes the mechanisms and pitfalls of functional city-planning the subject of his posters and collages. Although there is analytical criticism, it is obvious that the artist cannot escape the fascination of the spirit of modern, planned inner cities.

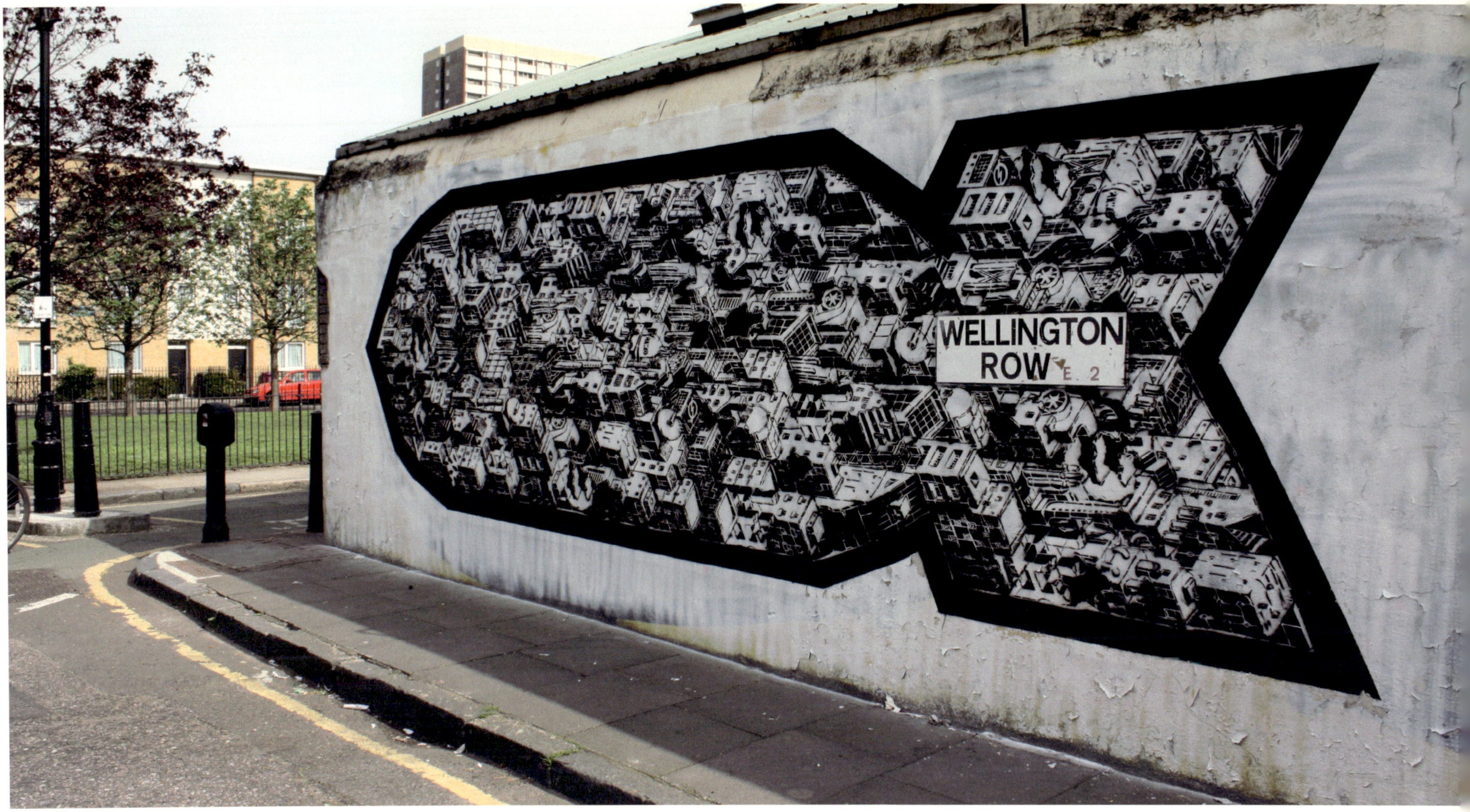

M-City / Mariusz Waras

UNTITLED

M-city is foremost a play with the form and space of the city, played on the walls, posters, billboards and stickers. All of the approximately 100 modular pieces of M-city are made as stencils. The resulting buildings can be joined and customized in multiple ways with parts of different stencils.

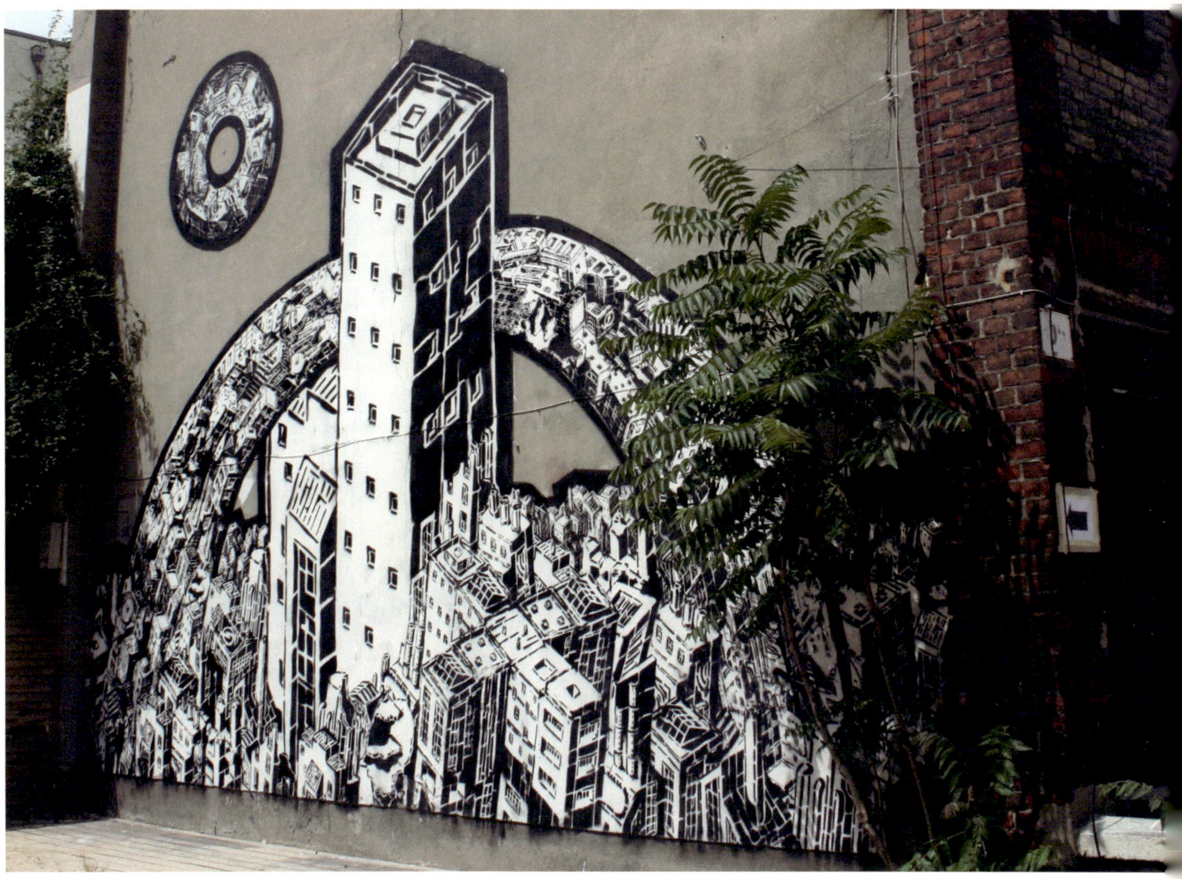

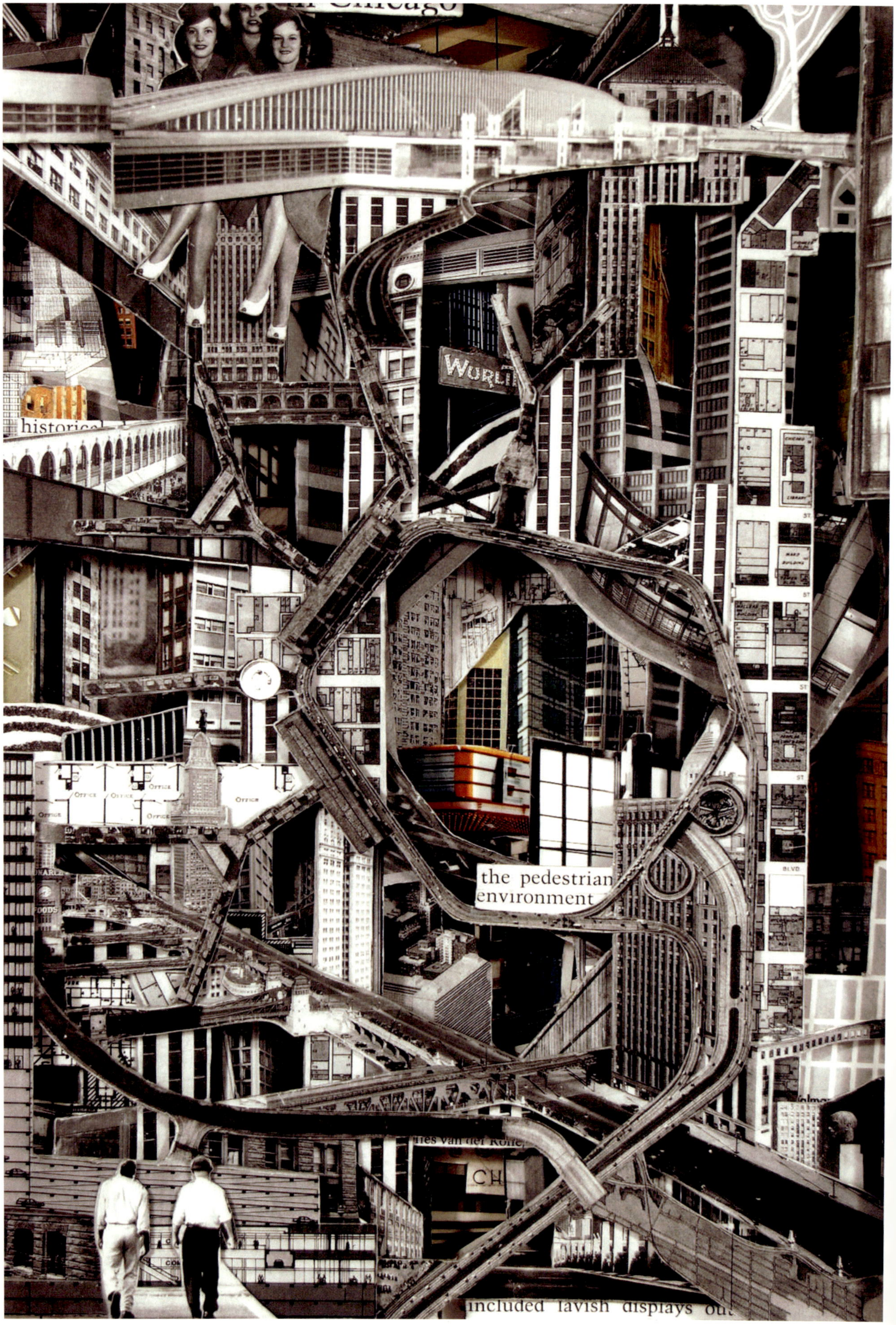

Brian Dettmer

CHICAGO ARCHITECTURE AND DESIGN

Dettmer is noted for his alteration of pre-existing media – such as old books, maps, record albums, and cassette tapes – to create new, transformed works of visual fine art.

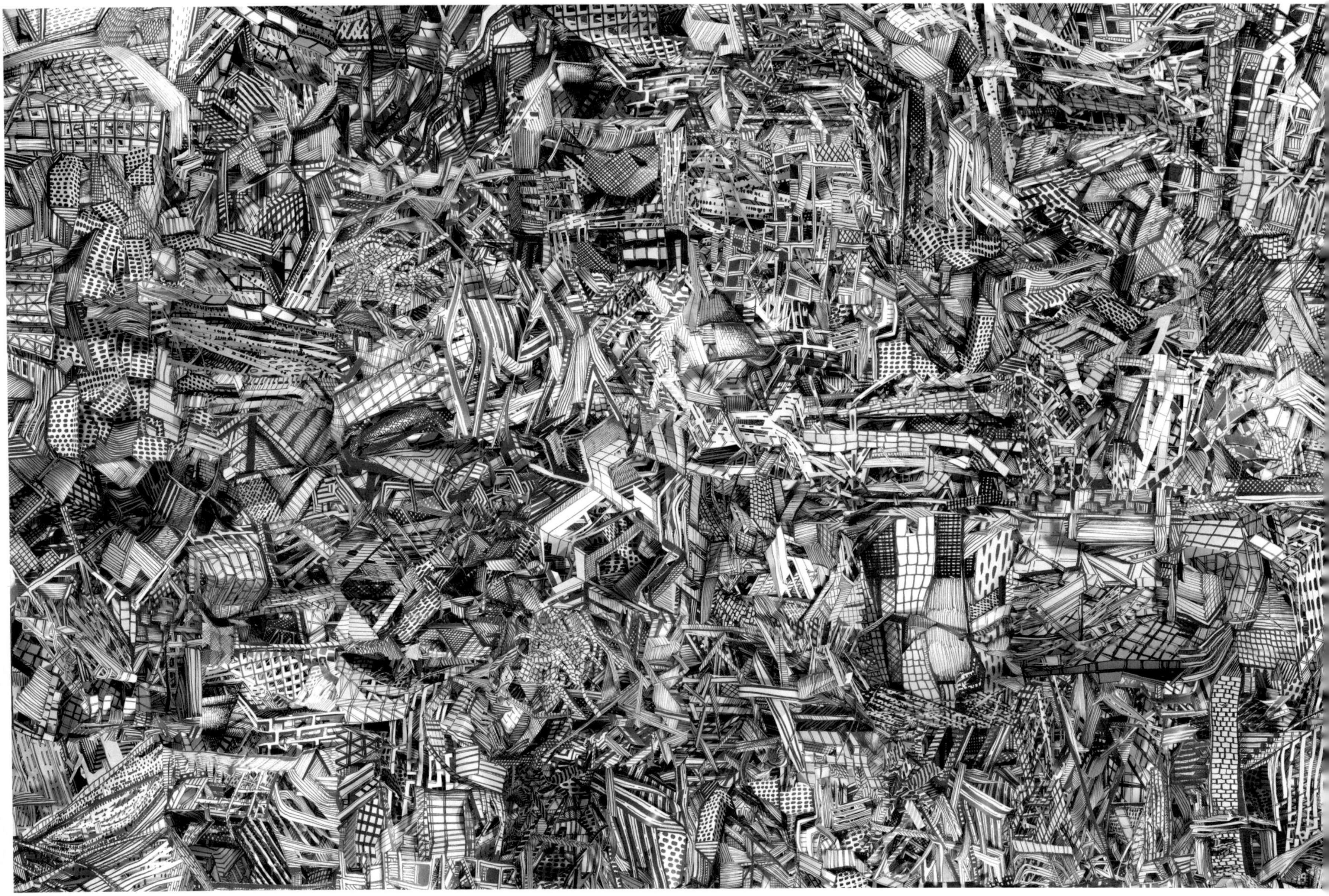

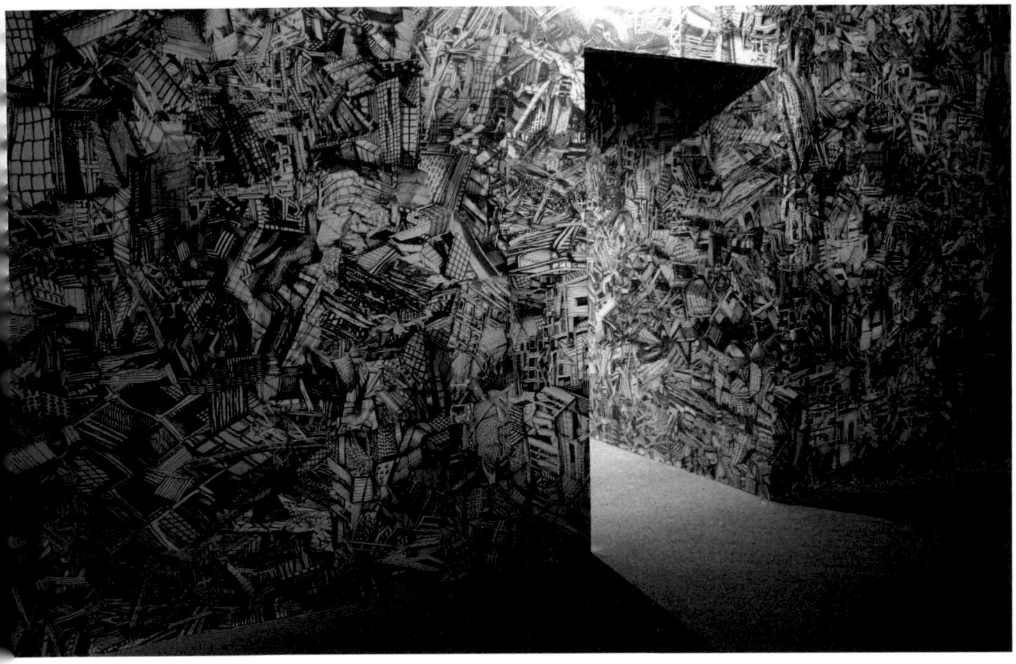

KramervanderVeer JEROEN KRAMER

CITY DUST

The drawing series City Dust is an intriguing collection of imaginary cuttings of the urban landscape: a patchwork of drawings, photographs, collages, structures and patterns. Images arising from a fascination for imaginary architecture: a hidden town beyond the tangible architecture.

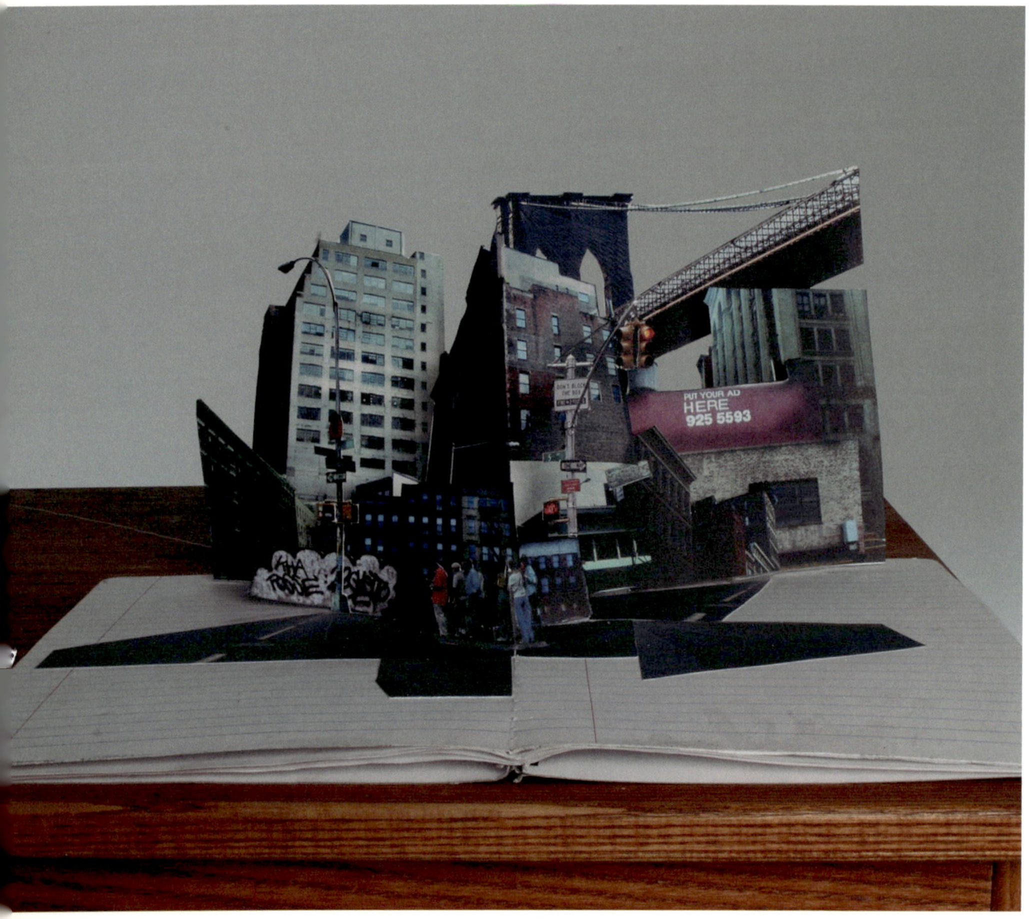

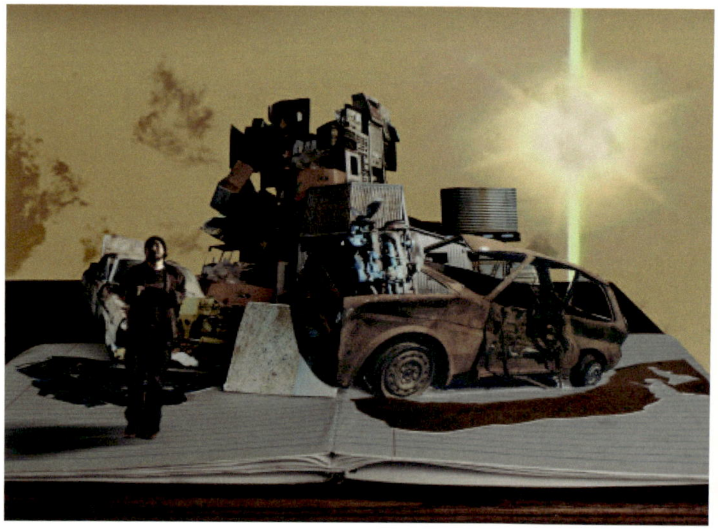

Asif Mian

AESOP ROCK: FAST CARS

A school notebook provides the theme for the flipbook animation video by designer and director Asif Mian for New York's Aesop Rock's single *Fast Cars* from the EP *Fast Cars, Danger, Fire & Knives* by Definitive Jux Records.

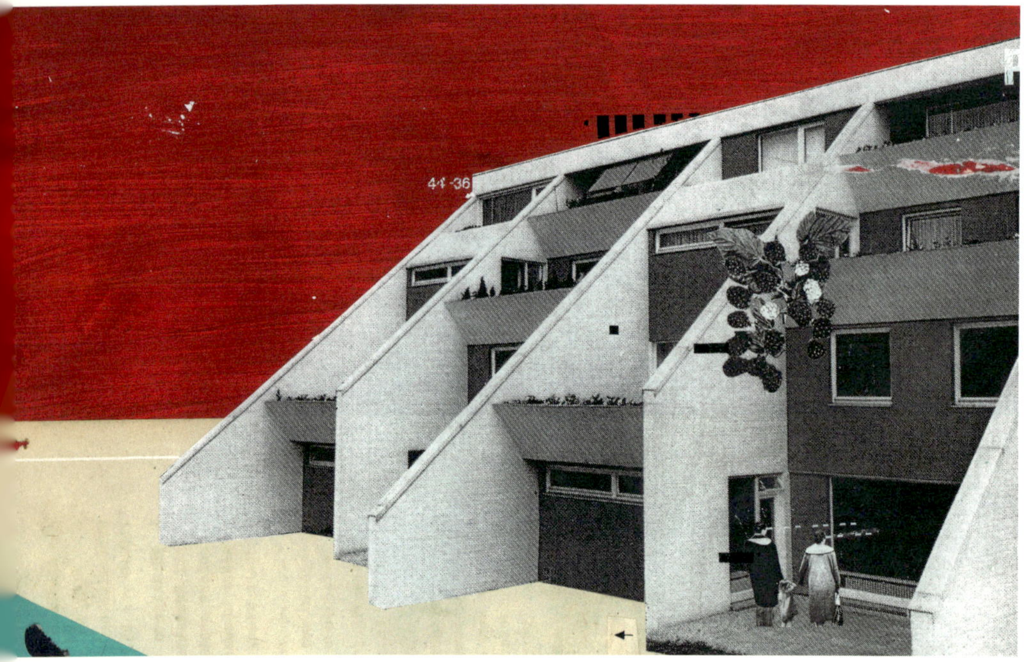

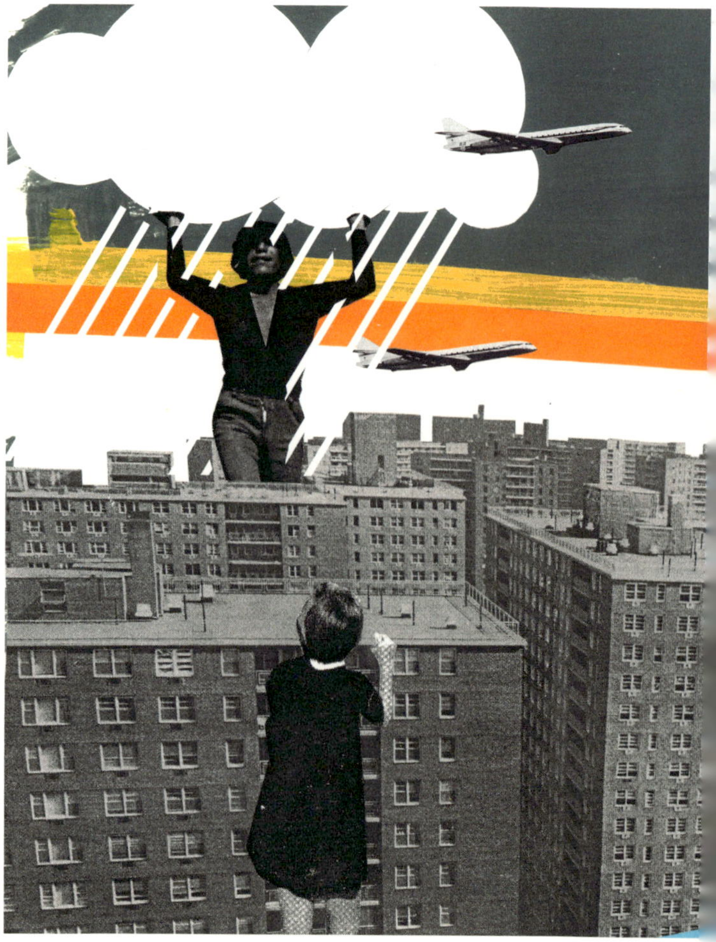

Mario Wagner

HOUSING *(top)*
WOLKEN *(right)*

German artist and illustrator Mario Wagner uses old magazines, scissor, glue, and acrylic to create his paper collage works.

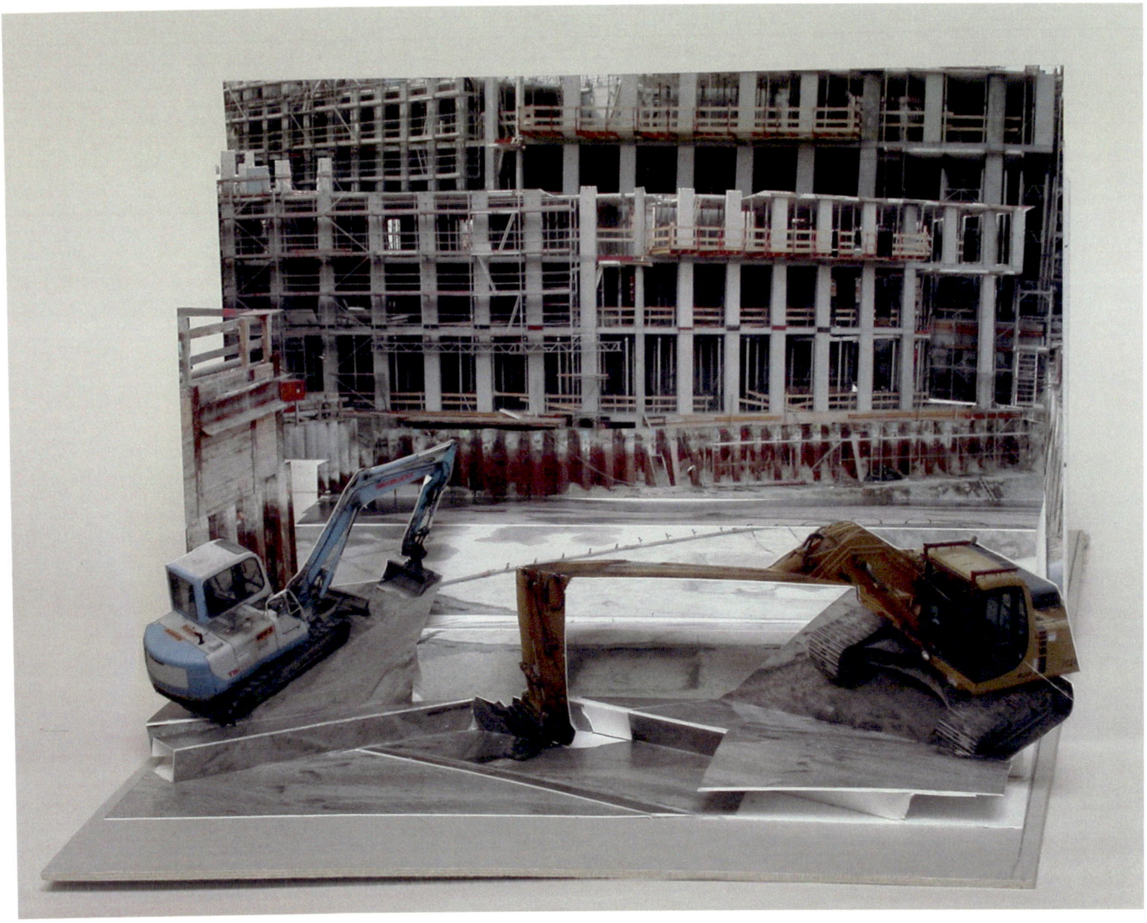

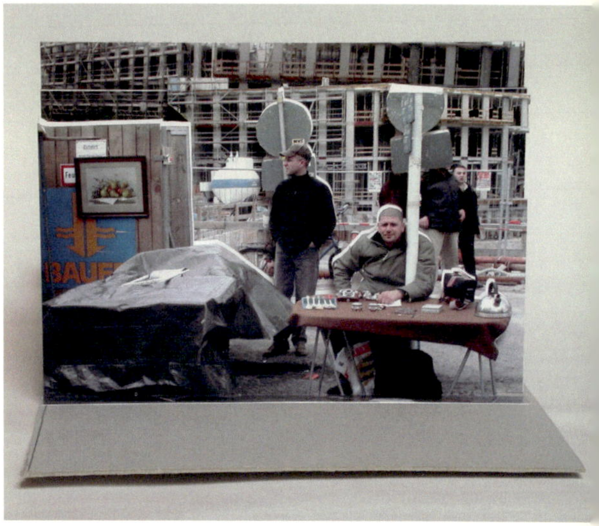

Philip Wiegard

SCAFFOLD *(bottom)*
JUNE 17TH *(top, left)*

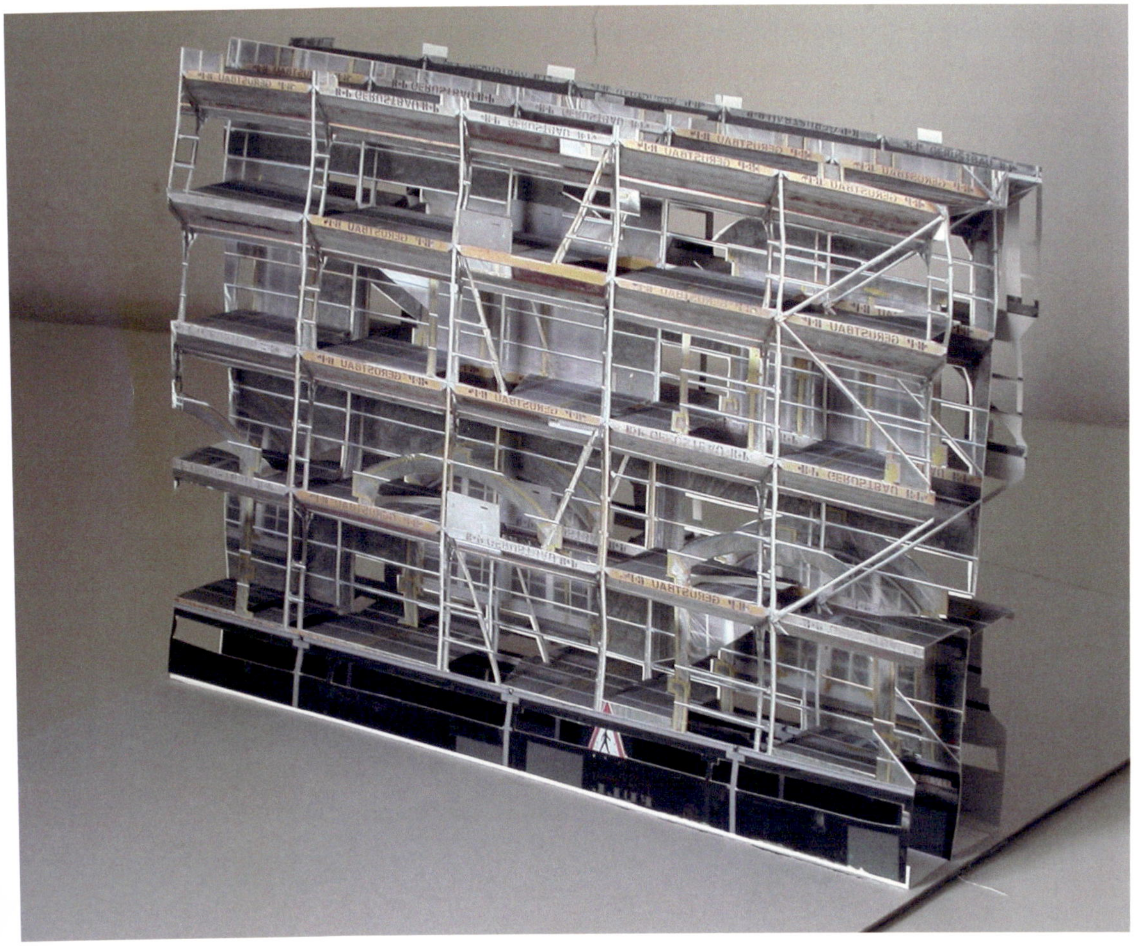

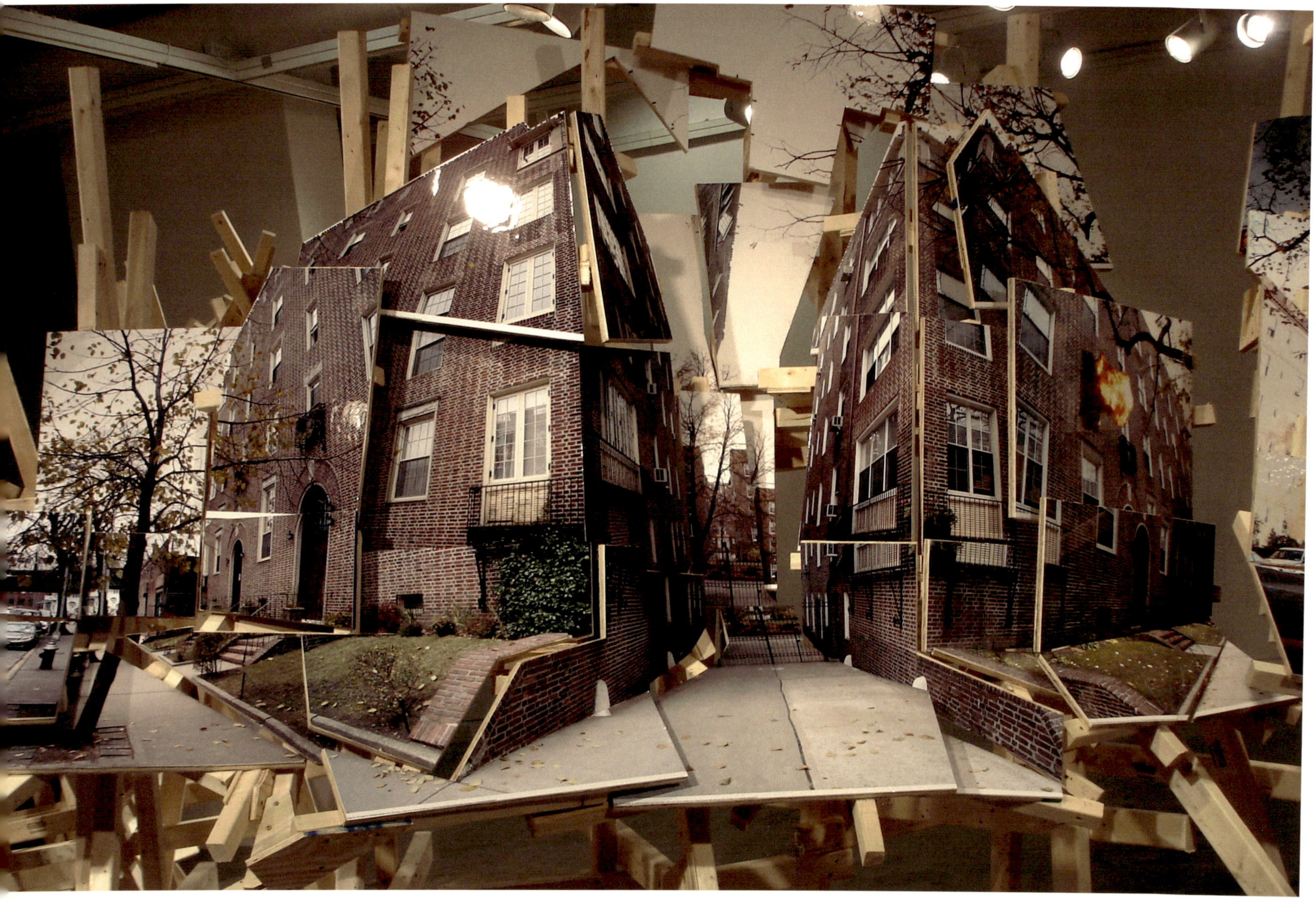

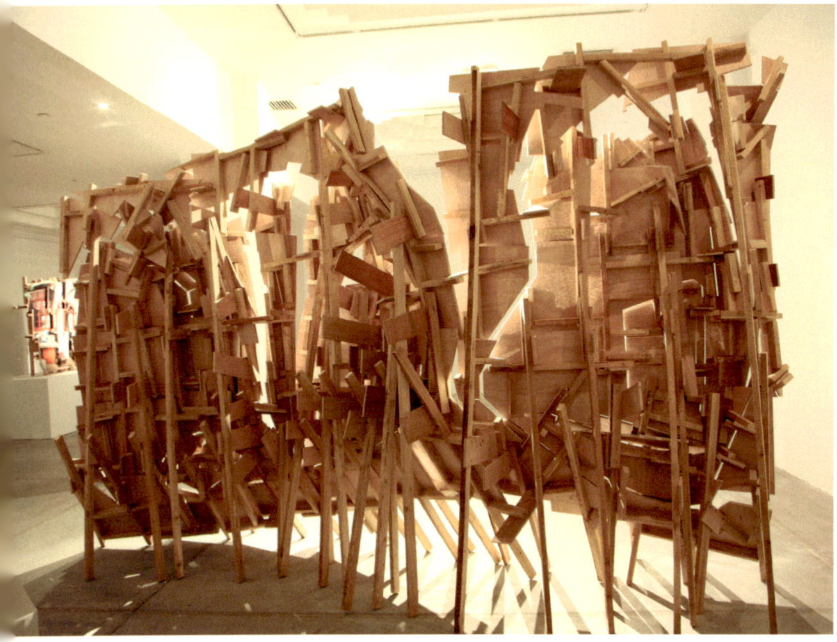

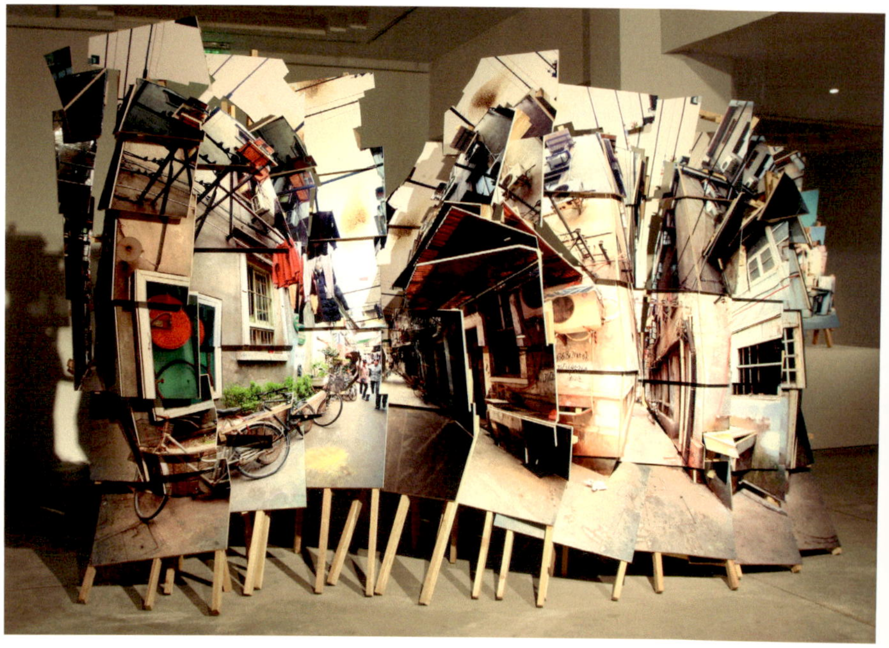

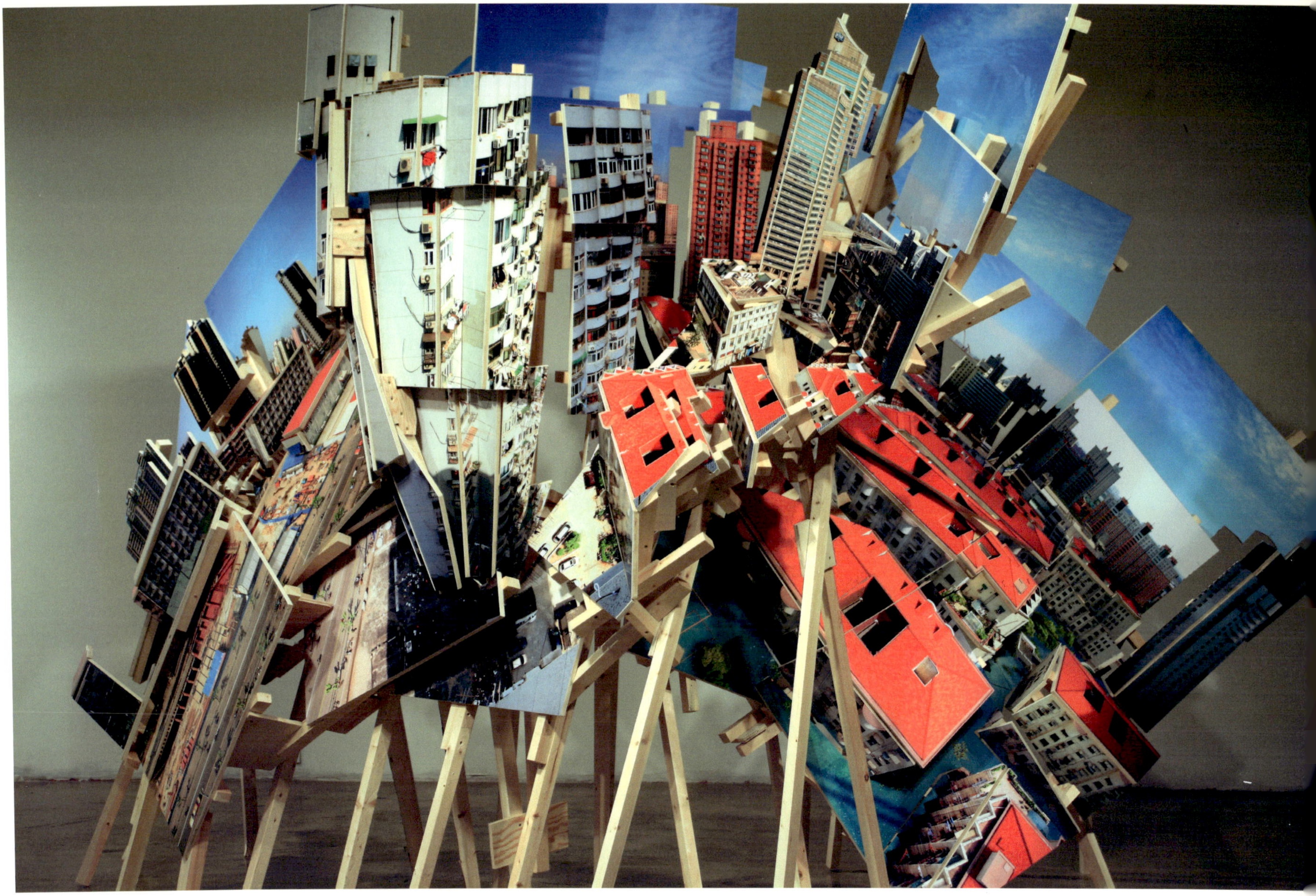

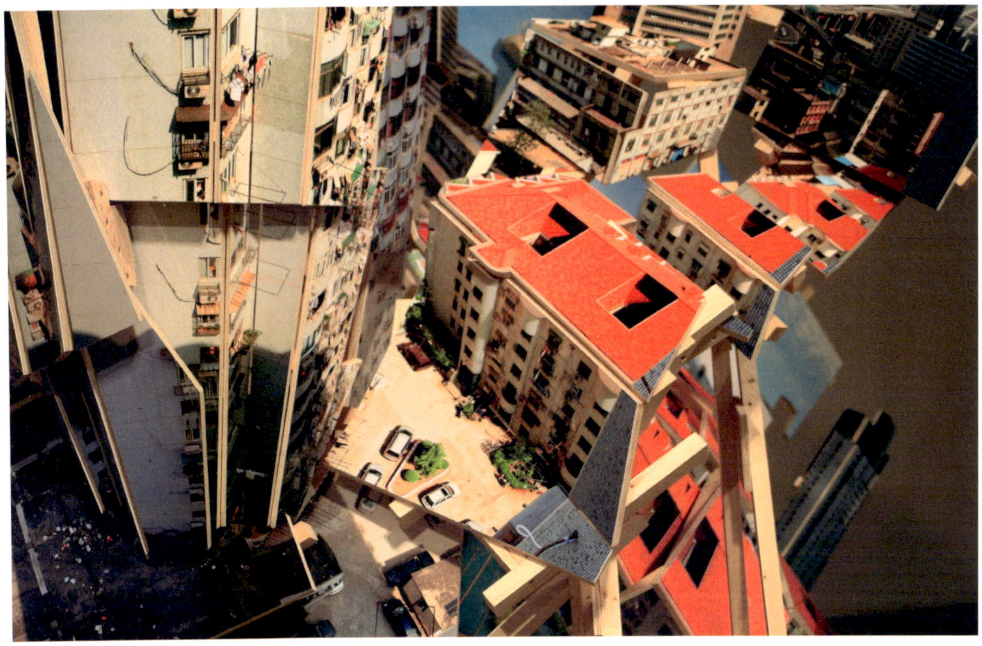

Isidro Blasco

Blasco designs architectural environments: Impressive large- and small-scale, intimate habitat-like structures that merge mental, perceptual and physical spaces, actively encouraging viewers to become adventurous participants.

UTICA ATLANTA *(left page, top)*
COURTYARD *(left page, bottom left + right)*
SHANGHAI AT LAST *(this page)*

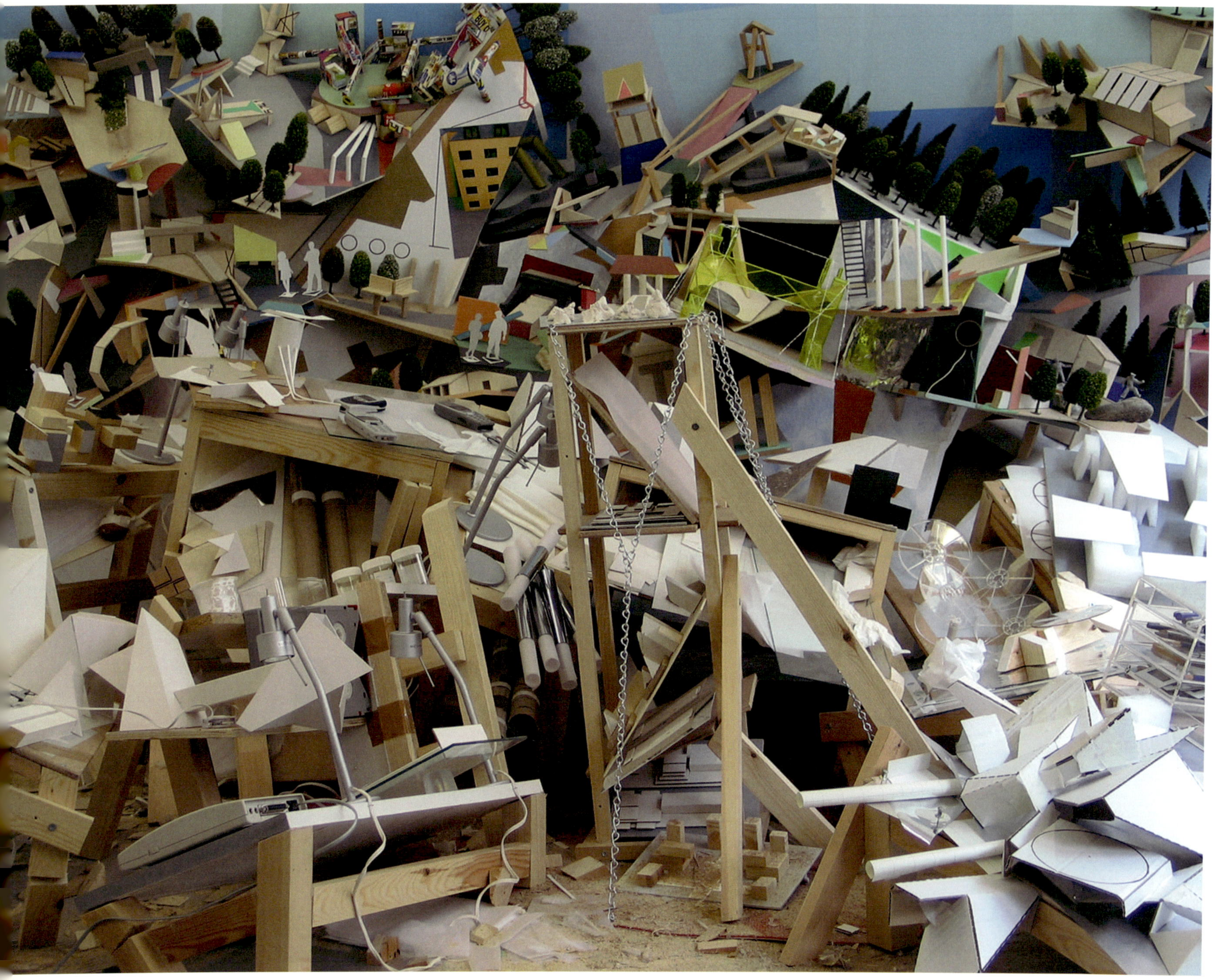

Paul Eachus

TREMOR

The photoworks of British artist Paul Eachus are large, almost the same size as the original subject matter, and present us with wholly constructed spaces that are overwhelming, excessive and fragmented.

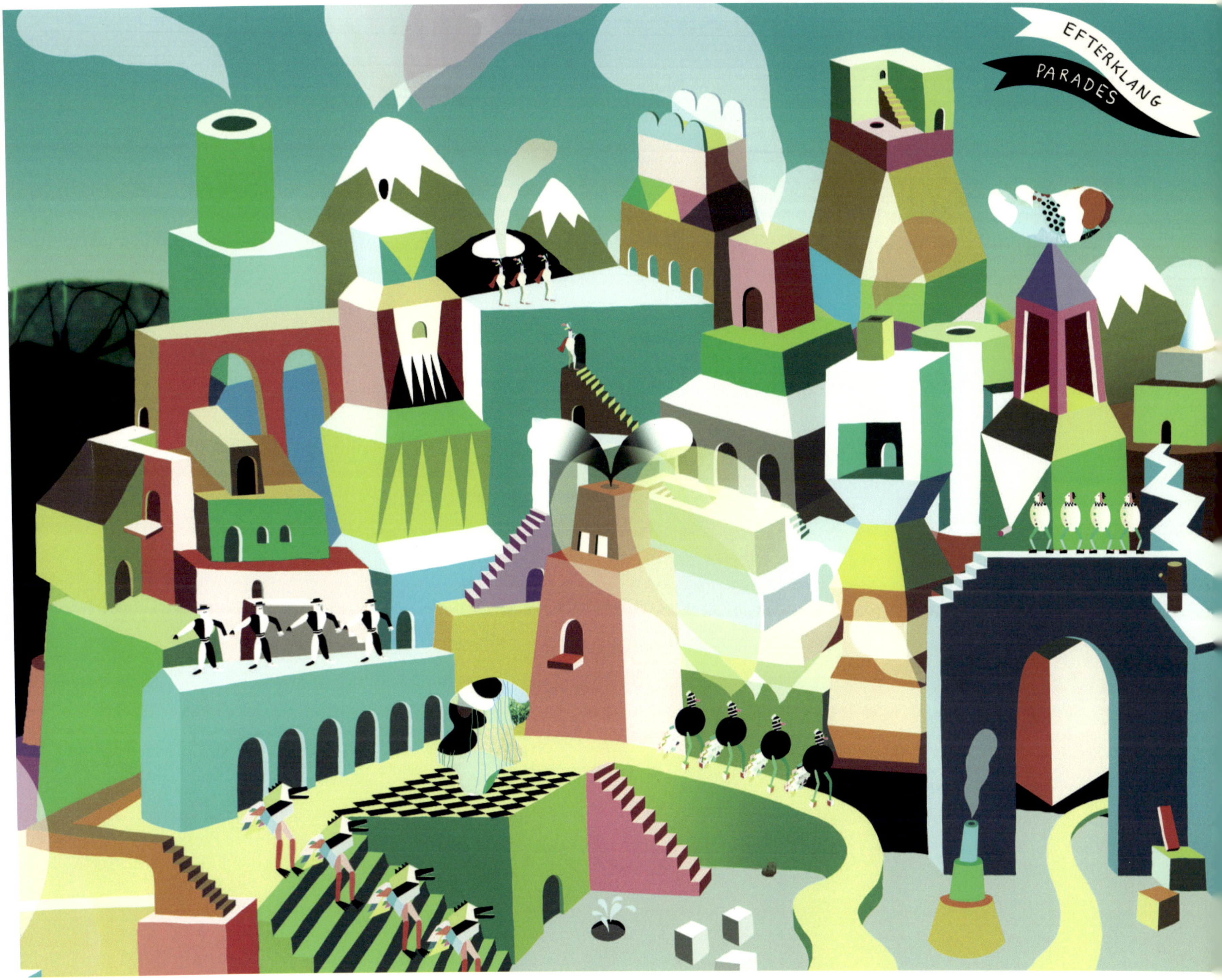

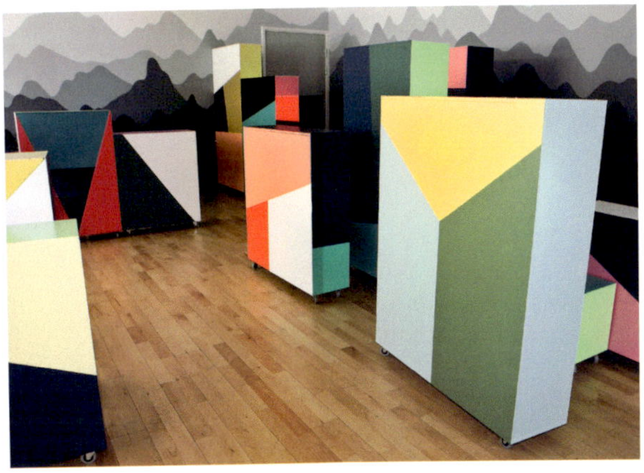

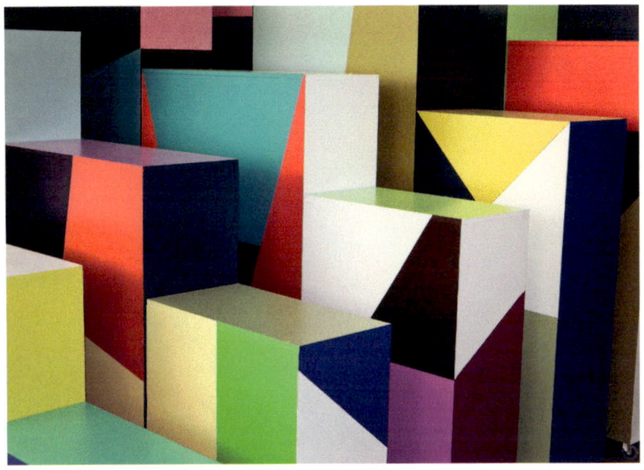

Nan Na Hvass WITH KASPER FJEDERHOLT, UFEX

EFTERKLANG *(top)*

This illustration is the cover artwork for album *Parades* by Danish Efterklangs.

Hvass&Hannibal

INTERIOR DESIGN OF A MEETING ROOM *(left)*

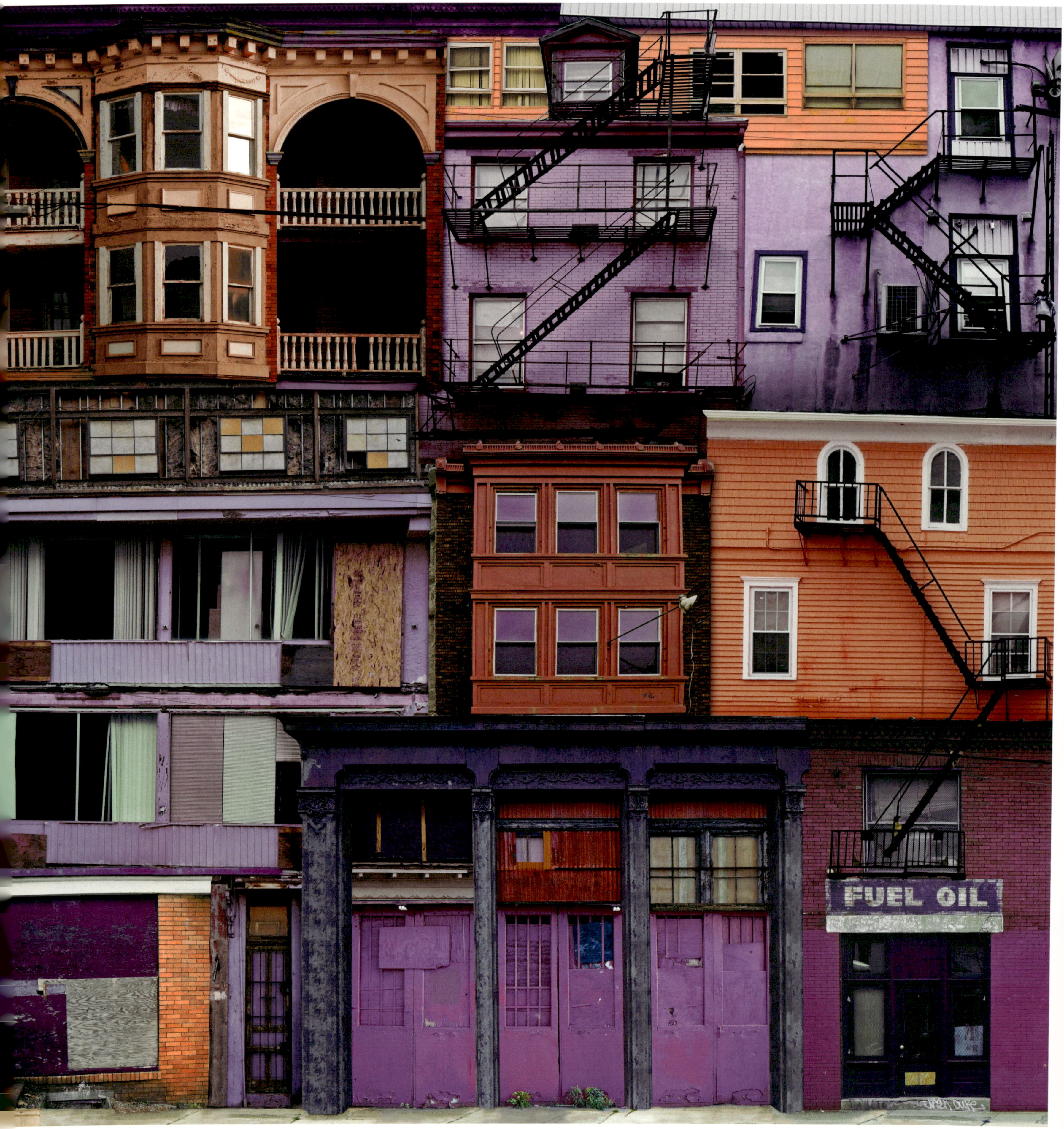
FUEL OIL

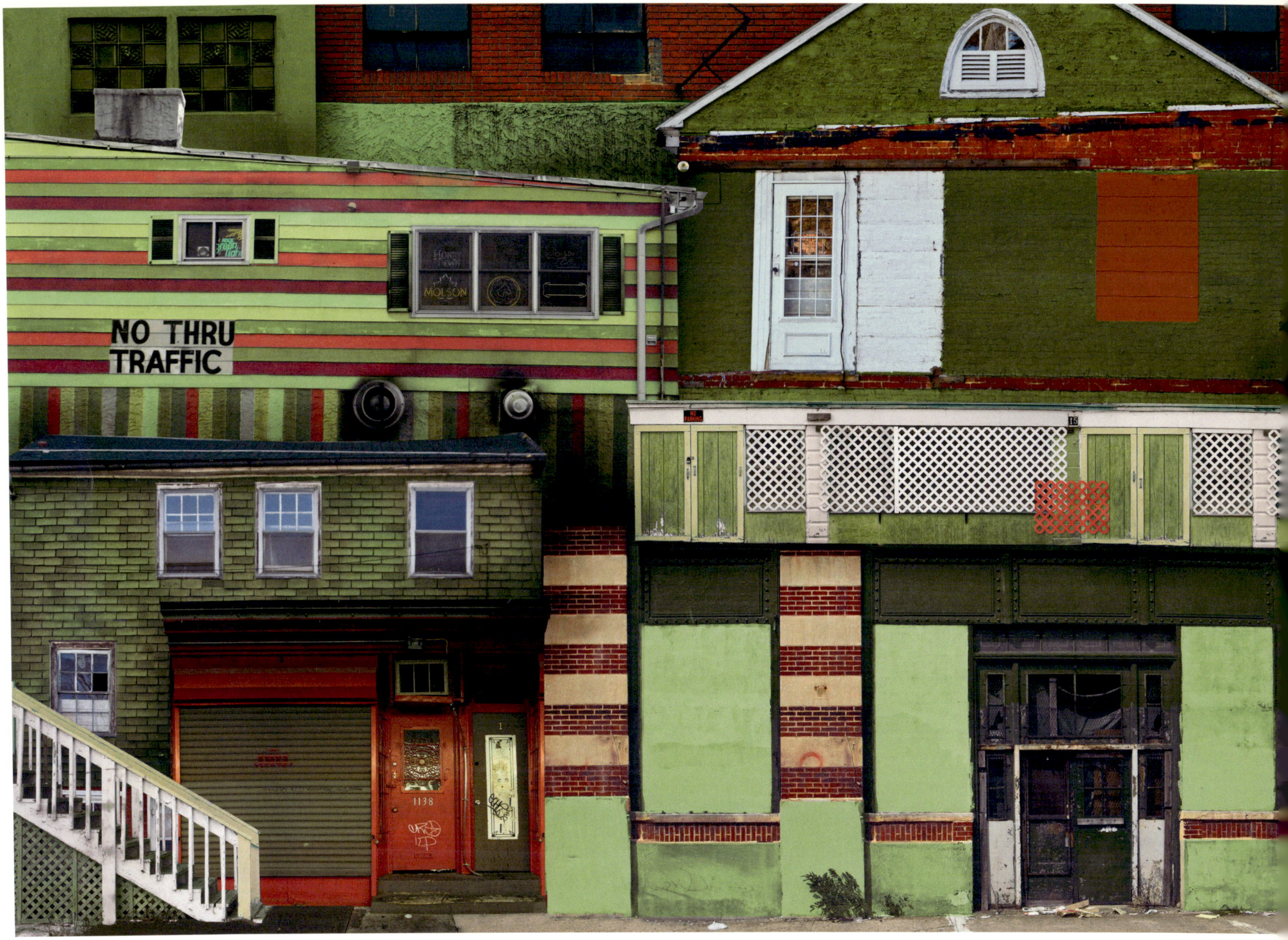

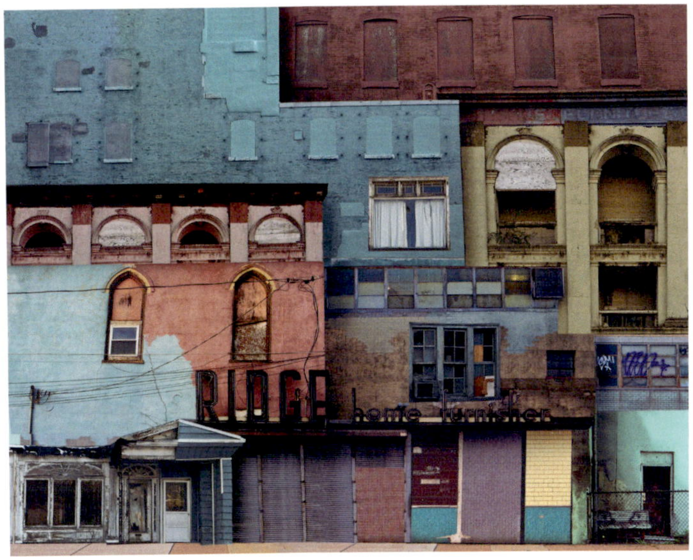

Laura S. Kicey

CONSTRUCT

The Construct series are images of places that do not exist. Their composite parts are the culmination of the ongoing photo-explorations of the artist. Using these photographic pieces, collected over three years, she blends together the intricate details of doors, bricks, peeling paint and mortar and gives them new colour and a place of their own.

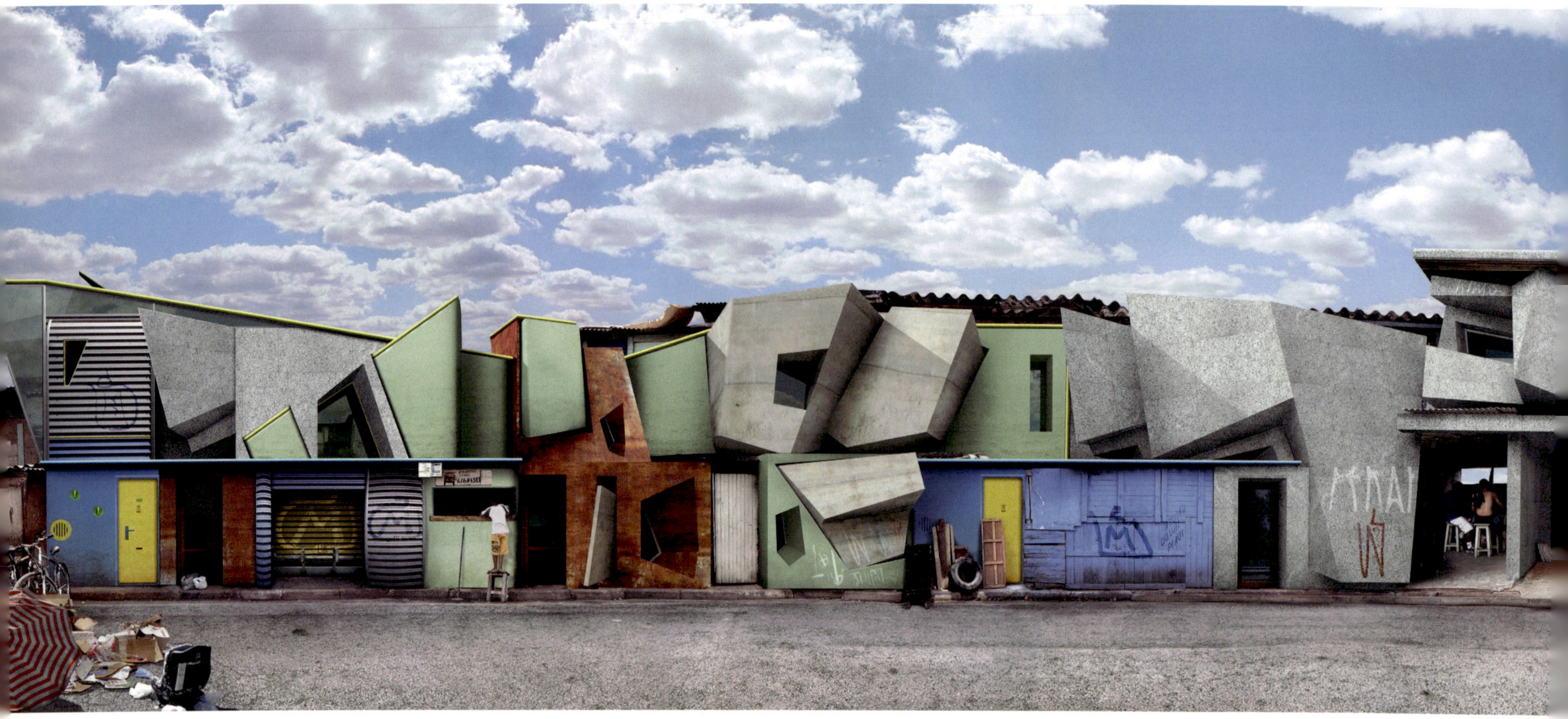

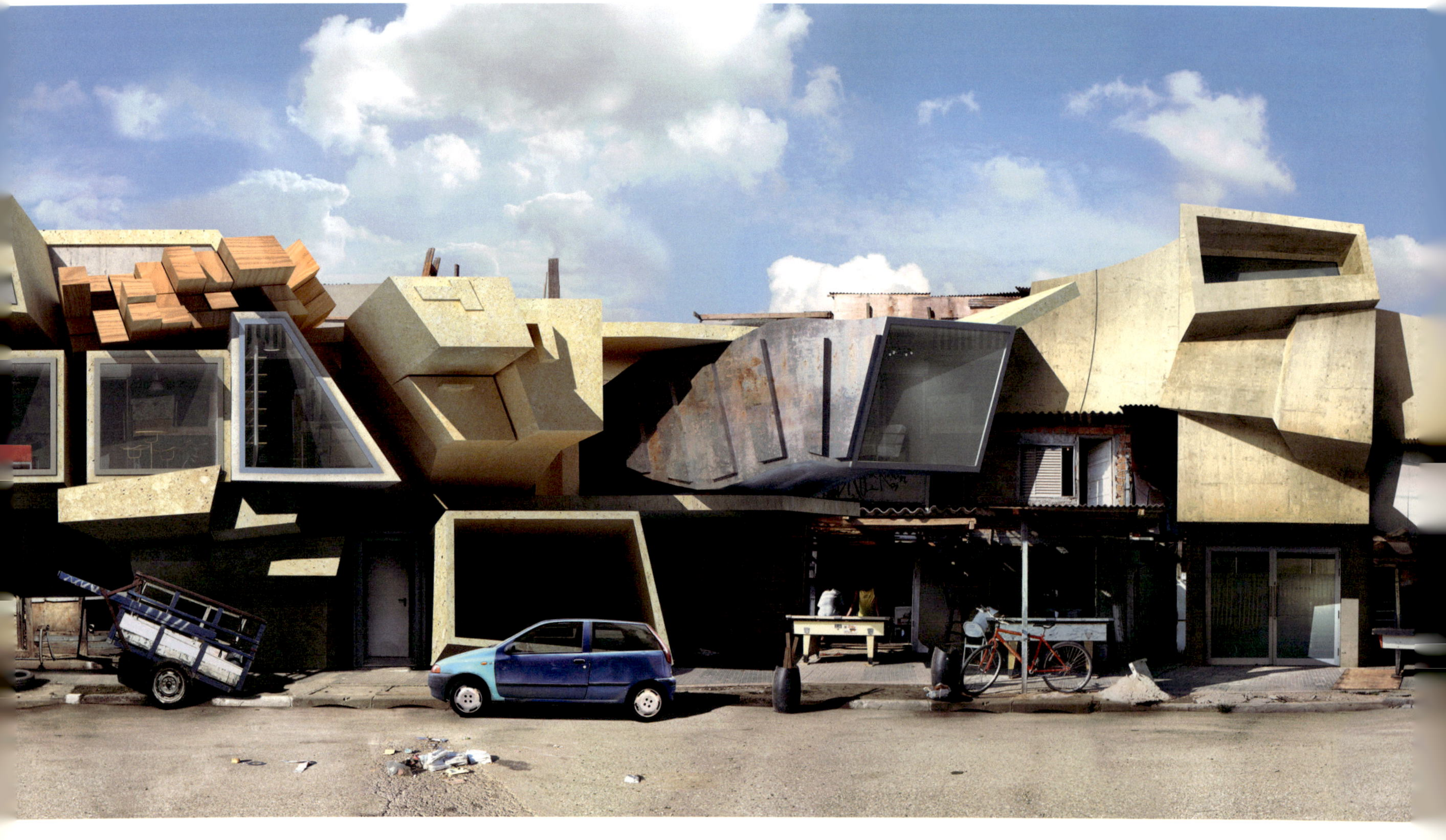

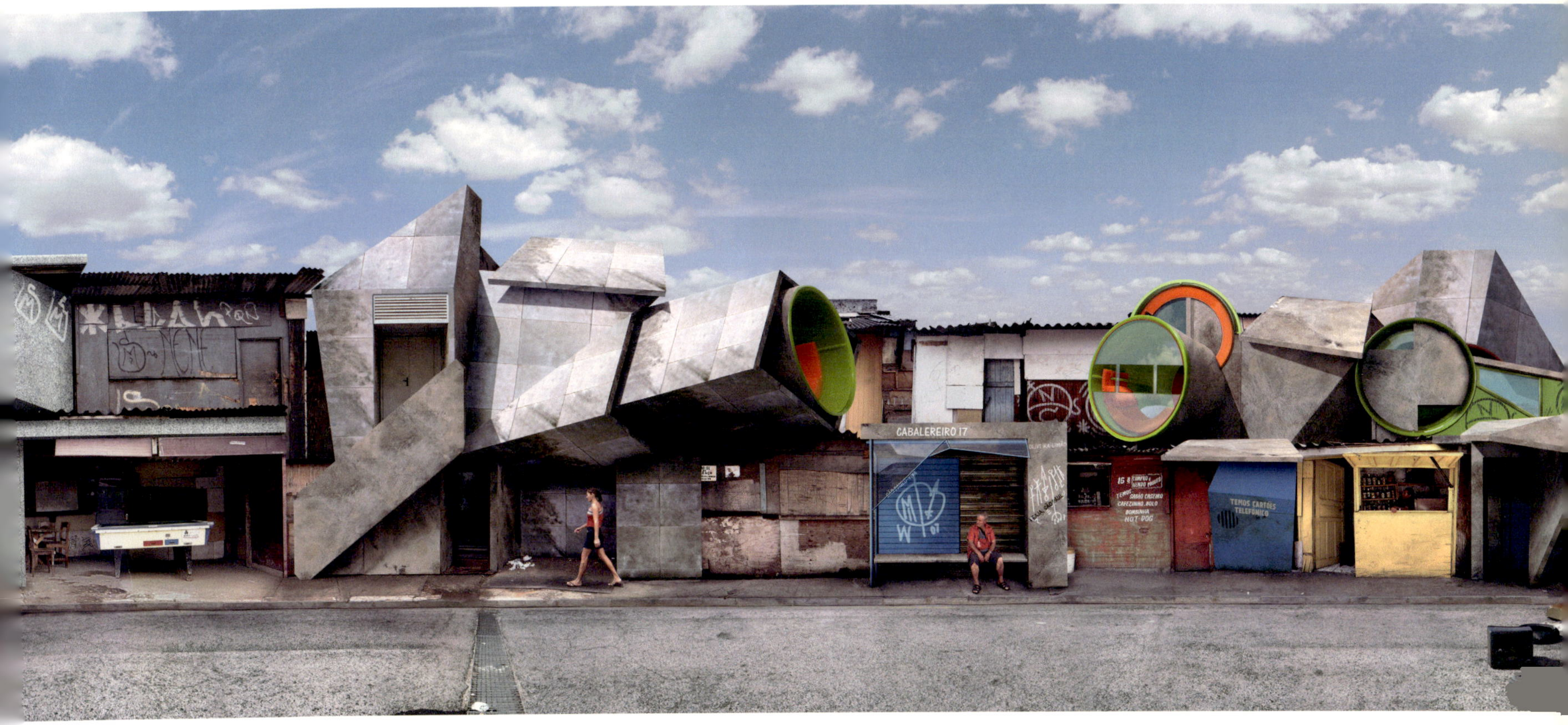

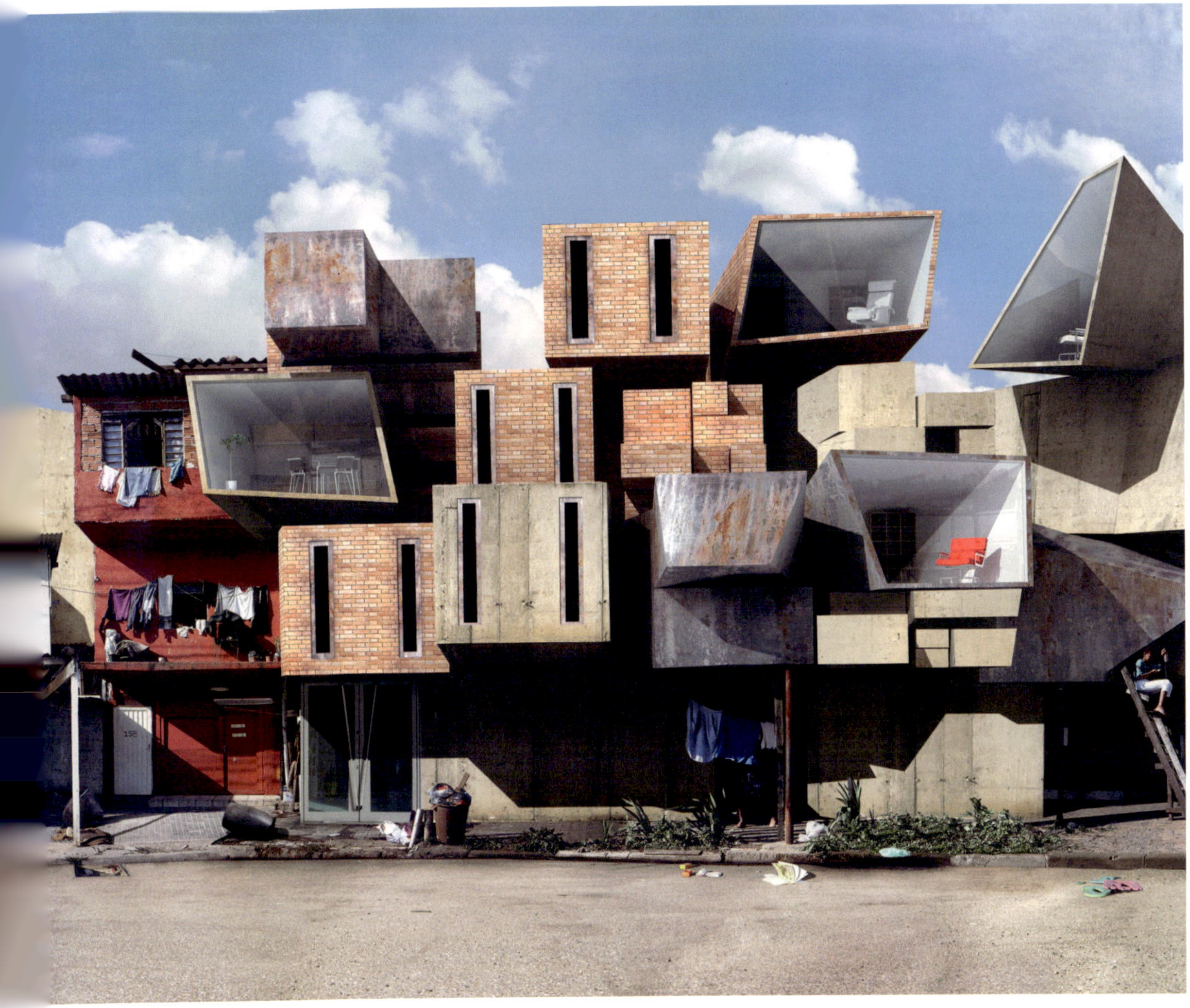

Dionisio González

NOVA IPIRANGA *(top)*
NOVA ACQUA GASOSA *(bottom)*

This series is the continuation of the project Arquitetura da sobra: A cidade subexposta, and is the result of several years of work traveling throughout the internal world of the shantytowns of São Paulo and Río de Janeiro.

After an exhaustive and exacting study of these massive unregulated settlements, the artist proposes a partial intervention in these chaotic spaces. Dionisio González proposes a radical restructuring of their constructural approach, improving precarious conditions of habitability.

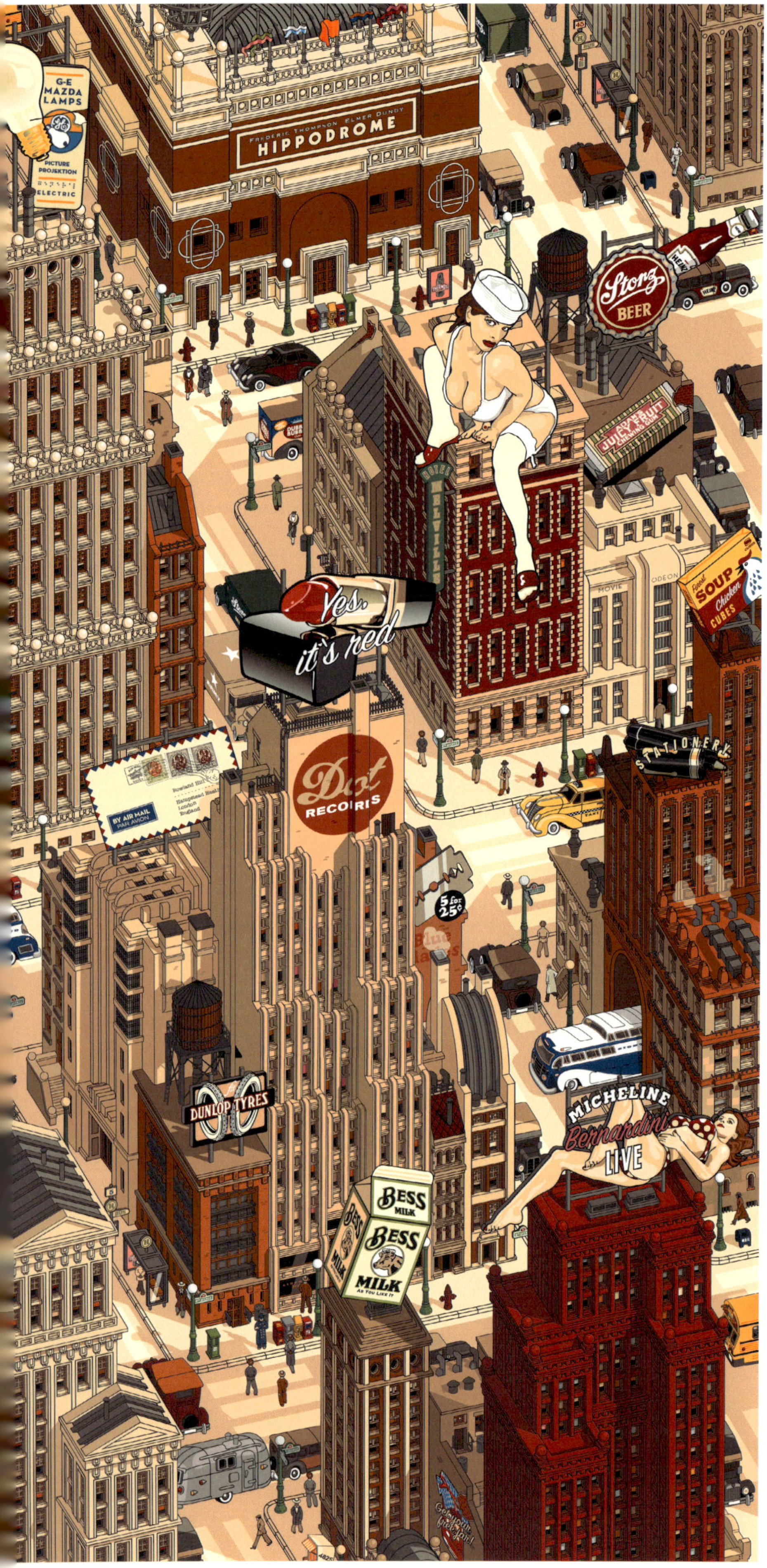

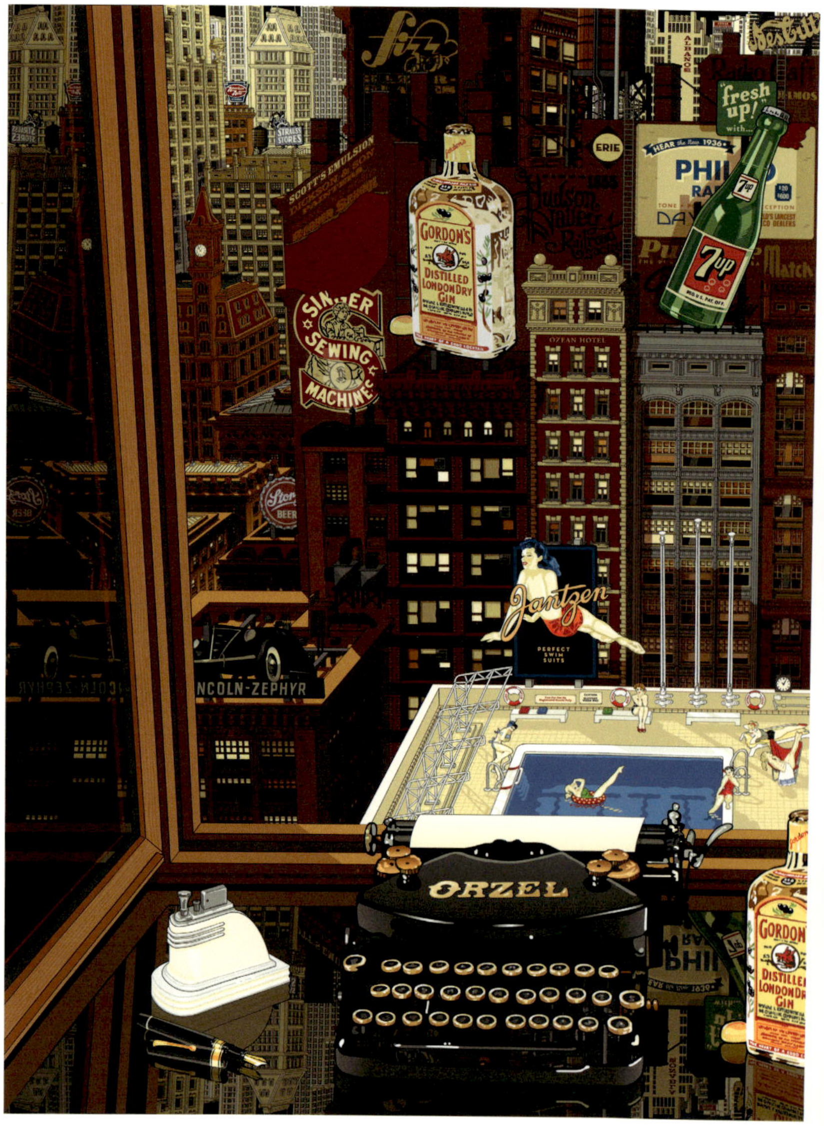

Apfel Zet

ANCIENT CITIES OF TOMORROW

The idea of this fictous city is a complet departure from the classic modernist visions of town planning of the 1920s until the 1970s: very tight, a lot of ornaments and details, very diverse styles – no invention of something new but quoting a lot of role models like Schinkel, Sullivan, Ferris, Hood, Dundy & Thompson.

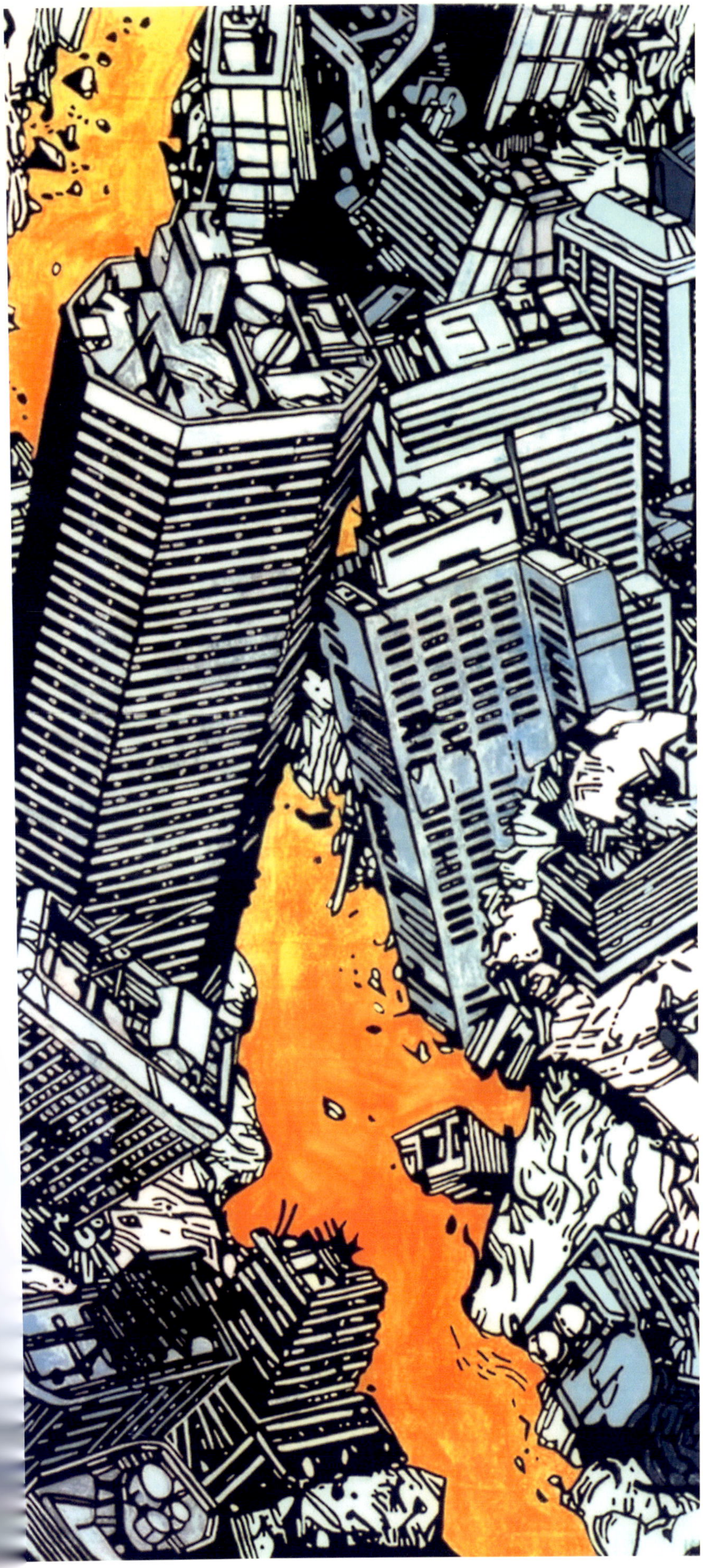

Alekos Hofstetter

ORANGE FLUSS
SPRECHBLASEN
TSUNAMI

The paintings and drawings of the Berlin painter Alekos Hofstetter use preexisting material as a primary source. The artist subjects his graphic material to an intricate process of disassembly in order to (re-)construct a single, unifying, synthetic, and universal reality. He works with background settings derived from comic books, architecture, philosophy or the international financial markets.

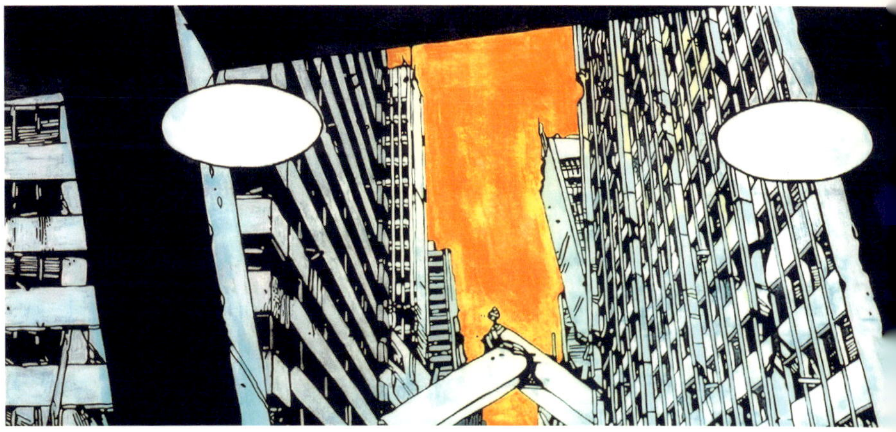

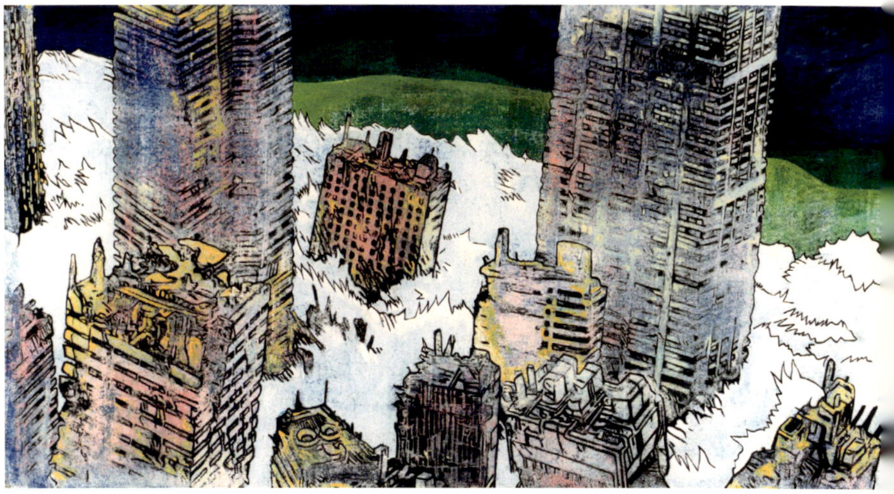

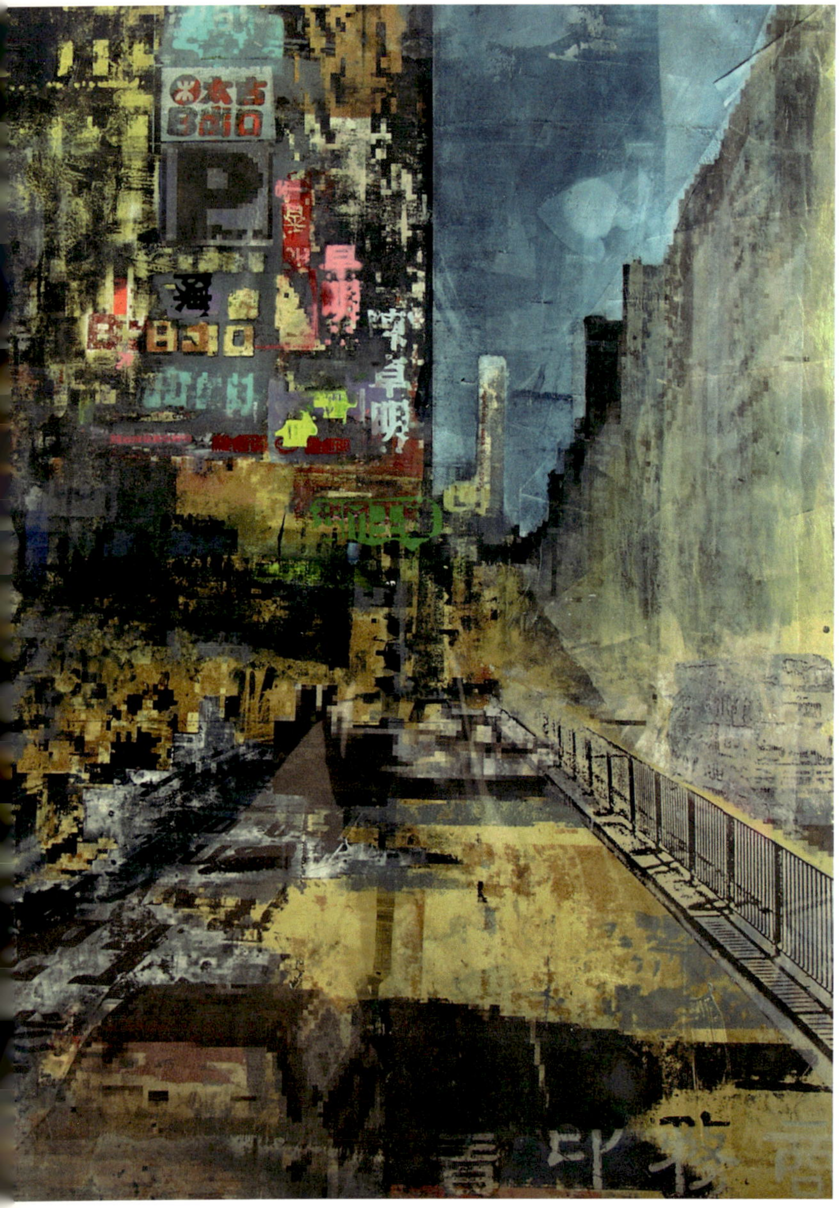

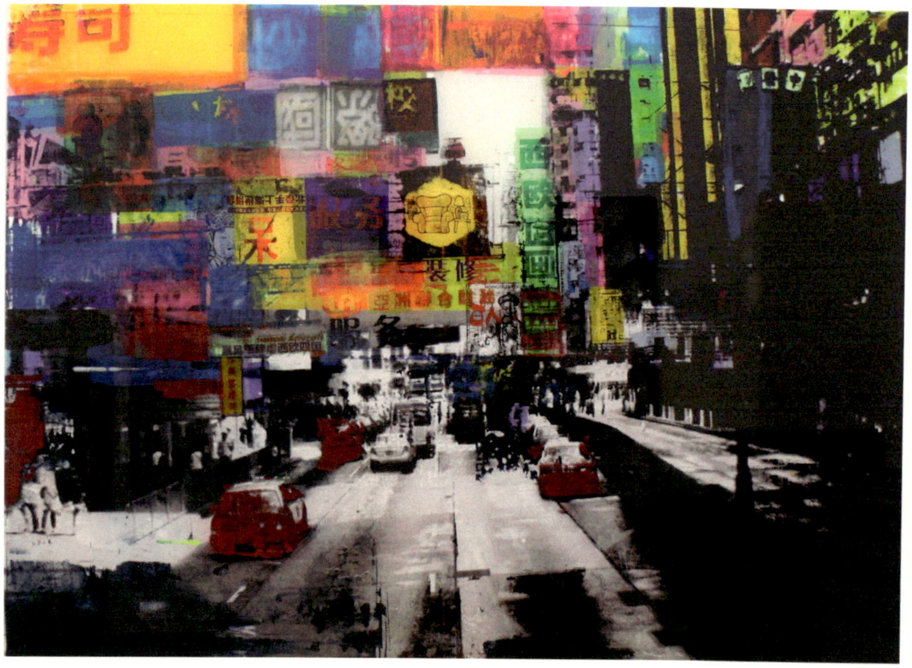

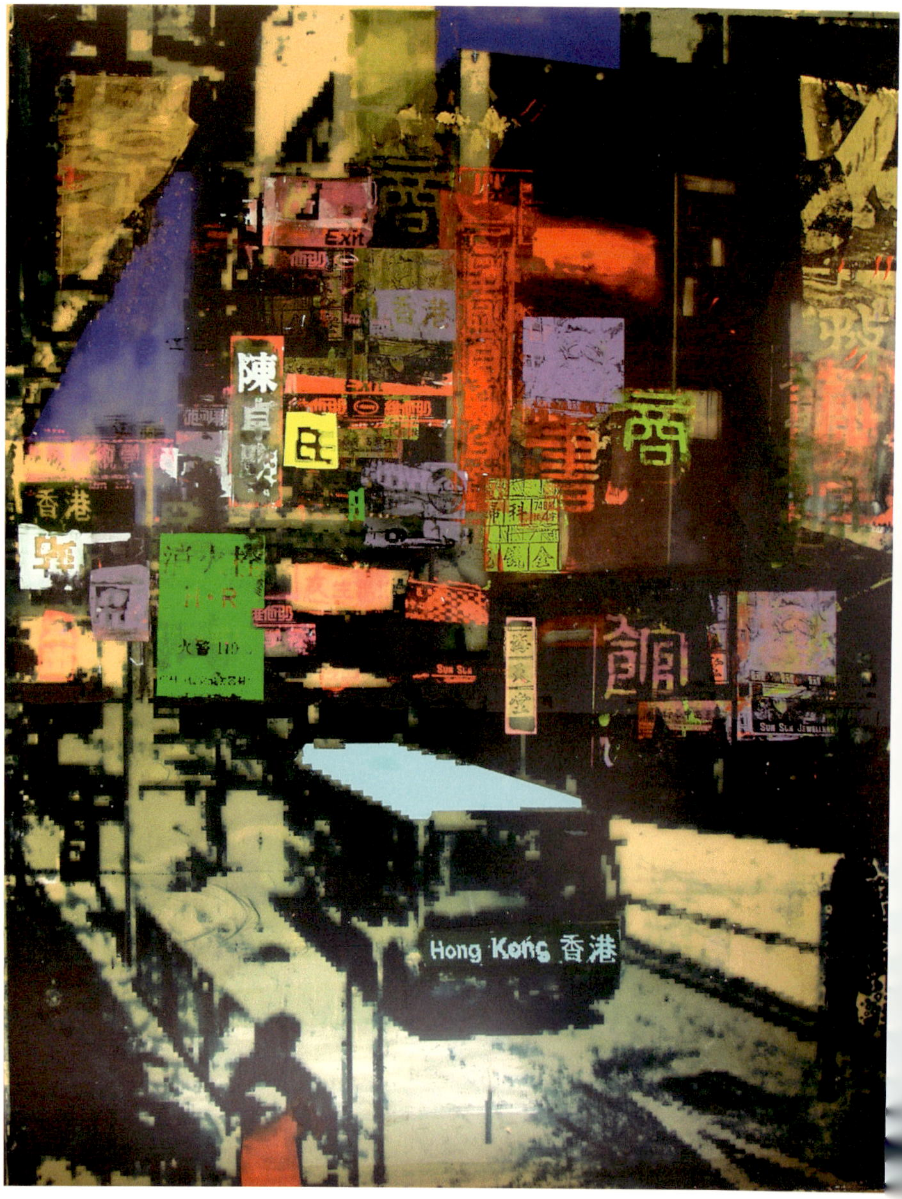

Sandra Rauch

The formally radical works of Sandra Rauch show the perception of living spaces and their effect on people. The "photomechanical light technology" procedure developed by Sandra Rauch allows a concentrated, compressed insight into an environment shaped by humanity.

HONG *(top)*
SUPERSTAR *(top, right)*
HONG KONG *(right)*
UNTITLED *(right page)*

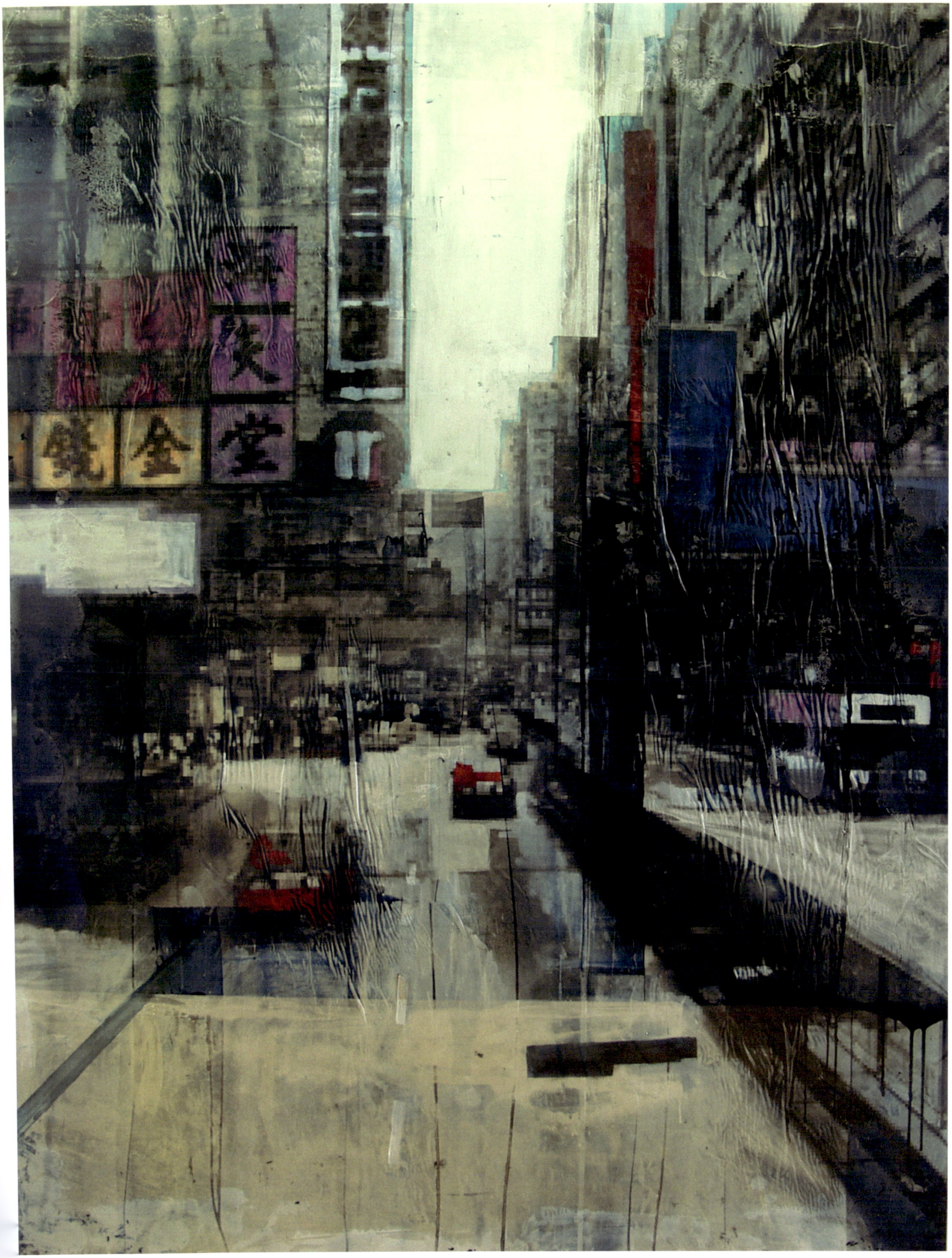
金
堂

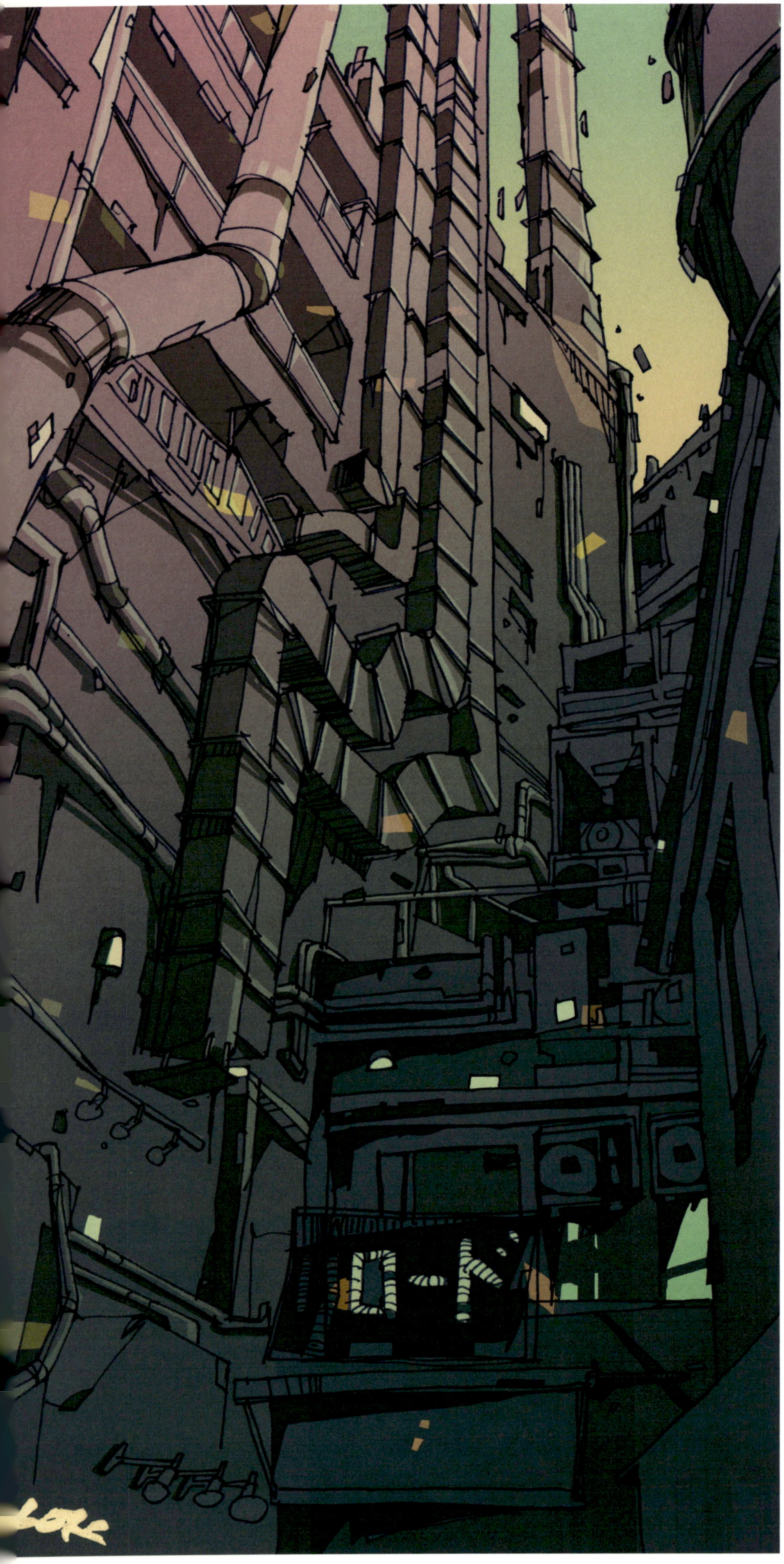

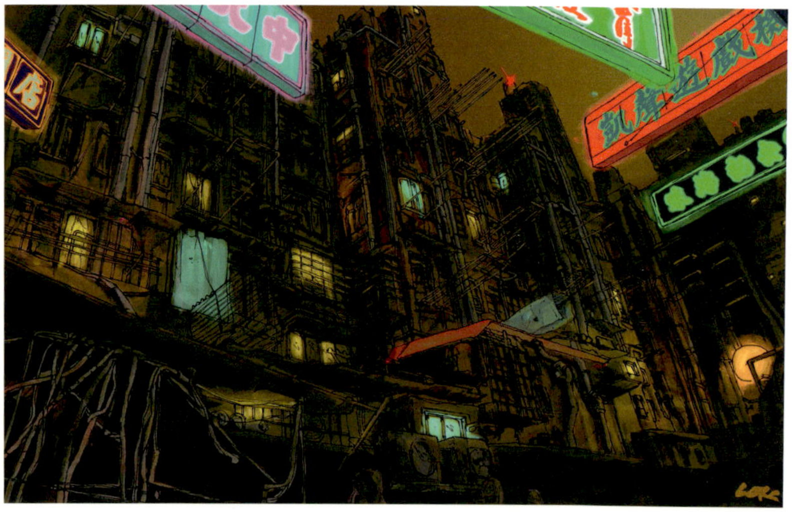

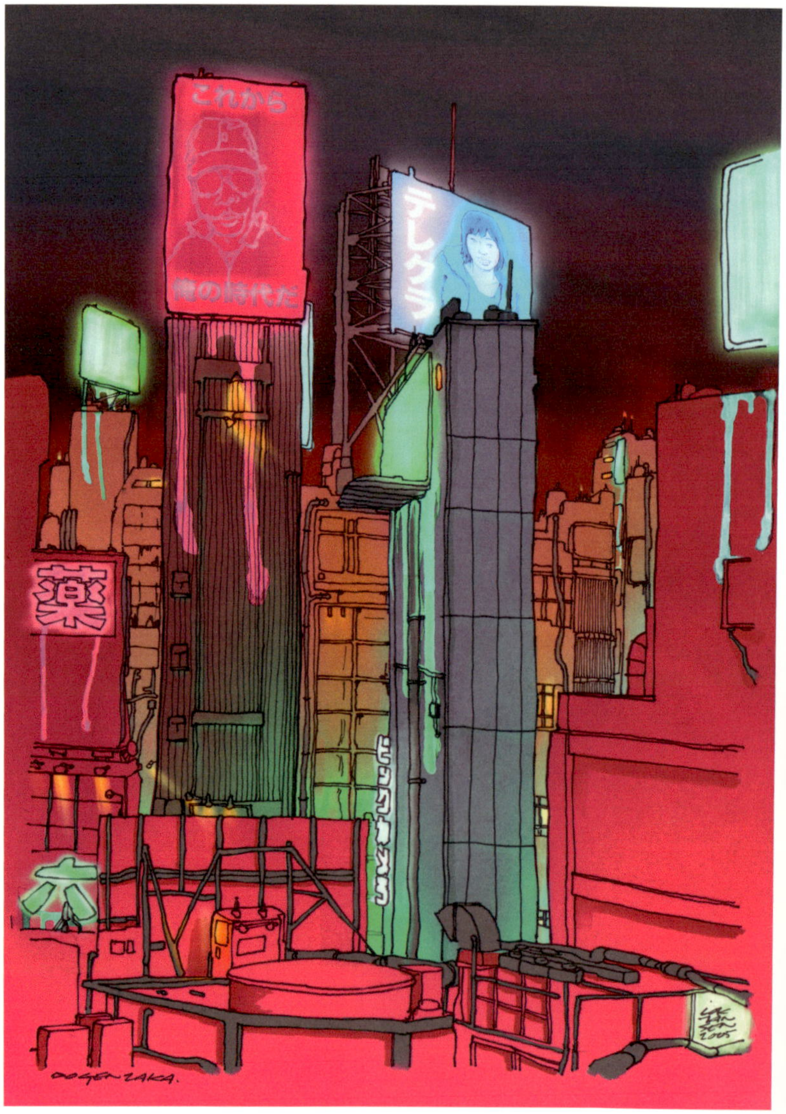

Lok Jansen

CITYSCAPES

This series of illustrations by Tokyo-based artist Lok Jansen is inspired by the city's seemingly wild, organic and extremely diverse look.

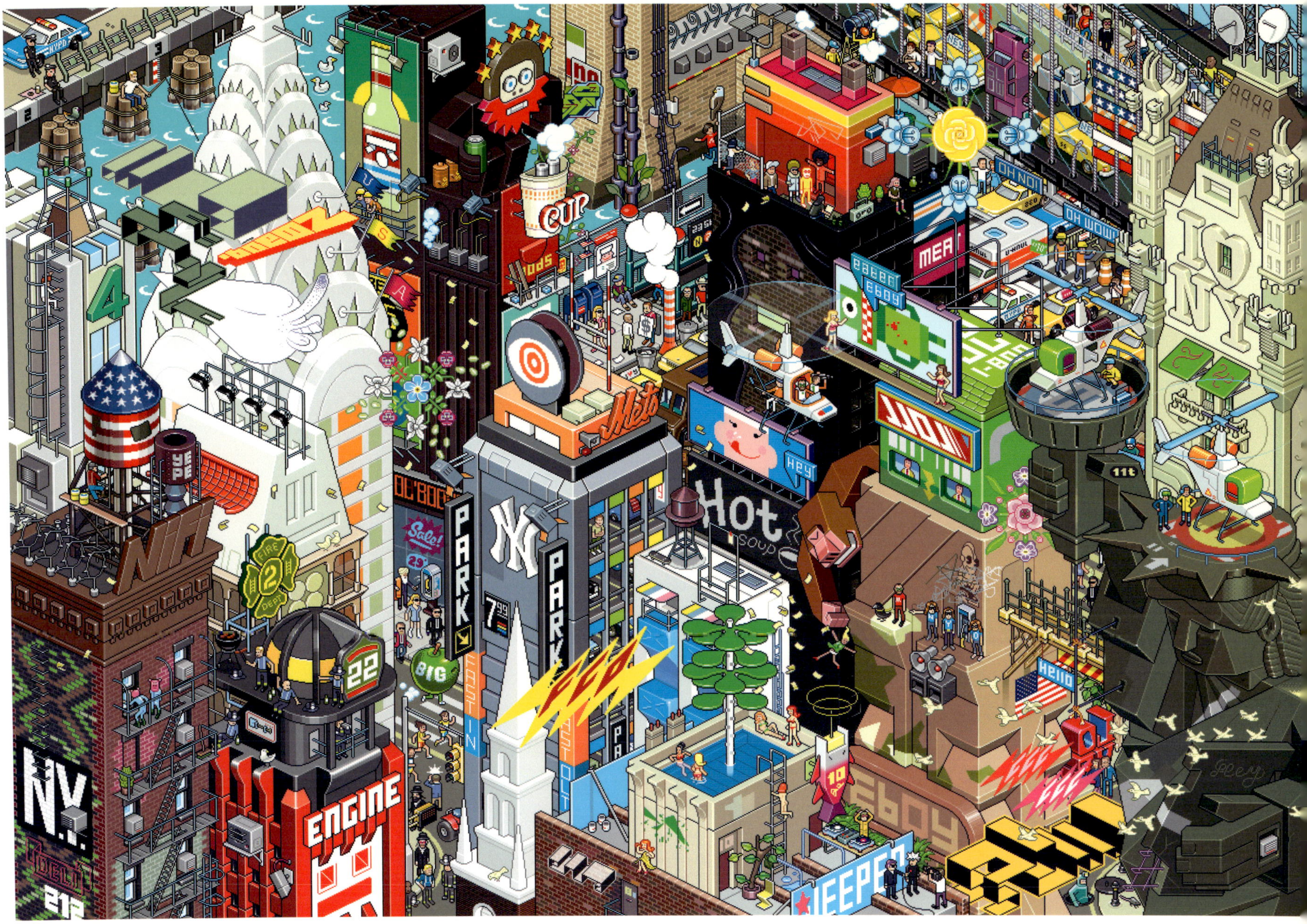

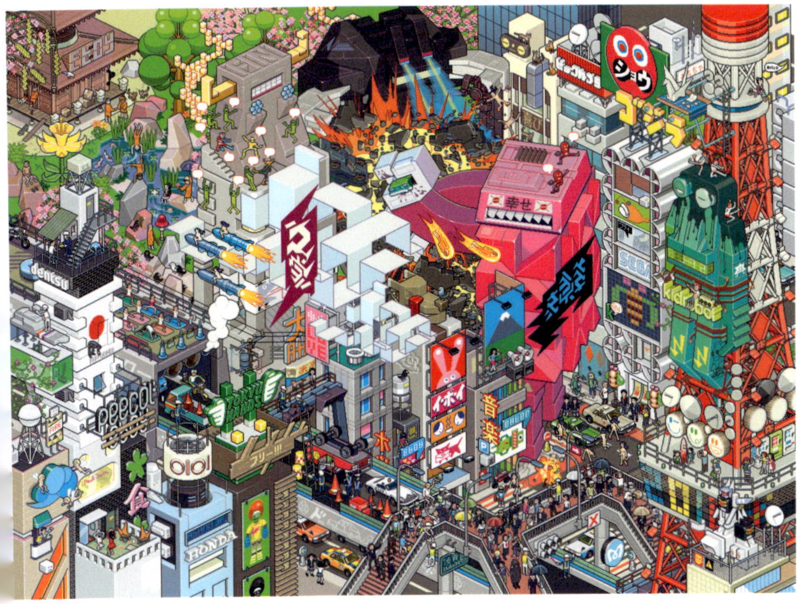

eBoy

NEW YORK *(top)*, TOKYO *(bottom)*

The eBoy collective, Steffen Sauerteig, Svend Smital and Kai Vermehr, creates re-usable pixel objects and deploys them to build complex and extensible artworks. The liveliness, density and variety of the urban environment is reflected in their famous eCity series.

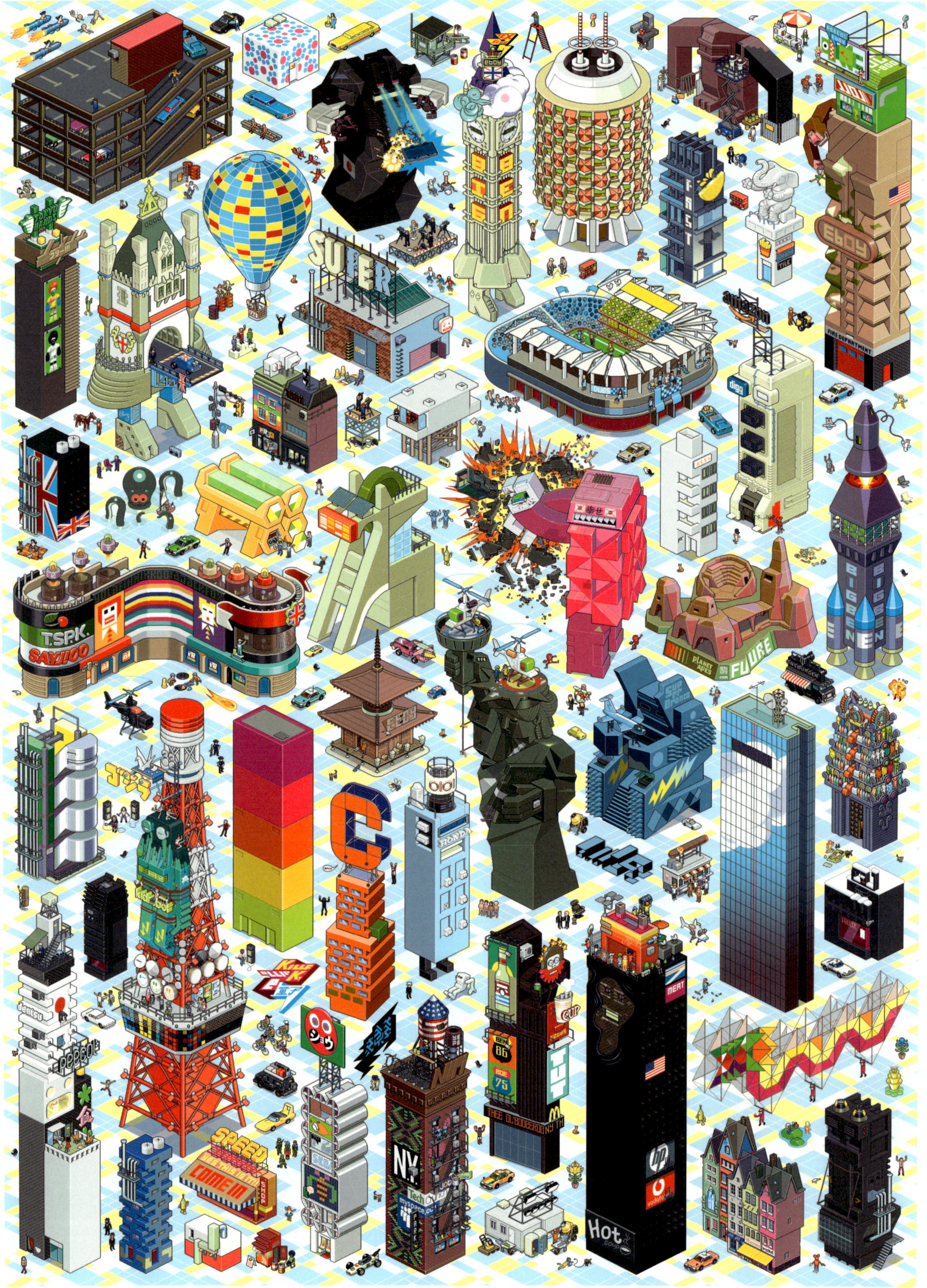

eBoy

PARTS POSTER

Mathilde Nivet

PATCH ALPHABET

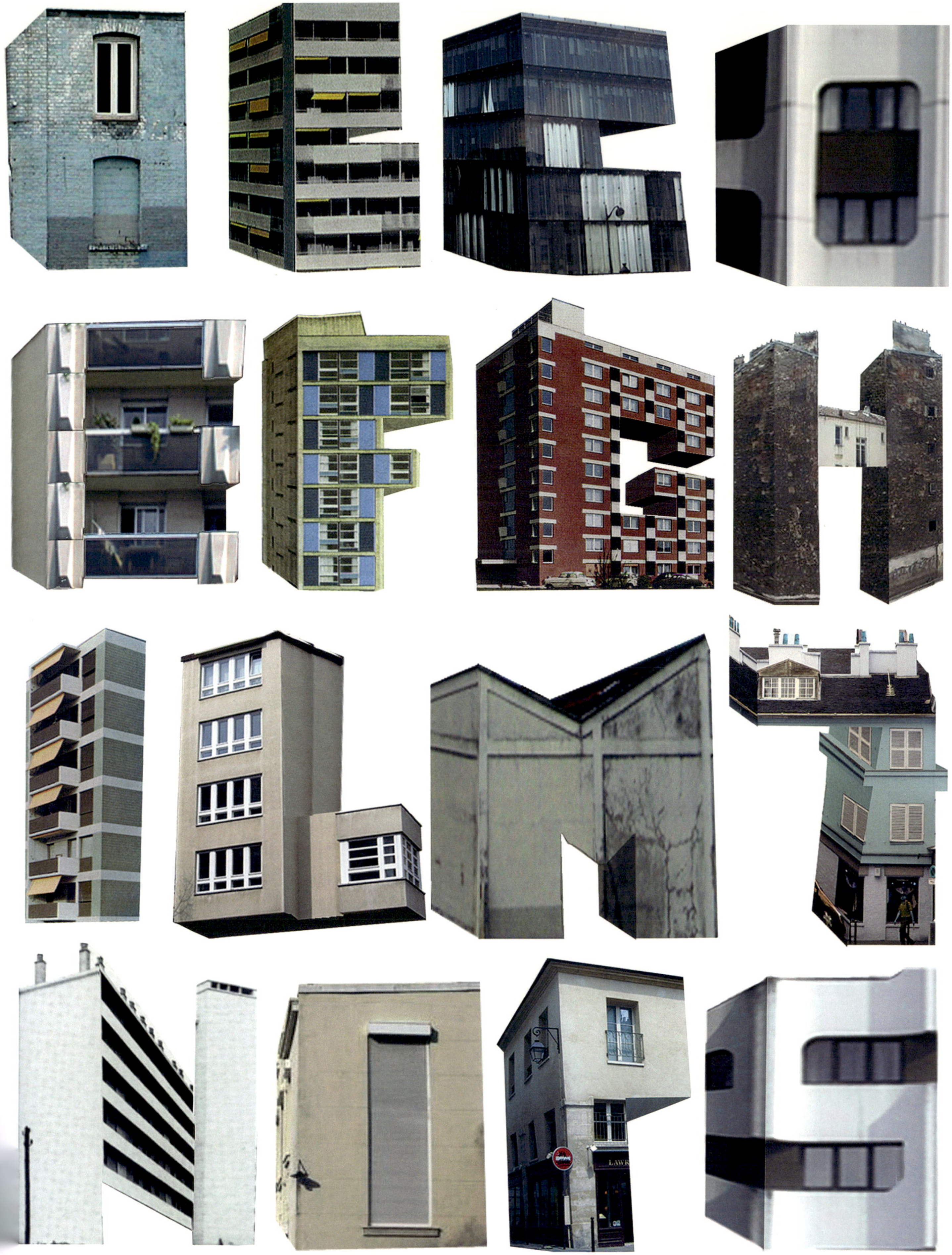

Evol / Ct'ink

CORRIDOR IN THE FLAMINGOBEACH LOTEL

Evol was invited, with many other artists, to design a room as part of the temporary Flamingo Beach Lotel project in Berlin, Neukölln. His installation transforms an ordinary apartment corridor into a deserted high-rise housing development at nighttime.

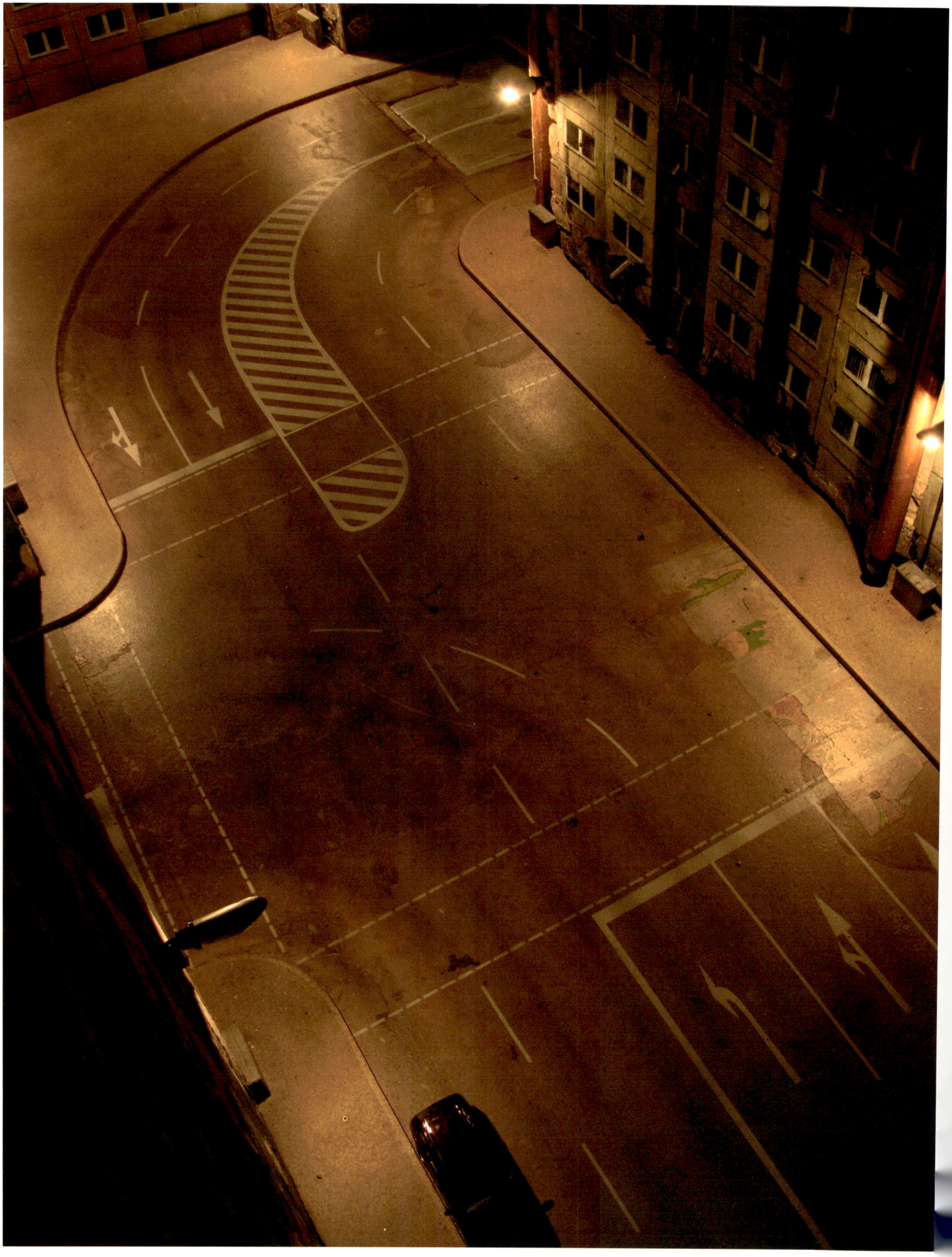

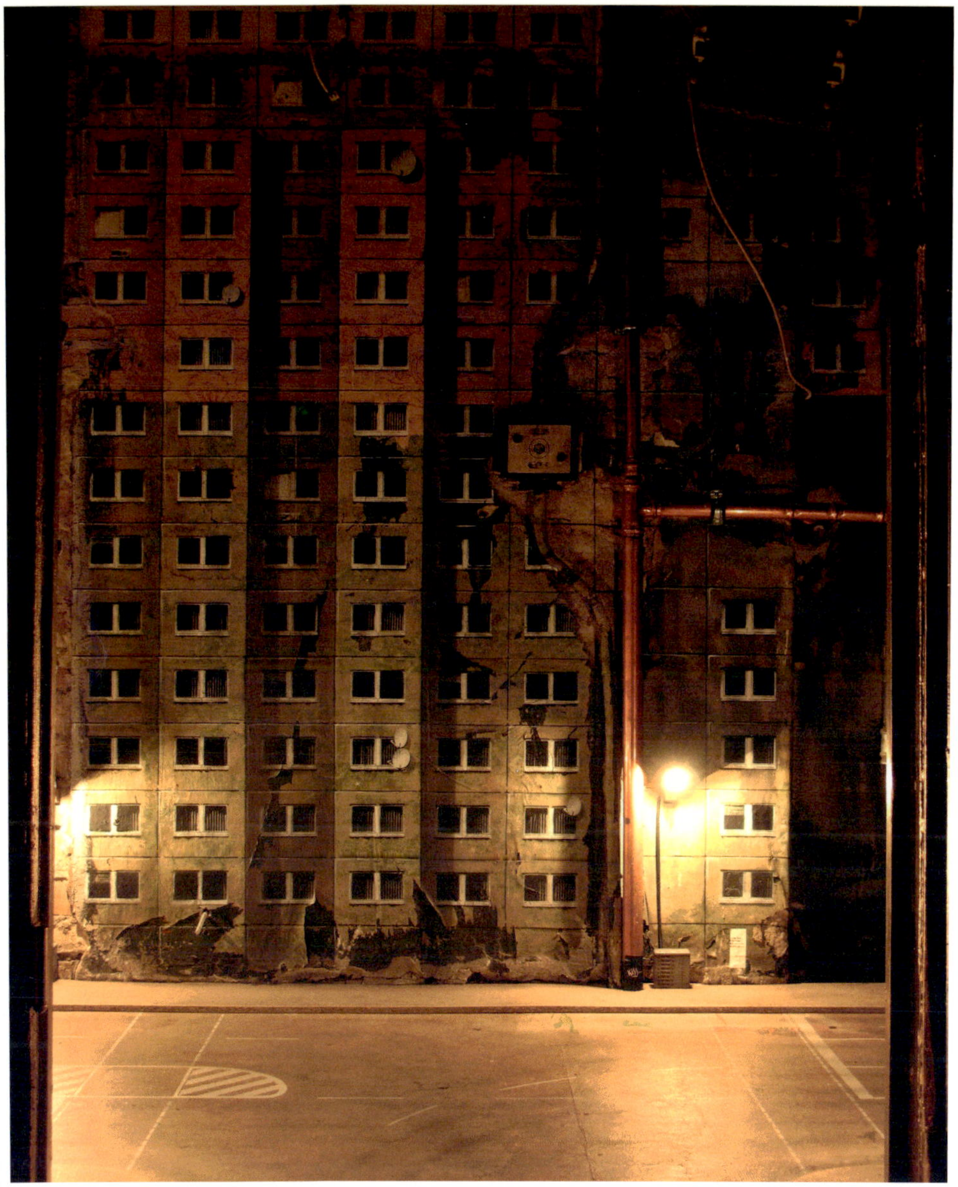

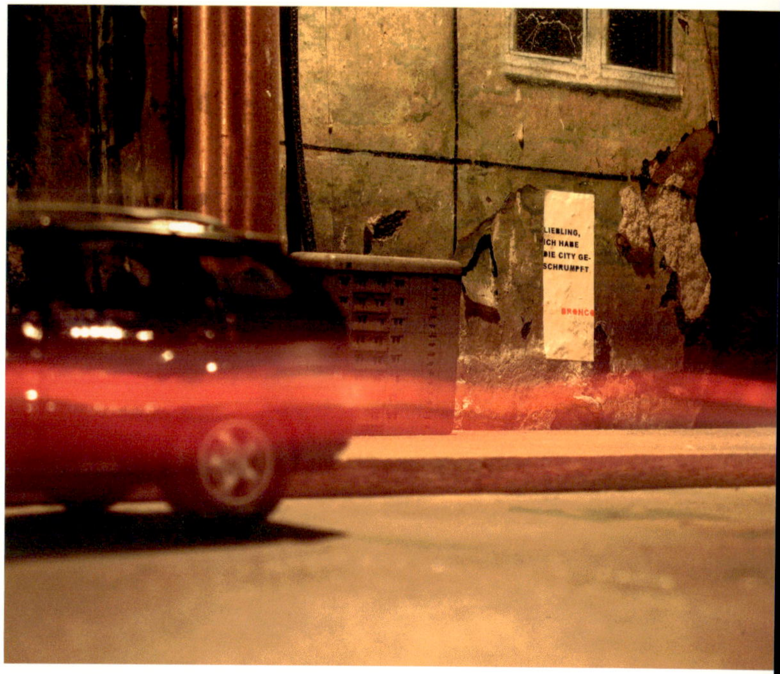
LIEBLING,
ICH HABE
DIE CITY GE-
SCHRUMPFT

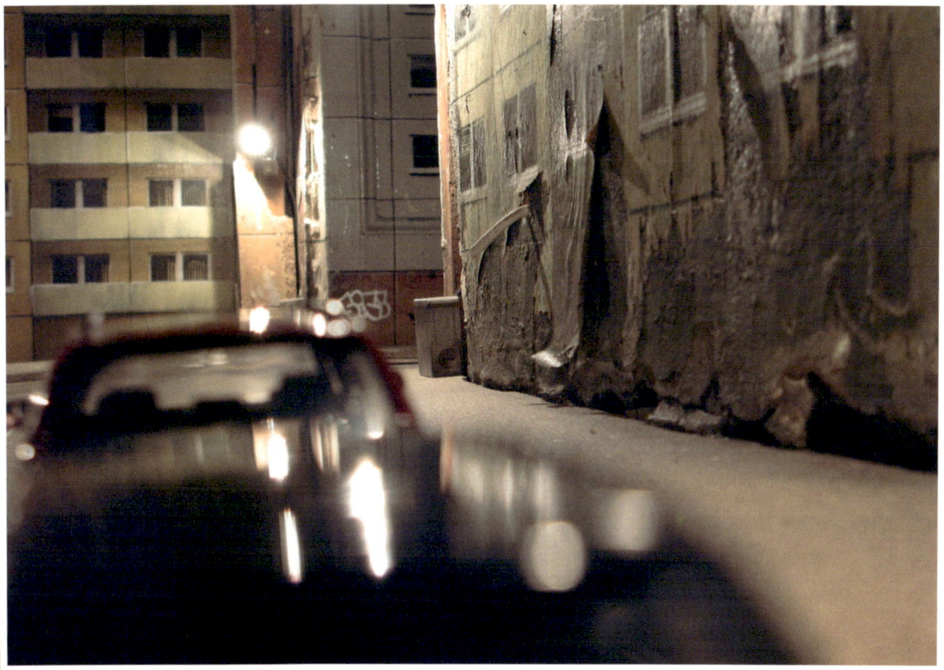

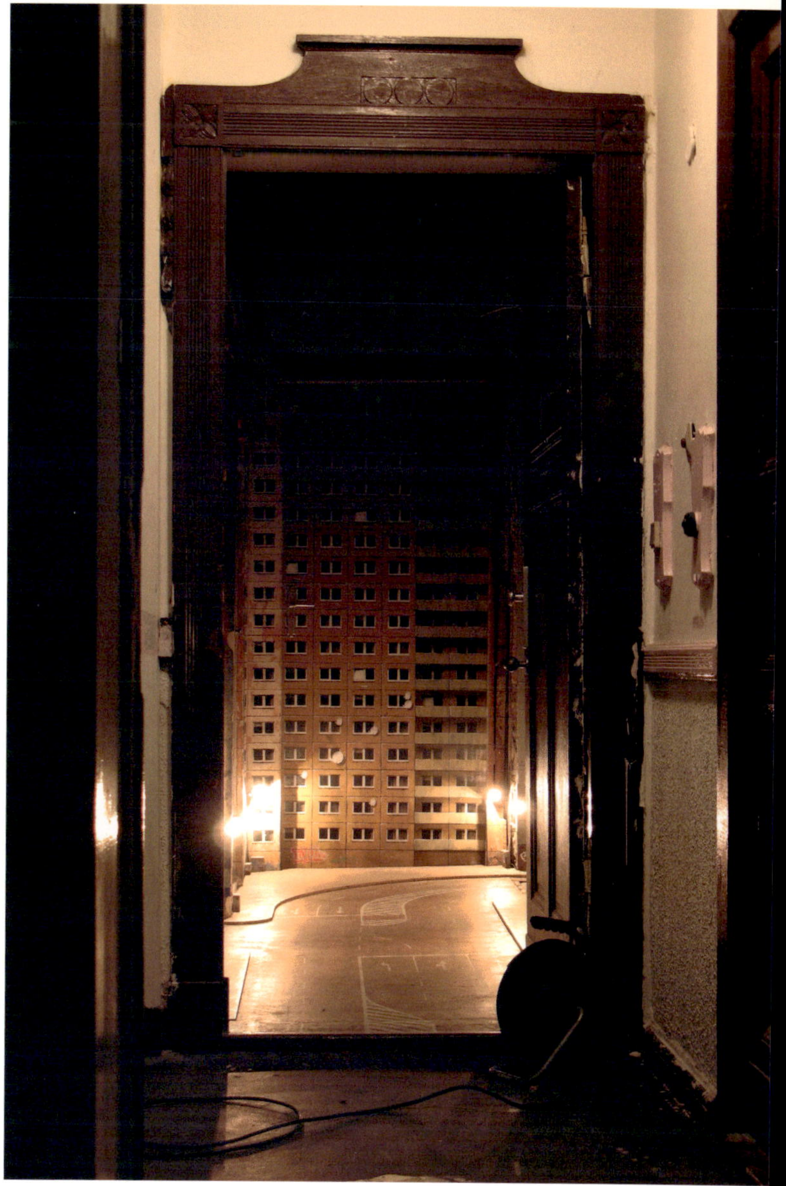

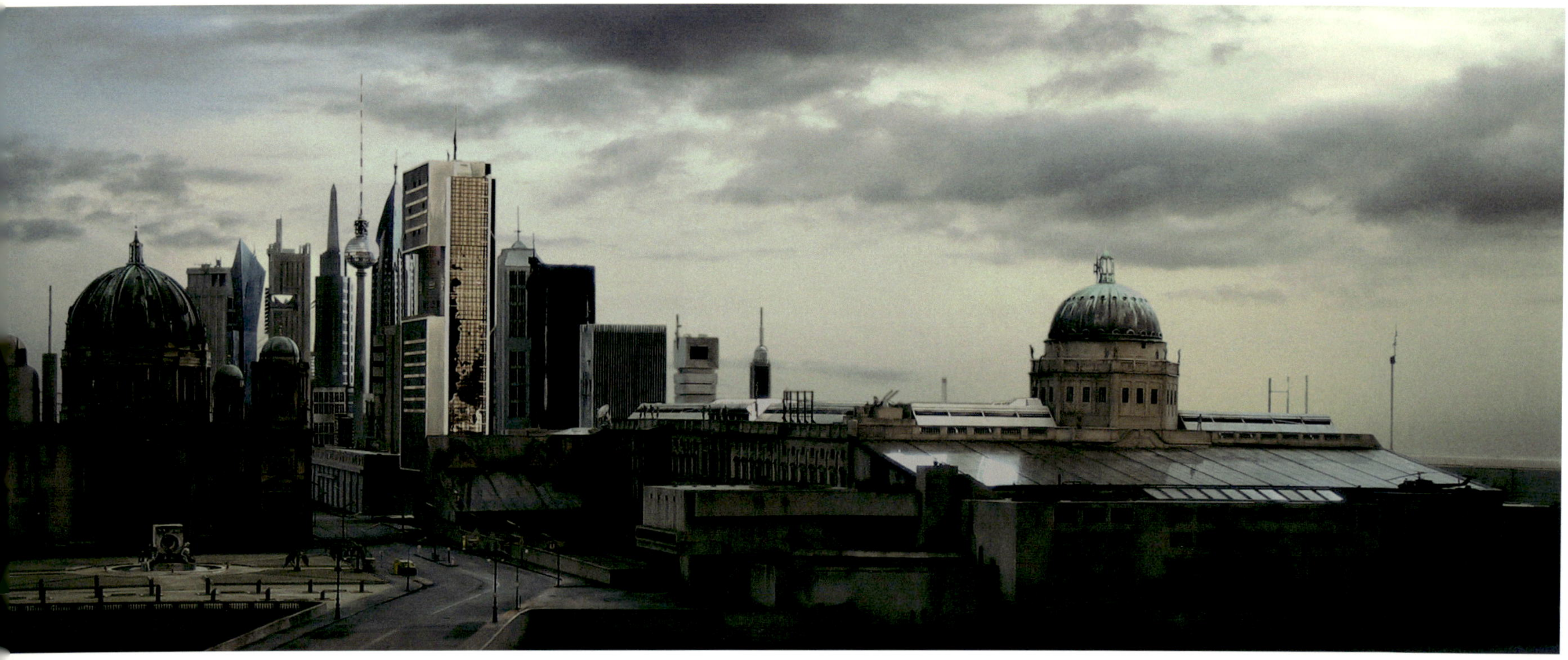

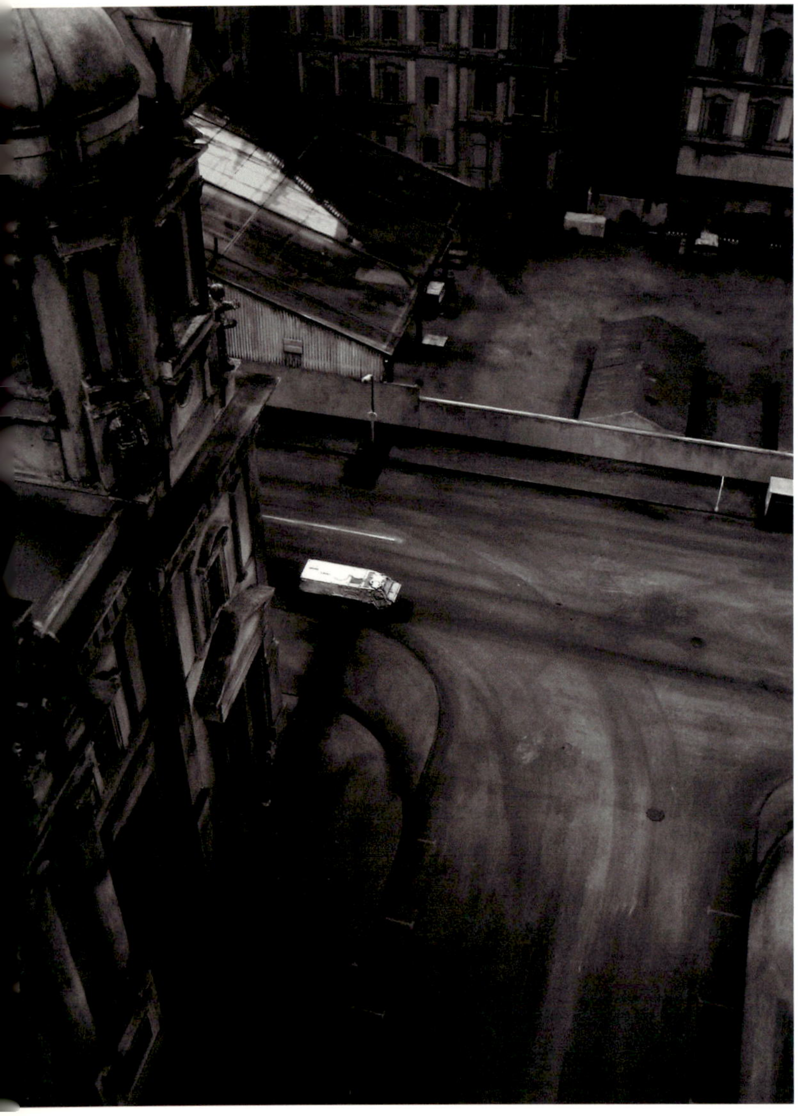

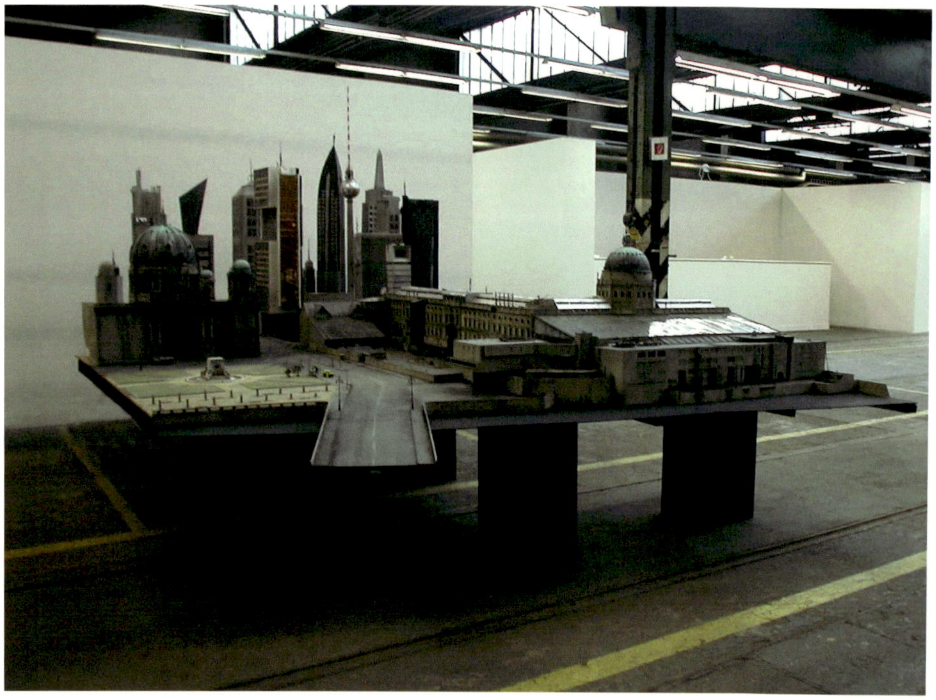

J. Michael Birn

A QUESTION OF LUST –
THE BERLIN LUSTGARTEN A.D. 2057

Architect and director J. Michael Birn's utopian installation offers an ironic vision for Berlin's Lustgarten in the city's centre.

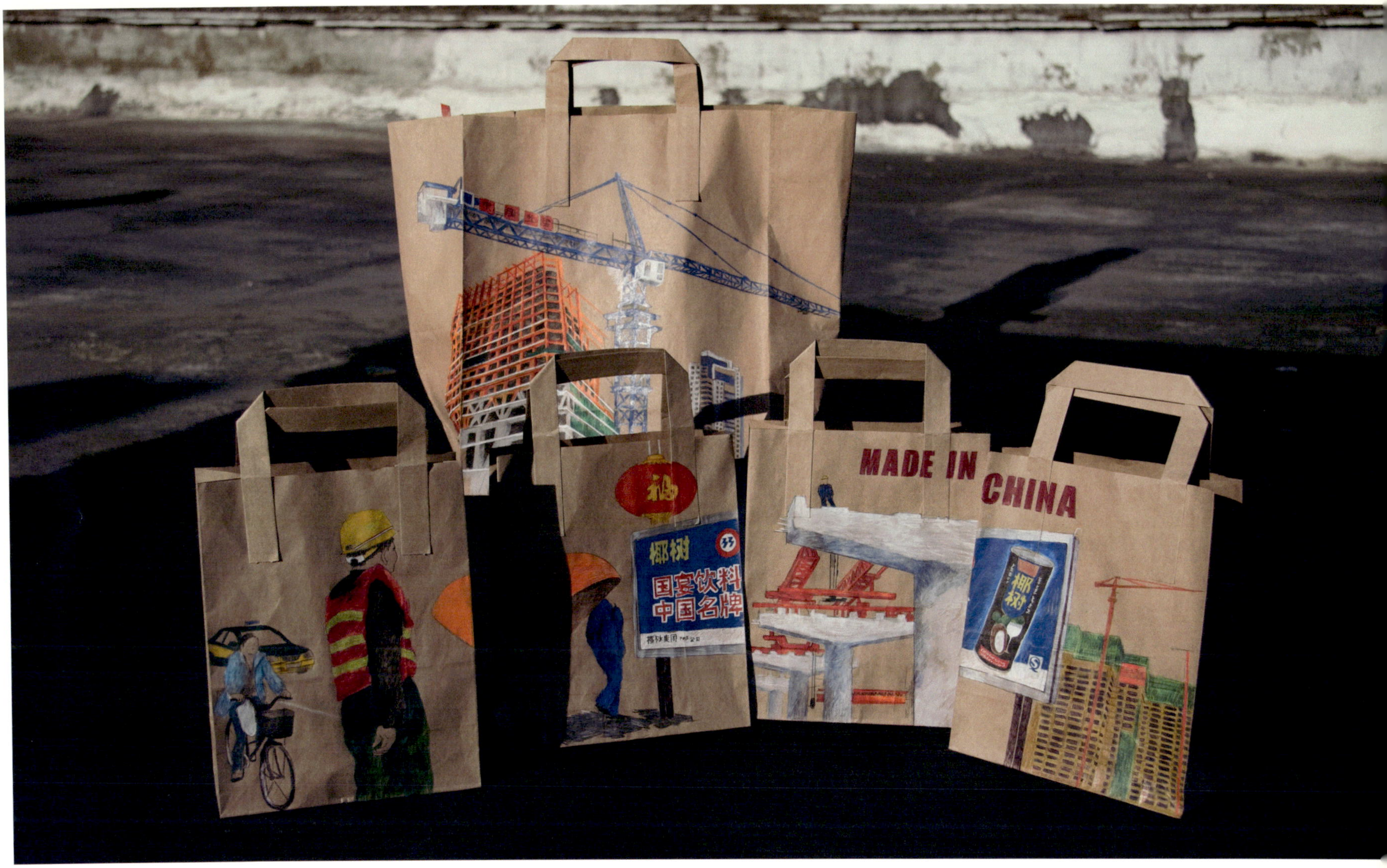

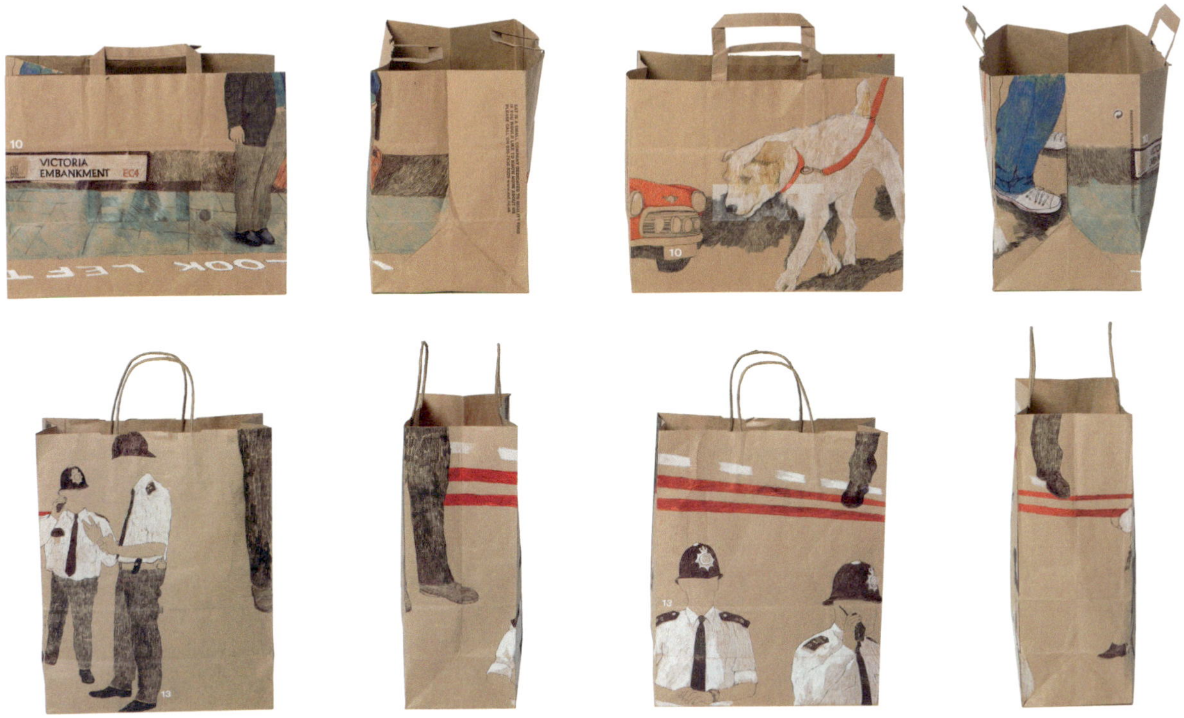

A B C D

Camille Rousseau

TRANSITION

Dealing with the preconception of this consumer icon, Rousseau took the surface of a carrier bag to capture a moment, taking the object as a passing reflection of the city. The ephemeral object becomes a witness of time and space.

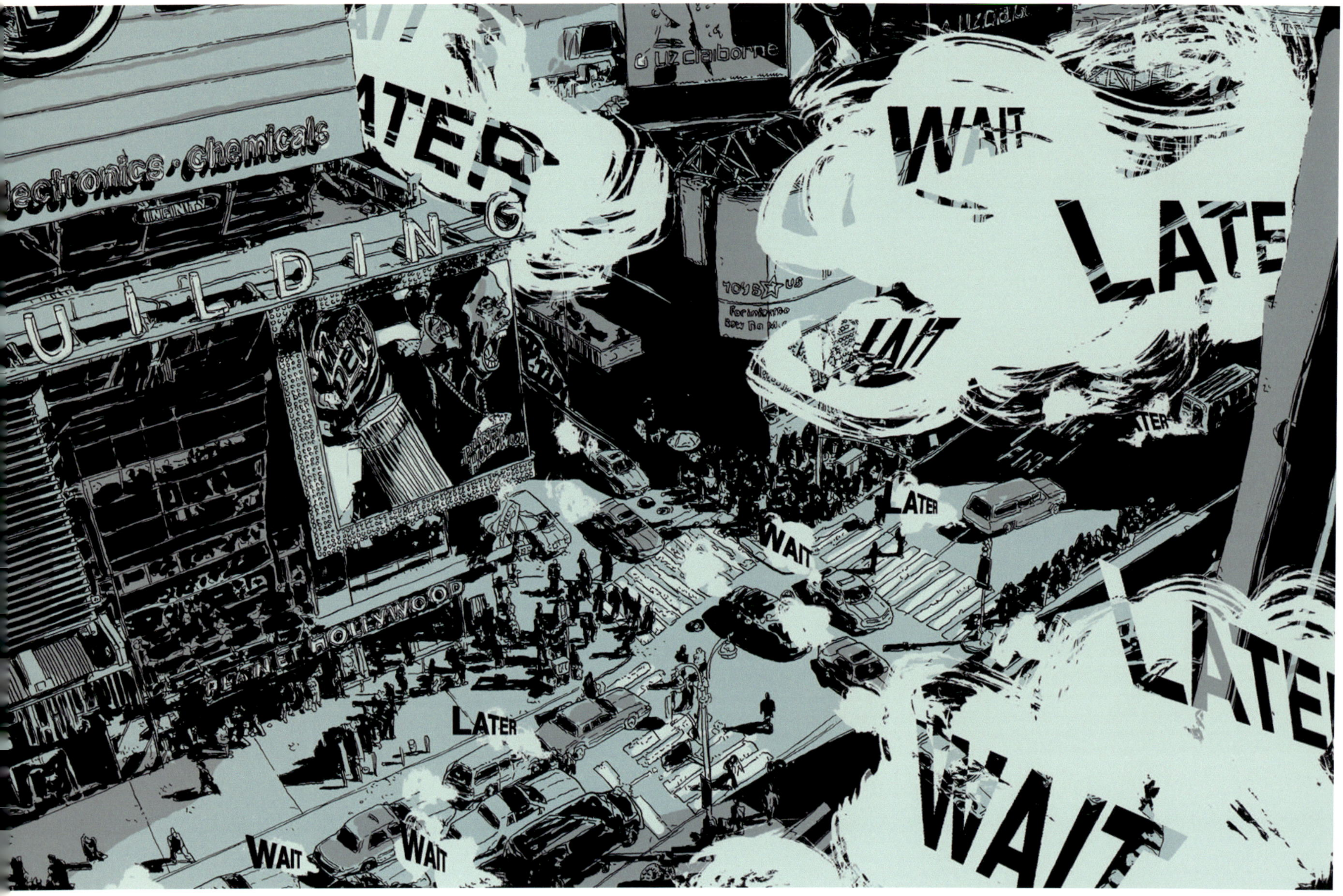

Jan Feindt

UNTITLED

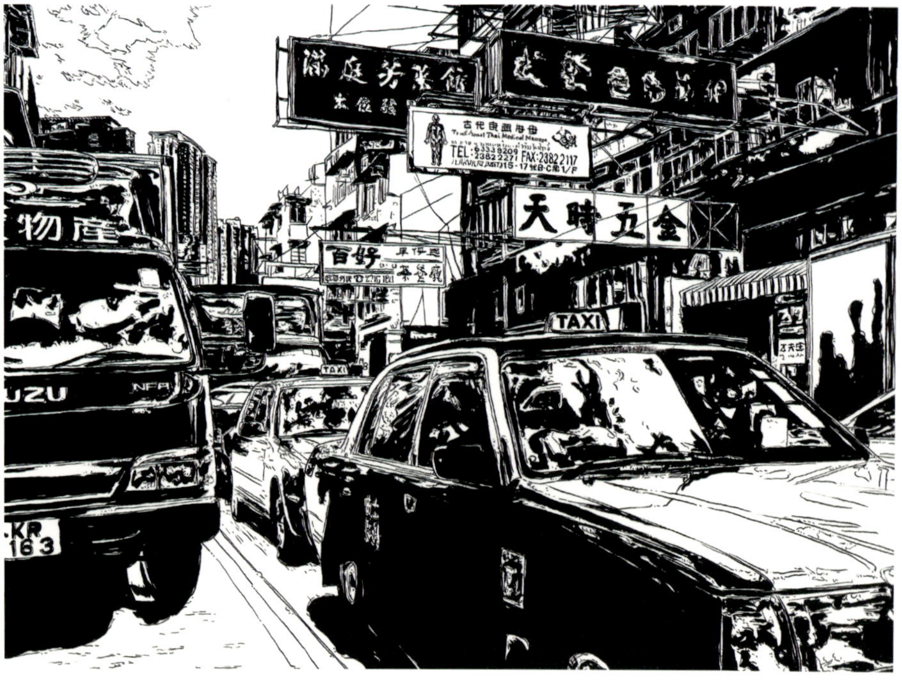

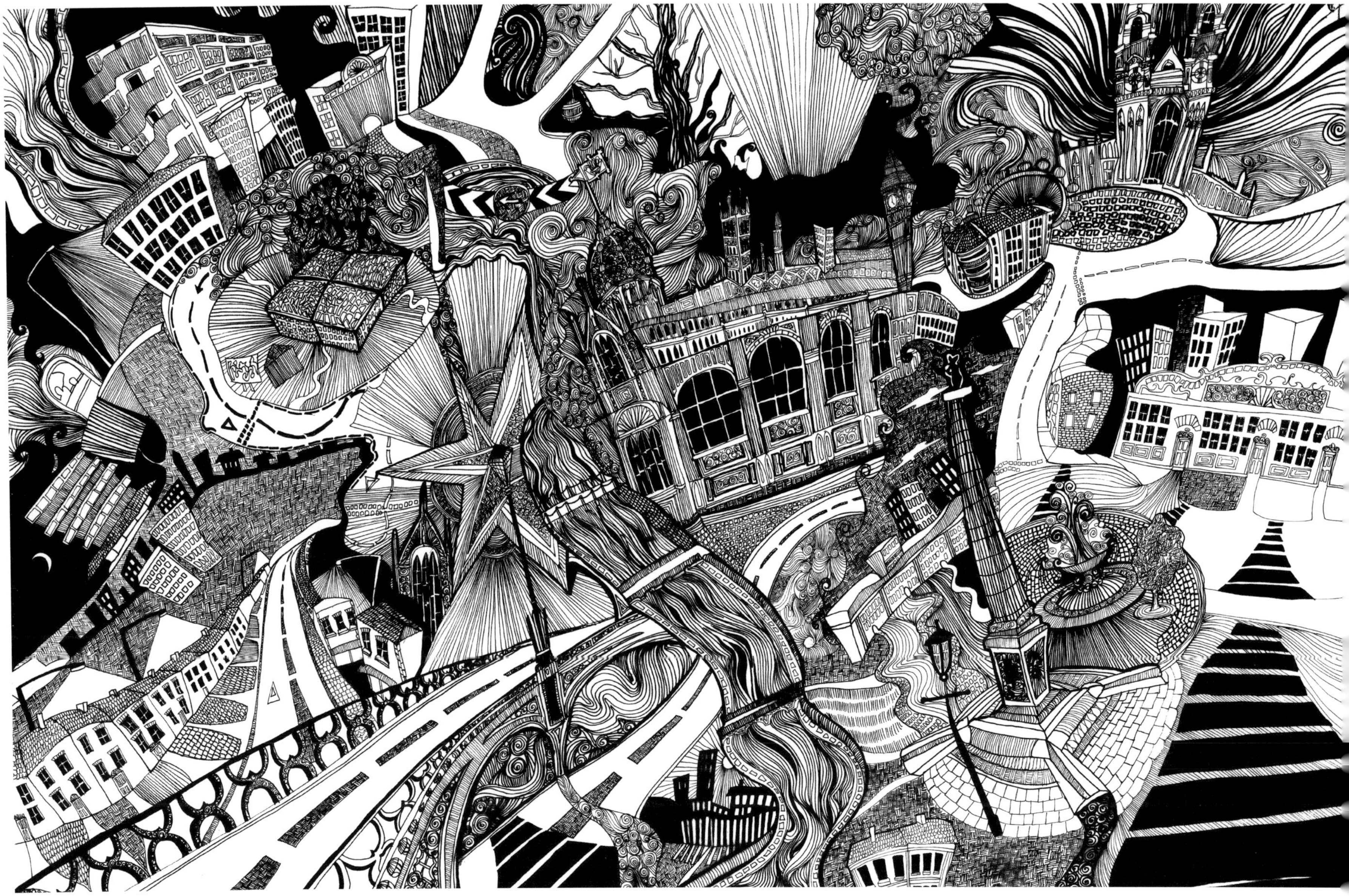

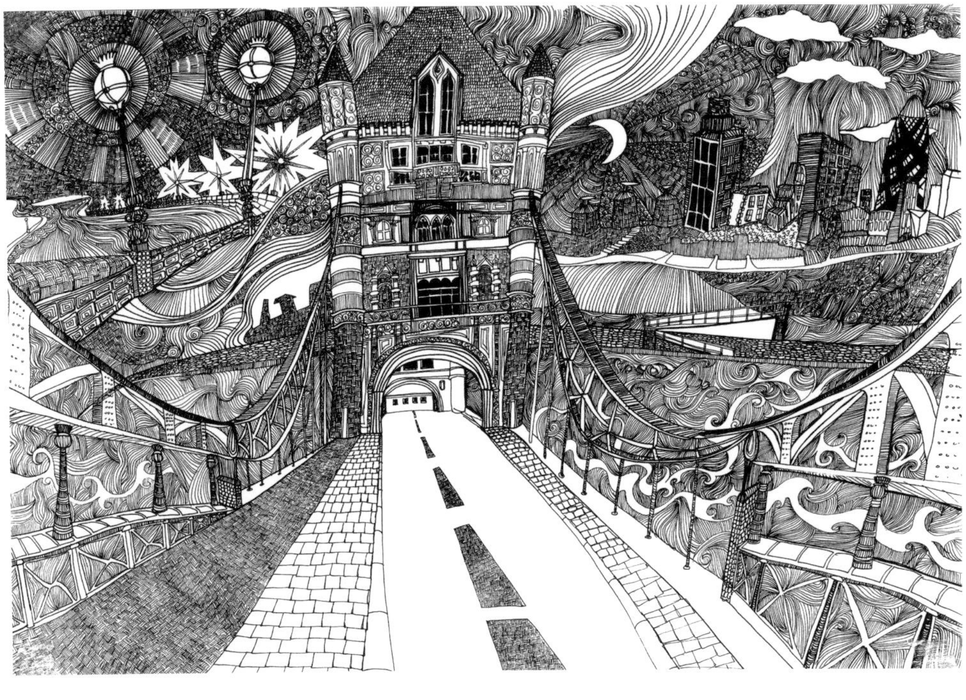

Lizzie Mary Cullen

453 BUS ROUTE *(top)*
TOWER BRIDGE *(left)*

Lizzie Mary Cullen's illustrations are inspired by psycho-geography and situationism in urban environments.

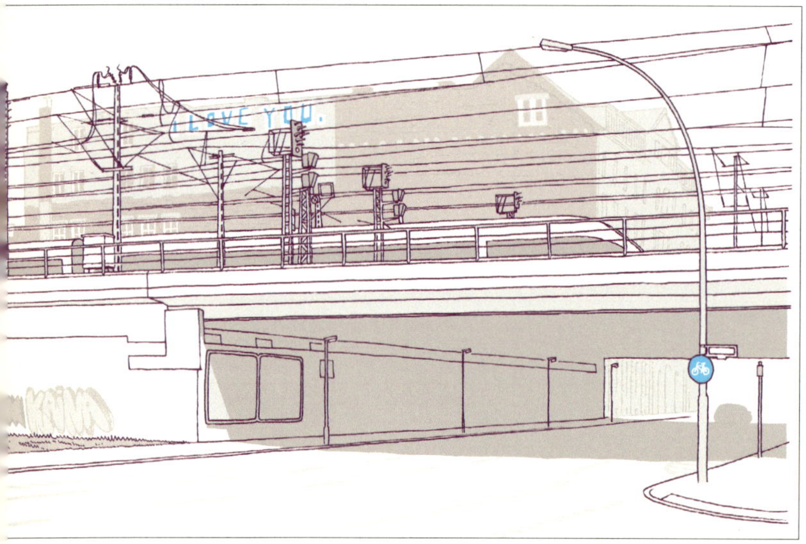

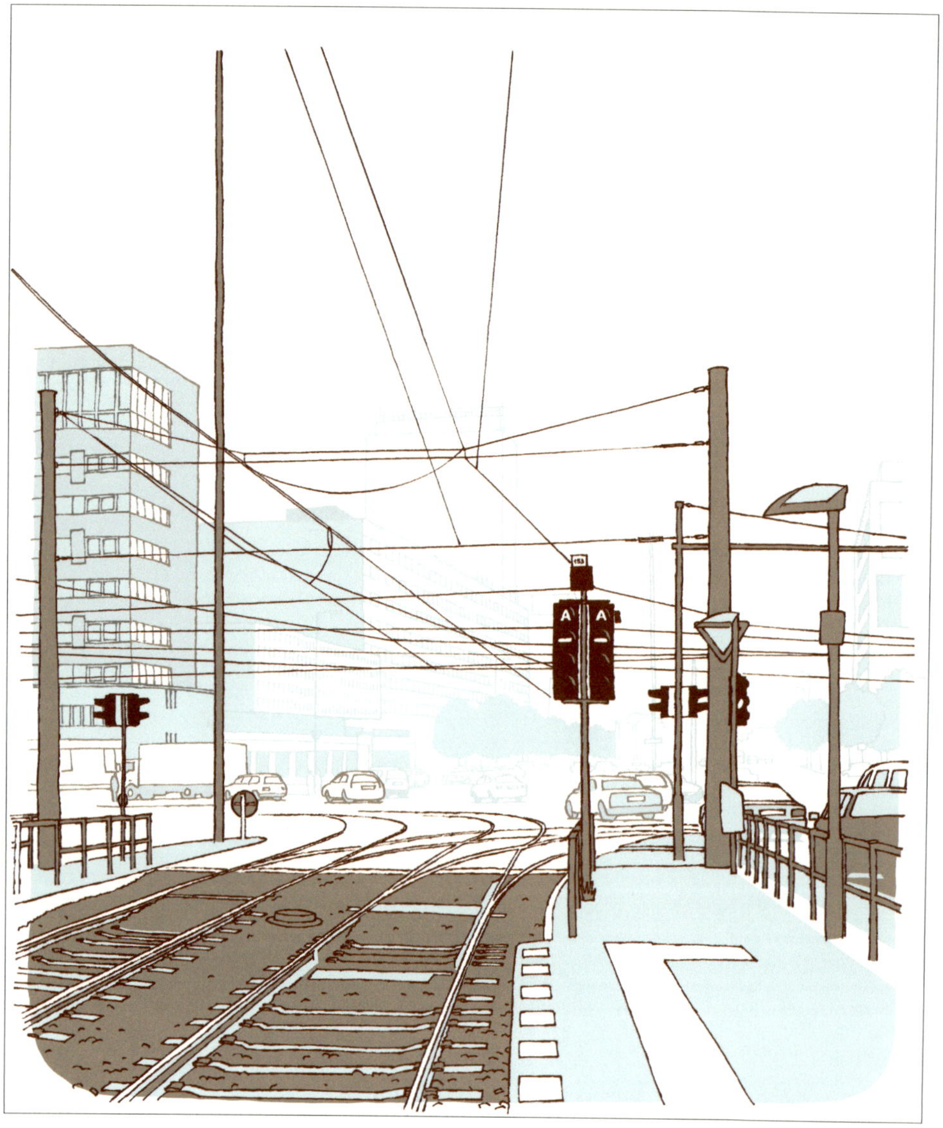

Tim Dinter

I LOVE YOU *(top)*
ALEX *(right)*
ROSA-LUXEMBURG-PLATZ *(bottom)*

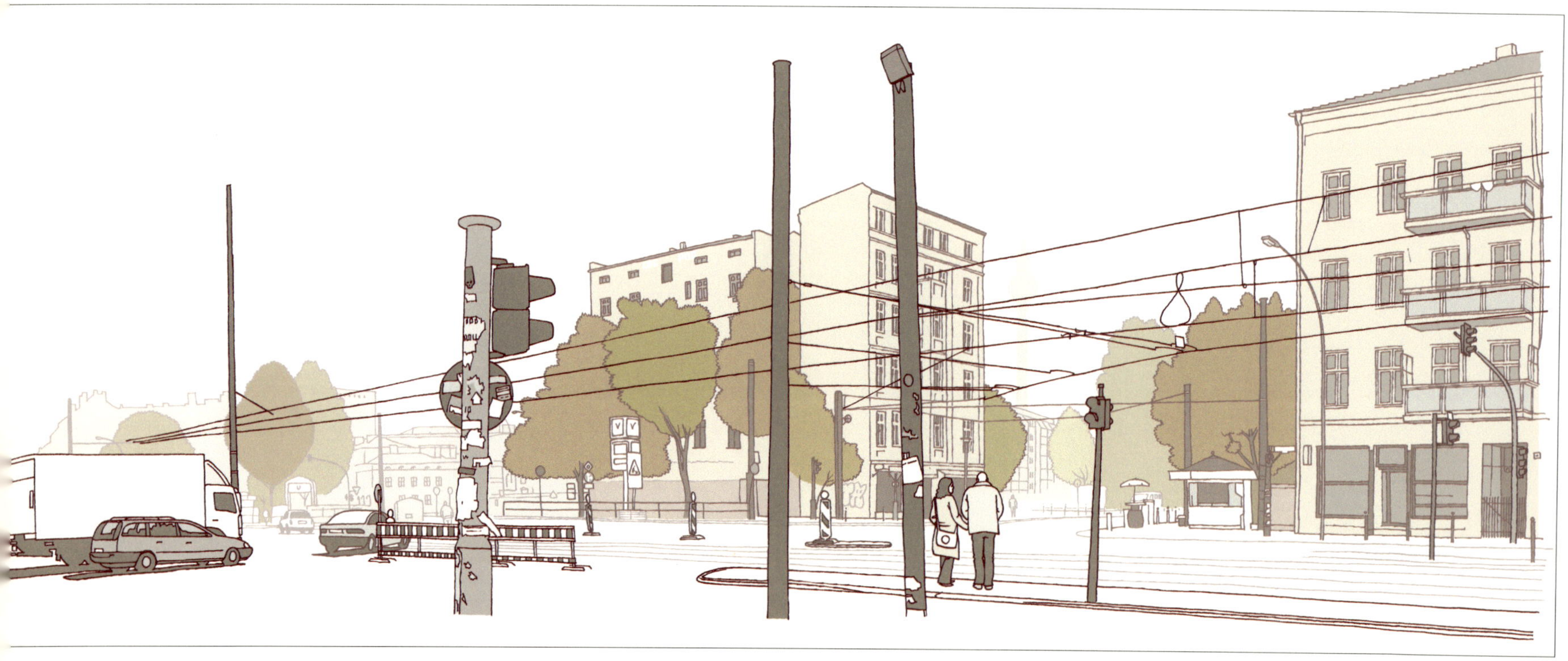

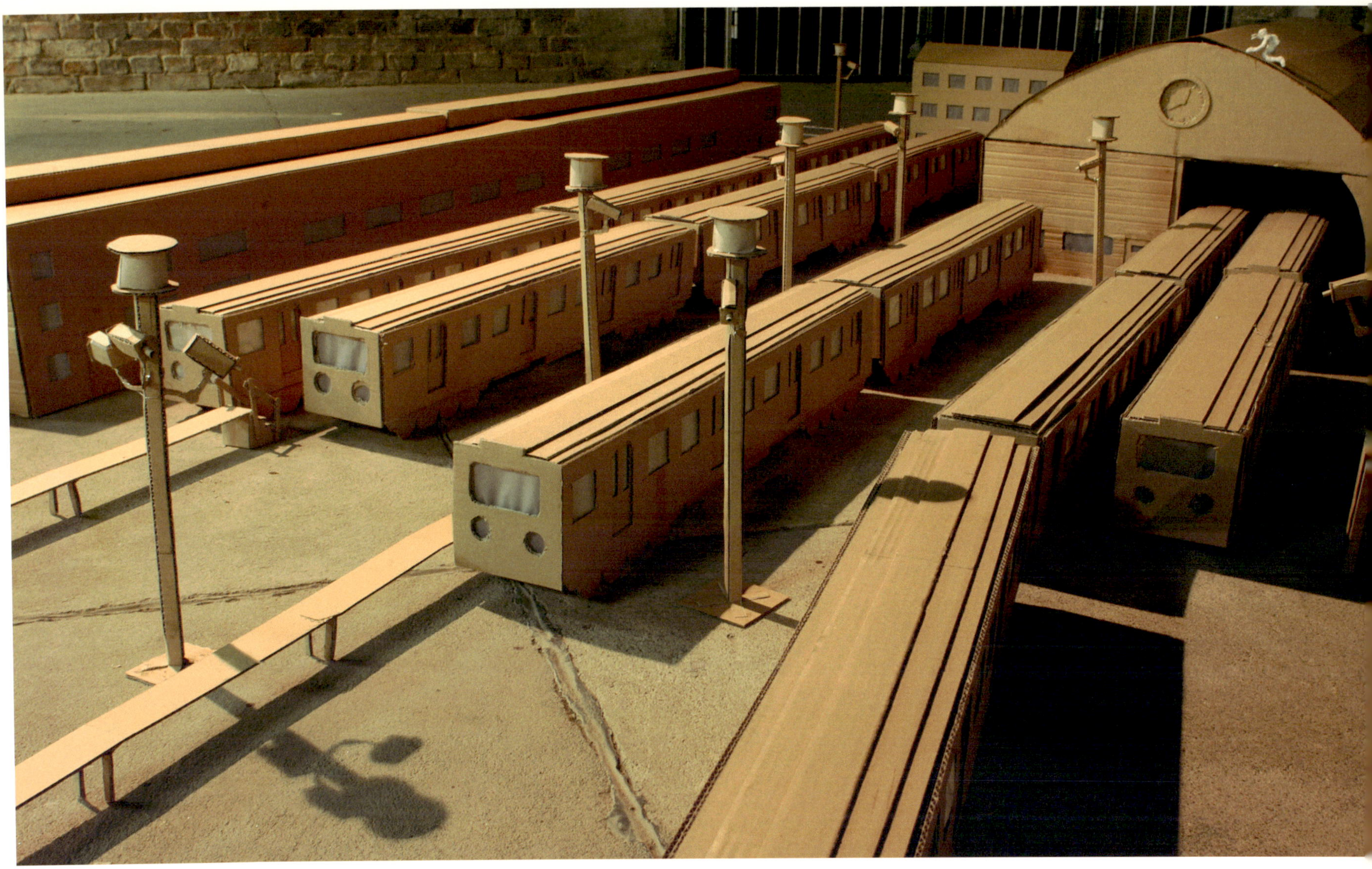

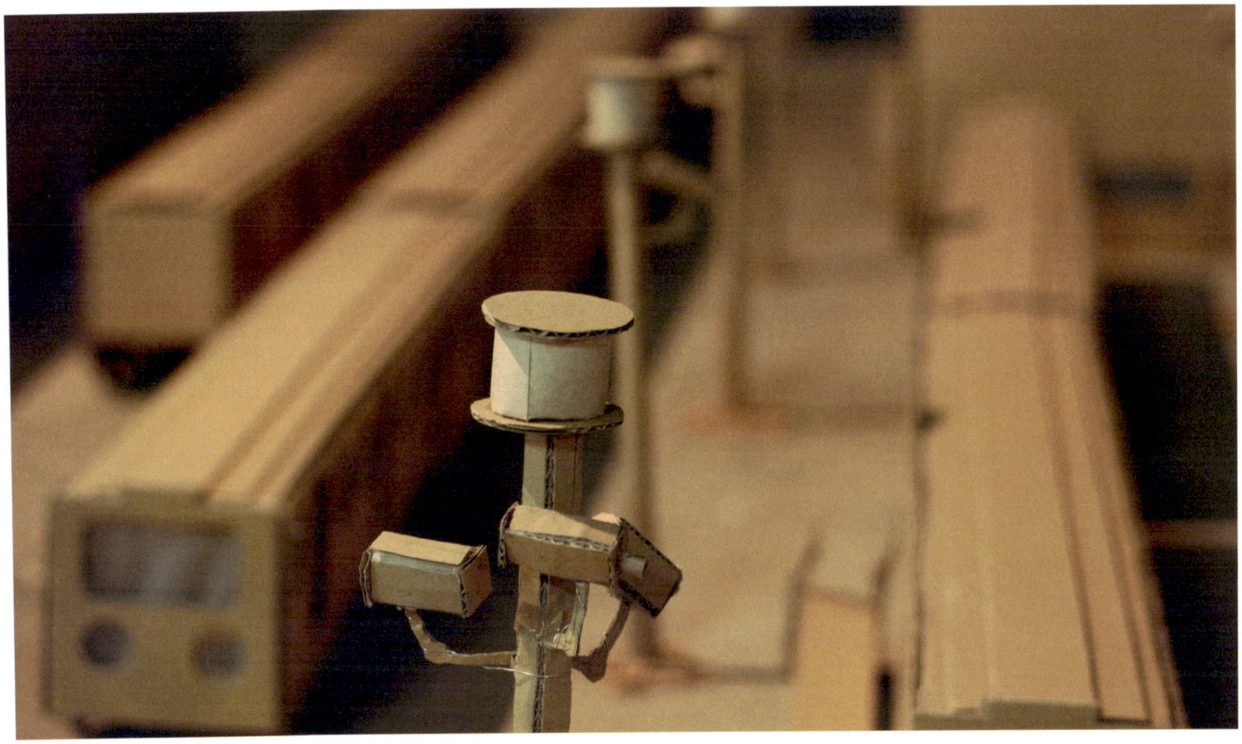

Jeremias Böttcher

CARDBOARD YARD

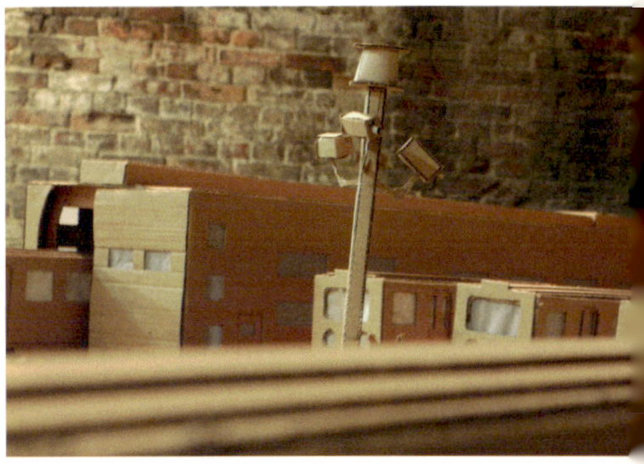

Larissa Fassler

HALLESCHES TOR

This is a model-like replica of a Berlin pedestrian underground tunnel linking platforms on the subway network. Here the transient space of an underground tunnel and its human traffic is transformed into a sculptural object. Working reproductions of the digital countdown clocks that announce arriving and departing trains are attached to both ends of the tunnel. The continuous music of the street musicians who play in the underground as well as the rushing footsteps of commuters can be heard over small speakers that have been installed inside the tunnel.

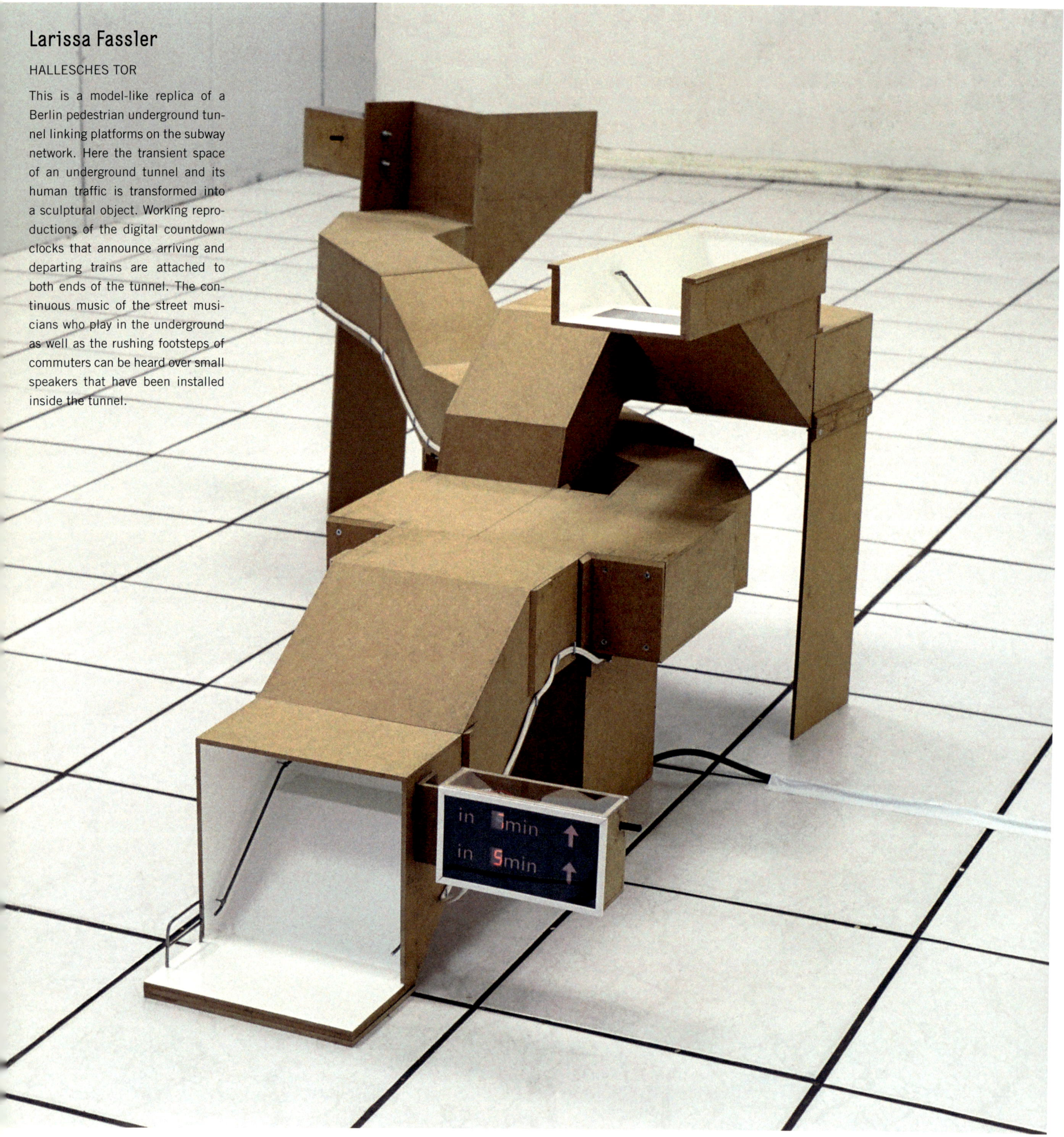

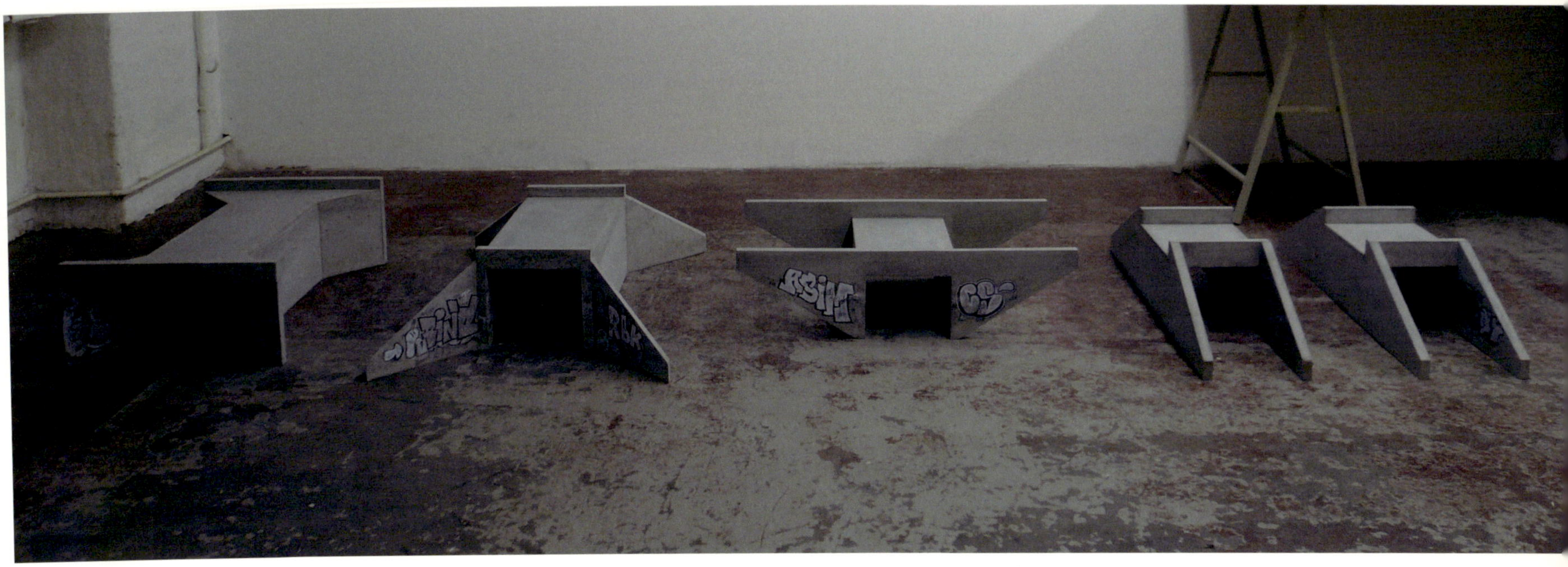

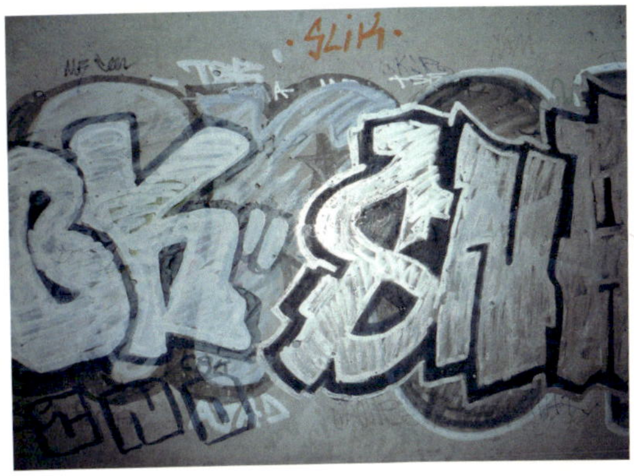

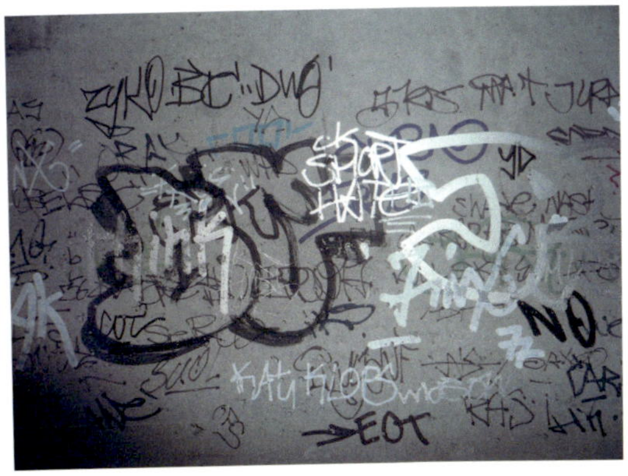

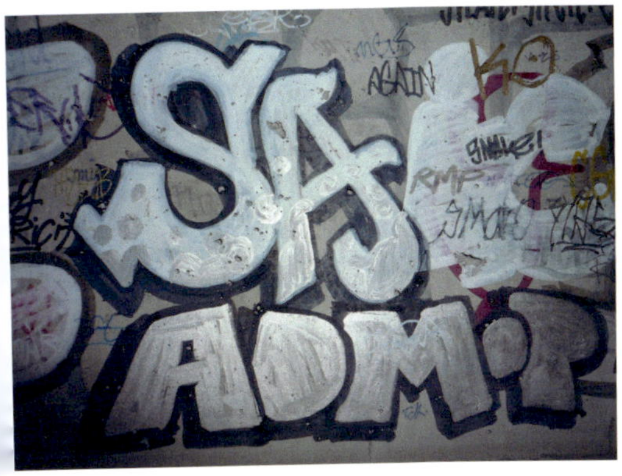

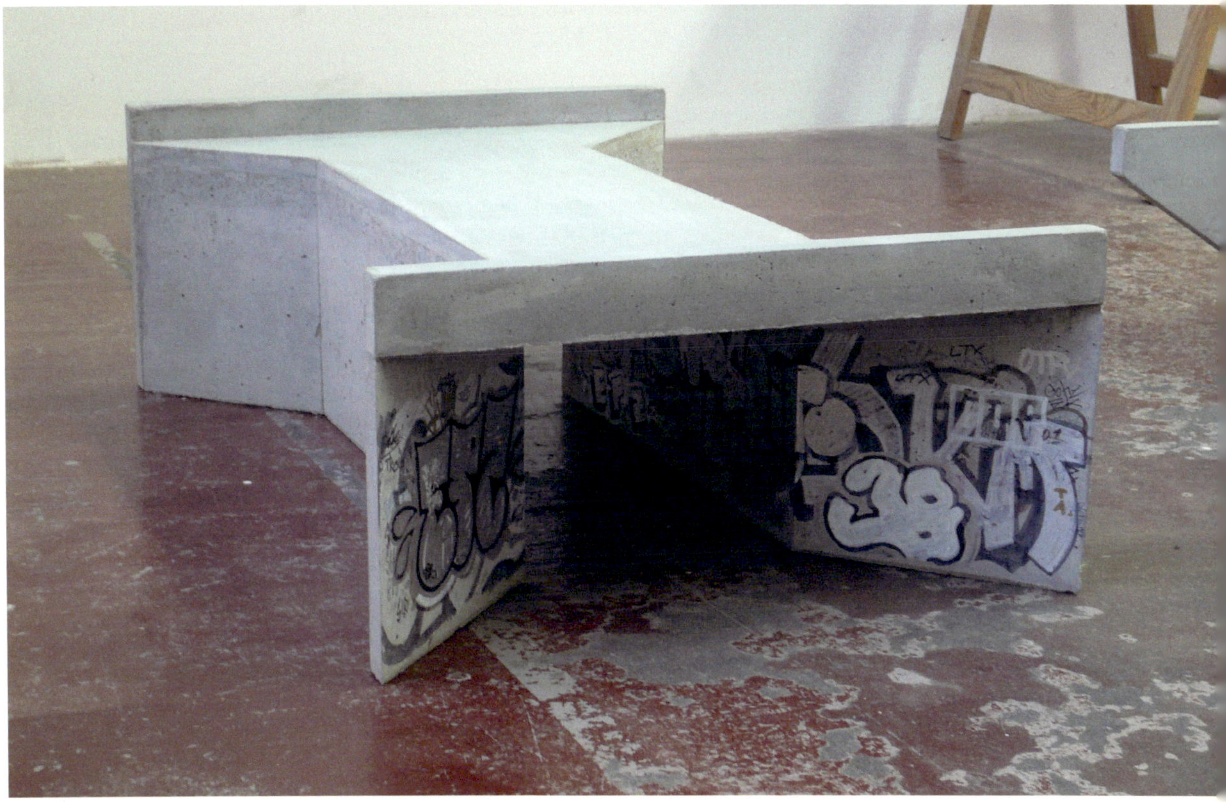

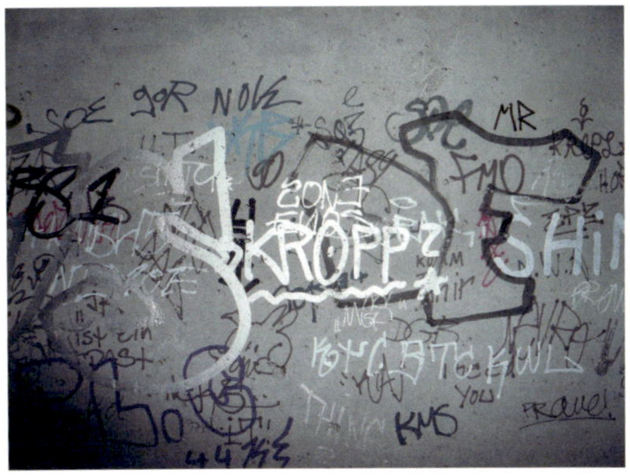

Jens Reinert

TUNNEL
GRAFFITI

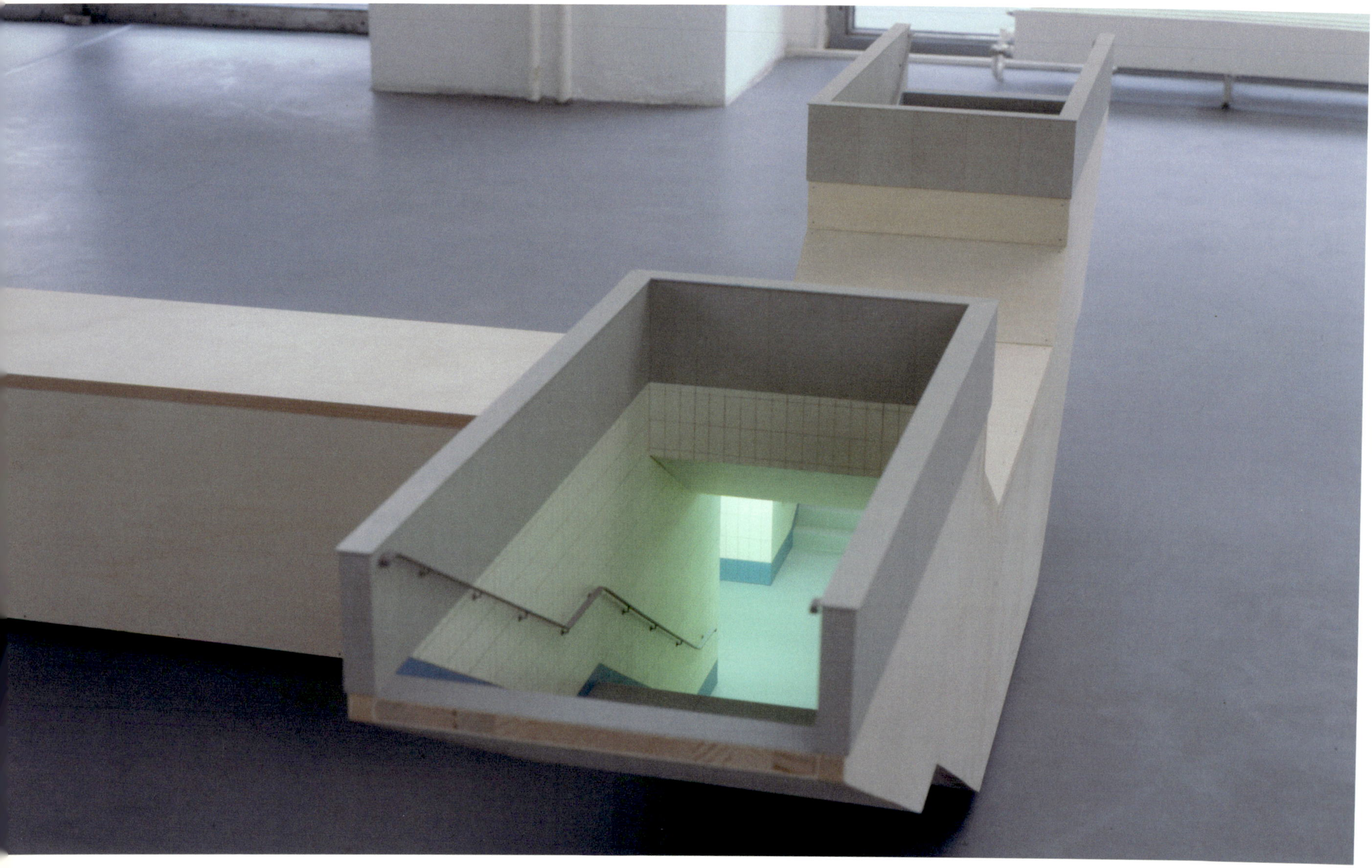

Jens Reinert

UNDERPASS *(top)*
BASEMENT GARAGE *(right)*

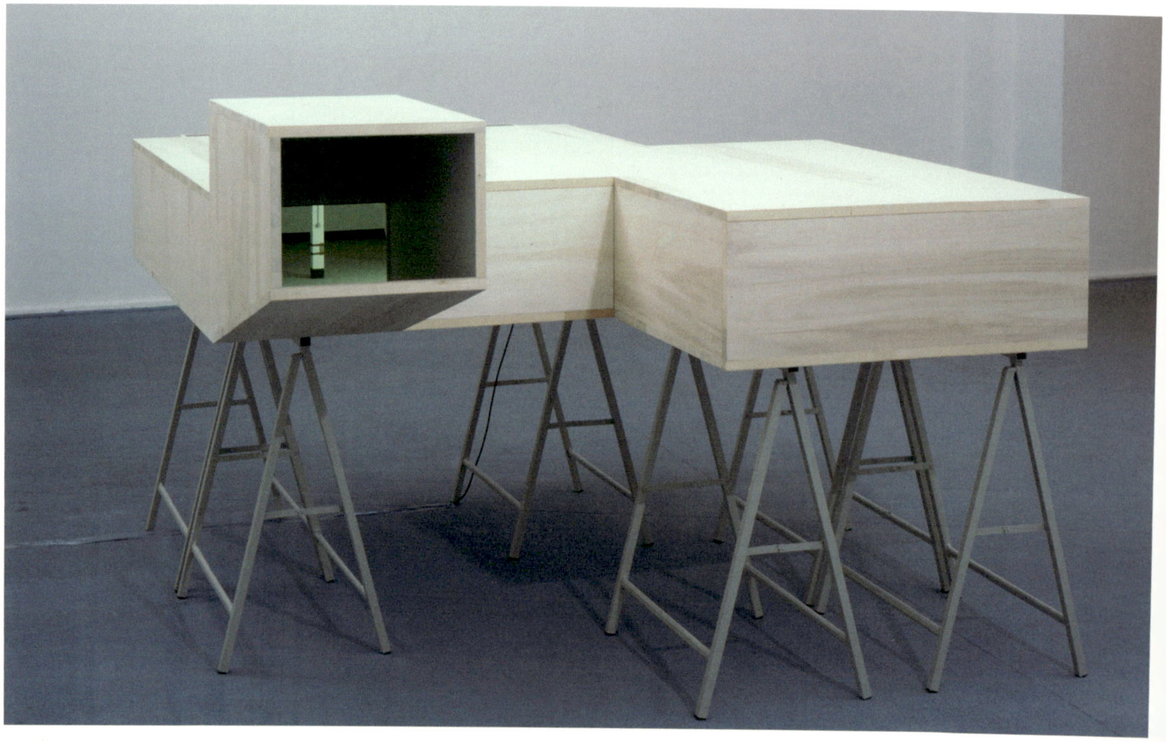

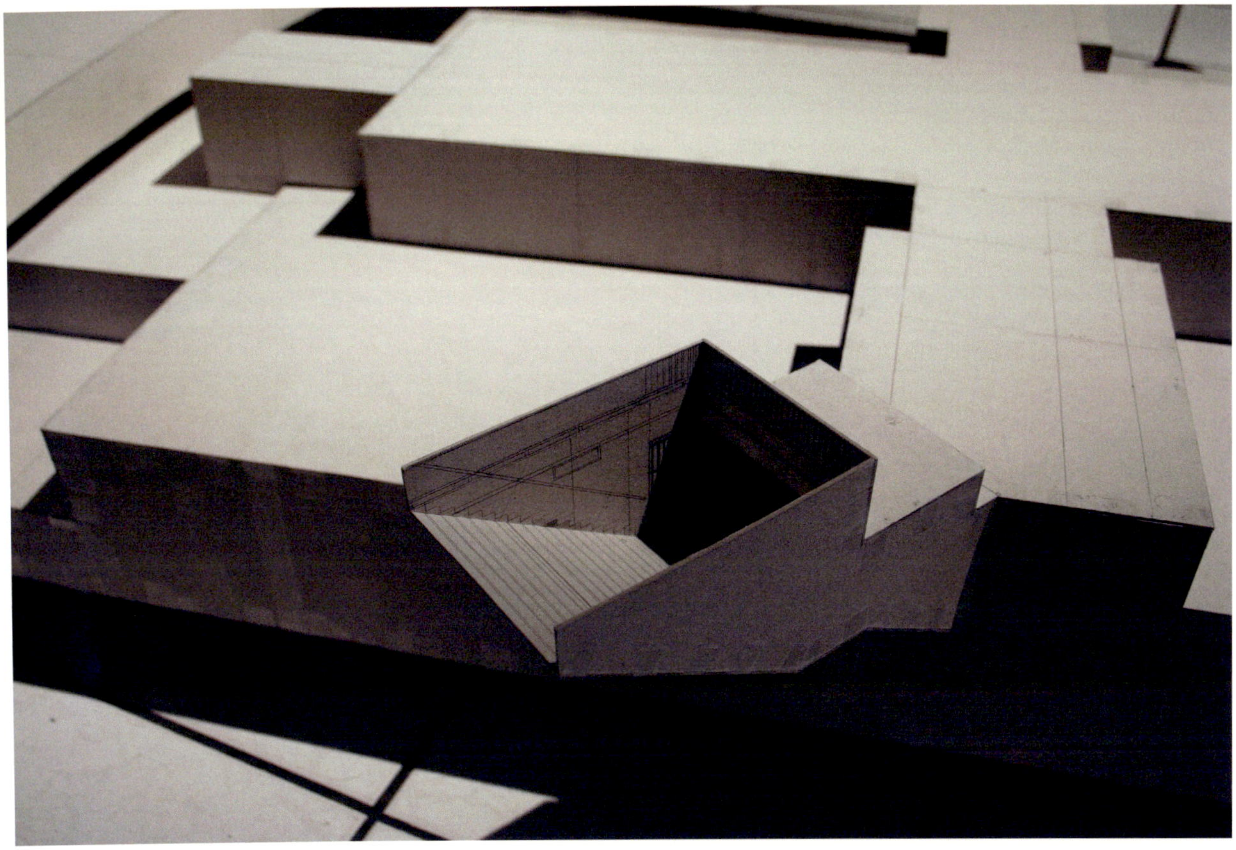

Larissa Fassler

ALEXANDERPLATZ

This large installation by Fassler is once again a model-like replica of a pedestrian underground system. It reveals the various abstract spaces we don't see, those that leave virtually no mark on the city's surface. Here, space is excavated: The complex carved-out corridors of the pedestrian tunnels become the "positive" of hidden space. The miniaturised scale and reconstruction of this busy public space is based on a subjective measuring system. Using finger lengths and counting footsteps, Fassler walked this network herself and gauged the internal dimensions and volumes of its platforms, halls, passageways, stairwells and elevator shafts.

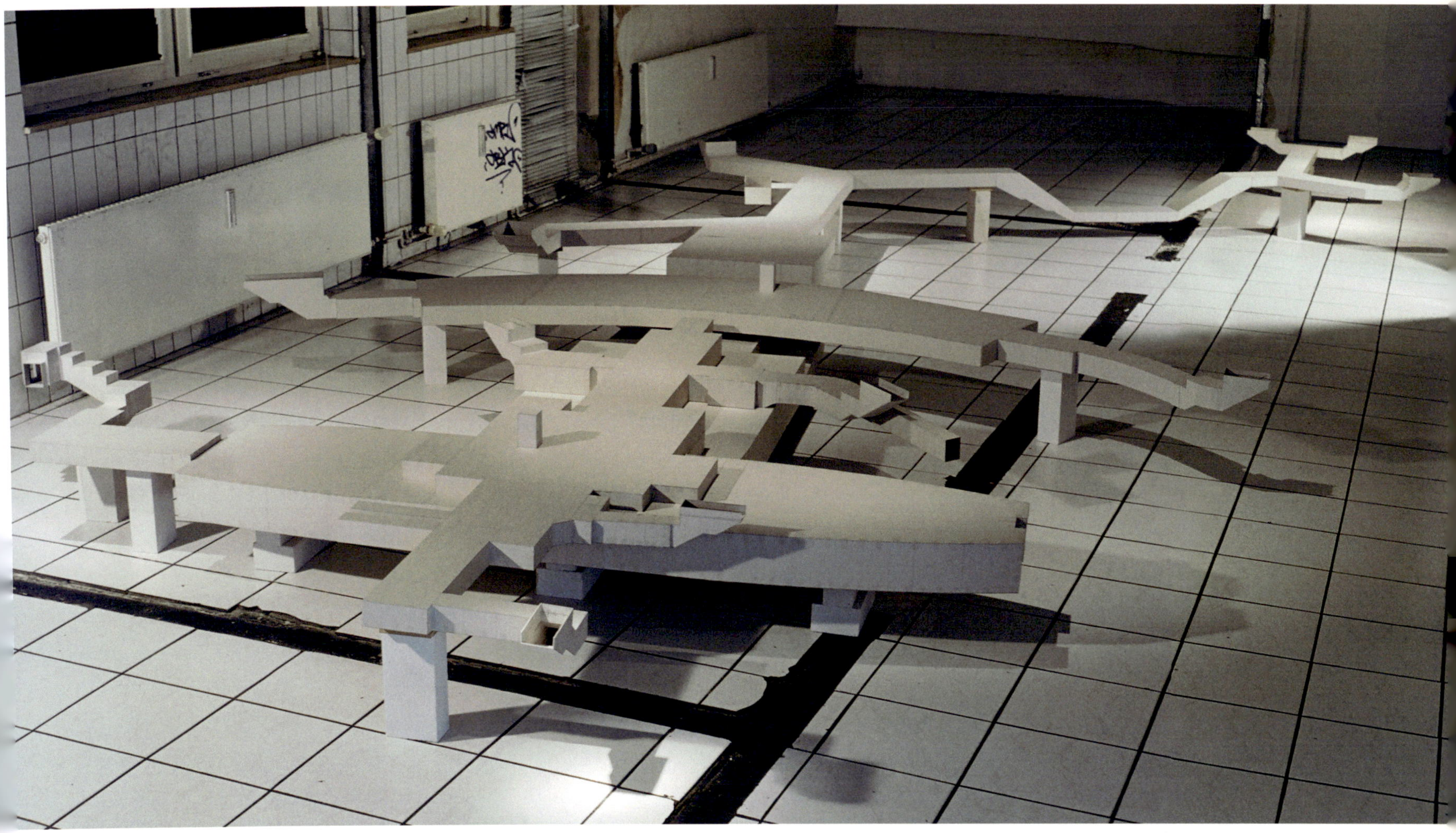

CITY HIGH

Taking a step back from the bustling scenes of inner-city life and moving high above the streets, the third and concluding chapter, City High, concentrates on extensive urban structures and far-reaching cityscapes.

The city offers a reality too complex and diverse, too disparate and plural, to be represented as a whole. This observation is valid for the city from its very beginning until this very day. And it holds all the more true for the numerous works presented in this chapter, such as the enthralling and many-layered Lego worlds by Andreas Zimmermann, Arne Quinze's interrogation of informal building formats in his *Bidonville* scultpure series or Jenny Berntsson's temporary Sandcity project for which the Swedish artist uses sand to construct cities: big and massive and fragile and changeable at the same time. Berlin-based artist Matias Bechtold literally invents pervasive mega cites from scratch with autistic meticulousness while Congolese artist Body Isek Kingelez's gives Dennis Scott Brown and Robert Venturi's seminal appeal *Learning from Las Vegas* a wholly new topicality with his psychedelic city models that seem to stop at nothing. The ever-changing nature of cities can also be traced in Eamon O'Kane's series of paintings on the development of a rural area into an industrial zone over time and its regeneration back to nature and Andy Council's humorous city-dinosaur illustrations. Raumlabor's responsive *Stick on City* calls upon the visitor to add their personal vision by drawing and sticking it into a large city image and the structural fabric of the city emerges in Matthew Picton's cartographic *City Sculptures*. Expanding in ever more complex patterns, Michael Najjar's multiple-exposure, black-and-white photo series *Netropolis* allows the complex organism that comprises each city to become visually transparent.

What we are witnessing here is the emergence of profoundly new city typologies that are shaped by creativity and curiosity beyond the blueprint.

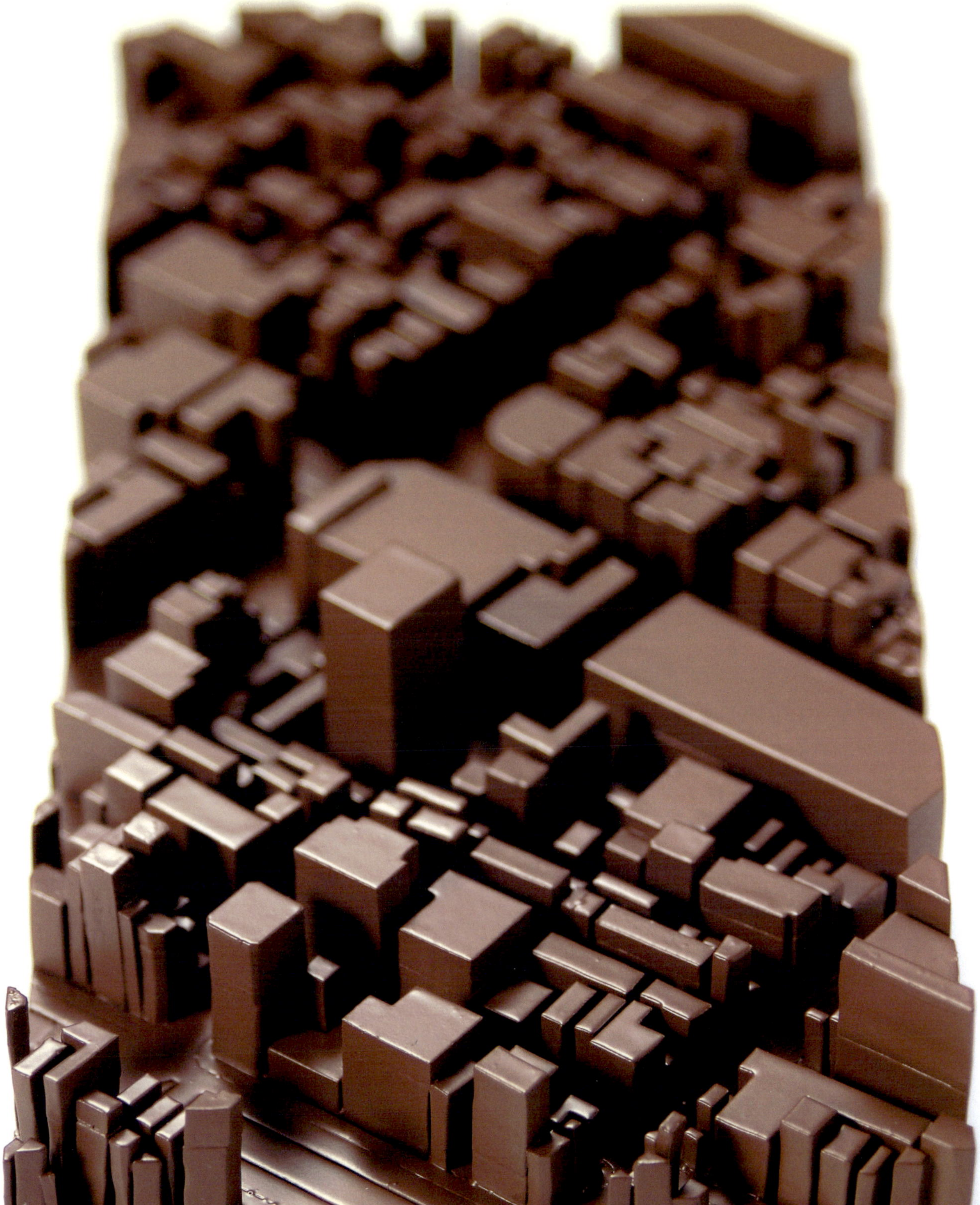

21_21 Design Sight NAOKO TONE + ATSUYOSHI IIJIMA

CITY MADE OF CHOCOLATE

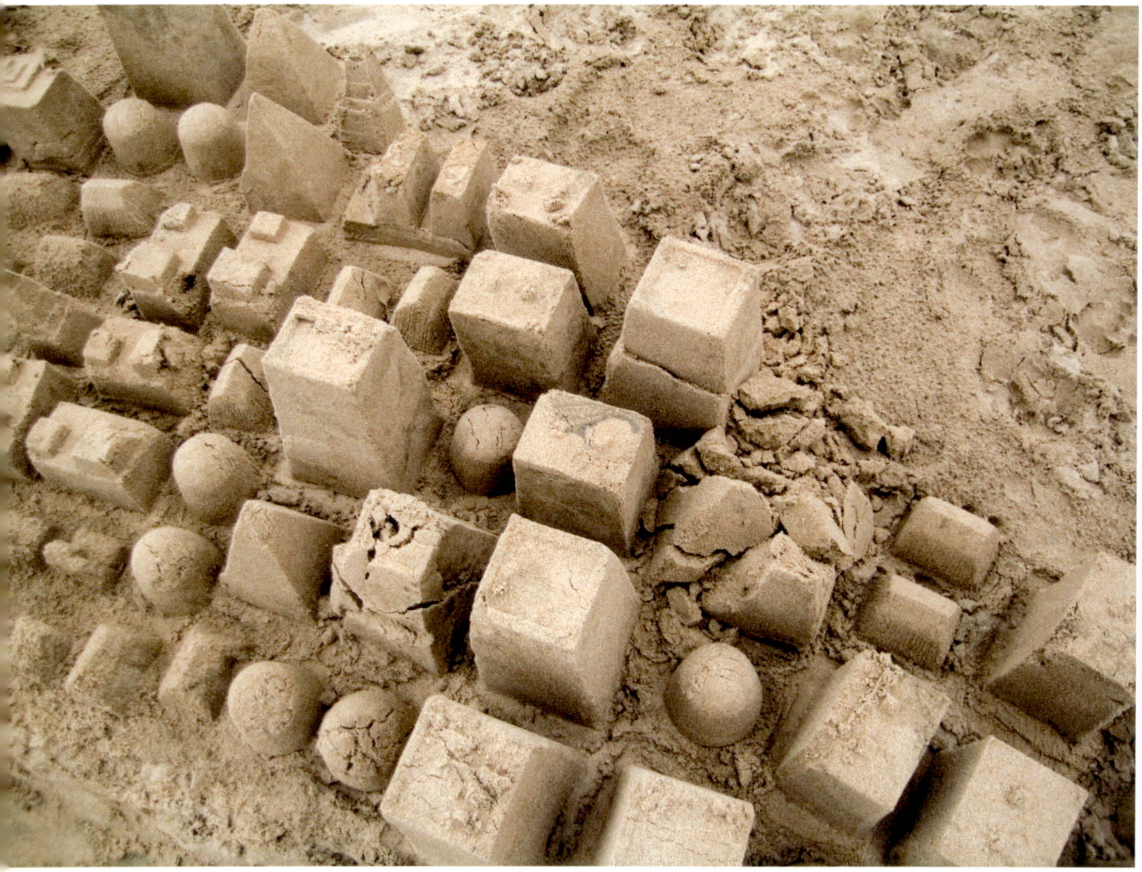

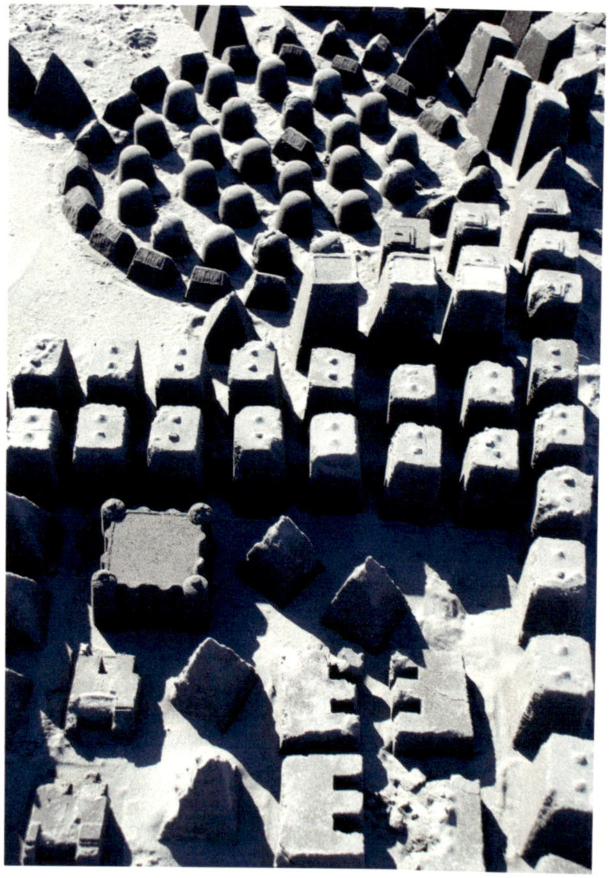

Jenny Berntsson

SANDCITY

Working within the framework of this temporary project, Jenny Berntsson travels to different places around the world, from Sweden to Iceland, India and Turkey, to build site-specific imaginary mega-cities that are gigantic as well as fragile and changeable.

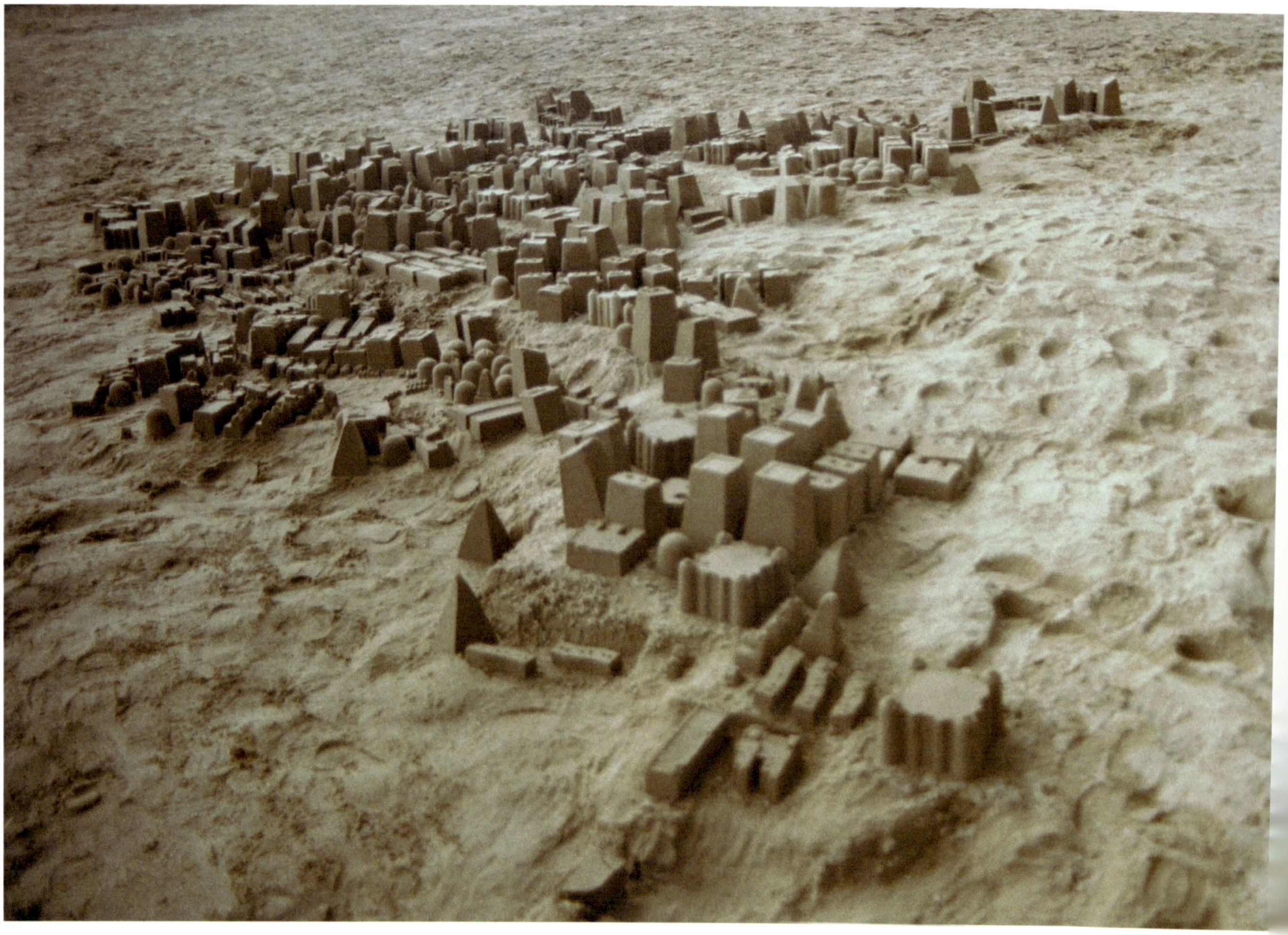

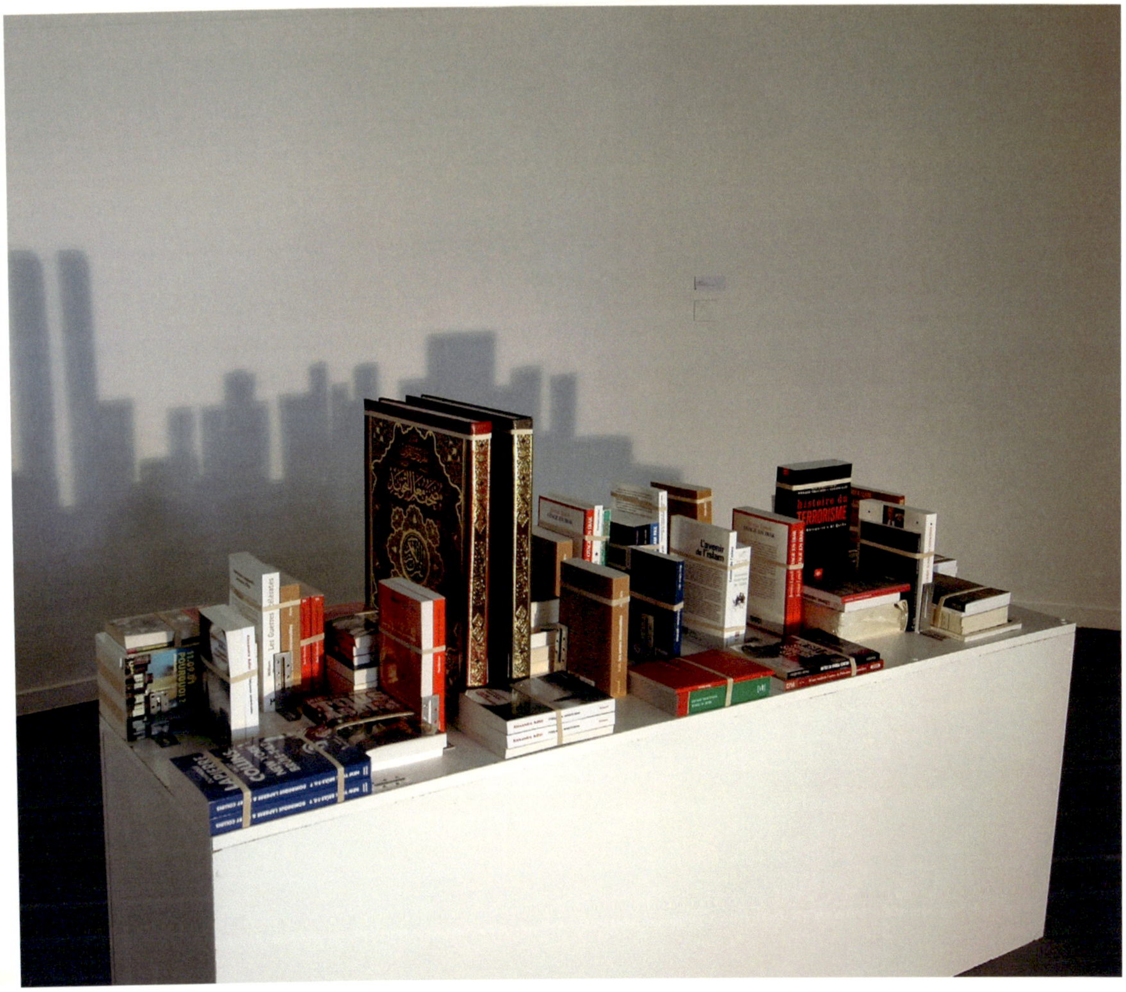

Mounir Fatmi

SAVE MANHATTAN 01 *(left)*

The project Save Manhattan is a reflection on the disaster of September 11, 2001. Save Manhattan 01, 2003–04, was composed of a variety of books all of which were written following the events of September 11th, except for the two copies of the Koran. The books are arranged on a table such that a light projected from a distance, creates a harsh outline of the pre 9/11 Manhattan skyline against the wall behind them. The two books of the Koran create the spectral image of the Twin Towers.

SAVE MANHATTAN 03: SOUND ARCHITECTURE *(bottom)*

This installation utilises sound as the essential element along with ninety speakers in varying shapes and sizes, which are arranged on the floor. This concert of noise is composed from real sounds that reflect the congestion of city life: horns, screeching tires, the subway and crashing cars, and also fictional sounds of explosions that were extracted from dozens of Hollywood blockbuster movies. A light is projected to create a sharply defined shadow of the pre-9/11 skyline of Manhattan. Here the viewer enters into the space and passes in front of the light, thereby becoming a part of the installation and, with that, a part of history.

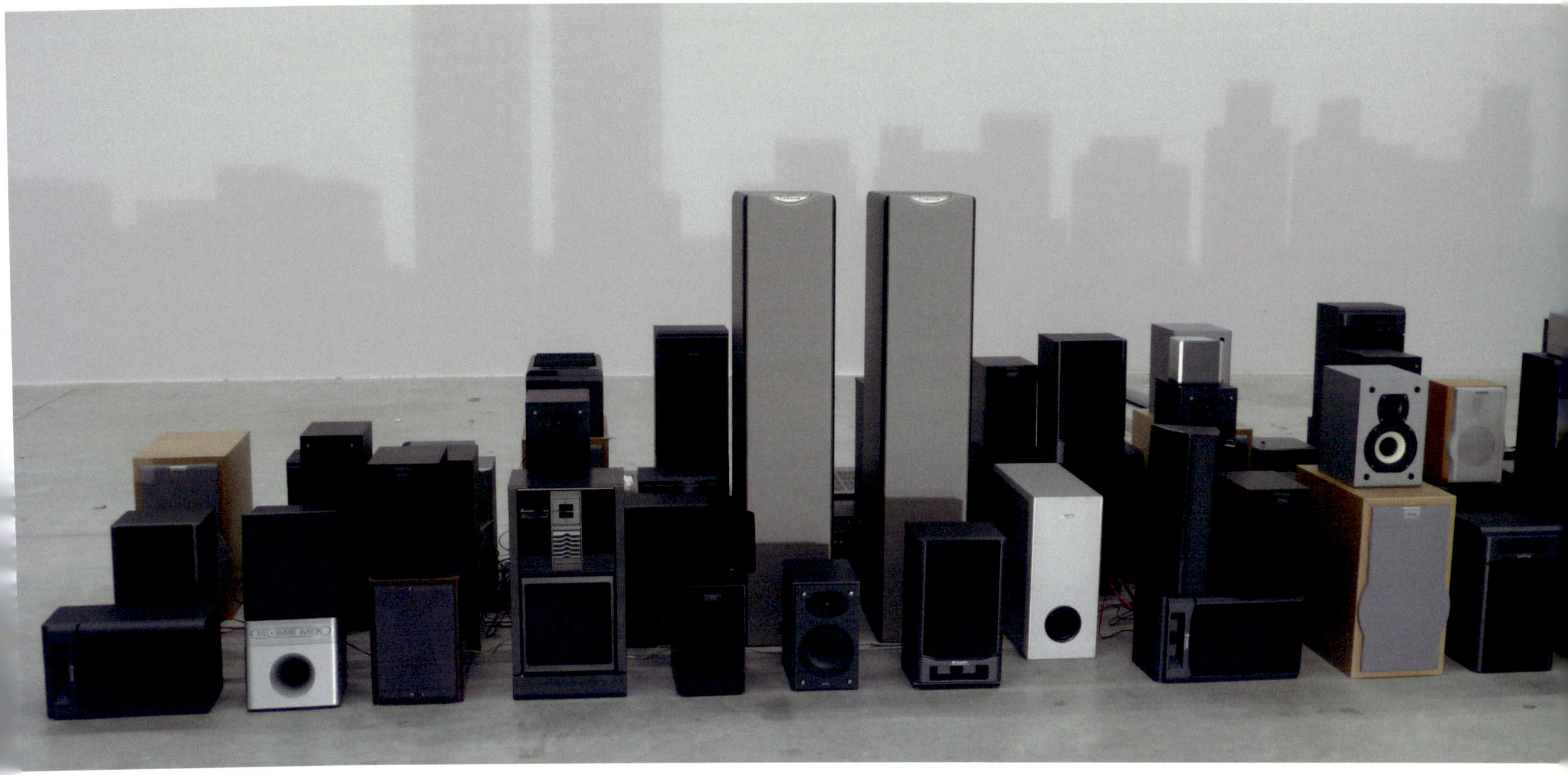

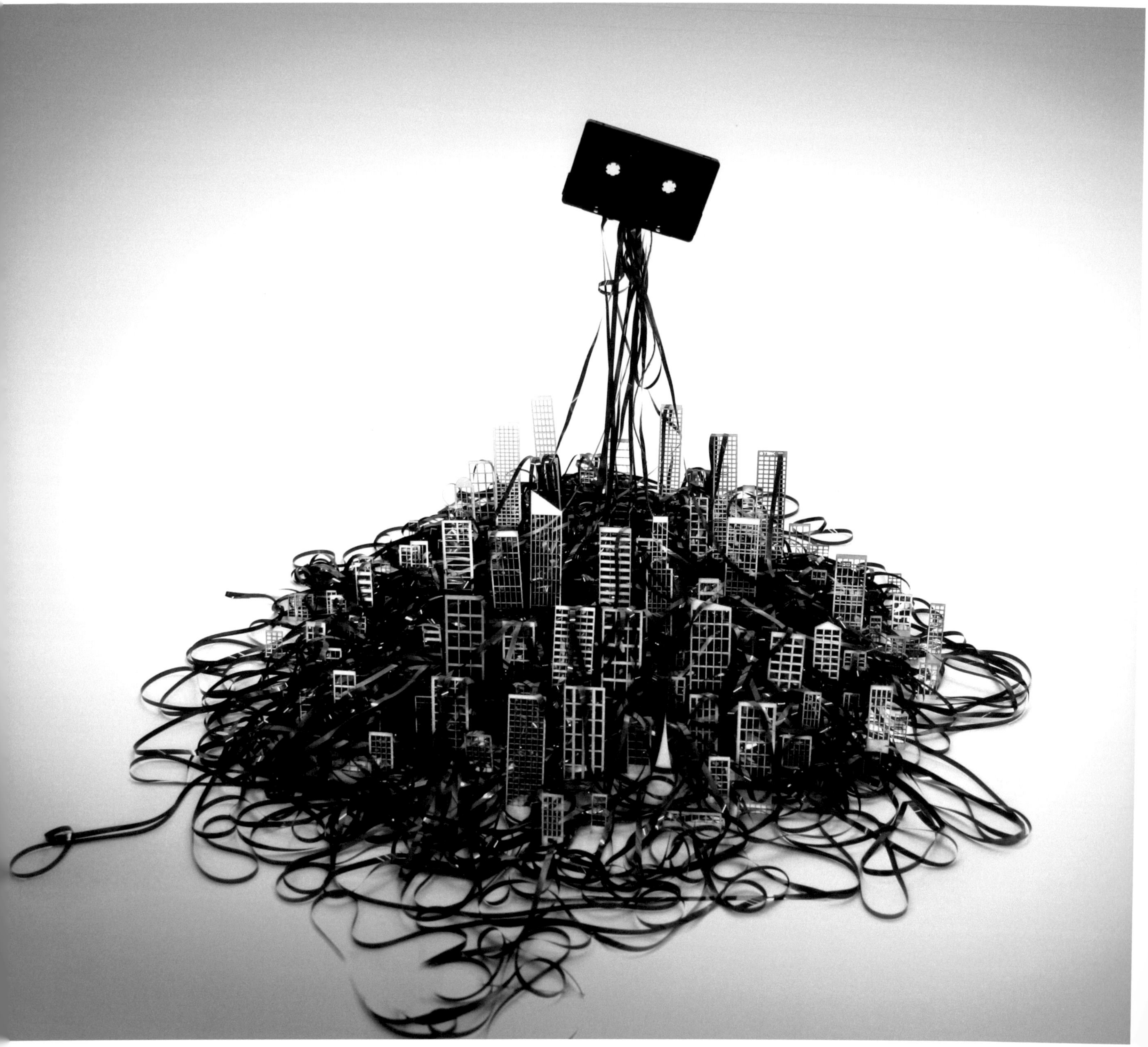

Simon Bent

MUSIC LANDSCAPE

Cover artwork for a CD mix by DJ Perplex. The idea behind this piece was to illustrate music flowing through the city and how music effects our lives.

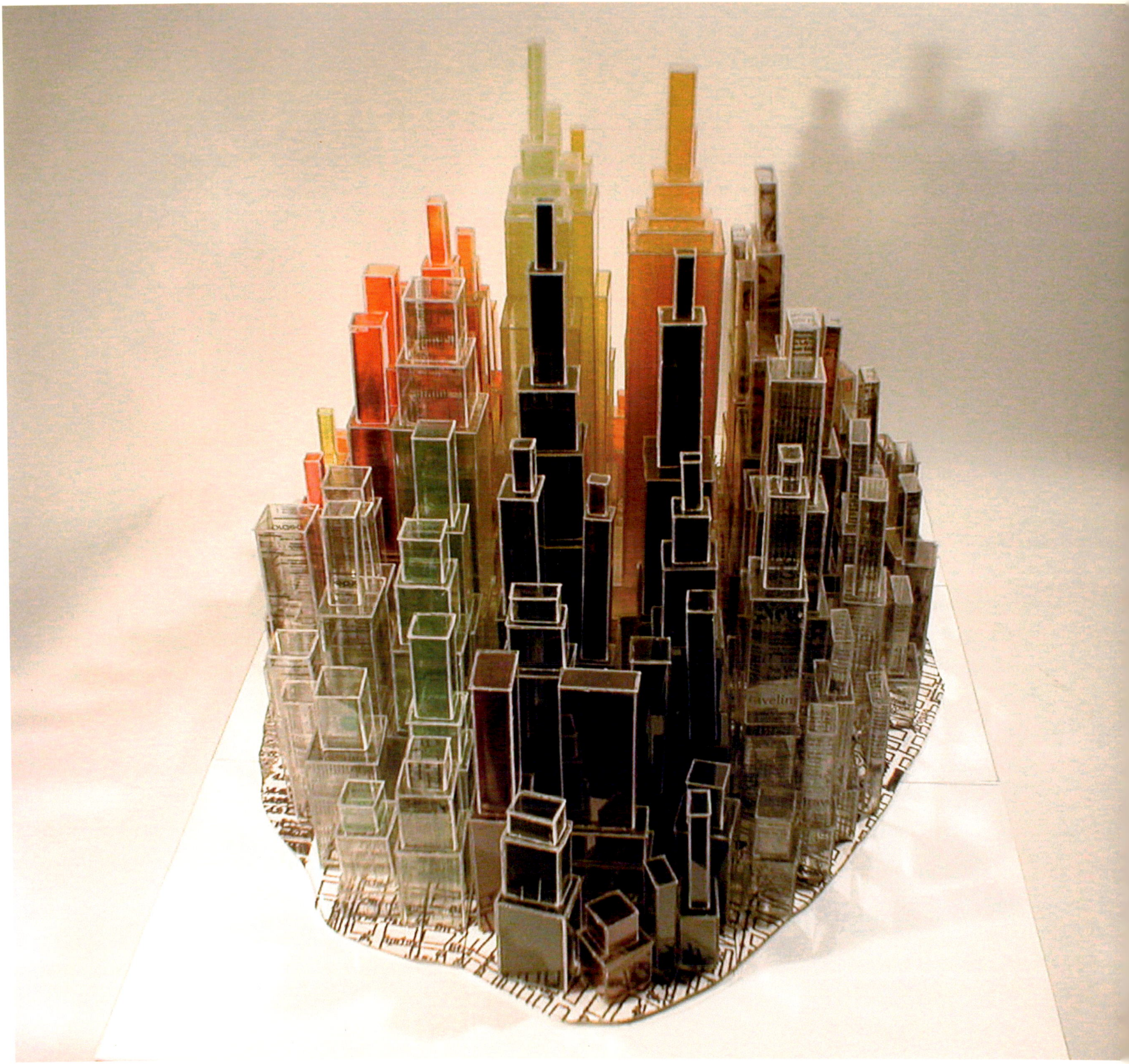

Faculty of Architecture / University of Technology Munich ANTJE LUCKHARDT AND NIKOLAUS WITTE

JOHN DOS PASSOS MANHATTAN TRANSFER

This model house for John Dos Passos's novel *Manhattan Transfer* was built as part of a seminar at the Faculty of Architecture of the University of Technology, Munich. The students were asked to replicate a building or piece of architecture from a literary text of their choice. Some of the resulting works were presented in an exhibition and accompanying publication entitled *Architektur wie sie im Buche steht* (a textbook example o farchitecture) edited by Winfried Nerdinger.

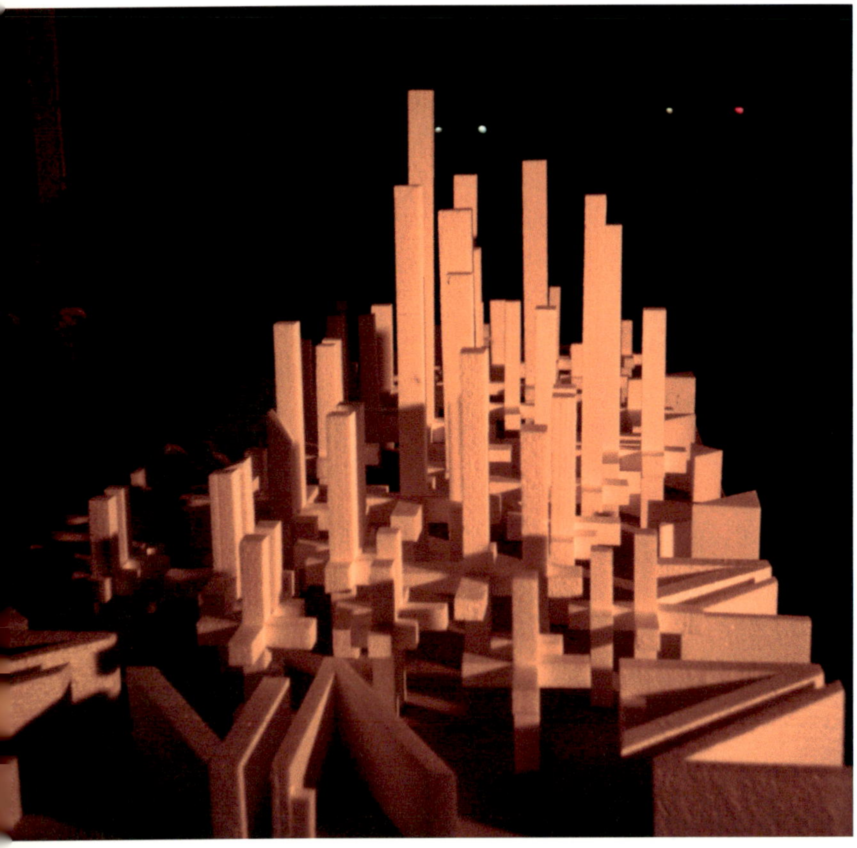

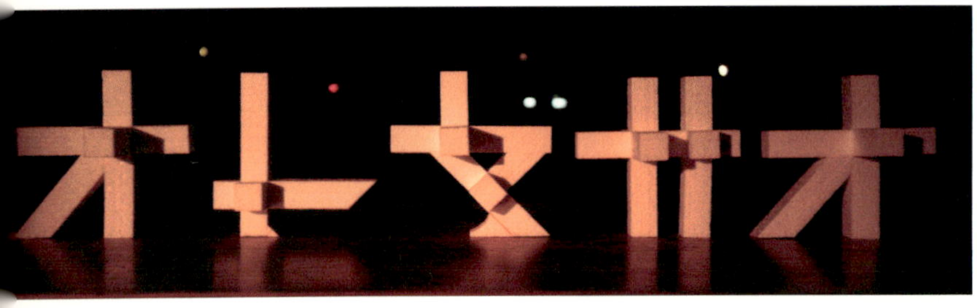

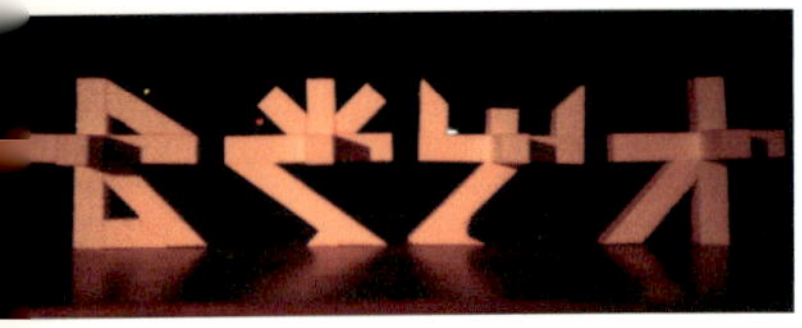

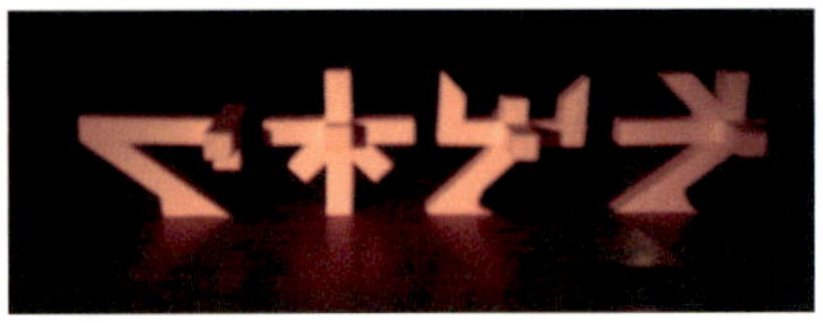

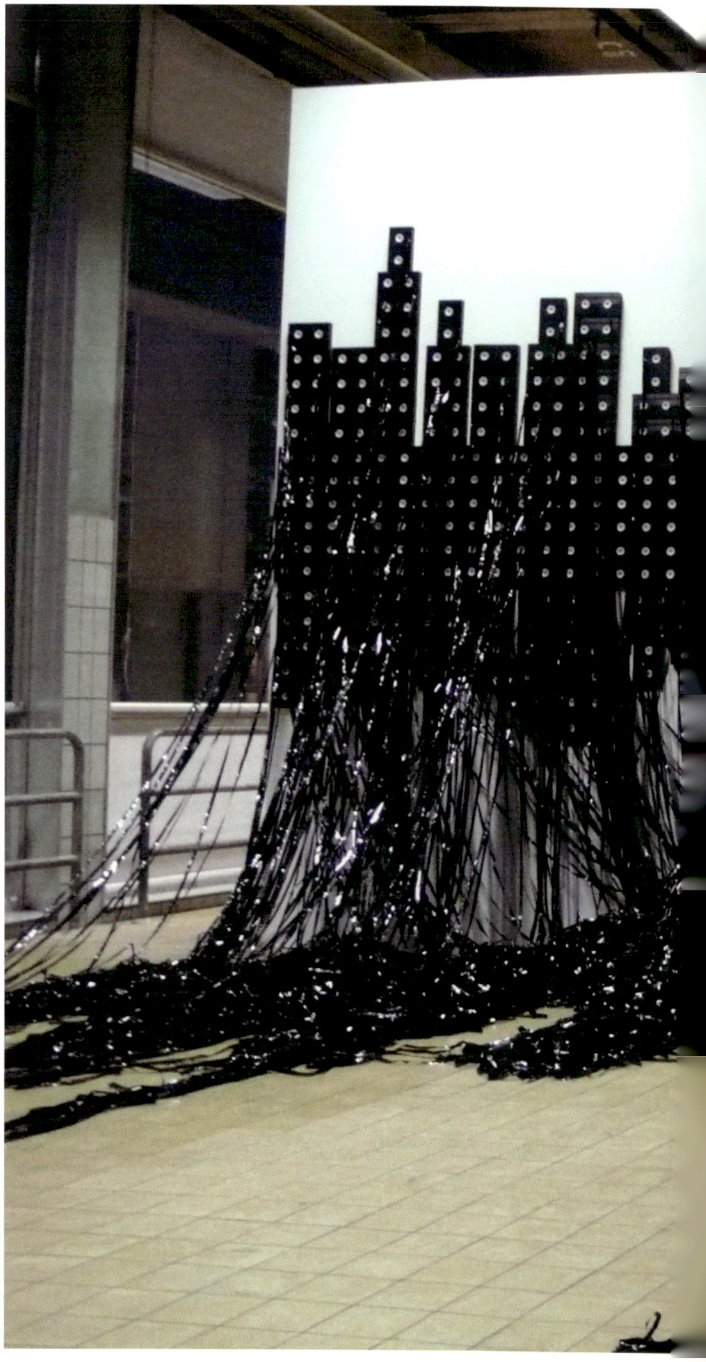

Akim

ALPHA BETA CITY

For Alpha Beta City, Berlin-based artist Akim created a city sculpture made of three-dimensional typographies.

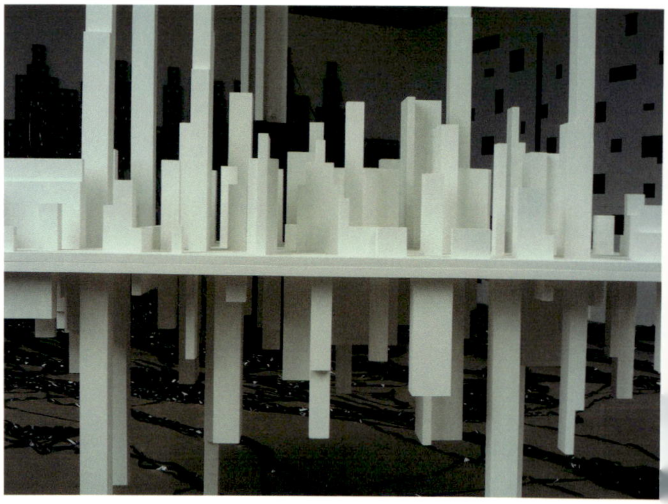

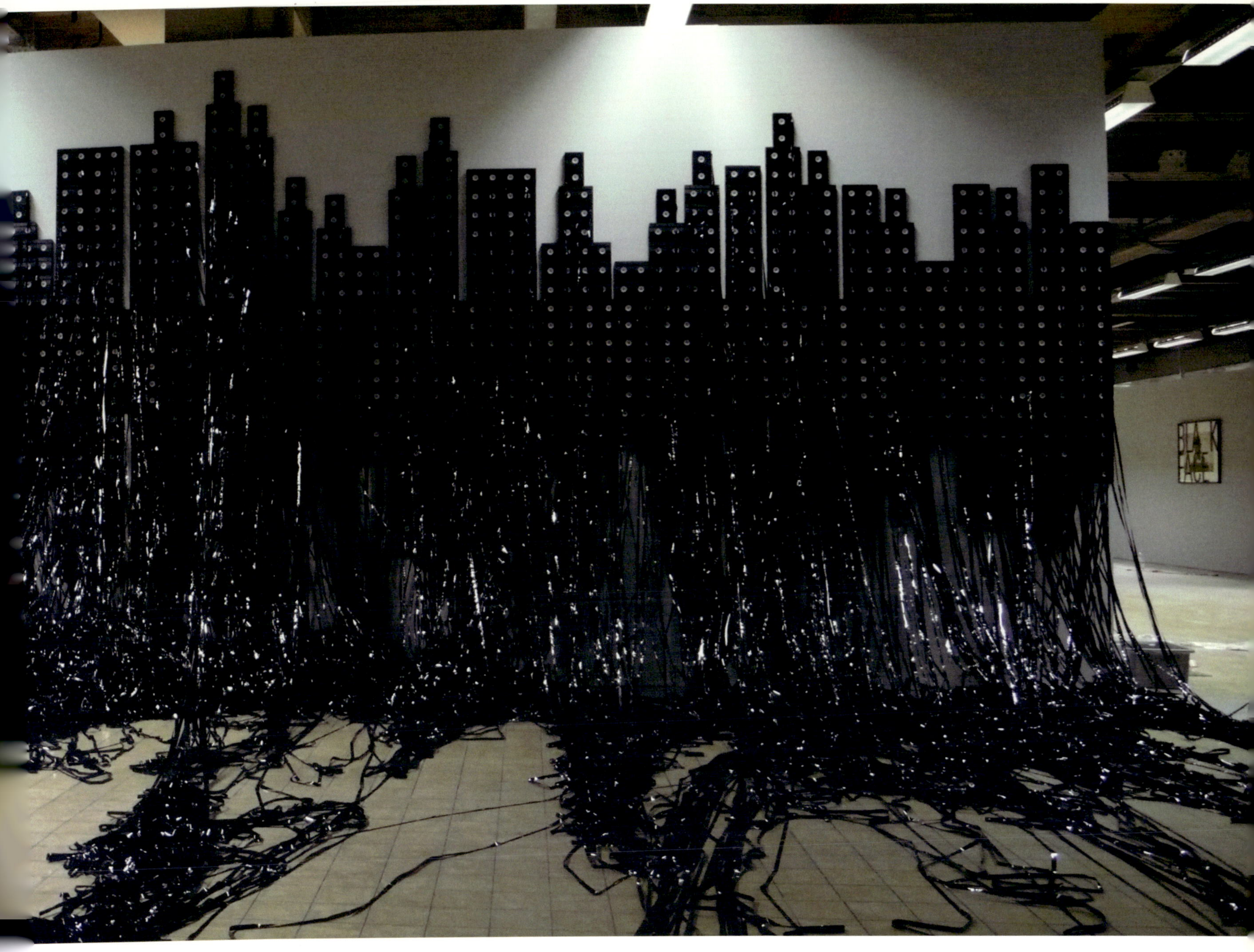

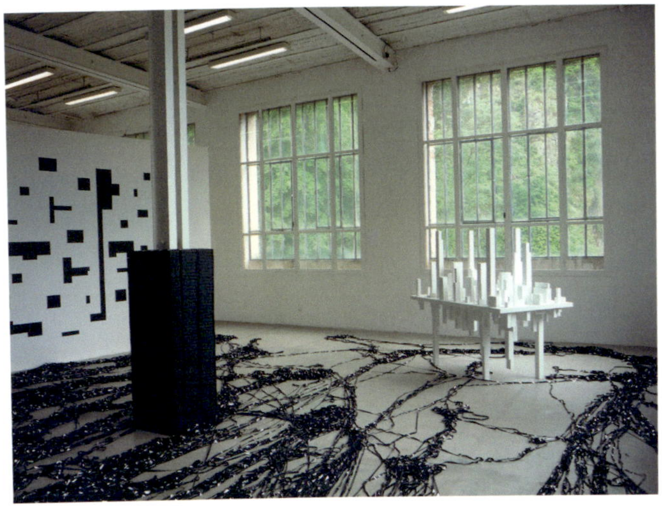

Mounir Fatmi

SKYLINE

This impressive skyline by Mounir Fatmi exhibited at the Brussels Biennial 2008 is made from numerous VHS tapes.

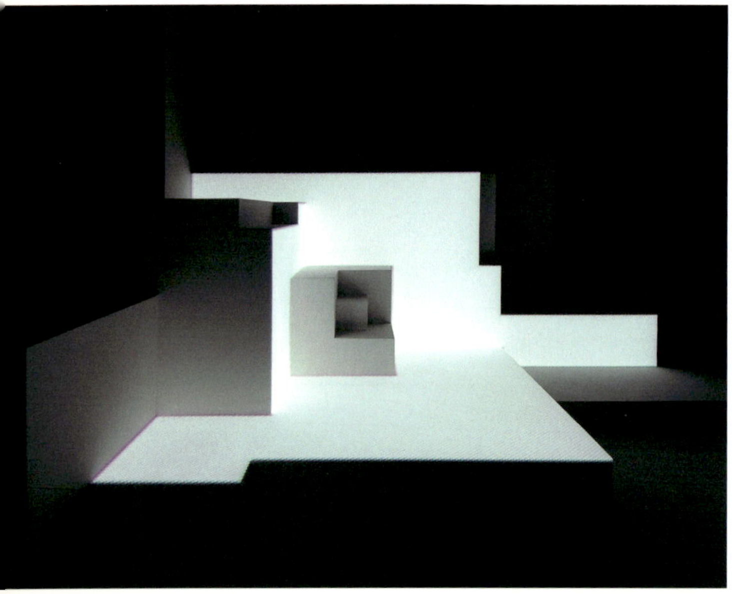

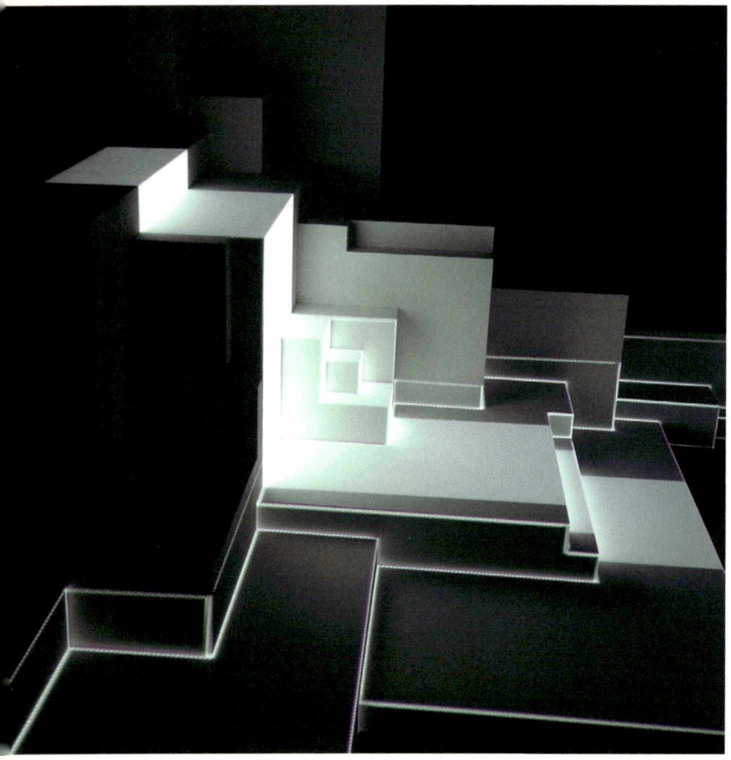

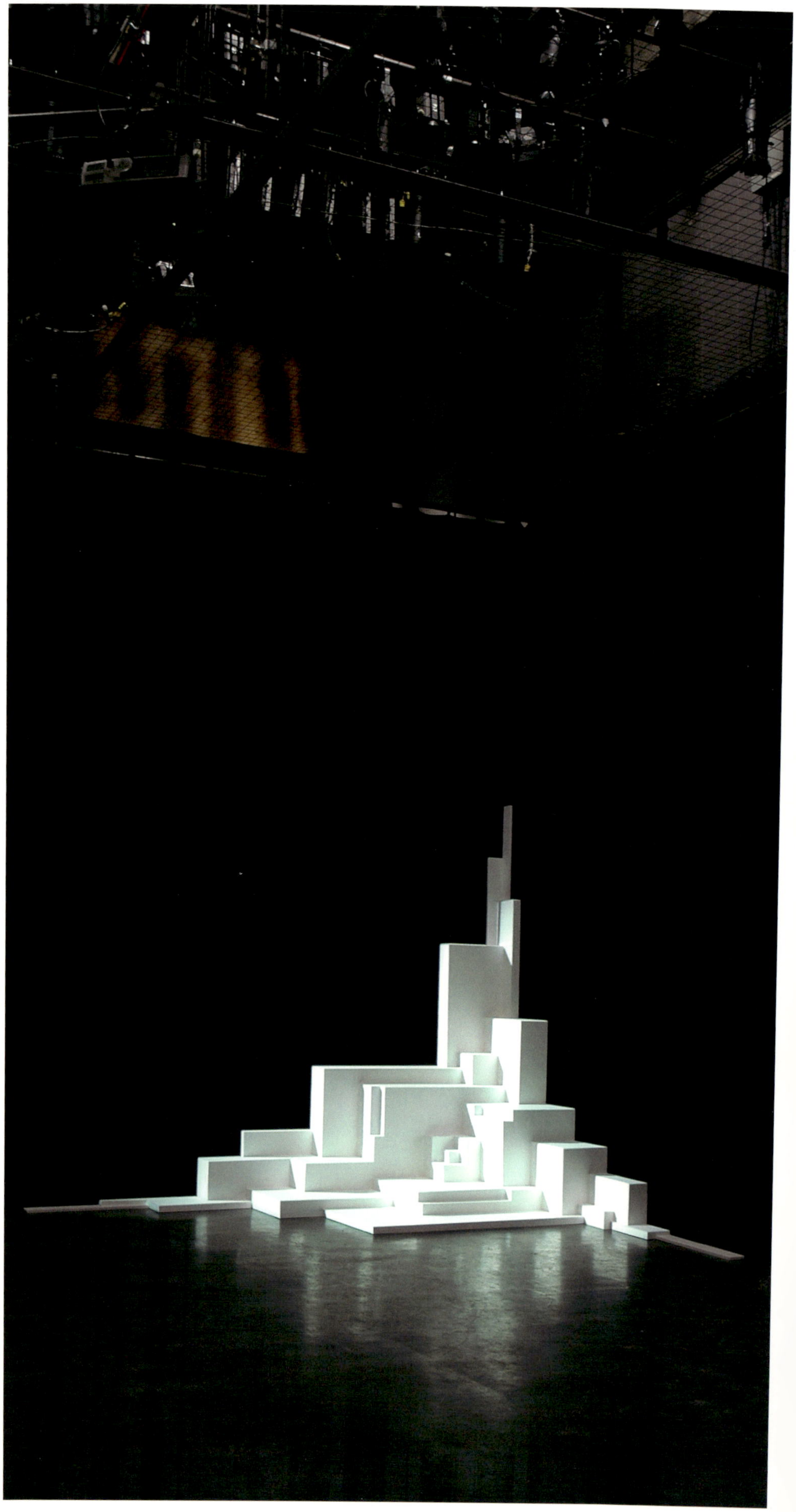

Pablo Valbuena

AUGMENTED SCULPTURE SERIES

This project investigates space-time not only as a three dimensional environment, but as a transformation of space as revealed by two layers that overlap each other. On the one hand, there is the physical layer, which controls the real space and shapes the volumetric base that serves as a support for the next level. The second level is a virtual projected layer that allows the control of the transformation and sequentiality of space-time. The blending of both levels gives the impression of physically transformable geometry.

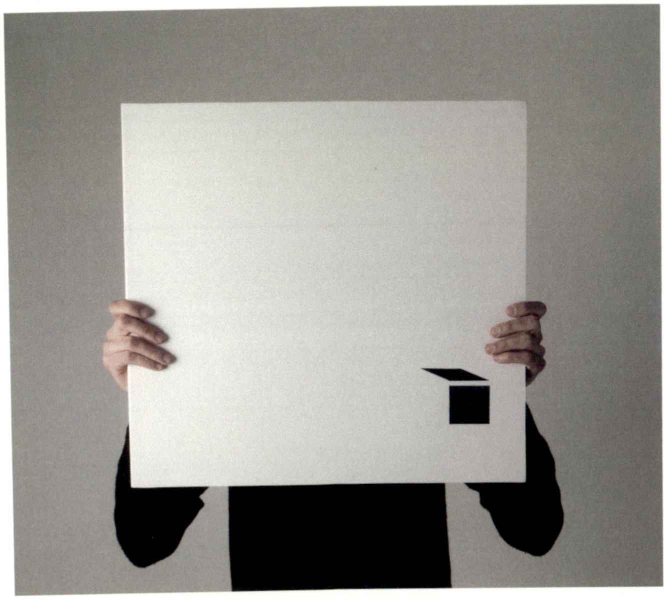

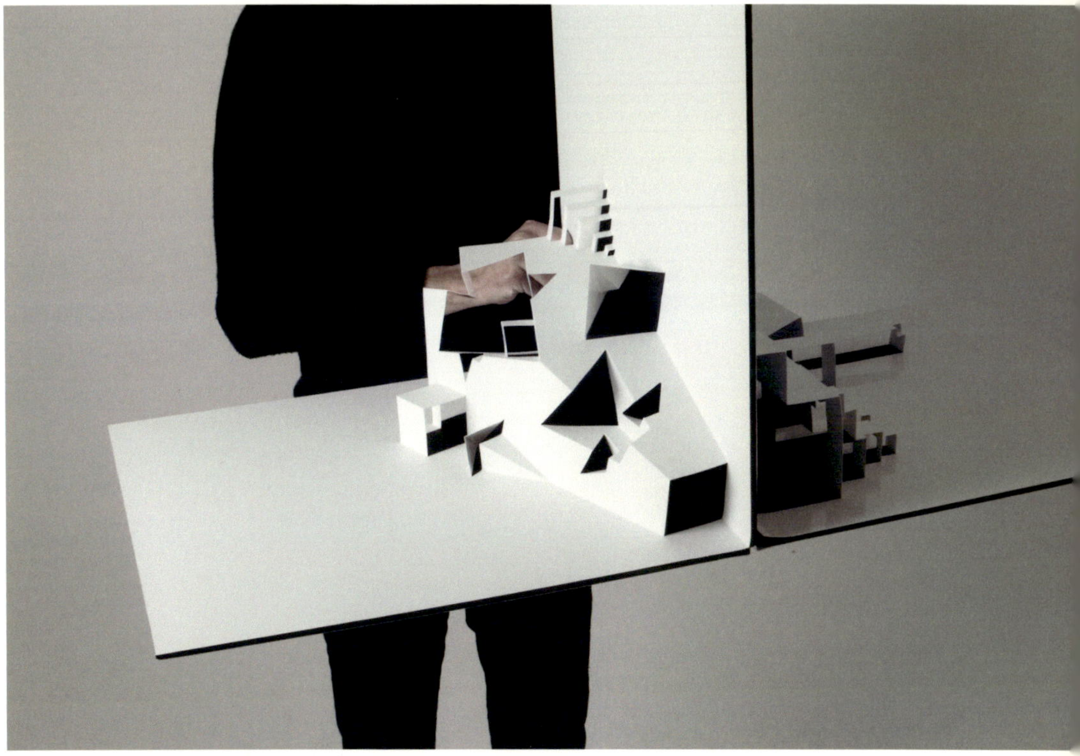

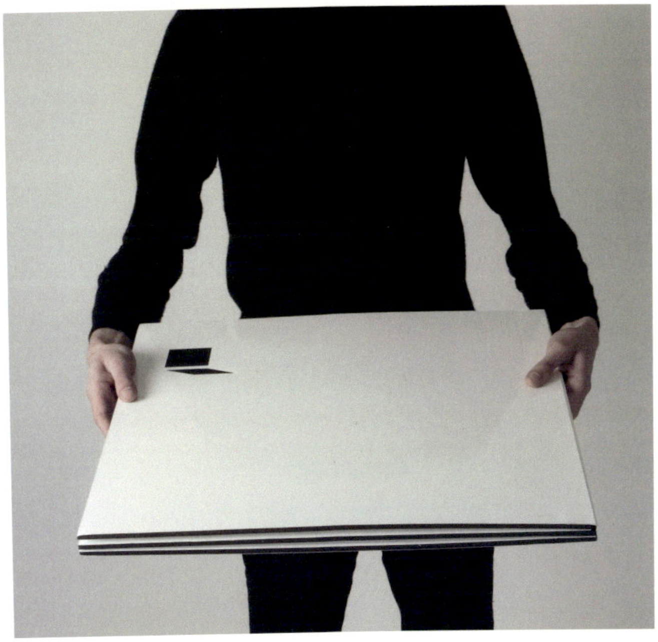

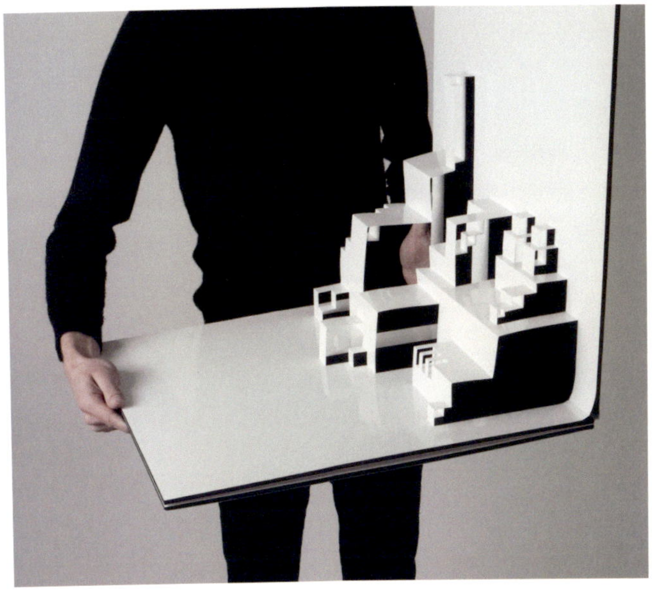

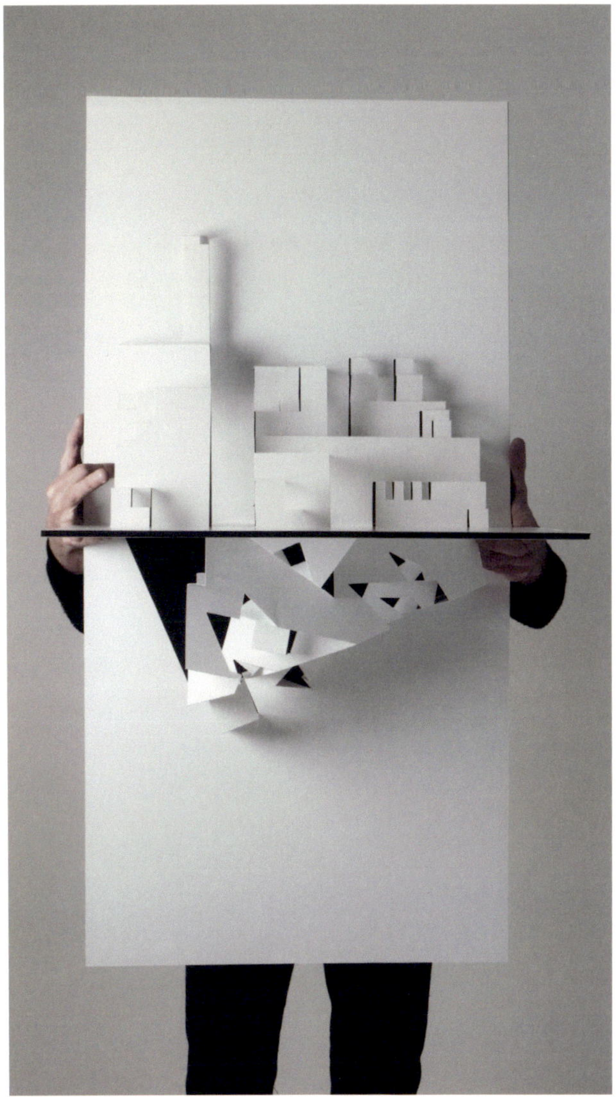

Olof Bruce, Tom Eriksson and Liv Wadström

INVISIBLE CITIES

A pop-up book that provides a tactile interpretation of Italo Calvino's *Invisible Cities*. The work is a handmade one-off piece consisting of folded and cut paper without any text or print.

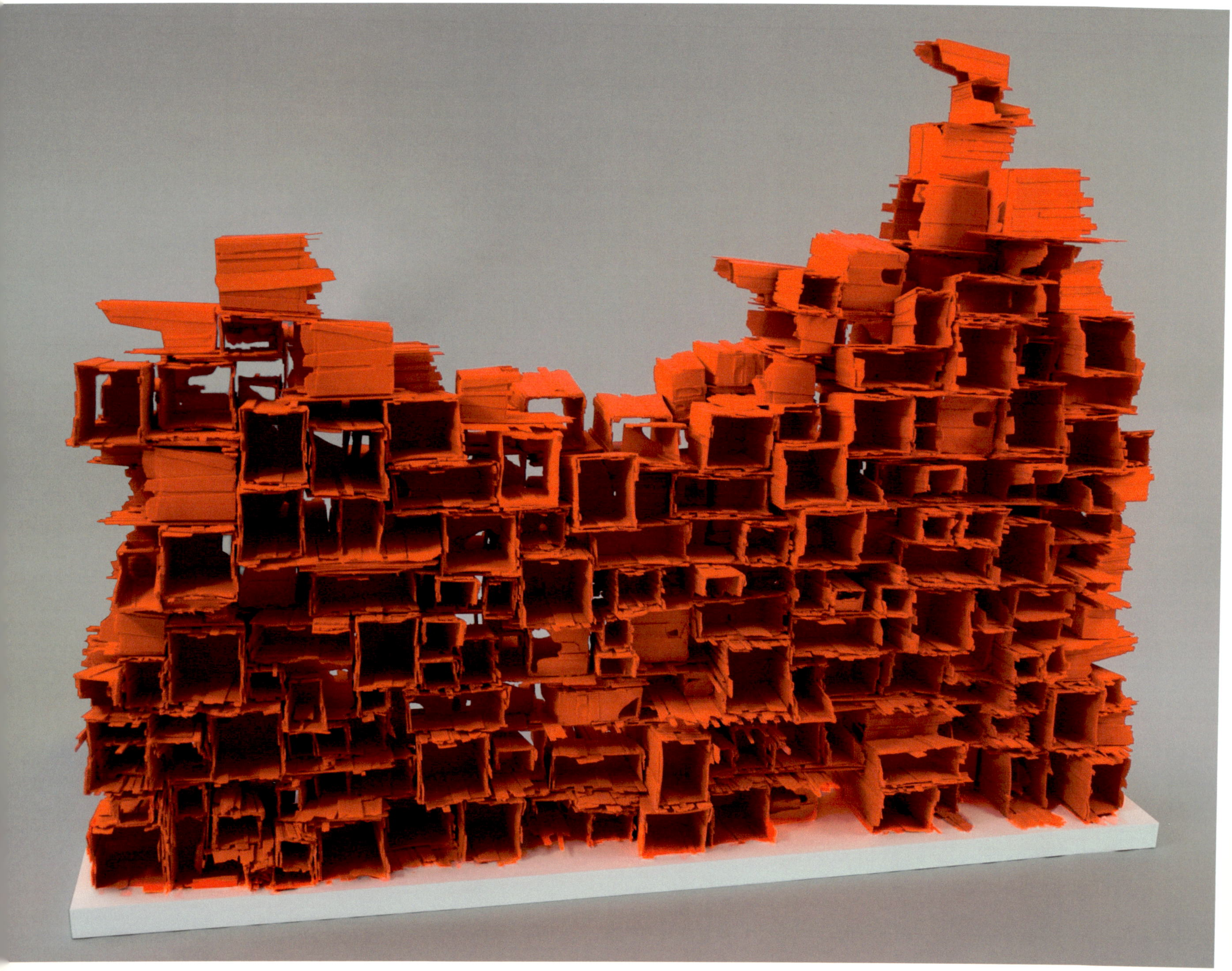

Arne Quinze BIDONVILLE *(top)*

The Bidonville sculpture series by Belgian artist Arne Quinze resembles shanty town-like structures competing with skyscrapers and parodies the speed in which cities today are being unreflectingly developed.

Andi Zimmermann HONG KONG *(right page)*

In his Spontaneous Random series, the photographer Andreas Zimmermann investigates the creative potential of the modular Lego building system. His digitally modified, large-scale photographs are reminiscent of abstract cityscapes.

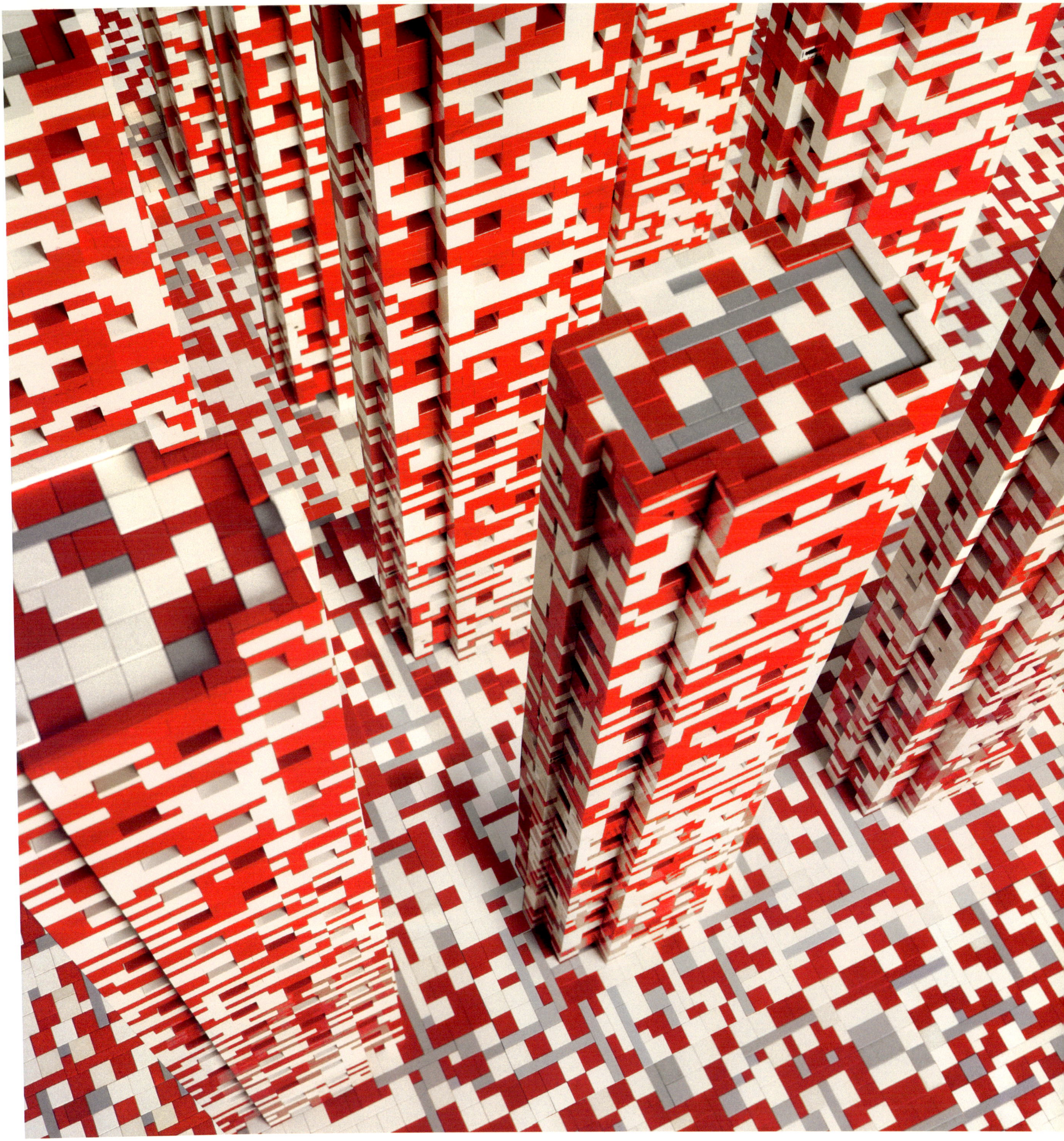

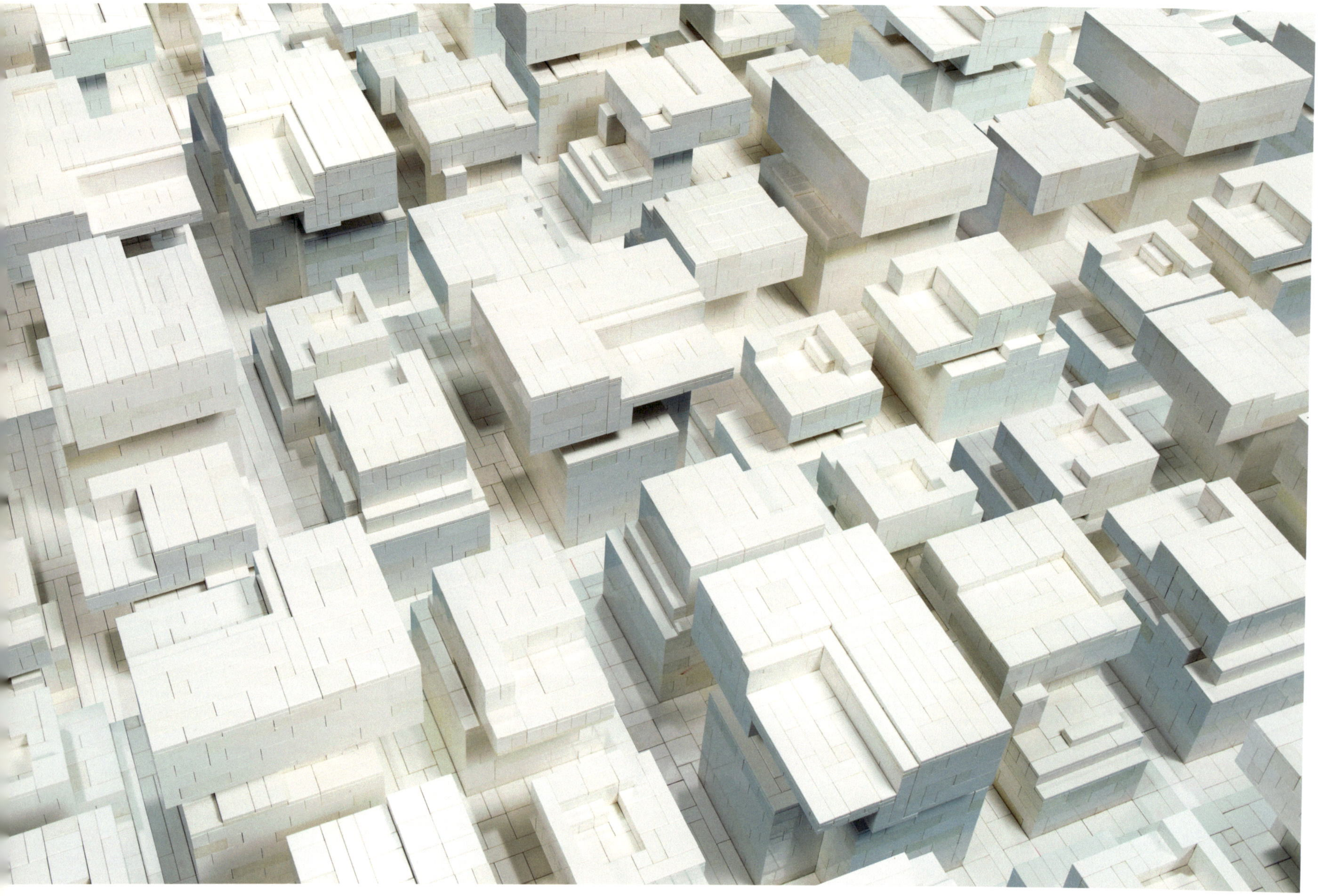

Andi Zimmermann

SCIFI *(top)*
TYPOLOGIE *(bottom)*

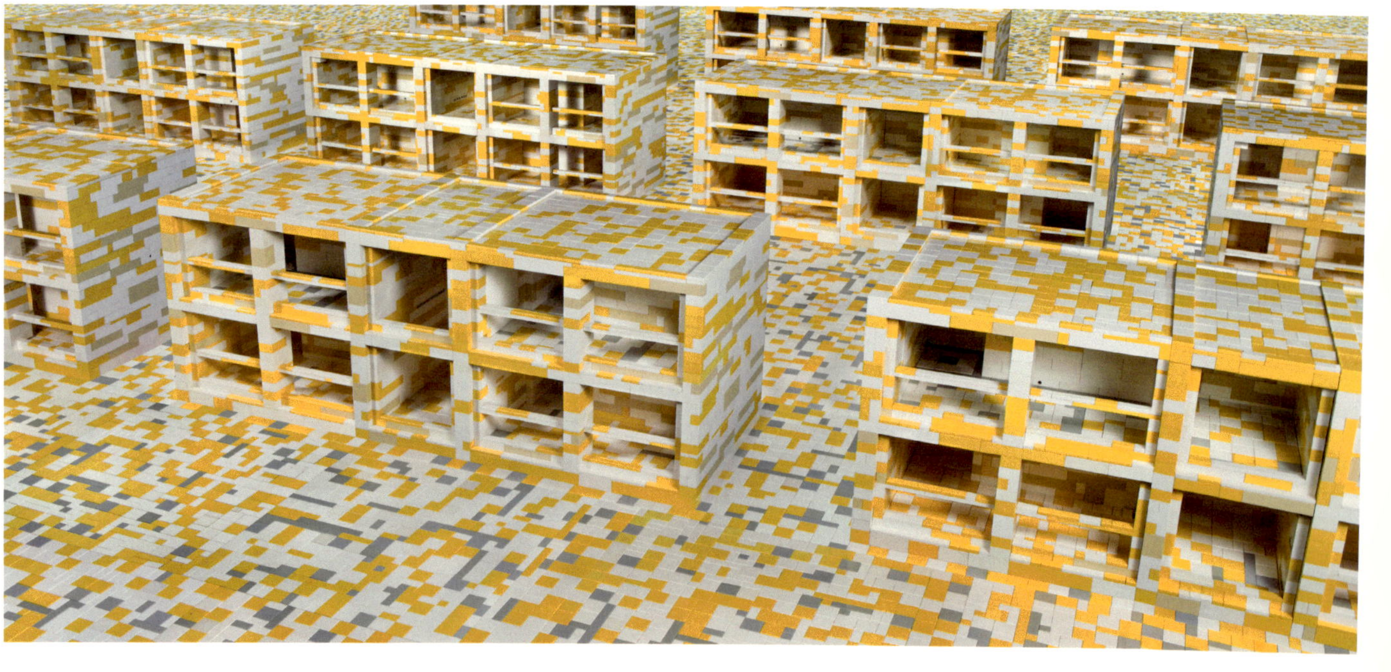

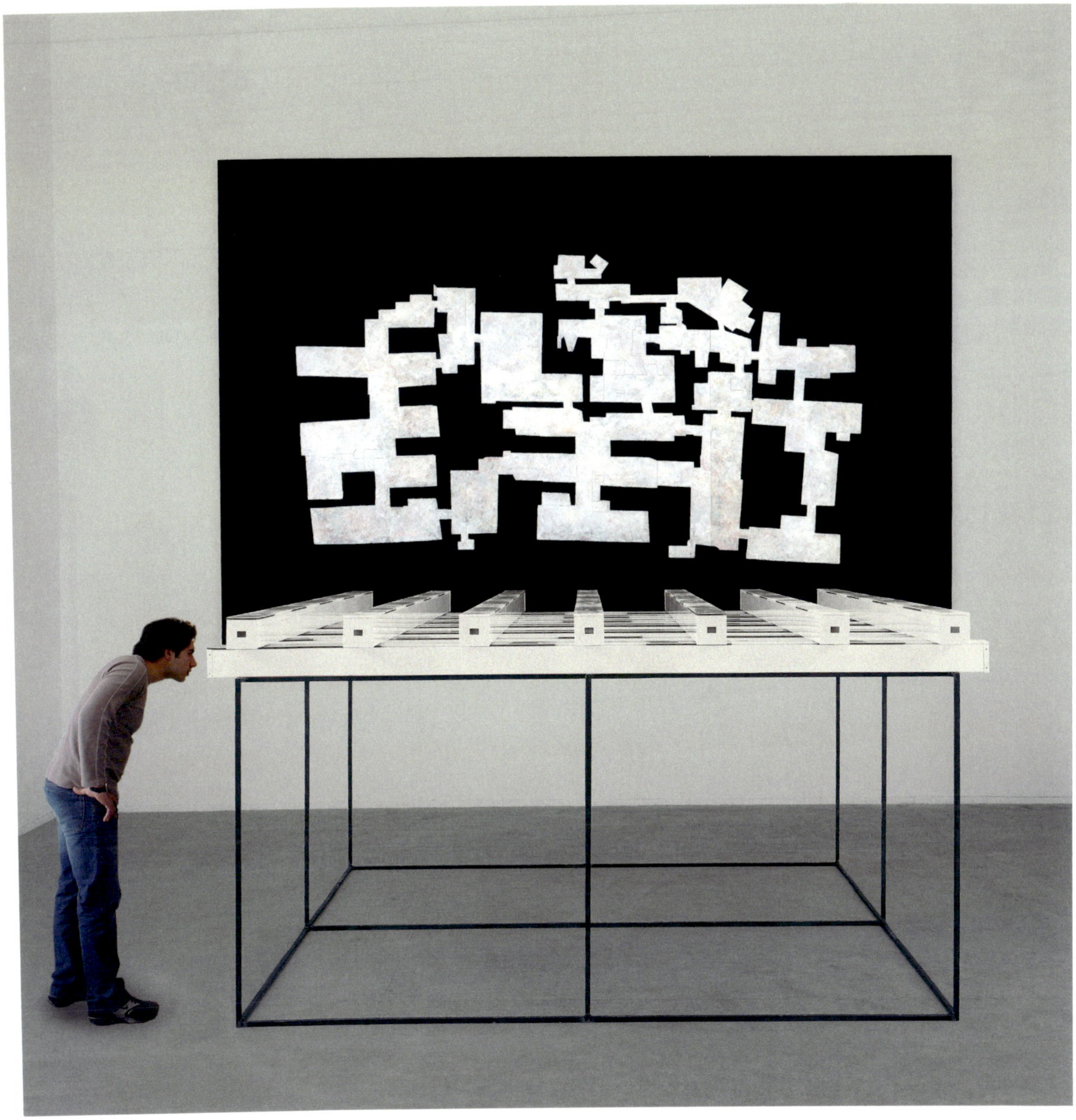

George Hadjimichalis

HOSPITAL THE BUILDING THE PLAN OF THE BUILDING

This multimedia installation is a philosophical inquiry into the nature of hospitals. A stylised architectural model entitled The Building is the installation's centrepiece. It is a simple structure, constructed from seven aluminium tubes, square in section and laid at right angles across seven others to make a grid of 14 corridors. Peering in through openings at the ends of the corridors, we glimpse a gleaming white interior populated by 125 tiny, cast bronze figures. A large canvas, The Plan of the Building, hangs on the wall behind the model. In contrast to the spatial simplicity of the model, this painted floor plan shows a labyrinthine layout.

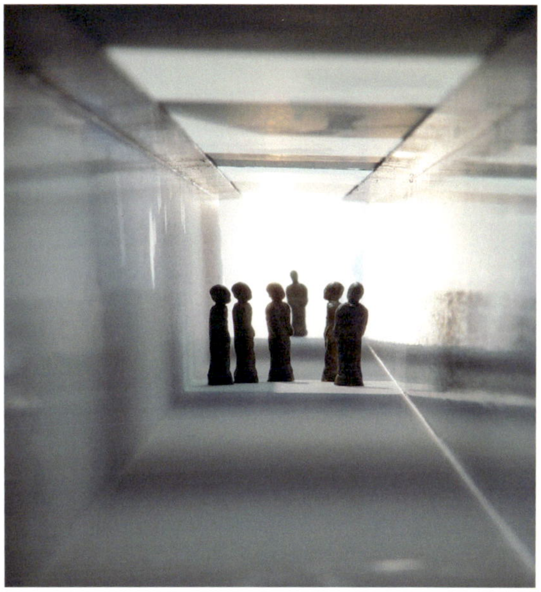

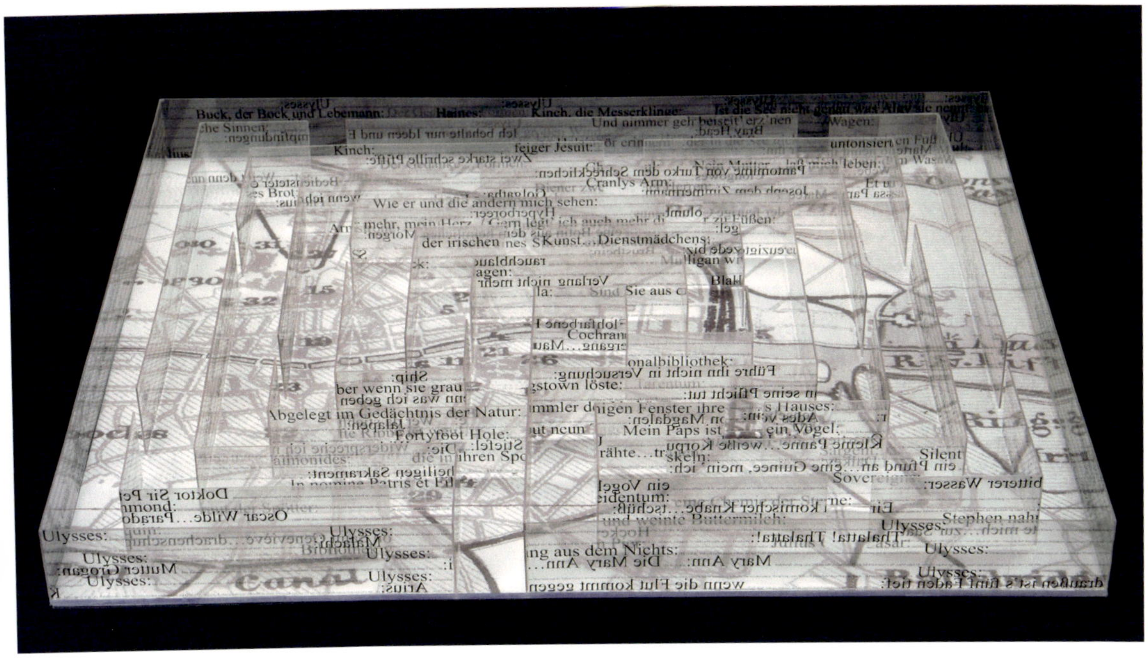

Faculty of Architecture / University of Technology Munich MONIKA GRANDL

JAMES JOYCE'S DUBLIN, ULYSSES

This model represents Dublin as described in James Joyce's seminal novel *Ulysses*. It was presented in an exhibition and accompanying publication entitled *Architektur wie sie im Buche steht* (a textbook example of architecture) edited by Winfried Nerdinger.

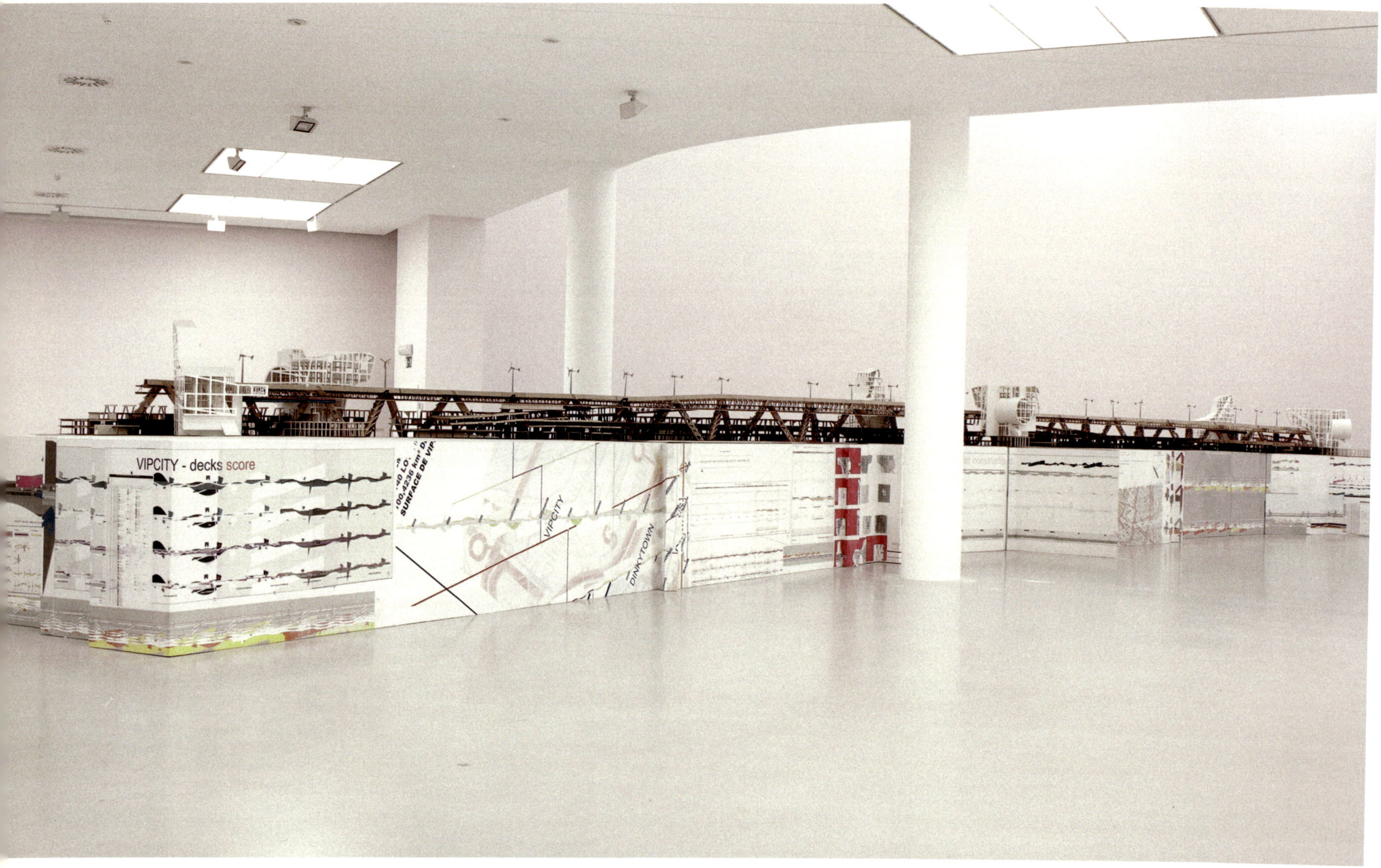

Luc Deleu & T.O.P. office

ONE NAUTICAL MILE,
AMENITIES FOR 9500 INHABITANTS

The nautical mile is the end result of a research by design into the necessary urban amenities relative to the number of inhabitants. In this concept for 76,000 occupants, half of which live in flats, the other half in freestanding houses on a lot with maximum dimensions calculated on the basis of the land available on earth per inhabitant at that moment (0.6633 ha per family).

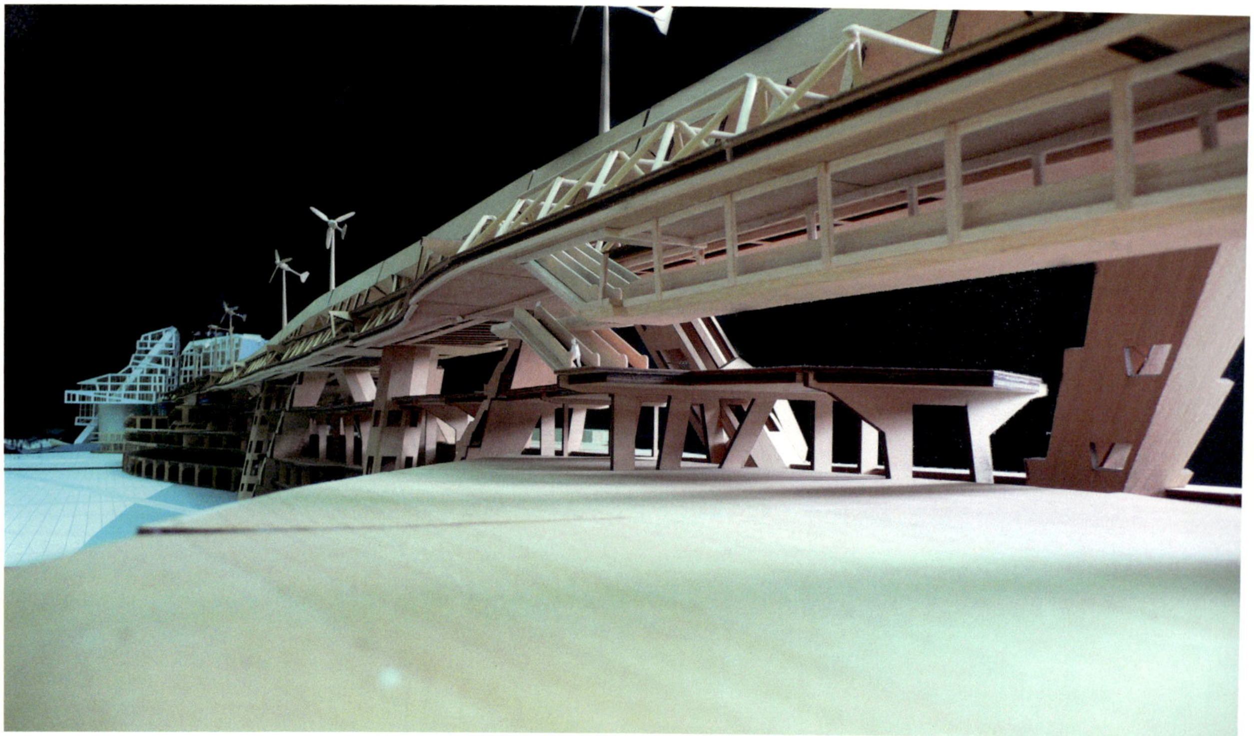

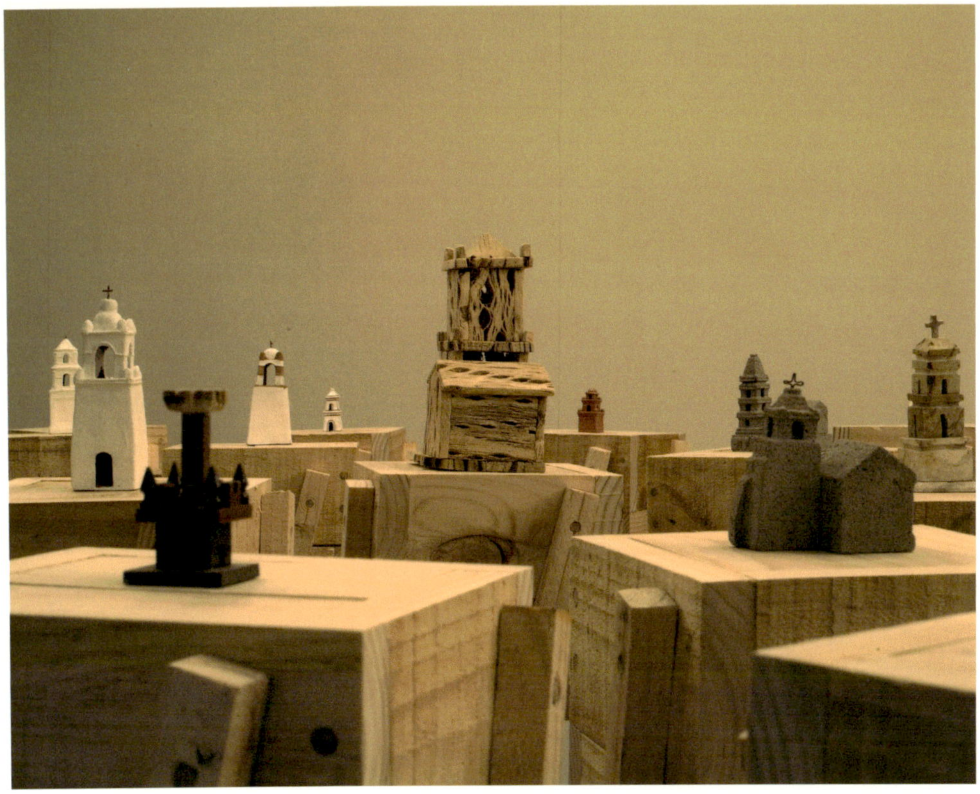

Pezo von Ellrichshausen

I WAS THERE, CHILEAN SOUVENIRS

This exhibition, curated by architects Mauricio Pezo and Sofia von Ellrichshausen, was conceived as the Chilean contribution to La Bienniale de Venezia, the 11th International Architecture Biennale. It is conceived as a platform to elaborate an unprecedented and detailed registry of icons of popular Chilean architecture; icons collectively assumed as emblems that stand for diverse local identities, then remade as miniature crafts figures (souvenirs), to then be finally offered as products of mass consumption. From a total of 100 pieces, the curators gathered 90 souvenirs of traditional architecture that can be found throughout Chile. Presented alongside these, and operating as a sort of curated simulacrum of representation, is a selection of 10 works of contemporary architecture built in Chile since the year 2000, which have been converted into the same miniaturised format.

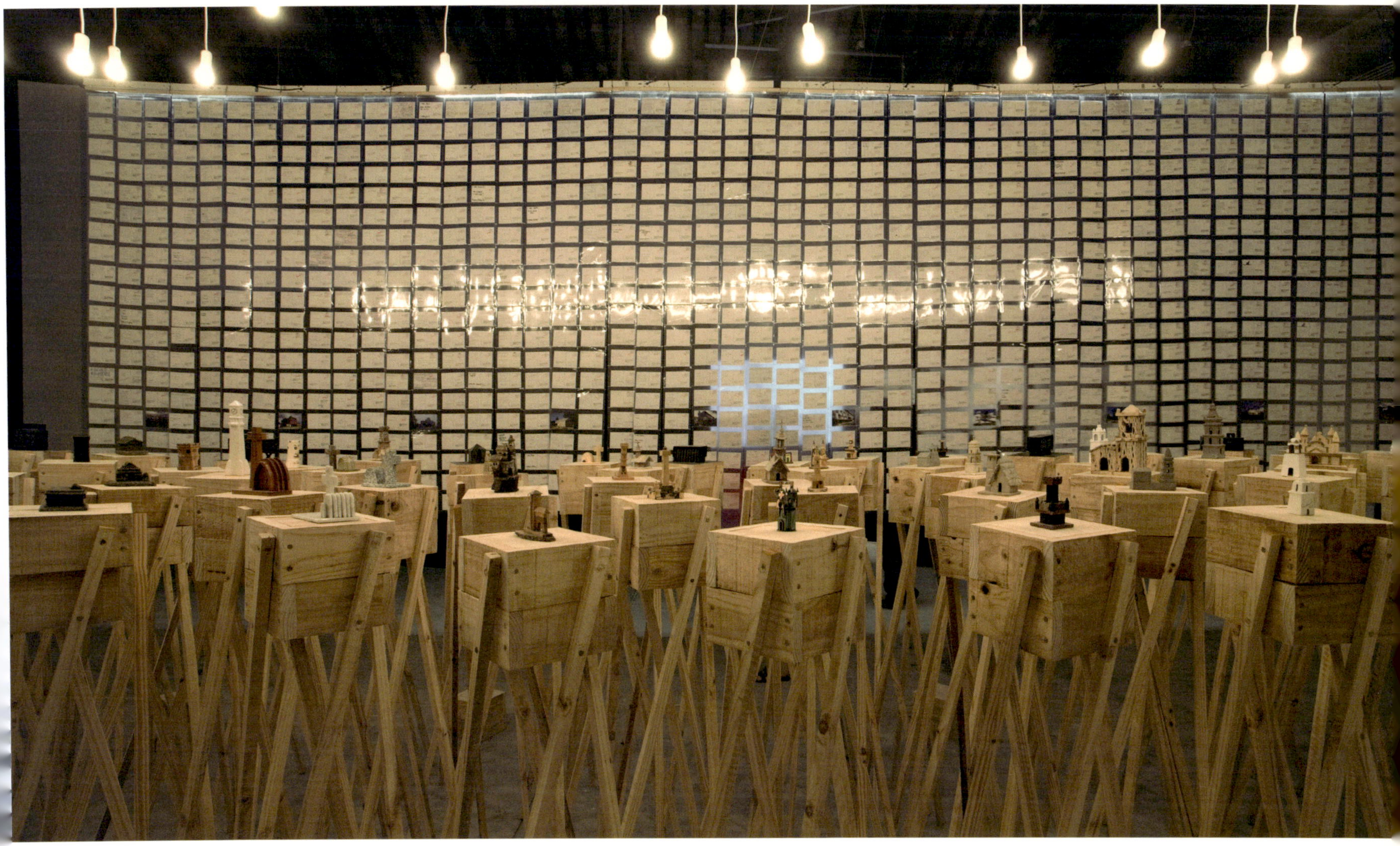

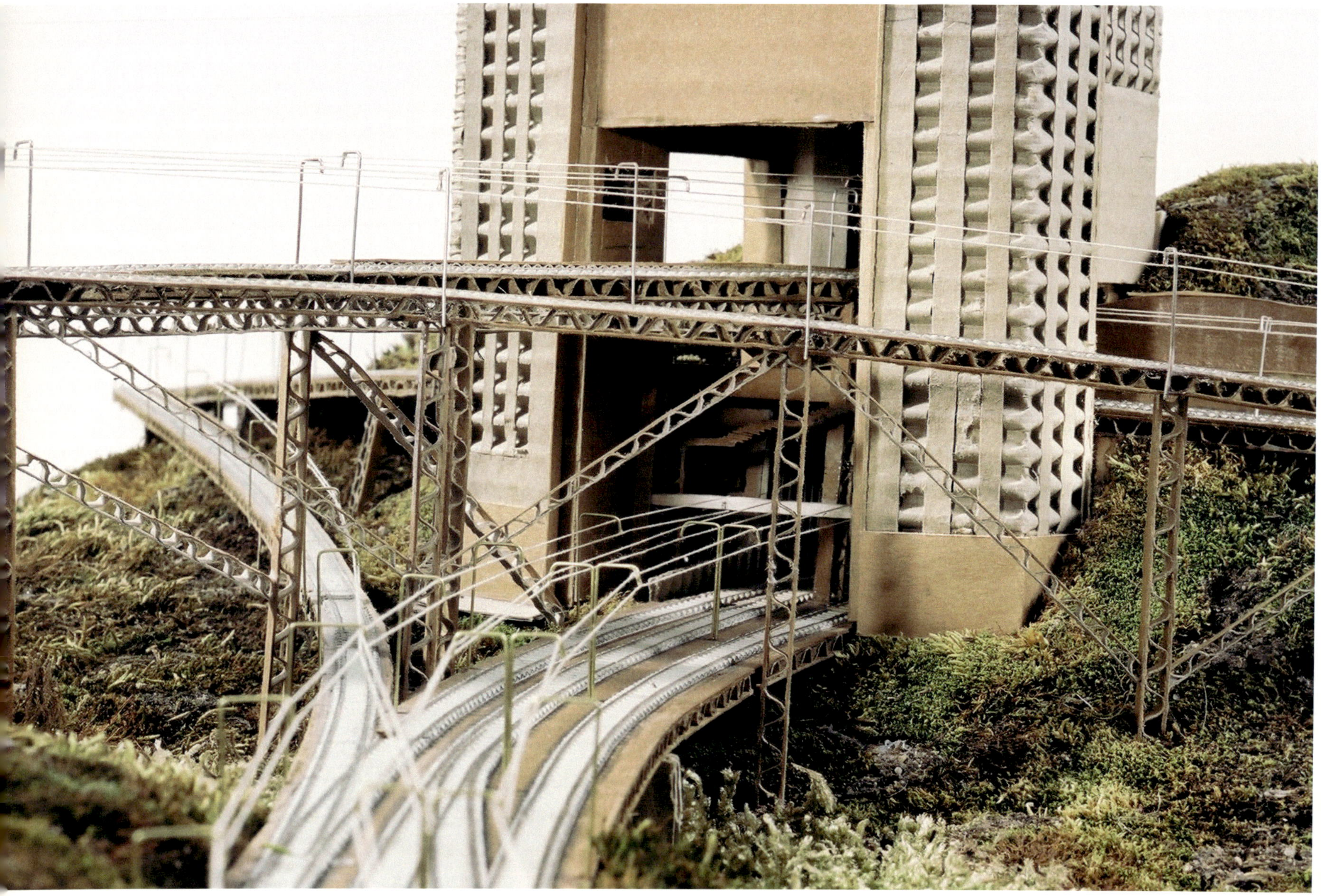

Matias Bechtold

OSTKREUZ

The artists's vision for Ostkreuz, a station on the Berlin suburban railway and one of the busiest in all Germany.

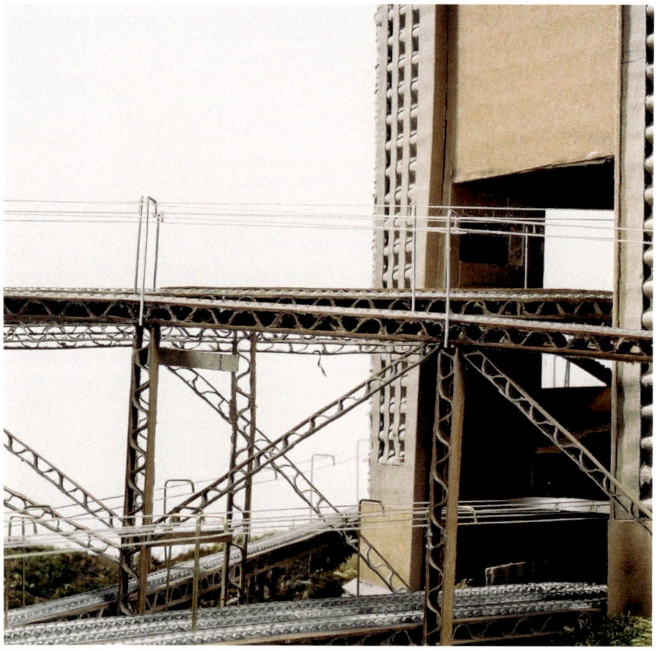

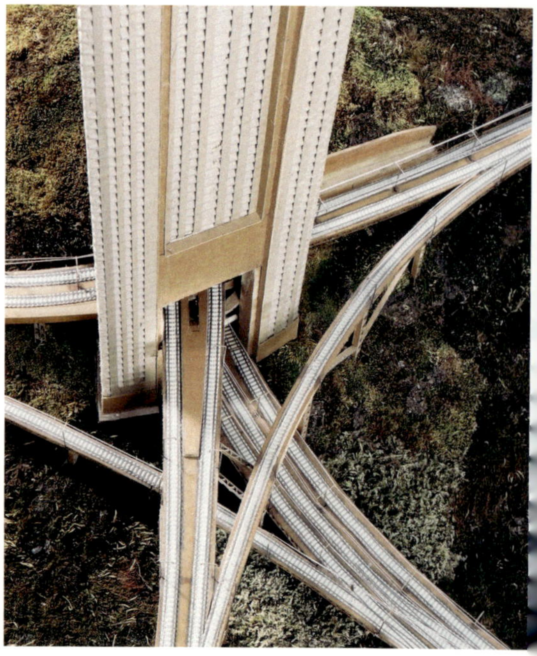

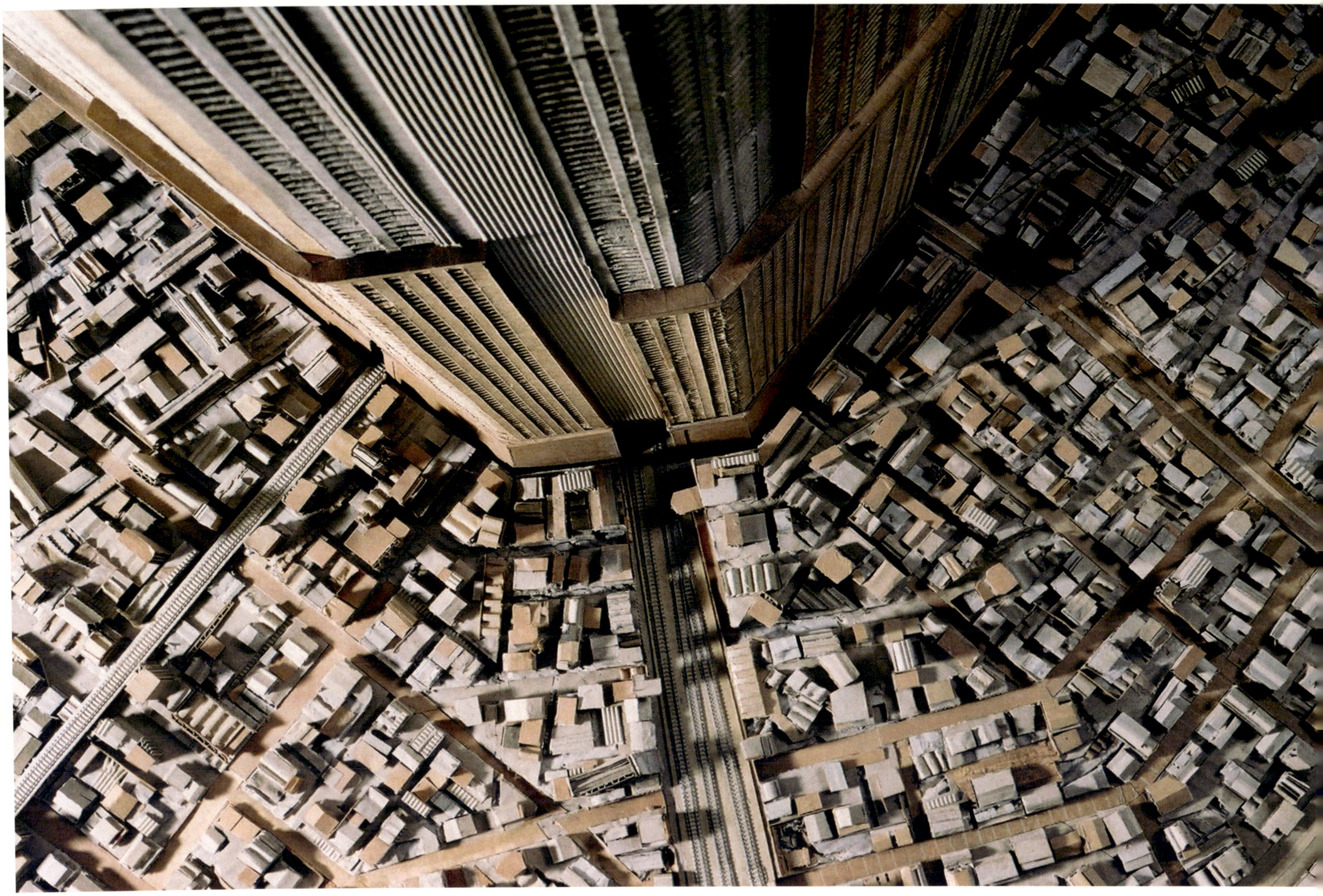

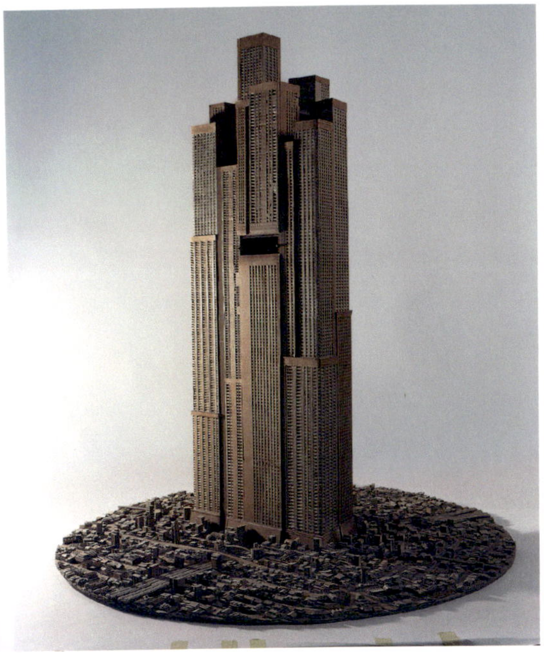

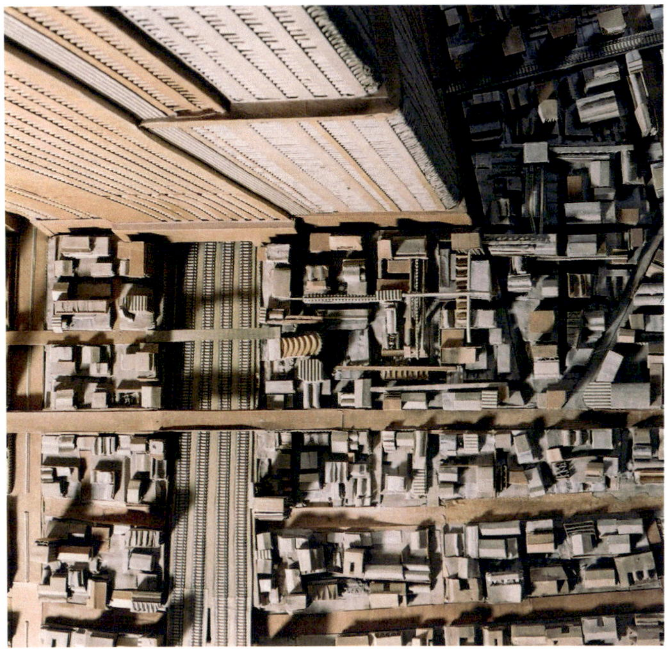

Matias Bechtold

BECHTOLD CITY

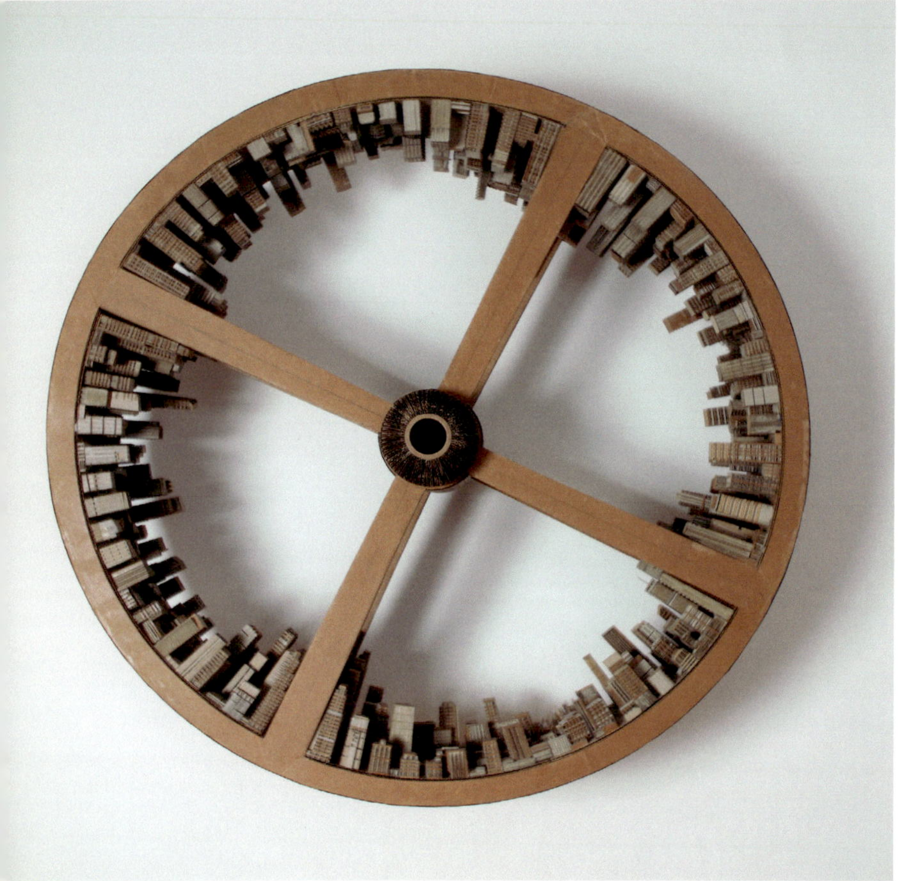

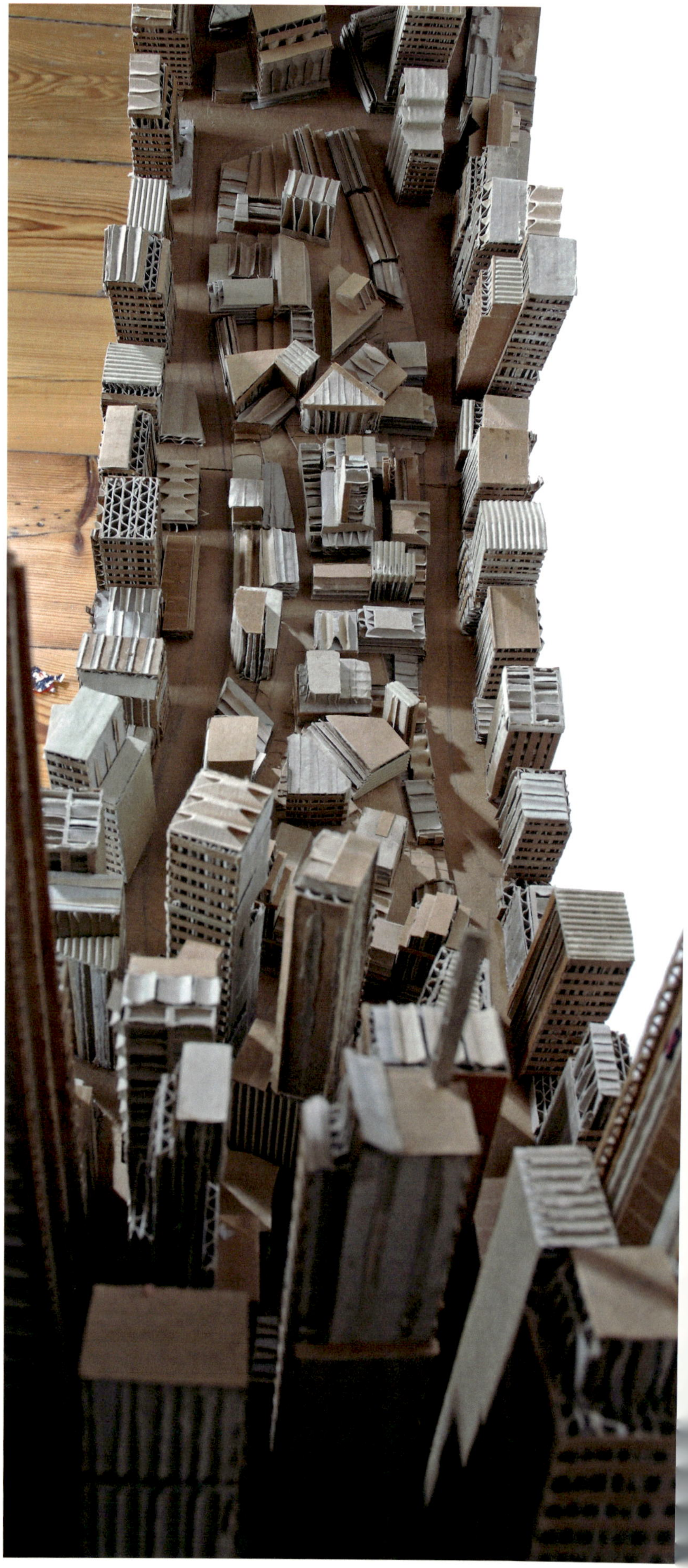

Matias Bechtold

ALLSTADT

Matias Bechtold's cardboard installation Allstadt (Spacecity) is an ironic take on the orbital satellites in Stanley Kubrick's enigmatic science fiction film *2001: A Space Odyssey* (1968). Human evolution, technology and metropolitan growth become intertwined.

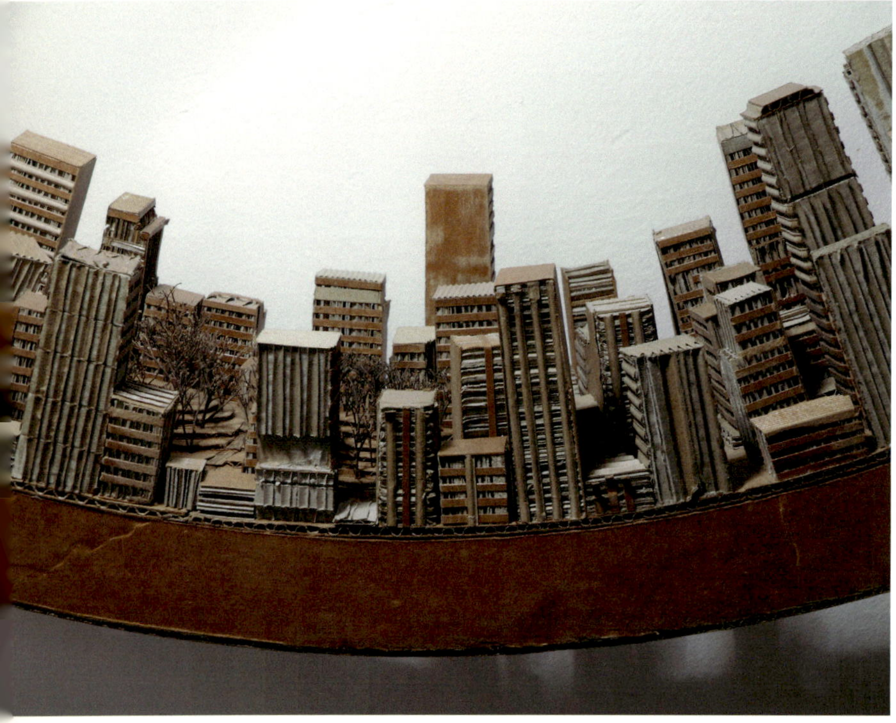

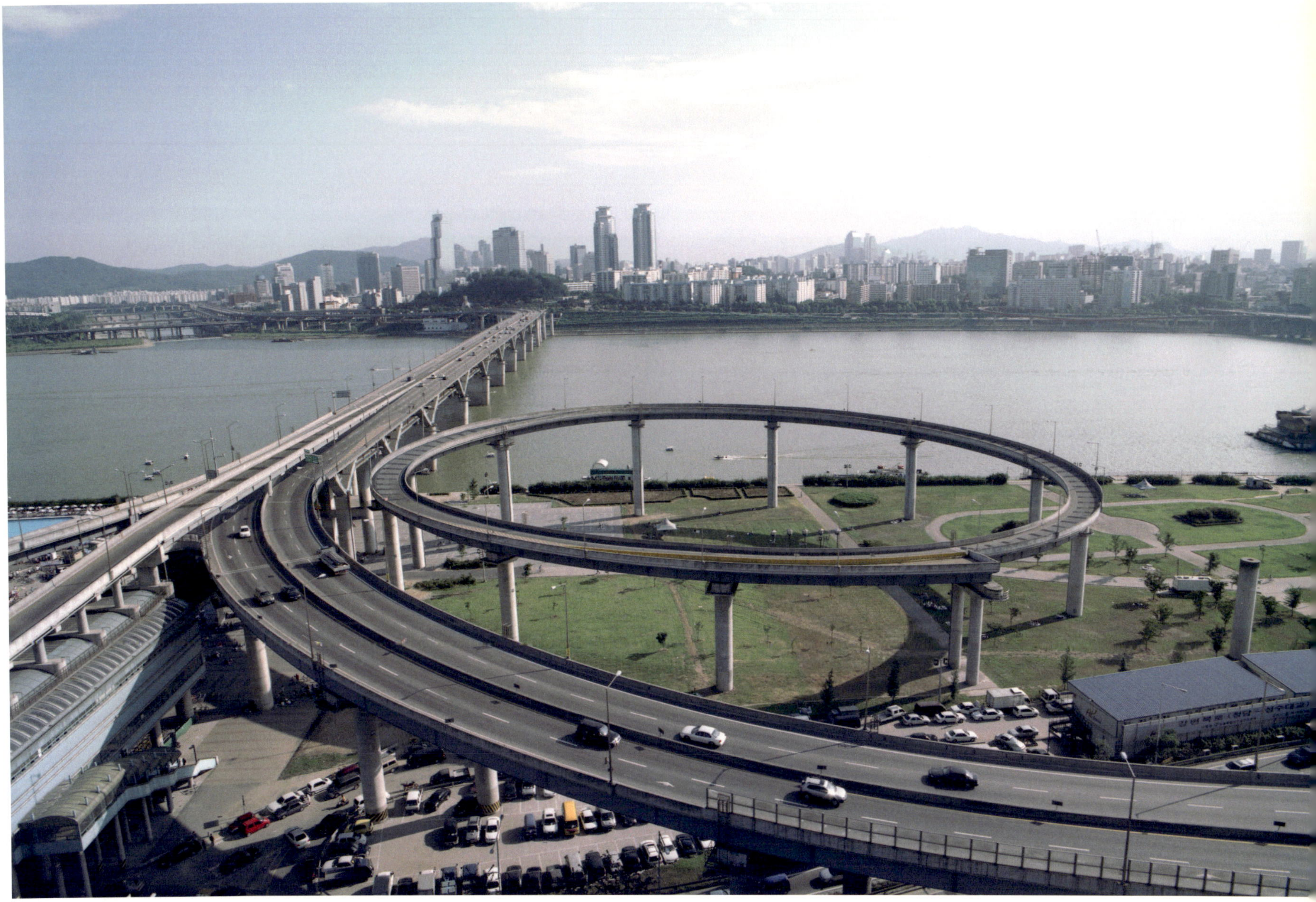

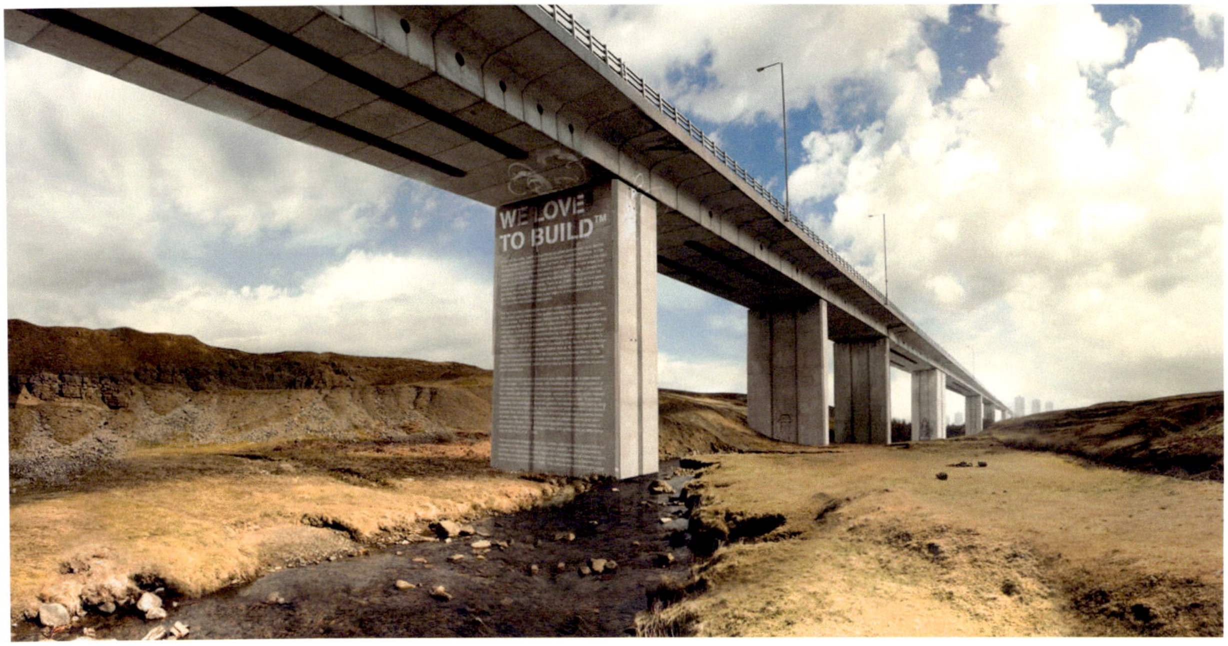

Simon Boudvin

TTUKSEOM *(top)*

Paul Hollingworth

WE LOVE TO BUILD *(left)*

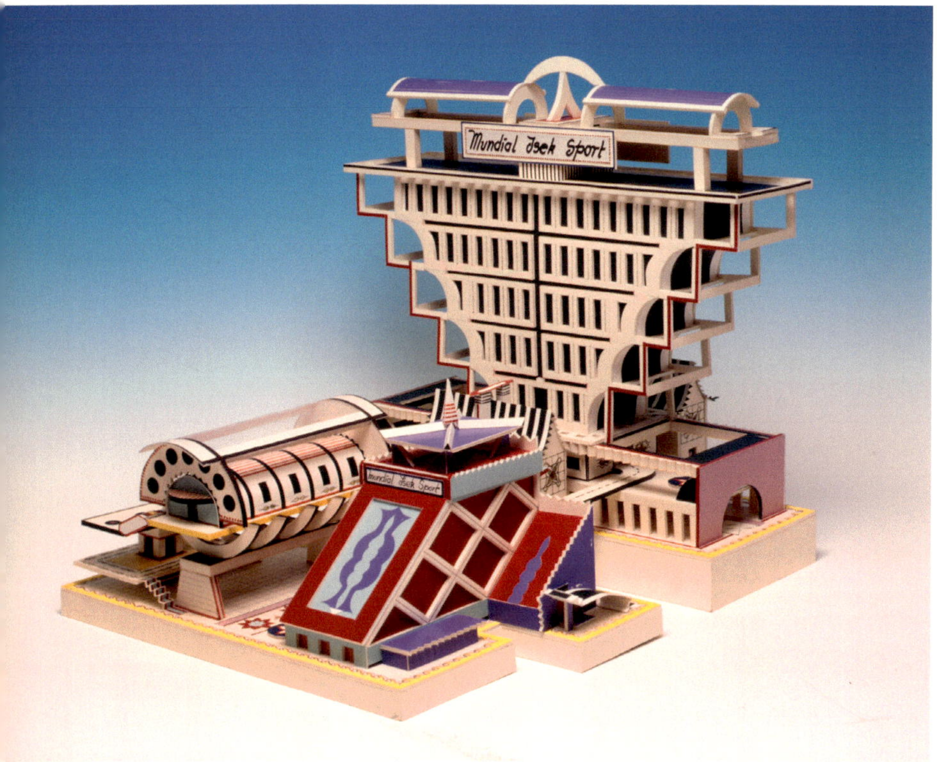

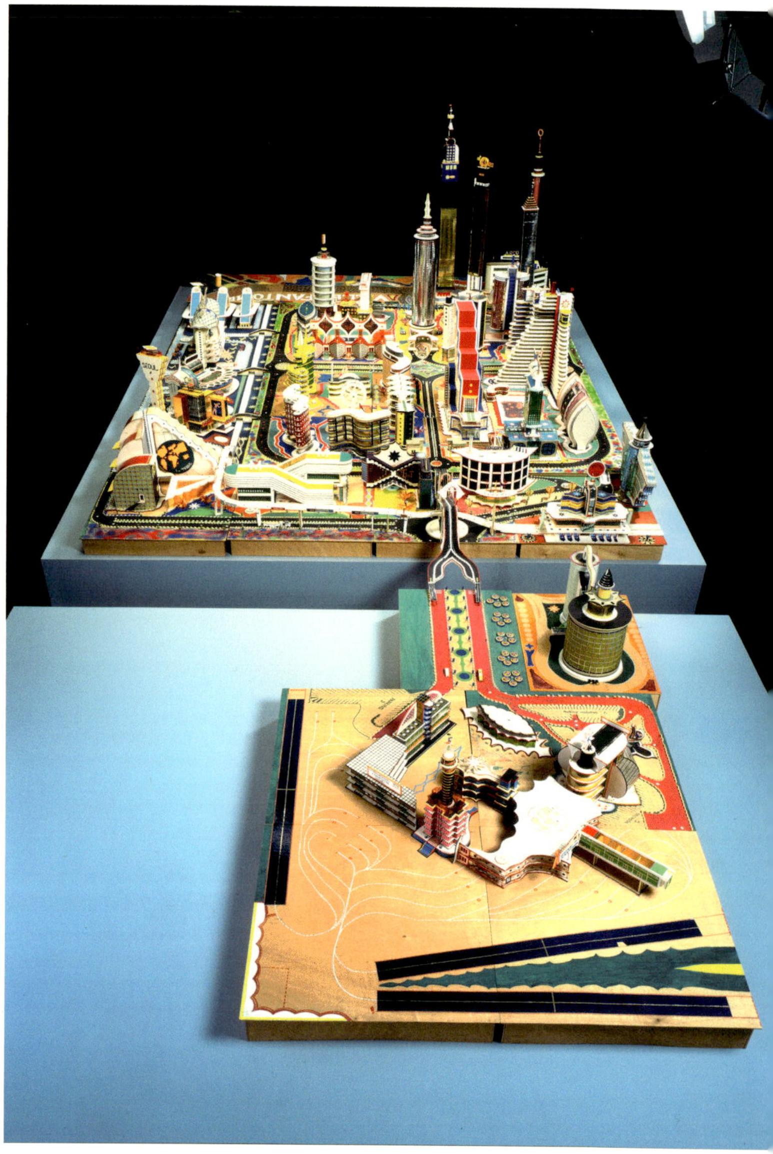

Body Isek Kingelez

This Congolese sculptor and artist is best known for his models of fantastic and utopian cities made of cardboard, paper and plastic that he calls "Extreme Models". His models of entire cites reflect the sprawling and anarchic metropolis of African megacities such as Kinshasa. Found materials such as bottle caps, corrugated cardboard or tinfoil are frequently incorporated in his works.

MUNDIAL ISEK SPORT *(top)*
ZAÏRE *(bottom)*
KIMBEMBELE IHUNGA *(right page)*
VILLE FANTÔME *(right)*
NEW MANHATTAN (MANHATTAN CITY 3021) *(bottom right)*

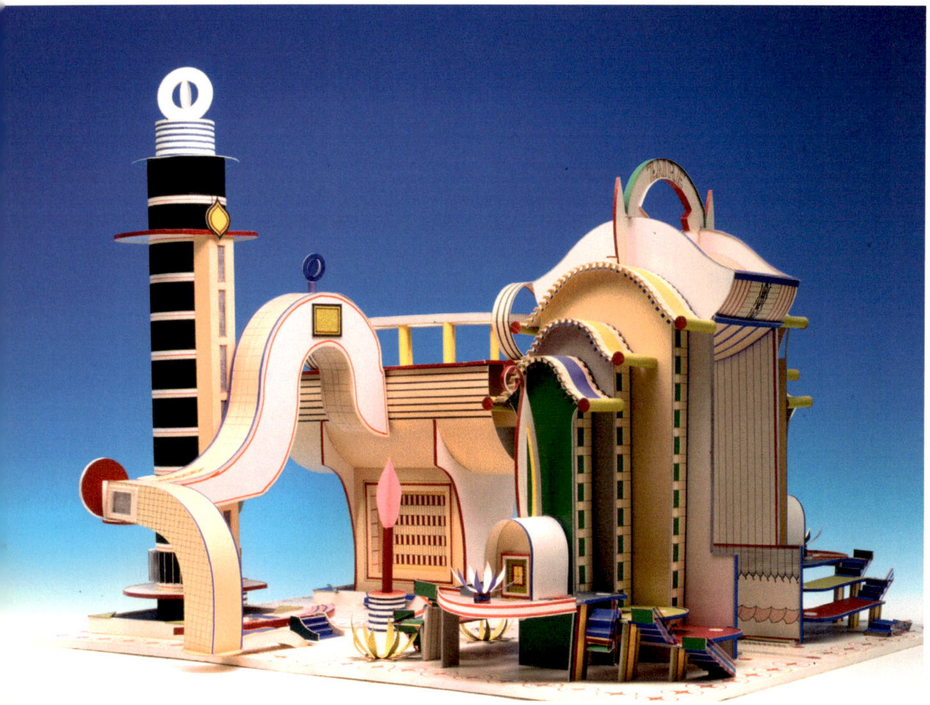

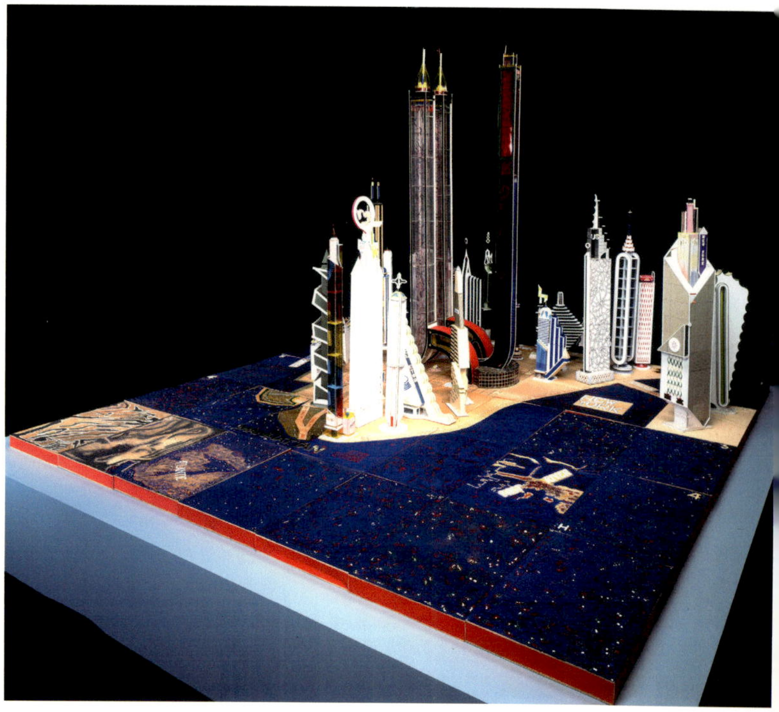

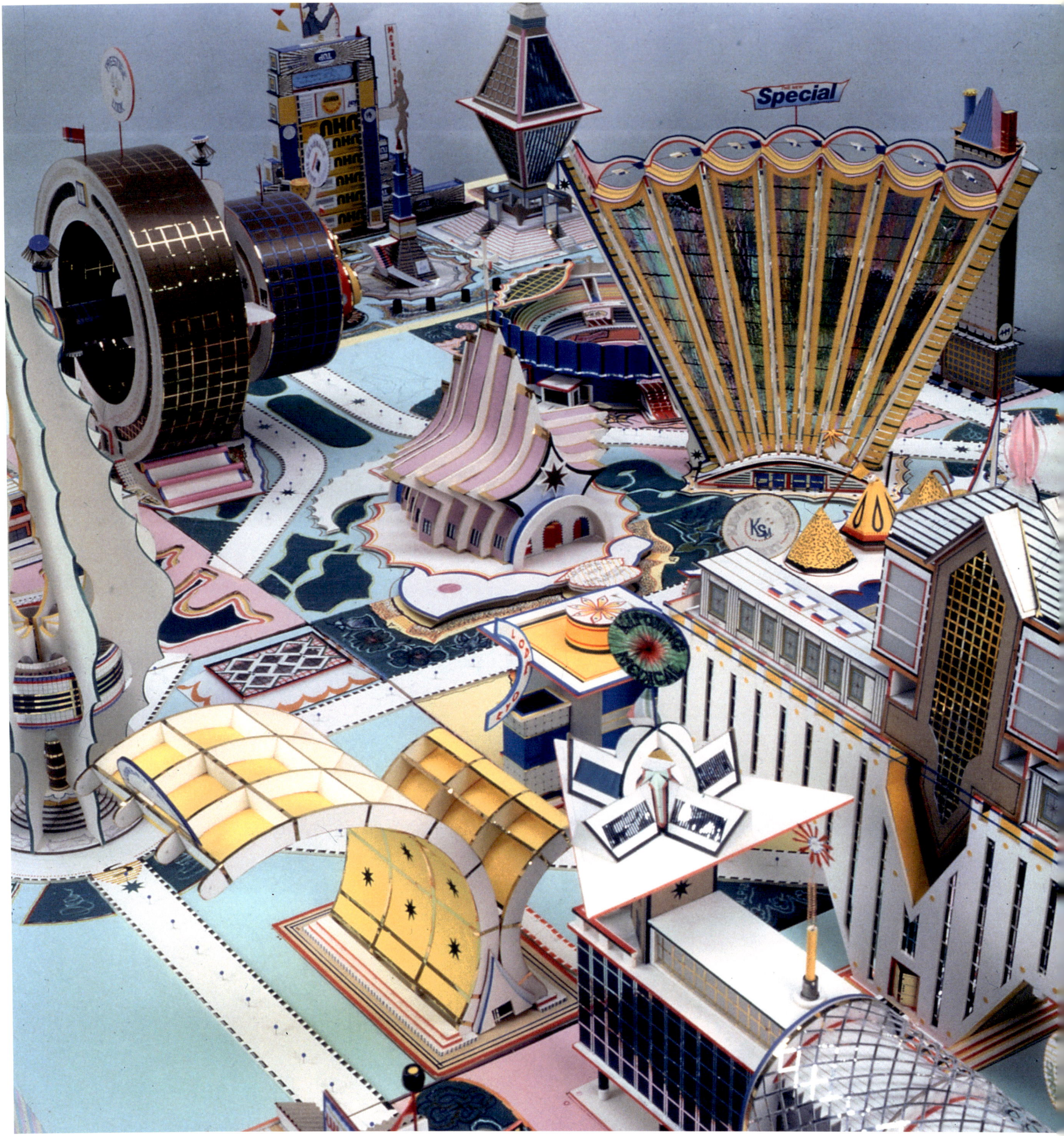
Special

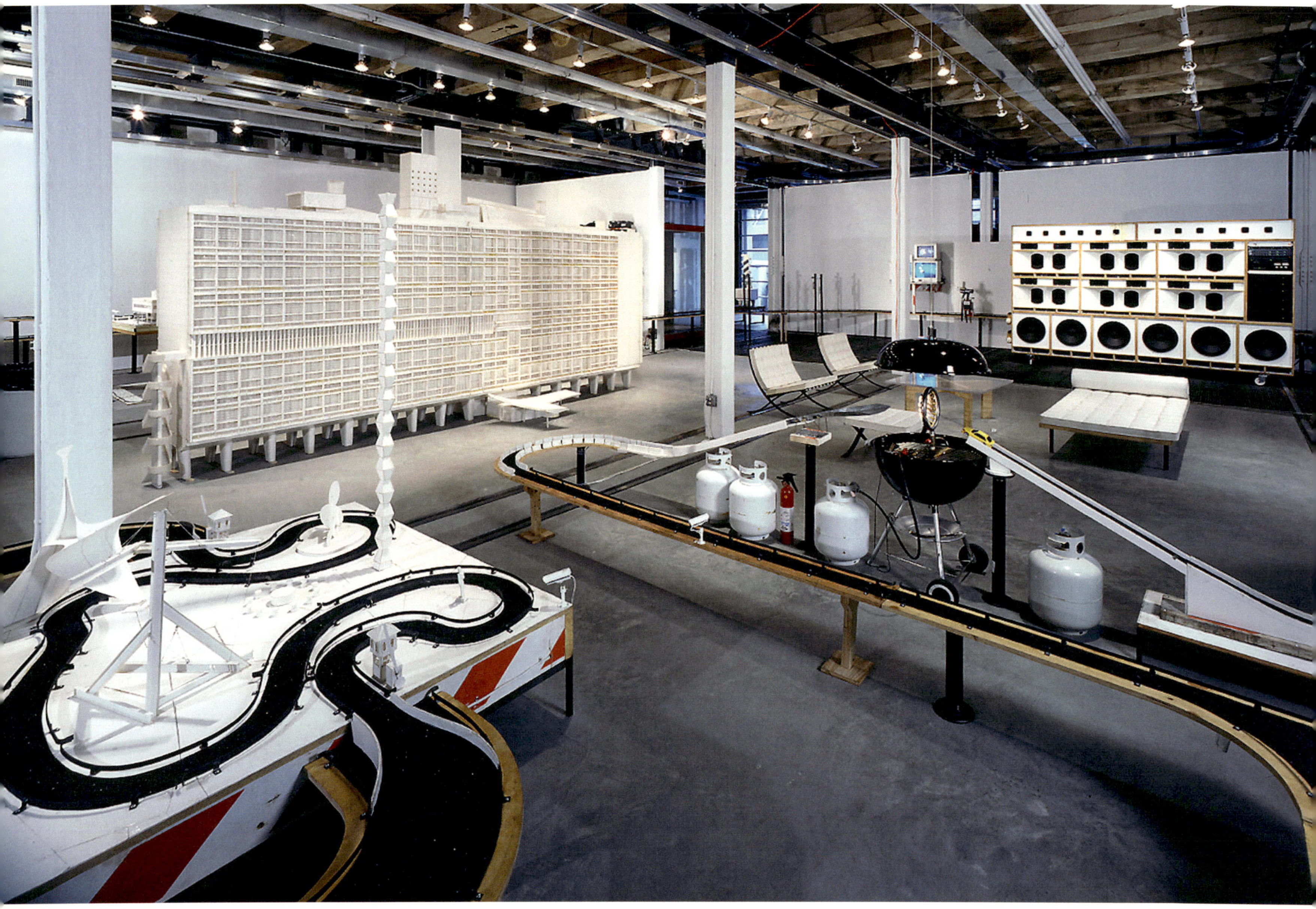

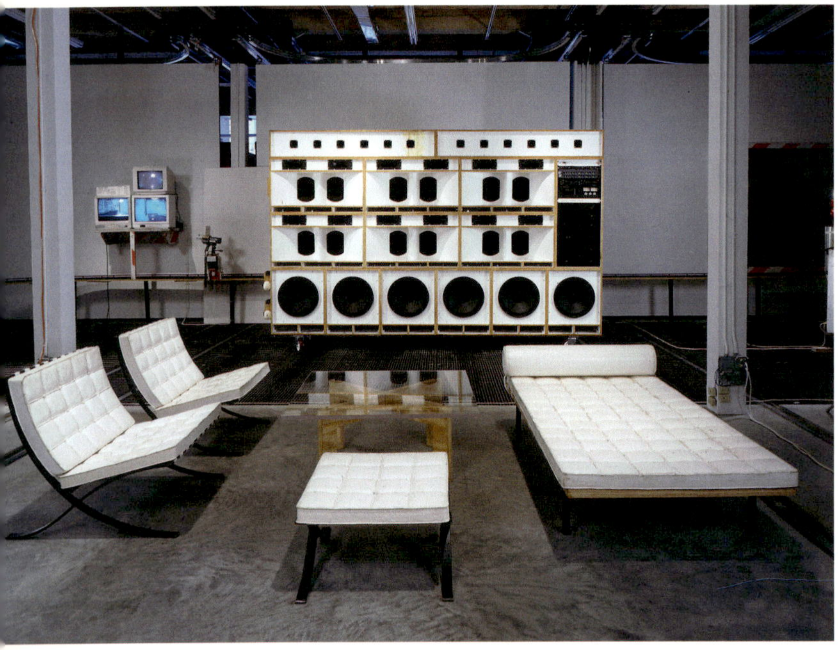

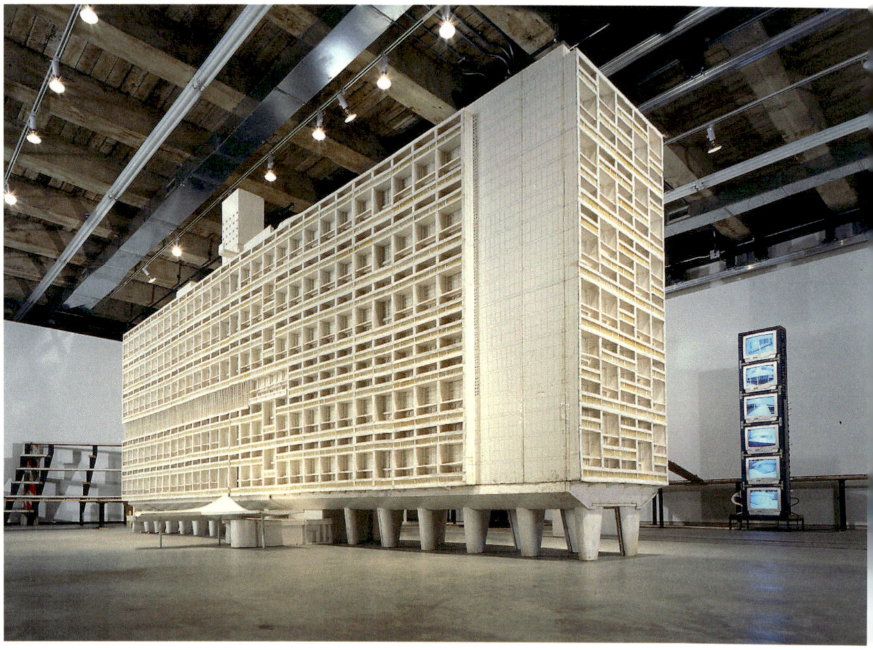

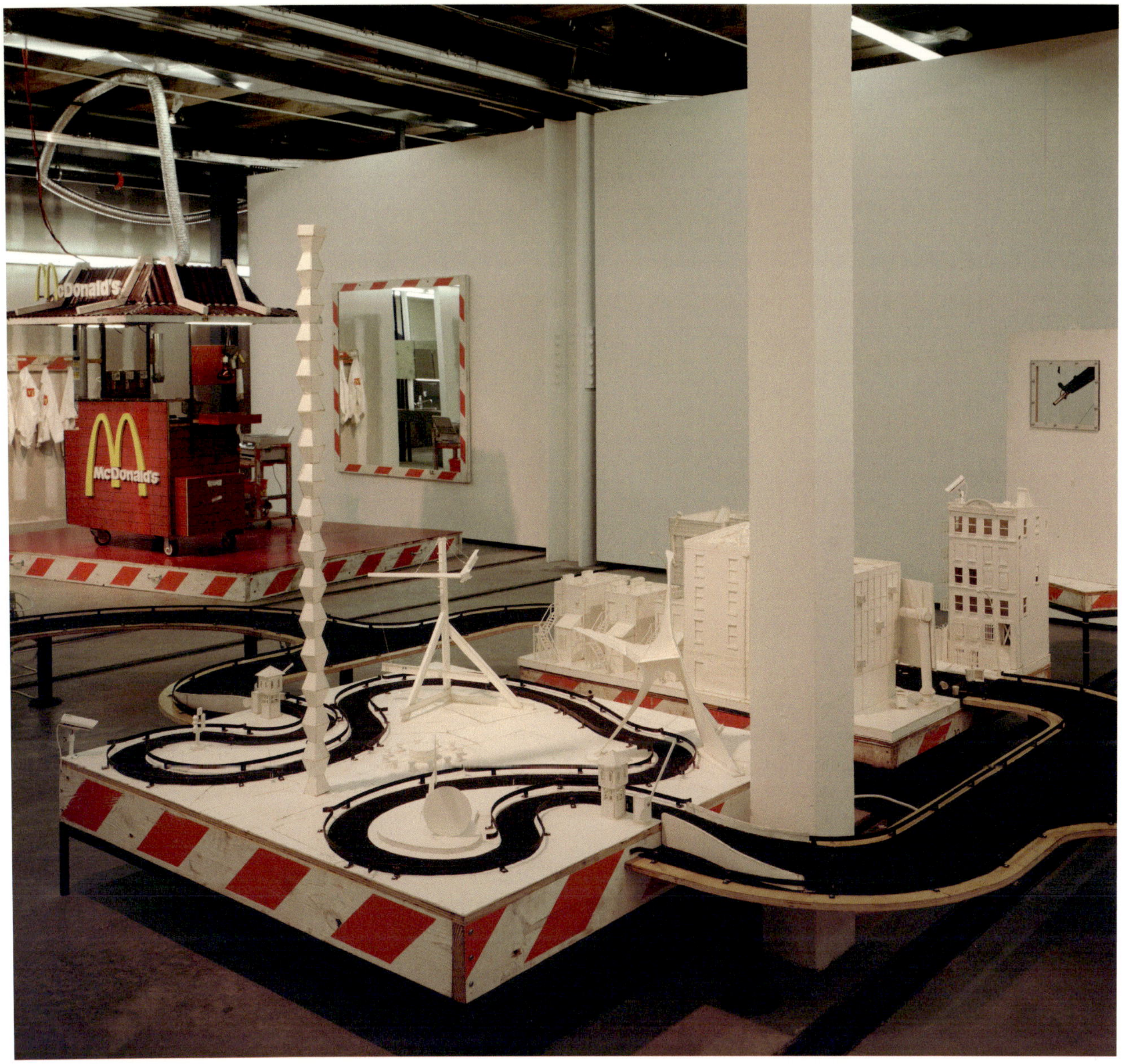

Tom Sachs

NUTSY'S

This chaotically sprawling installation by American artist Tom Sachs, based on culture and consumerism, is made up of sculptural, audiovisual, and performative elements connected by a roadway running the length and breadth of the installation. Security cameras connected to video monitors survey the scene as visitors move around the racetrack, marvelling at remote-controlled model cars zooming past the 1:25 scale reproductions of Le Corbusier's architecture, furniture by Mies van der Rohe, and other elements including a McDonald's restaurant, a 10,000-watt boom box, and a DJ station. Tom Sachs' Nutsy's entices visitors into this complex and chaotic world in which the idealistic modernism of Le Corbusier coexists alongside the commercial modernism of McDonald's.

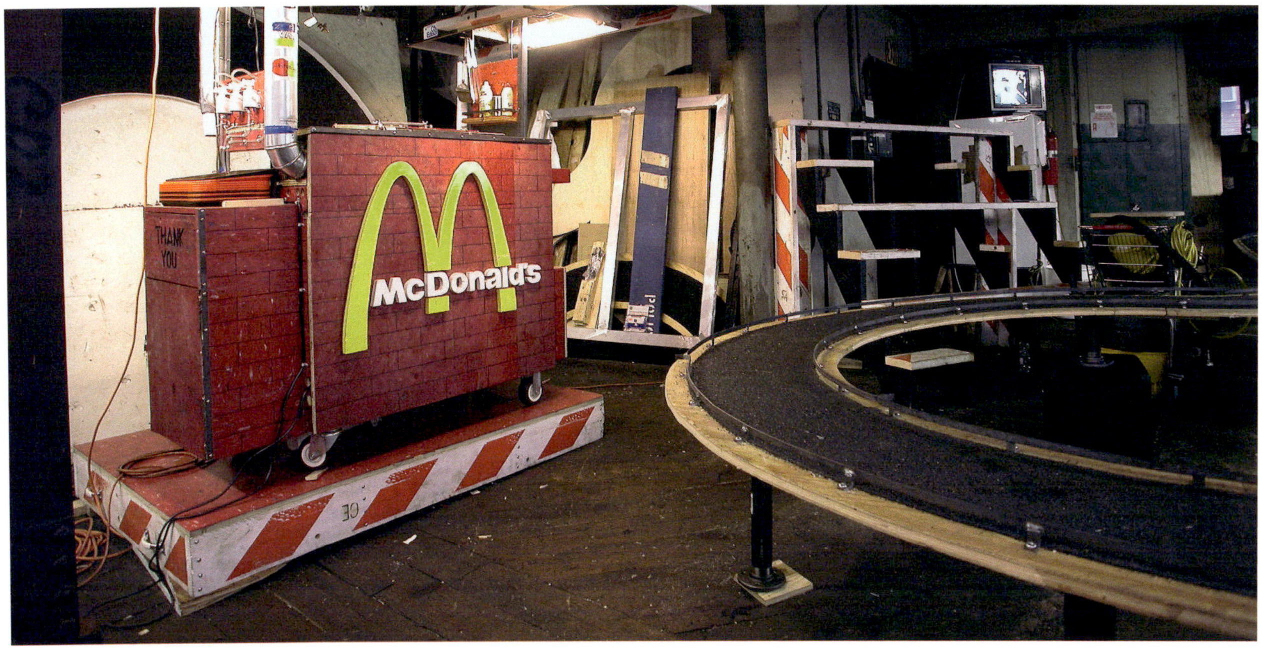

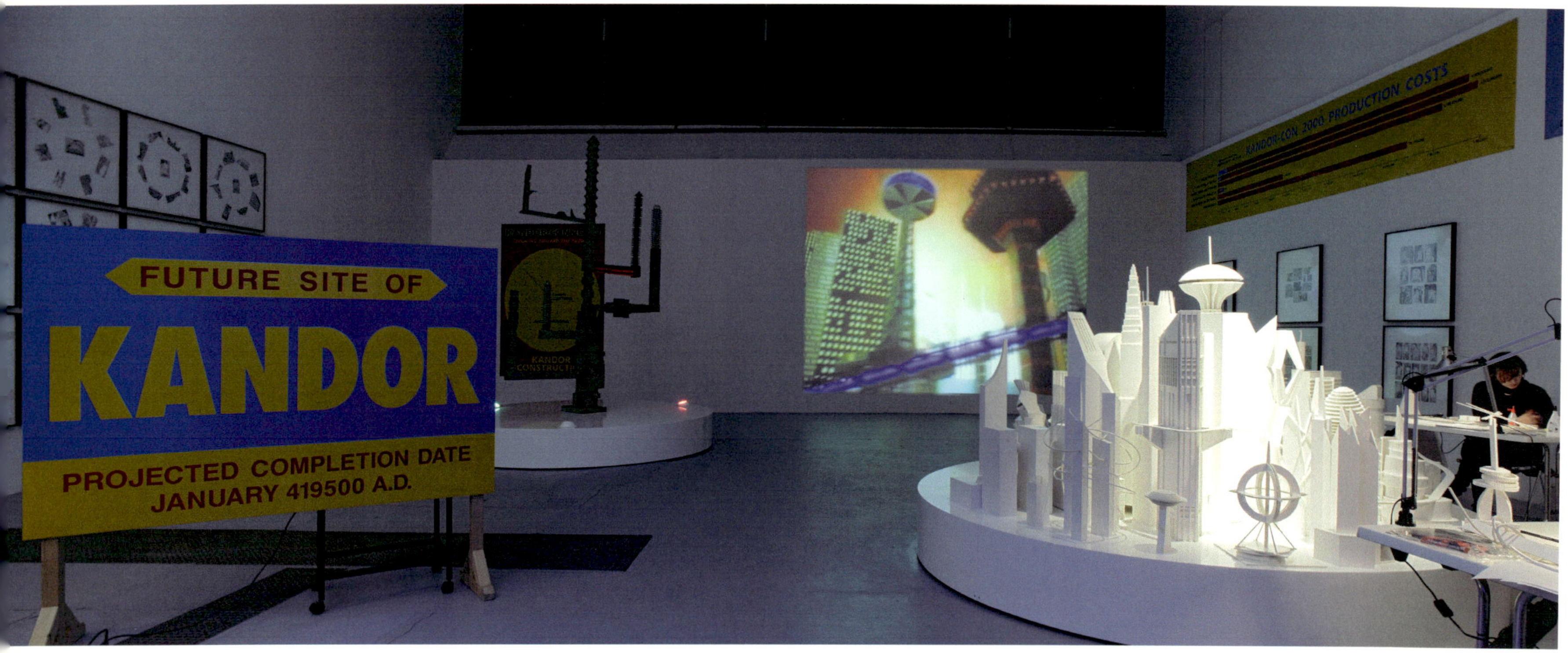

Mike Kelley

KANDOR-CON 2000

This exhibition of new works by Mike Kelley, shown in the Jablonka Gallery, features sculptures, lenticular lightboxes, and videos related to the fictional city of Kandor, the capitol of Superman's home planet Krypton. According to the Superman myth, Kandor is the only remaining vestige of the exploded Krypton, and the city is preserved, in a reduced state, in a bottle in Superman's possession.

Interestingly, the image of Kandor was never codified and the numerous representations of it in the comic book throughout the years vary widely in appearance. In this exhibition, Kelley reconstructs ten unique versions of Kandor, with its enclosing bottle, which, despite obvious differences, purport to depict the same city.

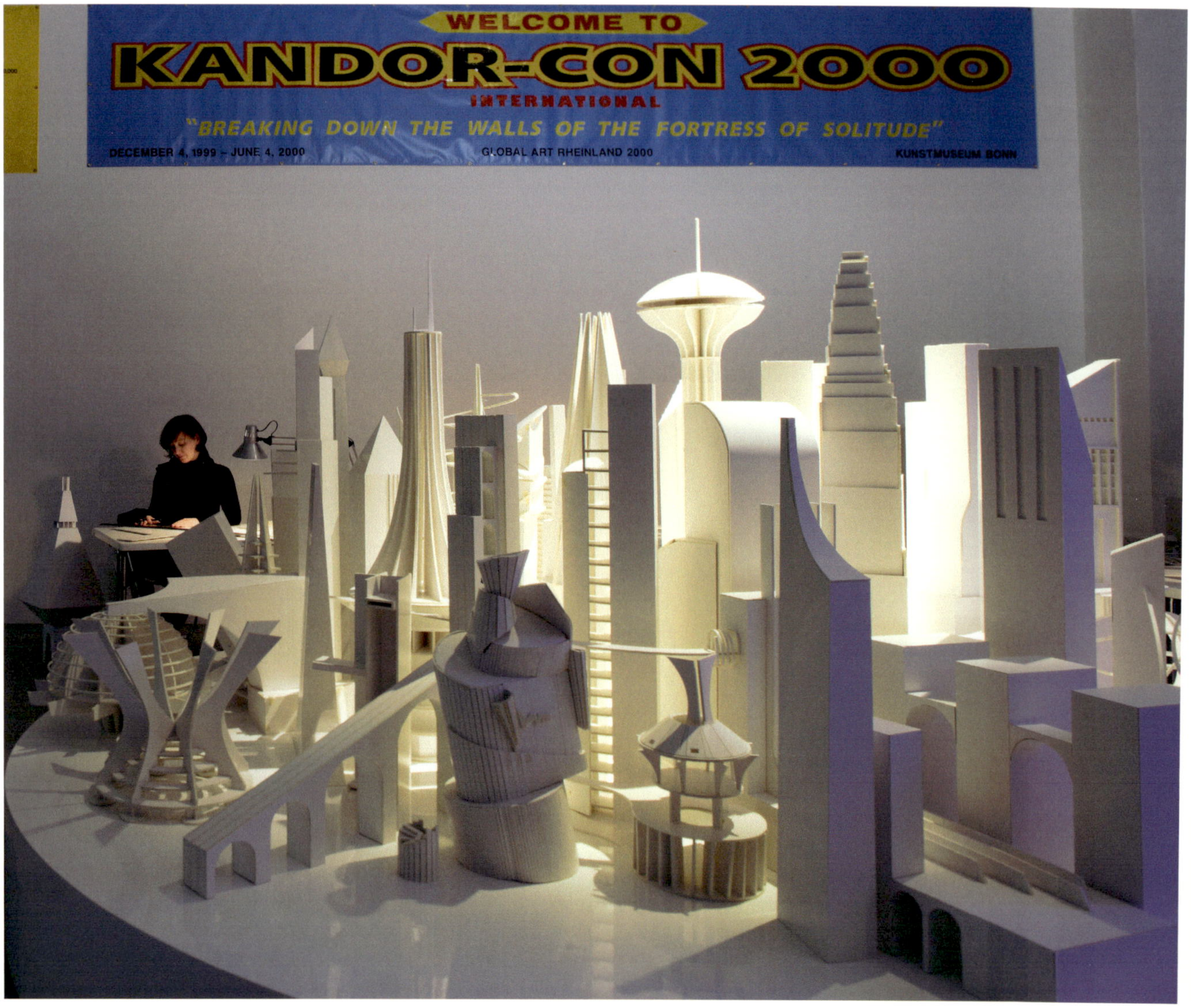

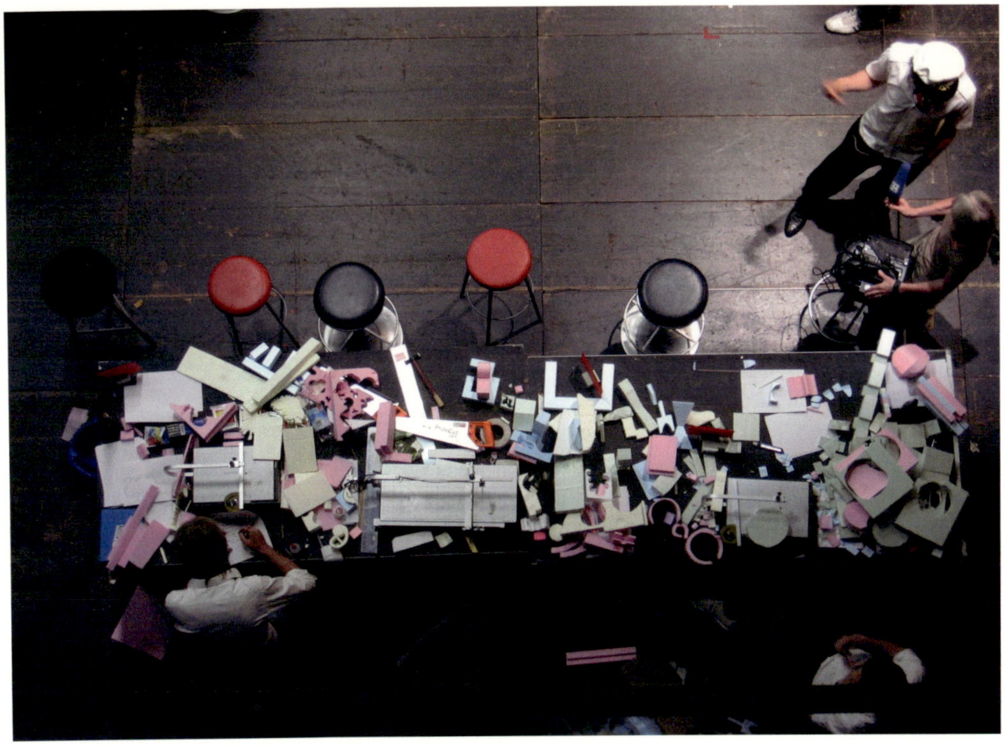

Raumlabor Berlin

BRANDHERDE

Commisioned by the Munich Kammerspiele, Berlin-based architecture collective raumlabor envisioned living scenarios for the future during a two-day workshop, by building a model of a new planet including hymns, pamphlets and poetry.

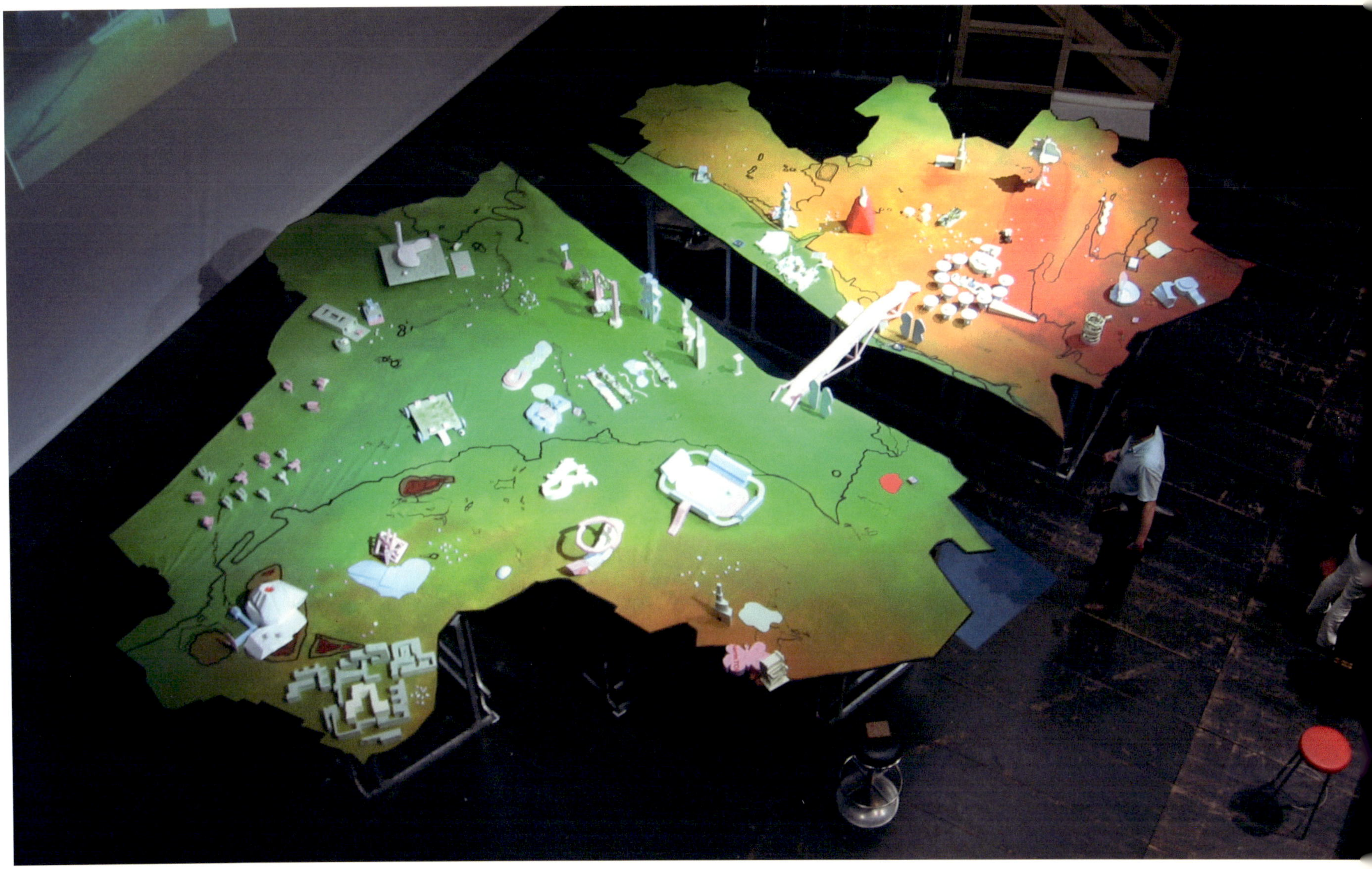

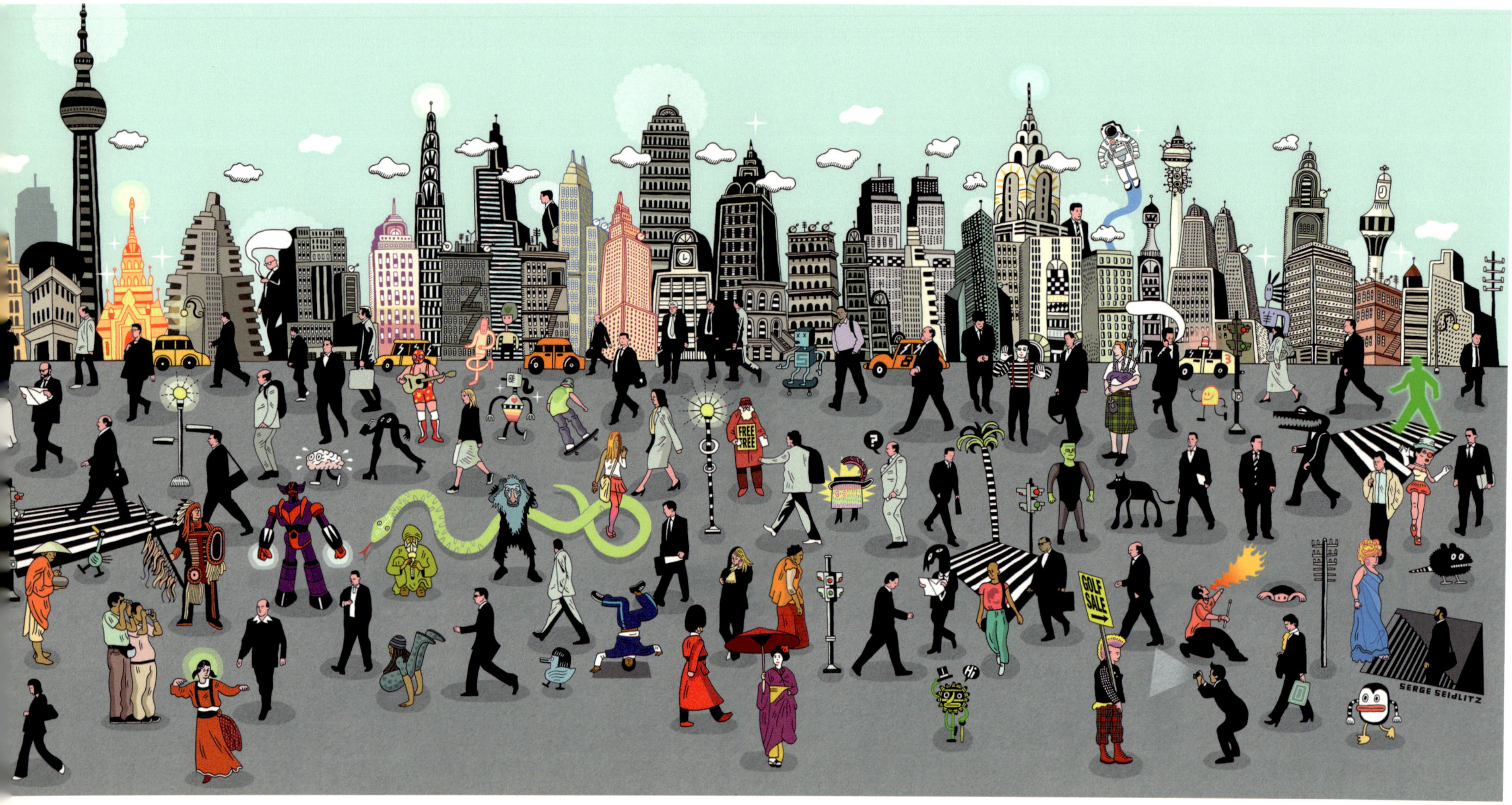

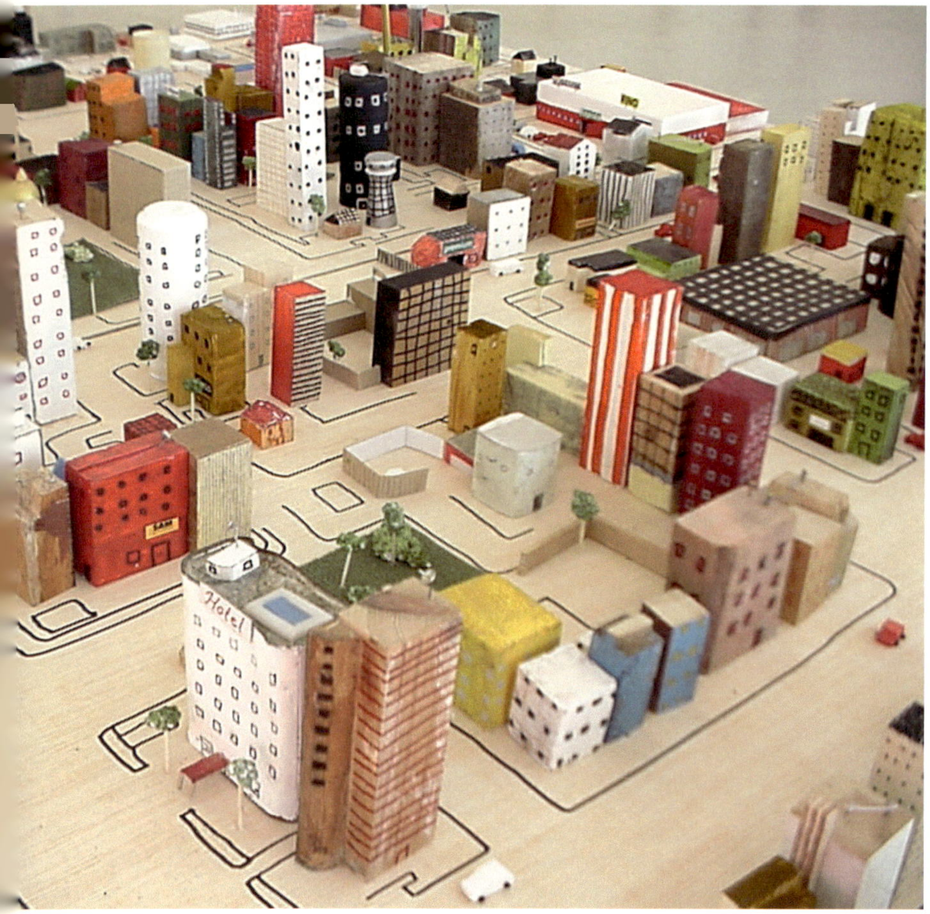

Jonas Liveröd

LOST & FOUND *(left + bottom)*

Relating to the quick and drastic changes of the neighbourhood Poble Nou in Barcelona, this model of a town is built from the left-overs found in the vast ruins of the old neighbourhood, torn down in order to give space for new construction. It was built specifically for the exhibition The best sky in Barcelona curated by Angelo Ferriera De Sousa at Sala Can Felipa in the heart of Poble Nou.

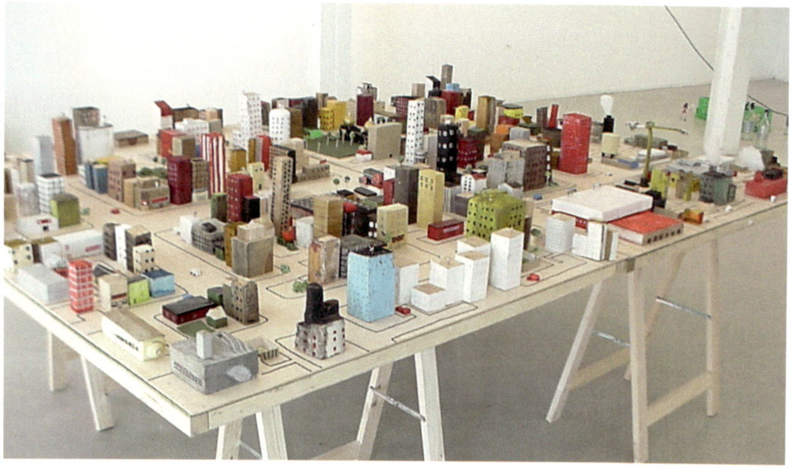

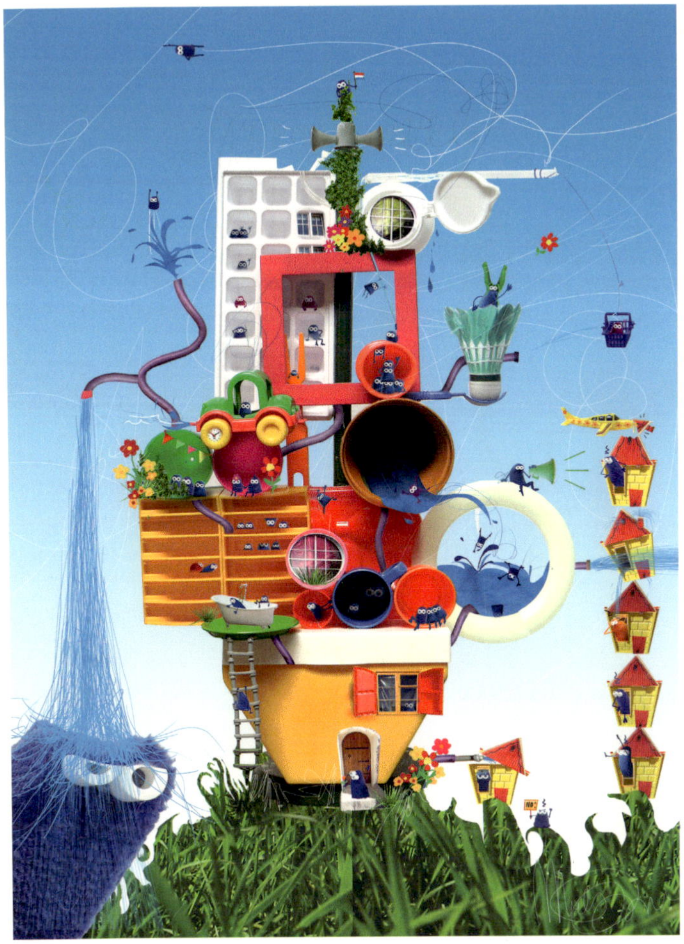

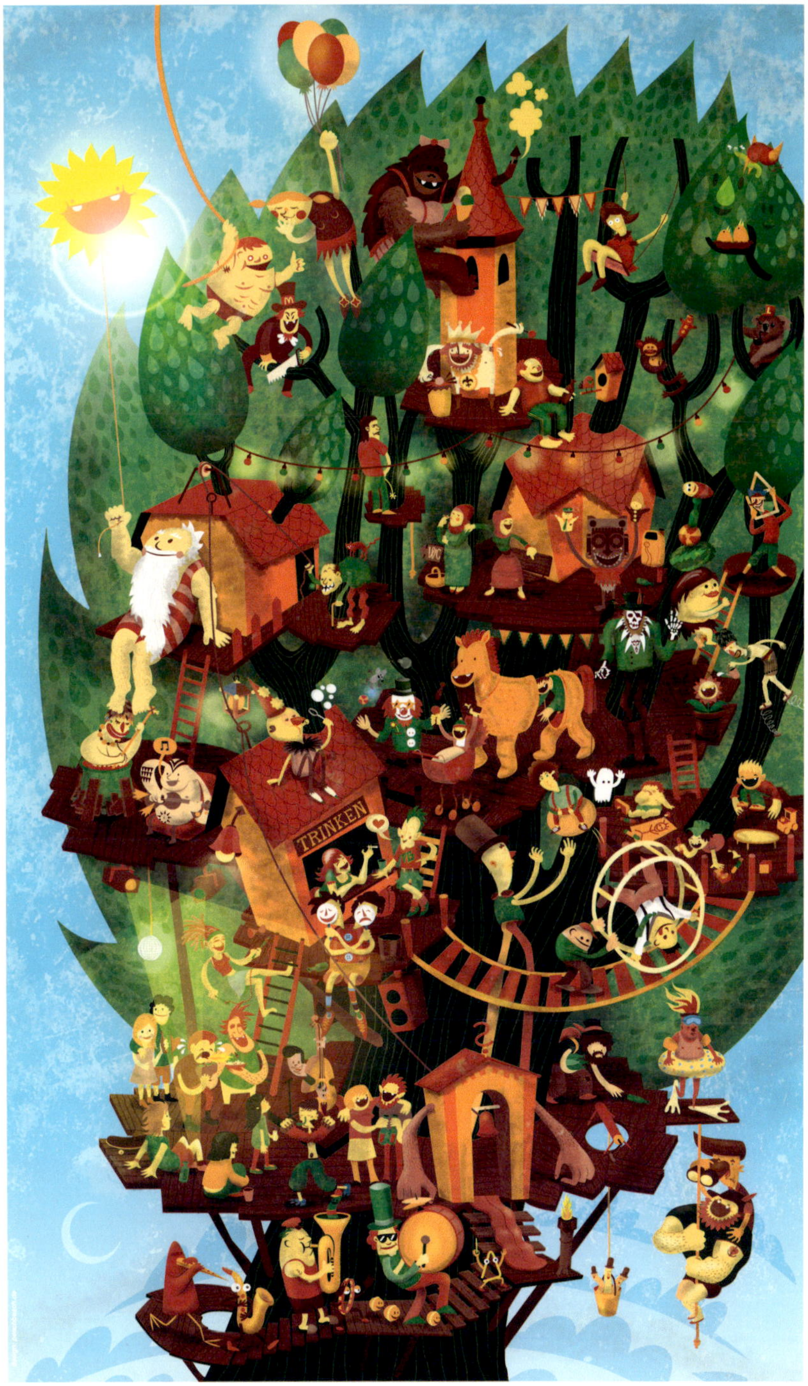

Mieke Driessen

DREAM HOUSE *(top)*

Peach Beach

BERLIN LACHT! (DETAIL) *(right)*

Serge Seidlitz

WORLD TRAVELLER *(left page, top)*
MONEY CITY *(bottom)*

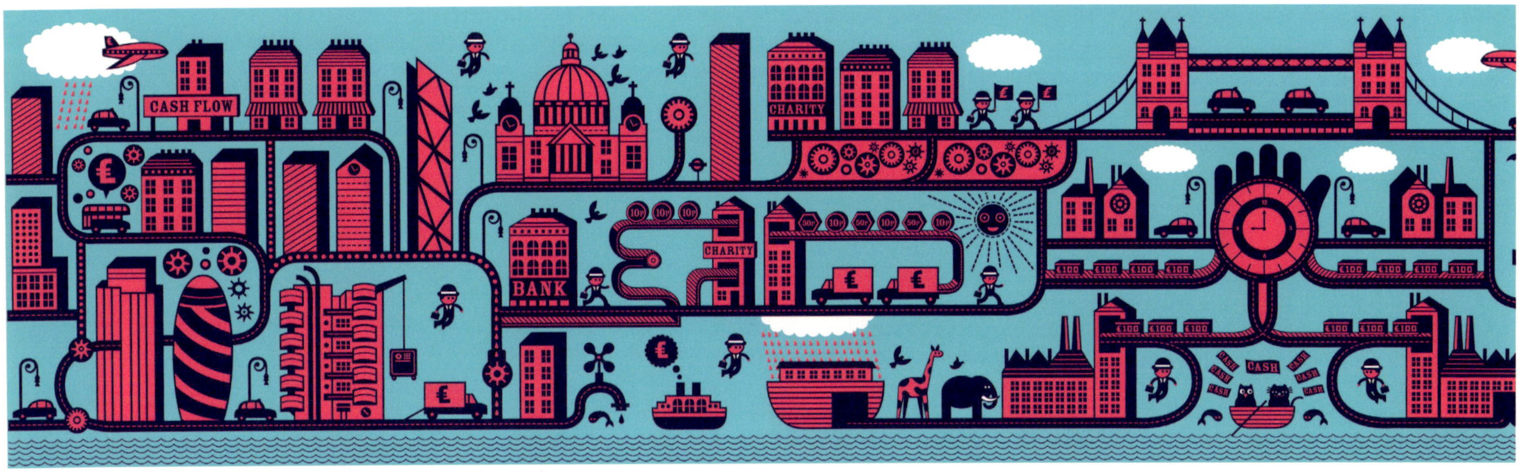

Andy Council

The various landscape-creatures by British artist Andy Council are made up of dinosaurs and local landmarks. The piece also touches on environmental issues – town taking over country.

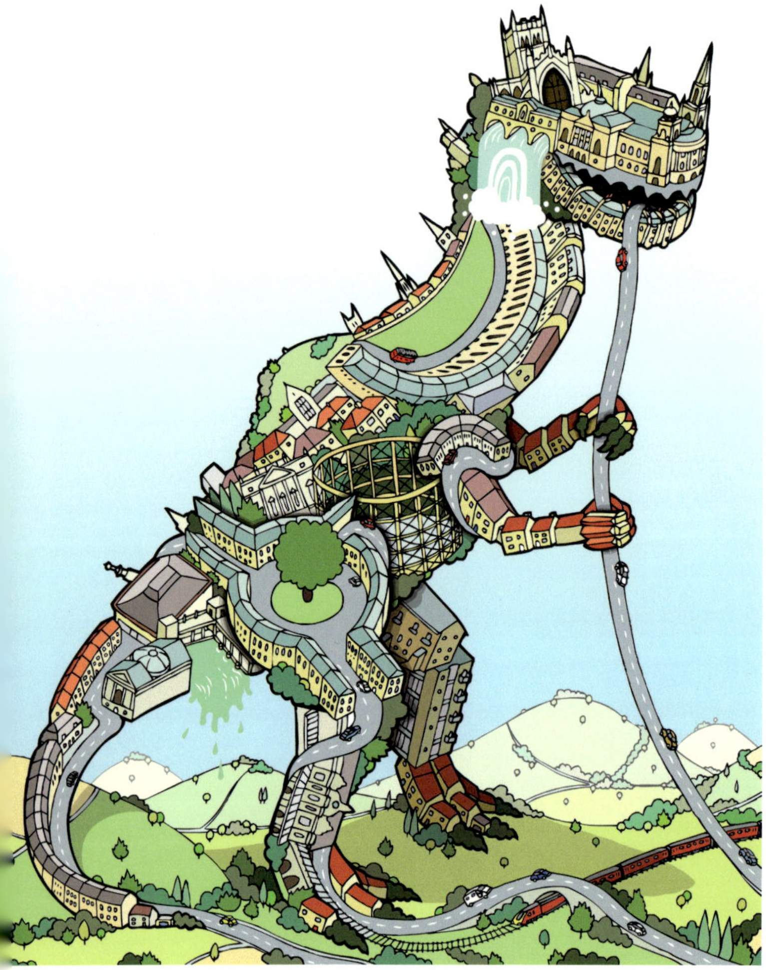

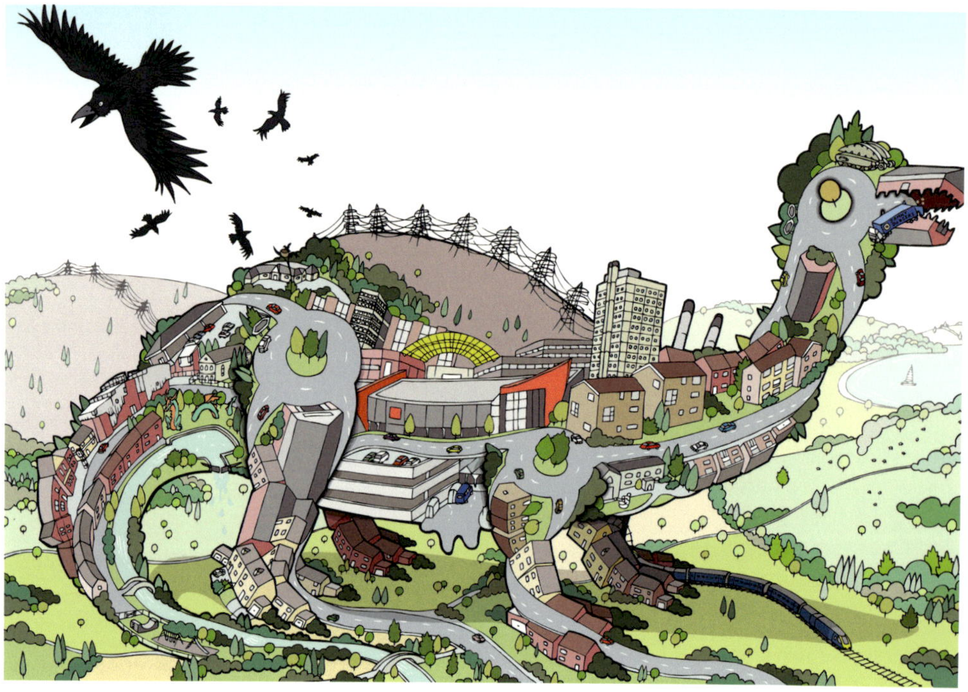

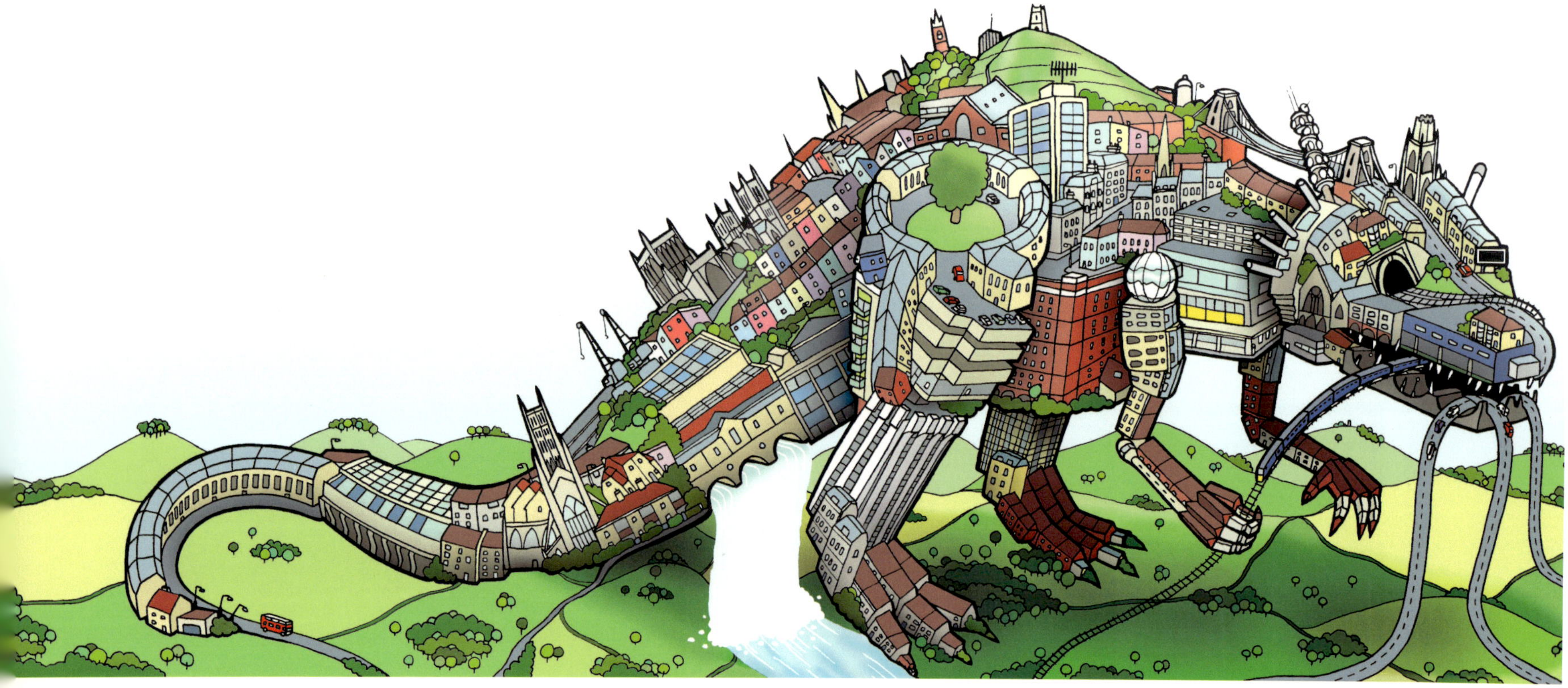

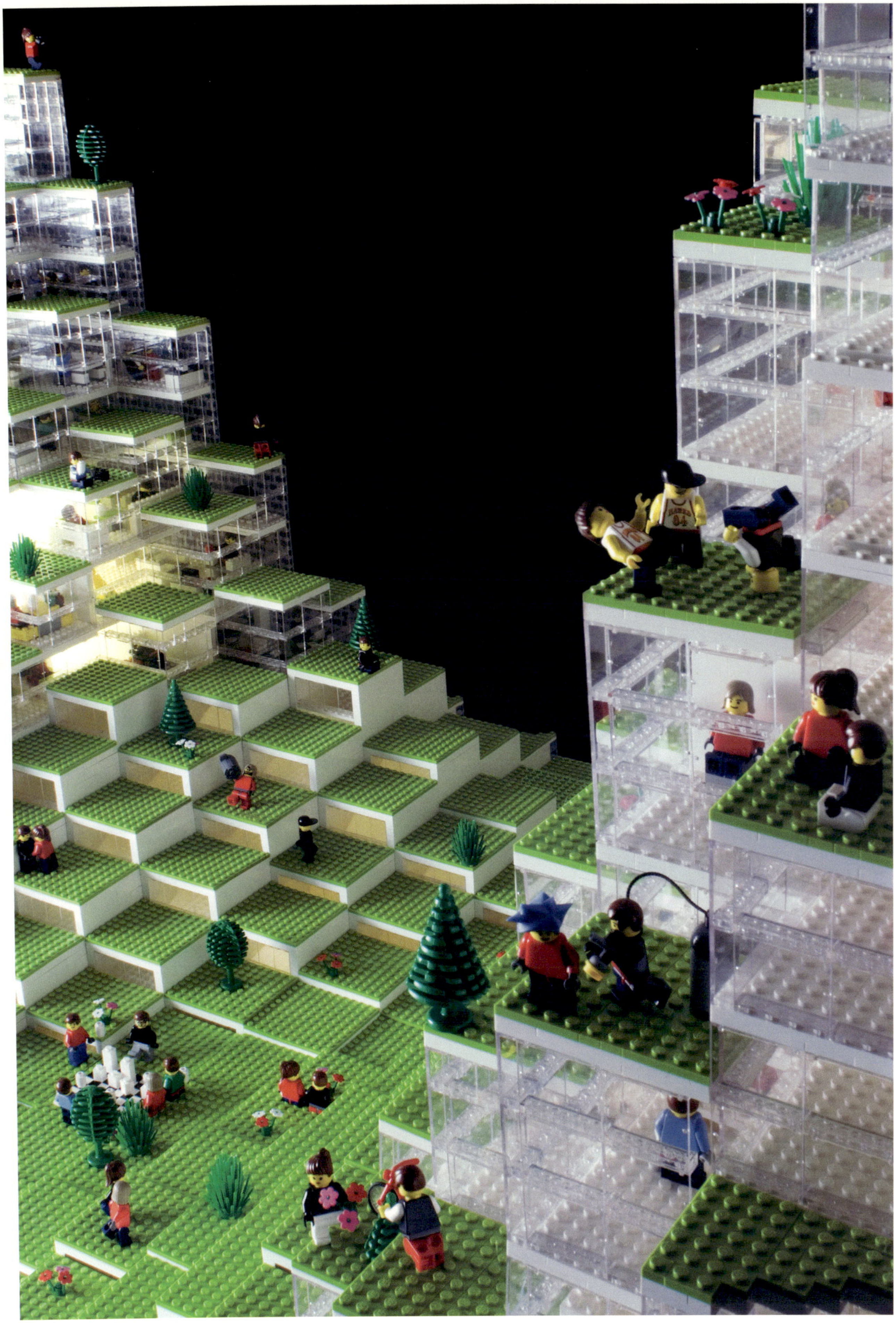

BIG / Bjarke Ingels Group

LEGO TOWERS

The terraced LEGO Towers model made out of 250,000 LEGO bricks by the Copenhagen-based architecture practice BIG/Bjarke Ingels Group, was originally conceived for Storefront for Art and Architecture in New York in 2007.

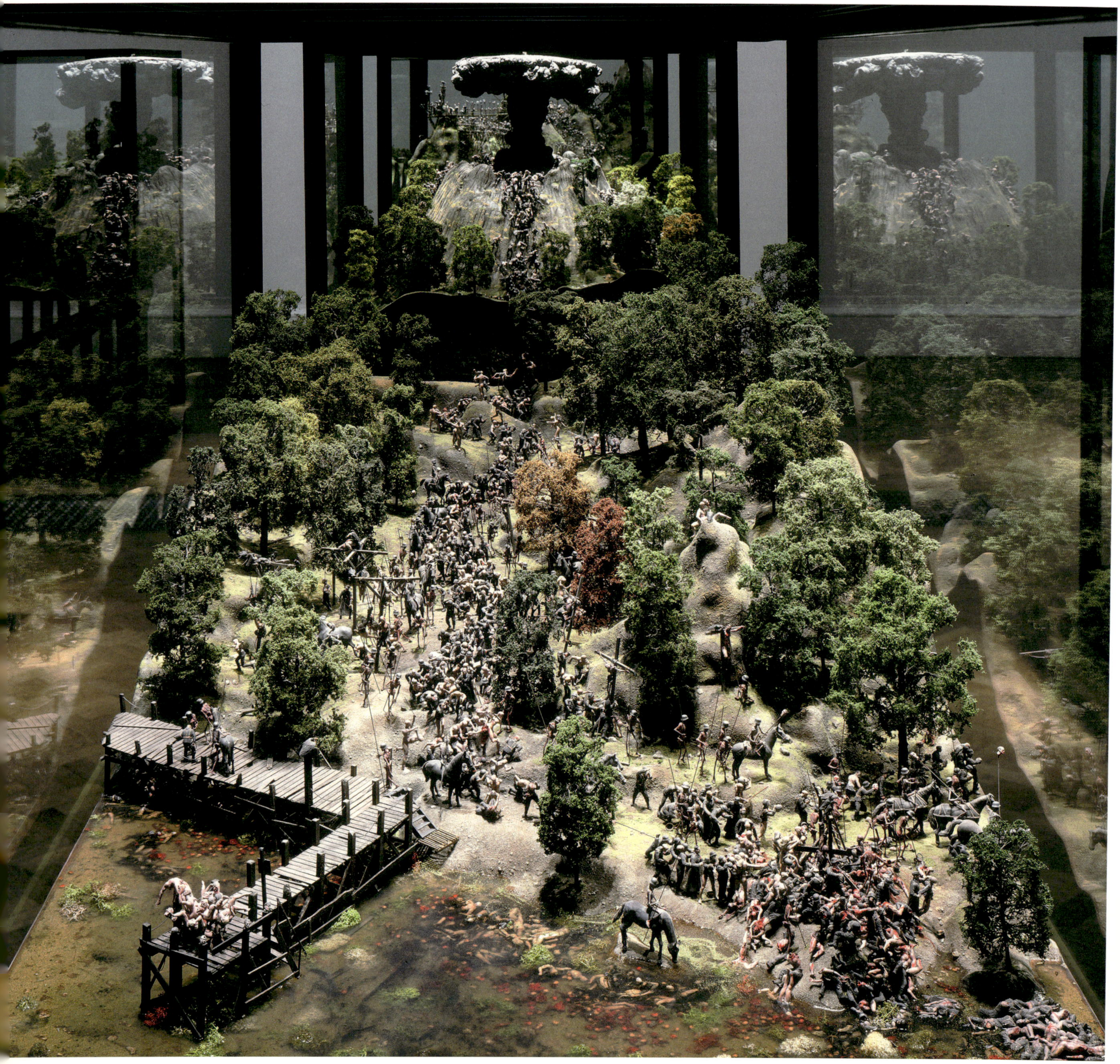

Jake & Dinos Chapman

HELL

This critically acclaimed installation in a glass case by the Chapman brothers features a series of miniature landscapes, showing thousands of Nazi soldier models committing atrocities.

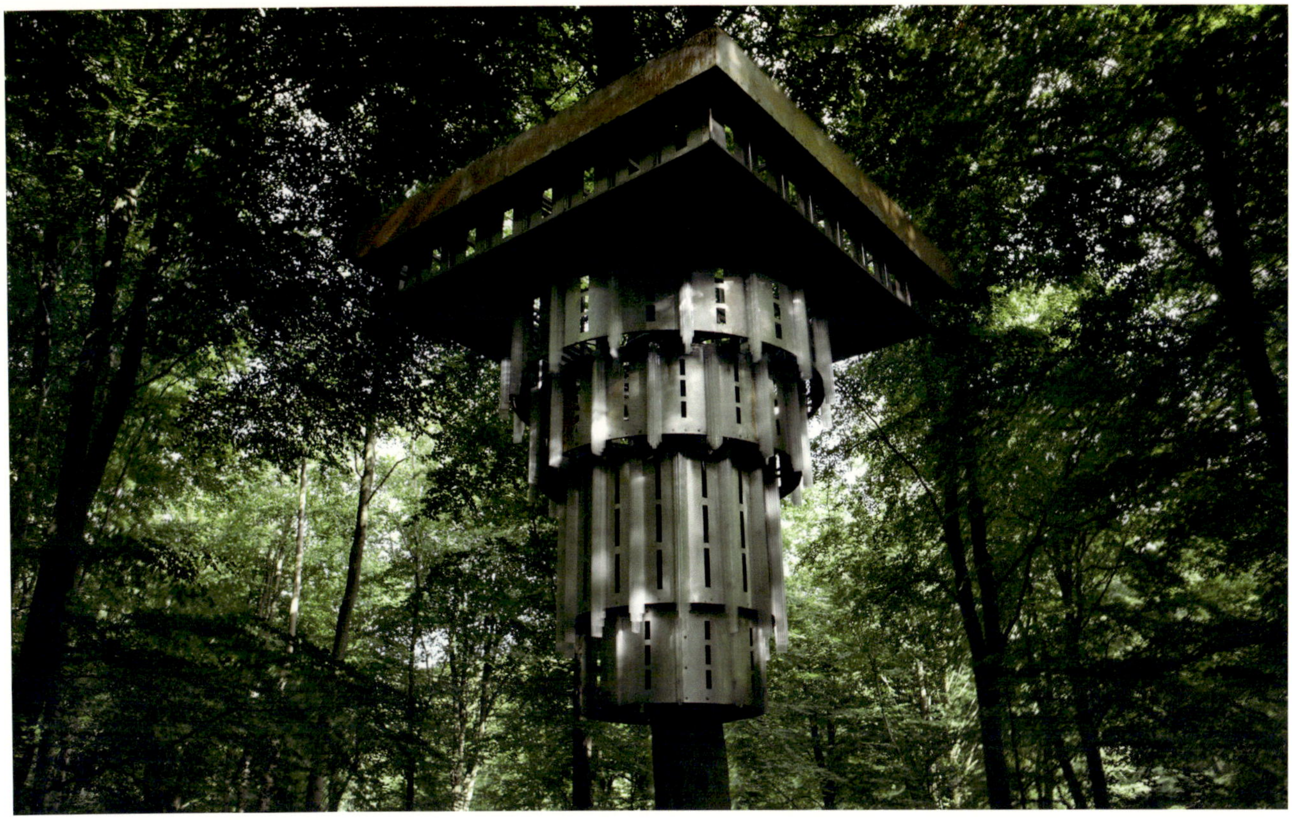

London Fieldworks

SUPER KINGDOM

This project by London Fieldworks is based on research into animal hibernation patterns in England's Kingswood Forest. The artists have presented a series of site-specific show homes in the forest. Super Kingdom can be viewed as a social engineering experiment for animals – a new community in the making referencing despot's palaces, gated community developments such as Alphaville in Brazil and the fortified exclusivity afforded to the wealthy and super-rich – all designed to keep urban reality at bay.

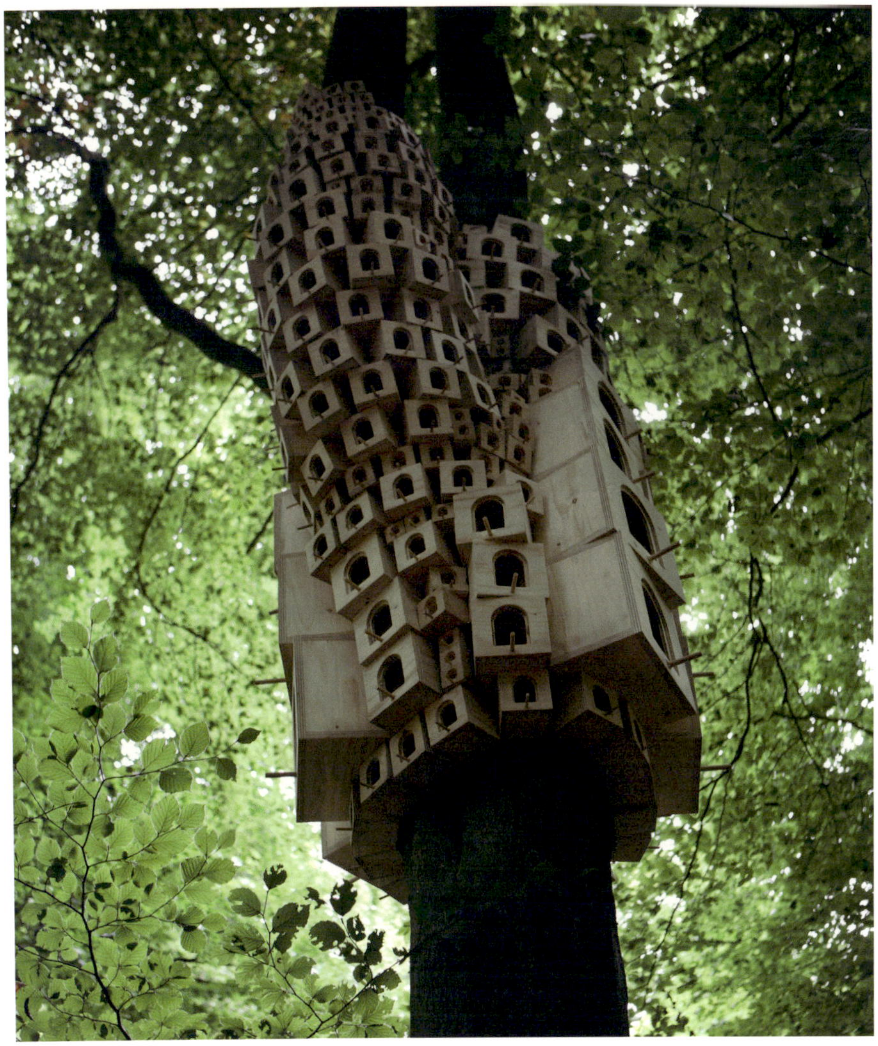

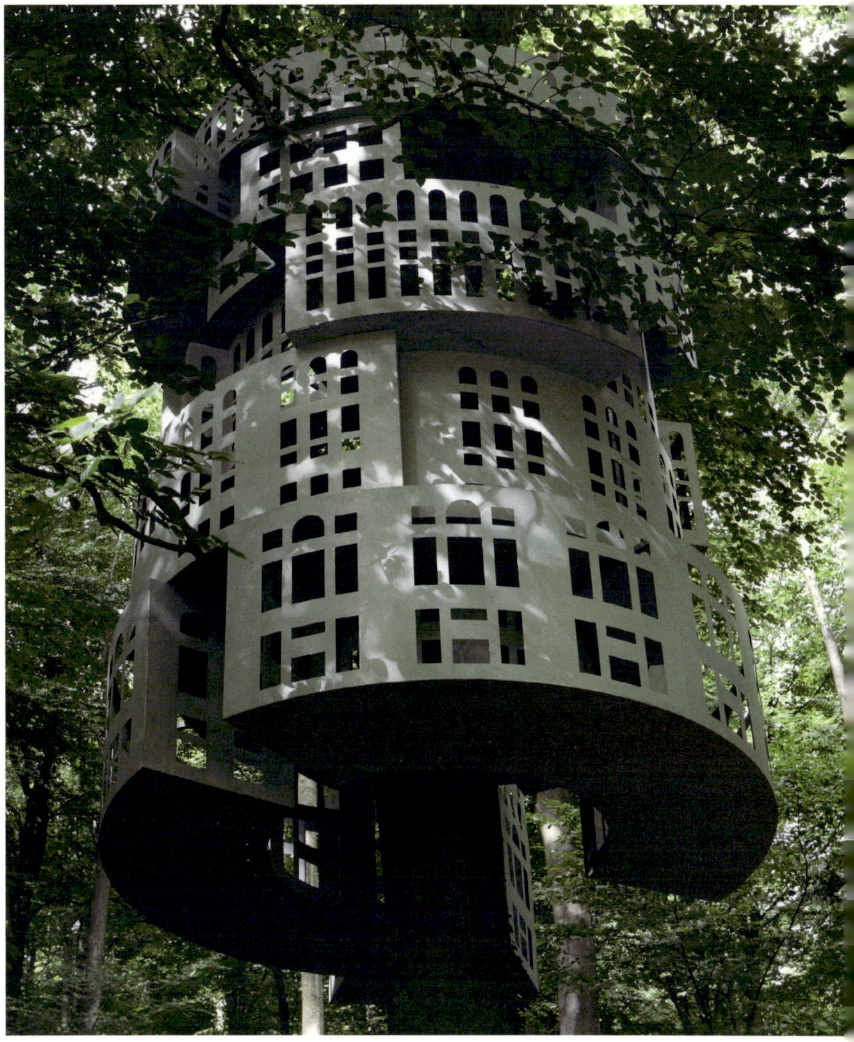

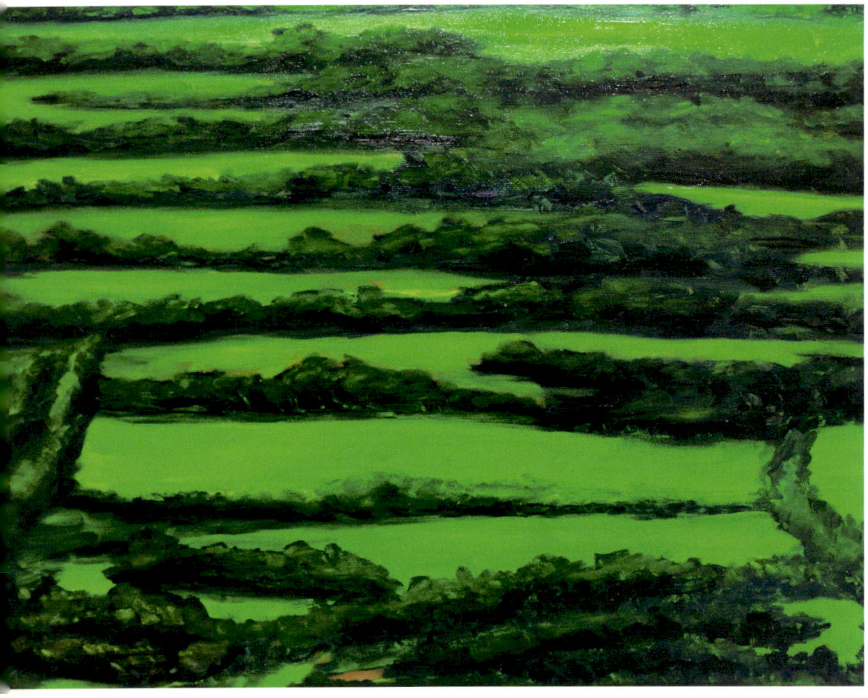

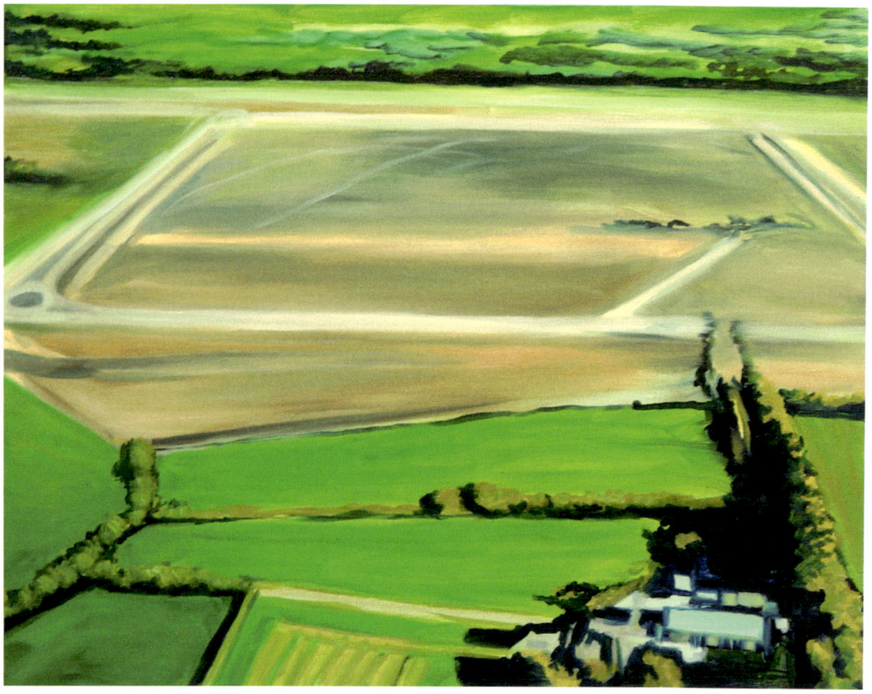

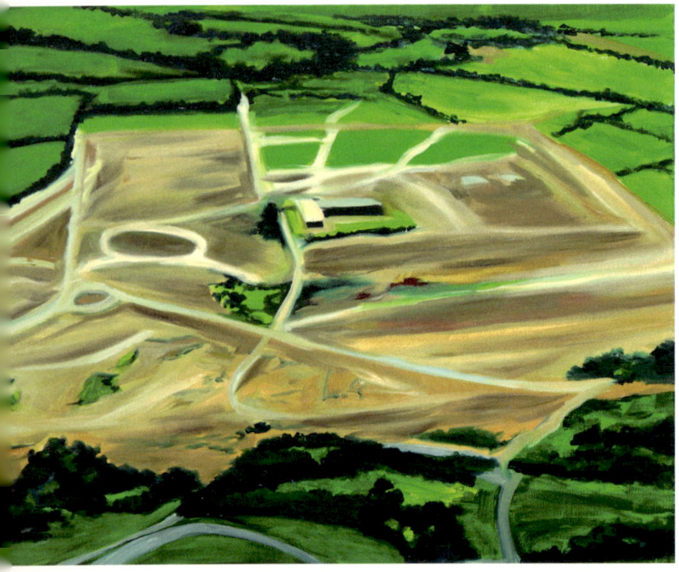

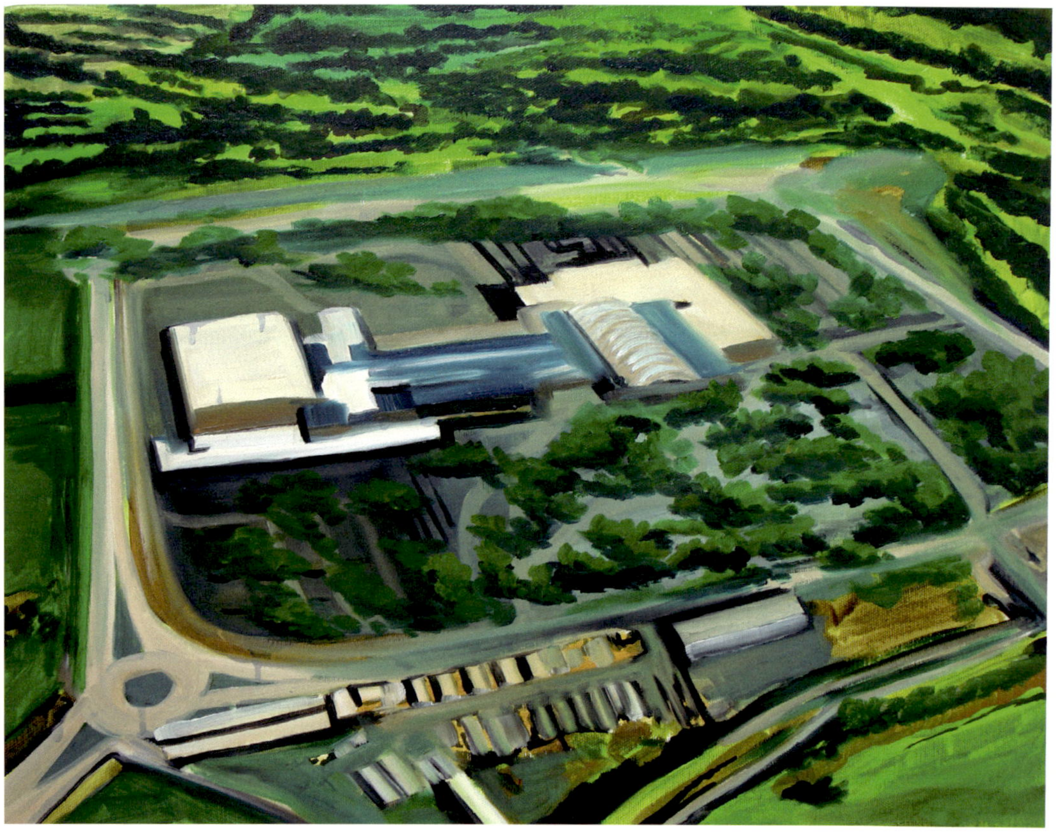

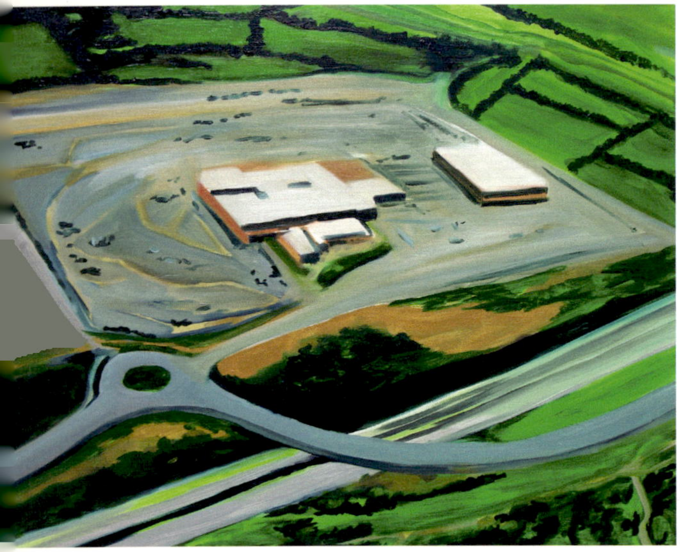

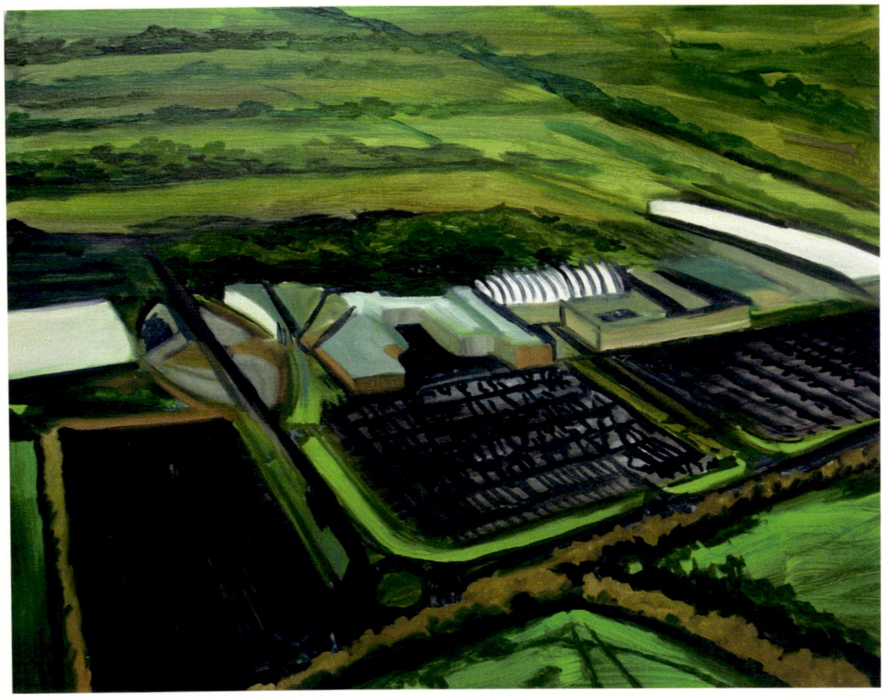

Eamon O'Kane

REGENERATION

Regeneration is a stop-motion animation created by filming the process of making a series of paintings based on the transformation of the Blanchardstown area (outside Dublin) over the last ten years. The process of painting echoes the construction of man-made interventions as the layers of paint chart the rapid build-up of an urban landscape. The animation then loops back to before the beginnings of this development when the area was farmland.

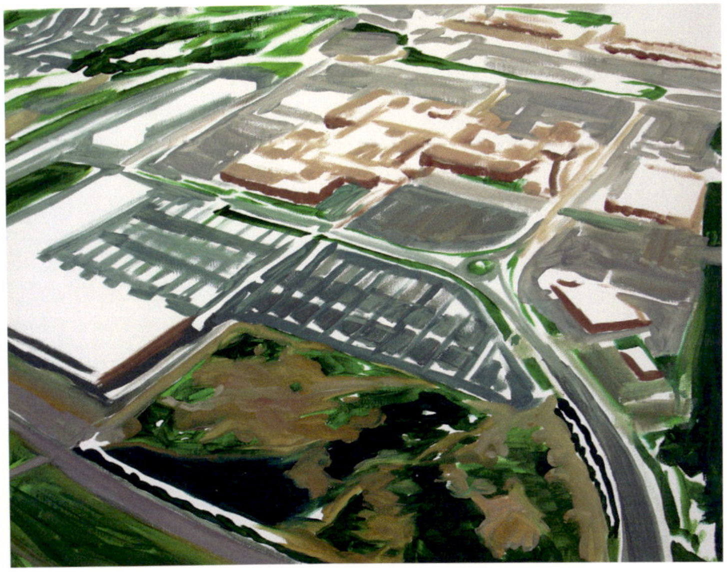

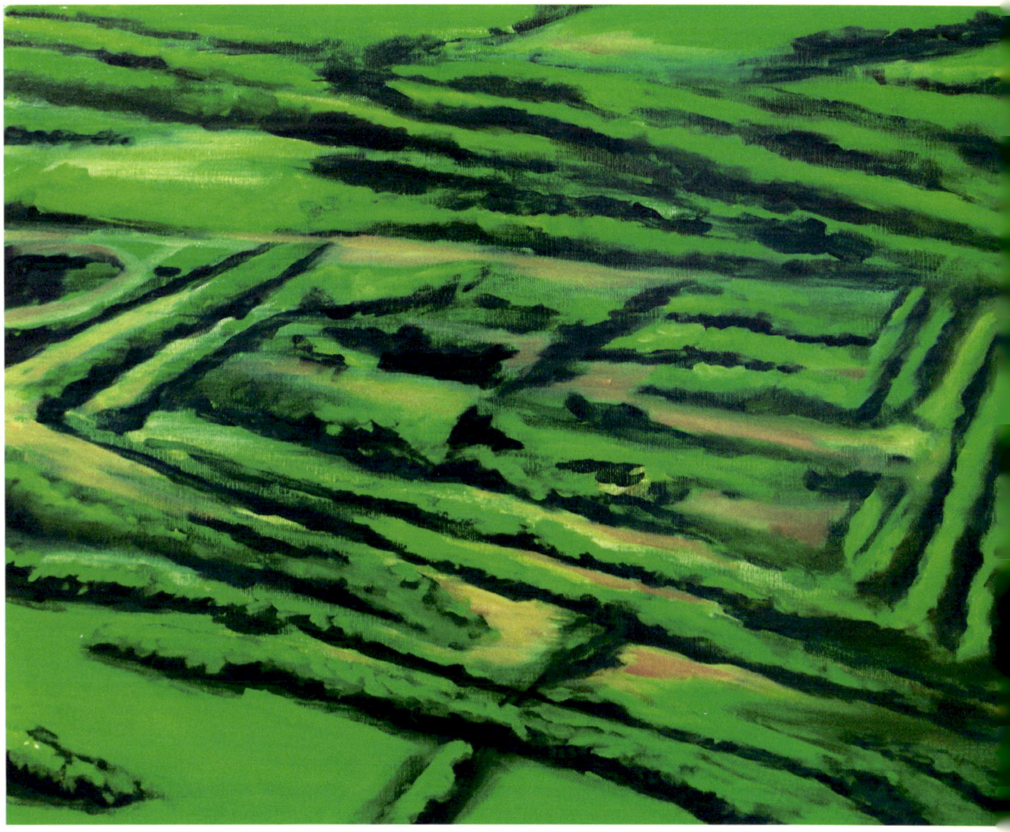

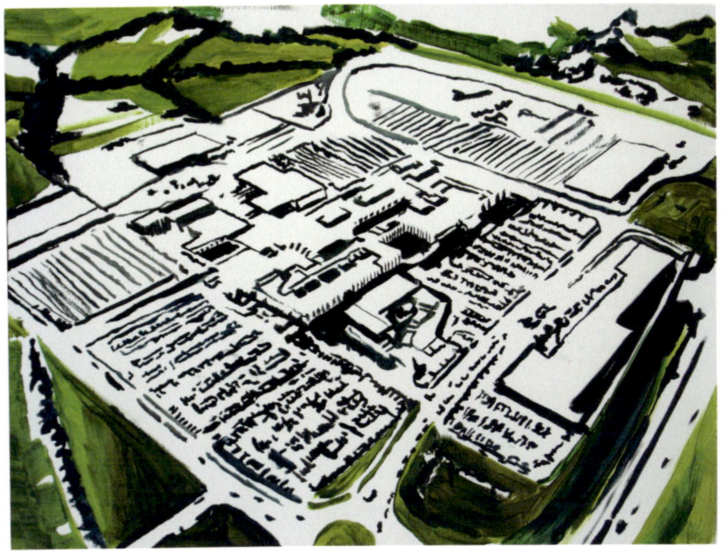

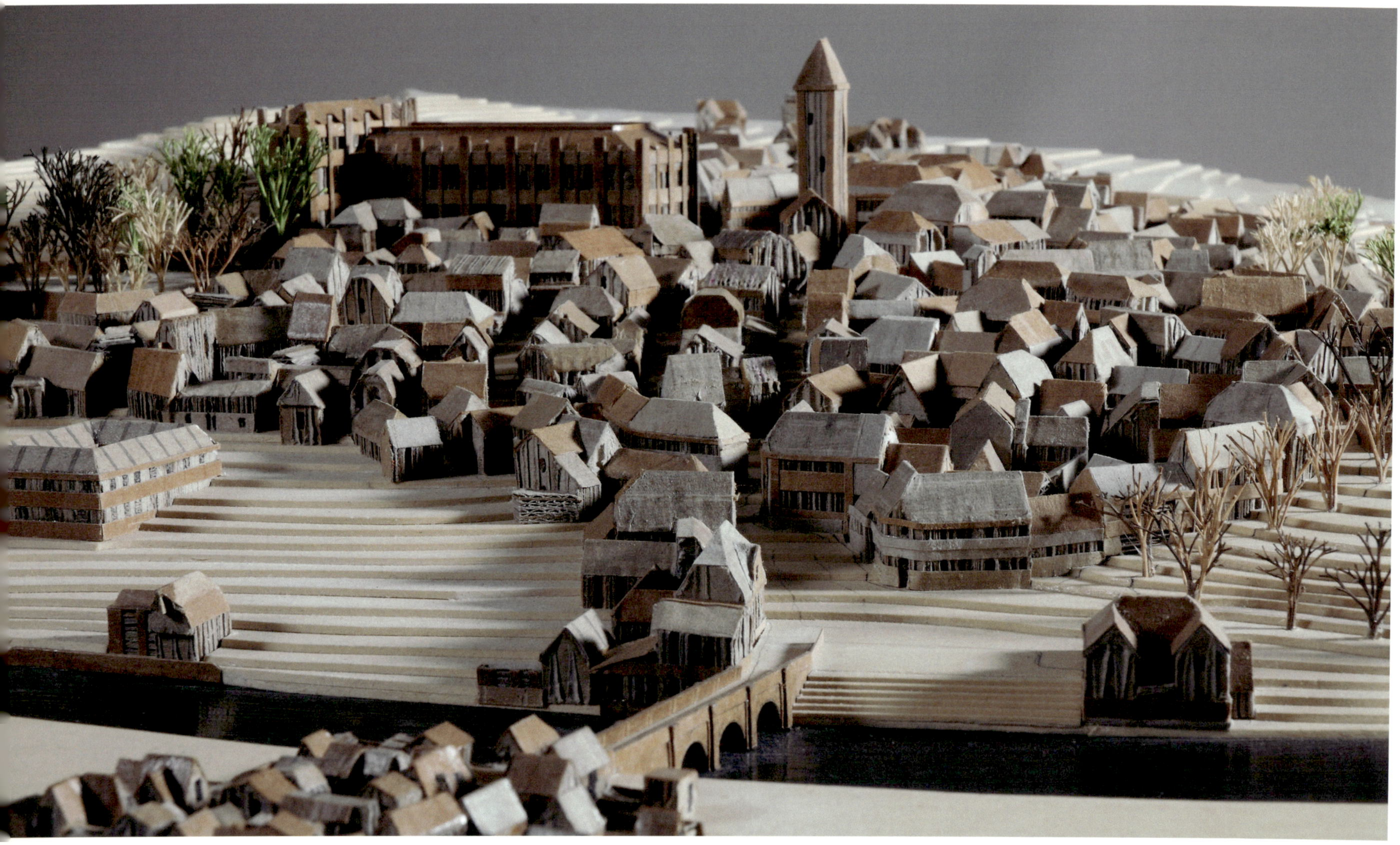

Matias Bechtold

STADT PERLE

Bechtold's Stadt Perle is based on the fictional city of Perle from Austrian Expressionist Alfred Kubin's novel *Die Andere Seite* (*The Other Side*, 1909), an apocalyptic fantasy set in an oppressive imaginary land which had an atmosphere of claustrophobic absurdity.

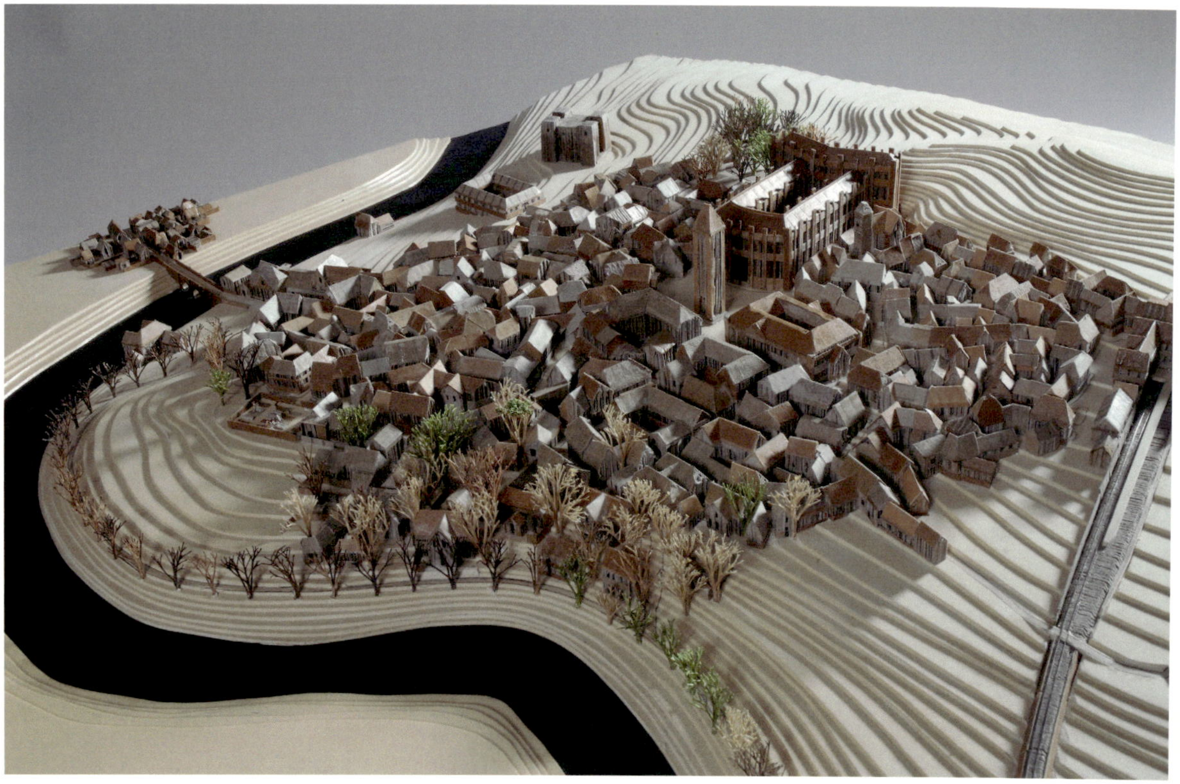

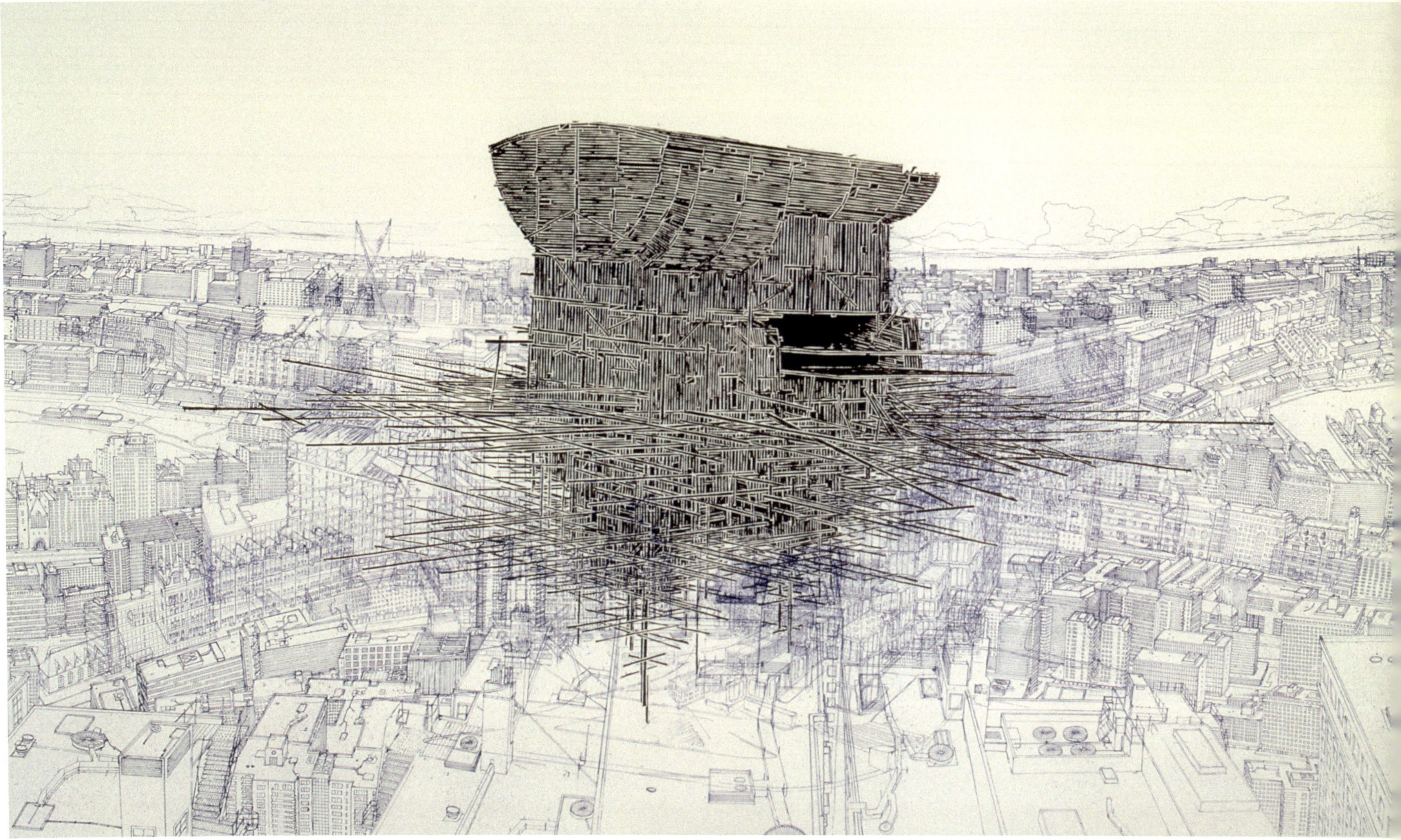

Rob Voerman

UNTITLED *(top)*

Peter Callesen

LIVING INSIDE MY HEAD *(right)*

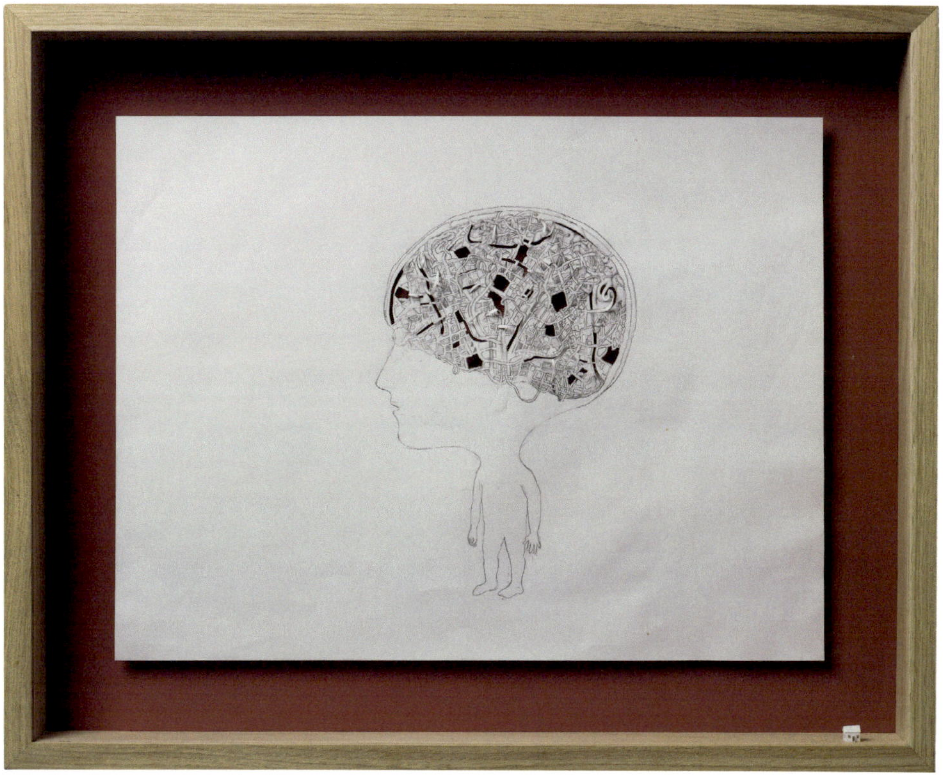

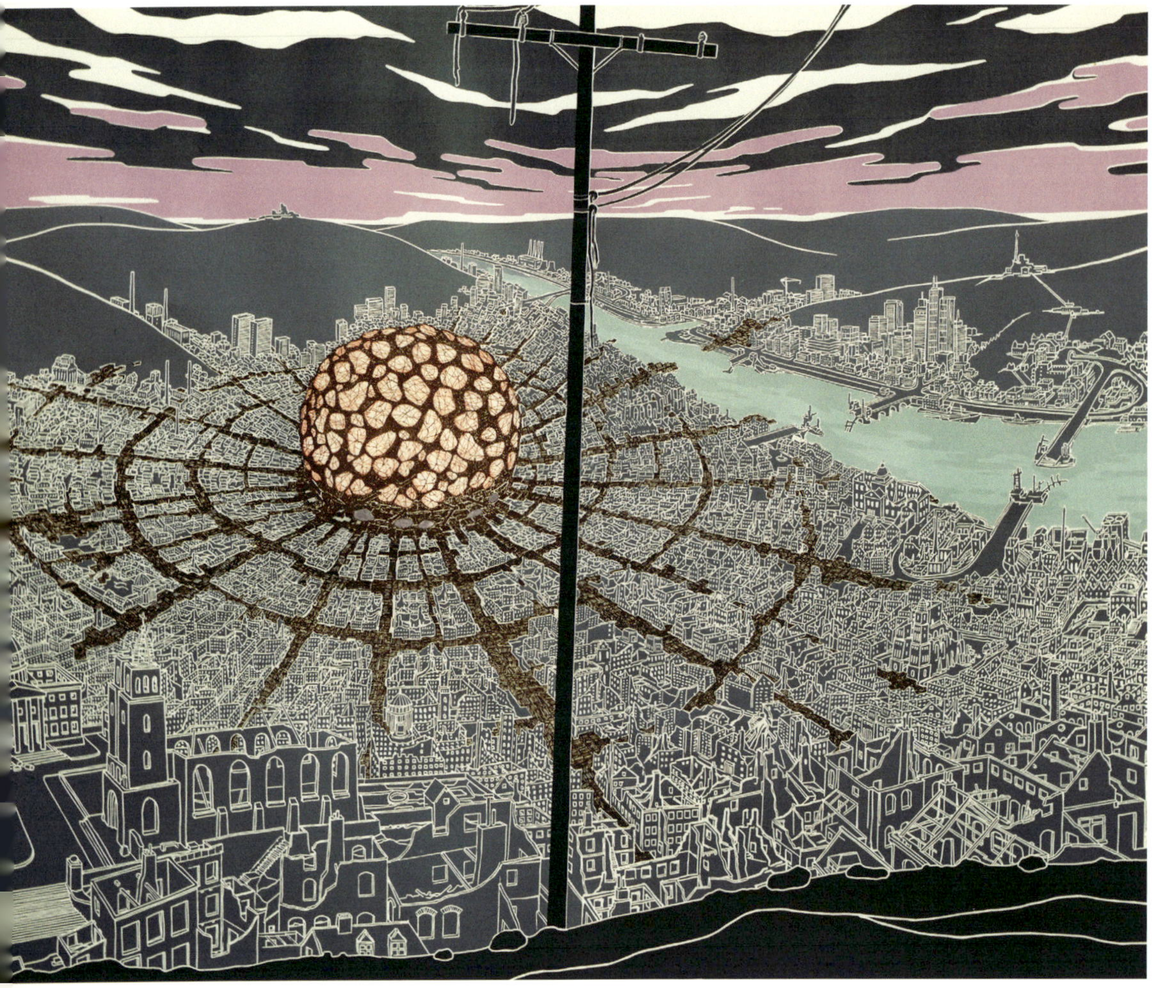

Rob Voerman

EPICENTRE *(top)*
ANNEX #3 *(bottom)*

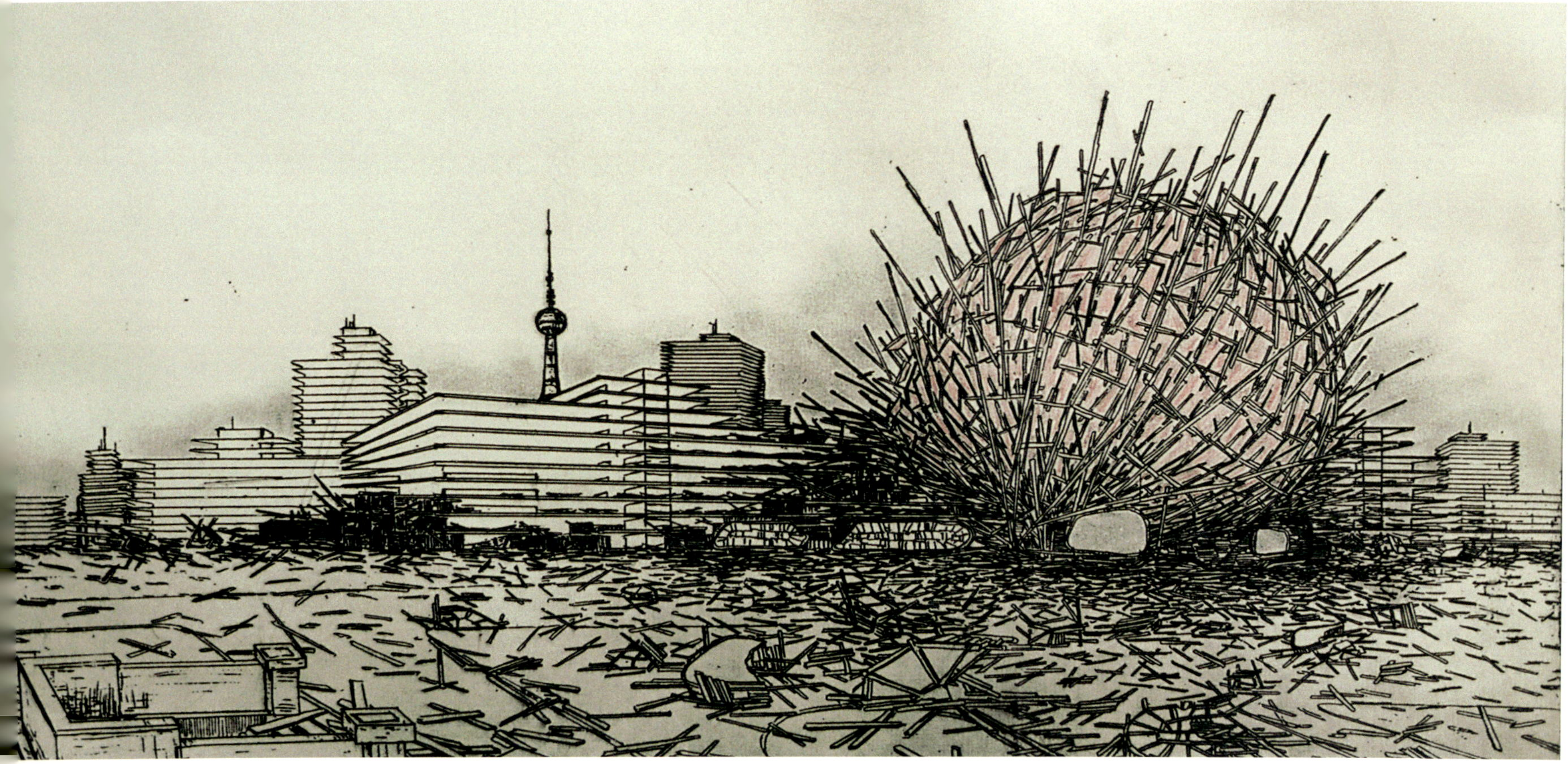

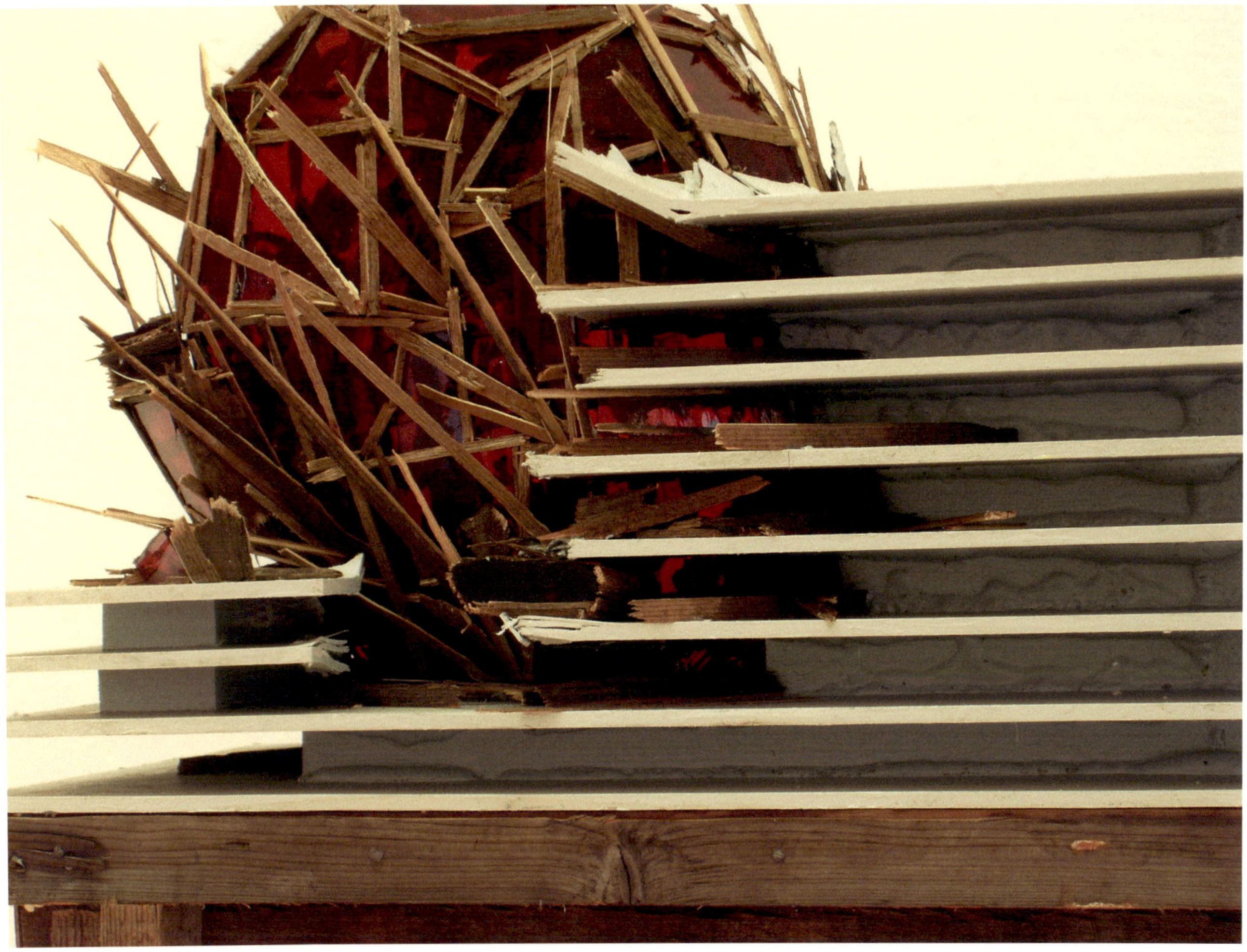

Rob Voerman

ANNEX #1

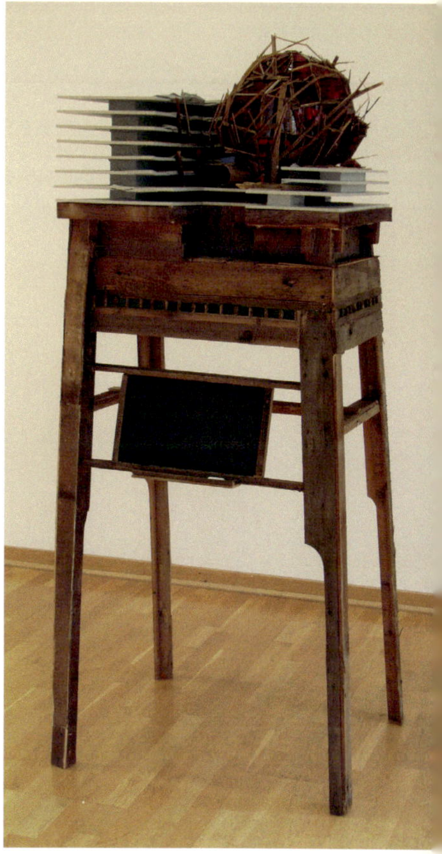

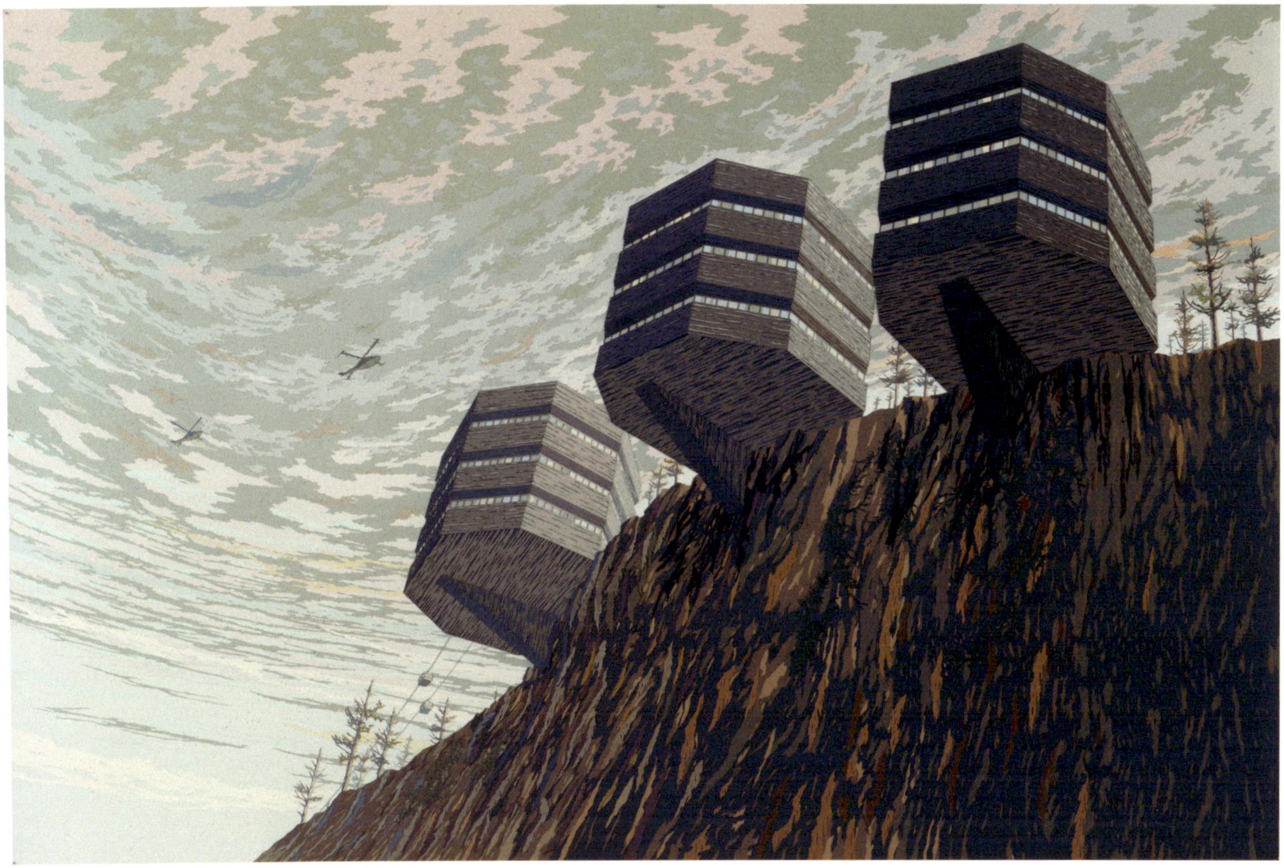

David Thorpe

PILGRIMS

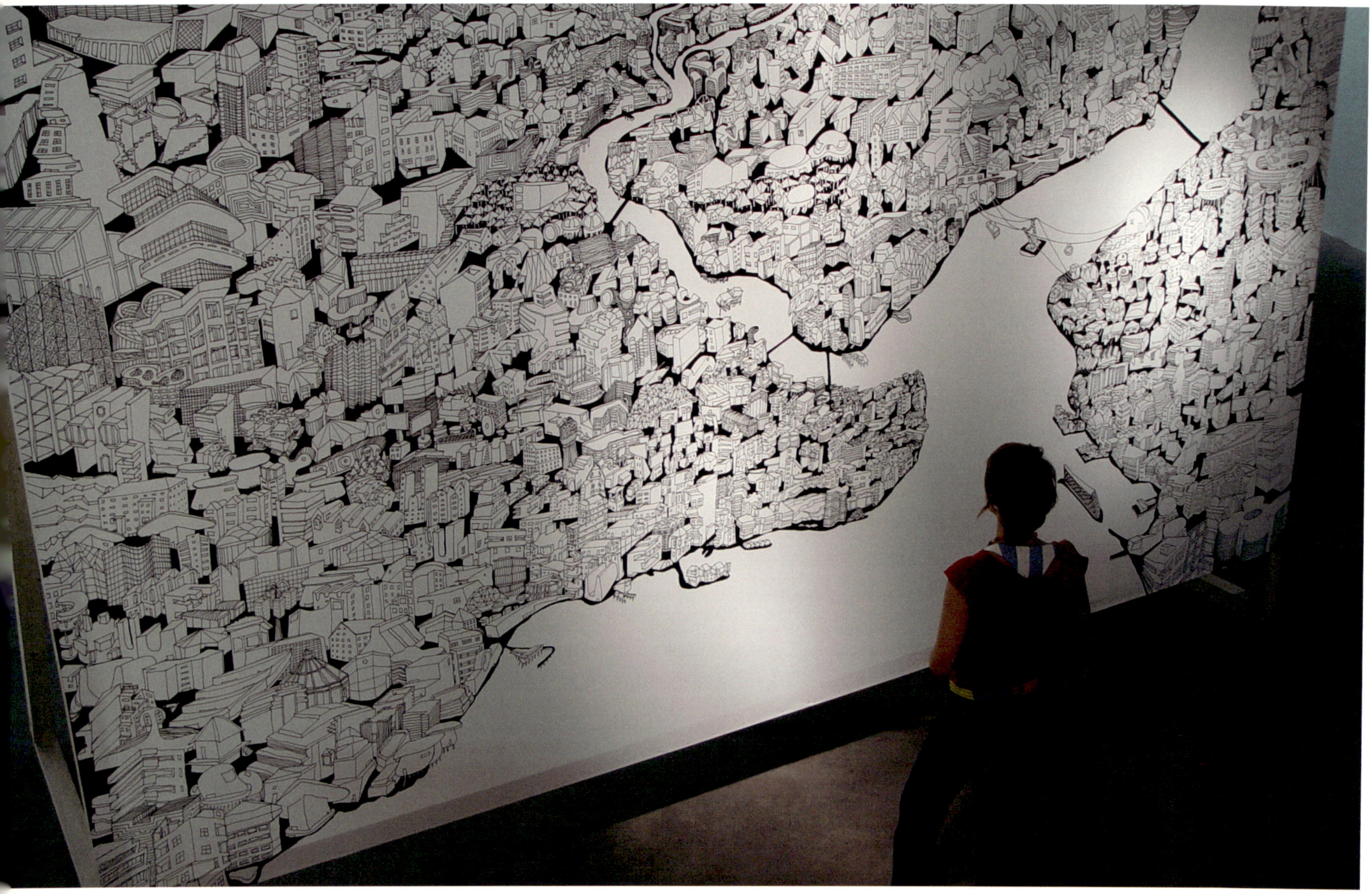

Erik Göngrich

NEW ISTANBUL

Erik Göngrich's intriguing display of his research into the city of Istanbul, Turkey, developed over multiple visits since 2000, was conceived for the 9th International Istanbul Biennial 2005. In the centre is a jagged wooden structure referring to the hills of Istanbul and providing seating to watch Göngrich's illustrations and video work.

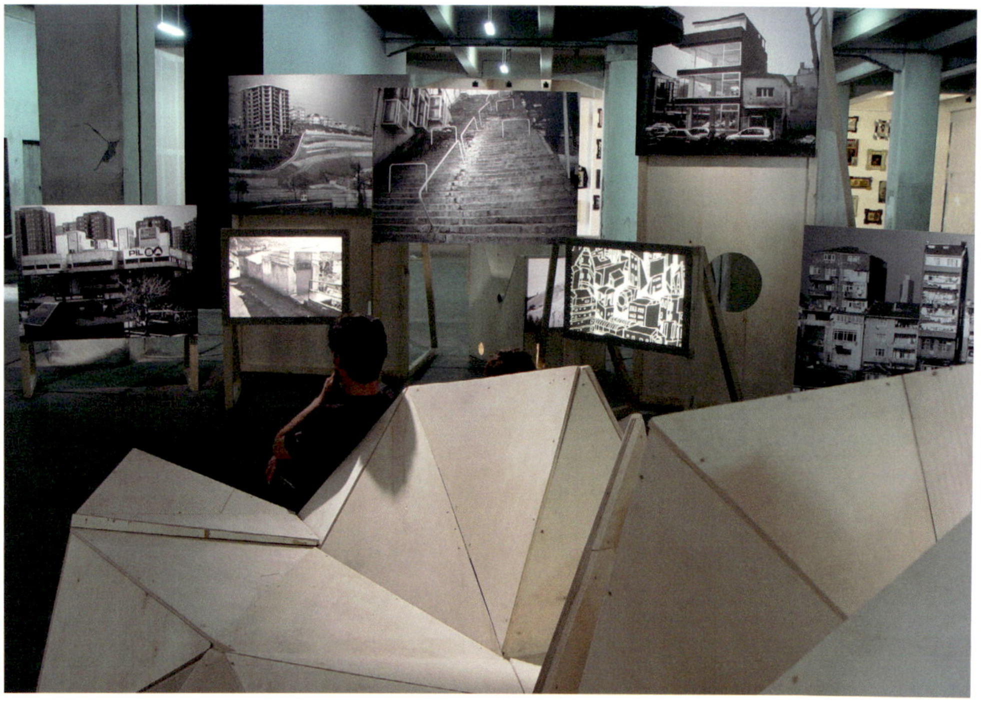

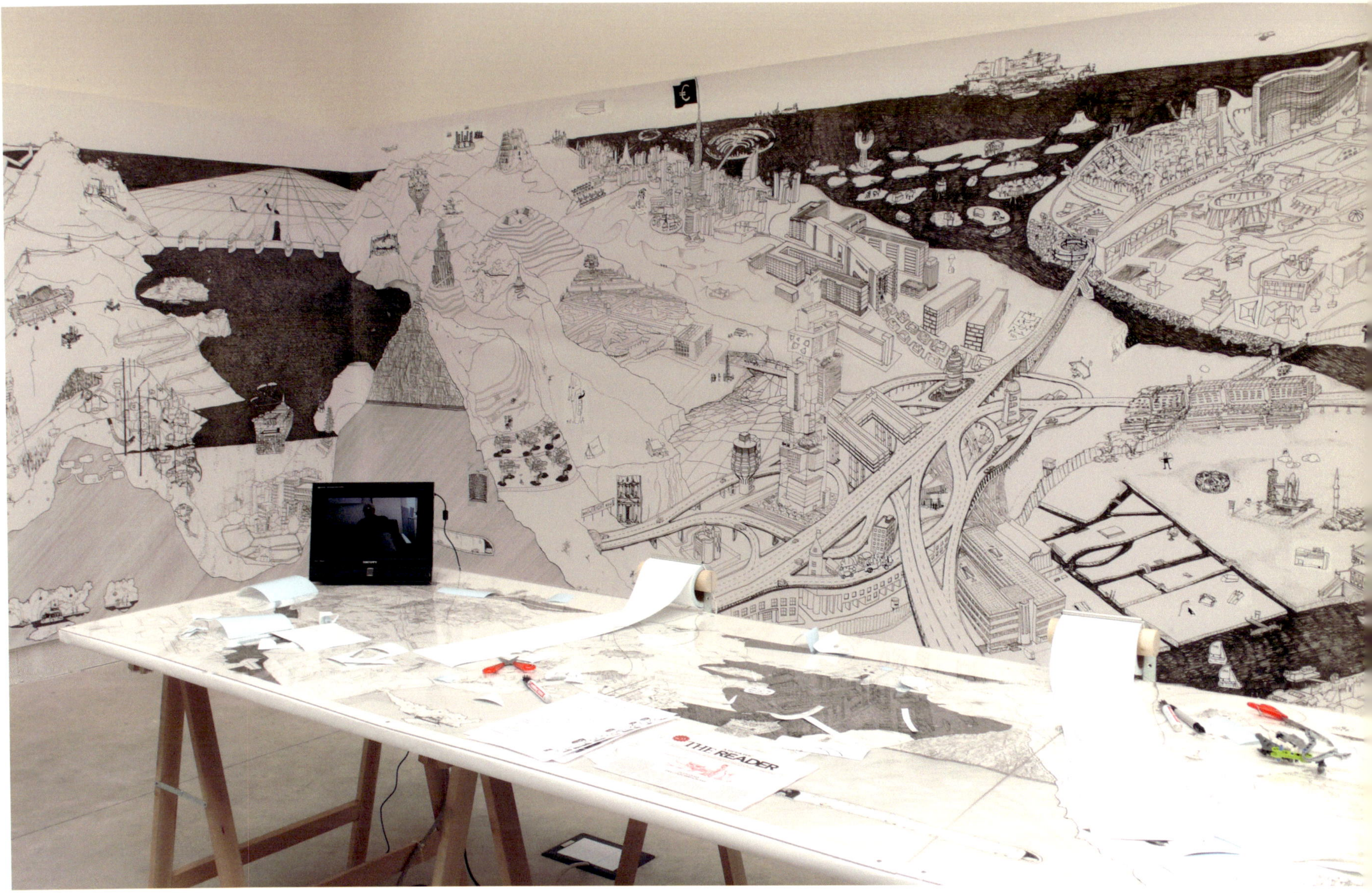

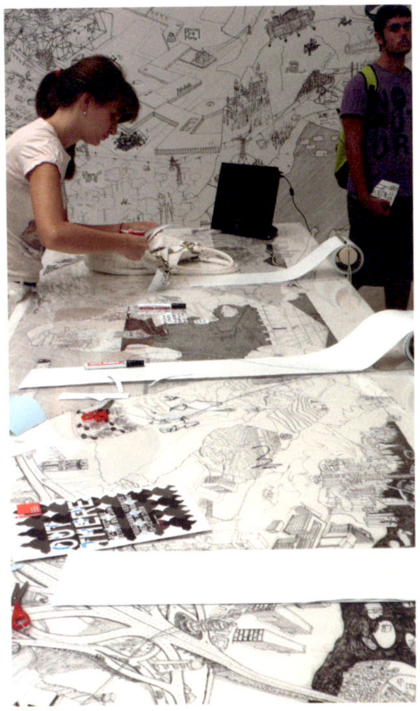

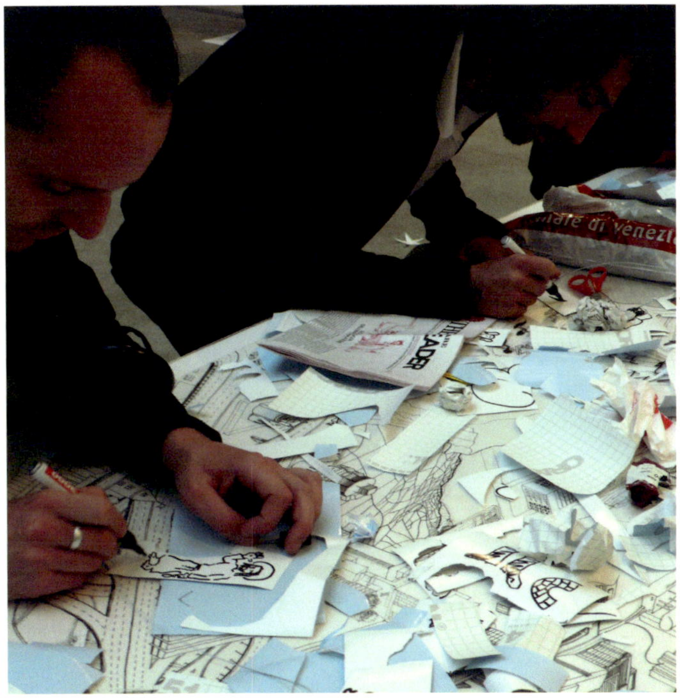

Raumlabor Berlin

STICK ON CITY

Stick on city is a responsive drawing, made to be permanently renewed. It is a training ground for utopians. Built and un-built iconic architectural designs assembled in an imaginary landscape. Visitors can take a tour, then add their own vision by drawing and simply sticking their work into the city.

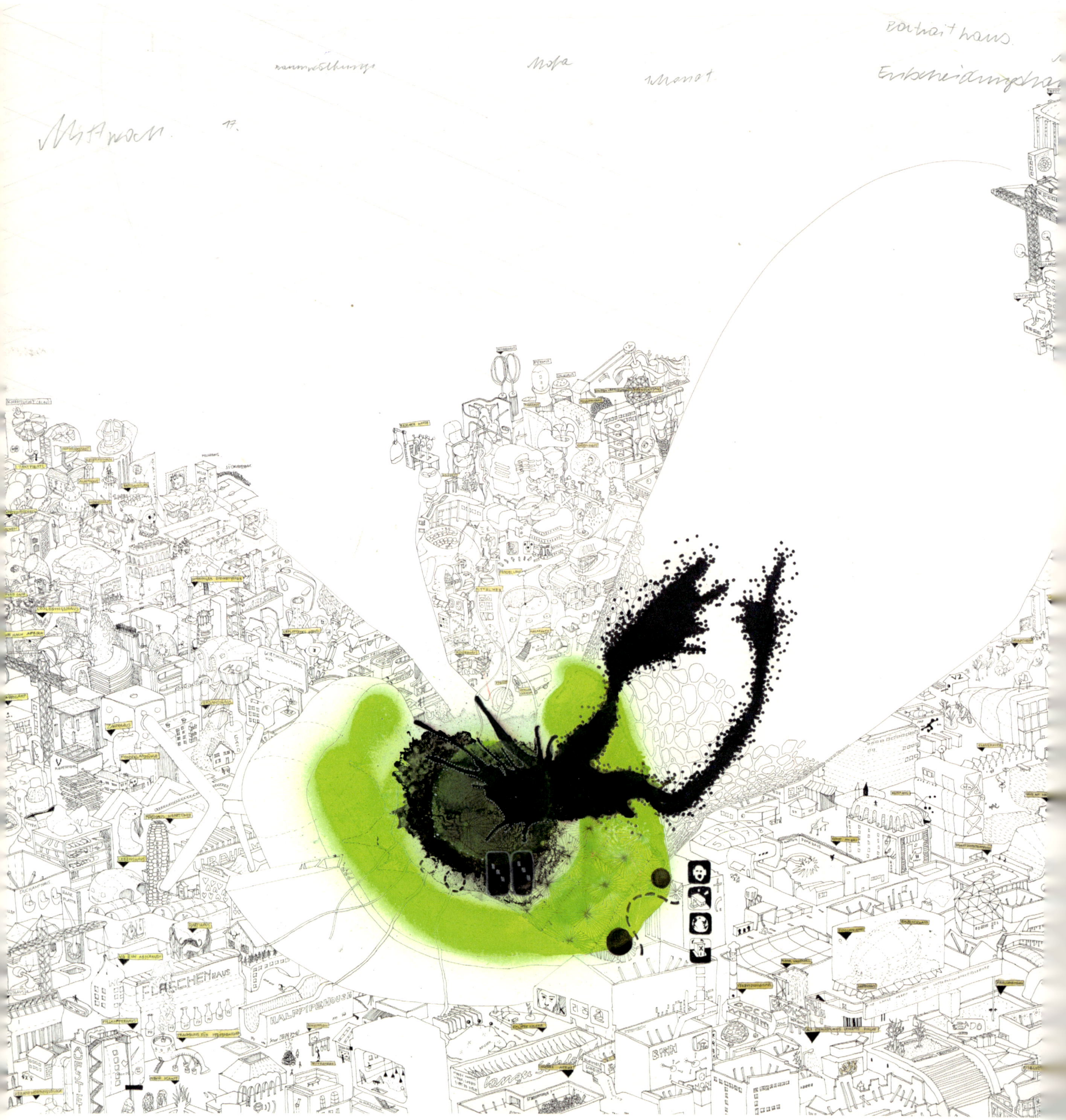
FLAECHENHAUS
HALFPIPEHOUSE

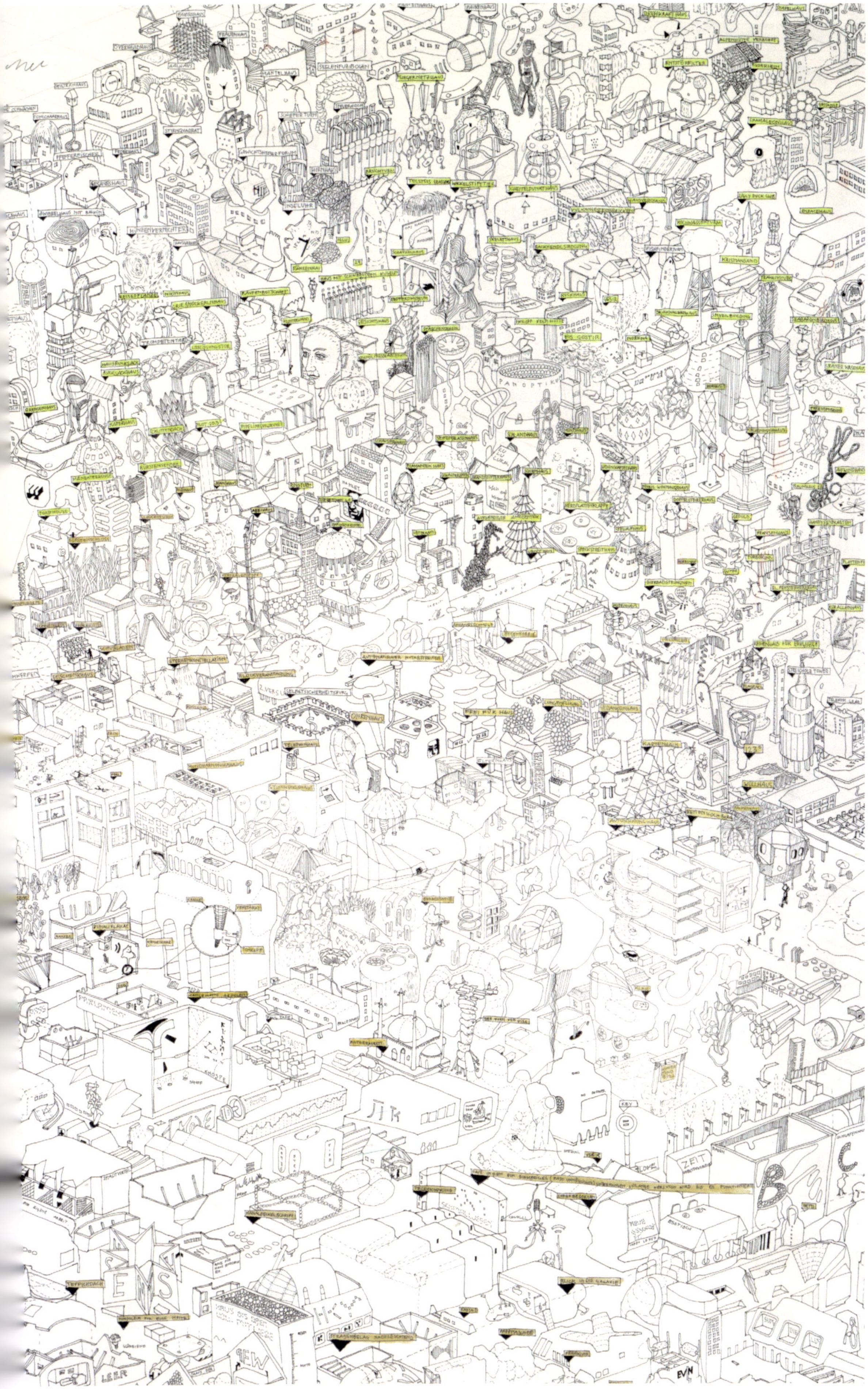

Constantin Luser

THE CITY

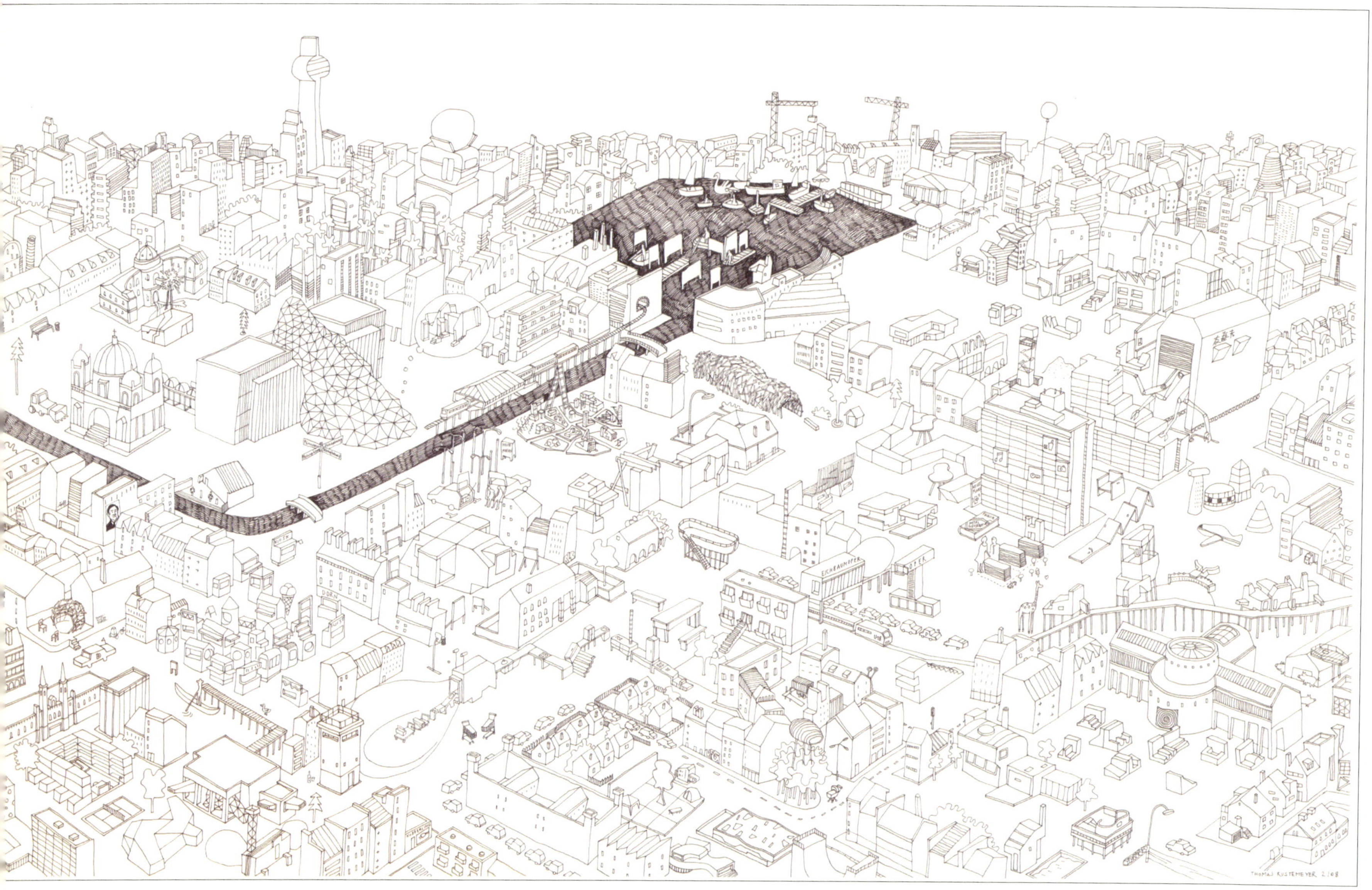

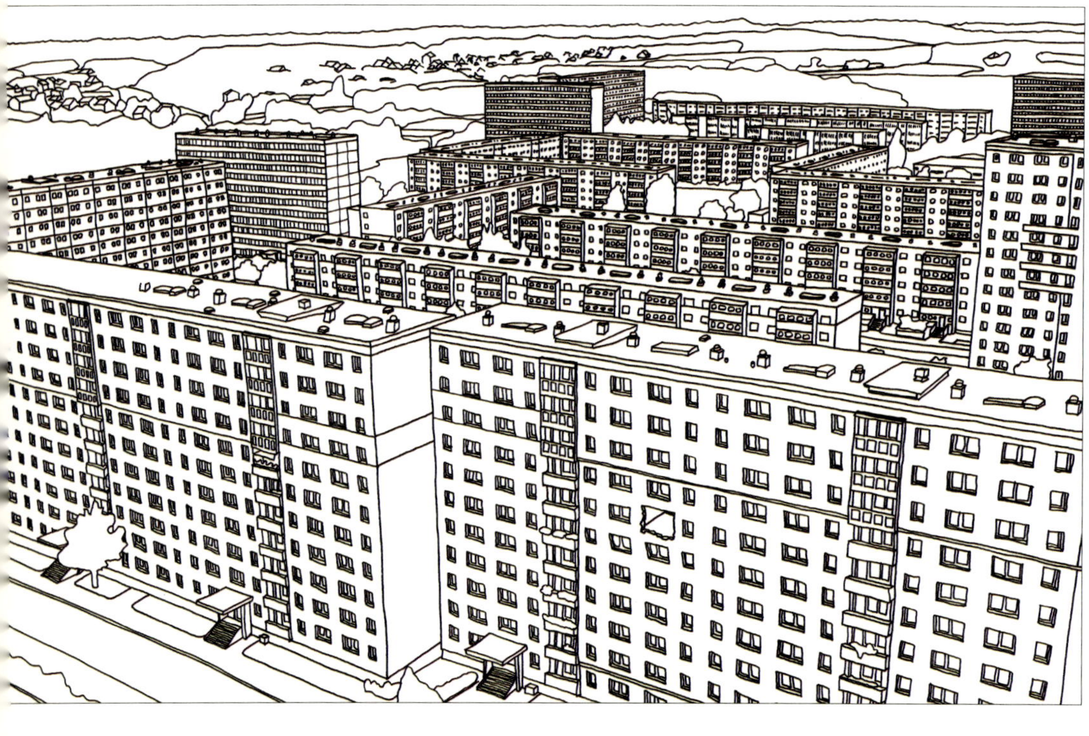

Raumlabor Berlin

RAUMLABORWELT *(top)*

Erik Göngrich

THEMROC *(left)*

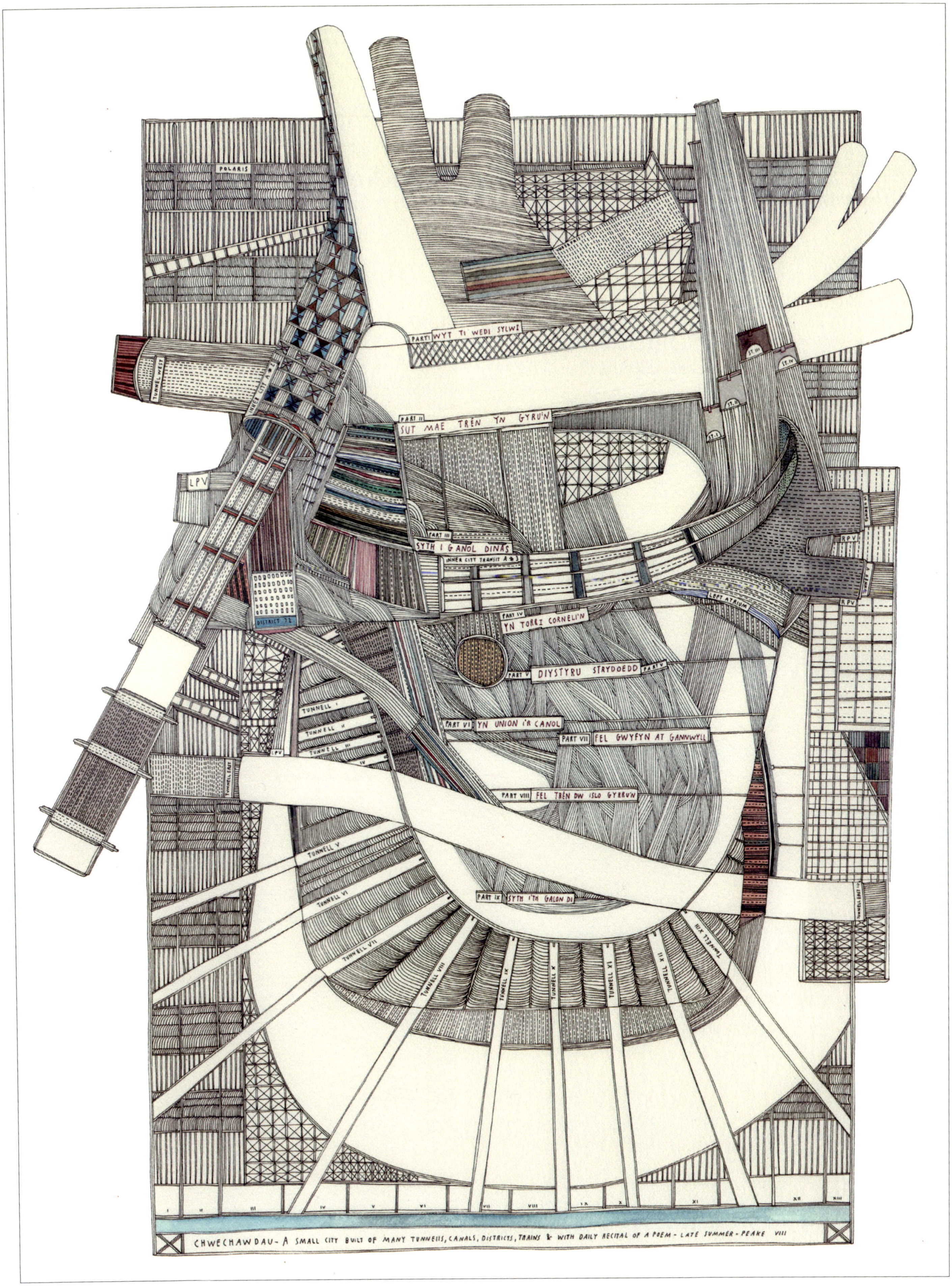

Nigel Peake

CITY OF TUNNELS

A proposed city constructed from a series of tunnels and underground arches.

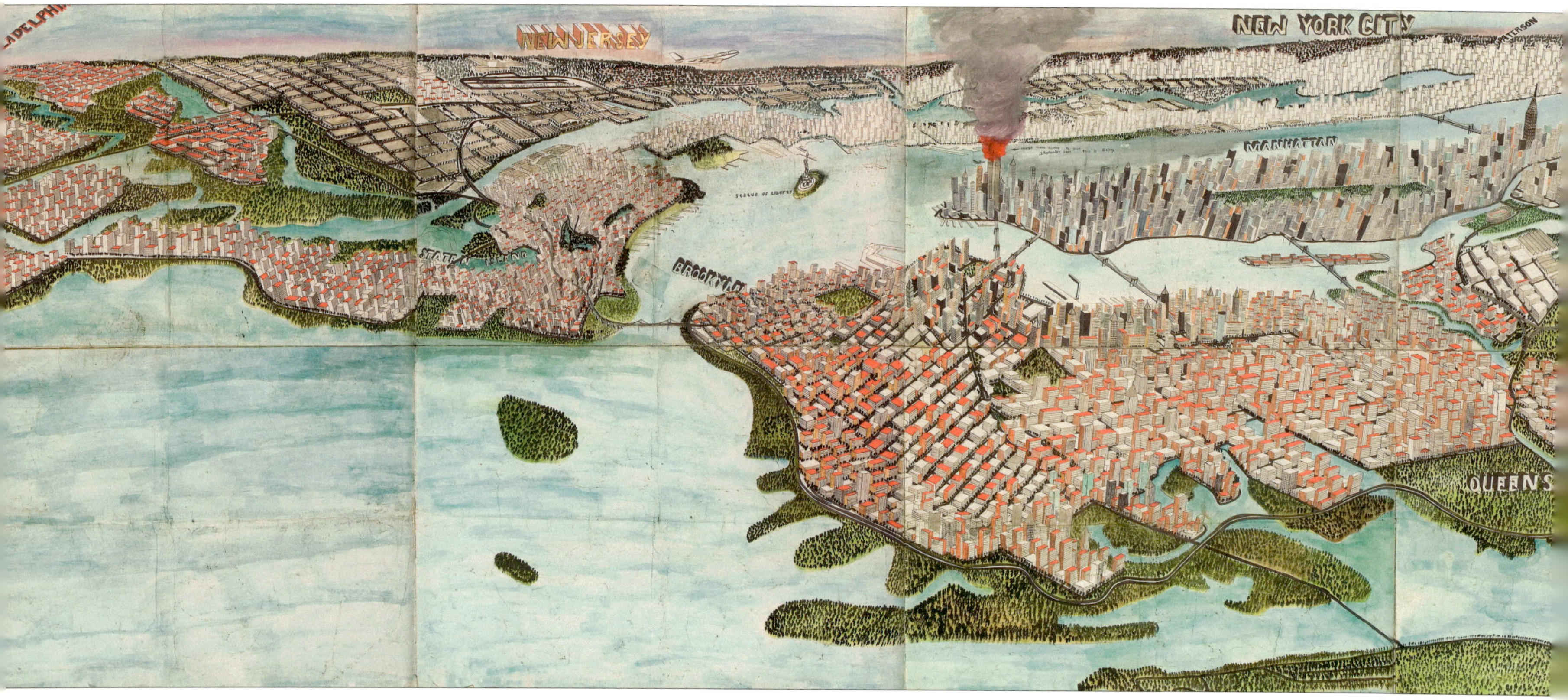
NEW JERSEY
NEW YORK CITY
MANHATTAN
BROOKLYN
QUEENS

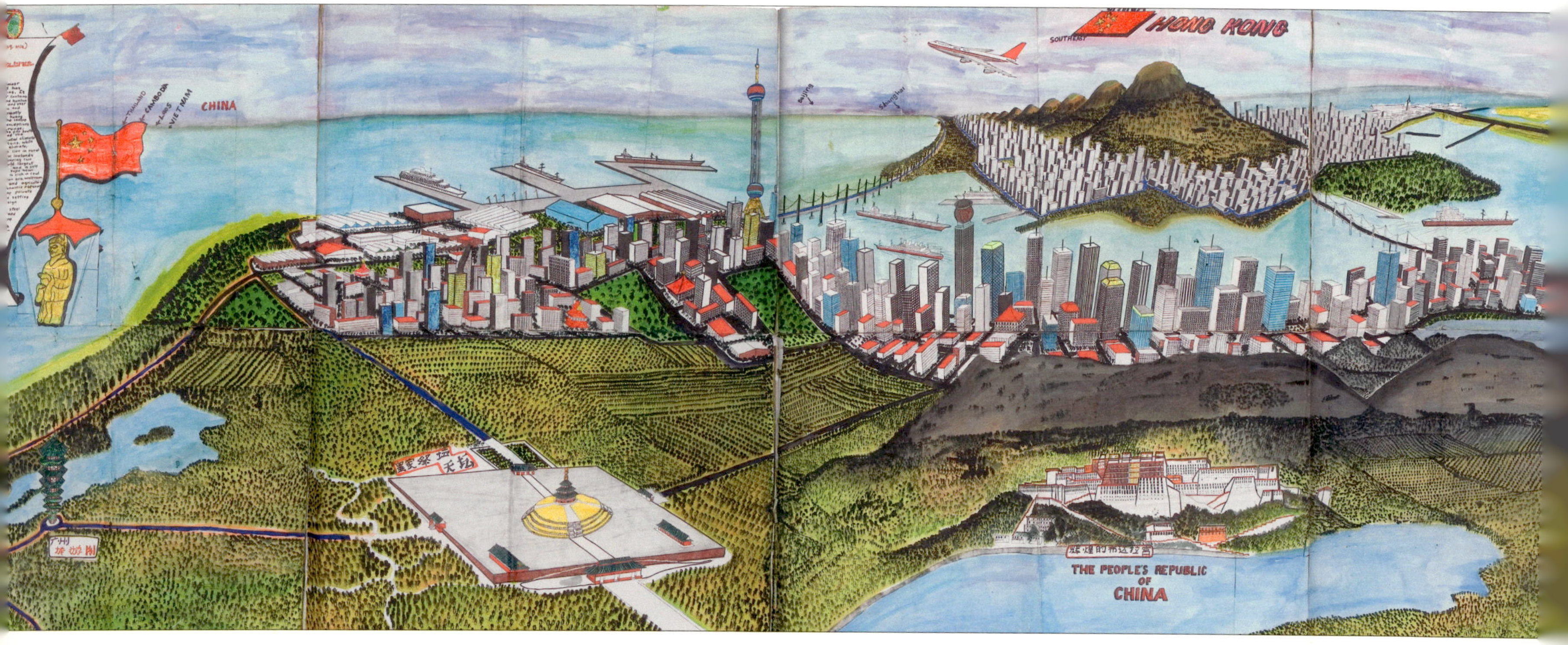
HONG KONG
CHINA
THE PEOPLE'S REPUBLIC
OF
CHINA

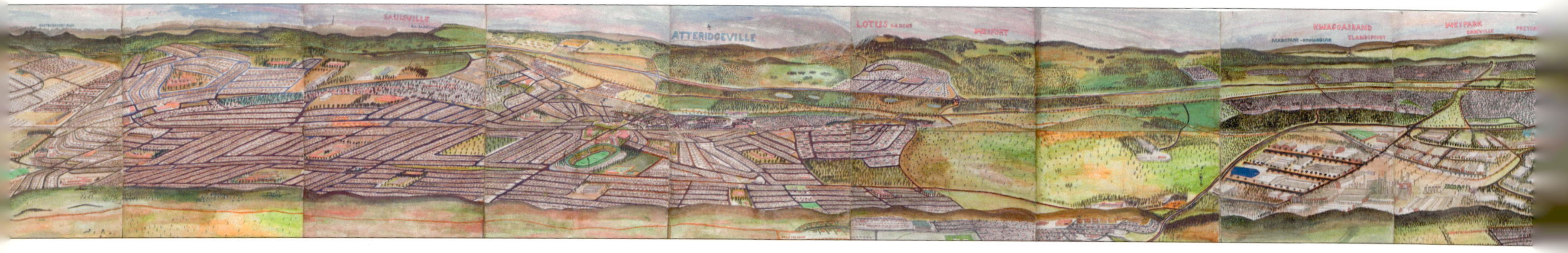
SAULSVILLE
ATTERIDGEVILLE
LOTUS GARDENS
WESFORT
KWAGGASRAND
WESPARK

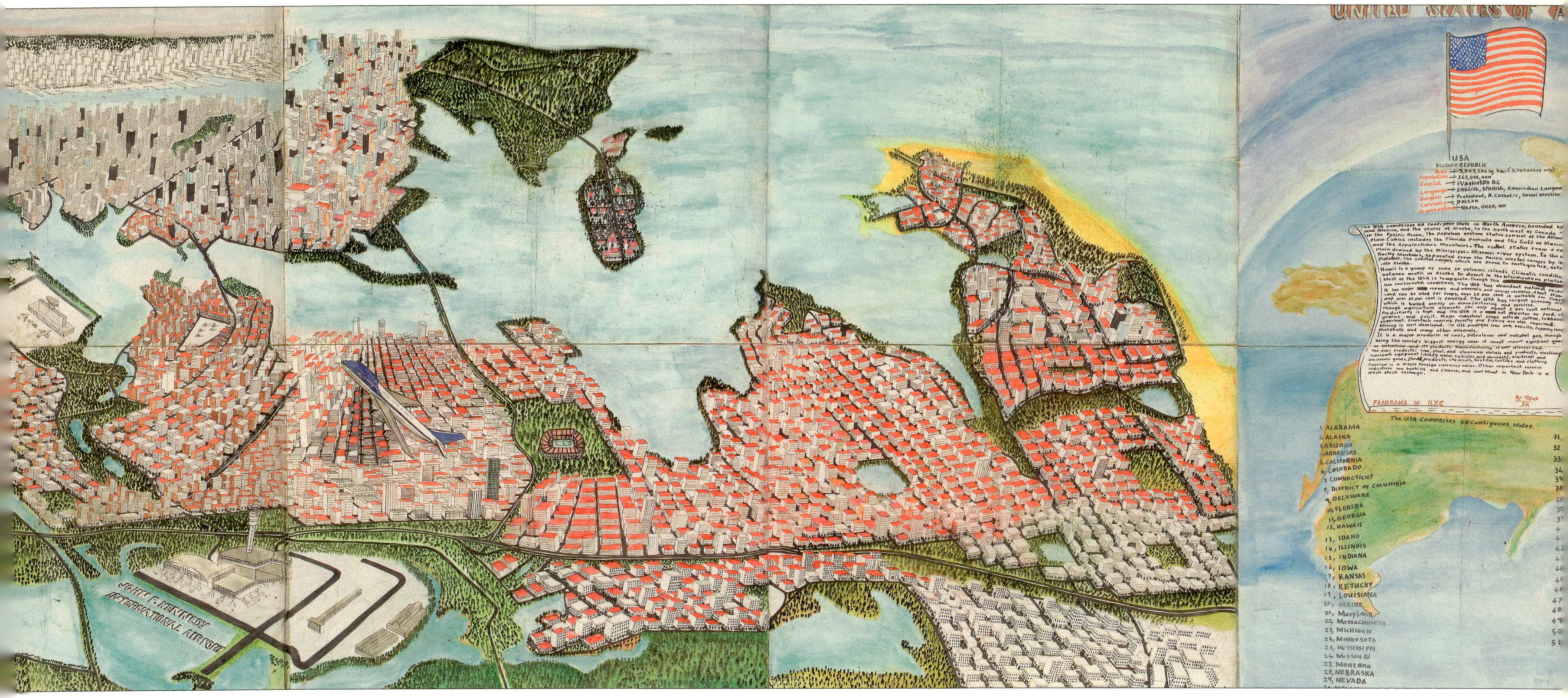

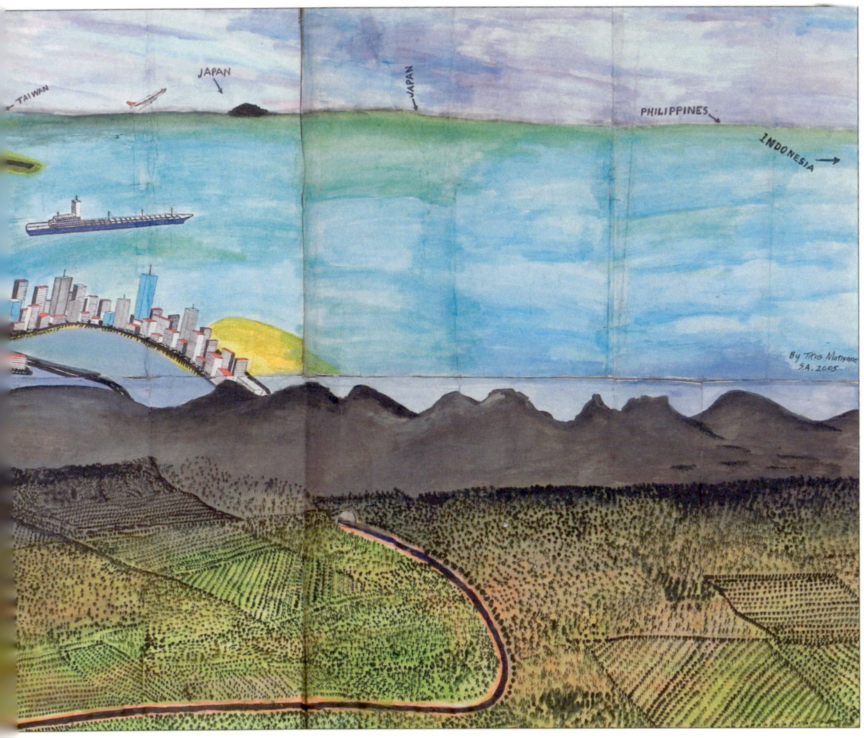

Titus Matiyane

South African sculptor, artist and musician Titus Matiyane creates huge panorama drawings of cities and landscapes from a bird's-eye view in his series Cities of the World. The panoramas, which he has been making since 1990, give the impression that the artist has observed the cities from the air, while in fact he only flew for the first time in 1998.

NEW YORK *(top)*
HONGKONG *(centre)*
TSHWANE *(bottom)*

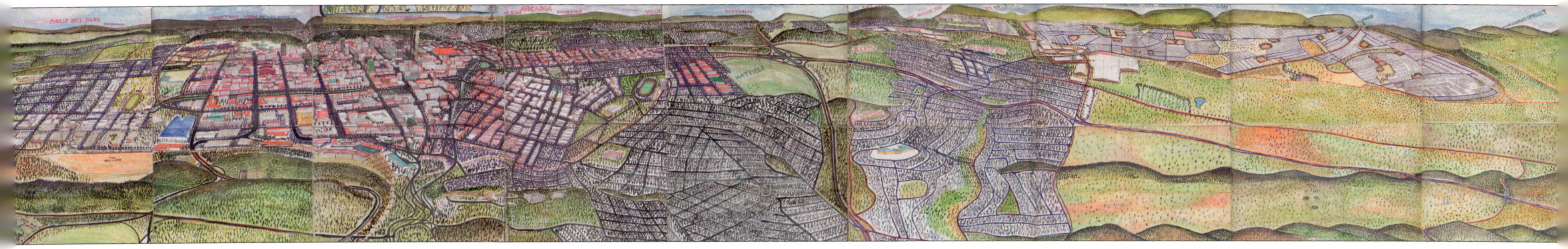

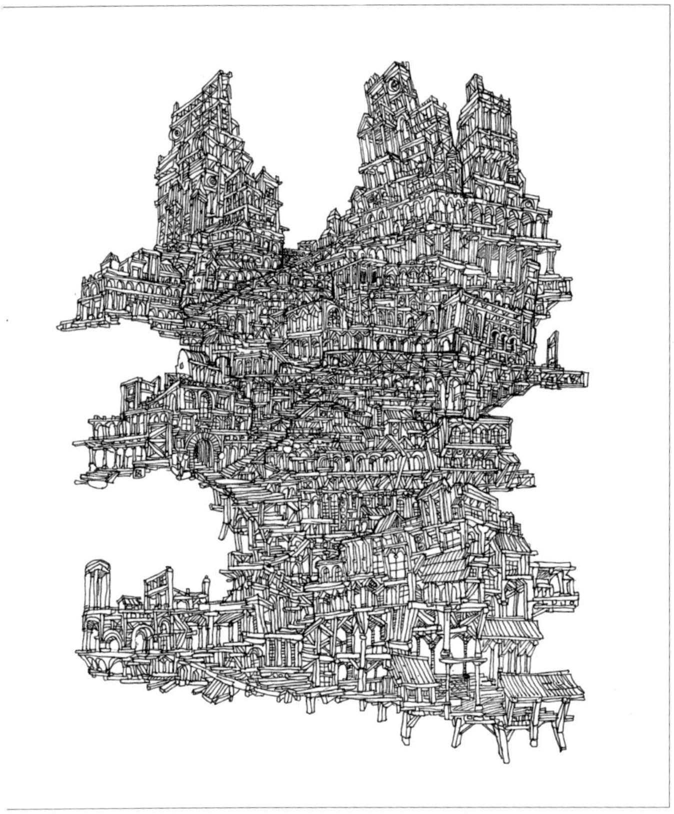

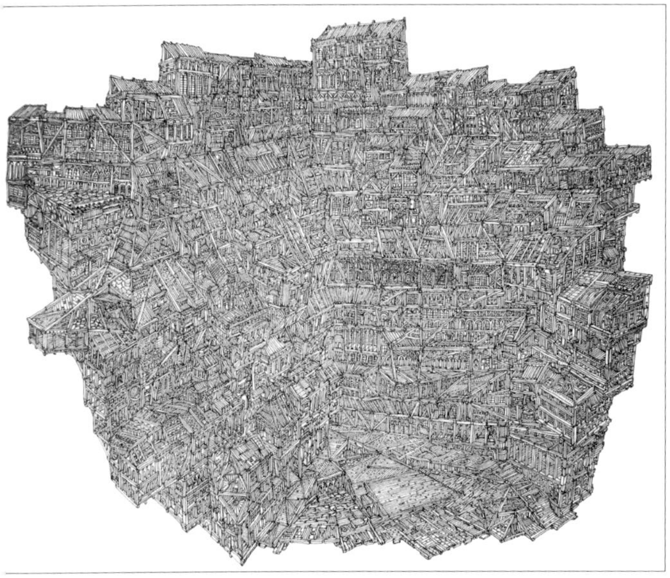

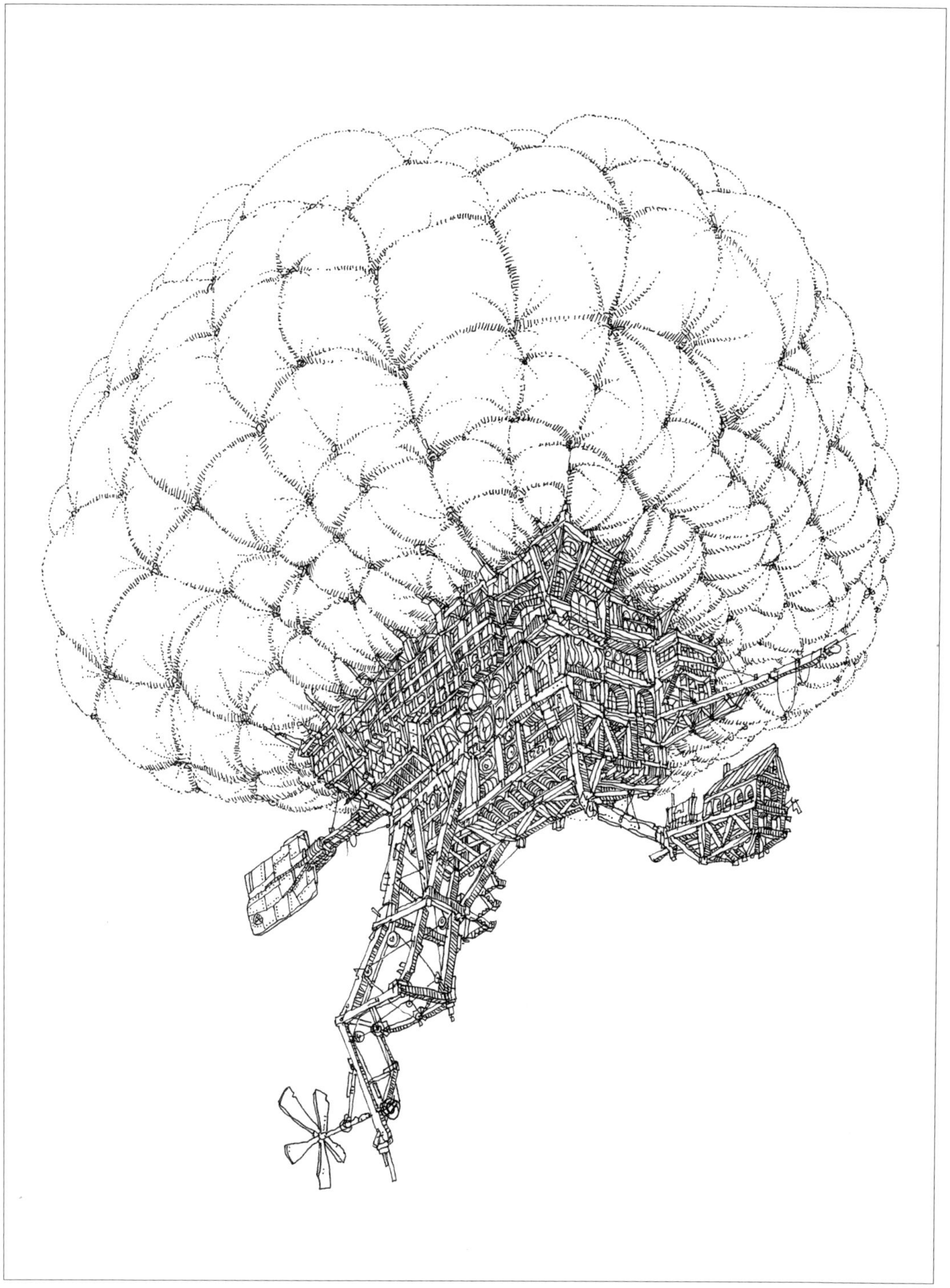

Vasco Mourão

DENSIDADE. CIUDAD *(top)*
DENSIDADE. REAL ESTATE *(bottom)*
DENSIDADE. ZEPPELIN *(right)*

Portuguese architect, illustrator and graphic designer creates in this series of impossible constructions drawings of subterranean cities, dirigble homes, and cliff-side housing.

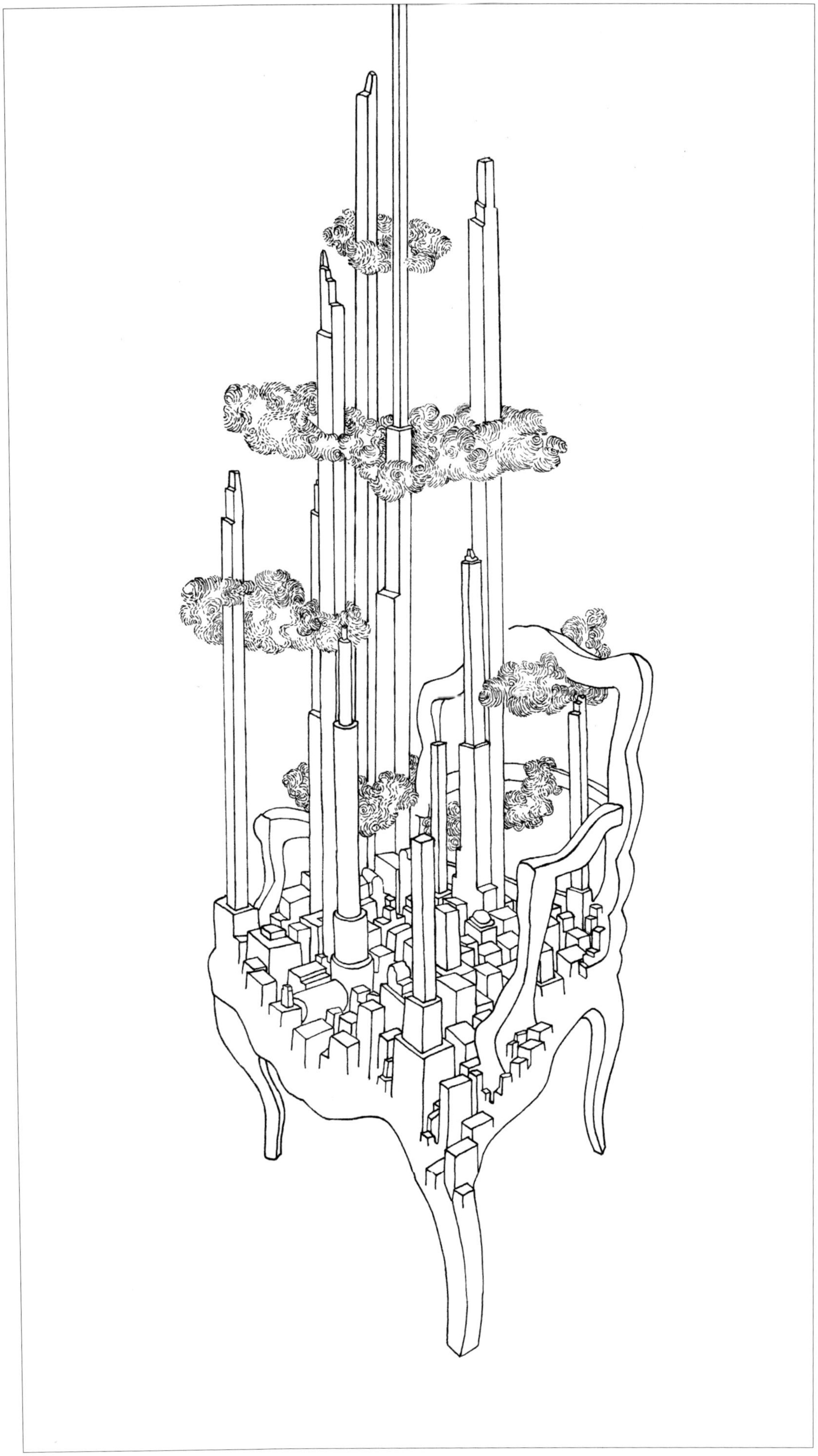

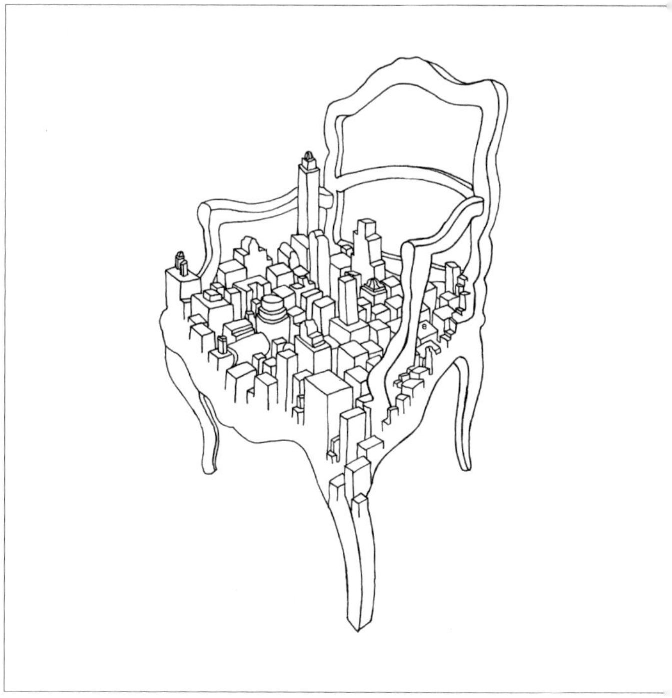

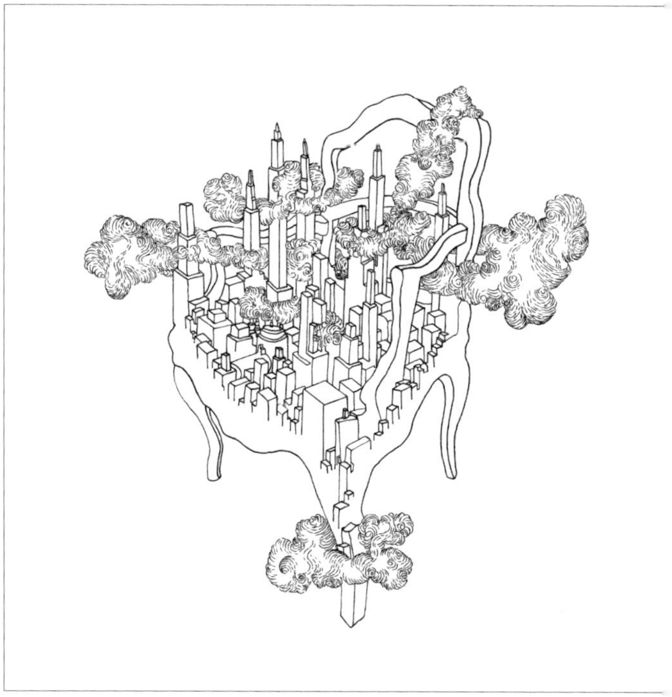

Bjorn Hegardt

CHAIR CITY

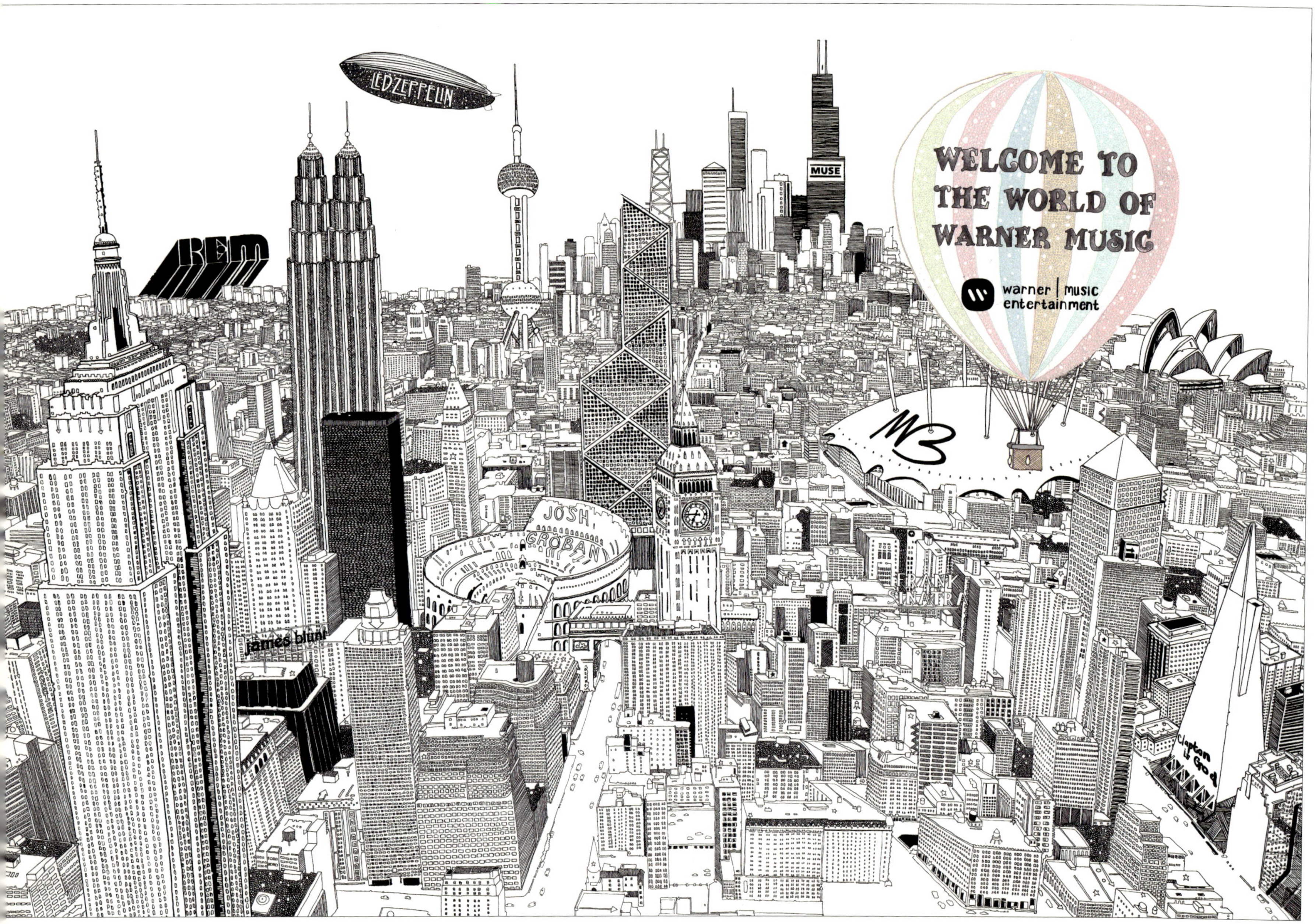

Chris Dent

WARNER WORLD *(top)*

Warner World incorporates some of the worlds most iconic buildings into one intense cityscape. This image was created for Warner Music Entertainment.

INTERGALACTIC *(right)*

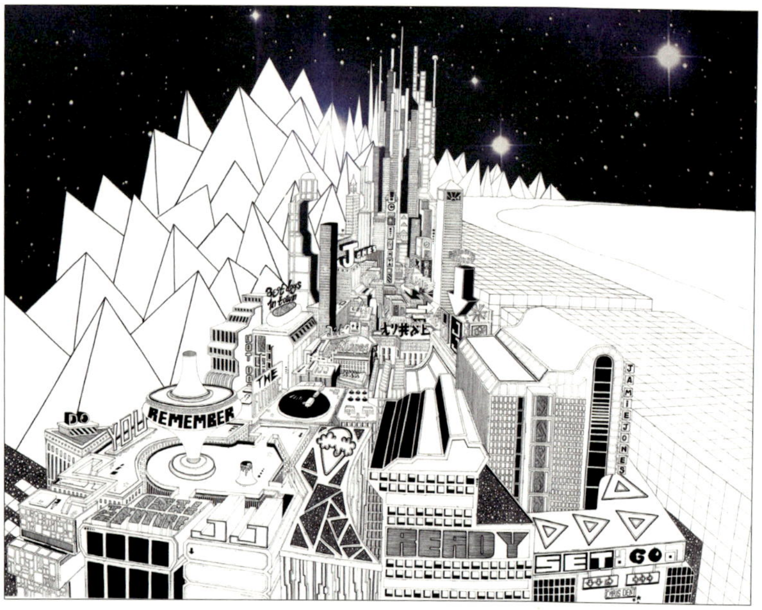

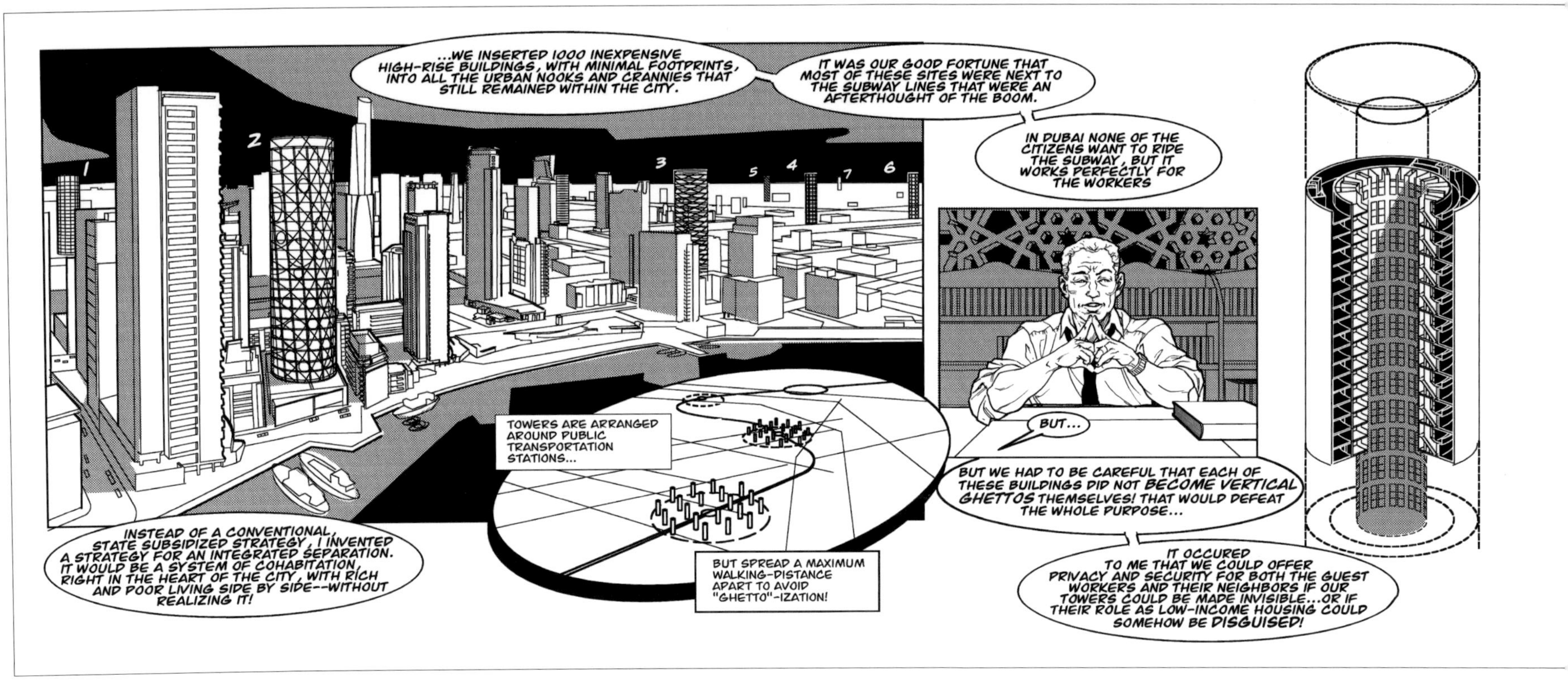

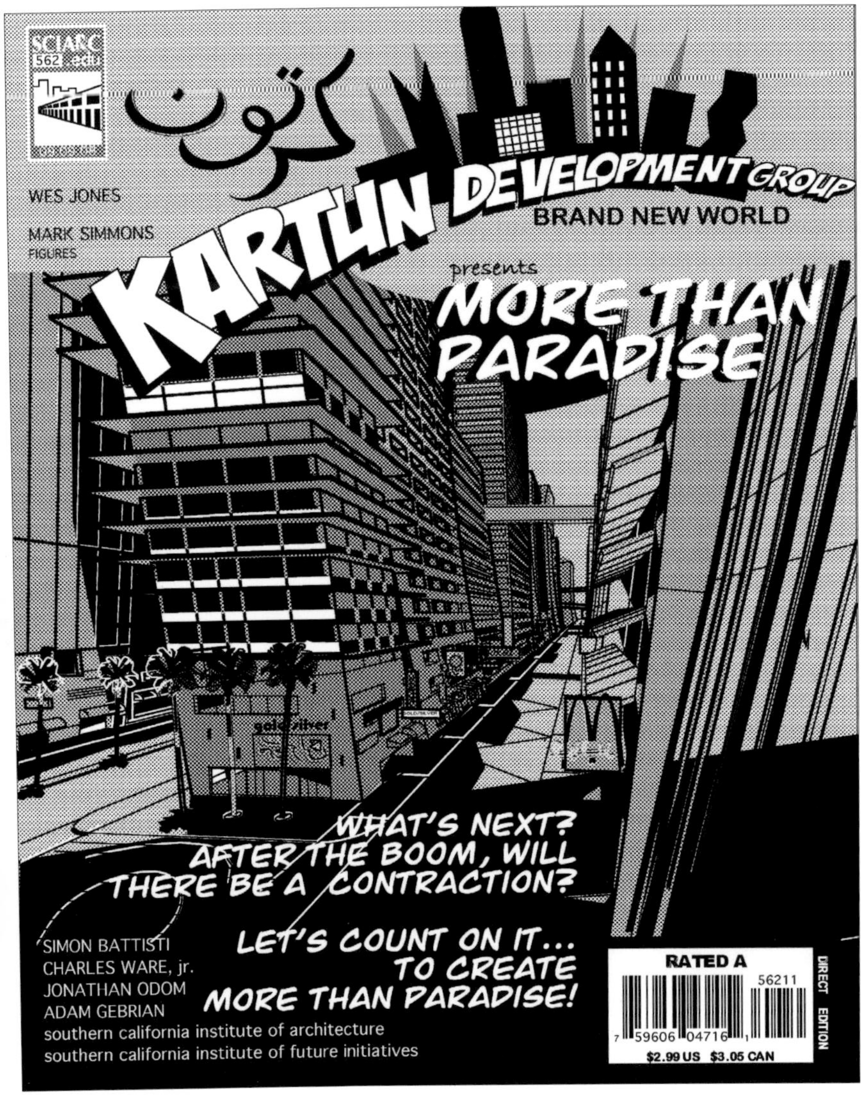

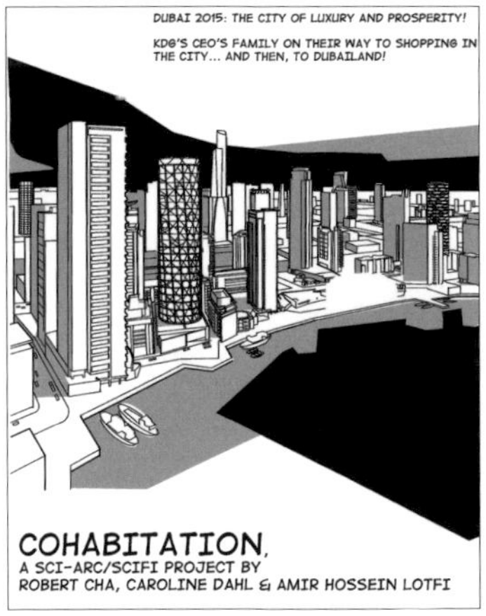

J, P: A Jones, Partners: Architecture

WITH SOUTHERN CALIFORNIA INSTITUTE OF ARCHITECTURE

RE:DOING DUBAI

As part of La Bienniale de Venezia, 11th International Architecture Biennale, Jones, Partners: Architecture offered a comic-strip interpretation/criticism/proposal for the future of Dubai. Dubai has become synonymous with excess and opportunity, its belligerent self-promotion a continuing challenge to conscience-plagued architects and critically-minded urbanists. This project asks how the good intentions of critical architecture can survive being co-opted, inevitably, by the power/capital structures that enable them.

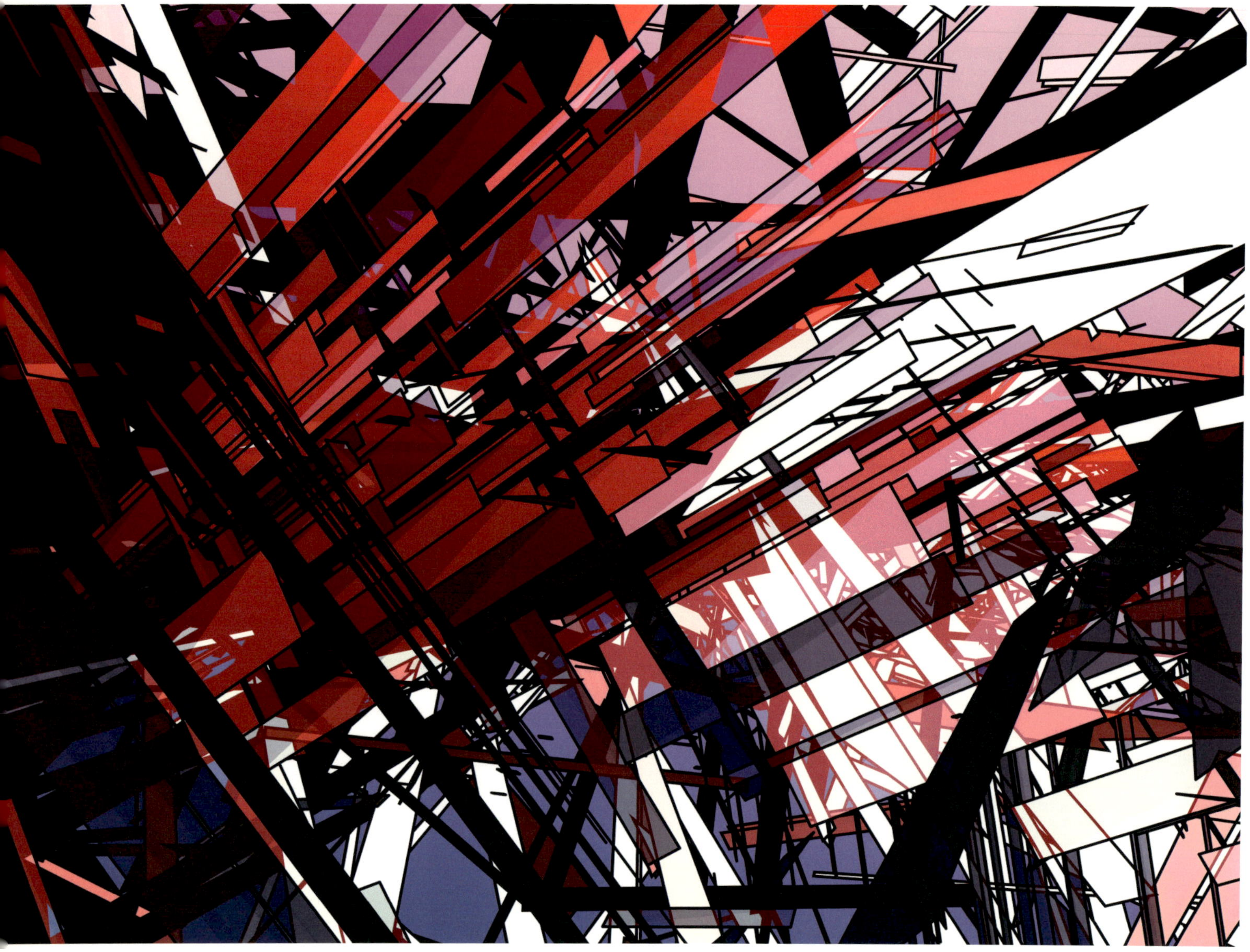

Holger Lippmann

DISINTEGRATION SERIES

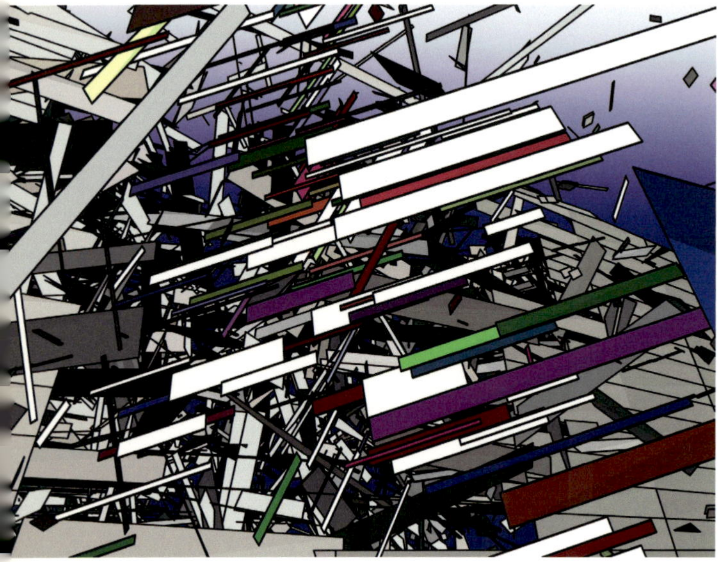

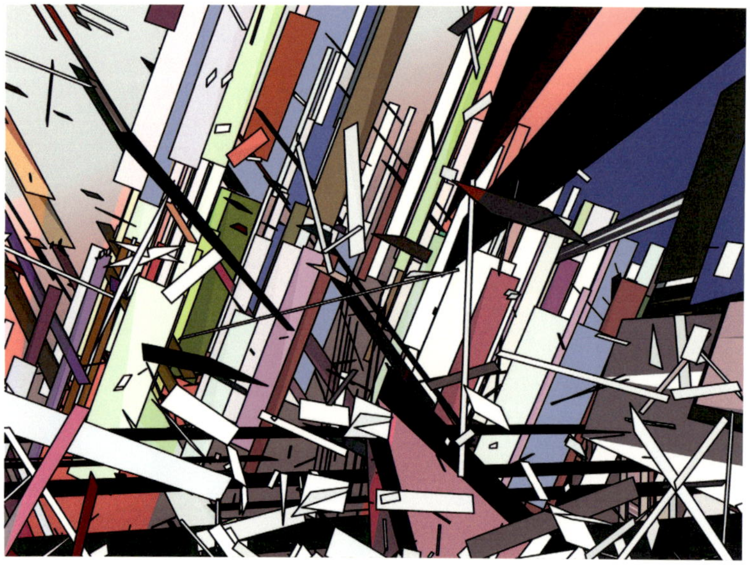

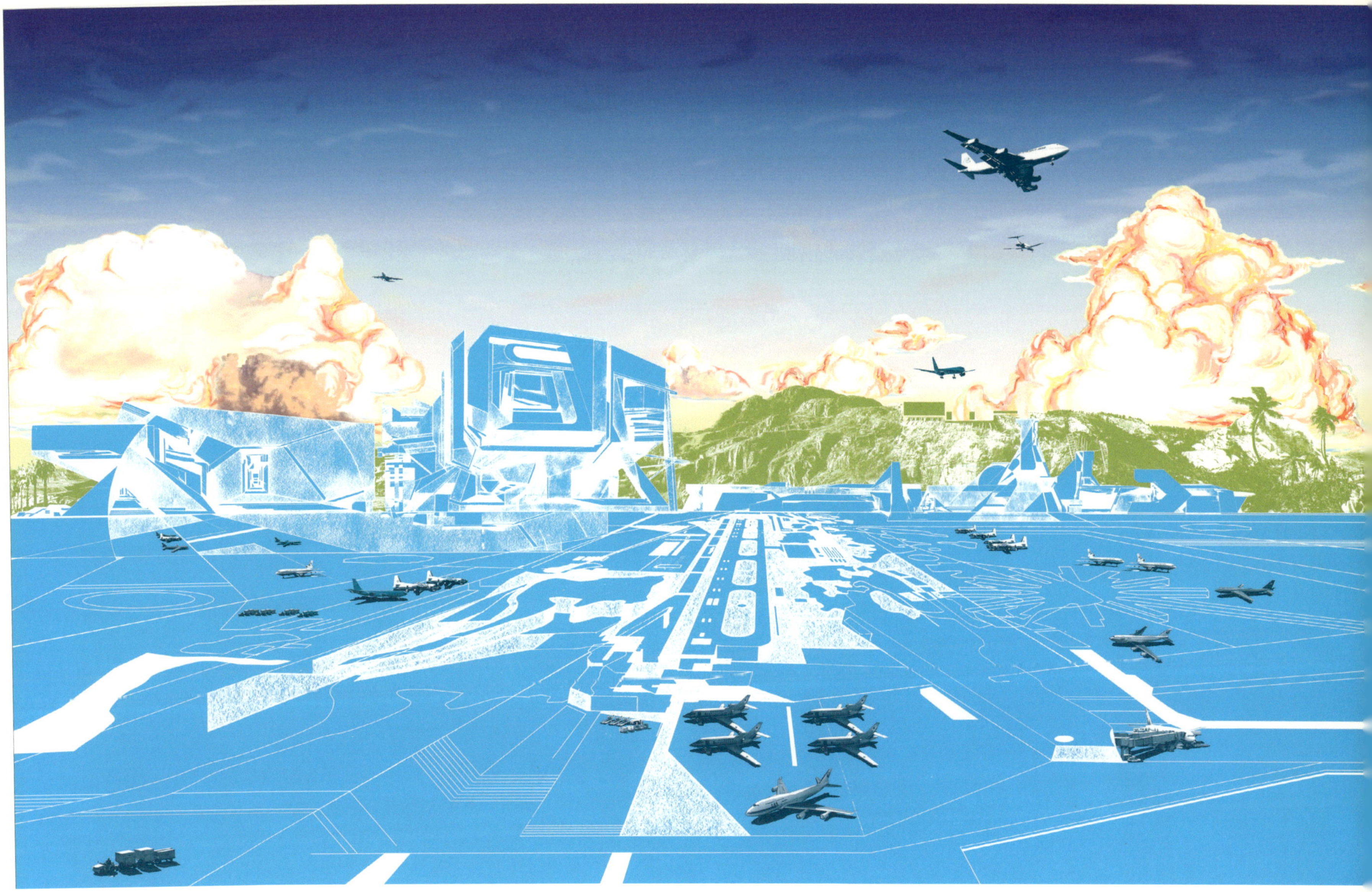

Hiroki Tsukuda

TERMINAL *(top)*, SONY MUSIC ILL [DEAD WONDERLAND] *(bottom)*

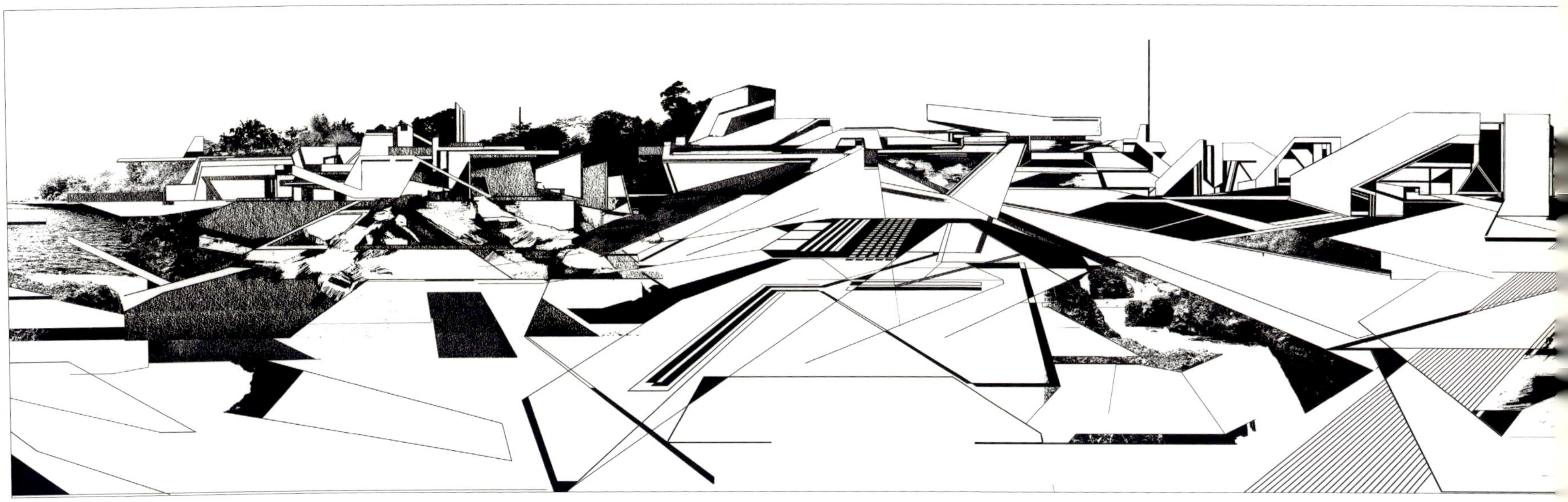

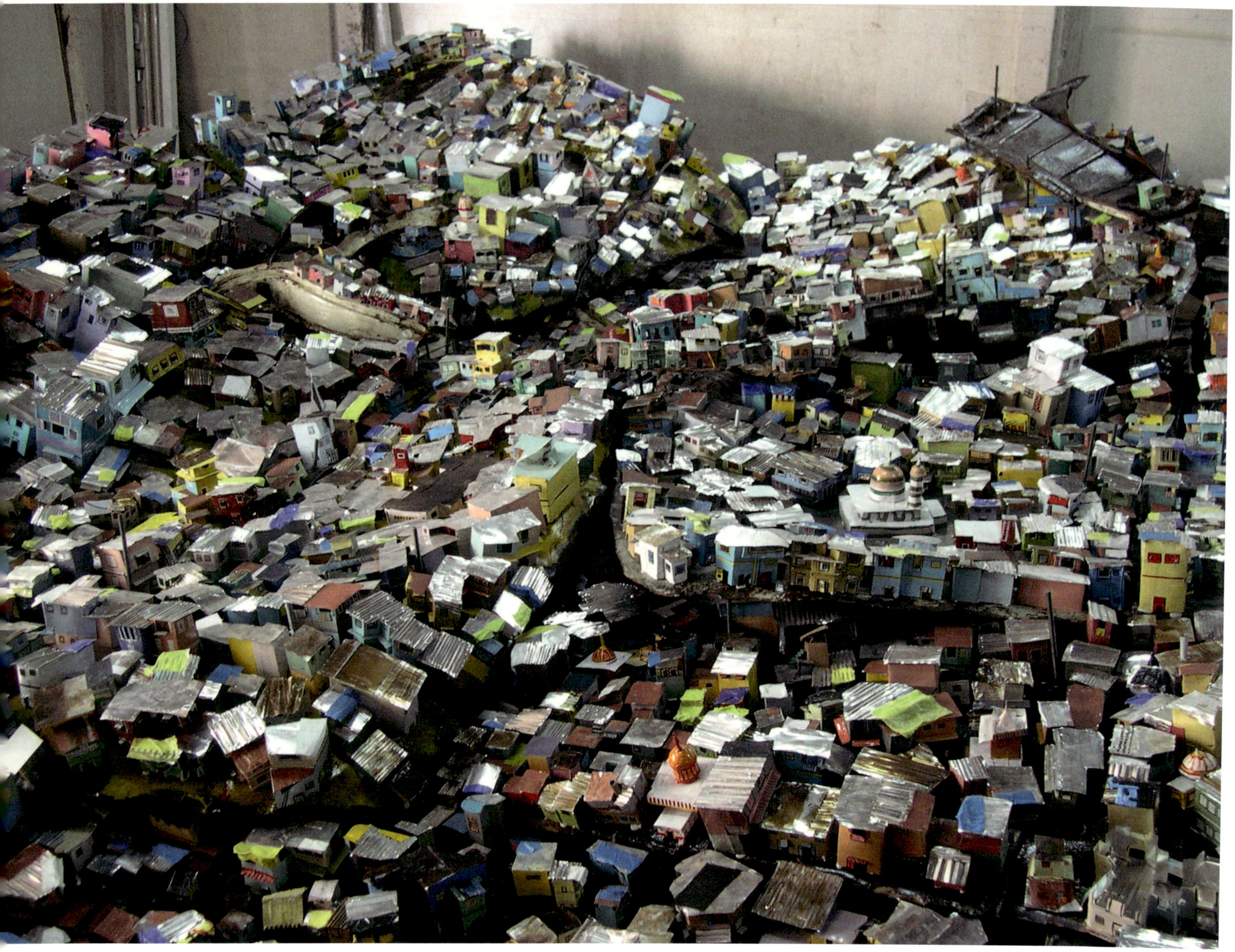

Hema Upadhyay

DREAM A WISH, WISH A DREAM

Upadhyay's installation Dream a Wish, Wish a Dream engineered a meticulous microcosm of Dharavi, the largest slum in Bombay and in Asia. Further developing earlier themes of space and urban quality, the artist fashioned and painted each element of the reconstruction using plastics and hardware materials, with recycled car scraps and sheet aluminium as a basis.

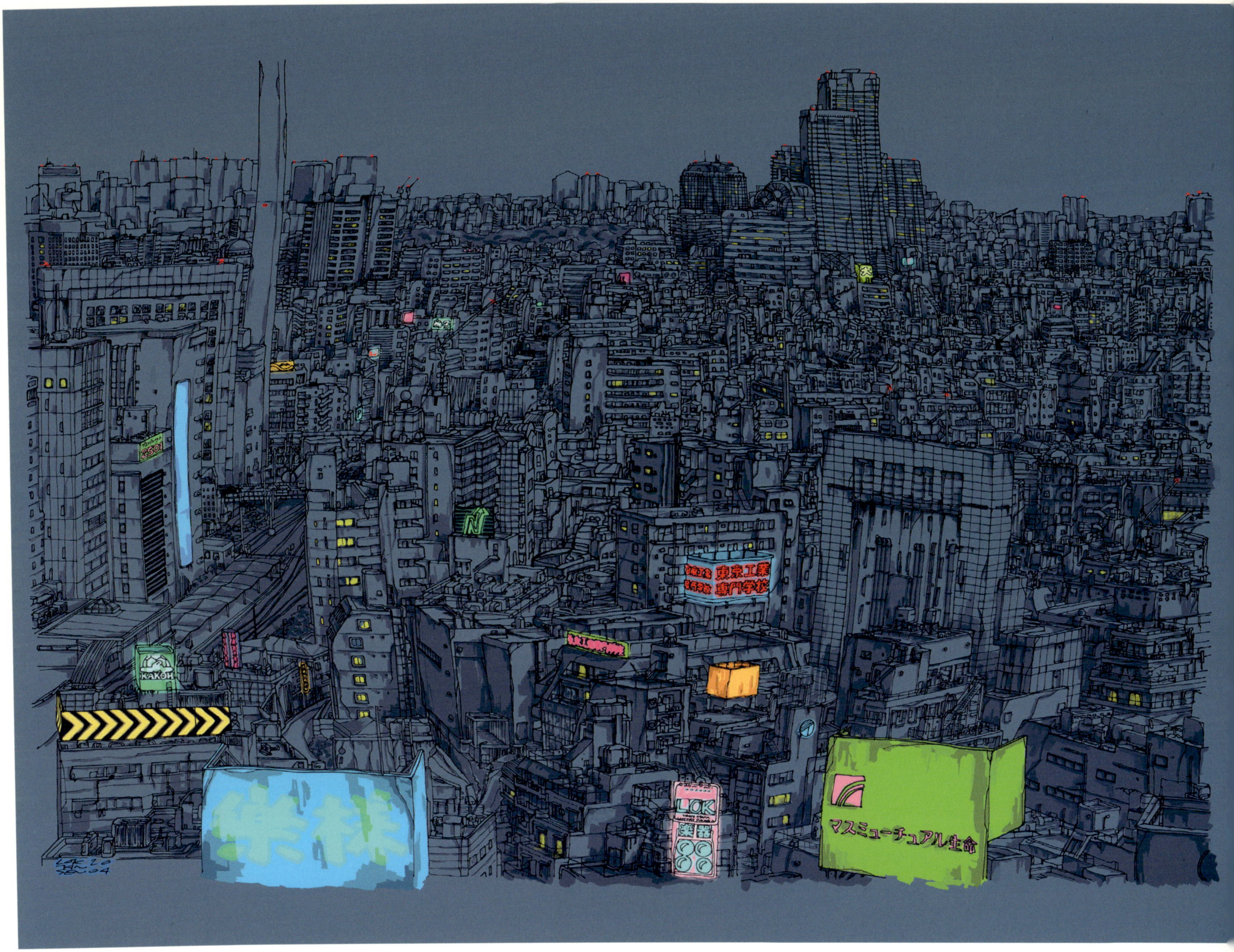

Lok Jansen

CITYSCAPE 2501

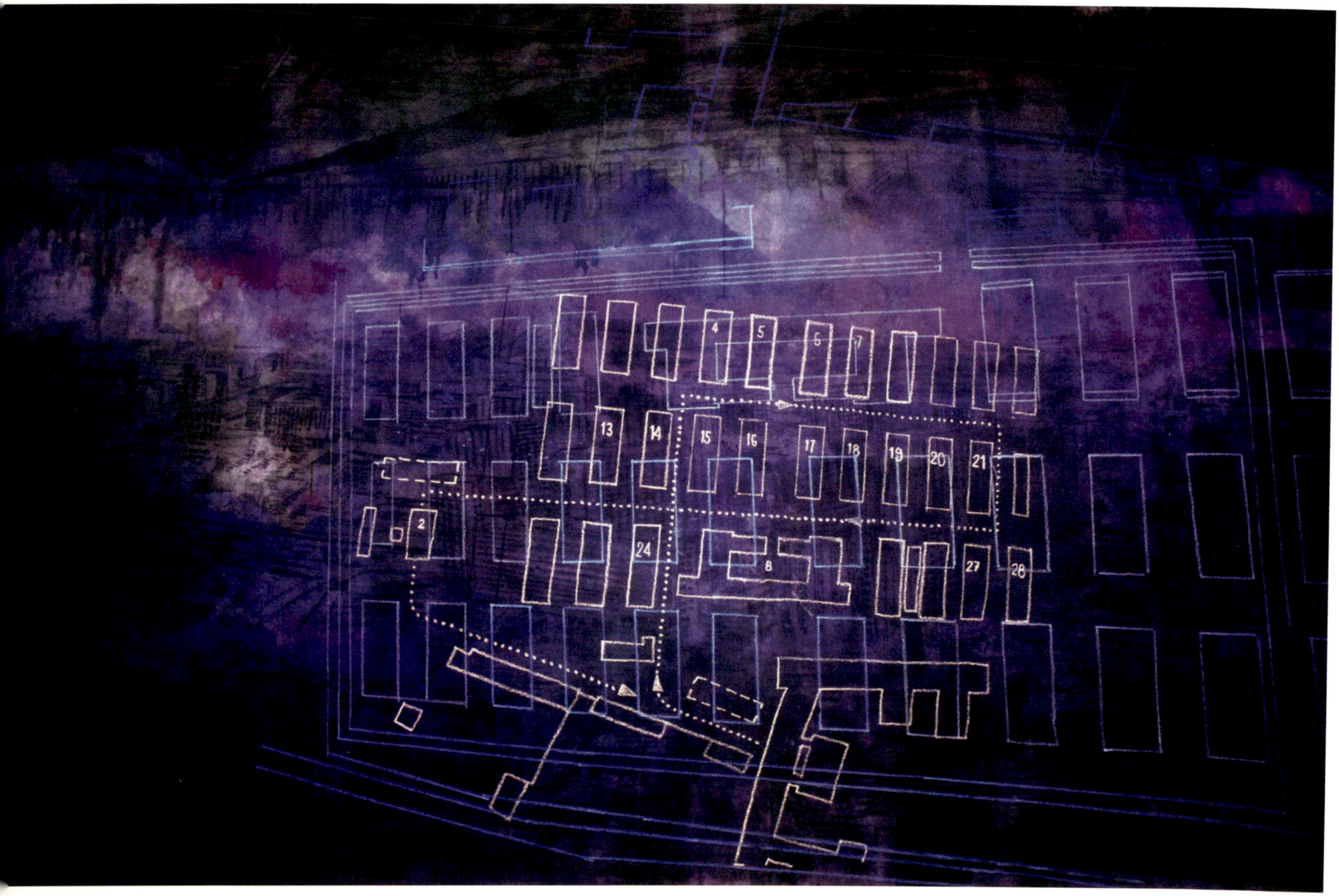

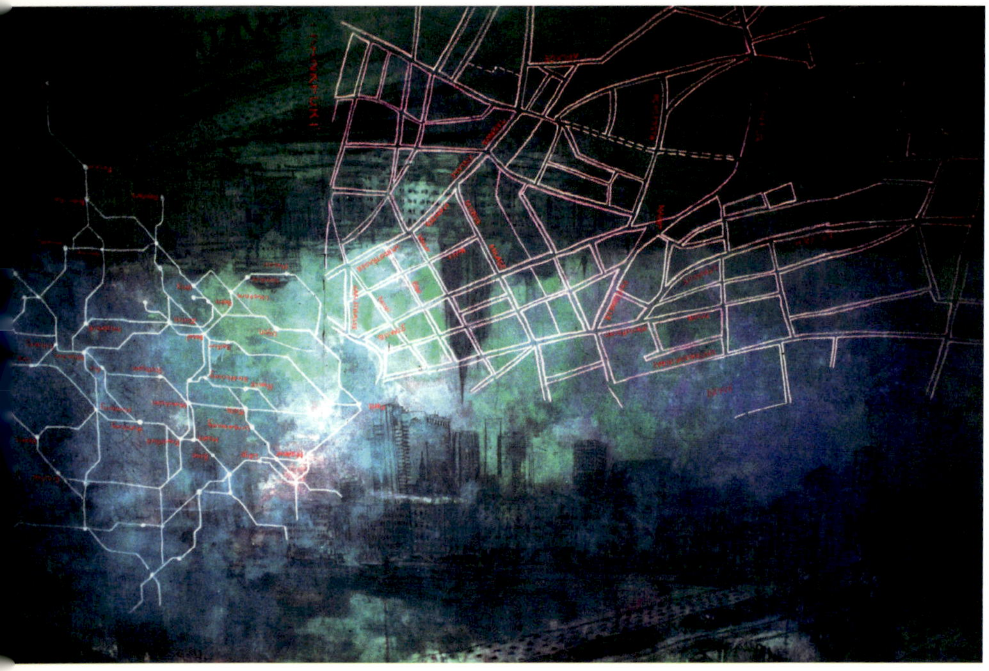

Eamon O'Kane

CITY PANORAMA SERIES

These large-scale City Panorama paintings depict cities from above. They are technically constructed by drawing the cityscape directly on raw canvas in charcoal and then applying consecutive layers of translucent acrylic paint. Numerous new and ancient maps are laid on top of each other.

CITY II – Warsaw *(top)*
CITY IV – Frankfurt *(bottom)*
CITY XII – Bagdad *(right page, top)*
CITY III – Rome *(right page, bottom)*

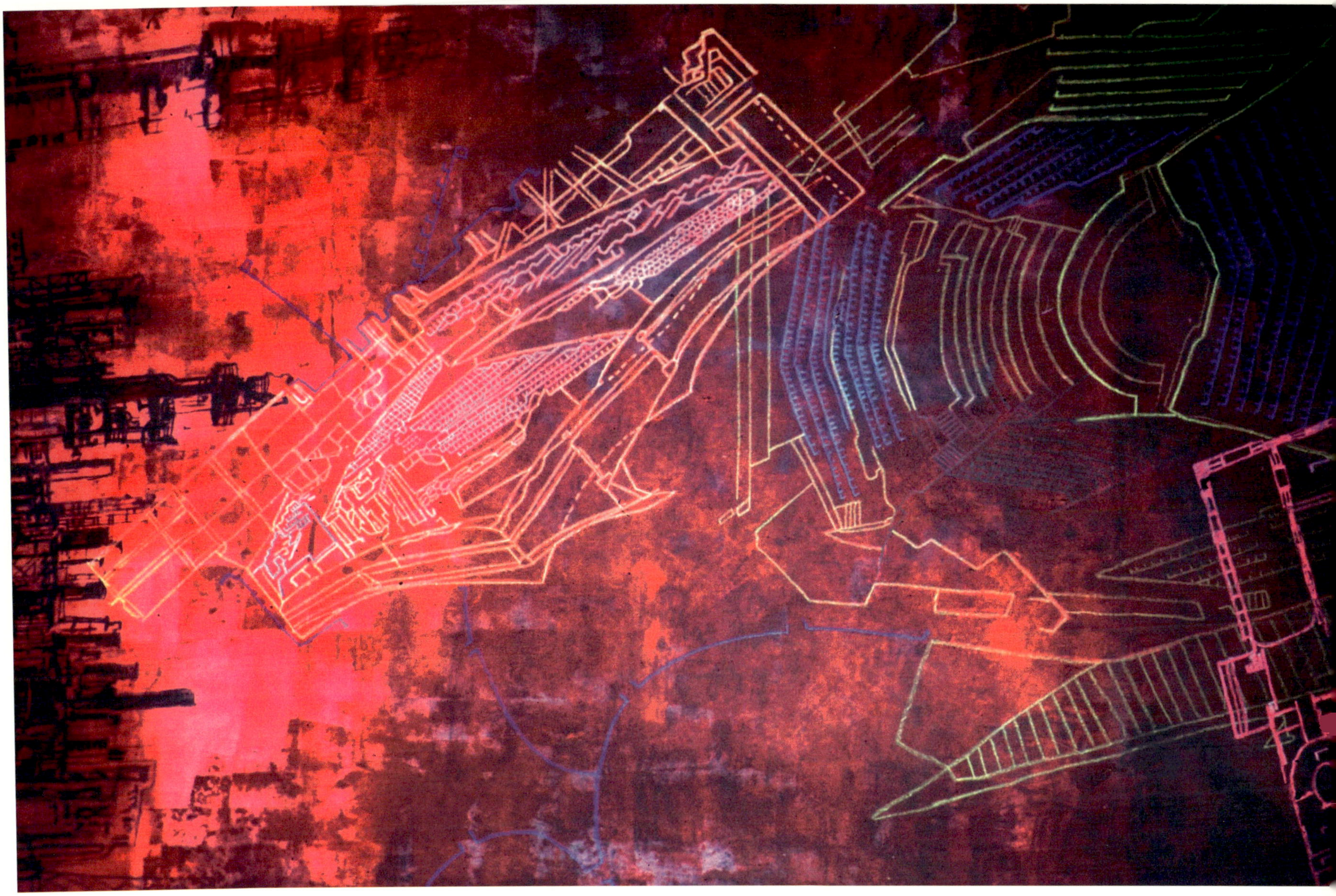

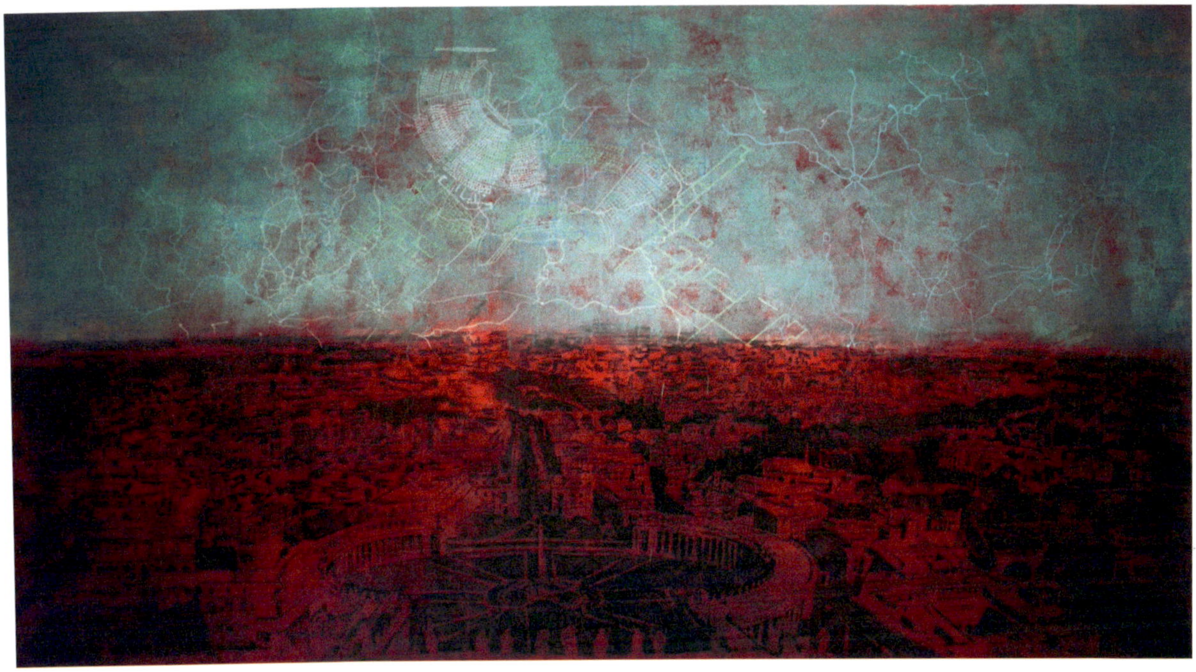

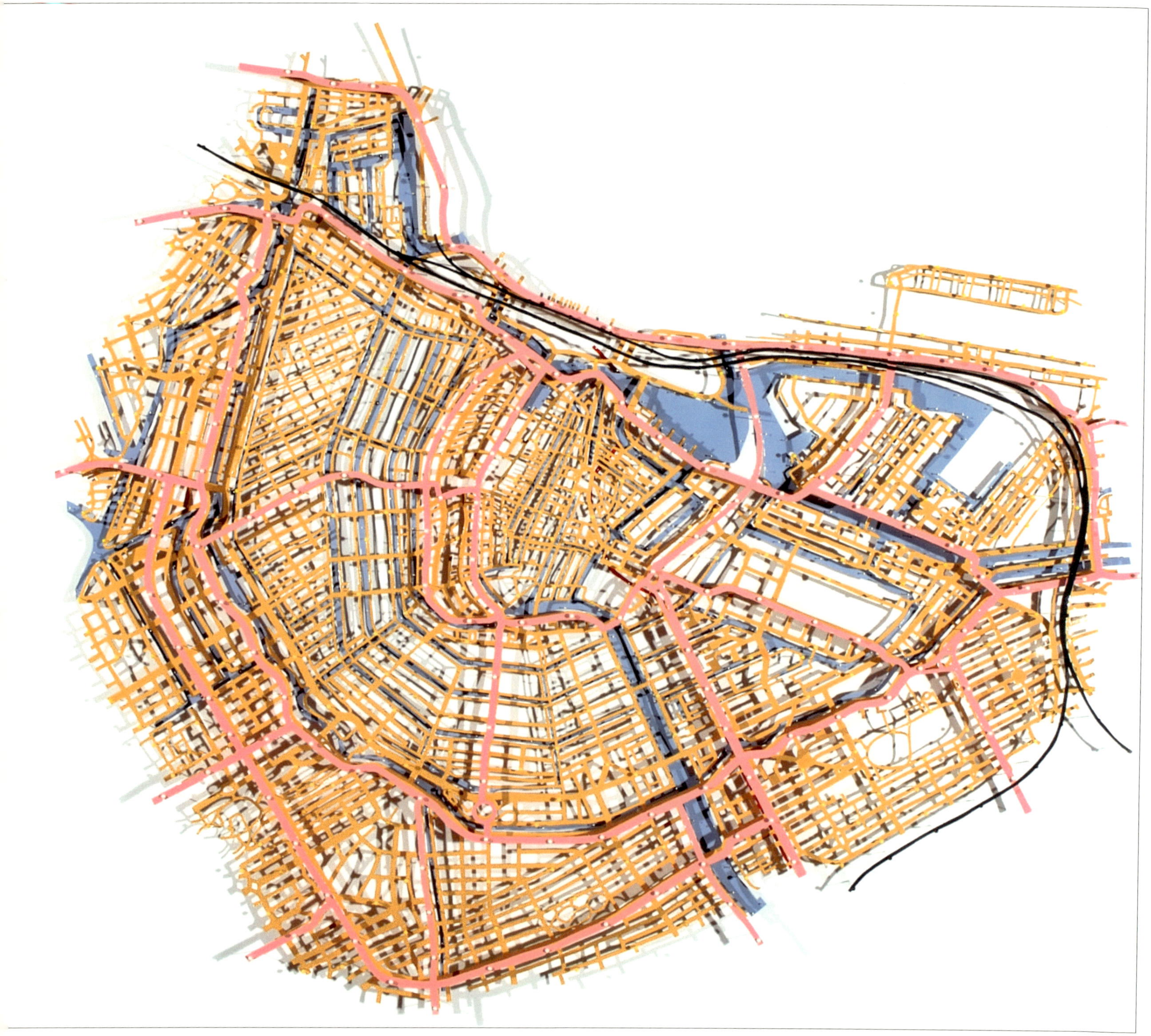

Matthew Picton

These works by Matthew Picton transform the two-dimensional mapped image into multi-layered sculptures, ommiting the layers of communication, transportation and river systems that comprise the current city. Extracting the lines of infrastructure from the background data renders the complex organism that comprises each city visually transparent.

AMSTERDAM – A sculpture of the infrastructure of Amsterdam, including the canals, roads, rail lines, subway.

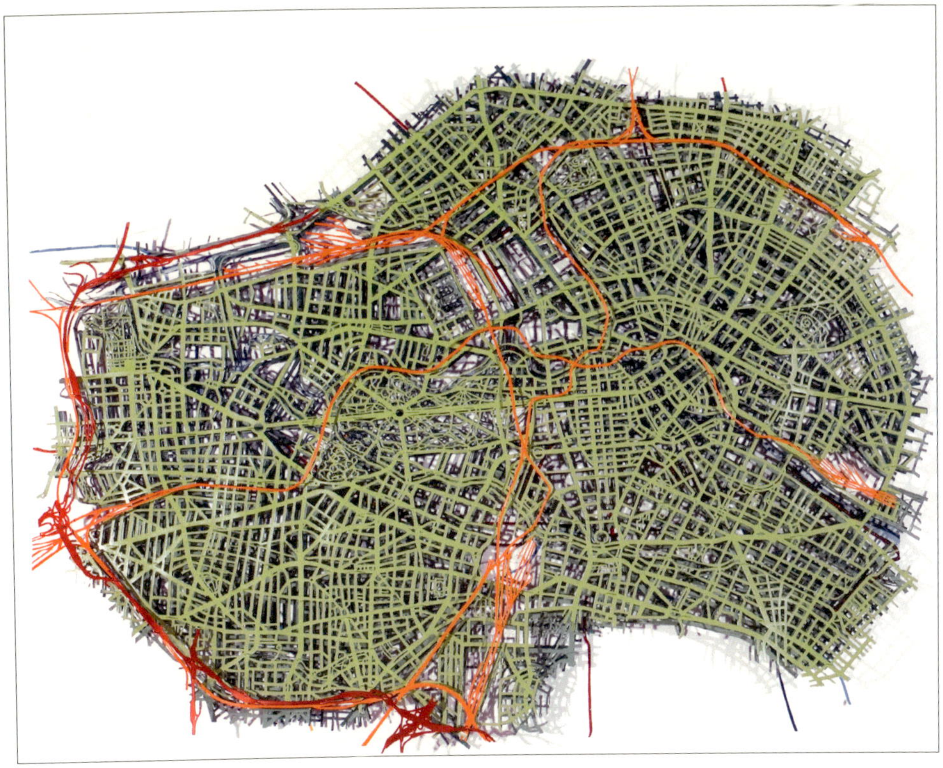

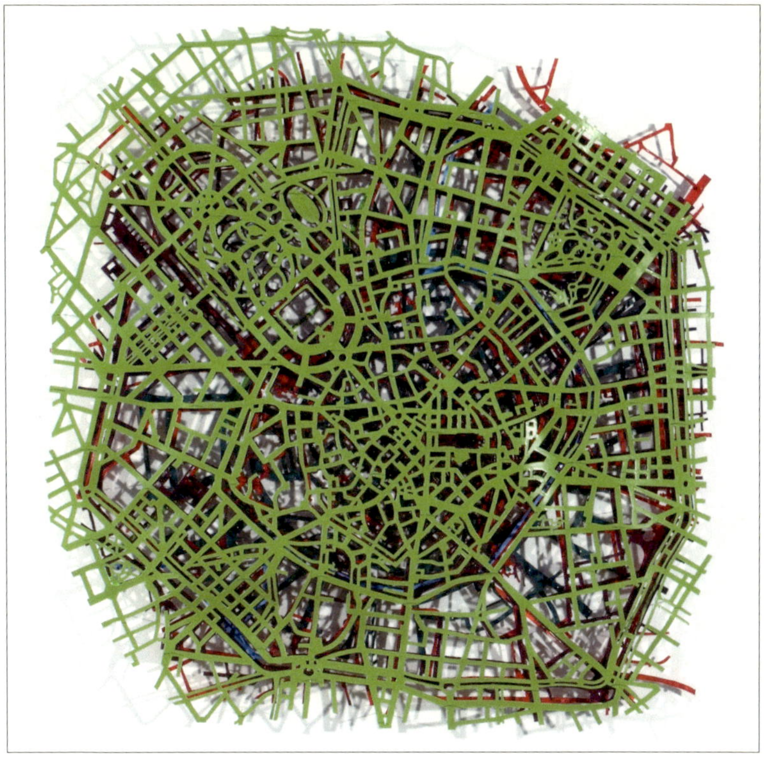

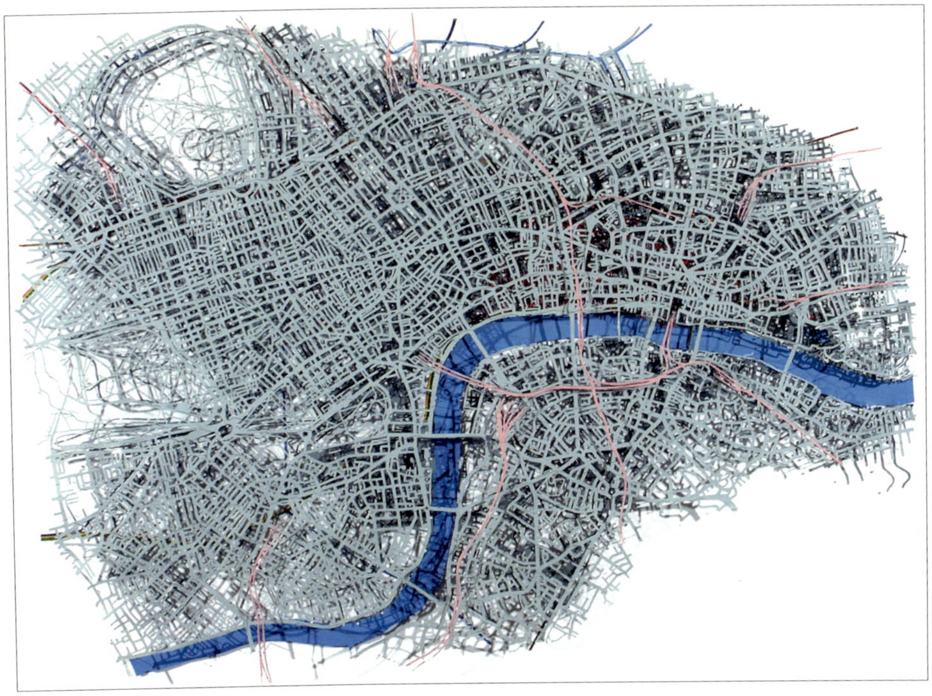

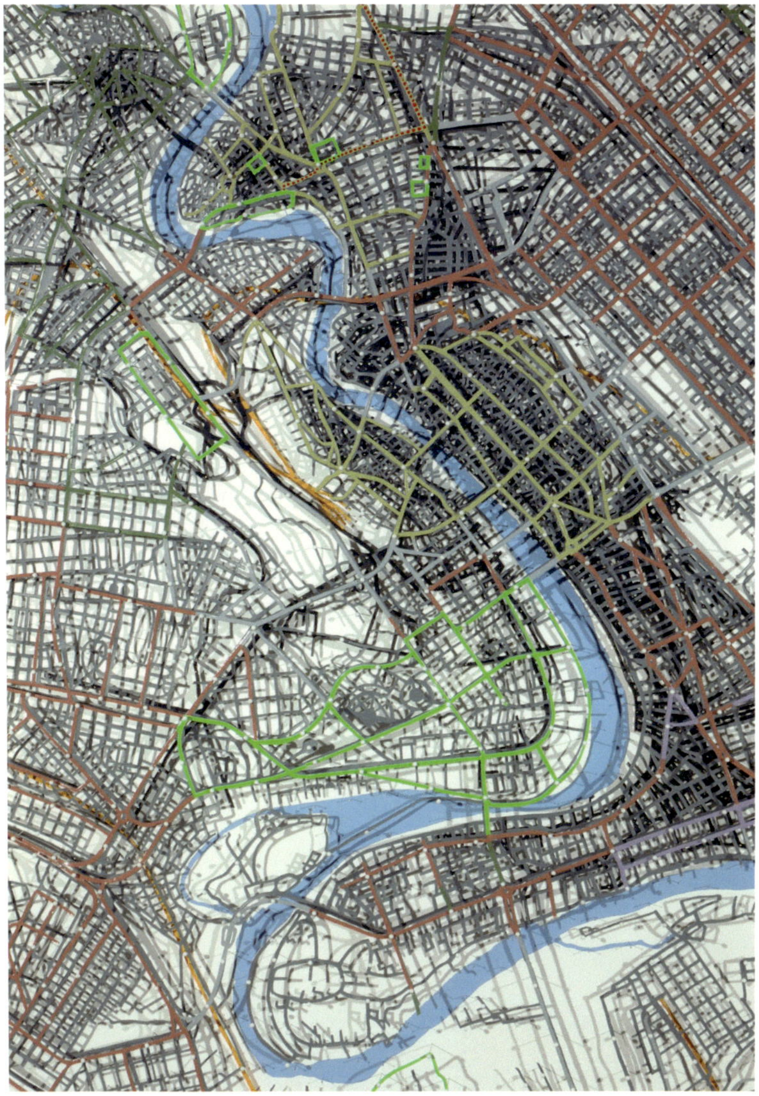

MILAN 1570, 1830, 1913, 2006 *(top left)*
BERLIN 1932, 1962, 2006 *(top right)* – A multi-layer sculpture of Berlin depicting the changes and developments that the 20th Century bought to the urban infrastructure of the city.
BAGHDAD 1944, 2007 *(bottom left)* – This work shows the development of current day Baghad since 1944; the sculpture reflects the current political and ethnic divisions within the city.
LONDON 1666, 1832, 2007 *(bottom right)* – A multi-layer sculpture returning historically to the Great Fire of London.

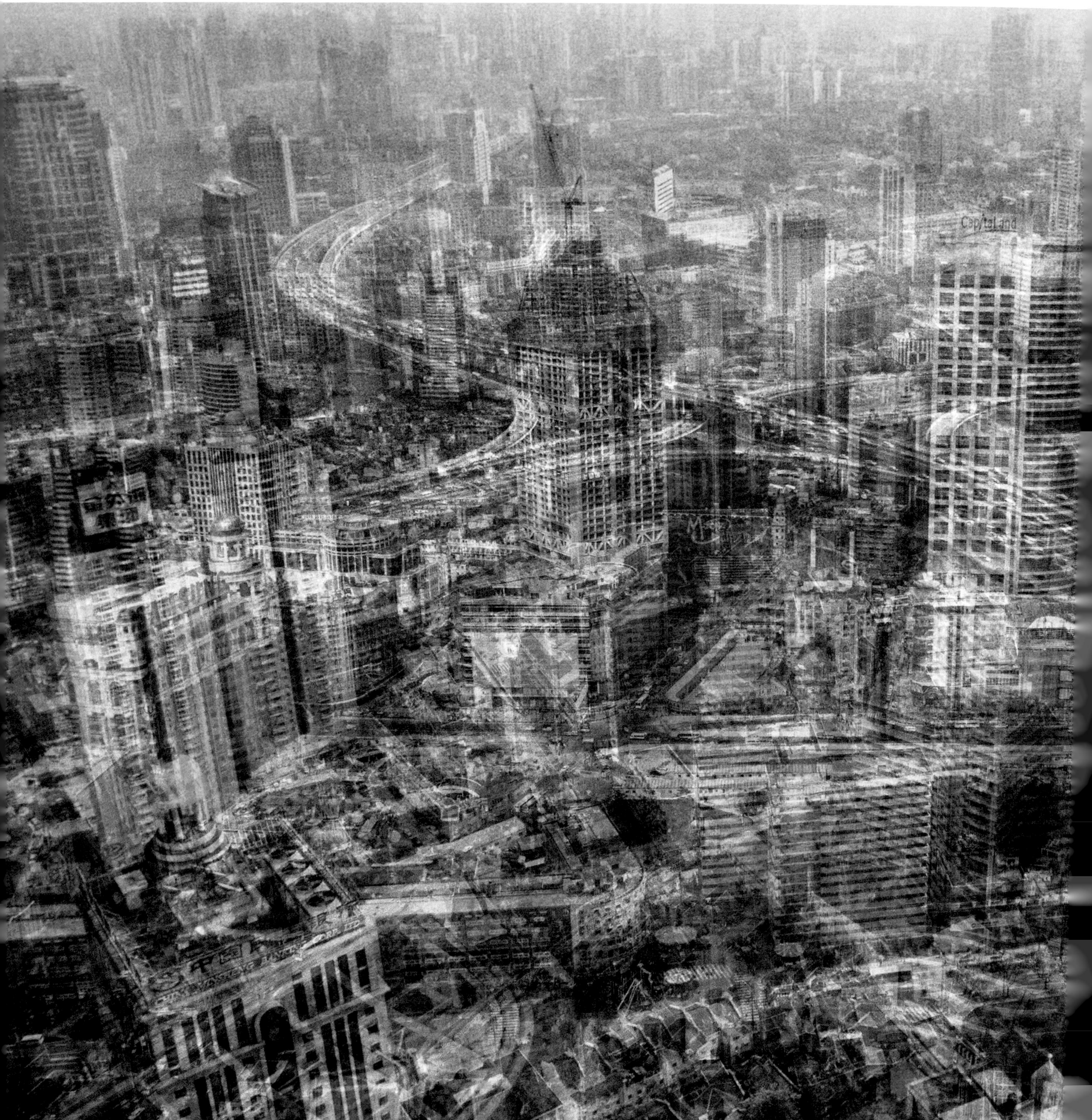
CapitaLand

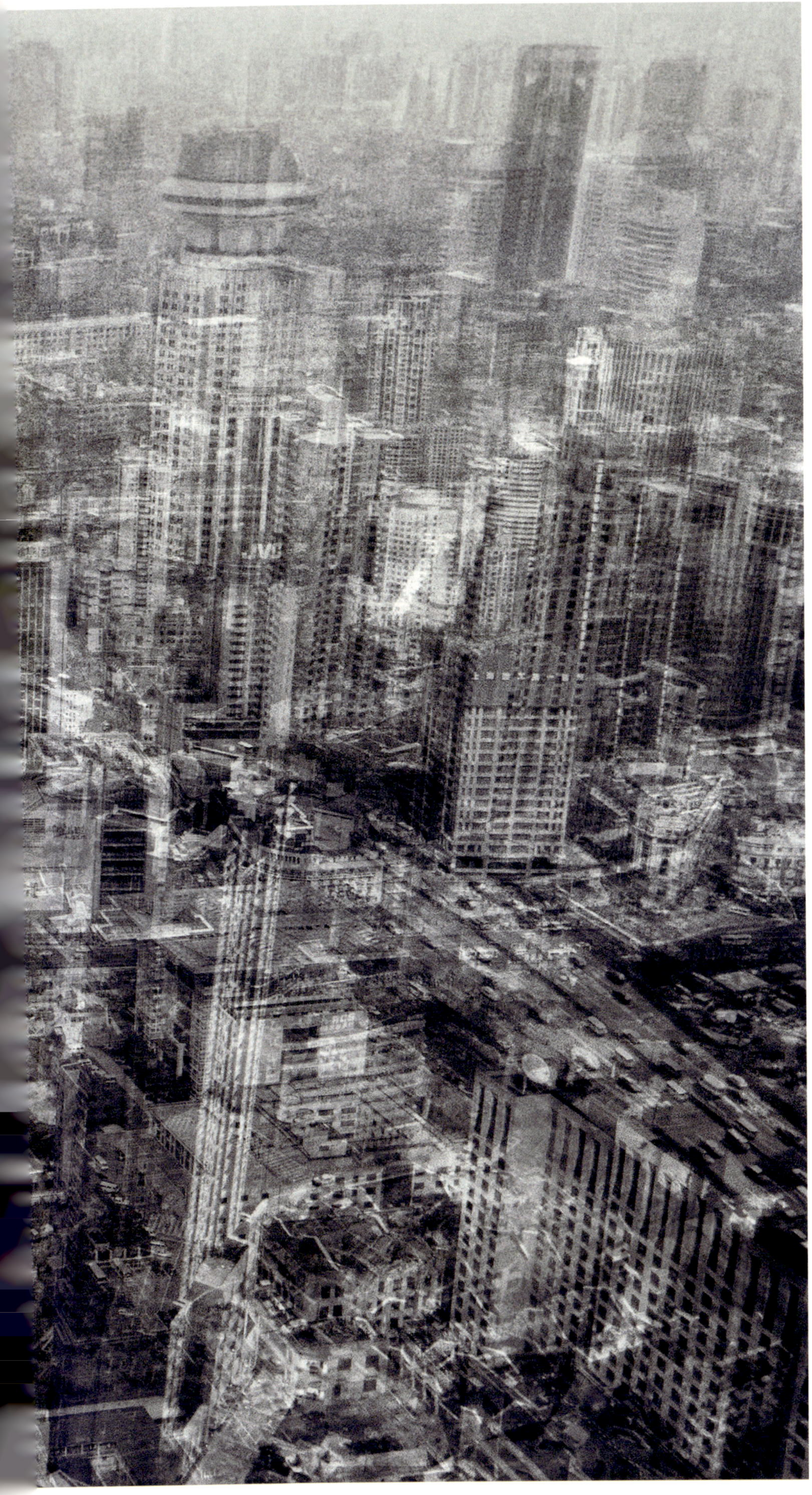

Michael Najjar

NETROPOLIS/SHANGHAI

This hybrid photo work series by Michael Najjar entitled Netropolis is an exploration of the way global cities will develop in the future. The panoramic view transforms the reality of urban spatial structure into landscape. The digital fusion of panoramic views taken from different angles transforms the landscape into a woven fabric of relationships that is abstract and multi-layered, yet still underpinned by a geographic reference point.

Erik Olofsen
• • • • Netherlands I www.erikolofsen.com, erikolofsen@gmail.com
p. 50 STATE OF DELUSION – Bilbao Arte, Bilbao, 2008.
p. 82 IN PLACES – Video installation on 1 screen, 4 min. looping. 2004.

Erwin Wurm
• • • • Austria I www.galerie-krinzinger.at, galeriekrinzinger@chello.at
p. 12 KUHFLADE – Aluminium + paint, 20x87x92cm, 2005.
p. 13 MIES VAN DER ROHE–MELTING – Resin + paint, 110x73x92cm, 2005.
p. 14 FAT HOUSE MOLLER/ADOLF LOOS – Resin + paint, 35x96x50cm, 34x47x48cm.
All © VG Bild-Kunst, Bonn 2008.

Evol / Ct'ink
• • • • Germany I www.evoltaste.com
p. 56 HANDLE WITH CARE [Lehmbruck 9-11 #3]
pp. 90–91 PLATTENBAUTEN: Blocks, Wohnmaschine, Alles wird gut, Concrete Wall
pp. 132–133 CORRIDOR IN THE FLAMINGOBEACH LOTEL
All Photos: © Evol courtesy of Wilde Gallery. Except photo Alles wird gut: © Boris Niehaus.

Faculty of Architecture / University of Technology Munich
• • • • Germany I www.architekturmuseum.de
p. 17 **Annika Sophie Dreyer:** VILLA KUNTERBUNT – Courtesy of the Architecture Museum of the University of Technology Munich, Germany.
p. 157 **Monika Grandl:** JAMES JOYCE'S DUBLIN, ULYSSES – Courtesy of the Architecture Museum of the University of Technology Munich, Germany.
p. 149 **Antje Luckhardt and Nikolaus Witte:** JOHN DOS PASSOS MANHATTAN TRANSFER – Courtesy of the Architecture Museum of the University of Technology Munich, Germany.

Filip Dujardin
• • • • Belgium I www.filipdujardin.be, filip.dujardin@pandora.be
pp. 86–88 FICTIONS – 2007, 2008.
All © VG Bild-Kunst, Bonn 2008.

Frank Kunert
• • • • Germany I www.frank-kunert.de, f-kunert@web.de
p. 24 SMALL WORLDS, ALMOST HEAVENLY, HOPE IS GREEN

Franz Höfner & Harry Sachs
• • • • Germany I www.skulpturenpark.org, info@skulpturenpark.org
p. 19 HAUSEN
p. 93 HONEY NEUSTADT

George Hadjimichalis
• • • • Greece I www.ghadjimichalis.gr, bernier@bernier-eliades.gr
p. 157 HOSPITAL THE BUILDING THE PLAN OF THE BUILDING – Courtesy of the artist and Gallery Bernier Eliadis.

Hans Op De Beeck
• • • • Belgium I www.hansopdebeeck.com, info@hansopdebeeck.com
p. 54 ACCUMULATION (design for The Building) – Sculptural model, mixed media, light (120x180x120cm), 2007. Courtesy of Caldic Collectie (Rotterdam) and Galleria Continua (San Gimignano – Beijing).
p. 68 OBSERVATORY, SOCIAL HOUSING, ARENA – Overall dimensions vary with installation. Courtesy of Galleria Continua, San Gimignano – Beijing; Galerie Krinzinger, Vienna; Xavier Hufkens, Brussels; Galerie Ron Mandos, Rotterdam – Amsterdam. 2008.
p. 69 PANORAMIC CONSTRUCTIONS – Three autonomous sculptures, mixed media (approx. 130x155x130cm; 106x115x185cm; 125x140x180cm). Courtesy of Galleria Continua, San Gimignano – Beijing; Galerie Krinzinger, Vienna; Xavier Hufkens, Brussels; Galerie Ron Mandos, Rotterdam – Amsterdam. 2008.

Hema Upadhyay
• • • • India I www.bodhiart.in, press@bodhiart.in
p. 196 DREAM A WISH, WISH A DREAM – Courtesy of the artist and Bodhi Art Gallery.

Hiroki Tsukuda
• • • • Japan I www.tsukudahiroki.com, voidvillage@snow.odn.ne.jp
p. 195 SONY MUSIC ILL [Dead Wonderland]
TERMINAL – © Hiroki Tsukuda, Courtesy of Nanzuak Underground.

Holger Lippmann
• • • • Germany I www.holgerlippmann.de, info@holgerlippmann.de
p. 194 DISINTEGRATION SERIES – 3D environment generated disintigration series, 2007.

Hvass&Hannibal
• • • • Denmark I www.hvasshannibal.dk, info@hvasshannibal.dk
p. 119 INTERIOR DESIGN OF A MEETING ROOM – Photo: Hans Kruse, Assistants: Nina Rasmussen and Lasse Gyrn, Copenhagen, DGI-byen, 2008.

Isidro Blasco
• • • • Spain I www.paellapans.com/isidroblasco, isidroblasco@pobox.com
pp. 116–117 UTICA ATLANTA, COURTYARD, SHANGHAI AT LAST

J. Davis Studio
• • • • USA I jdavisstudio.etsy.com, jdavisstudio@gmail.com
p. 14 NEIGHBORHOOD RING – Sterling Silver Ring, cast and hand fabricated. 4.6x1.9x0.6cm. 2009. Photo: Jens Look.
TINY HOUSE RING – Sterling Silver Ring House measures 0.6x0.6x0.6cm, 2008. Photo: Laura Desantis Olsson.

J. Michael Birn
• • • • Germany I www.jmbirn.de, jmb@berlin.de
p. 134 A QUESTION OF LUST – The Berlin Lustgarten a.d. 2057

Jake & Dinos Chapman
• • • • UK I www.whitecube.com, info@whitecube.com
pp. 26–27 ARBEIT MCFRIES – Glass Fibre, plastic & mixed media, dimensions variable (nine parts) © The Artist. Photo: Stephen White. Courtesy of Jay Joplin/White Cube (London). 2001.
p. 174 HELL – Mixed media 121.9x121.9x121.9cm, © The Artist. Photo: Stephen White. Courtesy of Jay Jopling/White Cube (London). 1999–2000.

Jakob Kolding
• • • • Germany I www.nicolaiwallner.com, nw@nicolaiwallner.com
p. 110 UNTITLED 1 – Poster 84x60cm. Courtesy of Galleri Nicolai Wallner. 2001.
UNTITLED 2 – Poster 84x41cm. Courtesy of Team Gallery. 2007/2008.
UNTITLED 3 – Lambda 140x200cm. Courtesy of Team Gallery. 2006.
UNTITLED 4 – Mixed media Dimensions variable Courtesy of Galleri Nicolai Wallner. 2007.
THE OUR-DIMENSIONAL NIGHTMARE – Collage and drawing on paper 70x100cm Courtesy of Galerie Martin Janda. 2008.

Jan Brokof
• • • • Germany I www.galerie-baer.de, kontakt@galerie-baer.de
p. 89 SYMMETRIE UND ALLTAG – Woodcut on wood (model), 47x83x64cm, 2007.
JUGENDZIMMER (Installation view) – Woodcut/ Installation, 262x310x368cm, 2005.
Courtesy of Galerie Baer/Raum für aktuelle Kunst.

Jan Feindt
• • • • Germany I www.janfeindt.de, janfeindt@gmx.de
p. 136 UNTITLED – Hand drawn 2007/2008.

Jenny Berntsson
• • • • Sweden I www.jennyberntsson.com, info@jennyberntsson.com
p. 146 SANDCITY – 2004–2008. Blijuburg, Amsterdam 2006, Photo: Charlott Markus. Egilstadir, Héraðsflói 2007. Photo: Frida Berntsson. Sicklastrand, Stockholm 2005.

Jens Reinert
• • • • Germany I jens-reinert.de, jens.reinert@snafu.de
p. 45 BUREAU – 75x22x36cm. Dienstraum, 2003. Photo: Marcus Schneider.
PAUL'S APARTMENT – 100x140cm, 2001.
PFÖRTNERLOGE – 65x40x35cm, 2001. Photo: Marcus Schneider.
3 DOORS – 48x35x40cm, 2004. Photo: Bernd Borchardt
ENTRY/EXIT – 40x36x36cm, 2006.
p. 55 COLOURFUL BALCONIES – 54x10x32cm. 2007.
p. 141 TAGS – 2008.
TUNNEL – concrete, magic markers, ca. 23cm, 2007.
GRAFFITI – 2007.
p. 142 UNDERPASS – Wood, balsa wood, MDF, polyurethane, acrylic, metal, cardboard, paper, acrylic paint, fluorescent tube lights, lightbulb, steel tables, steel supports, ca 250x360x60cm, 2003. Photo: Bernd Borchardt.
BASEMENT GARAGE – ca 190x180x50cm, 2004. Photo: Marcus Schneider.

Jeremias Böttcher
• • • • Germany I www.studiobrigant.com, ere@studiobrigant.com,
p. 139 CARDBOARD YARD – Station park, 2005. Photo: Uros Djurovic.

Jörn Gerstenberg
• • • • Germany I www.abelneuekunst.de, info@abelneuekunst.de
p. 43 PLATFORM – PVC print, 54.5x85cm, edition: 3 + 2 a.p., 2006. Abel Neue Kunst.
ELEPHANTHOUSE – PVC print, 70x130cm, edition: 4 + 1 a.p., 2006. Abel Neue Kunst.

Jonas Liveröd
• • • • Sweden I www.jonasliverod.com, hello@jonasliverod.com
p. 60 MELTING CATHEDRAL – Ink drawing on paper, approx. 130x110cm, 2008. Photo: Maja Atterstig.
p. 170 LOST & FOUND – Mixed media 2003. Sala Can Felipa, Barcelona. Exhibition curated by Angelo Ferriera De Sousa,

Jordi Colomer
• • • • Spain I www.jordicolomer.com, info@jordicolomer.com
pp. 94–95 ANARCHITEKTON

Joshua Callaghan
• • • • USA I www.joshuacallaghan.com, joshua@joshuacallaghan.com
pp. 104–105 CULVER-CITY TOWN SQUARE PROJECT – Culver-City, CA, 2005.
PLAYA VISTA PROJECT – Los Angeles, CA, 2007.
HOLLYWOOD PROJECT – Los Angeles, CA, 2007.

J, P: A Jones, Partners: Architecture with Southern California Institute of Architecture
• • • • USA I www.jonespartners.com, info@jonespartners.com
p. 193 RE:DOING DUBAI – La Bienniale de Venezia, 11th International Architecture Biennale, 2008.
Credits: Wes Jones Jones, Partners: Architecture, with Stefan Pfefferle, Jeixia Xu, Mark Daniels, Caroline Dahl, Hossein Lotfi Shemirani, Robert Cha, Charles Ware Jr., Simon Battisti, Jonathan Odom and (Mary Aramian, Jennifer Dinardo, Necmi Karaman, Ming Cheng Chang, Adam Gebrian) associated students. Figures by Mark Simmons, Academy of Art University. Sponsors: Southern California Institute of Future Initiatives (Jeffrey Inaba, Director), Southern California Institute of Architecture (Eric Moss, Director).

Karsten Konrad
• • • • Germany I www.loop-raum.de, loop@loop-raum.de
p. 33 IMMEUBLE SAR LE SABLE, DELTA 2 – © The Artist, Courtesy of Loop – Raum für aktuelle Kunst.
p. 35 ALDOS HAUS – © The Artist, Courtesy of Loop – Raum für aktuelle Kunst.
p. 56 APARTHOTEL ISTANBUL – © The Artist, Courtesy of Loop – Raum für aktuelle Kunst.
p. 96 DRESDEN – © The Artist, Courtesy of Loop – Raum für aktuelle Kunst.

Philip Wiegard
• • • • Germany | www.philipwiegard.com, philipwiegard@web.de
p. 89 BEROLINA – Pop-up, 31x19x15.5cm. 2003.
p. 115 SCAFFOLD – Pop-up, 46x26.5x23cm. Edition of 5. 2003.
JUNE 17TH – Berlin flea market. Pop-up, 31x19x15.5cm. Edition of 5. 2003.

Pipilotti Rist
• • • • Switzerland | www.pipilottirist.net
p. 20 SUBURB BRAIN – Audio/video installation at 48th Venice Biennial. Courtesy of the artist and Hauser & Wirth, Zürich London. Photo: A. Burger, 1999.

Rachel Whiteread
• • • • UK | luhringaugustine.com
pp. 77–78 PLACE (VILLAGE) – Courtesy of the artist, Luhring Augustine, New York and Gagosian, New York and London. Photo credit: Mike Bruce.
p. 83 EMBANKMENT – © Tate 2005. Photo credit: Marcus and Marcella Leith. Courtesy of the artist, Luhring Augustine, New York and Gagosian, New York and London.

Raumlabor Berlin
• • • • Germany | www.raumlabor-berlin.de, info@raumlabor-berlin.de
p. 169 BRANDHERDE – Benjamin Foerster-Baldenius with Cora Hegewald and Malte Jelden, Ingo Niermann, Tibor Bartholomä. Participating artists: Bernadette La Hengst, Knarf Rellöm.
p. 183 STICK ON CITY – Kindly supported by repro ringel Werkstätten für Farbvision und Kommunikation GmbH.
p. 186 RAUMLABORWELT – Illustration.

realities:united
• • • • Germany | www.realities-united.de, info@realu.de
p. 16 OPEN THE HOUSE: STADT – Jan Edler & Tim Edler Team: Milena Monssen, Erik Levander, Andreas Martini, Scientific Advisors: Markus Weder, Project Leader Clothing Physiology, EMPA St. Gallen, Switzerland; Ivo Locher, Wearable Computing Lab., ETH Zürich, Switzerland; Fashion: Textile Interfaces Alexandra Baum, Gotha, Germany Curated by Vitra Design Museum and Art Center College of Design, 2006.

Rhoads Clarke Design
• • • • UK | www.rhoadsclarke.com, rhoadsclarke@live.co.uk
p. 73 KITRADIO

Rob Voerman
• • • • Netherlands | www.robvoerman.nl, info@upstreamgallery.nl
p. 37 MEGAFARM – A.o. wood, glue, paint and display slides, Dimensions: 236x135cm, with a protuberance (length 130cm). 2004. Photo: Maarten Wetsema. Courtesy of Upstream Gallery.
p. 179 UNTITLED – Linoleum print and silkscreen on paper, 117x220cm. Edition of 4 + 1 A.P. 2004. Photo: Maarten Wetsema. Collection MoMA, Deutsche Bank, Arcadis, Coda Museum and private collection Athens. Courtesy of the artist and Upstream Gallery
pp. 180–181 EPICENTRE – Linoleumprint, silkscreen and watercolour on paper, 180x201cm. Editon of 5 + 1 A.P. 2007.
ANNEX #3 – Coloured etching on paper Dimensions: 30x40cm. Edition of 15. 2006. Courtesy of the artist and Upstream Gallery.
ANNEX #1 – Wood, cathedral glass, blackboard paint and piece of chalk. Dimensions: height 180x70x65cm. 2005. Tishman Speyer Art Collection, New York. Courtesy of the artist and Upstream Gallery.

Romain Laurent
• • • • France | www.romain-laurent.com, contact@romain-laurent.com
p. 106 WHAT IF TREES CAN DECIDE WHAT THEY REALLY WANT – 2007.

Sandra Rauch
• • • • Germany | www.sandra-rauch.de, contact@sandra-rauch.de
pp. 126–127 HONG – 150x200cm, acrylic.
SUPERSTAR – 200x150cm, acrylic.
HONG KONG STREET – 150x200cm, acrylic.
UNTITLED – 150x200cm, acrylic.

Serge Seidlitz
• • • • UK | www.sergeseidlitz.com, mail@sergeseidlitz.com
p. 170 WORLD TRAVELLER – Commissioned by Mark Reddy at BBH London, 2007.
p. 171 MONEY CITY – Brummel magazine, 2007.

Simon Bent
• • • • UK | www.volume2a.com, simon@volume2a.com
p. 148 MUSIC LANDSCAPE – Cover artwork for a CD mix by DJ Perplex, 2008.

Simon Boudvin
• • • • France | boudvin.free.fr, boudvin@free.fr
p. 17 SEMI-COLLECTIF – 2003.
p. 52 FACES – Courtesy of Galerie Corentin Hamel, 2005.
p. 57 HAUSMANN – 2005.
p. 163 TTUKSEOM – Seoul, South Korea, 2004.

Slinkachu
• • • • UK | little-people.blogspot.com, slinkachu@yahoo.co.uk
pp. 104–105 UNTITLED

Sotiria Kornaropoulou
• • • • Belgium | SotiriaKornaropoulou@51n4e.com
p. 34 THE HEART OF THE HOME: CUPBOARD HOUSE – IM masters, Design Academy Eindhoven, 2005.

Squint / Opera
• • • • UK | www.squintopera.com, info@squintopera.com
pp. 106–107 HONOR OAK – Suburban Bucolia/Flooded London. 2008.

Stephanie Backes
• • • • Germany | www.loop-raum.de, loop@loop-raum.de
p. 32 SCHWIMMER, KLAPPANZER, WANDLER – Courtesy of Loop – Raum für aktuelle Kunst.

Stephen Willats
• • • • UK | www.galeriethomasschulte.de, mail@galeriethomasschulte.de
p. 51 DEMOCRATIC GRID SERIES NO. 14 & 15
NETWORK INTERVENTIONS NO.7
pp. 102–103 SPACE TIME FRAGMENTS
MACRO TO MICRO
IMAGINARY JOURNEY
PERSON TO PERSON, PEOPLE TO PEOPLE

Studio Job – Job Smeets + Nynke Tynagel
• • • • Belgium | www.studiojob.be, office@studiojob.be
pp. 7–8 ROBBER BARRON: Clock, Table, Lamp. Photo: R. Kot Brussels.
p. 66 VASE OF BABEL – Pressed porcelain, 2006. Photo: Royal Tichelaar Makkum.

Sven Drühl
• • • • Germany | www.svendruehl.de, s.duehl@web.de
p. 41 S.D.F.L.W. II – Oil and lacquer on canvas, 150x150cm, 2007. Private collection South Germany, Courtesy of Galerie Michael Schultz, Berlin.
S.D.F.L.W. III – Oil and lacquer on canvas, 180x130cm, 2007. Private collection Norway, Courtesy of Galerie Michael Schultz, Berlin.
All © VG Bild-Kunst, Bonn 2008.

Theo Deutinger
• • • • Netherlands | www.td-architects.eu, tdeutinger@td-architects.eu
p. 101 VIVA LAS VEGAS – 2007.

Thomas Demand
• • • • Germany | www.thomasdemand.net, studio@thomasdemand.net
p. 38 EMBASSY – © Thomas Demand + VG Bild-Kunst, Bonn 2008.

Till Gerhard
• • • • Germany | www.galeriemichaeljanssen.de, berlin@galeriemichaeljanssen.de
p. 20 GLAUBE, HOFFNUNG UND LIEBE: Orakelstätte – Mixed media hut: 90x125x138cm, Photo: Alistair Overbruck, Köln, 30. Sep.–09. Nov. 2007.

Tim Dinter
• • • • Germany | www.timdinter.de, post@timdinter.de
p. 138 I LOVE YOU, ALEX, ROSA-LUXEMBURG-PLATZ – Illustrations, 2007.

Titus Matiyane
• • • • South Africa
pp. 188–189 Reproduced from Titus Matiyane. Cities of the World, 010 Publishers, Rotterdam (ISBN 978-90-6450-640-6).

Tom Sachs
• • • • USA | www.www.tomsachs.org, www.speronewestwater.com
pp. 166–167 NUTSY'S – Installation view of Nutsy's at the Bohen Foundation, New York, 2002-2003. Photo: Tom Powel. Courtesy of the artist and Sperone Westwater, New York.

Tonk
Taiyo Onorato & Nico Krebs
• • • • Switzerland | www.tonk.ch, taiyo-nico@gmx.net
p. 21 GROW HOMES

Unfold
Dries Verbruggen
• • • • Belgium | www.unfold.be, office@unfold.be
p. 15 XS,M,XL – 2002

Vangelis Vlahos
• • • • Greece | www.thebreedersystem.com, gallery@thebreedersystem.com
p. 36 BUILDINGS THAT PROCLAIM A NATION'S IDENTITY TO THE WORLD SHOULD NOT BE MISUNDERSTOOD – Scale model 1:150, dimensions of table with scale model 158x100x125cm, archive consisting of 5 binders Abo. Courtesy of the artist and The Breeder, Athens. Photos: Vivianna Athanassopoulou, Athens, 2003.

Vasco Mourão
• • • • Portugal | www.vascomourao.350.com, vascomourao@gmail.com
p. 190 DENSIDADE. CIUDAD
DENSIDADE. REAL ESTATE
DENSIDADE. ZEPPELIN
Series of drawings of impossible constructions. 2008.

Veron Urdarianu
• • • • Romania | www.arndt-partner.de, www.tanjapol.com
p. 33 SURVIVAL HOUSE, SCHUIFHUIS 3 – Sculpture wood, plexiglas, paint, 34x45x34cm, 2006. Photo: Gabriele Faber. Courtesy of Tanja Pol Gelerie, Munich/Arnt & Partner, Berlin, Zürich. © VG Bild-Kunst, Bonn 2008.

Wang Qingsong
• • • • China | www.wangqingsong.com
pp. 28–29 DREAM OF MIGRANTS – 170x400cm, C-Print, Beijing Film Studio, 2005.

INPRINT

Beyond Architecture
IMAGINATIVE BUILDINGS AND FICTIONAL CITIES

Edited by Robert Klanten and Lukas Feireiss
All texts written by Lukas Feireiss

Cover Photography by Filip Dujardin
Layout by Hendrik Hellige for Gestalten
Typeface (Typefaces):
Generika by Alexander Meyer; Foundry: www.gestalten.com/fonts
Trade Gothic by Jackson Burke

Project management by Elisabeth Honerla for Gestalten
Production management by Vinzenz Geppert for Gestalten
Text editing by Michael Robinson
Proofreading by Patricia Mehnert
Printed by Graphische Betriebe Eberl GmbH, Immenstadt im Allgäu
Made in Germany

Published by Gestalten, Berlin 2009
ISBN 978-3-89955-235-5

For more information, please check www.gestalten.com

Bibliographic information published by the Deutsche Nationalbibliothek.
The Deutsche Nationalbibliothek lists this publication in the Deutsche Nationalbibliografie; detailed bibliographic data is available on the Internet at http://dnb.d-nb.de.

This book was printed according to the internationally accepted FSC standards for environmental protection, which specify requirements for an environmental management system.

Mixed Sources
Product group from well-managed forests, controlled sources and recycled wood or fiber
www.fsc.org Cert no. GFA-COC-001446
© 1996 Forest Stewardship Council

Gestalten is a climate neutral company and so are our products. We collaborate with the non-profit carbon offset provider myclimate (www.myclimate.org) to neutralise the company's carbon footprint produced through our worldwide business activities by investing in projects that reduce CO_2 emissions (www.gestalten.com/myclimate).

myclimate
Protect our planet